Lecture Notes in Artificial Intelligence   8291

Subseries of Lecture Notes in Computer Science

LNAI Series Editors

Randy Goebel
University of Alberta, Edmonton, Canada
Yuzuru Tanaka
Hokkaido University, Sapporo, Japan
Wolfgang Wahlster
DFKI and Saarland University, Saarbrücken, Germany

LNAI Founding Series Editor

Joerg Siekmann
DFKI and Saarland University, Saarbrücken, Germany

Guido Boella Edith Elkind
Bastin Tony Roy Savarimuthu Frank Dignum
Martin K. Purvis (Eds.)

PRIMA 2013: Principles and Practice of Multi-Agent Systems

16th International Conference
Dunedin, New Zealand, December 1-6, 2013
Proceedings

 Springer

Volume Editors

Guido Boella
University of Turin, Department of Computer Science
Turin, Italy
E-mail: boella@di.unito.it

Edith Elkind
Nanyang Technological University, Division of Mathematical Sciences
Singapore
E-mail: eelkind@gmail.com

Bastin Tony Roy Savarimuthu
Martin K. Purvis
University of Otago, Department of Information Science
Dunedin, New Zealand
E-mail: {tony.savarimuthu; martin.purvis}@otago.ac.nz

Frank Dignum
Utrecht University, Department of Information and Computing Sciences
Utrecht, The Netherlands
E-mail: f.p.m.dignum@uu.nl

ISSN 0302-9743   e-ISSN 1611-3349
ISBN 978-3-642-44926-0   e-ISBN 978-3-642-44927-7
DOI 10.1007/978-3-642-44927-7
Springer Heidelberg New York Dordrecht London

Library of Congress Control Number: 2013951858

CR Subject Classification (1998): I.2.11, I.2.6, I.2.8, D.2, K.4.4, H.3.4, H.5.3, J.2

LNCS Sublibrary: SL 7 – Artificial Intelligence

Typesetting: Camera-ready by author, data conversion by Scientific Publishing Services, Chennai, India

Printed on acid-free paper

Springer is part of Springer Science+Business Media (www.springer.com)

Preface

PRIMA, the International Conference on Principles and Practice of Multi-Agent Systems, has emerged as one of the leading scientific conferences for research on multi-agent systems, attracting high quality, state-of-the-art research from all over the world. PRIMA endeavors to bring together researchers, developers, and academic and industry leaders who are active and interested in agents and multi-agent systems, their practices and related areas. The conference is specifically focused on showcasing work on foundations of agent systems, engineering agent systems as well as on promoting emerging areas of agent-research in several domains.

PRIMA 2013, the 16th International Conference on Principles and Practice of Multi-Agent Systems, was held in Dunedin, New Zealand, during December 1–6, 2013. The conference was hosted by University of Otago, co-located with AI 2013 (26th Australasian Artificial Intelligence Conference). PRIMA 2013 continued to build on the success of its predecessor conferences, held in Kuching (2012), Wollongong (2011), Kolkata (2010), Nagoya (2009), Hanoi (2008) and Bangkok (2007), as a high-quality forum for international researchers and practitioners to meet and share their work.

PRIMA 2013 received 81 submissions from 29 countries, each of which was assigned to three Program Committee (PC) members, who were overseen by a Senior PC (SPC) member. Each paper received at least three reviews. The review period was followed by an author response phase, and discussion amongst the PC, led by the SPC member assigned to the paper. Of the 81 submissions, PRIMA 2013 accepted 24 full papers (acceptance rate: 30 percent). Further 20 promising, but not fully mature contributions were accepted at reduced length as short papers; two of these were subsequently withdrawn by the authors. The papers that were submitted by one of the PC chairs were assigned to a separate track and were overseen by the other PC chairs in order to guarantee the integrity of the reviewing process.

Continuing the past trend, this conference showcased the impact of agents on the real world, across the spectrum from early research and prototypes to mature deployed systems. PRIMA 2013 featured two distinguished invited talks, by Aditya Ghose ("Agents in the era of big data: What the "end of theory" might mean for agent systems") and Nigel Gilbert ("Agents might not be people").

We would first like to thank all those who submitted papers to PRIMA 2013. Special thanks to the Program Committee members for their detailed reviews completed in a timely manner, and the Senior Program Committee for their considered judgements and recommendations on the papers. We are confident that this process has resulted in a high-quality diverse conference program.

Thanks also to EasyChair for the use of their conference management system to facilitate this complex process and the preparation of these proceedings. Our sincere thanks to the senior advisors of PRIMA 2013, Aditya Ghose, Sandip Sen, and Makoto Yokoo. A special thanks to Michael Winikoff for coordination, Heather Cooper and Lu Cox for organization, and the staff members and students of the department of Information Science and Computer Science for their efforts in local organization.

September 2013

Guido Boella
Edith Elkind
Bastin Tony Roy Savarimuthu
Frank Dignum
Martin K. Purvis

Organization

PRIMA 2013 was hosted by University of Otago, and was held in Dunedin, New Zealand, during December 1–6, 2013.

Conference Committee

General Co-chairs

Frank Dignum · Utrecht University, The Netherlands
Martin Purvis · University of Otago, New Zealand

Program Committee Co-chairs

Guido Boella · University of Torino, Italy
Edith Elkind · Nanyang Technological University, Singapore
Bastin Tony Roy
   Savarimuthu · University of Otago, New Zealand

Workshop Chairs

Virginia Dignum · Delft University, The Netherlands
Alistair Knott · University of Otago, New Zealand

Publicity Chairs

Tina Balke · University of Surrey, UK
Quan Bai · Auckland University of Technology,
   New Zealand

Sponsorship Chair

Mike Barley · University of Auckland, New Zealand

Local Arrangements Chairs

Maryam Purvis · University of Otago, New Zealand
Bastin Tony Roy
   Savarimuthu · University of Otago, New Zealand

Local Arrangements Advisors

Michael Winikoff · University of Otago, New Zealand
Stephen Cranefield · University of Otago, New Zealand

Senior Advisors

Aditya Ghose · University of Wollongong, Australia
Sandip Sen · University of Tulsa, USA
Makoto Yokoo · Kyushu University, Japan

Finance Chair

Stephen Hall-Jones   University of Otago, New Zealand

Web Masters

Mariusz Nowostawski   University of Otago, New Zealand
Heather Cooper   University of Otago, New Zealand

Senior Program Committee

Bo An   Chinese Academy of Sciences, China
Hoa Khanh Dam   University of Wollongong, Australia
Guido Governatori   NICTA, Australia
Katsutoshi Hirayama   Kobe University, Japan
Takayuki Ito   Nagoya Institute of Technology, Japan
Andrea Omicini   Alma Mater Studiorum Università di Bologna,
                                   Italy
Julian Padget   University of Bath, UK
Jeremy Pitt   Imperial College London, UK
David Pynadath   Institute for Creative Technologies, University
                                   of Southern California, USA
Paul Scerri   Carnegie Mellon University, USA
Paolo Torroni   University of Bologna, Italy
Pradeep Varakantham   Singapore Management University, Singapore
Harko Verhagen   Stockholm University/KTH, Sweden
Jie Zhang   Nanyang Technological University, Singapore

Program Committee

Tina Balke   University of Surrey, UK
Francesco Belardinelli   Universite d'Evry, France
Gauvain Bourgne   CRIL, CNRS UMR8188, Université d'Artois,
                                   France
Stefano Bromuri   University of Applied Sciences Western
                                   Switzerland, Switzerland
Nils Bulling   Clausthal University of Technology, Germany
Dídac Busquets   Imperial College London, UK
Arthur Carvalho   University of Waterloo, Canada
Shih-Fen Cheng   Singapore Management University, Singapore
Amit Chopra   Lancaster University, UK
Mehdi Dastani   Utrecht University, The Netherlands
Paul Davidsson   Malmö University, Sweden
Yves Demazeau   CNRS - Laboratoire LIG, France
Hiromitsu Hattori   Kyoto University, Japan

Reiko Hishiyama	Waseda University, Japan
Wan-Rong Jih	National Taiwan University, Taiwan
Ozgur Kafali	Royal Holloway, University of London, UK
Yoonheui Kim	University of Massachusetts at Amherst, USA
Yasuhiko Kitamura	Kwansei Gakuin University
Ramachandra Kota	Secure Meters Ltd., UK
Kazuhiro Kuwabara	Ritsumeikan University, Japan
Ho-Pun Lam	NICTA, Australia
Joao Leite	CENTRIA, Universidade Nova de Lisboa, Portugal
Churn-Jung Liau	Academia Sinica at Taipei, Taiwan
Maite Lopez-Sanchez	Universitat de Barcelona, Spain
Xudong Luo	Sun Yat-sen University, China
Sunilkumar Manvi	Basaveshwar Engg. College, India
Shigeo Matsubara	Kyoto University, Japan
Toshihiro Matsui	Nagoya Institute of Technology, Japan
Felipe Meneguzzi	PUCRS, Brasil
Tsunenori Mine	Kyushu University, Japan
Yohei Murakami	Kyoto University, Japan
Yuu Nakajima	Kyoto University, Japan
Hideyuki Nakanishi	Osaka University, Japan
Brendan Neville	University of Essex, UK
Mariusz Nowostawski	University of Otago, New Zealand
Nir Oren	University of Aberdeen, UK
Wojciech Penczek	IPI PAN and University of Podlasie, Poland
Duy Hoang Pham	Posts and Telecommunications Institute of Technology, Vietnam
Hongyang Qu	University of Oxford, UK
Franco Raimondi	Middlesex University, UK
Alessandro Ricci	University of Bologna, Italy
Juan Antonio Rodriguez Aguilar	IIIA-CSIC, Spain
Yuko Sakurai	JST, Japan
Mei Si	Rensselaer Polytechnic Institute (RPI), USA
Guillermo Ricardo Simari	Universidad Nacional del Sur, Argentina
Insu Song	James Cook University, Australia
Long Tran-Thanh	University of Southampton, UK
Wamberto Vasconcelos	University of Aberdeen, UK
Serena Villata	Inria Sophia Antipolis, France
Meritxell Vinyals	University of Southampton, UK
Gerhard Weiss	University Maastricht, The Netherlands
Brendon Woodford	University of Otago, New Zealand
Neil Yorke-Smith	American University of Beirut, Libanon

Additional Reviewers

Adam, Carole
Aitken, Jonathan
Cerutti, Federico
Chen, Siqi
Fossel, Joscha
Gabbriellini, Simone
Kacprzak, Magdalena
Kanamori, Ryo

Knapik, Michał
Morales, Javier
Oliehoek, Frans
Otsuka, Takanobu
Ranjbar-Sahraei, Bijan
Szreter, Maciej
Zhao, Dengji

Abstracts

Agents in the Era of Big Data: What the "End of Theory" Might Mean for Agent Systems

Aditya Ghose

Decision Systems Laboratory
School of Computer Science and Software Engineering
University of Wollongong, NSW 2522 Australia
aditya@uow.edu.au

Abstract. Our ability to collect, manage and analyze vast amounts of data has led some to predict the demise of theory. This has important implications for research in agent systems. It can mean that specifications of agent intent, or of agent behaviour, or the norms that constrain agent behaviour can be learnt from data and maintained in the face of continuous data streams. I will offer some examples of how the agents community is beginning to leverage data in this fashion, and what the challenges might be in the future.

Agents Might Not Be People

Nigel Gilbert

Centre for Research in Social Simulation, University of Surrey, UK
n.gilbert@surrey.ac.uk

Abstract. In most agent-based systems, the agents are intended to represent individual people. This is not surprising as we tend to think of the social world as being driven by the actions of individuals (so-called 'methodological individualism'). On occasion, however, we develop models in which the agents represent firms, nation states or other collectivities, without considering deeply the implications of doing so.

In this talk, I shall discuss the opportunities for agent-based models that are based on non-human agents, using several examples. First, I outline the defining features of an 'agent'. I then consider a model, the Simulating Knowledge dynamics of Innovation Networks (SKIN) model, in which the agents are firms, considering the ways in which the firms are similar to and different from human actors. Then I describe a simulation of academic science in which scientific papers, normally considered to be objects rather than actors, can usefully be represented as agents, and interpret this model in terms of actor-network theory. Finally, I describe recent work on modelling social practices for which theory sees people as being the substrate on which social practices are carried, and discuss the perennial issue of the extent to which it is useful to see the macro level emerge from the micro, and the micro being affected by the macro. I conclude by recommending that we should be readier to consider non-human agents when modelling the social world.

Table of Contents

Invited Paper

Full Papers

Short Papers

Agents in the Era of Big Data: What the "End of Theory" Might Mean for Agent Systems

Aditya Ghose

Decision Systems Laboratory
School of Computer Science and Software Engineering
University of Wollongong, NSW 2522 Australia
aditya@uow.edu.au

Abstract. Our ability to collect, manage and analyze vast amounts of data has led some to predict the demise of theory. This has important implications for research in agent systems. It can mean that specifications of agent intent, or of agent behaviour, or the norms that constrain agent behaviour can be learnt from data and maintained in the face of continuous data streams. I will offer some examples of how the agents community is beginning to leverage data in this fashion, and what the challenges might be in the future.

1 Introduction

The "data deluge" has been the topic of much recent discourse. Over the past decade (but, in some cases, even earlier) we have come to recognize that we have crossed a sort of tacit threshold in our capacity to collect, store and analyze large volumes of data. This has spawned a large industry in big data analytics, much of it focused on leveraging business insights (such as customer buying patterns) from large and real-time data streams. But we have also started asking whether the big data phenomenon might perhaps represent a more fundamental shift in the process of human inquiry. For one, we have the wherewithal to generate large bodies of statistical correlations from these data streams. That has not been without controversy (see, for instance, the recent Chomsky-Norvig debate [1]). For another, the statistically mined knowledge is turning out, in some cases, to be transient. The rules that we are able to mine change with the arrival of new data (although that is no surprise). This has led some to posit the "end of theory" [2]. The time-honoured scientific method of constructing largely stable predictive models on the basis of carefully curated data is being supplanted by machinery that generates and updates (potentially less reliable) models from data very quickly and without demanding as much effort from the human in the loop. To quote Anderson [2]: "Correlation supersedes causation, and science can advance without coherent models, unified theories, or really any mechanistic explanation at all"'.

My main argument here is that this is a game-changer for the agents research community. I will discuss some of the opportunities in broad outline, offer some specific examples, and list some challenges.

G. Boella et al. (Eds.): PRIMA 2013, LNAI 8291, pp. 1–4, 2013.

Much like the bulk of the AI community, agents researchers can now leverage the speed, scale and ubiquity of knowledge acquisition machinery. The devil, as always, is in the detail. The kinds of knowledge that agent systems rely on require specialized machinery, both for knowledge mining and by way of instrumentation for data collection. Let us consider a simple taxonomy for the types of knowledge that agent systems rely on. *Prescriptions* specify behaviour, and is to be found in constructs such as agent plans, policies, strategies and so on. *Drivers* specify agent motivation, and can be found in constructs such as goals, optimization objectives, event triggers and so on, *Constraints* circumscribe the space of valid behaviours, and can be found in constructs such as norms, commitments or even the constraint theories that multi-agent optimization techniques use. Each category in this taxonomy requires bespoke data and machinery. Prescriptions are typically mined from behaviour logs, process logs and their ilk. Drivers must be mined from data that describes the *impact* of agent behaviour (in our work, we have used *effect logs* that describe state transitions of objects impacted by agent behaviour). Sometimes, agent behaviour manifests as choices between competing alternatives, which can be captured in *decision logs*. Constraints must also be mined from a record of the impact of agent behaviour, or from a record of speech acts that contain clues about the commitments that an agent might have made [3].

In the following, I will offer two examples of our recent work in leveraging data in building and maintaining agent systems, before discussing some open questions.

2   Mining Agent Programs

In recent work [4], we addressed the knowledge acquisition bottleneck in the context of BDI agent programs. Given that organizations often avoid building agent-based solutions (even when there is a clear need and a good fit) because of the investment required and the perceived complexity of agent programming, we set out to build an *agent mining* tool that would simplify the task of building agent programs (and thus improve agent programmer productivity). The tool infers "first-cut" agent plans from *process logs* (time-stamped records of task execution) and plan contexts (preconditions) from *effect logs* (time-stamped records of object states). The tool also leverages norm mining techniques to refine agent plans from process log entries tagged as erroneous (either because of obligatory actions that were not performed or prohibited actions that were performed). Initial experimental results on the extent to which we could improve agent programmer productivity were promising.

More generally, this suggests that data-driven generation of agent behaviour (prescriptions) might become fairly standard in the future. Indeed, we might conceive of machinery that maintained agent programs to best fit the available data, incorporating human oversight at appropriate intervals and for key decision points.

3   The *Know-How Miner*

In recent work [5], we built the *Know-How Miner* to extract know-how descriptors (patterns of the form: to <GOAL>, <STEP1>, <STEP2>... - the steps to be separated by an AND or an OR) from the textual content of the web. Each know-how descriptor specifies the steps that (under conjunctive or disjunctive composition) help achieve a goal. The goal as well as the steps are extracted as text. The following is an example of a know-how descriptor that was extracted:

```
<to create a robust business plan>
take a comprehensive view of the enterprise
AND
incorporate management-practice knowledge from every first-semester
course
```

Implemented on fairly standard hardware, the tool is quite efficient. In one experiment, a single crawler, was able to produce 22 useful know-how descriptors in the space of about 30 minutes from 446 webpages.

The original intent of the *Know-How Miner* was harvesting process innovation. Organizations can use the tool to look outside their enterprise boundaries (and leverage, in the limit, all textual descriptions of know-how in the web) to identify alternative ways of doing things, which in turn would serve as triggers for process innovation.

It isn't hard to see that know-how descriptors can also be viewed as agent plans (or plan snippets). We can imagine a not-too-distant future where agent programmers would routinely rely on tools such as this to help them write better agent programs, or improve the quality of existing agent programs. We can also imagine a future where not just text, but multimedia content on the web could be mined for know-how.

4   Open Questions

For agent researchers in the era of big data, the possibilities are endless. Some of our other on-going work looks at how we might extract the objective functions that drive optimizing agents from *decision logs* (where each entry specifies the set of options available to an agent, plus the option selected). Norm learning machinery already exists. A future where data-driven agents become routine appears to be within reach.

There are some hard problems to solve, however. Unlike many other applications of knowledge mining, the knowledge comprising agent systems is not easily amenable to the traditional generate-evaluate-update cycle that is used to quality assure the knowledge that is mined. How much testing, verification or validation should we subject a mined body of behavioural knowledge to, before we are confident of deploying it in an operational agent system? If we spend too long, the "best-fit" behavioural specifications that can be mined from the data might have changed, requiring another evaluation cycle. If norms are to be data-driven, what would the evaluate-update part of the cycle for normative multi-agent systems look like? And finally, where and how should we position the human in the loop? How do we decide how much human oversight would be appropriate for an adaptive agent system?

The problem of *context* bedevils many big data applications. Much of the data that we have access to does not come with detailed specifications of the context within which the data was generated. Yet that contextual information makes all the difference to the quality of the theories (or agent programs, or customer insights) that we generate. Sometimes we may have the capability to deploy lightweight instrumentation to acquire some contextual information. How much is enough?

If we are staring at the end of theory, we will be left in a world with no constants. What kind of a world would that be for agents, both of the human and machine variety?

References

1. Norvig, P.: On chomsky and the two cultures of statistical learning. On-line essay in response to Chomsky's remarks in [2] (2011), http://norvig.com/chomsky.html
2. Anderson, C.: The end of theory. Wired Magazine 16 (2008)
3. Gao, X., Singh, M.P., Mehra, P.: Mining business contracts for service exceptions. IEEE Transactions on Services Computing 5, 333–344 (2012)
4. Xu, H., Savarimuthu, B.T.R., Ghose, A.K., Morrison, E., Cao, Q., Shi, Y.: Automatic bdi plan recognition from process execution logs and effect logs. In: Proc. of the EMAS-2013 Workshop, Held in Conjunction with AAMAS-2013. LNCS (LNAI). Springer (to appear, 2013)
5. Ghose, A.K., Morrison, E., Gou, Y.: A novel use of big data analytics for service innovation harvesting. In: Proc. of the 2013 International Conference on Service Science and Innovation. IEEE Computer Society Press (2013)

Norm Representation and Reasoning: A Formalization in Event Calculus

Wagdi Alrawagfeh

Computer Science Department
Memorial University of Newfoundland
St.John's, NL, Canada
Wagdi.alrawagfeh@mun.ca

Abstract. Norms play an important role in coordinating, regulating and predict-ing agents' behavior in open multi-agent societies. Much work has been done on modeling and developing normative multi-agent systems. Norms in open multi-agent societies are not fixed, they might emerge, change or vanish; there-fore agents need a mechanism to adapt their behavior accordingly. Using Event Calculus we propose a formal representation of prohibition and obligation norms. This includes the norm's context, rewards and sanctions. Using this formalization we propose a technique for BDI agents to reason at run time about their behavior taking into consideration current norms and past actions performed by the agent. In this work, we assume that the best behavior of an agent is the behavior with maximum utility. Our technique has been applied to a simple mining simulation.

Keywords: Norm-representation, normative-reasoning, Event Calculus.

1   Introduction

In open multi-agent societies heterogeneous agents designed by various people enter and leave while acting autonomously towards self-interested goals [1]. In such environments norms play an important role for regulating and predicting the agents' behavior. Norms have been used as behavior constraints that regulate and coordinate heterogeneous agents' behavior and foster cooperation and minimize conflicts among them [2]. Prohibition norms describe the behavior that agents should not perform. Obligation norms describe the behavior that agents have to perform. Permission norms describe the behavior that agents can perform [3].

Electronic Institutions [4] are an approach that often assumes agents that always comply and follow the norms. Although this makes their behavior more predictable and coordinated, this drastically decreases agents' flexibility and autonomy. Among self-interested agents, their highest priority is achieving their own goals; therefore they should not mindlessly obey social norms unless they benefit from such ob-edience. Thus, most researchers in normative multi-agent systems adopt another view where norms are considered as soft constraints in which agents have the choice to comply or to violate norms [5]. We are interested in the latter approach. Similar to human societies, agents that violate norms are subject to sanctions. Sanctions have

G. Boella et al. (Eds.): PRIMA 2013, LNAI 8291, pp. 5–20, 2013.
© Springer-Verlag Berlin Heidelberg 2013

been used as a norm enforcement tool to urge agents to respect norms and keep the system stable [6]. Thus we need agents able to adapt their behavior according to their society's norms to avoid potential punishments. We face at least two challenges in building such agents. Firstly, how do agents know the prevalent norms? Secondly, because norms are subject to change or emerge at run-time, and because agents might travel to different societies that have different norms, we need an application and society independent mechanism to help agents to consider dynamic norms in their practical reasoning. In order to address these two challenges, we need to design reasoning mechanisms able to identify dynamic norms, as well as consider these norms during an agent's practical reasoning. In this paper, we are concerned with the latter challenge, and focus on reasoning mechanisms for flexible norm compliance.

Here we are not concerned with modeling normative environments or describing the behavior of multi-agent systems rather, we are concerned with the impact of norms on an individual agent's behaviors at run time. We propose a norm's formal representation using Event Calculus and an application-independent strategy for reasoning about the effects of norms on an agent's behavior. The mechanism we develop in this paper allows an agent to choose the best plan from among multiple applicable plans.

Our contributions in this paper are the following: First, we develop a formal representation of norms, taking into consideration the fact that a norm may be composed of several actions. Second, we develop a strategy to reason about AgentSpeak plans taking into consideration the society's norms and the agent's past actions. The paper is structured as follows: we briefly review Jason and Event Calculus. Then we show our norm representation and our strategy of normative reasoning. Preliminary experiments and results are presented next. We review related work and draw the conclusion in the last Section.

2   Background

2.1   Jason

Deliberative agent architectures -e.g Beliefs, Desires and Intentions (BDI) based approaches such as PRS [7], DMARS [8] and AgentSpeak(L) [9]- use a plan library for the sake of goals achievement. BDI is one of the most identifiable and studied architectures to implement practical reasoning in multi-agent systems. It has proved to be effective in designing agents that operate properly in dynamic environments [10].

Jason [11][12] is a Java-based interpreter for an extended version of AgentSpeak(L) [9]. It implements the operational semantics of AgentSpeak(L) and provides a platform for developing multi-agent systems. AgentSpeak(L) is an extension of logic programming to provide an abstract framework for programming BDI agents. The belief base is represented as a fragment of first-order logic using a logic programming syntax. Two types of goals are defined in AgentSpeak(L): Achievement goals and test goals. An achievement goal is represented by a predicate prefixed with "!", e.g, !g states that agent has the goal to achieve a world state where g is true, and therefore the agent adopt plans that try to achieve g. A test goal is represented by a predicate followed by

"?", e.g, ?g means that the agent tries to unify g with predicates in the belief base and the goal succeeds only if the unification succeeds, otherwise it fails. A Jason-agent's basic architecture has the following components: belief base, set of events, plan library and set of intentions. For achieving a goal a plan needs to be selected. A plan is structured as follows: *Triggering-event: Context <- body.*

The events that may initiate the execution of a plan are triggering events. Triggering-events could be addition "+" or deletion "-"of goals or beliefs. When an event occurs it will be matched with the plans' triggering-event in the plan library. The matched plans are called relevant plans. The context part of the relevant plans is checked against the agent belief base. The relevant plans whose contexts are logical consequences of the current belief base are called applicable plans. The body part of plans is formed of actions and sub-goals. A plan is selected from the applicable plans and added to the agent intentions set. Here, we are using Jason notation in describing our work; the name of predicates begin with lowercase letter; variables begin with capital letter. The symbol ":" separates the triggering-event part from the context part of plans. In rules, the symbol ":-"separates a rule left and right hand sides; the symbols "&" and "|" indicate a conjunction and disjunction operators respectively. The context part is separated from the body part using the symbol "<-".   Consider the following Jason plan: **+clear(Block1): clear(Block2) <- !on(Block1,Block2).** The plan states that if Block1 is announced to be clear, then if Block2, clear, then we will have the new goal of putting Block1 on Block2.

2.2   Event Calculus

Event Calculus (EC) is a logical framework consisting of predicates and axioms to represent and reason about actions and their effects. It was originally proposed in logic programming by [13]. The basic idea of EC is to state that a particular fluent is initiated to be true in a particular time-point as a result of performing a particular action(s) and in the meantime no action occurred to terminate this fluent, where a fluent is a property whose values are subject to change at different points in time. EC is based on a many-sorted first-order predicate calculus. The basic components of EC are actions A, fluents F and time T.

Table 1. The predicates of the event calculus

Predicate	Meaning
happens(A,T)	Action A occurs at time T
holdsAt(F,T)	Fluent F is true at time T
terminate(A,F,T)	Occurrence of action A at time T will make fluent F false after time T
initiates(A,F,T)	Occurrence of action A at time T will make fluent F true after time T
clipped(T,F,Tn)	Fluent F is terminated between time T and Tn
<, >, <=, >=	Standard order relation for time

In addition to the above predicates we define the predicate **between(A,T1,T2)**, which means that action **A** occurred after time **T1** and before **T2**.

If the occurrence of action **A** at time **T1** initiates the fluent **F** at **T2** where **T1** is before **T2** then, the predicate **initiates(A,F,T1)** is not sufficient to represent the delayed effect. Therefore, we replaced the **initiates(A,F,T1)** predicate by **initiatesAt(A,F,T1,T2)** predicate, where *initiatesAt(A,F,T1,T2),* states that the occurrence of action **A** at **T1** will make fluent **F** true after **T2**, when **T1≤ T2**. However, **initiatesAt(A,F,T1,T2)** has the same semantics of **initiates(A,F,T1)** when **T1=T2**.

The basic event calculus axioms (with the slight modification on the initiates predicate) that are important to our work are as follows:

- **EC1**: *clipped (T1, F, T2) :- happens(A, T) & T1≤ T & T<T2 & terminates(A, F, T)*

This means that fluent **F** is terminated by the occurrence of action **A** between time **T1** and **T2**.

- **EC3'**: *holdsAt (F, T3) :- happens(A, T1) & initiatesAt(A, F, T1,T2) & T1≤ T2 & T2<T3 & not clipped (T2, F, T3)*

This means that the fluent **F** holds at Time **T3** if the action **A** occurs at time **T1** and the fluent **F** holds after time **T2** and **F** has not terminated between **T2** and **T3**.

Event Calculus is distinguished by its simplicity in describing concepts and it easily allows implementation for concept specifications since it is based on logic programming. Therefore, EC has been used for representing different concepts in multiagent systems; see for example [14] and [15].

3   Norm Representation Overview

In order to employ norms in an agent's practical reasoning a formal representation is needed. Our view of norm follows Anderson's reduction view of norm which states that norm's violation is necessarily followed by a sanction [16]. Sanctions and rewards which have been used as signals refer to norm-violation and norm-compliance [28]. Thus in our norm representation we define fluents for those signals. Using EC, norms are represented as a sequence of actions that make fluents true. We make the pivot of our norm representation to be the signals/fluents (sanctions/rewards). This is because agents' decision to comply or violate norms will be based on the sanctions and rewards.

3.1   Norms

We define a norm as a tuple **N = <D, C, Seq, S, R>** where:

- **D** ∈ {**F,O**} is the deontic type of the norm, **F** for prohibition and **O** for obligation.
- **C** is the norm's context. The specified sequence of actions is obliged/prohibited if **C** is a logical consequence of the agent's belief base. **C** is composed of (possibly empty) β, α or both. β is composed of **holdsAt** predicates which describe a particular world state. α is an event calculus formula to represent a sequence of actions.

- **Seq** is a sequence of action(s) that agents are not supposed to perform (or have to perform) in case of prohibition (obligation)[1].
- **S** is the sanction that will be applied if the norm has been violated or not fulfilled.
- **R** is the reward that agents may get if they fulfill an obligation norm.

Sanctions and rewards may have different forms such as, feel of shame, anxiety, greeting, respect, reputation, etc. In this work **S, R** $\in$ $_{\geq 0,}$ are non-negative integer numbers.

Prohibition Norms

In a particular context, if the occurrence of a sequence of action(s) is subject to punishment then this sequence of actions is prohibited in that context.

Obligation Norms

If the nonoccurrence of prescribed sequence of action(s) in a particular context is followed by punishment then this sequence of action(s) is obligated in that context. Also, the fulfillment of this sequence might be subjected to rewards.

The punishment or reward represents an incentive for agents to change their behaviors. For that purpose we will introduce Boolean fluents:

1. **fPun(Nid,S)** represents the punishment that may result from violating a prohibition norm , where **Nid** is norm identification number (unique number for each prohibition norms instance) and **S** is the punishment value. The prohibition norm is represented as follows:

initiatesAt(An,fPun(Nid,S),Tn,Tn):- C, happens(A1,T1) &...& happens(An,Tn)& T1<T2< & ...& <Tn .

- **D = F.**   // **fPun** refers to prohibition norm's violation
- **C**: the norm's context.
- **Seq = A1,..An**. // the prohibited sequence of actions.
- **S**:   the sanction.
- **R** is empty.

    This means that if **C** entailed from agent belief base and the sequence of actions **A1,..An** occurred at time **T1,..Tn** respectively, then after time **Tn** the sanction that may be applied is **S**. The fourth argument of the **initiatesAt** predicate does not have a role in representing the prohibition norms, but we need it for representing the obligation norms.

2. **oPun(Nid,S)** represents the punishments that may result from not fulfilling obligation norms , where **Nid** is norm identification number (a unique number for each obligation norms instance) and **S** is the punishment value.

3. **oRew(Nid,R)** represents the rewards that may be granted by fulfilling obligation norms, where **R** is the reward value.

---

[1]   If the order of actions was not important in a norm then in the norm representation we omit the dependencies among T1,T2..Tn-1. However T1,T2..Tn-1 should be less than Tn.

The obligation norm is violated in a particular context if δ occurred and then δ' did not occur, where δ is a sequence of actions, possibly empty, and δ' is a sequence of prescribed non occurred action(s). Fluent **oPun(Nid,S)** will hold when a violation occurred. The **initiates(A,F,T1)** predicate is not suitable to represent the violation of obligation norms. That because it is not suitable to represent the delayed effects of actions. Therefore, we replace it by the predicate **initiatesAt(A,F,T1,T2)**. The obligation norm is represented by two rules:

initiatesAt(Ai,oPun(Nid,S),Ti,Tn):- C & happens(A1,T1) & ... & happens(Ai,Ti) &...& not happens(Aj,Tj) | ... | not happens(An,Tn) & T1< &...& <Ti< &...& <Tj< &...& <Tn.

- **D = O**. // **oPun** refers to obligation norm's violation
- **C**: the context. (as specified before)
- **Seq = Aj,....An**. // the obligatory sequence of actions
- **S**: the sanction. (as mentioned before)
- **R** is empty.

This means that if **C** entailed from the agent's belief base and a sequence of actions (possibly empty) **A1,..Ai** occurred at time **T1,..,Ti** respectively, and a sequence of actions **Aj,..,An** did not occur at **Tj,..,Tn** then after **Tn** the sanction that may be applied is **S**.

initiatesAt(An,oRew(Nid,R),Ti,Tn):- C & happens(A1,T1) & ... & happens(Ai,Ti) &...& happens(Aj,Tj) & ... & happens(An,Tn) & T1< &...& <Ti< &...& <Tj< &...& <Tn.

Which means; if **C** entailed from agent's belief base and a sequence of actions (possibly empty) **A1,..Ai** occurred at time **T1,..Ti** respectively, and a sequence of actions **Aj,..,An** occurred at **Tj,..,Tn** then after **Tn** the reward that may be granted is **R**.

Example 1,
In a particular auction, if an agent bids and wins, then within 24 hours it should pay for the item and fill a survey. If so the agent will receive a discount code of $5 for the next purchase, otherwise, the agent will be added to the auction's black list.

Here the violation occurred if the agent performs the action "bid" and does not perform the actions "pay" or "fill_survey" (where the context is "win" after "bid"). Here, δ = **happens(bid,T1)**, δ'= **not happens(pay,T3) or not happens(fill_survey,T4)** where T1<T2<T3<T4 and the context is **holdsAt(win,T2)**.

The weight/value of being added to the black list is different from agent to agent. Therefore, we believe that this value should be assigned by the agent itself. This value could be based on agents' designed objectives and beliefs. Assume that for my agent this punishment value is equivalent to $10. This obligation norm will be represented as follows:

initiatesAt(bid,oPun(1,$10),T1,T4):- happens(bid,T1) & holdsAt(win,T2) & not happens(pay,T3) | not happens(fill_survey,T4) & T1<T2 & T2<T3 & T3<T4.

InitiatesAt(bid,oRew(1,$5),T1,T4):- happens(bid,T1) & holdsAt(win,T2) & happens(pay,T3) & happens(fill_survey,T4) & T1<T2 & T2<T3 & T3<T4.

As we saw above, norms might be composed of several actions. Consider another example:

Example 2,

In a particular society the obligation norm is "at Christmas you should call your parents, visit them and give them a gift. Otherwise they might feel disappointed. Here, Christmas is the norm's context, the person should do three actions to fulfill this obligation norm; call, visit and give. The punishment of violating this norm is parents' disappointment. In this example, δ is empty (in this case the first and third arguments of the predicate **initiatesAt** are always variables) and δ'= **not happens(call,T1) or not happens(visit,T2) or not happens(give,T3)** where T1<T2<T3. Assuming that there are no rewards of this norm's fulfillment then we need one rule to represent the norm:

initiatesAt(A,oPun(normID, disappointed),T0,T3):- holdsAt(christmas,T1) &
not happens(call,T1) | not happens(visit,T2) | not happens(give,T3) &
T1<T2<T3 .

3.2 Normative Reasoning Strategy

In this section we present a strategy that helps our agent to adapt its behaviors according to the society's norms. After the applicable plans are selected our strategy utilizes them and finds the best plan to be added to the agent's intention set. Our strategy could be added to the BDI interpreter to add the normative reasoning ability. In Fig.1, an overview of the basic BDI interpreter is illustrated as white boxes, while our proposed additions are presented as gray boxes. In order to deal with dynamic norms (new and abrogated norms) our normative reasoning strategy should be combined with the norm identification process. The norm identification process enables the agent to discover new and abrogated norms and represents the new norms as beliefs in the belief base. However, the norm identification process is outside of the scope of this paper [17].

To the best of our knowledge, previous work in normative reasoning does not take an agent's history into consideration. Most of the previous work checks whether a plan under investigations separately respects the norms or not. An agent may have a plan P1 and a plan P2, and both of them separately respect norms. However performing P1 and then P2 may violate norms if P1 has one or more actions that, when combined with one or more actions from P2, violates norms. Our strategy enables the agent to discover such potential violation. For example, suppose that the sanction of crossing a red light three times is driver license suspension. Thus, without taking the

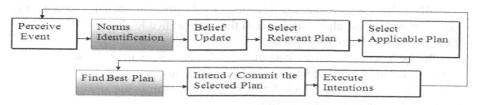

Fig. 1. Reasoning processes flow

driver/agent past actions into consideration in the normative reasoning, agent will not be able to discover such violations.

We introduce the following fluent that states whether a plan has more profits than losses. The fluent **help(Plan)** will be true if the execution of **Plan** has more rewards than punishments. The rewards value comes from achieving the goal that is associated with **Plan** and fulfilling obligation norms. The punishments value comes from violating prohibition norms or not fulfilling obligation norms. We define a predicate **goal-preference(G,Points)** to describe the preference of achieving goal **G**, where **Points** is an integer number refer to the importance of **G** and the goal importance is determined according to the agent's designed objectives. For the sake of normative reasoning our agent uses the following application-independent axioms:

EC1 & EC3' from Section 3

Ax1:   between(A,T1,T2) :- happens(A, T) & T1<T & T<T2

Ax2: terminates(*,help(P),T):- happens(*,T)

Ax3: terminates(*,fPun(I,S),T):- happens(*,T)

Ax4: terminates(*,oPun(I,S),T):- happens(*,T)

Ax5: terminates(*,oRew(I,S),T):- happens(*,T)

Where * is an application-independent special event that refers to the fact that the associated fluents becomes false after **T**. In addition to the above application-independent axioms, we introduce the following rule (we call it helpful-rule).

Helpful-Rule:

initiatesAt(K,help(Plan_i),T1,T2):-.findall(V1,holdsAt(oRew(_,V1),T2+1), Wins)   &   .findall(V2,holdsAt(fPun(_,V2),T2+1),   Loses1)   & .findall(V3,holdsAt(oPun(_,V3),T2+1),   Loses2)   & goalpreference(G,Points) & Points + sum(Wins)- sum(Loses1) - sum(Loses2)> 0.

by asserting action **K** (see algorithm-1), we pretend that **K** has occurred). **findall(V,P,S)** function -as in Prolog and Jason- return all the values of **V** where predicate **P** is true and variable **S** instantiates with the sum of values **V**. **sum(Wins)** will have the rewards that may be granted if **Plan_i** was executed. **sum(Loses1)** and **sum(Loses2)** will have the sanctions that may result if the plan was executed. We can now define how our agent finds a best plan. We need the following additional definitions:

— Let *act(Π)* be a function that returns the sequence of actions of the plan Π, (**A1,A2,...An**). Before the agent takes the decision of intending/committing planΠ, it will use the algorithm-1 to find the most profitable plan.
— Let Γ be the set of applicable plans.
— Let **Bel** be a belief base represents the agent's knowledge about the society along with the society's norms represented in Event Calculus.
— Let Ω = EC1, EC3', Ax1, Ax2, Ax3, Ax4, Ax5, helpful-rule and Bel.
These are used in the following algorithm.

```
Algorithm -1 //find best plan
Input: applicable plans.
Output: best plan. // the plan with the highest utility.
```

```
1:   function FindBestPlan(Γ)
2:   for all Π in Γ do
3:       for all θ ∈ act(Π) do
4:           Bel ← Bel ∪ happens(θ,T++).
     // T is the current time.   // Next action will be as-
serted at T+1, etc.
5:       end for
6:       T← current time.
7:       if Ω ⊢ holdsAt(help(Π),T) then
8:           utility(Π)← Points + sum(Wins) - sum(Loses1)-
sum(Loses2).   // see helpful-rule.
9:       end if
10:    delete the asserted predicates at 2,3 and 4 above.
11:  end for
12:  Bestplan ← max { utility(Γ) }.
13:  End Function
```

As we see in the algorithm above, lines 3-5 the agent will add the predicates **happens** (see Table-1) starting from time **T1** which represent the current time. The actions specified in the predicate **happens** have not occurred yet. By adding them, the agent pretends that he has executed them in order to reason if the current plan Π is helpful or not. Plan Π is helpful if the predicate **holdsAt(help(Π),T)** is deduced from current belief base; hence, the rewards are more than losses. The plan of maximum utility will be ready for execution by adding it to the intentions. When the intended plan is executed the **happens** predicate for each executed action will be added to the belief base (same as in lines 3-5 in the algorithm above). If the last action is asserted at time **Tn** then predicate **happens(*,Tn+1)** will be asserted. The purpose of this addition is to terminate the fluents (**help, fPun, oPun** and **oRew**) after **Tn+1**. Thus, if the past executed plans were causing norm violation/ fulfilling then we do not want this violation/fulfillment to be discovered again in the future.   However, our strategy discovers the violation/fulfillment that results from combining the current plan (under investigation) with the past executed plans. As we see in Fig.2. Our strategy discovers violation2/fulfillment2 and violation3/fullfilment3. Violations-1/fulfillments-1 does not have to be included because they are already discovered in the past. In other words, the agent should not be punished or rewarded more than one time for the same act.

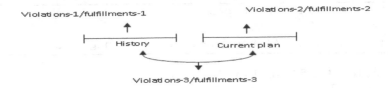

Fig. 2. The actions that are included in the normative reasoning

4   Experiments

We applied our work to a mineral mining society which has been adapted from the Gold Miners scenario[2]. In this scenario, gold and silver pieces are scattered in a grid-like territory and the agents collect the scattered pieces to their respective depot (one for silver and one for gold). Our agent is associated with goals and engaged in this society. We assume that there are a set of norms which govern the society. By providing our agent with the proposed norm representation and the normative reasoning strategy, it should be able to choose the profitable behavior (the behavior of highest utility).

The society has five agents: Our agent is equipped with our normative reasoning strategy and one other agent chooses a plan randomly from the applicable plans. The remaining three agents do not have direct roles in our current comparison. They exist in the society just to reflect the fact that other agents are sharing the society; therefore if the two agents (under comparison) spend a long time in reasoning then other agents may race them and collect all or most of the pieces. In our experiments, the game has 25 gold pieces and 15 silver pieces. Once the gold and silver have been collected the game is over. The comparison is done between our agent and the second agent (call it OtherAgent). We assume that the norms are already identified and represented in the belief base. Since the work in this paper is in its preliminary stages the aim of the experiment is to show that our agent is able to utilize our reasoning strategy and choose the best available behavior in the presence of norms.

4.1   Mineral Mining Society

We add our agent and OtherAgent to this society to achieve their goals taking into consideration the society's norms. Agents in this society can do the actions: **pick(-)**, **drop(-,-) and moveto(-,-)**.
The two agents have one continuous goal, **!collect(gold)**, and the following plan library for achieving the goal:

```
@plan1-1 // the agent will collect gold to the silver de-
pot.
  +!collect(gold): free <- !find(gold,X,Y); moveto(X,Y) ;
pick(gold); moveto(silver_depotX,silver_depotY) ;
drop(gold,silver_depot).
```

---

[2] http://jason.sourceforge.net/Jason/Examples

```
@plan1-2// the agent will collect gold to the gold depot.
+!collect(gold): free <- !find(gold,X,Y); moveto(X,Y) ;
pick(gold); moveto(gold_depotX,gold_depotY);
drop(gold,gold_depot).
```

```
@plan1-3 // the agent will collect gold to the gold depot
and collect silver to silver depot.
+!collect(gold): free <- !find(gold,X,Y); moveto(X,Y) ;
pick(gold); moveto(gold_depotX,gold_depotY);
drop(gold,gold_depot); !find(silver,X1,Y1); pick(silver);
moveto(silver_depotX,silver_depotY);
drop(silver,silver_depot).
```

```
@plan1-4 // the agent will collect gold to the gold depot
and collect another gold to the gold depot.
+!collect(gold): free <- !find(gold,X,Y); moveto(X,Y) ;
pick(gold); moveto(gold_depotX,gold_depotY);
drop(gold,gold_depot);  !find(gold,X1,Y1); moveto(X1,Y1)
; pick(gold); moveto(gold_depotX,gold_depotY);
drop(gold,gold_depot);
```

For the goal "!collect(gold)" we define its achievement importance using the predicate **goalpreference(collect(gold), 10)**. We suppose that the mineral mining society has the following norms. The norms are represented as we specified in Section 3.1

Prohibition Norms

- It is prohibited to drop gold in the silver's depot if the gold's depot is not full, the sanction value is 5.

initiatesAt(drop(gold,silver_depot),fPun(1,5),T,T):-   not   holdsAt(full(gold_depot),T) happens(drop(gold,silver_depot),T).

- It is prohibited to drop silver in the gold's depot if the silver's depot is not full, the sanction value is 10.

initiatesAt   (drop(silver,gold_depot),fPun(2,10),T,T):-   not   holdsAt(full(silver_depot),T) & happens(drop(silver,gold_depot),T).

- It is prohibited to carry more than one gold piece at the same time, the sanction value is 10

initiatesAt(pick(gold),fPun(3,10),T2,T2):- happens(pick(gold),T1) & happens(pick(gold),T2) & T1<T2 & not between(drop(gold,_),T1,T2).

Obligation Norms

- It is obligatory to collect silver immediately after collecting gold, the sanction value is 10. The reward for adhering is 10.

initiatesAt(pick(gold),oPun(1,10),T1,T3):-happens(pick(gold),T1) & happens(drop(gold,_),T2)& happens(pick(gold),T3) & not between(pick(silver),T2,T3) & T1<T2 & T2<T3.

initiatesAt(pick(gold),oRew(1,10),T1,T3):- happens(pick(gold),T1) & happens(drop(gold,_),T2)& happens(pick(gold),T3) & between(pick(silver),T2,T3) & T1<T2 & T2<T3.

In Fig.3, the experiment results show that our proposed normative reasoning strategy helps our agent to achieve his goal as well as maximize its accumulative profits. As we see at the X axis the two agents under comparison collected at most 12 pieces of gold and silver out of 40. That because the other three agents do not rely on the plan library, but just collect any piece they find.   The experiment was repeated ten times and the average results were recorded.

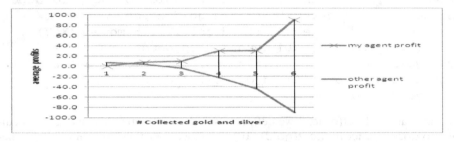

Fig. 3. Comparison Results

5   Related Work

In this section we review some work that deals with the impact of norms in autonomous agent reasoning. In [18] a normative agent architecture was proposed and a programming language was used in their investigation of normative practical reasoning. The architecture was more concerned with fulfilling specific norms than goals. The architecture was driven by norms instead of mental states (as in traditional BDI agents). They studied the problem of norm inconsistency that may result when agents adopt new norms. In [19] the researchers extended BDI based agents to allow them to change their behaviors in response to newly accepted norms. In their work a new plan is created to comply with obligation norms, and suppressing a plan when it violates a prohibition norm. In their reasoning strategy a plan is suppressed if it has at least one action that violates a norm. However it could be beneficial for an agent to execute a particular plan even if it has an action that violates a norm.   For example the rewards of achieving a goal and the rewards of fulfilling obligation norms could be more than the value of the punishment of violating some prohibition norms. In our approach we take this point into consideration; therefore, a plan could be chosen for execution even if it violates norms. In our model all the applicable plans' actions have been taken into consideration in reasoning about norms and at the same time agents' behaviors are still driven by goals.

Researchers in [20] proposed a technique for taking norms into consideration in describing how to execute a plan. They define norms as constraints on the values of variables in the actions descriptions. Our work here differs from their work in the view and the definition of norms. Their norms are constraint based, so norms describe the manner in which the action should be executed when this action is selected for execution. Researchers in [21] extended BDI programming language 2APL [22] to support normative concepts, prohibition, obligation, sanction, duration and deadline. An exogenous organization sends the prohibition and obligation norms to the agent. Similar to [23] the obligation norm is stored as a goal to be fulfilled with a priority related to the violation's sanction. The prohibition norms are stored in the agent event base. They define deadline execution for plans and they investigate plans scheduling based on the deadline. Feasible plans are checked against the norms. If a plan has an action that violate prohibition norm of a priority greater than or equal the priority of the plan then the plan was not selected. Similar to [19] a plan is checked against one prohibition, but here if the goal preference is greater than the sanction the plan is adopted. However, based on this a plan is adopted even if it violates several prohibitions if each prohibition sanction separately is less than the goal preference.

In [24] a methodology for normative reasoning at run-time was proposed. They develop a design-time and run-time institution (normative system) in the context of BDI agents. They assume agents can query a special agent (InstitutionKeeper) about the normative states. They used Jason interpreter to implement their work. Their agent do reasoning as follows: the agent gets percepts from the environment and normative percepts from a special agent called InstitutionKeepr. The InstitutionKeeper stores the normative state and handle all institution instantiation. Before an agent executes an action it asks the InstitutionKeeper whether it is forbidden to perform it. In contrast to our model their agent is dependent in a special agent in the institution to help him do normative reasoning.

In spite of the fact that planning is outside of the scope of BDI practical reasoning, some interesting work [19][25] adds planning capabilities to the normative reasoning strategy. Researchers in [26] proposed v-BDI as an extension to the BDI architecture to enable normative reasoning, selecting and customizing plan to ensure norm compliance. The normative process is applied on the entire plan library. However, the efforts of this process will be wasted if a plan was irrelevant or inapplicable. In our technique the agent does the normative reasoning just for the applicable plans (the plan that has context logically consequent to the agent current beliefs). Also in our norm representation we deal with sanctions and rewards.

Researchers in [14] used EC for representing normative positions. They restrict their attention to obligation and permission. They assumed that any action not permitted is prohibited. The work in [15] supposed that any action that is not prohibited nor obliged is permitted. In our work we did not add permission norms in our reasoning model. This will be part of our future work to improve our proposed normative reasoning strategy. To the best of our knowledge, previous normative reasoning strategies do not take into consideration the agent's past actions as we do here in this work. Also, in the norm representation, nobody explicitly discusses the ability of representing norms that are composed of several actions. When we designed our model we took into consideration the fact that the future work for our model supposes that our agent does not know norms beforehand but it identifies norms of the society at run-time. Therefore, we do not have that freedom in representing norms. Norm identification is outside of the scope of this paper so we started our work in this paper assuming that norms have been identified and represented by EC. The norm representation method that we have adopted (EC) is powerful enough to represent more complex norms than those identified in [27][28]. This implies that the development that could be applied on norm identification approach in [17][27] such as identifying the world state, agents role, more detailed context, etc, could be added to our representation method.

Work in [14] and [26] did not differentiate punishment severity. They do count the number of times a violation occurred. It is clear that decision making based on the number of violations will not be a precise decision because a punishment for one violation could be more severe than several accumulated punishments. For example the punishment of killing a person is more severe than the punishments of shouting in a library or not returning a book.

6   Conclusion

Using Event Calculus we developed a new norm representation formalism to enable agents to use norms in their practical reasoning. For norm representation, we introduced three fluents: fPun and oPun to refer to prohibition norm violation and obligation norm violation respectively, and oRew for obligation norm fulfillment. The proposed norm representation is able to represent norms that are composed of several actions along with the norm's context. Our proposed normative reasoning strategy helps our agent in choosing the most profitable plan. It takes into consideration the potential violations/fulfilling with the current plan and the potential violation/fulfillments that may result from the combination of agent's past actions and the actions of the current plan. The most profitable plan is the plan with the highest utility. Therefore, our agent might choose a plan that has some norms violations if the profits of performing that plan are more than the losses.

We have implemented our work using the Jason BDI interpreter [12]. However, we believe that our approach is general enough to allow us to use any BDI interpreter. We have shown the applicability of our approach by developing a simple mineral mining scenario. As future work, we plan to complete the picture by adding the norm identification ability to our agent. We believe that adding permission norms to our proposed normative reasoning strategy will improve agent rationality especially in uncertain environment.

Acknowledgements. I would like to very gratefully acknowledge the enthusiastic help of Dr. Felipe Meneguzzi with both technical and presentational aspects of this work. I would also like to thank Dr. Todd Wareham for his advice that improved the presentation of the paper.

References

1. Ramchurn, S.D., Huynh, T.D., Jennings, N.R.: Trust in multi-agent systems. The Knowledge Engineering Review 19(1), 1–25 (2004)
2. Boella, G., van der Torre, L.: A Game-Theoretic Approach to Normative Multi-Agent Systems. In: Dagstuhl Seminar Proceedings 07122 - Normative Multi-Agent Systems. LZI, Dagstuhl (2007)
3. Boella, G., van der Torre, L.: Regulative and constitutive norms in normative multi-Agent systems. In: Proceedings of 9th International Conference on the Principles of Knowledge Representation and Reasoning (KR 2004), pp. 255–265. AAAI Press (2004)
4. Esteva, M., Rodríguez-Aguilar, J.-A., Sierra, C., Garcia, P., Arcos, J.-L.: On the formal specification of electronic institutions. In: Sierra, C., Dignum, F.P.M. (eds.) AgentLink 2000. LNCS (LNAI), vol. 1991, pp. 126–147. Springer, Heidelberg (2001)
5. Aldewereld, H., Dignum, F., García-Camino, A., Noriega, P., Rodríguez- Aguilar, J.A., Sierra, C.: Operationalisation of norms for usage in electronic institutions. In: Proceedings of the Fifth International Joint Conference on Autonomous Agents and MultiAgent Systems (AAMAS 2006), pp. 223–225. ACM Press, New York (2006)
6. Castelfranchi, C.: Formalizing the informal?: Dynamic social order, bottom-up social control, and spontaneous normative relations. JAL 1(1-2), 47–92 (2004)
7. Rao, A.S., Georgeff, M.: BDI Agents: from Theory to Practice. In: Proceedings of the 1st International Conference on Multi-Agent Systems, San Francisco, CA, pp. 312–319 (1995)
8. d'Inverno, M., Kinny, D., Luck, M., Wooldridge, M.: A formal specification of dMARS. In: Singh, M.P., Rao, A.S., Wooldridge, M. (eds.) ATAL 1997. LNCS, vol. 1365, pp. 155–176. Springer, Heidelberg (1998)
9. Rao, A.S.: AgentSpeak(L): BDI agents speak out in a logical computable language. In: Van de Velde, W., Perram, J. (eds.) MAAMAW 1996. LNCS, vol. 1038, pp. 42–55. Springer, Heidelberg (1996)
10. Dignum, F., Morley, D., Sonenberg, E., Cavedon, L.: Towards socially sophisticated BDI agents. In: Durfee, E. (ed.) Proceedings of the International Conference on Multi-agent Systems (ICMAS 2000), pp. 111–118. IEEE Press (2000)
11. Bordini, R.H., Hübner, J.F.: BDI Agent Programming in AgentSpeak Using *Jason*. In: Toni, F., Torroni, P. (eds.) CLIMA 2005. LNCS (LNAI), vol. 3900, pp. 143–164. Springer, Heidelberg (2006)
12. Bordini, R.H., Huebner, J.F., Wooldridge, M.: Programming Multi-Agent Systems in AgentSpeak using Jason. Wiley (2007)
13. Kowalski, R.A., Sergot, M.J.: A logic-based calculus of events. New Generation Computing 4(1), 67–95 (1986)
14. Artikis, A., Kamara, L., Pitt, J., Sergot, M.: A Protocol for Resource Sharing in Norm-Governed Ad Hoc Networks. In: Leite, J., Omicini, A., Torroni, P., Yolum, P. (eds.) DALT 2004. LNCS (LNAI), vol. 3476, pp. 221–238. Springer, Heidelberg (2005)
15. Fornara, N., Colombetti, M.: Specifying artificial institutions in the event calculus. In: Dignum, V. (ed.) Handbook of Research on Multi-agent Systems: Semantics and Dynamics of Organizational Models, pp. 335–366. IGI Global, Hershey (2009)
16. Soeteman, A.: Pluralism and Law: Amsterdam. In: Proceedings of the 20th IVR World Congress of the International Association for Philosophy of Law and Social Philosophy (IVR), Legal Reasoning, vol. 4, p. 104 (2001)
17. Alrawagfeh, W., Brown, E., Mata-Montero, M.: Identifying norms of behaviour in multi-agent societies. In: The Seventh Conference of the European Social Simulation Association (ESSA), Montpellier, France, September 19-23 (2011)

18. Kollingbaum, M.: Norm-governed Practical Reasoning Agents. Ph.D. Dissertation, University of Aberdeen (2005)
19. Meneguzzi, F., Luck, M.: Norm-based behaviour modification in BDI agents. In: Proceedings of the Eighth International Joint Conference on Autonomous Agents and Multiagent Systems (AAMAS 2009), Budapest, pp. 177–184 (2009)
20. Oren, N., Vasconcelos, W., Meneguzzi, F., Luck, M.: Acting on Norm Constrained Plans. In: Leite, J., Torroni, P., Ågotnes, T., Boella, G., van der Torre, L. (eds.) CLIMA XII 2011. LNCS, vol. 6814, pp. 347–363. Springer, Heidelberg (2011)
21. Alechina, N., Dastani, M., Logan, B.: Programming norm-aware agents. In: Procs. 11th Int'l Conf. on Autonomous Agents & Multiagent Systems (AAMAS 2012), Valencia, Spain, vol. 2, pp. 1057–1064. IFAAMAS (2012)
22. Dastani, M.: 2APL: A practical agent programming language. Autonomous Agents and Multi-Agent Systems 16(3), 214–248 (2008)
23. Criado, N., Argente, E., Botti, V.: Rational Strategies for Norm Compliance in the n-BDI Proposal. In: De Vos, M., Fornara, N., Pitt, J.V., Vouros, G. (eds.) COIN 2010. LNCS, vol. 6541, pp. 1–20. Springer, Heidelberg (2011)
24. Balke, T., De Vos, M., Padget, J.A., Traskas, D.: Normative run-time reasoning for institutionally-situated BDI agents. In: Proceedings - 2011 IEEE/WIC/ACM International Joint Conferences on Web Intelligence and Intelligent Agent Technology, vol. 3, pp. 1–4. IEEE Computer Society, Piscataway (2011)
25. Panagiotidi, S., Vázquez-Salceda, J.: Towards Practical Normative Agents: A Framework and an Implementation for Norm-Aware Planning. In: Cranefield, S., van Riemsdijk, M.B., Vázquez-Salceda, J., Noriega, P. (eds.) COIN 2011. LNCS, vol. 7254, pp. 93–109. Springer, Heidelberg (2012)
26. Meneguzzi, F., Vasconcelos, W., Oren, N., Luck, M.: Nu-BDI: Norm-aware BDI Agents. In: Proceedings of the 10th European Workshop on Multi-Agent Systems, Dublin, Ireland (2012)
27. Alrawagfeh, W., Brown, E., Mata-Montero, M.: Norms of Behaviour and Their Identification and Verification in Open Multi-Agent Societies. International Journal of Agent Technologies and Systems (IJATS) 3(3), 1–16 (2011), doi:10.4018/jats.2011070101.
28. Savarimuthu, B.T.R.: Mechanisms for norm emergence and norm identification in multi-agent societies (Thesis, Doctor of Philosophy). University of Otago (2011)

Evaluating the Cost of Enforcement by Agent-Based Simulation: A Wireless Mobile Grid Example

Tina Balke[1,2], Marina De Vos[2], and Julian Padget[2]

[1] University of Surrey, Centre for Research in Social Simulation
t.balke@surrey.ac.uk
[2] University of Bath, Dept. of Computer Science
{mdv,jap}@cs.bath.ac.uk

Abstract. The subject of this paper is the cost of enforcement, to which we take a satisficing approach through the examination of marginal cost-benefit ratios. Social simulation is used to establish that less enforcement can be beneficial overall in economic terms, depending on the costs to system and/or stakeholders arising from enforcement. The results are demonstrated by means of a case study of wireless mobile grids (WMGs). In such systems the dominant strategy for economically rational users is to free-ride, i.e. to benefit from the system without contributing to it. We examine the use of enforcement agents that police the system and punish users that take but do not give. The agent-based simulation shows that a certain proportion of enforcement agents increases cooperation in WMG architectures. The novelty of the results lies in our empirical evidence for the diminishing marginal utility of enforcement agents: that is how much defection they can foreclose at what cost. We show that an increase in the number of enforcement agents does not always increase the overall benefits-cost ratio, but that with respect to satisficing, a minimum proportion of enforcement agents can be identified that yields the best results.

1 Introduction

Open systems that are sustained by the contributions, in whatever form, of the participants are fragile because of their susceptibility to free-riding. Ostrom [1] has famously documented and analysed many such scenarios, a pre-dominant feature of which is their reliance on zero or low participant turnover. Ostrom's work focuses on (semi-)closed systems in which contributions can be reinforced through mechanisms such as identity and sanctions such as ostracism. Identity is a more slippery notion in open systems, and both that and high turnover, render ineffective sanctions depending on long-term relationships and individual need for the resource created by the system. Open systems tend to rely upon other means to protect themselves and their participants, amongst which is the use of enforcement agents – a kind of police. The important distinction between such systems and Ostrom's is that behaviour is no longer self-regulating, but rather there are agents whose responsibility it is to observe behaviour, detect infractions and mete out punishment. This task then has a cost for these agents and a benefit to the system as a whole. Consequently, it is common for the system somehow to reward such agents.

G. Boella et al. (Eds.): PRIMA 2013, LNAI 8291, pp. 21–36, 2013.

As a result of the costs incurred by enforcement agents, for each such system, the questions to be answered are in particular: how many enforcement agents are needed? how much will they cost? and, how much free-riding can be tolerated? All these questions are related to the concept of "satisficing" [2] which suggests a decision-making strategy that attempts to meet criteria for adequacy, rather than optimality. We will describe the concept in more detail later in this paper.

An analytical initial estimate to answer the issues above might be possible, but begs many questions of the assumptions made about participant behaviour and effectively ignores how behaviour may change in response to system rules: will participants continue current behaviour – in the case of a rule change in an existing system – and what behaviour will participants adopt – in the case of a new system? Analytical solutions, such as game theory, also have problems in other areas such as: (1) identifying implicit but unknown effect in models, (2) enabling the testing of alternative settings and parameter sweeps, [3] which is why we opt for simulation as tool to explore the parameter space of a system that is open to free-riding and to evaluate different approaches to encouraging system sustaining behaviour.

The subject of this paper is how agent-based simulation can help answer the above kinds of questions and to illustrate the approach we take the scenario of the wireless mobile grid (WMG) [4], without prejudice as to the concept's viability. In situations where several people are interested in the same content or data (e.g. financial news, sports events,...) there are two aspects to the WMG:

1. Mobile devices download (some parts of) a resource over 3G, but opportunistically share (to acquire the whole) using peer-to-peer protocols over ad-hoc wireless networks, and
2. Infrastructure contention is lowered in densely populated situations, due to local sharing reducing the demand on 3G access.

There are individual and system benefits to each of these. The first, as well as potentially offering a speed advantage, also uses less power (the energy cost per bit for WLAN transmission is much lower than for 3G [5]) which results in longer handset standby times. The second means that network providers do not have to build infrastructure to allow for total peak demand, which may be occasional and volatile (e.g. sports events, financial districts, airports), yet can still deliver large volumes of digital content – demand for which is rising rapidly – to large numbers of users. With these benefits, WMGs contribute to a better utilization and thus sustainable handling of resources (i.e. battery capacity and networks).

The effectiveness of the WMG depends on user participation and collaboration, which raises the question of how that may be realized. The strategic user may place their own benefit above that of the collective. This matters because collaboration in a WMG comes at the cost of battery consumption. Hence, a rational user will choose to access resources without commitment from themselves. However, if a substantial proportion of users take this path, the network is unsustainable and all users are deprived of the benefits arising from cooperation [6].

However, since collaboration is essential for WMG to work and beneficial to the participants as a whole, it may be desirable to encourage it and even enforce it. Since purely technical solutions for enforcement are frequently subverted (see [7] for example), costly to implement and difficult to replace, the WMG designers have sought to employ non-technical enforcement mechanisms in addition to potential hardware solutions. Balke [8] sets out a taxonomy of approaches for non-hardware dependent enforcement in a WMG-like environment, from which we select one particular mechanism, namely encouraging cooperation through *enforcement agents*. These enforcement agents are given the task of policing the WMG. For this purpose they participate in the system with normative power [9] and permission from the system owner to punish negative behaviour (i.e. free-riding) when detected, by imposing sanctions. Police officers are an example of enforcement agents in the real world: in contrast to "normal" citizens, they are empowered by the state to – in their function as police officers – carry out actions like arrests, etc.

This paper presents results from a social simulation developed for the purpose of analysing the effect of enforcement agents on the above outlined cooperation problem, which we situate in the context of WMGs, i.e. an example of an open-distributed system[1]. In the next section (Sec. 2), to make this paper self-contained, we summarize the key elements of WMG, how cooperation may occur, how enforcement agents help and discuss related work on mobile grids and on enforcement. Sec. 3 describes how WMGs and participating and enforcement agents are modelled in the simulation. The simulation results, their analysis and the discussion of the "satisficing" criterion are presented in Sec. 4, where the focus is strictly on the costs of enforcement related to energy consumption and cooperation benefits in the WMG.

2 Enforcement and WMGs

As noted earlier, Fitzek et al. [4] have proposed the WMG concept in order to address both energy and scalability issues arising from the high consumer up-take of edge devices utilising digital services.

The key activity in WMG is the creation of ad-hoc networks between temporarily co-located devices, in which they use short-range communication, such as wireless LAN or Bluetooth. One advantage of such communications is that, compared to 3G cellular HSDPA/LTE infrastructure communication, the energy cost per transmitted bit is much lower – approximately 1/25th or 4% of the 3G cost. For the discussion here, we assume the use of the IEEE802.11 WLAN specification, which has the highest energy saving potential and according to [5] the best potential for WMG applications.

The intrinsic weakness of the WMG proposal is that energy consumption benefits are only achievable through cooperation. In Ostrom's terms, the participants contribute resources to form a common pool [1], which all may then use to achieve a common goal, say through the downloading of part of map, video or other data fragments, which they are all interested in and which can then be combined into a whole[2]. From a utility maximisation perspective, it should be better to cooperate than act individually, but

---

[1] A preliminary and limited version of these results has been presented at a workshop. Those proceedings have not been archived.

[2] For the WMG situation situation this implies that instead of each downloading the same files, mobile phone users interested in the same data – e.g. financial news or videos from big sports events – each only download part of the files and obtain the remaining parts via the more battery efficient WLAN connection, instead of 3G.

there is a risk that the cost of subscription to the WMG outweighs the gains. Thus, a (bounded) rational actor should free-ride on the WMG, except that if all actors do the same, there is no WMG.

Given that the WMG is proposed as a potential real business concept, free-riding is particularly problematic for parties trying to advance its commercial value and investing in its development. These parties are namely the telecommunications providers which, for the sake of simplicity, we assume are the same as the infrastructure providers. For these parties it is important to assess at an early stage of development of the WMG whether it is worth investing in the idea or not, by assessing:

1. Whether mechanisms can be put in place to reduce/prevent free-riding, or at least limit its impact, and
2. Whether it is possible to assess the associated costs of those mechanisms.

Enforcement agents are one such approach (others are discussed shortly), but such services are not going to be without cost themselves. Thus, it is necessary to analyse both the monetary costs (to the service providers) of employing enforcement agents, and the costs in terms of total resource consumption (in particular energy) in the system.

Having decided to examine the viability of enforcement agents in WMG, some choices are required about the form of reward and the powers they shall have within the system. It is useful to make an analogy with police officers:

1. They are paid by a state to help to ensure that the law is upheld,
2. They do not have any greater physical abilities than a "normal" citizen, but
3. They do have special rights and powers to carry out their job.

Similarly, enforcement agents participate in the WMG to observe whether free-riding is taking place, and in return receive free or reduced price phone services. We assume that the enforcement agents always report honestly, when free-riding is observed, and it is for the service provider to apply a sanction to the offending users. Sanctions could take several forms, such as limitation of the contract, contractual fines or sending battery-intensive messages to violators. This last is the option taken in this study.

2.1 Combating Free-Riding

There is a large literature in economics and social sciences on cooperation and free-riding and the mechanisms to overcome the latter. One of the most well-known analyses is by Ostrom [10], who shows that in small (relatively closed) communities these "tragedies" can be overcome. However, as noted in the introduction, open systems are qualitatively different and typically require quite different solutions, for which the literature can be broken into four broad classes of solutions which can be applied separately or in combination with one another:

1. **Technological Approaches:** In WMG, this means "hard-wiring and/or hard-coding restrictions" into the technological components (hardware and software) of mobile phones or into the protocols [11]. Drawbacks to technological solutions are that:
   (a) adaptations at run-time can be difficult or impossible to implement,
   (b) users might feel too restricted and not adopt WMG at all

(c) user modifications may render technological solutions ineffective [12, Ch.16].

2. **Formal Normative Concerns:** In this group works typically range from the analysis of structural relationships between system entities [13] to the discussion of operational semantics of the norms present in free-riding-like settings [14].

3. **Cognitive Aspects:** Includes the adoption or internalization of norms, the role or modes of learning and adaptation that may be associated with punishment of free-riding, or the effectiveness of punishing free-riders depending on the cognitive make-up of participants [15][3].

4. **Economics-Inspired Approaches:** Most of the works in this category focus on punishing free-riding as a deterrent to the rational behaviour of utility-based participants (e.g. [16]). Thus, a punishment is a fine taken from the the participant's benefits. Effectiveness is usually measured against the system equilibria, that is the points where the competing (cooperation *versus* punishment) influences balance out [17]. Methodology has been either game-theoretic (see [18] for example) or experimental (including agent-based simulations) [19,20]. Reputation mechanisms are one example here, on the grounds that a bad reputation may lead to future negative utilities (e.g. if no cooperation partners can be found due to a bad reputation) [21].

The approach adopted in this study falls into the last category above: the sanctions are fines on the free-riding agents, for which they must account in their utility considerations. In contrast to [22], we account for the costs of enforcement. These are primarily the energy costs of the enforcement agents in using their phones, but we also account for fixed overhead costs to network providers in paying each enforcement agent for its service. One paper simulating enforcement and its costs is by [23], who investigate enforcement costs in ostracism situations. For reasons already given we believe their closed world ostracism assumption is problematic for open distributed systems. Consequently, we take both the simulation approach and the proposals for which enforcement costs to consider in [23] as a starting point and adapt and extend it to account for features of the WMG domain. Agent-based simulation is the vehicle for our analysis for two reasons:

1. Simulation allows the testing of different hypotheses and parameter settings in a controlled environment, and
2. The scenario requires a heterogeneous population of phone users, whose proportions and individual behaviours can be varied.

The users are mobile, have limited information about the system and are assumed to make bounded rational decisions on the basis of their goals and the environment they operate in. This highly complex setting is inappropriate for analytical modelling, so an empirical approach remains the best way to test our hypotheses about the cost and effectiveness of enforcement.

---

[3] As such, reputation mechanisms have a place here, if the participants are cognitive agents that are affected by poor reputation. We discuss the economic perspective of reputation under the next heading.

3   The WMG Simulation

To describe the experimental set-up of our agent-based simulation, we explain the three component models of which it is comprised:

1. The technical model of the WMG,
2. The model of the actors in the system represented as agents,
3. The cost model for the introduction of enforcement agents

Subsequently, we present the simulation environment, its controlling parameters and the hypotheses to test.

3.1   The Technical Model

The design of the technical model is based on a few assumptions commonly known together as the "Flat Earth" model [24]. This is widely used and accepted as 'best practice' in communication simulations, hence we adopt it here. The relevant assumptions are symmetry (if node A can hear node B, B can hear A), perfect signal strength, no external interference, no obstacles and limited communication range. Furthermore, we assume that all participants in the system have a mobile phone with the same technical specifications, that is having equal battery consumption rates for equal actions performed. This assumption is supported by [5] which states that for representative phones with features for WMG communication, the differences between different mobile phones are only marginal. We use his measurements of mobile phone battery consumption for sending and receiving on 3G and WLAN respectively.

3.2   The Agent and Interaction Model

We distinguish two types of system participants: "normal" users and enforcement agents. Both types move randomly and at any given point of time can interact with the agents that are in their communication radius, as determined by the operational range of the WLAN connection.

For the normal agents in the system, we assume bounded rationality and (personal) utility maximization. The latter means that when deciding what to do, the agents consider the utility of the available actions and choose the one with the highest utility. Utilities may vary from agent to agent. An agent could for example assign cooperation a high utility, whereas another might assign a higher utility to the reduction of their battery consumption. Bounded rationality specifies that the agents do not necessarily know the whole system and thus cannot base their decision on complete (system) knowledge. That is why they can only optimize their local (current location bound) utility, which may be different from the global one. The procedure for the decision-making process for normal agents and their utility considerations is described in Figure 1, which we will now explain in more detail: The normal agent decision-making procedure is:

1. At simulation start, normal agents are randomly assigned the task of downloading a specific file. On receiving this task, the agents can decide on how to obtain this file, that is either by downloading it themselves or by trying to find a collaboration

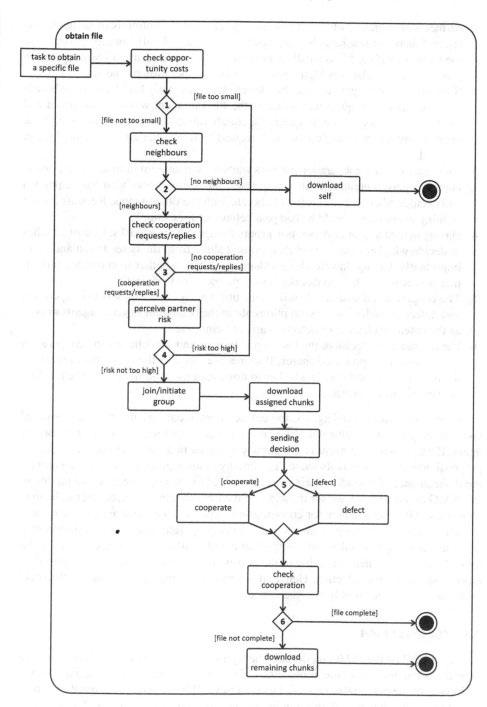

Fig. 1. The Agent Decision Making Process. The numbers in the decision nodes correspond with the item numbers in the decision-making procedure described in section 3.2.

partner with which to obtain the file jointly. The former option is of particular interest if there are few neighbouring agents (i.e. potential collaboration partners) in the vicinity or if the file is small, as both situations could result in low cooperation gains as well as relatively high costs for finding cooperation partners.

2. If the number of neighbours and the file size are sufficiently high[4], the agent broadcasts cooperation request that specifies the file the agent wants to download and its request for cooperation. Requests for collaboration do not need to be sent if the agent receives a matching cooperation request from another agent, to which it can respond.

3. An agents seeking cooperation partners waits a fixed amount of time for responses. Having received enough positive responses, the agent checks who has responded and decides whether it wants to collaborate with the other agents. Reasons for not wanting to cooperate could be bad past behaviour for example.

4. Having agreed to join a cooperation group, the agent has two tasks. First of all it has to decide whether to download its promised share from the base-station and more importantly, having downloaded its share, to decide whether to cooperate further, that is to send the share to its cooperation partners, or to defect.

5. The cooperation decision is based on the utilities the agent assigns to cooperation and defection including is assumptions about the behaviour of other agents as well as the potential chances of detection and of being fined.

6. Having made its decision, the last step is to wait and see whether the cooperation partners send the promised shares. If shares are missing, the agent must repeat the decision process and decide whether to download the missing shares itself or find new cooperation partners.

In contrast to the normal agents, the enforcement agents are not given a download task, but only become active when they receive a collaboration proposal from another agent. If an enforcement agent is not already engaged in an interaction, it accepts the proposal and always sends its share. The energy consumption costs that the enforcement agents incur for sending their share, are added to the total energy consumption in the WMG in order to account for the additional energy that the enforcement mechanism consumes. After the deadline for cooperation has passed, the enforcement agent identifies the cooperation group members that did not cooperate. These agents are reported and a sanction applied to them. It is important to note with respect to defection from the agreed cooperation, that according to the current rules, an agent may not be punished more than once for a defection. Hence, if several enforcement agents detect the same violation, the violator is only punished once.

3.3   The Cost Model

Having described the WMG model and the agent (decision) model, the last aspect we consider is the analysis of the implications of the employment of enforcement agents.

In view of the potential commercial interest in WMGs, from the large number of possible factors to evaluate with the simulation, we concentrate on two linked to business:

---

[4] This value is agent-specific. It is based on an agent's attitude to risk and preference for cooperation.

Table 1. Simulation Variables

Name	Simulation Parameter
# Normal Agents	400
Enforcement Agents as % of Normal Agents	0%, 1%, 2%, 3%, 4%, 5%
Fine percentage	100%, 200%, 300%, 400%, 500%, 600%, 700%, 800%, 900%, 1000%
# Consecutive Tasks	50
Movement Pattern	Random Walk

financial implications – what are the financial overheads associated with the mechanism, as well as the potential benefits – and overall battery consumption – potential reduced consumption and extended handset cycles make this attractive for user. To do so, the following two assumptions are made:

1. The one universal mobile phone provider offers its customers the option to join the WMG or not. If they join and the cooperation is successful, they can reduce their battery consumption according to the specifications given earlier. Customers can opt not to participate – that is never accept a collaboration request – without penalty. However if a user does accept a collaboration request, but fails to contribute, he/she runs the risk of being penalised.

2. The costs of the enforcement agents are two-fold: firstly, as mentioned earlier, enforcement produces additional battery consumption that needs to be accounted for. Secondly, in this paper, we assume that in return for their support in controlling the wireless mobile grid and as incentive to report truthfully, they can use their mobile phones free of charge and thus can save an amount c_{eAg} which is the average level of a mobile phone bill. In consequence, for each enforcement agent employed, the infrastructure provider loses c_{eAg} of potential revenue. Here, we account for both types of costs, starting with the energy consumption and afterwards extend it to the reward costs for enforcement agents. This includes a discussion of the significance of the level of c_{eAg} in Section 4, where we analyse the results of the simulation experiment. As also mentioned earlier, for the sake of simplicity and because they benefit from honesty by saving c_{eAg} we assume that the enforcement agents always try to fulfil their duty. It can however happen that because agents move out of range of one other, they sanction agents that act honestly, that is produce statistical false-positives. We are able to check for these and consider them in the analysis of the success of the enforcement mechanism.

3.4 Simulation Parameters

The implementation of the above components, namely the agents and the technical and the financial model, is realized using the Jason simulation platform [25]. The agent reasoning is encoded in AgentSpeak, and all remaining parts of the simulation are programmed in Java. Table 1 gives an overview of the simulation configuration parameters used in the experiments.

The simulation parameters specify the number of the normal agents, the duration of the simulation (i.e. the number of tasks – the number of files to obtain – per agent in the simulation). We use a random walk to determine where an agent is located at each cycle and thus which neighbours and potential cooperation partners it has. The communication radius is based on WLAN specifications and is the same for all agents (including the enforcement ones).

The purpose of the simulation is to test not only the impact of enforcement agents, but also the sensitivity of the cooperation problem to the number of such agents in proportion to the normal population. Furthermore we investigate the effect of the level of the fine issued by the enforcement agent in case of a violation. The primary performance indicator is taken to be the total battery consumption across the entire population, from which we exclude the effect of fines following a violation, to be able concentrate on the energy required for downloading and sharing files (as well as policing the system) in our analysis. We identify a measure we call the *average energy consumption (AEC) ratio*, which is the ratio of the actual battery costs of the interactions that take place, over the theoretical costs of downloading if each participant downloads everything themselves. As more sharing occurs, this ratio tends to 0, conversely, less sharing and the ratio tends to 1 (or theoretically even above 1, if the defection rate is high). Consequently, the simulation experiments test the following hypotheses:

Hypothesis 1: The employment of enforcement agents increases cooperation and decreases the AEC ratio.

Hypothesis 2: An increase in the percentage of enforcement agents results in a reduction of the AEC ratio.

Hypothesis 3: An increase in the fine value results in an increase in cooperation and a reduction of the AEC ratio.

In order to test these hypotheses we run factorial experiments, in which each parameter ranges over a discrete set of possible values and the set of experiments cover all the combinations of values across the factors. Each experiment consists of 50 simulation runs for each of the parameter combinations in Table 1. For each run, each agent has the task of downloading a file – and hence making cooperation decisions – 50 times. Each time, the file assigned to the agent is randomly chosen from a pool of files. The results of these runs are then analysed using Matlab. We use ANalysis Of VAriance (ANOVA) to test the significance relationship between the parameters in the simulation (independent variables) and the number and ratio of defections and the AEC ratio (dependent variables). This informs us whether specific input parameters (or parameter combinations) influence the outputs[5]. As a post-hoc test to ANOVA, we also use Tukey's test, which identifies the impact of specific variables on the overall result.

4   Results and Evaluation

Following the presentation of our hypotheses and the experimental set-up, we now turn to the analysis of the simulation results in order to confirm or refute the proposed hypotheses.

---

[5] We performed the Shapiro-Wilk test as well as Levene's test to ensure the applicability of the ANOVA.

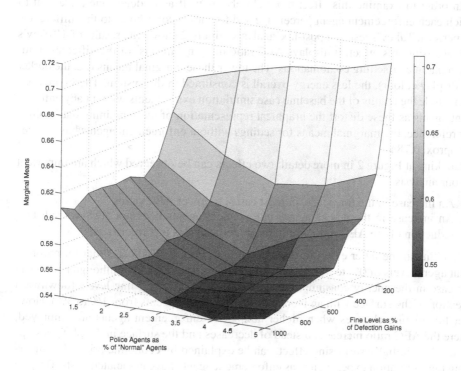

Fig. 2. Marginal Means for Comparing Simulation Experiments with different Percentages of Enforcement Agents for different Fine Levels. In a design with several factors (e.g. battery capacity, police agent percentage and fine level), the marginal means for one factor are the means for that factor averaged across all levels of the other factors.

We start with hypothesis one which states that the introduction of enforcement agents increases cooperation and reduces the overall AEC in the system. To test this hypothesis we look at differences in the AEC rates in the simulation experiments with and without enforcement agents and compare these for the different fine values. With the help of ANOVA, we test whether the null hypothesis that the enforcement agents account for no difference can be rejected or not. We performed this test for all fine levels and get significant p-values (< 0.0001) for all of them, that is, we can reject the null hypothesis and conclude that the utilisation of enforcement agents results in a difference in the AEC rates. This is true even for low fine levels and indicates the deterrent effect of fining. We use one-tailed t-tests to establish the nature of the difference between having enforcement agents and having none and confirm that lower AEC ratios are dominant in the simulation experiments with enforcement agents. This confirms Hypothesis 1. However, when performing the ANOVA, high error rates for all fine levels are detected. This typically indicates that a difference exists between the rates of enforcement agents and fine levels that are grouped in the ANOVA.

In order to examine this effect more closely, as well as to determine the extent to which each enforcement agent percentage and fine level contributes to this difference, we perform Tukey's test as a post-hoc analysis. Figure 2 shows the results of a Tukey's test analysing this effect. It displays AEC ratio marginal means for the different simulation parameter setting combinations. The lower these marginal means (i.e. the darker the display colour), the less energy overall is consumed in the system. The figure does not include the results of the baseline case simulation experiments without any enforcement agents as these distort the graphical representation of the remaining data-points. For reference, the marginal means for settings without enforcement agents have values of approx. 0.7843.

Looking at Figure 2 in more detail: two effects can be observed which are important for our analysis:

1. An increase in the fine leads, in most cases, to lower AEC ratios
2. An increase in the percentage of enforcement agents does not always result in a reduction of the AEC ratio, implying Hypothesis 2 is incorrect.

Looking at the latter effect in more detail first, Figure 2 indicates that for enforcement agent levels of 0% to 3%, Hypothesis 1 seems true: a steady (although not linear) decrease in the energy consumption ratios can be seen for all fine levels (downward direction of the surface with an increase of enforcement agents from 1% to 3%). However this picture changes when higher number of enforcement agents are employed, where the AEC ratio increases instead of decreases and the surface in the plot goes upwards. This initially surprising effect, can be explained by economic principles underlying the simulation experiments, as enforcement agents have associated costs. Despite the reduction of battery usage when more enforcement agents are employed, this additional reduction – and the detection of violations – does come at a price, which must be summed across all the enforcement agents. In contrast, the detection of violations follows the economic principle of the law of diminishing marginal utility (also known as "Gossen's First Law"). This law states that for any good or service, its marginal utility decreases as the quantity of the good or service increases, *ceteris paribus*. In terms of our simulation this implies that: with increasing numbers of enforcement agents, the number of additional detections ($\Delta(D)$) decreases with each additional enforcement agent ($\Delta(x)$). This can be explained by:

1. The larger the number of enforcement agents, the higher the probability that several enforcement agents are in the same location and observe the same violation. We pointed out earlier that – in accordance with general legal principles – an agent can only be held accountable once. Thus, an agent can only be punished once regardless of how many enforcement agents observe the violation. As a result, additional observations of the same event do not produce any additional benefit. Nevertheless, the costs for the enforcement agents need to be paid: that is, their battery consumption still counts towards the total battery consumption across the system.
2. In the case of successful enforcement, that is a high number of detections, rational agents will attempt to cooperate in order to avoid a possible detection of violations and consequent fine. So, the total number of violations decreases, automatically reducing the number of potential detections, resulting in the same enforcement agent cost problem.

As a consequence, instead of aiming for absolute enforcement, economic theory suggests using "satisficing" [2], that is *minimizing* $\Delta(D)/\Delta(x)$, which can be determined by means of the factorial experiments, and the best result approximated. Additionally, a simulation can also be used for testing thresholds, for example, how many enforcement agents are needed on average to detect 90% of all violations. Thus, quality of service requirements can be stated and the associated costs determined *a priori*.

In our experiments – comparing 3%, 4% and 5% enforcement agents – the lower percentage of enforcement agents performs better for satisficing cooperation with respect to the AEC ratio. Conversely, for between 0% and 3% enforcement agents, the gains made by additional units of enforcement agents *are* beneficial, suggesting there is a minimum in this region. Thus, although not optimal with regard to the detection of violations (3% enforcement agents will detect less than 5%) the costs associated with them, that is the energy they consume for performing their observation and punishing actions, are significantly lower, making them more advantageous in terms of the overall energy saving. However, as pointed out earlier, the WMG is a real world business case study and additional costs/losses might be incurred. When first describing the idea of enforcement agents, we explained that one incentive for them to help control the system could be financial benefits, such as free mobile phone contracts. This incentive can be quantified. Currently, mobile telecommunication providers have an average monthly revenue per user of approximately $c_{eAg} = €$ 15 [26], which is mainly generated through contracts. For 3% enforcement agents, for a provider like T-Mobile with 35,403,000 customers in Europe in 2011 [27, p.90], this implies a monthly loss of revenue of approximately € 15.9 million. This cost needs to be weighed against the benefits of the WMG, such as energy savings or possibly higher subscriptions numbers if users embrace the WMG idea and potential capital savings on network infrastructure. Based on these figures, 3% enforcement agents seems a rather high price, and a lower number of enforcement agents or a less generous incentive for their service (e.g. only covering the marginal costs of their contracts) might seem more affordable.

One other means to decrease the AEC ratio is to increase the fine level and thereby indirectly decrease the number of defections. In Figure 2, we can observe that the increase in the fine level indeed decreases the mean values (confirming Hypothesis 3), however the decrease has a diminishing nature. This suggests a saturation effect with respect to the fine level, that is the higher the fine gets, the lower the additional gains from it. Consequently, we observe that high fine levels do not yield high benefits and can even increase battery consumption, as energy used by the enforcement agents does not result in the detection of violations. On a social level, they could also result in acceptance problems by the wireless grid users, which in turn is counter-productive if infrastructure providers want to promote WMGs as part of their business concept.

The feared problem of false-positives in our simulation (e.g. false accusations due to agents moving out of each other reception range) did not have a major impact in the simulation experiments. Over all experiments we had 0.007% false positive rate, i.e. 7 in 100,000 users were wrongly accused.

5 Conclusion and Future Work

We have presented an analysis of the costs of enforcement, depending on two factors: the amount of enforcement and the fine level imposed in case of sanction.

We use our analysis to examine the facilitation of cooperation in WMGs – a kind of large-scale open distributed system. For the WMG case study we are able to confirm two out of our three hypotheses, namely that enforcement agents help to reduce the AEC ratio and that an increase in the fine level is aligned with this effect. We furthermore establish, that the increase in both the number of enforcement agents and the fine level have diminishing returns, which in the case of the number of enforcement agents can even lead to negative battery consumption results. Hence, in combining the two concepts it is important to get the right balance between the deterrent effect of the enforcement mechanisms and the costs associated with it. Although these results are based on a case-study specific agent-based simulation, our experiments clearly demonstrate that the costs associated with enforcement are important to consider in any enforcement mechanism, as they can significantly alter its benefit. Clearly each scenario has its own key parameters, so while the results of this study cannot be applicable in another domain, we believe the approach offers useful methodological lessons for the modelling and evaluation of mechanisms for the maintenance of open system common pool problems in general.

As part of future work, we intend to investigate further the effect of the movement of agents, by implementing more realistic movement patterns than random walk. We also plan to explore a wider range of evaluation parameters. On a different level, the introduction of coordination between the enforcement agents also seems sensible. Currently, the individual enforcement agents act independently. Despite this lack of coordination, we only recorded a very few occasions in which two enforcement agents observed the same interaction, which is not surprising given the relatively small percentages of these agents in the population. Nonetheless, a natural human assumption, which may be overturned by the results, would be that for more effective enforcement, a limited level of coordination between these agents could be useful.

Finally, our case-study in based on direct reciprocation, in which collaboration always focuses on an immediate quid pro quo. This neglects the idea that the contribution of an agent to the system and its benefit from the system might have a time discrepancy, such as in routing scenarios. Accounting for a lack of direct interaction is therefore also a part of future work.

References

1. Ostrom, E.: Understanding Institutional Diversity. Princeton University Press (2005)
2. Simon, H.A.: Rational choice and the structure of the environment. Psychological Review 63(2), 129–138 (1956)
3. Conte, R., Gilbert, N.: Computer simualtion for social theory. In: Artificial Societies: The Computer Simulation of Social Life. Routledge (1995)
4. Fitzek, F.H.P., Katz, M.D.: Cellular controlled peer to peer communications: Overview and potentials. In: Fitzek, F.H.P., Katz, M.D. (eds.) Cognitive Wireless Networks, pp. 31–59. Springer (2007)

5. Perrucci, G.P., Fitzek, F.H., Petersen, M.V.: Energy saving aspects for mobile device exploiting heterogeneous wireless networks. In: Heterogeneous Wireless Access Networks. Springer US (2009)
6. Wrona, K., Mähönen, P.: Analytical model of cooperation in ad hoc networks. Telecommunication Systems 27(2-4), 347–369 (2004)
7. Leibowitz, N., Ripeanu, M., Wierzbicki, A.: Deconstructing the kazaa network. In: Proceedings of the Third IEEE Workshop on Internet Applications. IEEE Computer Society (2003)
8. Balke, T.: A taxonomy for ensuring institutional compliance in utility computing. In: Boella, G., Noriega, P., Pigozzi, G., Verhagen, H. (eds.) Normative Multi-Agent Systems. Dagstuhl Seminar Proceedings, vol. 09121, Schloss Dagstuhl - Leibniz-Zentrum für Informatik, Germany (2009)
9. Jones, A.J.I., Sergot, M.J.: A formal characterisation of institutionalised power. Logic Journal of the IGPL 4(3), 427–443 (1996)
10. Ostrom, E.: Coping with tragedies of the commons. Annual Review of Political Science 2, 493–535 (1999), Workshop in Political Theory and Policy Analysis; Center for the Study of Institutions, Population, and Environmental Change, Indiana University, Bloomington, USA
11. Chen, W., Guha, R.K., Kwon, T.J., Lee, J., Hsu, Y.Y.: A survey and challenges in routing and data dissemination in vehicular ad hoc networks. Wireless Communications & Mobile Computing 11(7), 787–795 (2011)
12. Schneier, B.: Liars and Outliers. Wiley (2012) ISBN13:978-1-118-14330-8
13. Boella, G., Pigozzi, G., van der Torre, L.: Normative framework for normative system change. In: AAMAS (1), pp. 169–176 (2009)
14. Grossi, D., Aldewereld, H., Dignum, F.: *ubi lex, ibi poena*: Designing norm enforcement in E-institutions. In: Noriega, P., Vázquez-Salceda, J., Boella, G., Boissier, O., Dignum, V., Fornara, N., Matson, E. (eds.) COIN 2006. LNCS (LNAI), vol. 4386, pp. 101–114. Springer, Heidelberg (2007)
15. Conte, R., Andrighetto, G., Campenni, M.: Internalizing norms. A cognitive model of (social) norms' internalization. The International Journal of Agent Technologies and Systems (IJATS) 2(1), 63–73 (2010)
16. Feldman, M., Papadimitriou, C., Chuang, J., Stoica, I.: Free-riding and whitewashing in peer-to-peer systems. In: Proceedings of the ACM SIGCOMM Workshop on Practice and Theory of Incentives in Networked Systems. ACM (2004)
17. Becker, G.S.: Crime and punishment: An economic approach. The Journal of Political Economy 76(2), 169–217 (1968)
18. Coleman, J.S.: Foundations of Social Theory. Belknap Press (August 1998)
19. Gurerk, O., Irlenbusch, B., Rockenbach, B.: The competitive advantage of sanctioning institutions. Science 312(5770), 108–111 (2006)
20. Perreau de Pinninck Bas, A.: Techniques for Peer Enforcement in Multiagent Networks. PhD thesis, Universitat Autónoma de Barcelona, Spain (2010)
21. König, S., Balke, T., Quattrociocchi, W., Paolucci, M., Eymann, T.: On the effects of reputation in the internet of services. In: Proceedings of the 1st Int. Conference on Reputation (ICORE 2009), pp. 200–214 (March 2009)
22. Andrighetto, G., Villatoro, D.: Beyond the carrot and stick approach to enforcement: An agent-based model. In: European Conference on Cognitive Science (2011)
23. El Mouden, C., West, S.A., Gardner, A.: The enforcement of cooperation by policing. Evolution 64(7), 2139–2152 (2010)
24. Kotz, D., Newport, C., Gray, R.S., Liu, J., Yuan, Y., Elliott, C.: Experimental evaluation of wireless simulation assumptions. In: Proceedings of the 7th ACM International Symposium on Modeling, Analysis and Simulation of Wireless and Mobile Systems, pp. 78–82. ACM (2004)

25. Bordini, R.H., Hübner, J.F., Wooldridge, M.: Programming Multi-Agent Systems in AgentSpeak using Jason. Wiley Series in Agent Technology. John Wiley & Sons (2007)
26. ie Market Research: 3q10 germany mobile operator forecast, 2010–2014 (2010), `https://www.iemarketresearch.com/Members/Reports/3Q10-Germany-Mobile-Operator-Forecast-2010--2014-Germany-to-have-118-million-mobile-subscribers-in-2014-with-market-share-of-T-Mobile-declining-to-34--RID1590-1.aspx`
27. T-Mobile: Geschäftsbericht, annual report (2011), `http://www.telekom.com/static/-/103442/10/120223-ar2011-pdf-si`

Reaching Your Goals without Spilling the Beans: Boolean Secrecy Games

Nils Bulling[1], Sujata Ghosh[2], and Rineke Verbrugge[3]

[1] Clausthal University of Technology
Clausthal, Germany
bulling@in.tu-clausthal.de
[2] Indian Statistical Institute
Chennai, India
sujata@isichennai.res.in
[3] University of Groningen
Groningen, Netherlands
L.C.Verbrugge@rug.nl

Abstract. Inspired by the work on Boolean games, we present turn-based games where each of the players controls a set of atomic variables and each player wants to achieve some individual goal in such a way that the other players remain unaware of the goal until it is actually achieved. We present definitions of winning such games with hidden goals for different non-cooperative settings, and discuss in which types of situations players have winning or equilibrium strategies. We also provide some complexity bounds on deciding whether a player has a winning strategy.

1 Introduction

In many intelligent interactions, there are some goals that are commonly known to all concerned, while individuals may also attempt to achieve a secret or *hidden goal* of their own. For example, in a purportedly 'win-win' *negotiation* between two companies, they aim to settle on certain issues in a way that is advantageous to both. Still, while negotiating, both parties also consider their individual benefits, possibly unknown to the other party [14,18]. Thus, in the resulting settlements, in addition to some goals commonly known to all, some hidden goals are often achieved as well. Sometimes, these goals become common knowledge once they are reached, whereas in other cases, they remain secret forever. It may also happen that the secret goal is revealed before the actual settlement, which may even lead to the cancellation of the settlement.

Such hidden individual goals occur not only in the mixed-motive negotiations described above, where participants have both cooperative and adversarial motives. Even in the case of *teamwork*, individual team members may try to secretly achieve some individual goal while being involved in achieving the team's collective intention [6,4]. As an example, consider *The Count of Monte Cristo* by Alexandre Dumas (père) [5]. In this story, two of the 'bad guys', Fernand Mondego and the deputy public prosecutor Villefort, achieve their common goal of

G. Boella et al. (Eds.): PRIMA 2013, LNAI 8291, pp. 37–53, 2013.

imprisoning the book's hero Edmond Dantès for life in Château d'If. However, both men are driven by entirely different secret goals that they do not divulge to one another: Fernand Mondego has the hidden goal to marry Edmond Dantès' fiancee Mercédès, while Villefort is secretly driven by the goal to save his reputation and career by preventing Dantès from delivering a treasonous letter from Napoleon to Villefort's father.

Of course in openly *competitive* situations, there is even more reason to hide one's goals from opponents than in mixed-motive negotiations or seemingly cooperative cases of teamwork. For example, during the Second World War, the allied forces prepared an elaborate scheme, Operation Fortitude, to deceive the Germans into thinking that the allies were going to invade Norway and Pas de Calais, rather than Normandy [2]. The scheme to hide their real goal involved faked armies, faked wireless traffic, faked information passed on by double agents, and much more. Even after the actual landing in Normandy on June 6, 1944, the allied forces managed to delay German reinforcement in Normandy by convincing them that the landings in Normandy were meant as a diversionary attack to take attention away from Pas de Calais. In summary, from fictional adventure stories through tales of deception in wars to modern day negotiations, hidden goals may drive individuals involved in intelligent interactions.

In this paper, we aim to formalize the idea of achieving secret goals. Inspired by the work on Boolean games [10,3], we present turn-based games where each player controls a set of atomic variables and wants to achieve some goals in such a way that its opponents do not know which goals it pursues until those goals are actually reached. This paper forms an initial investigation, intended to lead to a better understanding of ways to obtain vital information from rivals without revealing much of one's own positions; after all, knowledge is power (cf. [1]). The idea is to use very simple tools of logic and game theory to express hiding as well as gaining information in an interactive process.

2   Boolean Secrecy Games

In this section we introduce the basic definitions. A *Boolean secrecy frame* (BSF) is the basic model of our static setting. We use a *game base* for representing a specific evolution of the BSF. Finally, a *Boolean secrecy game* (BSG) consists of a BSF and a game base.

2.1   Boolean Secrecy Frames

Let *Props* be a non-empty finite set of propositional variables and let $\mathcal{L}(Props)$ denote the set of formulas of propositional logic over *Props*, constructed with the usual propositional connectives together with the propositional constants $\top$ (truth) and $\bot$ (falsity). In the following we will simply write $\mathcal{L}$ if the set of propositions is clear from context.

We use *Players* to refer to the set of players. Players are denoted by $1, 2, 3, \ldots$. In the following, if not said otherwise, we assume that *Players* $= \{1, \ldots, n\}$ and use $i, j, \ldots$ to refer to players. We use $\bar{i}$ to refer to "the opponents of i", i.e. to the set of players $Players \setminus \{i\}$. Players can decide on the truth values of specific propositions they control.

We want to model the question whether one player can achieve a certain goal formula, without the other player(s) knowing what the goal is until it becomes true. Let Γ be the set consisting of all possible goals that any of the players might want to achieve. It is common knowledge among all the players that these are the possible goals. However, these goals will certainly not all become collective goals or collective intentions [6,4]. We consider the case where players may not be certain of the exact goal(s) that their opponents would like to achieve. The subset of the *secret goals* of a player i is given by $\Gamma_i \subseteq \Gamma$.

Similarly to [8], achieving goals may involve some costs, and sometimes players need to minimalize the cost. To this effect, we introduce costs associated with players' actions and give restraining conditions by considering cost limits.

Definition 2.1 (Boolean secrecy frame). *The sets $\mathcal{P}_i \subseteq Props$ of propositional variables stand for each player i's set of propositions, such that $\mathcal{P}_i \cap \mathcal{P}_j = \emptyset$ for all $i, j \in Players$ with $i \neq j$. Furthermore, $\neg \mathcal{P}_i$ stands for $\{\neg p : p \in \mathcal{P}_i\}$.*

For $i \in Players$, we define the set $\Sigma_i := \mathcal{P}_i \cup \neg \mathcal{P}_i \cup \{skip_i\}$ and for any $C \subseteq Players$, we define $\Sigma_C := \bigcup_{i \in C} \Sigma_i$. The set Σ_i represents the actions of player i. We refer to actions in $\mathcal{P}_i \cup \neg \mathcal{P}_i$ as propositional actions.

A Boolean secrecy frame (BSF) is a tuple

$$F = (Players, Props, (\mathcal{P}_i)_{i \in Players}, \Gamma, (\Gamma_i)_{i \in Players}, (c_i)_{i \in Players}, (C_i)_{i \in Players}),$$

where $Players$ and $Props$ are as given above; function $c_i : \Sigma_i \to \mathbb{R}^+$ represents the costs associated with the moves of player i; $C_i \in \mathbb{R}^+$ is the cost limit for player i; $\Gamma \subseteq \mathcal{L}$ is the set of possible goals for the players, which is commonly known to all players; and $\Gamma_i \subseteq \Gamma$ is the set of secret goals of player i, not known among the other players.

In contrast to [8] and similarly to [9], we do not require that the players' sets of propositions form a partition of $Props$, so not necessarily $\bigcup_{i \in Players} \mathcal{P}_i = Props$. Propositions not contained in $\bigcup_i \mathcal{P}_i$ are controlled by some external entity not being part of the game. We also refer to the elements of $\mathcal{P}_i \cup \neg \mathcal{P}_i \cup \{skip_i\}$ as *actions* of player i. An action $p \in \mathcal{P}_i$ corresponds to agent i making p true, and action $\neg p \in \neg \mathcal{P}_i$ corresponds to i making p false; alternatively, when agents have run out of propositions—a proposition can only be set once—they can *skip*.

As a running example for our subsequent discussions, let us consider the misinformed German high command and the British command during Operation Fortitude. We can set variables p_1 for the British troops preparing for some attack, p_2 for the British attacking Normandy, and p_3 for the British attacking Pas de Calais, p_4 for the German troops preparing for defending Normandy, p_5 for the German troops preparing for defending Pas de Calais.[1] Here follows the relevant Boolean secrecy frame.

---

[1] For simplicity, we leave out Norway from the example.

Example 2.1 (Boolean secrecy frame). We consider a BSF with two players $\{1$ *(British)*, 2 *(German)*$\}$ and the set of propositions $Props = \{p_1, \ldots, p_5\}$. The set of propositions controlled by the players are given by $\mathcal{P}_1 = \{p_1, p_2, p_3\}$, and $\mathcal{P}_2 = \{p_4, p_5\}$. The set of possible goals $\Gamma = \{p_1 \wedge (p_4 \rightarrow p_3) \wedge (p_5 \rightarrow p_2), (p_1 \wedge p_4 \wedge p_2) \vee (p_1 \wedge p_5 \wedge p_3)\}$. Player 1's set of secret goals is given by $\Gamma_1 = \{(p_1 \wedge (p_4 \rightarrow p_3) \wedge (p_5 \rightarrow p_2)\}$; player 2's secret goal set is empty.

The first goal formula, which is also the secret goal for the British, says that wherever the Germans put up their defense, the British will attack at the other point. The other goal formula says that the troops from both sides will meet at one of the regions, which corresponds more to the assumed (non-secret) German goal. In this way, we represent a simplification of Operation Fortitude.

In the dynamic Boolean secrecy games that we will define, agents do not win simply by reaching their goals: they must do so without spilling the beans; that is, without the others knowing about their secret goals.

2.2   Histories and Propositional Truth Assignments

In the following, if not said otherwise we assume that $F = (\mathcal{P}layers, \mathcal{P}rops, (\mathcal{P}_i)$ $_{i \in \mathcal{P}layers}, \Gamma, (\Gamma_i)_{i \in \mathcal{P}layers}, (c_i)_{i \in \mathcal{P}layers}, (C_i)_{i \in \mathcal{P}layers})$ is a Boolean secrecy frame (BSF). A BSF models the initial setting and the player characteristics. Now, the players try to realize their hidden goals by following a specific course of action. The performance of all players over time yields a finite sequence of actions which we call a *history*. Histories encode possible dynamic evolutions in the given BSF. We only impose the restriction that the action of making a particular atomic proposition p in $\mathcal{P}rops$ true or false can be executed at most once along any history. Histories that contain a propositional action p or $\neg p$ for each proposition p in $\bigcup_{i \in \mathcal{P}layers} \mathcal{P}_i$ are of particular interest and are called *complete*.

Definition 2.2 (History, subhistory, complete history). *An F-history is a finite sequence $h = (a_j)_{j=0,\ldots k} \in (\bigcup_{i \in \mathcal{P}layers} \Sigma_i)^*$, $k \geq 0$ (or, $h = \epsilon$) such that:*

1. *if $a_l \in \{p, \neg p\}$ for some $p \in \bigcup_{i \in \mathcal{P}layers} \mathcal{P}_i$ and $0 \leq l \leq k$, then there is no $l' \neq l$ with $0 \leq l' \leq k$ and $a_{l'} \in \{p, \neg p\}$;*
2. *if $a_l = skip_i$, then for all $p \in \mathcal{P}_i, \exists j : 0 \leq j < l$ and $(a_j = p$ or $a_j = \neg p)$.*

The length of h, $|h|$, is defined as $|h| = k + 1$. We write $h[l]$ to refer to the lth action a_l on h where $0 \leq l < |h|$. For two histories h, h' we say that h' is a subhistory of h, denoted by $h' \leq h$, if h' is an initial segment of h. We write $h' < h$ if $h' \leq h$ and $h' \neq h$. The set of propositions occurring in h is referred to as $\mathcal{P}rops(h)$; i.e. $\mathcal{P}rops(h) = \{p \mid \exists j : 0 \leq j < |h| and (a_j = p$ or $a_j = \neg p)\}$. The concatenation of two finite sequences $h, h' \in (\bigcup_{i \in \mathcal{P}layers} \Sigma_i)^*$ is denoted by hh'.

Let $C \subseteq \mathcal{P}layers$. A history h is said to be C-complete if $\bigcup_{i \in C} \mathcal{P}_i \subseteq \mathcal{P}rops(h)$. As abbreviations, we say that h is i-complete if h is $\{i\}$-complete, and that h is complete if it is $\mathcal{P}layers$-complete.

According to the definition, each history can consist of at most $|\mathcal{P}rops|$-many propositional actions, and never contains a literal p or $\neg p$ for which $p \in \mathcal{P}rops \setminus \bigcup_{i \in \mathcal{P}layers} \mathcal{P}_i$.

A history is one possible evolution of a BSF; usually, there are many possible evolutions. Firstly, a player i can select any action from Σ_i. Secondly, the order in which players act need not be fixed. One option, although not always realistic in dynamic environments, would be to fix such an ordering. Instead, we impose some constraints on the possible dynamic evolutions. A sensible requirement could for instance be that each player is allowed to make all her controlled propositions true or false, that is, each history could be *Players*-complete. A player being allowed to make all her controlled propositions true or false in one block of actions—,one after the other—is not sensible, however, as then she might reveal what her secret goal is. In a two-player setting one could assume that the players act alternately. We propose two possible intuitive fairness conditions:

Definition 2.3 (Fair and alternating histories). *Let h be an F-history. (a) h is said to be* fair *if it is $\mathcal{P}layers$-complete. (b) h is said to be π-alternating where π is a permutation on $\mathcal{P}layers$ if for all $i \in \mathcal{P}layers$ and all $l \in \mathbb{N}$ with $l \cdot |\mathcal{P}layers| + \pi(i) \leq |h|$, we have $h[l \cdot |\mathcal{P}layers| + \pi(i)] \in \Sigma_i$.*

Finally, we relate histories to valuations of propositional variables. Each history gives rise to a *partial valuation* of the propositions occurring in it. A complete history corresponds to a complete valuation of $\bigcup_{i \in \mathcal{P}layers} \mathcal{P}_i$.

As a reminder, a (truth) *valuation* is a function $v : \mathcal{P}rops \rightarrow \{\mathbf{t}, \mathbf{f}\}$ which assigns a truth value to each proposition in $\mathcal{P}rops$. In order to evaluate Boolean formulas we lift a valuation v to formulas in the standard way. We write $v(\varphi) = \mathbf{t}$ (resp. $v(\varphi) = \mathbf{f}$) to denote that valuation v makes φ true (resp. false). A *P-valuation* is a partial valuation defined on a subset $P \subseteq \mathcal{P}rops$. Clearly, a valuation is a $\mathcal{P}rops$-valuation and vice versa.

In order to check whether a player i can achieve a given goal, we introduce an *i-extension* of a partial valuation, which extends it to a partial valuation that specifies truth values for all propositions controlled by i. Thus, an i-extension fixes all of i's variables. Finally, a *completion* of a partial valuation extends it to a *complete* one by assigning truth values to *all* propositions from $\mathcal{P}rops$ not yet specified by the original partial valuation:

Definition 2.4 (Induced valuation, i-extension, completion). *Given an F-history h, the h-induced valuation is the $\mathcal{P}rops(h)$-valuation v_h with $v(p) = \mathbf{t}$ (resp. $v(p) = \mathbf{f}$) if $p = a_j$ (resp. $\neg p = a_j$) for some j with $0 \leq j < |h|$. Let $P, P' \subseteq \bigcup_{i \in \mathcal{P}layers} \mathcal{P}_i$. We say that a P-valuation v agrees with a P'-valuation v' if for all $p \in P \cap P'$, we have that $v(p) = v'(p)$. An i-extension v' of a P-valuation v is a $(P \cup \mathcal{P}_i)$-valuation that agrees with v on P. A completion v' of a P-valuation v is a $\mathcal{P}rops$-valuation v' that agrees with v on P.*

Note that an i-extension of an h-induced valuation is indeed a partial valuation (see Definition 2.2). It is not difficult to see that for any fair history h and any players i, j with $i \neq j$, history h gives a j-extension for a $\mathcal{P}_i$-valuation agreeing with the $\mathcal{P}rops(h)$-valuation v_h. If $\bigcup_{i \in \mathcal{P}layers} \mathcal{P}_i = \mathcal{P}rops$ then any fair history h gives a completion for each $\mathcal{P}_i$-valuation agreeing with $\mathcal{P}rops(h)$-valuation v_h.

2.3   Extensive Form Boolean Secrecy Game

We have just introduced Boolean secrecy frames (BSF) and histories. Each history represents one possible course of action, corresponding to some specific combination of strategies (strategy profile) of the players. Initially, if there are no fixed strategies, many histories may still be possible. We call the set that contains all possible evolutions a *game base*.

Definition 2.5 (Game base, i-history). *Let H be a non-empty set of F-histories. We say that H is an F-game base if it satisfies the following conditions:*

1. *$\epsilon \in H$ (i.e., H contains the empty history);*
2. *if $h \in H$ then every subhistory h' of h is in H (i.e., H is downwards closed);*
3. *for all histories $h \in H$ there is a player $i \in \mathcal{P}$layers such that for each history h' that has h as strict subhistory (i.e., $h < h'$), we have that $h'[|h|] \in \Sigma_i$; for this player i who is about to play, we call h an i-history; and*
4. *all maximal histories $h \in H$ are complete; here, a history h is maximal if there is no history $h' \in H$ with $h < h'$.*

We use H_i to denote the set of all i-histories in H. Moreover, H is π-alternating if all histories $h \in H$ are π-alternating. Note that all maximal histories are fair.

In particular, requirement 3 ensures that the game base can be seen as the underlying structure of a turn-based extensive form game. At each history (h), it is the turn of the player who "owns" all the directly succeeding nodes $(h'[|h|])$. Requirement 4 enforces that players eventually assign a truth value to all the variables they control.

Definition 2.6 (Full-branching game base). *An F-game base H is said to be full-branching if for all $i \in \mathcal{P}$layers, the following holds for the set H_i of all i-histories in H: If $h \in H_i$, then for all $p \in \mathcal{P}_i \setminus \mathcal{P}rops(h)$, both $hp \in H$ and $h\neg p \in H$.*

Note that in every F-game base H there is a unique player $i \in \mathcal{P}$layers such that $\epsilon \in H_i$. We refer to i as the *initial player*. It is also easy to see that each combination of a BSF F and permutation π gives rise to a unique π-alternating full-branching game base H.

Finally, we are ready to introduce *Boolean secrecy games*. They model all possible evolutions of a BSF regarding a given F-game base without fixing any truth assignment of any player in advance. Essentially, a *Boolean secrecy game* (BSG) encodes an extensive form game, well-known from game theory [12]. However, in order to define the players' preference relations, we need some additional notions.

Definition 2.7 (Boolean secrecy game). *A Boolean secrecy game (BSG) is given by $G = (F, H)$, where F is a Boolean secrecy frame and H is a full-branching F-game base. We say that G is the H-based game over F. Moreover, we lift the properties of H given in Definition 2.5 and Definition 2.6 to G.*

A Boolean secrecy game $G = (F, H)$ gives rise to a canonical extensive form game frame $E(G)$. Histories of H correspond to nodes in $H(G)$. A player function, indicating which player's turn it is, can be extracted from the set of i-histories: it is player i's turn at history h if and only if h is an i-history.

Example 2.2 (Boolean secrecy game). The BSF F in Example 2.1 and the order $(1, 2)$ give rise to a unique full-branching $(1, 2)$-alternating BSG $G = (F, H)$, as shown in Figure 1(a).

The strategy s_1 for player 1 makes her play p_1 at the first node, and then allows her to respond with p_2 to all possible moves for player 2. Player 1 could have given different responses to different moves of player 2. Note that decisions are irreversible. Thus, after a player chooses to play p_i or $\neg p_i$, these possibilities disappear from the subsequent play, while literals corresponding to not-yet-played controlled variables remain possible for that player.

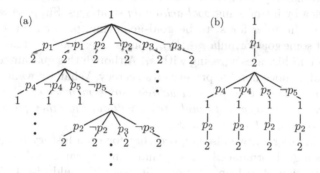

Fig. 1. (a) A diagrammatic representation of the full branching F-game base, with F given in Example 2.2. (b) A strategy s_1 for player 1 and corresponding game base $H|_{s_1}$.

2.4   Strategies, Histories, and Winning Criteria

We introduce the notion of *strategy*, prescribing how a player acts.

Definition 2.8 (Strategy). *Let $G = (F, H)$ be a Boolean secrecy game. An i-strategy (in G) is a function $s_i : H_i \to \Sigma_i$ such that if $s_i(h) \in \{p, \neg p\}$ then $s_i(h') \notin \{p, \neg p\}$ for all histories h' that strictly extend h (i.e., $h < h'$); and such that if $s_i(h) = skip_i$, then h is i-complete.*

A C-joint strategy for a coalition $C \subseteq Players$ is a tuple of strategies, one for each player in C. A strategy profile is a $Players$-joint strategy.

Now, not all histories are compatible with a player's strategy, only those that respect the actions specified by it. We say that such histories *agree* with a strategy. Formally, we have:

Definition 2.9 (Agreeing, $H|_s$). *A history $h = (a_j)_{j=0,\dots,k}$ agrees with an i-strategy s_i if for all $h' < h$ with $h' \in H_i$ we have that $h[|h'|] = s_i(h')$ (i.e. the* *action prescribed at h' by s_i is the next action extending h' in h). Similarly, for $C \subseteq$ Players, we say that h agrees with a C-joint strategy $s_C = (s_{i_1}, \ldots, s_{i_{|C|}})$ if h agrees with s_{i_j} for $j = 1, \ldots, |C|$. We use $H|_{s_C}$ to denote the set of all histories from H agreeing with s_C and we write $H|_{s_i}$ for $H|_{\{s_i\}}$.*

Note that, if s_i is a member of the tuple s_C, then $H|_{s_C} \subseteq H|_{s_i}$.

Example 2.3 (Strategy).
A 1-strategy in the BSG given in Example 2.2 is shown in Figure 1(b).

The idea of the player 1 (British) strategy is to attack wherever the player 2 (Germans) is not building up their defense. The play given by the sequence $p_1, p_5, p_2, \ldots$ models the actual history to some extent [2].

When is a strategy "winning" for a player? We are interested in strategies that keep the set of its intended goals secret, in the sense that the opponents should not become fully aware of a subset of goals before they are achieved. We capture this idea by introducing *goal-achieving* strategies. Suppose we are given an i-strategy s_i. In order for s_i to be goal-achieving, player i must be able to guarantee that some goal formula $\varphi \in \Gamma_i$ becomes true; that is, φ must eventually become true on *all* histories agreeing with s_i. Although this guarantees the truth of a secret goal, it does not yet preserve its secrecy. What we want to model is the following question: *"Can player i achieve some member of Γ_i, that is, can the agent make a certain goal formula true, without the other players knowing what the goal is until it becomes true?"*

For preserving secrecy, we also require that for each history h agreeing with s_i there is a non-goal formula $\varphi' \in \Gamma \backslash \Gamma_i$ that can be guaranteed by i to become true at an extension of h: from $\bar{i}$'s point of view, φ' could also be a goal of i. Formally, there should exist an appropriate i-extension extending the choices made so far.

Although these points capture the basic idea of keeping the goals secret, we are not yet done. Consider the case where $\Gamma = \{a \rightarrow (b \lor c), (b \lor c)\}$, $\Gamma_i = \{b \lor c\}$, $s_i(\epsilon) = a$ and $s_i(ad) = b$, where d is a move of a player in $\bar{i}$ during their turn. Clearly, s_i satisfies both conditions mentioned above. After the first step, however, it should be clear for $\bar{i}$ that i has the *subgoal* to make $b \lor c$ true. Although $\bar{i}$ is still not sure whether i's actual goal is $a \rightarrow (b \lor c)$ or $b \lor c$, they have a clear idea of what comes next. To avoid this, we require that the deceiving goal φ' is sufficiently different from the actual goal at each step. Finally, we capture these ideas formally:

Definition 2.10 (Goal-achieving). *Let $G = (F, H)$ be a BSG. An i-strategy s_i is goal-achieving if the following holds. For all F-histories $h \in H|_{s_i}$ there is a subhistory $h' \leq h$ and a formula $\varphi \in \Gamma_i$ such that:*

1. $v(\varphi) = \mathbf{t}$ for all completions v of the h'-induced valuation (i.e. goal φ is guaranteed to become true);

and for all $h'' < h'$ the following conditions hold:

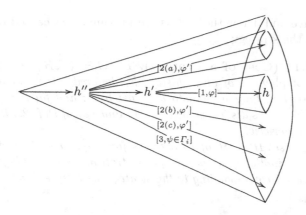

Fig. 2. Goal-achieving strategies as described in Definition 2.10. The figure shows some history $h \in H|_{s_i}$ and a subhistory h'. All completions of h' (cf. the part labeled $[1, \varphi]$) make φ necessarily true. Moreover, before h', at any subhistory h'' of h', no secret goal formula of i is allowed to be necessarily true (existence of such completions shown by the arrow labeled $[3, \psi \in \Gamma_i]$); in particular, φ is not allowed to be necessarily true at h''. Finally, there must also be a potential goal formula φ', sufficiently different from φ (cf. arrow labelled $[2(c), \varphi']$), that is not a secret goal of i (cf. arrow labeled $[2(b), \varphi']$) and that can be made true by i (cf. arrow labelled $[2(a), \varphi']$).

2. *there is a formula* $\varphi' \in \Gamma \backslash \Gamma_i$ *such that*

   (a) *there is an i-extension* v_1 *of the* h''-*induced valuation* $v_{h''}$ *such that for all completions* v_2 *of* v_1, *we have* $v_2(\varphi') = \mathbf{t}$ *(i.e.* φ' *is a possible goal that* i *could enforce);*

   (b) *there is at least one completion* v_3 *of the* h''-*induced valuation* $v_{h''}$ *such that* $v_3(\varphi') = \mathbf{f}$ *(i.e.* φ' *is not yet guaranteed to be true);*

   (c) *there is a completion* v_4 *of the* h''-*induced valuation* $v_{h''}$ *such that* $v_4(\varphi') \neq v_4(\varphi)$ *(i.e.* φ' *is sufficiently different from* φ).

3. *for all* $\psi \in \Gamma_i$ *there exists a completion* v_5 *of the* h''-*induced valuation* $v_{h''}$ *such that* $v_5(\psi) = \mathbf{f}$ *(i.e. no goal of agent* i *has been guaranteed to be true before* φ *at* h').

Figure 2 illustrates the definition of goal-achieving strategies. There can be more than one goal-achieving strategy. Naturally, which one to choose should also depend on the costs of executing a strategy; in particular, the execution may exceed the cost limit of a player.

Before defining the cost of a strategy, we observe that a strategy profile s_C for $C \neq$ *Players* usually identifies a *set* of histories in the secrecy game, namely $H|_{s_C}$. Furthermore, note that although a complete profile s fixes all players' choices, the variables controlled by the environment are not yet set–again, resulting in a set of possible histories. As a consequence, when defining a player's *costs* of a strategy we need to consider a set of possible histories. We take on the worst-case perspective and define the cost as the maximal cost caused by any history agreeing with the strategy.

Definition 2.11 (Cost of a strategy). *Let $G = (F, H)$ be a BSG. We define the* cost *of player i of an F-history h, denoted $c_i(h)$, inductively as follows: $c_i(\epsilon) = 0$ (i.e., the empty history is cost-free); and for $h'a \le h$, $c_i(h'a) = c_i(h')$ if $a \in \Sigma_{\bar{i}}$ or h' satisfies conditions (1) and (2) of Def. 2.10; and $c_i(h'a) = c_i(h') + c_i(a)$ otherwise.*

The cost of a set $H' \subseteq H$ of F-histories for player i is defined as $c_i(H') := \max_{h \in H'} c_i(h)$. Finally, if s_C is a C-joint strategy for $C \subseteq$ Players, we define the cost of player i corresponding to the strategy s_C as $c_i(s_C) = c_i(H|_{s_C})$. Thus, $c_i(s_i) = c_i(H|_{s_i})$.

Note that, if s_i is a member of the tuple s_C, then $c_i(s_C) \le c_i(s_i)$. We have used the intuitive additive model to define costs of strategies in terms of cost of individual actions. The effect of different kinds of cost functions on the determination of winning strategies is left for future work.

Definition 2.12 (Winning). *Given a BSG $G = (F, H)$, an i-strategy s_i is* winning *in G iff it is goal achieving and $c_i(s_i) \le C_i$. Player i is* winning *iff there is a winning i-strategy.*

Note that more than one player can have a winning strategy in a given game G. Also, it is possible that no player can win, see Section 2.5.

One could think of different kinds of winning conditions, for example: one that guarantees that nobody else's goal is satisfied; one that finds out another player's goal before the goal becomes true; one that satisfies one's goal formulas (while possibly allowing others to satisfy theirs); one that satisfies one's goal formula and nobody else does; and various other possibilities. For now, we restrict ourselves to the winning condition of Definition 2.12. Ultimately, we are interested in the question whether players have a strategy to keep their hidden goals secret given a (static) BSF. This crucially depends on the order in which players move. Formally, this is captured by game bases.

Definition 2.13 (Winning in Boolean secrecy frames). *We say that a player i wins in the Boolean secrecy frame F if i wins in the H-based game of F for every full-branching F-game base H. If we consider complete π-alternating game bases only, then we say that i wins in the π-alternating Boolean secrecy frame F.*

2.5 Non-determinacy and Importance of Order

We show the existence of a Boolean secrecy game $G = (F, H)$ in which no player has a winning strategy. We consider a real-life situation. A hiring committee for a faculty position, consisting of a mathematician with some expertise of biology and a physicist. The committee has to hire a theoretical biology expert with good managerial skills. Both committee members, however, are commonly known not to be able to evaluate candidates' managerial skills (there is an outside expert for that). If the two committee members want to hire a candidate in their own expert area, there is no chance of keeping that secret in committee discussions, as they can only mention someone's scientific expertise as argument in favor of a candidate. We now construct a BSF with as intuitive meanings of the propositional atoms: p_1 means that the chosen candidate is an expert on mathematics and biology; p_2 means that the chosen candidate is an expert on bio-physics; and p_3 means that the chosen candidate has good managerial skills. Consider the frame $F = (\mathcal{P}layers, \mathcal{P}rops, (\mathcal{P}_i)_{i \in \mathcal{P}layers}, \Gamma, (\Gamma_i)_{i \in \mathcal{P}layers}, (c_i)_{i \in \mathcal{P}layers}, (C_i)_{i \in \mathcal{P}layers})$, instantiated as follows: $\mathcal{P}layers = \{1, 2\}$; $\mathcal{P}rops = \{p_1, p_2, p_3\}$; $\mathcal{P}_1 = \{p_1\}$; $\mathcal{P}_2 = \{p_2\}$; $\Gamma = \{p_1 \wedge p_3, p_2 \wedge p_3\}$; $\Gamma_1 = \{p_1 \wedge p_3\}$; $\Gamma_2 = \{p_2 \wedge p_3\}$; $c_i : \Sigma_i \to \{1\}$ for each i; $C_i = 2$ for each i.

Because neither player has control over p_3, it can be shown that neither player has a winning strategy in any full-branching F-game base H. Note that the non-determinacy depends on the fact that $\bigcup_{i \in \mathcal{P}layers} \mathcal{P}_i$ is a proper subset of $\mathcal{P}rops$.

Perhaps surprisingly, it turns out that the order of the players' moves matters a lot when it comes to winning. One might think that for a full-branching π-alternating game-base H, if i is winning in (F, H) then i could also win in all π'-alternating game bases H', as long as π and π' are equivalent with respect to i, that is $\pi(i) = \pi'(i)$. But this is not the case, as we now show by an example.

Consider a BSF with three players $\{1, 2, 3\}$ and set of propositions $\mathcal{P}rops = \{p_1, \ldots, p_5\}$. The set of propositions controlled by the players are given by $\mathcal{P}_1 = \{p_1, p_3\}$, $\mathcal{P}_2 = \{p_2\}$, $\mathcal{P}_3 = \{p_4, p_5\}$. The set of possible goals $\Gamma = \{p_1 \wedge p_2, p_3 \wedge \neg p_2, p_4 \vee p_5\}$. Player 1's set of secret goals is given by $\Gamma_1 = \{p_1 \wedge p_2, p_3 \wedge \neg p_2\}$; player 2's and player 3's secret goal sets are empty. We let $C_1 = C_2 = C_3 = 10$ and $c_i : \Sigma_i \to \{1\}$ for $i \in \{1, 2\}$. If player 2's first move is before player 1's first move, then player 1 has a winning strategy: "if player 2 has made p_2 true, then make p_1 true; if player 2 has made p_2 false, then make p_3 true".[2] However, if player 1 has her first move before player 2, then player 1 has no winning strategy. So, in this three player frame F, if H is the $(2, 1, 3)$-alternating full branching game base, then player 1 will have a winning strategy in $G = (F, H)$, whereas she will not have any winning strategy in $G = (F, H')$ where H' denotes the $(3, 1, 2)$-alternating game base. Note that the position of player 1 is the same in both cases.

3   Computational Complexity

An interesting question is whether a player can win in a BSG (see Definitions 2.12 and 2.13). Here, we present some results on the complexity of such problems.

Firstly, let us consider the representation of the input. We measure the size $|F|$ of a BSF,

$$F = (\mathcal{P}layers, \mathcal{P}rops, (\mathcal{P}_i)_{i \in \mathcal{P}layers}, \Gamma, (\Gamma_i)_{i \in \mathcal{P}layers}, (c_i)_{i \in \mathcal{P}layers}, (C_i)_{i \in \mathcal{P}layers})$$

---

[2] Note that different histories agreeing with this strategy may incur different costs for player 1.

as the sum of the sizes of all elements in F; that is, $|F| = |\mathcal{P}layers| + |\mathcal{P}rops| + \sum_{i=1}^{|\mathcal{P}layers|} \mathcal{P}_i + \sum_{\gamma \in \Gamma} |\gamma| + \sum_{\gamma \in \Gamma_i, i \in \mathcal{P}layers} |\gamma| + \sum_{i \in \mathcal{P}layers}(|c_i| + |C_i|)$, where $|\gamma|$ denotes the length of the formula γ and we assume, omitting the details, that $|c_i|$ and $|C_i|$ refer to some reasonable encoding of the functions c_i and numbers C_i, respectively. $|H|$ refers to the cardinality of set H.

The *size* of a BSG $G = (F, H)$ is defined as $|F| + |H|$. In this representation, the size of H is usually exponential in the size of F. Hence, *compact representations* are of more interest. Instead of taking H as input, we only fix the *structure* of the game base according to Definition 2.3; for example, we can consider only π-alternating game bases. Then, following Definition 2.13, we would like to determine whether a player is winning in a frame together with a structural description of the game base. For example, the input might be given by (F, π) and the question to be answered is whether a player is winning in all BSG's (F, H) where H is a π-alternating F-game base. In the case of π-alternating game bases, we even have that the BSG (F, H) is unique and that in most non-trivial cases the size of the input (F, π) is exponentially smaller than the size of the corresponding explicit input (F, H), where H is the unique π-alternating F-game base. Naturally, complexity results for input (F, π) are more insightful than for (F, H).

To start with, we show that the question whether a player is winning can be solved efficiently for the class of games $G = (F, H)$ for which the input is given in explicit form *and* all propositions are controlled by the players, that is, $\mathcal{P}rops = \bigcup_{i \in \mathcal{P}layers} \mathcal{P}_i$. We denote this class of games by $\mathcal{G}^-$. The general case, in which not necessarily $\mathcal{P}rops = \bigcup_{i \in \mathcal{P}layers} \mathcal{P}_i$, is more complex. We have the following complexity results:

Proposition 3.1. *The problem whether a player is winning in $G \in \mathcal{G}^-$ (in explicit form) is in $\mathbf{P}$ with respect to the size of G.*

Proof. Let $F = (G, H)$ and player i be given. We propose a labeling procedure to determine whether i has a winning strategy. For ease of understanding, we interpret the game base H as a tree and use standard vocabulary: each history h represents a *node* and each minimal extension ha of h is a (direct) *child* of h, the empty history ϵ is the root, etc. We use four types of labels for nodes $h \in H$, where $\varphi \in \Gamma$: φ, standing for "φ is true on all completions of v_h"; $[\varphi]$, for "there is an i-strategy in h that guarantees that φ will be true"; $\langle \neg \varphi \rangle$, for "there is a completion of v_h that makes φ false"; and G_φ, for "a node labelled φ is reachable". We use $L(h)$ to denote the set of labels of node h. We apply the following steps to H. For each formula $\psi \in \Gamma$:

(1) Label all leaf nodes h (i.e. maximal histories) with $[\psi]$ and ψ if $v_h(\psi) = \mathbf{t}$ and with $\langle \neg \psi \rangle$ if $v_h(\psi) = \mathbf{f}$. (This is possible because $\mathcal{P}rops = \bigcup_{i \in \mathcal{P}layers} \mathcal{P}_i$.)

Now, we apply the following steps as long as possible:

(2) Let $h \in H \backslash H_i$. Label h with $[\psi]$ (resp. ψ) if all children (i.e. direct successors) h' of h are labelled with $[\psi]$ (resp. ψ); otherwise, label h with $\langle \neg \psi \rangle$.

(3) Let $h \in H_i$. Label h with $[\psi]$ (resp. $\langle \neg \psi \rangle$) if there is a child labelled $[\psi]$ (resp. $\langle \neg \psi \rangle$) (i.e. player i can make ψ (resp. $\neg \psi$) true) and with ψ if all children are labelled with ψ .[3]

Now we have for $\varphi \in \Gamma$: *There is an i-strategy s_i such that for all F-histories* $h \in H|_{s_i}$ *we have* $v_h(\varphi) = \mathbf{t}$ *iff the root node is labeled* $[\varphi]$, i.e. $[\varphi] \in L(\epsilon)$.

The following steps label some subtrees as invalid (we use a label $\bot$)—we cannot immediately delete these trees due to technical reasons. For all nodes h in the tree do the following:

(4) If $\varphi \in L(h) \cap \Gamma_i$, then label all children of h with $\bot$. [This ensures Condition 3 of Def. 2.10, identifies the lowest occurrence of a node labelled $\varphi \in \Gamma_i$.]

(5) If there is no $\psi \in \Gamma \backslash \Gamma_i$ with $\{[\psi], \langle \neg \psi \rangle\} \subseteq L(h)$, then label all children $\bot$. [Condition 2(a) and 2(b) of Def. 2.10.]

(6) If $\varphi \in L(h) \cap \Gamma_i$ and $\bot \notin L(h)$, then label all predecessors of h with G_φ.

(7) Check whether there is a $\varphi \in \Gamma_i$ and $\psi \in \Gamma \backslash \Gamma_i$ with $\{G_\varphi, [\varphi], [\psi], \langle \neg \psi \rangle\} \subseteq L(h)$ and a leaf node h' reachable from h with $\{\langle \neg \psi \rangle, [\varphi]\} \subseteq L(h')$ or $\{[\psi], \langle \neg \varphi \rangle\} \subseteq L(h')$. If this is not the case, then label h and all children with $\bot$ [Condition 2(c) of Def. 2.10.]

(8) Remove all labels G_φ from all nodes and apply the following again: For all h, if $\varphi \in L(h) \cap \Gamma_i$ and $\bot \notin L(h)$, then label all predecessors of h with G_φ.

Now, we remove all nodes labelled $\bot$ from H and observe: *There is a goal-achieving i-strategy s_i iff* $\{[\varphi], G_\varphi\} \subseteq L(\epsilon)$ *for some* $\varphi \in \Gamma_i$.

Finally, we need to consider costs. We introduce new labels C_x^φ for the nodes where $\varphi \in \Gamma_i$ and $x \in \mathbb{R} \cup \{\infty\}$.[4] The intuitive reading is that φ can be guaranteed with cost x.

(9) If h is a leaf node with $\varphi \in L(h) \cap \Gamma_i$, then label it with $C_{\hat{c}_i(h)}^\varphi$ where $\hat{c}_i(a_1 \ldots a_n) = c_i(a_1) + \cdots + c_i(a_n)$; otherwise with C_∞.

In the following we say that a node is labelled with $C_?^\varphi$ if it is labelled with a label of the above type C_x^φ for some $x \in \mathbb{R} \cup \{\infty\}$. Finally, we apply the following steps to H for as long as possible:

(10) If $h \in H \backslash H_i$ is not labelled $C_?^\varphi$ and all children of h are labelled with $C_?^\varphi$, then label h with $C_{\max\{x | h' \in S \text{ and } h' \text{ is labelled } C_x^\varphi\}}^\varphi$, where S is the set of all children of h. [Computes the costs, cf. Def. 2.12.]

(11) If $h \in H_i$ is not labelled $C_?^\varphi$, and all children of h are labelled $C_?^\varphi$, then label h with $C_{\min\{x | h' \in S \text{ and } h' \text{ is labelled } C_x^\varphi\}}$, where S is the set of all children of h labelled $C_?^\varphi$. [Ensures Def. 2.12.]

Now, s_i *is winning iff* $\{[\varphi], G_\varphi, C_x^\varphi\} \subseteq L(\epsilon)$ *with $x \leq C_i$ for some* $\varphi \in \Gamma_i$. The described algorithm runs in time polynomial in $|G|$. □

Proposition 3.2. *The general problem whether a player is winning in a BSG G is in Δ_2^P and is* **coNP***-hard with respect to the size of G.*

Proof. We modify the algorithm given in the proof of Proposition 3.1. We observe that we only need to modify step 1 of the algorithm, since the propositions in

---

[3] If for some formula ψ both $\psi, \neg \psi \in \Gamma$, a node could have all labels $[\psi], [\neg \psi], \langle \neg \psi \rangle$, $\langle \neg \neg \psi \rangle$; double negations cannot be removed! Also, $\psi \in L(h)$ iff $\langle \neg \psi \rangle \notin L(h)$.

[4] ∞ has its standard meaning; in particular, $x < \infty$ for all $x \in \mathbb{R}$.

$Props \backslash \bigcup_{i \in Players} \mathcal{P}_i$ never occur on a history. Now, let $\psi[v_h]$ be ψ but with each proposition $p \in \bigcup_{i \in Players} \mathcal{P}_i$ in ψ replaced by $\top$ (resp. $\bot$) if $v_h(p) = \mathbf{t}$ (resp. if $v_h(p) = \mathbf{f}$). Then in step 1, we replace $v_h(\psi) = \mathbf{t}$ by $\models \psi[v_h]$ and $v_h(\psi) = \mathbf{f}$ by $\not\models \psi[v_h]$. The modified algorithm can be implemented by a deterministic Turing machine with **NP**-oracle.

coNP-hardness is shown by a reduction of SAT to the complement of our problem. Suppose $\psi \equiv \exists x_1, \ldots x_n \varphi(x_1, \ldots, x_n)$ is a SAT instance. We define $Props = \{x_1, \ldots, x_n\}$, $Players = \{1\}$, $\mathcal{P}_1 = \emptyset$, $\Gamma = \Gamma_1 = \{\neg\varphi\}$, omitting the other elements of F. Then there is only a single game base $H = \{\epsilon\}$ and we have that i is not winning iff $v(\neg\varphi) = \mathbf{f}$ for some valuation of $Props$ iff ψ is true [cf. condition 1 of Def. 2.10[5]].   □

The next result sheds light on the interesting case of compact representations. In this paper, we only consider the case of π-alternating (full-branching) game bases. Note that there is a gap between lower and upper bound.

Proposition 3.3. *The problem whether a player is winning in a frame F over π-alternating F-game bases is in Σ_4^P and is Σ_2^P-hard in the size of F and π.*

Proof. **Membership**: Firstly, we sketch an algorithm checking whether i is winning in (F, π) (cf. Def. 2.10). We proceed bottom-up and assume that h, h', h'' are given as in Definition 2.10.

The problem given in item 3 of Def. 2.10, denoted as the language L_3, can be solved by a non-deterministic TM in polynomial time by guessing a completion v'' of the h''-induced valuation and because Γ_i is part of the input and can be traversed in polynomial time. The same holds for the problem given in item 2(b) of Def. 2.10, which we denote by L_{2b}. Thus, $L_{2b}, L_3 \in \mathbf{NP}$.

The problem given in 2(a) of Def. 2.10, denoted L_{2a}, can be solved by a non-deterministic **NP**-oracle TM in polynomial time by first guessing an i-extension v' of the h''-induced valuation and checking whether for all completions v of v', $v(\varphi') = \mathbf{t}$. The latter can be implemented by an oracle guessing a completion v, checking whether $v(\varphi') = \mathbf{f}$ and reverting the answer. This shows that $L_{2a} \in \Sigma_2^P$.

Problem L_{2c} corresponding to 2(c) can also be solved analogously to 2(b) by guessing an appropriate completion; thus, $L_{2c} \in \mathbf{NP}$.

Summing up, item 2, denoted by problem L_2, can be solved by a deterministic TM with an oracle solving L_{2a}, L_{2b}, L_{2c}. Thus, $L_2 \in \Sigma_2^P$.

Analogously, the complement of the problem in item 1 of Def. 2.10, $\bar{L}_1$, can be solved by a non-deterministic TM in polynomial time: firstly, a completion v of the h'-induced valuation is guessed and then it is verified whether $v(\varphi) = \mathbf{f}$. Hence, $L_1 \in \mathbf{coNP}$.

Now, for a given s_i the question whether for all F-histories $h \in H|_{s_i}$ there is a subhistory $h' \leq h$ and a formula $\varphi \in \Sigma_i$ such that the conditions 1, 2 and 3 hold and can be solved in Σ_3^P. We denote the problem by L. To see this we construct a non-deterministic TM with a Σ_2^P oracle accepting the complement of L. $(\star)$

---

[5] Note that in this case conditions 2 and 3 of Def. 2.10 are vacuously true, as ϵ has no proper subhistories.

Firstly, the machines guesses an F-history h and checks whether for all $h' \leq h$ (there are only polynomially many) and all $\varphi \in \Gamma_i$ (Γ_i is part of the input), conditions 1, 2 or 3 are violated. The latter can be determined by a query to a $\Sigma_2^{\mathbf{P}}$ oracle following our previous considerations. So, $L \in \mathbf{coNP}^{\Sigma_2^{\mathbf{P}}} = \mathbf{\Pi}_3^{\mathbf{P}}$.

Finally, to check whether i is winning we use a non-deterministic $\mathbf{\Pi}_3^{\mathbf{P}}$-oracle TM to guess a strategy s_i and to verify whether it satisfies the conditions of Definition 2.10 and whether $c(s_i) \leq C_i$. We have just shown the verification of the former can be done in $\mathbf{\Pi}_3^{\mathbf{P}}$. Whether s_i adheres to the cost limit can be incorporated in $(\star)$. This shows that whether there is a winning strategy can be solved in $\Sigma_4^{\mathbf{P}}$.

Hardness: Next, we prove $\Sigma_2^{\mathbf{P}}$-hardness by a reduction of Q_2SAT [13]. Let $X = \{x_1, \ldots, x_n\}$, $Y = \{y_1 \ldots y_m\}$ and let $x \notin X \cup Y$ be a fresh variable. Suppose that $\psi \equiv \exists X \forall Y \varphi(X, Y)$ is a Q_2SAT instance.[6] We define $\textit{Players} = \{1\}$, $\Gamma = \{x\} \cup \Gamma_1$, $\Gamma_1 = \{\varphi\}$, $\textit{Props} = X \cup Y \cup \{x\}$, $\mathcal{P}_1 = X \cup \{x\}$, and no cost limits.

"$\Rightarrow$:" Suppose 1 is winning. Then, on all histories (there is only one for a given strategy!) there is a (sub)history $h' = x_{i_1}, \ldots, x_{i_k}$ such that it is true that $\forall X \backslash \{x_{i_1}, \ldots, x_{i_k}\} \forall Y \varphi[v_{h'}]$; here, $\varphi[v_{h'}]$ is φ but with proposition $p \in \{x_{i_1}, \ldots, x_{i_k}\}$ in φ replaced by $\top$ if $v_{h'}(p) = \mathbf{t}$ and by $\bot$ if $v_{h'}(p) = \mathbf{f}$. However, this implies that $\exists X \backslash \{x_{i_1}, \ldots, x_{i_k}\} \forall Y \varphi[v_{h'}]$ holds and thus that ψ is true.

"$\Leftarrow$:" Suppose ψ is true and let v_X be a witnessing truth assignment of the variables in X. Let s_X be the strategy that assigns truth values to propositions according to v_X with respect to the order $x_1, \ldots, x_n$ and makes x true afterwards. We show that s_X is a winning strategy (again, note that there is only one history for a fixed s_X). Then there is a minimal subsequence $h' = x_1, \ldots, x_k$ with $\forall X \backslash \{x_1, \ldots, x_k\} \forall Y \varphi[v_{h'}]$. Such a sequence exists because the history $h = x_1, \ldots, x_n, x$ satisfies φ (for, ψ is true). We need to show that all the other conditions of a goal-achieving strategy are satisfied. We consider h' and first assume that $h \neq h'$ (i.e. $x_k \neq x$) and consider $x \in \Gamma$. In this case, 3 of Def. 2.10 is true by definition. Condition 2(a) of Def. 2.10 holds because the 1-extension in which x is set $\mathbf{t}$ is a witness. For condition 2(b), any completion where x is set $\mathbf{f}$ is sufficient; and for 2(c), payer 1 has to choose an appropriate truth value for x. For $h = h'$, the same argument holds for all subhistories, and in the last step the goal of 1 is already true. $\square$

4   Conclusion

In this article, we propose a game-like model to describe how an agent can go about trying to achieve a goal without letting the others know until the goal has been reached. The turn-based Boolean games used in our setting facilitate modeling situations where a player can play and strategize based on how the others have acted in the history of the game, in order to keep the player's intended goals secret. The point of *trying to achieve something in secret* would be lost if we considered normal form games instead of turn-based ones.

---

[6] Here, $\exists X \xi(X)$ abbreviates $\exists x_1 \ldots \exists x_n \xi(x_1, \ldots, x_n)$.

Various recent work [9,8] has focused on variants of cooperative Boolean games, introduced in [7]. The current work has taken some inspiration from those articles, but we used the idea of Boolean games that was introduced in [10] for modeling interactive situations.

We have addressed the question whether a player is winning in a game and have analyzed the computational complexity with respect to explicit and compact game representations. In our future research, we would like to close the gaps in the complexity results and to consider more sophisticated solution concepts. We also plan to elaborate on other compact game representations, not only π-alternating game bases.

For future work, it would also be interesting to combine the notion of secret goals with other forms of uncertainty; for example, agents could have incomplete information about which other agent controls which variables, as in [16]. One issue that has not been touched in this work is that of 'cooperativeness' [7]. In what ways can some of the players cooperate to achieve their goals? We would like to propose characterizations and complexity results for cooperativeness in our setting. Finally, it would be interesting to investigate whether one can adapt a dynamic framework similar to [11] to model the idea of achieving secret goals.

Acknowledgements. We would like to thank the three anonymous reviewers for their useful suggestions. This research was supported by Vici grant NWO 277-80-001 awarded to Rineke Verbrugge.

References

1. Ågotnes, T., van der Hoek, W., Wooldridge, M.: Scientia potentia est. In: Sonenberg, et al. (eds.) [15], pp. 735–742
2. Barbier, M.: D-Day Deception: Operation Fortitude and the Normandy Invasion. Greenwood Press, Westport (2007)
3. Bonzon, E., Lagasquie-Schiex, M.-C., Lang, J., Zanuttini, B.: Boolean games revisited. In: Brewka, G., Coradeschi, S., Perini, A., Traverso, P. (eds.) ECAI. Frontiers in Artificial Intelligence and Applications, vol. 141, pp. 265–269. IOS Press (2006)
4. Dignum, F., Dunin-Keplicz, B., Verbrugge, R.: Creating collective intention through dialogue. Logic Journal of the IGPL 9(2), 289–304 (2001)
5. Dumas, A.: Le Comte de Monte-Cristo. Gallimard, Paris (1844)
6. Dunin-Kęplicz, B., Verbrugge, R.: Teamwork in Multi-Agent Systems: A Formal Approach. Wiley, Chichester (2010)
7. Dunne, P.E., van der Hoek, W., Kraus, S., Wooldridge, M.: Cooperative boolean games. In: Padgham, L., Parkes, D.C., Müller, J.P., Parsons, S. (eds.) 7th International Joint Conference on Autonomous Agents and Multiagent Systems (AAMAS 2008), pp. 1015–1022. IFAAMAS (2008)
8. Endriss, U., Kraus, S., Lang, J., Wooldridge, M.: Incentive engineering for Boolean games. In: Walsh (ed.) [17], pp. 2602–2607
9. Grant, J., Kraus, S., Wooldridge, M., Zuckerman, I.: Manipulating Boolean games through communication. In: Walsh (ed.) [17], pp. 210–215

10. Harrenstein, P., van der Hoek, W., Meyer, J.-J., Witteveen, C.: Boolean games. In: van Benthem, J. (ed.) Proceedings of the 8th Conference on Theoretical Aspects of Rationality and Knowledge, pp. 287–298. Morgan Kaufmann Publishers Inc., San Francisco (2001)
11. Herzig, A., Lorini, E., Moisan, F., Troquard, N.: A dynamic logic of normative systems. In: Walsh (ed.) [17], pp. 228–233
12. Osborne, M., Rubinstein, A.: A Course in Game Theory. MIT Press, Cambridge (1994)
13. Papadimitriou, C.: Computational Complexity. Addison-Wesley, Reading (1994)
14. Raiffa, H., Richardson, J., Metcalfe, D.: Negotiation Analysis: The Science and Art of Collaborative Decision Making. Belknap Press of Harvard Univ. Press, Cambridge (2002)
15. Sonenberg, L., Stone, P., Tumer, K., Yolum, P. (eds.): Proceedings 10th International Conference on Autonomous Agents and Multiagent Systems (AAMAS 2011). IFAAMAS (2011)
16. van der Hoek, W., Troquard, N., Wooldridge, M.: Knowledge and control. In: Sonenberg, et al. (eds.) [15], pp. 719–726
17. Walsh, T. (ed.): Proceedings of the 22nd International Joint Conference on Artificial Intelligence, IJCAI 2011, Barcelona, Catalonia, Spain, July 16-22. IJCAI/AAAI (2011)
18. Zlotkin, G., Rosenschein, J.S.: Incomplete information and deception in multi-agent negotiation. In: Proceedings of the Twelfth International Joint Conference on Artificial Intelligence, pp. 225–231 (1991)

Incorporating PGMs into a BDI Architecture

Yingke Chen[1], Jun Hong[1], Weiru Liu[1], Lluís Godo[1,2],
Carles Sierra[1,2], and Michael Loughlin[1]

[1] Queen's University Belfast, Belfast, UK
[2] IIIA, CSIC, Bellaterra, Spain

Abstract. In this paper, we present a hybrid BDI-PGM framework, in which PGMs (Probabilistic Graphical Models) are incorporated into a BDI (belief-desire-intention) architecture. This work is motivated by the need to address the scalability and noisy sensing issues in SCADA (Supervisory Control And Data Acquisition) systems. Our approach uses the incorporated PGMs to model the uncertainty reasoning and decision making processes of agents situated in a stochastic environment. In particular, we use Bayesian networks to reason about an agent's beliefs about the environment based on its sensory observations, and select optimal plans according to the utilities of actions defined in influence diagrams. This approach takes the advantage of the scalability of the BDI architecture and the uncertainty reasoning capability of PGMs. We present a prototype of the proposed approach using a transit scenario to validate its effectiveness.

1 Introduction

SCADA (Supervisory Control And Data Acquisition) systems have proved to be a powerful and successful technology in various application domains, including power generation, power transmission, transportation, and military applications [1]. However, the complexity of such systems increases too rapidly to be handled by traditional software engineering approaches. This complexity comes from the large number of subsystems needed to implement business process requirements [2]. Moreover, trained experts who supervise the entire system also face the challenge of dealing with explosively growing amounts of sensory data, especially in emergency situations. Current SCADA systems lack autonomous and intelligent capabilities to meet these pressing requirements and are difficult to scale up to larger and more complex deployments [3,4].

As SCADA systems are situated in dynamic environments, not all sensory data can be deemed completely accurate. Nevertheless, human experts are capable of estimating the state of the world even if the sensory data has inherent errors/noise or uncertainty, is incomplete or in conflict with data acquired from other sources. Experts also have to make decisions based on uncertain and incomplete information. Therefore, an autonomous SCADA system requires an adequate framework to reason about uncertainty and model decision making based on uncertain information.

G. Boella et al. (Eds.): PRIMA 2013, LNAI 8291, pp. 54–69, 2013.

The belief-desire-intension (BDI) agent architecture is a successful paradigm for modeling rational agents [5]. BDI agents have been used to develop SCADA systems by treating system components as autonomous agents, to provide better scalability, autonomy and intelligence [6,7,2]. Each agent's beliefs (knowledge about the environment), desires (goals), and intentions (commitments to act) are explicitly represented. These beliefs, desires, and intentions are also known as the agent's mental states. Using the BDI architecture, one can specify, design and verify different types of agents in different application domains. AgentSpeak [8] is an agent-oriented programming language for specifying agents within the BDI framework.

In this paper, motivated by the need to address the scalability and noisy sensing issues in SCADA systems, our main contribution is the incorporation of two probabilistic graphical models (PGMs) (Bayesian networks (BNs) and influence diagrams (IDs)) into a BDI architecture. Specifically, we introduce an agent's epistemic state [9] in the hybrid BDI-PGM framework, and define that based on PGMs which model the stochastic environment where the agent is situated. Sensory observations in the environment are first fed into the PGMs, and the corresponding belief sets are derived after uncertainty propagation in the PGMs. Since it is possible that an agent may be *ignorant* about the environment because of the inherent uncertainty, we take into account the utilities of actions, and maximize the utility in such situation. For example, when a train agent does not know the actual state of a signal, it prefers to *stop* rather than keeping *moving*. We specify utilities of actions in various situations using influence diagrams (IDs), and formulate plan selection as a utility-based decision problem. The hybrid BDI-PGM framework takes the advantage of the scalability of the BDI architecture and increases its uncertainty reasoning capability by incorporating PGMs (BNs and IDs) into it. In addition, a prototype of the proposed approach applied in a transit scenario is designed and implemented to validate its effectiveness.

The rest of the paper are organized as follows. Section 2 reviews the related work. Section 3 presents the essentials of the techniques we use, including the AgentSpeak framework, BNs, and IDs. Section 4 discusses how to embed PGMs into a BDI architecture, and propose a utility-driven plan selection approach. In Section 5, we describe the design and implementation of the transit scenario with noisy sensing to validate our approach. Section 6 concludes the paper and describes future work.

2   Related Work

In [2], the advantages of applying MAS (multi-agent systems) technologies to address the challenges of traditional control systems are discussed. The advantages (e.g., scalability, autonomy and intelligence) are illustrated through a case study describing a SCADA system for electricity transportation management. In [6,7] the authors focus on the application of MAS to power engineering, where problems are formalized, technologies are discussed, and several implementation issues are addressed. In [10] it is reported that MAS technologies outperform classical technologies in the protection of power distribution systems.

There have been several approaches to modeling uncertainty in MAS. In [11] the degrees of beliefs that a BDI agent has are quantified using Dempster-Shafer theory. The graded BDI architecture [12] uses uncertain beliefs (as probabilities) and graded preferences (as expected utilities) to rank plans. Bayesian networks have been widely used for modeling uncertain environments [13]. There have been studies about combining BNs with the BDI architecture to handle the uncertainty in beliefs and select appropriate plans in a dynamic environment. In [14] the agent deliberation process is modeled by a BN. Both causality and quantitative relations between beliefs are taken into account, and applicable plans are sorted so that the plan whose context has the highest likelihood to be valid is selected. Its threshold-based plan selection approach is further extended in [15] by adding bias and randomness to all applicable plans. In [16] a tool connecting an MAS development framework (Jason [17]) with a BN constructor is developed. These approaches essentially focus on selecting plans based on the likelihood of their contexts. However, the acquisition of uncertain beliefs has not been addressed. In this paper, we consider a more realistic situation, where an agent makes observations by performing sensing actions. The sensory observations are first fed into PGMs, leading to an agent's epistemic state being revised after uncertainty propagation in the PGMs. Beliefs may be derived from the revised epistemic state and such beliefs are then added to an agent's belief set.

Autonomous agents have to make rational decisions to pursue their goals (i.e., selecting appropriate plans) in a stochastic environment. Markov decision processes (MDP) and partially observable MDPs (POMDPs), as well as their graphical representations, IDs [18], are popular frameworks to model an agent's decision making processes in stochastic environments. In [19] POMDPs and the BDI architecture are compared, and the correspondences between desires and intensions on the one hand, and rewards and policies on the other hand are illustrated. In [20] the relationship between the policies of MDPs and the intentions in the BDI architecture is further discussed. In particular, it shows that intentions in the BDI architecture can be mapped to policies in MDPs. The performance and scalability of (PO)MDPs and the BDI architecture are compared in [21]. In particular, (PO)MDPs have a better performance when the domain size is tractable since the BDI architecture uses a heuristic planning approach. The BDI architecture has better scalability since the state space in (PO)MDPs grows explosively when modeling complex application domains (e.g., SCADA systems). A hybrid BDI-POMDP framework [22] has been proposed for quantitatively analysing the teaming behaviours of agents in an uncertain environment. Different from this approach, our proposed approach embeds PGMs into the BDI architecture to model the uncertainty about the environment and reason about optimal decisions of agents.

3   Preliminaries

In this section, we describe the basics of the techniques we use in the paper.

3.1   AgentSpeak

An AgentSpeak agent $\mathbb{A}$ can be represented as a tuple $\langle \mathsf{BB}, \mathsf{PLib}, \mathsf{E}, \mathsf{A}, \mathsf{I}, \mathcal{S}_\varepsilon, \mathcal{S}_\mathcal{O}, \mathcal{S}_\mathcal{I} \rangle$, where $\mathsf{BB}, \mathsf{PLib}, \mathsf{E}, \mathsf{A}, \mathsf{I}$ are its belief base, plan library, event set, action set and intention stack, respectively. $\mathcal{S}_\varepsilon, \mathcal{S}_\mathcal{O}, \mathcal{S}_\mathcal{I}$ are the selection functions for events, plans and intentions, respectively. We define beliefs, goals, triggering events, and plans for an AgentSpeak agent following the notation in [8]. We use Φ to denote a finite set of symbols for predicates, actions, and constant, and $\mathcal{V}$ to denote a set of variables. We use $a, b, \ldots$ to denote elements in Φ and $X, Y, \ldots$ to denote elements in $\mathcal{V}$. A term t is a constant symbol in Φ or a variable in $\mathcal{V}$.

Definition 1. *Let b be a n-ary predicate symbol, and $t_1, \ldots, t_n$ be terms (collectively referred as t thereafter), then $b(t)$ is a belief atom. Given belief atoms $b(t)$ and $c(t)$, then $b(t)$, $c(t)$, $b(t) \wedge c(t)$, and $\neg b(t)$ are beliefs.*

Definition 2. *Let g be a predicate symbol, and $t_1, \ldots, t_n$ be terms, then $!g(t)$ and $?g(t)$ are goals. Specifically, $!g(t)$ is an achievement goal and $?g(t)$ is a test goal.*

Definition 3. *Let $b(t)$ be a belief atom, and $!g(t)$ and $?g(t)$ be goals, then $+b(t)$, $-b(t)$, $+!g(t)$, $-!g(t)$, $+?g(t)$ and $-?g(t)$ are triggering events. Here operators $+$ and $-$ denote addition and deletion of a belief or goal, respectively.*

Definition 4. *Let a be an action symbol, and $t_1, \ldots, t_n$ be terms, then $a(t)$ is an action.*

Definition 5. *Let e be a triggering event, $b_1, \ldots, b_m$ be beliefs, $h_1, \ldots, h_n$ be goals or actions, then $e : b_1 \wedge \ldots \wedge b_m \leftarrow h_1; \ldots; h_n$ is a plan. Here, $b_1 \wedge \ldots \wedge b_m$ is referred as the context of the plan.*

The belief base represents an agent's knowledge about the environment in which it is situated. The plan library PLib contains a set of plans for either achieving the agent's goals or responding to changes in the environment. In AgentSpeak, an agent's behaviour is specified by a set of beliefs and plans. Each plan may specify a set of actions to be performed, a set of subgoals to be achieved and a set of conditions under which the plan is applicable. A plan is applicable, when its *triggering event* occurs and its *context* is valid. The applicable plan can be executed by performing actions and achieving subgoals specified in its *body*. The execution of a plan is the agent's response to changes in the environment and the means to achieve its goals.

In a reasoning cycle as shown in Fig. 1, agent $\mathbb{A}$ responds to the triggering event e at the top of its event stack, by selecting and executing a plan p, which is referred to as an intention. A set of plans, whose contexts are valid according to the belief base BB, will be identified from the plan library PLib. Only one plan will be selected and executed. Performing an action may change the environment and consequently change the agent's belief base. The execution of the chosen plan may also add new events to the event stack, which will be handled in future reasoning cycles.

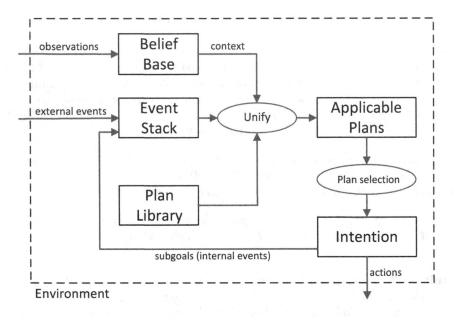

Fig. 1. The reasoning cycle of an AgentSpeak agent

Example 1. Assume that agent $\mathbb{A}$ represents an autonomous train. In train agent $\mathbb{A}$'s belief base BB, some of its belief atoms can be:

- Sig(red): the signal is red;
- Moving: the train is moving;
- Train($\mathbb{A}$, 100): agent $\mathbb{A}$'s own position;
- Train($\mathbb{B}$, 300): another train's position;
- Station(central, 1000): the location of the train station named central.

The train agent can perform the following actions:

- stop: stop from normal speed;
- accel: accelerate from still to normal speed;
- move(X, Y): move from the current position X to the new position Y with normal speed;
- senseSignal: observe the signal within its sensing range;
- openDoor: open doors on the train for passengers to board;
- closeDoor: close doors after boarding;
- senseBoarding: observe whether boarding is completed;

The following plans in PLib specify the train agent A's behaviours under different contexts. P1 and P2: if a signal is sensed either green or red while the train is moving, it will either keep moving or stop, and keep checking the signal. P3 and P4: while the train is still, it will move when the signal becomes green; otherwise it will stay still and keep sensing.

- (P1)+!drive : Moving ∧ Sig(green) ← move; senseSignal; !drive;
- (P2)+!drive : Moving ∧ Sig(red) ← stop; senseSignal; !drive;
- (P3)+!drive : ¬ Moving ∧ Sig(red) ← senseSignal; !drive;
- (P4)+!drive : ¬ Moving ∧ Sig(green) ← move; senseSignal; !drive;

3.2 Probabilistic Graphical Models

Probabilistic graphical models (PGMs) are a combination of graph theory and probability theory by encoding probabilistic dependency relations in the graphical structures. Bayesian networks (BNs) and influence diagrams (IDs) are two popular PGMs. They provide a natural specification language for various problem domains with inherent uncertainty. Over the past decades, a set of efficient algorithms and sophisticated tools have been developed for PGMs [13].

A Bayesian network $\mathcal{B}$ over a set of random variables $\overrightarrow{\mathbf{X}} = \{X_1, \ldots, X_n\}$ is defined by a pair $\mathcal{B}(\overrightarrow{\mathbf{X}}) = \langle G, \Theta \rangle$. G is a directed acyclic graph, in which each node represents a random variable X_j, with edges representing the dependencies between variables. Θ is a set of parameters $\theta_{x_{j,i}|\pi_{j,i}} = P(x_{j,i} \mid \pi_{j,i})$ for each instantiation of $x_{j,i}$ of variable X_j given $\pi_{j,i}$ which is the instantiation of the parents of X_j. These conditional probabilities are used to quantify dependencies between variables. Given a BN $\mathcal{B}$, a joint probability distribution over $\{X_1, \ldots, X_n\}$, $P(X_1, \ldots, X_n)$, is defined.

As an example, the Bayesian network as shown in Fig. 2(a) represents the dependency relation between the observation of a signal and the actual state of the signal. It shows that the observation (O, a binary variable with two states 'oR' (for observed 'red') and 'oG' (for observed 'green')) is determined by the actual state of the signal (S, a binary variable with two states 'red' and 'green'). The conditional probability table in the Fig. 2(b) shows the probability distribution over observations given different states of the signal. Each number in this table represents the conditional probability of seeing an observation given the actual state. For example the probability of observing 'oR' given the signal is 'red' is denoted as $P(\text{oR} \mid \text{red}) = P(O = \text{oR} \mid S = \text{red}) = 0.7$.

The uncertainty reasoning in BNs is carried out by applying the Bayes' rule. Assuming the initial prior probability distribution over the states of the signal (S node) is uniform, i.e., $(0.5, 0.5)$, the posterior probability distribution can be inferred from its prior probability distribution, the conditional probabilities and the new observation. For example, the probability of the signal being 'red' given 'red' is observed ($P(\text{oR}) = 1$) is computed as follows:

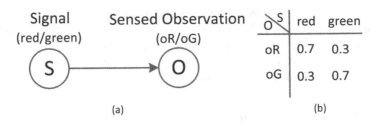

Fig. 2. (a) The Bayesian network for a signal and its observation. (b) The condition probability table for $P(O \mid S)$.

$$P(\text{red} \mid \text{oR}) = \frac{P(\text{red}, \text{oR})}{P(\text{oR})} = \frac{P(\text{red}, \text{oR})}{P(\text{red}, \text{oR}) + P(\text{green}, \text{oR})}$$

$$= \frac{P(\text{oR}|\text{red})P(\text{red})}{P(\text{oR}|\text{red})P(\text{red}) + P(\text{oR}|\text{green})P(\text{green})}$$

$$= \frac{0.7 \cdot 0.5}{0.7 \cdot 0.5 + 0.3 \cdot 0.5} = 0.7.$$

Influence diagrams (also known as decision graphs) are extended from Bayesian networks by introducing actions and their utilities. They can model the problem of making optimal decisions in an uncertain environment given incomplete information. An influence diagram $\mathcal{D}$ is defined by a pair $\mathcal{D}(\vec{\mathbf{X}}, \vec{\mathbf{D}}, \vec{\mathbf{U}}) = \langle G, \Theta \rangle$, which models a set of random variables $\vec{\mathbf{X}}$, a set of actions $\vec{\mathbf{D}}$, and the utilities of actions $\vec{\mathbf{U}}$ in various situations. There are three types of nodes in G: chance nodes (representing the environment), decision nodes (representing actions), and utility nodes (representing the utilities of actions). In Fig. 3(a), D ($\vec{\mathbf{D}} = \{D\}$) and U ($\vec{\mathbf{U}} = \{U\}$) are a decision node and a utility node, respectively. The parameter of the U node $\theta_{U|D,S} = U(D, S)$ is set in the utility table as shown in Fig. 3(b). For example, $U(D = \text{stop}, S = \text{red}) = 10$ indicates that 10 reward points can be obtained if the train stops when the signal is red. Thereafter, we will denote $U(D = \text{stop}, S = \text{red})$ as $U(\text{stop}, \text{red})$ for simplicity.

The optimal decision is selected from a set of possible decisions based on their expected utilities (EU), which takes into account the actions utilities and the probability distribution over the state of the world. For example, assuming the initial prior probability distribution of S is uniform and 'red' is observed ('oR'), $EU(\text{stop})$ is calculated as follows:

$$EU(\text{stop}) = \sum_{s \in S} P(s \mid \text{oR})U(\text{stop}, s)$$

$$= P(\text{red} \mid \text{oR})U(\text{stop}, \text{red}) + P(\text{green} \mid \text{oR})U(\text{stop}, \text{green})$$

$$= 0.7 \cdot 10 + 0.3 \cdot -1 = 6.7.$$

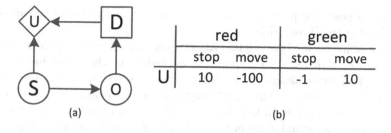

	red		green	
	stop	move	stop	move
U	10	-100	-1	10

(a)   (b)

Fig. 3. (a) The influence diagram for decision making based on information observed from a signal. (b) The utility table for $U(D, S)$.

IDs (more specifically, dynamic IDs) are graphical representations of MDPs and POMDPs, all of which can be used to reason about an agent's actions given incomplete information about the environment. Different from (PO)MDPs, the computational complexity of reasoning under uncertainty in PGMs can be reduced by making use of the defined graphical structures, in particular, the conditional dependencies among random variables [18].

4   Incorporating PGMs into a BDI Architecture

In this section, we describe how to incorporate PGMs into a BDI architecture to model the uncertainty about the situated stochastic environment and an agent's decision making process. First, an agent's epistemic states for random variables, which model the uncertainty about the stochastic environment, and the corresponding belief sets of the epistemic state are defined. The possible states of the environment, sensory observations, and their relationships are modeled using PGMs. The uncertainty propagation is carried out by BNs. The belief sets derived from the epistemic states will trigger the selection of relevant plans. When more than one plan is applicable due to uncertainty in an agent's beliefs, we formulate the plan selection as a decision making process, which models utilities of actions in influence diagrams, and propose a utility-driven approach for plan selection.

4.1   Reasoning about Beliefs under Uncertainty

In a foggy day, the signal may not be as clear as in a normal day. We cannot be certain about the colour of the signal based on a sensory observation. More specifically, we cannot be sure whether the signal is red ('Sig(red)') when a certain sensory observation is given ($P(oR) = 1$), let alone with given an uncertain evidence about the sensory observation, such as $P(oR) = 0.8$ and $P(oG) = 0.2$. The relationship between the actual state of the signal and a sensory observation can be modelled by a BN as shown in Fig. 2(a). Inferring the actual state (S node) from an observation (O node) is carried out by the standard reasoning procedure in BNs. In other words, an observation is seen as evidence on O

node, and the posterior probability distribution over the states of the signal is calculated using the Bayes' rule.

In the reasoning cycle of the original AgentSpeak agent, given an event, usually a set of applicable plans will be identified according to the belief base. As an autonomous and rational agent, in addition to considering uncertainty about the stochastic environment, the agent may also need to take into account the utilities of actions in plans. In the signal example, when the train agent has no clear idea about the actual state of the signal, it will perform according to the utilities of possible actions. The train agent will be rewarded if it stops, or may face a penalty for violating the traffic regulations. In addition to specifying the uncertainty about the state of a variable and its relationship with its sensory observation in a BN, the relevant actions and their corresponding utilities in various situations are specified in an ID as shown in Fig 3. The plan which include actions with the highest utility will be selected and executed.

First, we formally define the epistemic state [9] to link PGMs to the belief base of an AgentSpeak agent.

Definition 6. *Given a set of discrete random variables* $\vec{\mathbf{X}} = \{X_1, \ldots, X_n\}$*, a set of actions* $\vec{\mathbf{D}}$*, and the corresponding utilities of actions in various situations* $\vec{\mathbf{U}}$*, modeled by an ID* $\mathcal{D}(\vec{\mathbf{X}}, \vec{\mathbf{D}}, \vec{\mathbf{U}})$*, an agent's epistemic state about the states of random variable* X_i *is defined as* $\Phi(X_i) = \langle P_{X_i}, \mathcal{D}(\vec{\mathbf{X}}, \vec{\mathbf{D}}, \vec{\mathbf{U}}) \rangle$*, where* $P_{X_i} : S_{X_i} \to [0, 1]$ *is a prior or marginalized probability distribution obtained via* $\mathcal{D}(\vec{\mathbf{X}}, \vec{\mathbf{D}}, \vec{\mathbf{U}})$ *on the state space* S_{X_i} *of variable* X_i*.*

$\mathcal{D}(\vec{\mathbf{X}}, \vec{\mathbf{D}}, \vec{\mathbf{U}})$ will be referred as $\mathcal{D}$ thereafter if the context is unambiguous. Note that, the ID $\mathcal{D}$ included in the definition of the epistemic state can be simplified into a BN when the utilities of actions are not available.

Definition 7. *Let* $\Phi(X)$ *be an epistemic state for a discrete random variable* X *with its state space* $S_{X_i} = \{x_1, \ldots, x_n\}$*, the belief set of* $\Phi(X)$*, denoted as* $Bel(\Phi(X))$*, is defined as*

$$Bel(\Phi(X)) = \begin{cases} x_i, \text{ when } P_X(x_i) \geq \delta_i \\ \mathsf{T}, \qquad \text{ohterwise} \end{cases}$$

Here δ is a pre-defined threshold for accepting that x_i represents the real world concerning X. Notation T is a special constant representing an agent's *ignorance*, that is, an agent is not certain about the state of variable X.

Definition 8. *Given an epistemic state* $\Phi(X_i) = \langle P_{X_i}, \mathcal{D}(\vec{\mathbf{X}}, \vec{\mathbf{D}}, \vec{\mathbf{U}}) \rangle$*, and a new observation on* X_j*, represented by a probability function* P_{X_j}*, the revision of* $\Phi(X_i)$ *by* P_{X_j} *is defined as*

$$\Phi(X_i) \circ P_{X_j} = \langle P'_{X_i}, \mathcal{D}(\vec{\mathbf{X}}, \vec{\mathbf{D}}, \vec{\mathbf{U}}) \rangle$$

Here, P'_{X_i} *is the posterior probability distribution on state space* S_{X_i} *after the propagation of an uncertain input modeled by* P_{X_j} *using* $\mathcal{D}(\vec{\mathbf{X}}, \vec{\mathbf{D}}, \vec{\mathbf{U}})$*.*

Example 2. In the signal example, given the ID $\mathcal{D}(\{S, O\}, \{D\}, \{U\})$ as shown in Fig. 3, we have an epistemic state $\Phi(S) = \langle P_S, \mathcal{D} \rangle$ to represent the probability distribution over the states of the signal. Assuming we initially have the probability distribution $P_S(\text{red}) = 0.15$ and $P_S(\text{green}) = 0.85$, a new sensory observation $P_O(\text{oR}) = 0.15$ and $P_O(\text{oG}) = 0.85$ will revise the epistemic state to get $\langle P'_S, \mathcal{D} \rangle$ where $P'_S(\text{red}) = 0.09$ and $P'_S(\text{green}) = 0.91$. Given a threshold $\delta = 0.9$, the belief set of the revised epistemic state $\Phi(S) \circ P_O$ is 'green'. Consequently, a belief atom 'Sig(green)' will be added into the agent's belief base.

The posterior probability distribution based on an sensory observation, can be used as the prior probability distribution of the next sensory observation. This process repeats until an agent has reached some state that it no-longer needs to make another observation.

4.2   Utility-Driven Plan Selection

After reasoning about beliefs under uncertainty in the PGMs, beliefs will be added into an agent's belief base and these beliefs are consistent with the original AgentSpeak framework. In the signal example, when either 'Sig(green)' or 'Sig(red)' is added, the existing plans (P1-P4 in Example 1)) are still applicable.

Note that, when obtaining the belief sets from epistemic states, the pre-defined threshold may not be exceeded. In this case, the belief with the special constant T will be added to the belief base. In the signal example, when the certainty degree on any state of the signal is not high enough, we will have belief 'Sig(T)' to represent the agent's *ignorance* about the actual state of the signal. In this case, the agent can either 'stop' or 'move'. Here, we have two additional plans (P5 and P6) in the plan library.

- (P5)+!drive : Moving $\wedge$ Sig(T) $\leftarrow$ move; senseSignal; !drive;
- (P6)+!drive : Moving $\wedge$ Sig(T) $\leftarrow$ stop; senseSignal; !drive;

According to the ID $\mathcal{D}$ as shown in Fig. 3(a) and the utility table of the utility node as shown in Fig. 3(b), the train agent's plan selection shall also take into account the utilities of actions. After inferring the probability distribution over the states of the signal from sensory observations, the expected utility of each possible action is calculated. In addition to considering the contexts of plans, the expected utilities of actions in the plans will affect the plan selection of the train agent.

Example 3. In the signal example, two plans are applicable (P5 and P6) when the certainty degree on any state of the signal is not high enough, and we want to select a plan which is more reasonable in terms of the utility. First, the probability distribution over states of the signal (e.g., $P_S(\text{red}) = 0.2$ and $P_S(\text{green}) = 0.8$) will be transferred to the ID $\mathcal{D}$. Afterwards, the expected utilities of actions are calculated: $EU(\text{stop}) = 1.2$ and $EU(\text{move}) = -12$. In this case, since 'stop' is considered as more beneficial than 'move', plan P6 will be selected.

Specifically, when the probability of a particular state s_i is over a threshold, a single plan can still be selected in the first place. In this case, the expected utility is only calculated for the action in this particular plan, and the action will be selected (since its expected utility will be the maximum one). Therefore, the problem of selecting a plan with normal beliefs is a special case of plan selection when a special belief atom represents the agent's *ignorance* about the state of the variable in the environment.

Now, we extend the definition of an AgentSpeak agent as follows.

Definition 9. *An extended AgentSpeak agent* $\mathbb{A}'$ *is defined by a tuple* $\langle \mathsf{BB}, \mathsf{PLib}, \mathsf{E}, \mathsf{A}, I, \mathcal{S}_\varepsilon, \mathcal{S}_\mathcal{O}, \mathcal{S}_\mathcal{I}, \mathsf{EpS} \rangle$, *where* EpS *is a set of epistemic states, with all other items being the same as defined in Section 3.*

It should be noted that we allow an agent to have multiple epistemic states, each for a different variable (or a set of variables). This assumption is reasonable since an agent may have beliefs (which could be uncertain) and knowledge about different parts of the environment (we assume these parts are *localized* or *isolated*). For each part, the knowledge, which is represented by a BN or an ID, and its associated beliefs constitute one *localized* or *isolated* epistemic state.

The reasoning cycle of an extended AgentSpeak agent is shown in Fig. 4. Compared to the original reasoning cycle as shown in Fig. 1, the observations containing uncertain information go through epistemic states before affecting the belief base. The PGMs included in the epistemic states are used to reason about uncertain observations and derive belief sets. After applicable plans have been identified, in order to select a unique one to execute, expected unities of possible actions are calculated using the PGM.

5   MAS Transit Scenario

We use a transit scenario to validate the effectiveness of the hybrid BDI-PGM framework. We describe how to use Jason [17] to implement this scenario. Jason is an open-source interpreter for AgentSpeak which implements AgentSpeak's operational semantics and thus provides a platform for developing MAS. We use Hugin [23] to reason over the embedded PGMs. Hugin provides a friendly user interface to create, edit and manipulate BNs and IDs, and it also wraps up all functionalities (e.g., inserting evidence and propagating uncertainty) as an API for further development purposes. The implemented prototype can be considered as a proof of concept of the feasibility of applying advanced MAS technology for developing SCADA systems in the presence of uncertainty about the dynamic environment.

5.1   Transit Scenario

There are two transit trains running in the same direction on a one directional rectangle track that links two stations (as shown in Fig. 5). There are two train stations and two signals. Each train starts moving and keeps checking the signal

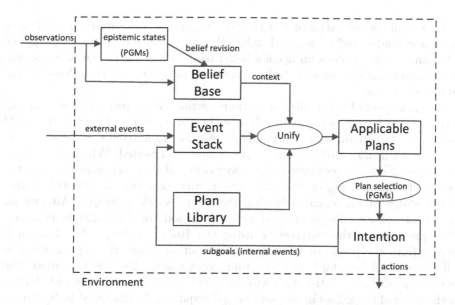

Fig. 4. The reasoning cycle of the hybrid BDI-PGM framework

when it is within the sensing range. After a train sees a red signal, it stops and keeps checking the signal. When a trains sees a green signal, it either keeps moving if it is already moving or starts moving if it is still, and it keeps checking the signal.

We assume that the weather is foggy, therefore the signal cannot be sensed with certainty. The rest of this scenario is assumed to be certain (i.e., trains do not fail and the agent always succeed in closing the door).

There is a PGM (specifically, the ID shown in Fig. 3) specified by Hugin, including the graphical structure and the parameters, to represent the knowledge about the noisy sensing situation.

5.2 MAS Implementation

Each agent's belief base contains both static information (i.e., the location of the stations and the signal) and dynamic information (i.e., the locations of both trains). Here is a snapshot of the belief base of the train agent $\mathbb{A}$.

- Train($\mathbb{B}$, 300): train $\mathbb{B}$'s position;
- Signal(1, 500): the signal 1's position;
- Moving: train $\mathbb{A}$ is moving;
- Sig(red): the signal ahead is red.

The train agents can perform the actions listed in Example 1. The goal of the entire system is to run trains safely and smoothly. The two train agents require communication with each other about their current positions.

As part of the infrastructure of the transit system, the environment class in Jason is extended and customized to handle the action of each train agent. The environment class revises an agent's belief base as a consequence of an action. The communication between train agents are also treated as actions by the environment class.

The most part of this transit scenario is certain. With respect to sensing the signal, we implemented the approach described in Section 4. Initially, the PGM specified in the Hugin format is included into the train agent's epistemic state, and a uniform prior distribution on the S node is inserted. When the sensory action 'senseSignal' is performed, an sensory observation is first sampled from the probability distribution on the observations given the probability distribution on the states of the signal, following the Monte Carlo principle. Afterwards, the sensory observation is inserted into the O node of the PGM as evidence. After propagating the uncertainty using the Hugin engine, a belief atom is derived from the posterior probability distribution about the signal, and this belief atom will be added into the train agent's belief base. Furthermore, the posterior probability distribution will serve as the prior probability distribution on the state of the signal in the next step if required. As discussed in Section 4, the original AgentSpeak plan selection procedure is still applicable.

When the train agent received the belief 'Sig(T)' for the *ignorance* about the actual state of the signal, it will further consider the utilities of actions. Besides the observation sampling and uncertainty propagation, the expected utility of each action is calculated. In this case, the difference between two applicable plans (P5 and P6) comes from their first actions. Other items in these plans are ignored since they are not relevant to the actions in the PGM. The plan, which has the action with the highest utility, will be selected.

In the customized environment class, there is also a visual panel showing the entire scenario as shown in Fig. 5. All agents (the ones for the trains, the signal, and the train stations) are located on a rectangular track. The belief base and the information from the epistemic state of each train agent are listed in the left bottom. The environment also receives input from the buttons on the right bottom (e.g. switching the signals and informing that the passengers boarding is complete). These buttons simulate the events generated by the agents for signals and train stations. The probability distribution about the signals included in agents' epistemic states are shown near the track.

5.3   Testing Scenarios

Based on the defined actions, a rich class of behaviours of the transit scenario can be specified. For example,

- When the train is approaching the train station, it stops first and opens its doors for passenger boarding. Afterwards, the train keeps sensing whether the boarding is complete. The train will then close its doors and start moving again.
- The safe distance between trains is always kept.

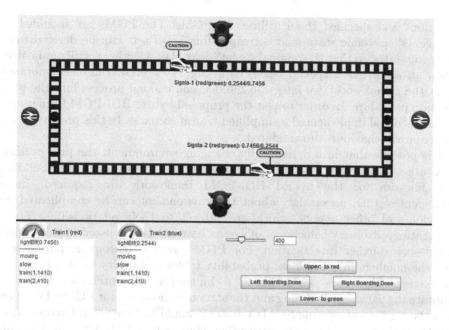

Fig. 5. The transit train scenario

With respect to the noisy sensing of the signal, we considered the following two situations:

- When one train is entering the sensing range of a signal which is green, it keeps sensing the signal and moving forward at a normal speed. Its epistemic state about the actual state of the signal keeps changing until leaving the sensing range.
- Assume the signal is initially green, and the train proceeds at a normal speed. When the train is approaching the signal, we switch the signal to red. The train's epistemic state and its belief base will change after making several observations. Additionally, since the train is close to the signal, the belief is updated quickly since the noise is small (we implicitly encoded this information into the conditional probability tables in the BNs). A sudden break stops the train.

All these behaviours have been validated by the implemented prototype.

6   Conclusions

In this paper, we addressed the problem of handling uncertainty about a stochastic environment in a BDI architecture by presenting a hybrid BDI-PGM framework. In particular, we used PGMs to model the uncertainty about the environment and their relationships. We further took into account the utilities of actions and specified these utilities in PGMs. The PGMs are included in the agents' epistemic state, and corresponding belief sets can be derived from epistemic states, so that the original AgentSpeak plan selection is still applicable. When an agent has a special belief, e.g., 'Sig(T)', representing the *ignorance* about the actual world, we integrate the decision making process into the plan selection procedure. In order to test the proposed hybrid BDI-PGM framework, we designed and implemented a simplified transit scenario. In this prototype, all the required behaviours are validated.

It is possible that in a dynamically changing environment, the pre-specified plans are not complete. As future work, algorithms for automatically building plan libraries for the hybrid BDI-PGM framework are required. In a multiagent setting, uncertainty about the environment can be complicated by behaviours of other agents, which are subject to their relationships. These cooperating/adversary behaviours of agents have not be discussed in this paper, and deserve further investigation. For PGMs, setting reasonable parameters (i.e., the numbers in conditional probability tables and utility tables) is always challenging. There are sophisticated techniques in the literature that can facilitate the parameter learning and the structure discovery for PGMs. Learning from the log data of existing SCADA systems would be beneficial. Furthermore, quantitative comparison study with other uncertain BDI architectures is also necessary.

Acknowledgment. The authors are grateful to Kim Bauters for his helpful comments and anonymous reviewers for their constructive comments and insights.

References

1. Boyer, S.A.: SCADA: Supervisory Control And Data Acquisition. International Society of Automation (2009)
2. Jennings, N.R., Bussmann, S.: Agent-based control systems. IEEE Control Systems Magazine 23, 61–74 (2003)
3. Guilherme, I., Pedrosanto, R., Teixeira, A., Morooka, C.K., Sierra, C.: A multiagent architecture for supervisory and control system. In: CIMCA/IAWTIC/ISE, pp. 98–103 (2008)
4. Valckenaers, P., Sauter, J., Sierra, C., Rodriguez-Aguilar, J.: Applications and environments for multi-agent systems. JAAMAS 14(1), 61–85 (2007)
5. Rao, A.S., Georgeff, M.P.: An abstract architecture for rational agents. In: KR, pp. 439–449 (1992)
6. McArthur, S., Davidson, E., Catterson, V., Dimeas, A., Hatziargyriou, N., Ponci, F., Funabashi, T.: Multi-agent systems for power engineering applications - part I: Concepts, approaches, and technical challenges. IEEE Trans. on Power Systems 22(4), 1743–1752 (2007)
7. McArthur, S., Davidson, E., Catterson, V., Dimeas, A., Hatziargyriou, N., Ponci, F., Funabashi, T.: Multi-agent systems for power engineering applications - part II: Technologies, standards, and tools for building multi-agent systems. IEEE Trans. on Power Systems 22(4), 1753–1759 (2007)

8. Rao, A.S.: Agentspeak(L): BDI agents speak out in a logical computable language. In: Perram, J., Van de Velde, W. (eds.) MAAMAW 1996. LNCS, vol. 1038, pp. 42–55. Springer, Heidelberg (1996)

9. Ma, J., Liu, W.: A framework for managing uncertain inputs: An axiomization of rewarding. IJAR 52(7), 917–934 (2011)

10. Baxevanos, I., Labridis, D.: Implementing multiagent systems technology for power distribution network control and protection management. IEEE Trans. on Power Delivery 22(1), 433–443 (2007)

11. Parsons, S., Giorgini, P.: On using degrees of belief in BDI agents. In: IPMU (1998)

12. Casali, A., Godo, L., Sierra, C.: A graded BDI agent model to represent and reason about preferences. AIJ 175(7-8), 1468–1478 (2011)

13. Jensen, F.V., Nielsen, T.D.: Bayesian Network and Decision Graphs. Springer (2007)

14. Fagundes, M.S., Vicari, R.M., Coelho, H.: Deliberation process in a BDI model with Bayesian networks. In: Ghose, A., Governatori, G., Sadananda, R. (eds.) PRIMA 2007. LNCS, vol. 5044, pp. 207–218. Springer, Heidelberg (2009)

15. Luz, B., Meneguzzi, F., Vicari, R.: Alternatives to threshold-based desire selection in Bayesian BDIagents. In: EMAS, pp. 208–223 (2013)

16. Kieling, G., Vicari, R.: Insertion of probabilistic knowledge into BDI agents construction modeled in Bayesian networks. In: CISIS, pp. 115–122 (2011)

17. Bordini, R.H., Hübner, J.F., Wooldridge, M.: Programming Multi-agent Systems in AgentSpeak using Jason. Wiley Interscience (2007)

18. Doshi, P., Zeng, Y., Chen, Q.: Graphical models for interactive POMDPs: representations and solutions. JAAMAS 18(3), 376–416 (2009)

19. Schut, M., Wooldridge, M., Parsons, S.: On partially observable MDPs and BDI models. In: d'Inverno, M., Luck, M., Fisher, M., Preist, C. (eds.) UKMAS Workshops 1996-2000. LNCS (LNAI), vol. 2403, pp. 243–260. Springer, Heidelberg (2002)

20. Simari, G.I., Parsons, S.: On the relationship between MDPs and the BDI architecture. In: AAMAS, pp. 1041–1048 (2006)

21. Simari, G.I., Parsons, S.D.: On approximating the best decision for an autonomous agent. In: GTDT (2004)

22. Nair, R., Tambe, M.: Hybrid BDI-POMDP framework for multiagent teaming. JAIR 23, 367–420 (2005)

23. Andersen, S.K., Olesen, K.G., Jensen, F.V., Jensen, F.: HUGIN - a shell for building Bayesian belief universes for expert systems. In: IJCAI, pp. 1080–1085 (1989)

A Multi-agent Based Migration Model for Evolving Cooperation in the Spatial N-Player Snowdrift Game

Raymond Chiong[1] and Michael Kirley[2]

[1] School of Design, Communication and Information Technology,
Faculty of Science and Information Technology,
The University of Newcastle, Callaghan, NSW 2308, Australia
[2] Department of Computing and Information Systems,
Melbourne School of Engineering,
The University of Melbourne, Parkville, VIC 3010, Australia

Abstract. In recent years, there has been an increased interest in using agent-based simulation models to investigate the evolution of cooperative behaviour in spatial evolutionary games. However, the relationship between individual player mobility (or migration) and population dynamics is not clear. In this paper, we investigate the impacts of alternative migration mechanisms in the spatial N-player Snowdrift game. Here, agents occupy sites in a two-dimensional toroidal lattice. Specific game instances are created by nominating N sites from each of the local neighbourhoods. We use a genetic algorithm to evolve agent game-playing strategies. In addition, agents have an opportunity to migrate to different sites in the lattice at regular intervals. Key parameters in our model include the migration rate, the actual dispersal distance, the "take-over" scheme, the group size N, and the relative cost-to-benefit ratio of the game. Detailed simulation experiments show that the proposed model is able to promote cooperation in a population of mobile agents. However, the magnitude of the dispersal distance plays a significant role in determining population dynamics. Our findings help to further understand how migratory (mobility) patterns affect evolutionary processes.

1 Introduction

Spatial evolutionary games have attracted considerable interest across a variety of disciplines including social science, biology, economics, statistical physics and computer science [31,32,23,24,36,40,13]. Previous studies have shown that spatial structures ranging from regular lattices to different types of complex networks can promote high levels of cooperation (see [41] for a comprehensive review). A key characteristic of the spatial extension is the short-range interactions that restrict the number of players who can interact with a given player at a particular site. This enables cooperators to form clusters, in which the benefits of mutual cooperation can outweigh losses against defectors. The general understanding is therefore that cooperative behaviour arises when interactions between players are confined to local neighbourhoods.

G. Boella et al. (Eds.): PRIMA 2013, LNAI 8291, pp. 70–84, 2013.
© Springer-Verlag Berlin Heidelberg 2013

Clearly, interaction topology affects population dynamics [33,10,12,21]. However, the implications of employing mobile individuals in spatial evolutionary games are not well understood. A number of theoretical investigations (e.g., [28,35,27,37,26]) have demonstrated the selective advantage of migration under a variety of circumstances, such as to avoid kin competition, inbreeding, or to escape local catastrophes. Migration has also been shown to be a driving force of urban and interregional dynamics [43,5]. Moreover, an increasing number of recent studies have revealed that it is actually possible to evolve and sustain cooperation in a population of mobile individuals using two-player spatial games (see Section 2).

In this paper, we investigate the effects that alternative migration mechanisms have on the evolution of cooperation in the spatial N-player Snowdrift (SD) game. Here, we focus on the case where agents in the population are mapped onto a two-dimensional regular lattice with periodic boundary conditions. The focal agent participates in a game instance with $N - 1$ other agents drawn from its local neighbourhood at each iteration, and the interaction topology within the local neighbourhood is based on the number of players playing the game. We use a genetic algorithm (GA) to evolve agent game-playing strategies over a fixed number of generations. After strategy update, each agent in the population is given an opportunity to make a move to a randomly selected lattice site. We have adopted the *time*-based migration scheme from [15]: the probability that an agent moves from its current location to a new site is based on the amount of time it has occupied a given position. When an agent moves, its movement is constrained to within a certain migration range. Whether the move is successful or not depends on the relative fitness of the agent occupying the destination position.

Comprehensive numerical simulations across a range of parameter settings show that cooperation can be maintained, and even enhanced, in a population of mobile agents, when compared to the case where the agents never move at all. However, the enhancement is strictly dependent on the cost-to-benefit ratio as well as the range of movement. A further analysis of the population dynamics suggests that migration also promotes higher levels of diversity in the population.

The remainder of this paper is organised as follows: Section 2 reviews related work studying the role of migration on the evolution of cooperation. In Section 3, we present the details of our agent-based migration model. Section 4 describes the experimental settings and results. Finally, we draw conclusions in Section 5 and highlight some potential future work.

2   Related Work

Generally, migration in the context of evolutionary games can occur in two forms. The first is based on spatial lattices with empty sites, in which mobile agents can move to sites that are not occupied by other individuals. The second approach is to divide the population into distinct groups, and migration takes place between groups. The migration issue has been an extremely well-studied topic in ecological and social sciences.

In computer science, migration has been studied in the context of *distributed* GAs [7] and *cellular* GAs [2]. In distributed GAs, individuals are "swapped" or "exchanged" between groups/populations (also known as *island* models, see [6,3]). As for cellular GAs, empty sites in the population may be "colonised" by individuals from nearby local neighbourhoods (e.g., see [25]). However, the role of migration on the evolution of cooperation has received relatively little attention. This may be attributed to the fact that early work in this area had found that mobility could undermine cooperative behaviour by allowing defectors to invade cooperators and avoid retaliation (e.g., see [16,17]).

Several recent studies, however, have shown that it is actually possible to evolve and sustain cooperation in a population of mobile agents in two-player spatial games. For example, Vainstein et al. [42] studied the minimal conditions for sustaining cooperation in the spatial Prisoner's Dilemma (PD) game with the presence of unbiased, non-contingent mobility using a two-dimensional lattice with empty sites. They found that given a certain parameter range, such random movement can maintain or even enhance the level of cooperation compared to the "never-move" case. Subsequently, random mobility has also been shown to be able to promote cooperative behaviour in different kinds of evolutionary games [18,38] and spatial structures (e.g., two-dimensional planes [30] and complex networks [44]). More recently, random mobility within heterogeneous view radii [47] (where players play with those within their vision fields) or in the form of biological flocks [9,8] (where players move in groups) has been examined and shown to be favourable to cooperation too.

In addition to random mobility, the effectiveness of alternative movement mechanisms has been investigated. Notable examples include success-driven migration [19,20], adaptive migration [22] and aspiration-induced migration [45,29]. Success-driven migration is based on the idea that players can elect to move to sites with higher expected payoffs. The challenge of success-driven migration, however, is to determine in advance the potential payoff of the "non-local" site. In contrast, in the adaptive migration model players only make use of local information when attempting a move. In the study presented by Jiang et al. [22], adaptive migration took place probabilistically in proportion to the number of defectors in the neighbourhood. Aspiration-induced migration is a third alternative, where players move to a new site if their payoff is below a certain aspiration level. Each of these migration schemes has been shown to enhance the extent of cooperative behaviour considerably, even in a noisy environment [20] or in an environment dominated by defectors [22].

To date, only a limited number of studies have considered the migration issue in N-player games. In the study carried out by Zhang et al. [48], they proposed a model of evolutionary Public Goods (PG) games where individuals were divided into groups. Migration to a neighbouring group was allowed if an individual's payoff does not meet or surpass the local expectation (similar to aspiration-induced migration). In another study based on the PG game, Aktipis [1] proposed a simple "walk-away" strategy that enables individuals to leave their group if they cannot gain high returns (due to too many defectors) in the group. Both studies have shown that such contingent movements can promote cooperative behaviour in the multi-player context. Instead of the PG game, Suzuki and Kimura [39] considered the co-evolution of cooperation and mobility using the N-player PD game. They observed oscillations in the numbers of cooperators and defectors when the cost-to-benefit ratio of cooperation is small.

Despite the increasing number of studies on migration and the evolution of co-operation in recent years, including some that have covered multi-player games, we are not aware of any previous work that has examined the effects of migration in the N-player SD game. Our aim here is therefore to build this gap.

3 The Model

3.1 Game Structure and Payoffs

We consider the spatial N-player SD game, where interacting agents are placed on the sites (x) of an $L \times L$ square lattice with periodic boundary conditions. Each site is occupied by one agent at a time. Every agent – the focal agent a_x – plays an iterative game in each generation with $N - 1$ other individuals (recall that N is the group size) from its local neighbourhood. The interaction topology is determined by the group size in place [13]. In the cases of $N = 5$ and $N = 9$, the non-focal sites are based on the von Neumann and Moore neighbourhood structures respectively. For other N values (e.g., $3 \leq N \leq 8$), the non-focal sites are randomly picked from within the Moore neighbourhood at the start of the game. These sites, which form the focal agent's group, do not change over the course of the game.

The payoff of agent a_x after each game instance is calculated according to the following utility function [11]:

$$U = \begin{cases} b \times i - c \times (N-1)/i & \text{for cooperators,} \\ b \times i & \text{for defectors.} \end{cases} \tag{1}$$

where b is the benefit, c is the cost of cooperation, and i is the number of cooperators among the group members.

3.2 Agent Strategy

We use a GA to model the simultaneous evolution of a large set of possible strategies in the population. This GA approach was first used by Axelrod [4] for the two-player Iterated PD game. Here, we have adopted a variant proposed by Yao and Darwen [46] since Axelrod's representation scheme does not scale well with the increase in the number of players for N-player games.

Every agent a_x is initialised with a randomly created strategy s_x (encoded in the form of a binary string). During the course of interactions, each agent uses its own unique strategy to decide on the action (decoded from its past history) to be played. An agent's decision of whether to cooperate or defect at a particular iteration is based on the outcomes of its previous three actions. When a game history is not available, the agent's decision to either cooperate or defect is based on some randomly hard-coded actions in its strategy (see [46] for details).

After every generation, the agents are presented with an opportunity to update their strategies synchronously according to the cumulative payoffs received. Here, each generation consists of T iterations. Following the findings from [13], we have set $T = 25$ for the simulation experiments in this paper. Using a form of rank-based selection, agents with lower rankings (i.e., those ranked $< 50\%$ in their group) are given the opportunity to copy the fittest strategy in their group. Crossover and mutation events, with probabilities of 0.7 and 0.05 respectively, take place at the same time to allow the creation of new strategies in the population.

3.3 Agent Movement

After updating their strategy, the focal agent a_x has an opportunity to "migrate" to a randomly selected lattice site. The rationale behind this migration mechanism is based on the idea that if an agent has stayed at its current location for a long time, it is more likely that the agent will attempt to move to a new site. This type of movement can be thought of as a form of random mobility (see [42,15]).

The probability that an agent attempts to move is based on the following sigmoid dispersal function:

$$Prob(a_x \rightarrow a_{x'}) = \frac{1}{1 + \exp^{-z \times g}} \qquad (2)$$

where z is the number of times the agent has failed to move away from its current site, and g is the ratio of current time step t to the total number of time steps T (i.e., $g = t/T$).

Finally, the range of movement is constrained by a *distance* parameter d ($0 \leq d \leq L/2 - 1$), which determines how far an agent can move. For example, when $d = 1$ the focal agent a_x can only move one step within the local (von Neumann) neighbourhood; when $d = 2$ the agent can move up to two steps, and so on. The movement can be either vertical or horizontal in the lattice (see Figure 1). The base-case or "no mobility" case corresponds to $d = 0$. As there are no empty sites, agent a_x will "take over" the new randomly selected site only if its cumulative utility is greater than that of the agent at the new location ($a_{x'}$). Otherwise, the position of agent a_x remains unchanged. For each successful movement, the vacated site will be filled by a copy of a randomly selected individual from $N - 1$ other agents of the original group of agent a_x.

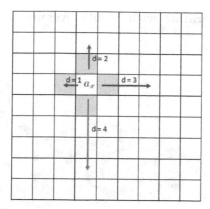

Fig. 1. An illustration of agent movement based on the von Neumann neighbourhood: after each generation, the focal agent a_x will be given an opportunity to move either vertically or horizontally. The movement range allowed is dependent on the value of d.

4   Experiments and Results

We have carried out extensive numerical simulations to compare equilibrium proportions of agents playing cooperatively in the population when mobility is allowed. The underlying hypothesis tested was that cooperation levels can still be maintained in a population of mobile agents playing the spatial N-player SD game, if the migration range is limited. In the subsequent sections, we describe the model parameters and report experimental results for the following scenarios:

1. We compare equilibrium proportions of agents playing cooperatively in the population across the spectrum of d values and cost-to-benefit ratios r as well as different group sizes N.
2. We examine the impact of different "take-over" schemes on the levels of cooperation observed.

4.1   Experimental Settings and Parameters

All simulation experiments were performed with a population size of $30 \times 30 = 900$ agents (i.e., $L = 30$). Different values of N (and thus local neighbourhood sizes) were examined: the von Neumann ($N = 5$) and Moore ($N = 9$) neighbourhoods; and then variable neighbourhood sizes ranging from $N = 3$ to $N = 8$. The initial population was randomly assigned with approximately 50% of cooperators and 50% of defectors. Every agent played iteratively for a total of 500 generations, and the simulation results were obtained by averaging the number of cooperators over the total number of generations. Payoffs of agents were calculated based on Equation 1, using a range of b and c values normalised to a function of cost-to-benefit ratios $r \in [0...1]$. The values used for the GA parameters were described in Section 3.2. All the simulations were repeated for 100 independent trials with appropriate statistical tests.

4.2   Levels of Cooperation with Mobile Agents

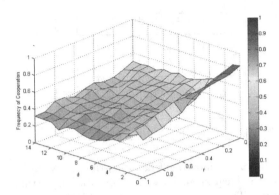

Fig. 2. The frequency of cooperation as a function of $r = c/b$ across different d values for the spatial N-player SD game with time-based migration, where $N = 5$ (von Neumann). All data points are averages over 100 realisations.

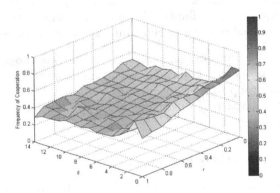

Fig. 3. The frequency of cooperation as a function of $r = c/b$ across different d values for the spatial N-player SD game with time-based migration, where $N = 9$ (Moore). All data points are averages over 100 realisations.

Figures 2 and 3 show the equilibrium frequency levels of cooperation achieved for the N-player SD game with von Neumann and Moore neighbourhoods respectively, when the values of d and r were varied. The general trend we can see is that the levels of cooperative behaviour decrease as the values of d and r increase. This trend is consistent across a wide range of d and r, although at times we also observe that the extent of cooperation can be enhanced when agent movement is allowed. It is worth noting that even for high r, the populations can still maintain an intermediate level of cooperation.

Focusing on two distance parameter values $d = 0$ and $d = 1$ in Figure 2, we notice that the proportions of cooperators in the case $d = 0$ appear to be higher than the case $d = 1$ when r values are small. For intermediate to high r, however, we see in the figure that cooperative behaviour is greatly promoted. Moving our attention to Figure 3, we observe that the proportions of cooperators in the never-move case (i.e., $d = 0$) are slightly higher than the case of $d = 1$ when r is less than or equal to 0.1. From $r = 0.2$ onwards, however, the levels of cooperation achieved with $d = 1$ become considerably higher than $d = 0$.

To test for statistical differences between the levels of cooperation observed in the two cases, we have applied pair-wise t-tests with significance levels of $\alpha = 0.05$ to the results obtained for the N-player SD game with $d = 0$ and $d = 1$. The null hypothesis tested was that the mean frequency of cooperation values at each value of r were the same for the two cases. In Table 1, the cases being compared are represented by a symbol in each cell. Three different symbols are used: "$=$" indicates that there is no statistical significance between the two cases, "$+$" means that one case has yielded a significantly higher level of cooperation than the other case, and "$-$" is used if otherwise.

From the statistical test results presented in Table 1, it is clear that cooperative behaviour can be maintained in a population of mobile agents. Moreover, we see that the levels of cooperation can even be significantly enhanced across a wide range of r values. This is particularly evident in the cases of high r for the N-player SD game with both von Neumann and Moore neighbourhoods. The results suggest that it is actually better to allow players to move around (within a limited migration range) in the more "difficult" portion of the games (e.g., larger r and N values).

Table 1. Statistical tests for $d = 0$ and $d = 1$ on the spatial N-player SD game at specific r intervals with time-based migration

| | Spatial N-player SD | | | |
| | von Neumann | | Moore | |
r	$d = 0$	$d = 1$	$d = 0$	$d = 1$
0.0	$=$	$=$	$=$	$=$
0.1	$=$	$=$	$=$	$=$
0.2	$=$	$=$	$=$	$=$
0.3	$+$	$-$	$=$	$=$
0.4	$+$	$-$	$=$	$=$
0.5	$=$	$=$	$=$	$=$
0.6	$-$	$+$	$-$	$+$
0.7	$-$	$+$	$-$	$+$
0.8	$-$	$+$	$-$	$+$
0.9	$-$	$+$	$-$	$+$
1.0	$-$	$+$	$-$	$+$

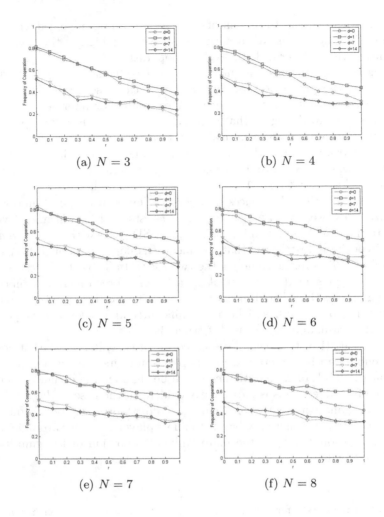

Fig. 4. The frequency of cooperation as a function of $r = c/b$ for the spatial N-player SD game with time-based migration and different group sizes. Each data point is an average over 100 realisations.

To help explain these results in more detail, we have extended our simulation experiments from the von Neumann and Moore cases to other values of N. Despite the differing interaction topologies of these neighbourhoods, it is worth noting that the randomly-picked local sites for agent a_x (selected at the beginning of the game) do not change over the course of the game. However, the agents occupying those sites may in fact change as a consequence of the migration.

Figures 4 (a)–(f) confirm that our findings with the von Neumann and Moore cases are consistent across different N values within the immediate local neighbourhood. From the figures, we see that the extent of cooperative behaviour

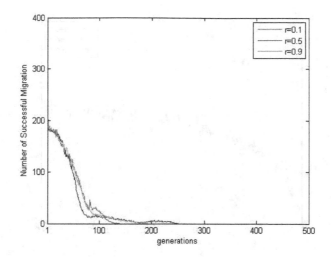

Fig. 5. The number of successful migration as a function of time (generations) for the spatial N-player SD game with the default better-take-over scheme, based on the von Neumann neighbourhood and $d = 1$, averaged over 100 trials

with $d = 1$ is again higher than $d = 0$ but this time for high r. Statistical tests show that the differences are significant in most cases (t-tests, $p < 0.05$).

To verify that the system size does not adversely affect the findings reported in this section, we have also tested the simulation results using larger population sizes ($L = 50$ and $L = 100$). The simulation experiments with larger L values confirmed that, although the exact levels of cooperation do vary slightly between different population sizes (the differences are not statistically significant), the results are fully consistent with our observation based on $L = 30$.

4.3   An Analysis of the "Take-Over" Schemes

The simulation results described so far have demonstrated that cooperative behaviour can be significantly enhanced, when limited mobility is allowed in a population of agents playing the spatial N-player SD game iteratively. These results have been achieved based on the condition that agents "on the move" are required to have higher payoffs than those occupying the possible destination positions for successful migration to realise (hereafter we call this the *better-take-over* scheme). This condition dictates that migration activities in the population are active within the first 100 generations, as shown in Figure 5. Thereafter, only a small number of agents, if any, succeed in moving to other locations.

To explore what the outcomes would be if alternative take-over schemes are in place, we have repeated the simulation experiments but this time we have allowed the moving agents to take over the destination location probabilistically. That is, the agents no longer need to have greater payoffs than individuals at randomly

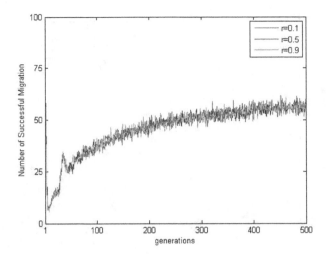

Fig. 6. The number of successful migration as a function of time (generations) for the spatial N-player SD game with probabilistic take-over ($\rho = 0.1$), based on the von Neumann neighbourhood and $d = 1$, averaged over 100 trials.

selected new locations for successful migration to happen. They simply take over the destination position with a certain probability ρ. This kind of probabilistic take-over enables migration activities to remain active until the end of every run, as can be seen in Figure 6.

Figure 7 shows the equilibrium frequency levels of cooperation achieved for the N-player SD game, based on the von Neumann neighbourhood and $d = 1$, when the values of ρ were varied. The results confirm that our findings are robust against different take-over schemes. In the figure, we see that the extent of cooperative behaviour can be maintained for a wide range of r regardless of the value of ρ. As r increases, the level of cooperation decreases, which is unavoidable and fully expected given the nature of the game. However, an interesting observation here is that, comparing to the never-move case ($d = 0$) there is actually a significant increase (t-tests, $p < 0.05$) in the cooperation level for higher r values. It is also worth noting that the levels of cooperation obtained here are consistently higher than those reported previously with the better-take-over scheme. This suggests that diversity introduced to the population via constant migration can further improve the extent of cooperative behaviour.

The results presented in this section reinforce our conclusion that the promotion and maintenance of cooperation is possible with a population of mobile agents, and the prerequisite is that the migration range has to be kept small. Notably, this conclusion holds irrespective of the take-over scheme. A small amount of stable migration throughout a run is found to enhance the cooperation levels significantly in the most challenging part of the game (i.e., high r).

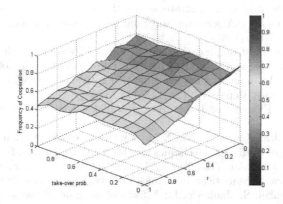

Fig. 7. The frequency of cooperation as a function of $r = c/b$ across different take-over values for the spatial N-player SD game based on the von Neumann neighbourhood and $d = 1$. All data points are averages over 100 realisations.

5   Conclusion and Future Work

In this paper, we have investigated the effects of migration on the evolution of co-operation in the spatial N-player SD game. Migration activities are widespread in biological and social systems. Including migration scenarios in models of cooper-ation may therefore help us to understand why and how cooperative behaviour can be established. Our detailed computational simulations across a range of cost-to-benefit ratios and group sizes have clearly shown that cooperation can be promoted in a population of mobile agents. This conclusion is robust with respect to the take-over schemes used. The constraint, however, is that the move-ment range has to be kept small. Our results are consistent with those reported by recent studies along this line of research. Significantly, we have taken the current understanding of mobility issues in spatial evolutionary games one step further by considering the N-player SD game.

Future work will consider the impacts that alternative strategy update mecha-nisms have (e.g., those based on stigmergic interactions [34,14]) on the evolution of cooperation with mobile agents in place.

References

1. Aktipis, C.A.: Is cooperation viable in mobile organisms? Simple walk away rule fa-vors the evolution of cooperation in groups. Evolution and Human Behavior 32(4), 263–276 (2011)
2. Alba, E., Dorronsoro, B.: Cellular Genetic Algorithms. Springer, Berlin (2008)
3. Alba, E., Tomassini, M.: Parallelism and evolutionary algorithms. IEEE Transac-tions on Evolutionary Computation 6(5), 443–462 (2002)

4. Axelrod, R.: The evolution of strategies in the iterated prisoner's dilemma. In: Davis, L. (ed.) Genetic Algorithms and Simulated Annealing, pp. 32–41. Morgan Kaufmann, Los Altos (1987)
5. Batty, M.: Cities and Complexity: Understanding Cities with Cellular Automata, Agent-Based Models, and Fractals. The MIT Press, Cambridge (2005)
6. Cantú-Paz, E.: A survey of parallel genetic algorithms. Calculateurs Parallèles, Réseaux et Systòmes Répartis 10(2), 141–171 (1998)
7. Cantú-Paz, E.: Efficient and Accurate Parallel Genetic Algorithms. Kluwer, Norwell (2000)
8. Chen, Z., Gao, J.X., Cai, Y.Z., Xu, X.M.: Evolution of cooperation among mobile agents. Physica A: Statistical Mechanics and its Applications 390, 1615–1622 (2011)
9. Chen, Z., Gao, J.X., Cai, Y.Z., Xu, X.M.: Evolutionary prisoner's dilemma game in flocks. Physica A: Statistical Mechanics and its Applications 390, 50–56 (2011)
10. Chiong, R., Dhakal, S., Jankovic, L.: Effects of neighbourhood structure on evolution of cooperation in N-player iterated prisoner's dilemma. In: Yin, H., Tino, P., Corchado, E., Byrne, W., Yao, X. (eds.) IDEAL 2007. LNCS, vol. 4881, pp. 950–959. Springer, Heidelberg (2007)
11. Chiong, R., Kirley, M.: Evolving cooperation in the spatial N-player snowdrift game. In: Li, J. (ed.) AI 2010. LNCS, vol. 6464, pp. 263–272. Springer, Heidelberg (2010)
12. Chiong, R., Kirley, M.: Iterated N-player games on small-world networks. In: Krasnogor, N., Lanzi, P.L. (eds.) Proceedings of the Genetic and Evolutionary Computation Conference (GECCO 2011), pp. 1123–1130. ACM Press, New York (2011)
13. Chiong, R., Kirley, M.: Effects of iterated interactions in multi-player spatial evolutionary games. IEEE Transactions on Evolutionary Computation 16(4), 537–555 (2012)
14. Chiong, R., Kirley, M.: The evolution of cooperation via stigmergic interactions. In: Proceedings of the IEEE Congress on Evolutionary Computation (CEC 2012), pp. 1052–1059. IEEE Press, Piscataway (2012)
15. Chiong, R., Kirley, M.: Random mobility and the evolution of cooperation in spatial N-player iterated prisoner's dilemma games. Physica A: Statistical Mechanics and its Applications 391, 3915–3923 (2012)
16. Dugatkin, L.A., Wilson, D.S.: ROVER: A strategy for exploiting cooperators in a patchy environment. The American Naturalist 138(3), 687–701 (1991)
17. Enquist, M., Leimar, O.: The evolution of cooperation in mobile organisms. Animal Behaviour 45(4), 747–757 (1993)
18. Guan, J.-Y., Wu, Z.-X., Wang, Y.-H.: Evolutionary snowdrift game with disordered environments in mobile societies. Chinese Physics 16(12), 3566–3570 (2007)
19. Helbing, D., Yu, W.: Migration as a mechanism to promote cooperation. Advances in Complex Systems 11(4), 641–652 (2008)
20. Helbing, D., Yu, W.: The outbreak of cooperation among success-driven individuals under noisy conditions. Proceedings of the National Academy of Sciences of the United States of America 106, 3680–3685 (2009)
21. Hofmann, L.-M., Chakraborty, N., Sycara, K.: The evolution of cooperation in self-interested agent societies: A critical study. In: Sonenberg, L., Stone, P., Tumer, K., Yolum, P. (eds.) Proceedings of the 10th International Conference on Autonomous Agents and Multiagent Systems (AAMAS 2011), Taipei, Taiwan, pp. 685–692 (2011)
22. Jiang, L.-L., Wang, W.-X., Lai, Y.-C., Wang, B.-H.: Role of adaptive migration in promoting cooperation in spatial games. Physical Review E 81(3), 36108 (2010)

23. Killingback, T., Doebeli, M.: Spatial evolutionary game theory: Hawks and doves revisited. Proceedings of the Royal Society of London: Biological Sciences 263, 1135–1144 (1996)
24. Kirchkamp, O.: Spatial evolution of automata in the prisoners' dilemma. Journal of Economic Behaviour and Organization 43(2), 239–262 (2000)
25. Kirley, M.: A cellular genetic algorithm with disturbances: Optimisation using dynamic spatial interactions. Journal of Heuristics 8(3), 321–342 (2002)
26. Kümmerli, R., Gardner, A., West, S.A., Griffin, A.S.: Limited dispersal, budding dispersal, and cooperation: An experimental study. Evolution 63(4), 939–949 (2009)
27. Kun, A., Scheuring, I.: The evolution of density-dependent dispersal in a noisy spatial population model. Oikos 115, 308–320 (2006)
28. Lambin, X., Aars, J., Piertney, S.B.: Dispersal, intraspecific competition, and kin facilitation: A review of the empirical evidence. In: Clobert, J., Danchin, E., Dhondt, A.A., Nichols, J.D. (eds.) Dispersal, pp. 110–122. Oxford University Press (2001)
29. Lin, Y.-T., Yang, H.-X., Wu, Z.-X., Wang, B.-H.: Promotion of cooperation by aspiration-induced migration. Physica A: Statistical Mechanics and its Applications 390, 77–82 (2011)
30. Meloni, S., Buscarino, A., Fortuna, L., Frasca, M., Gómez-Gardeñes, J., Latora, V., Moreno, Y.: Effects of mobility in a population of prisoner's dilemma players. Physical Review E 79(6), 067101 (2009)
31. Nowak, M.A., May, R.M.: Evolutionary games and spatial chaos. Nature 359, 826–829 (1992)
32. Nowak, M.A., May, R.M.: The spatial dilemmas of evolution. International Journal of Bifurcation and Chaos 3, 35–78 (1993)
33. Ono, M., Ishizuka, M.: Prisoner's dilemma game on network. In: Lukose, D., Shi, Z. (eds.) PRIMA 2005. LNCS, vol. 4078, pp. 33–44. Springer, Heidelberg (2009)
34. O'Reilly, G.B., Ehlers, E.: Synthesizing stigmergy for multi agent systems. In: Shi, Z.-Z., Sadananda, R. (eds.) PRIMA 2006. LNCS (LNAI), vol. 4088, pp. 34–45. Springer, Heidelberg (2006)
35. Perrin, N., Goudet, J.: Inbreeding, kinship, and the evolution of natal dispersal. In: Clobert, J., Danchin, E., Dhondt, A.A., Nichols, J.D. (eds.) Dispersal, pp. 123–142. Oxford University Press (2001)
36. Santos, F.C., Pacheco, J.M.: Scale-free networks provide a unifying framework for the emergence of cooperation. Physical Review Letters 95, 098104 (2005)
37. Schtickzelle, N., Fjerdingstad, E.J., Chaine, A., Clobert, J.: Cooperative social clusters are not destroyed by dispersal in a ciliate. BMC Evolutionary Biology 9, 251 (2009)
38. Sicardi, E.A., Fort, H., Vainstein, M.H., Arenzon, J.J.: Random mobility and spatial structure often enhance cooperation. Journal of Theoretical Biology 256, 240–246 (2009)
39. Suzuki, S., Kimura, H.: Oscillatory dynamics in the coevolution of cooperation and mobility. Journal of Theoretical Biology 287, 42–47 (2011)
40. Sysi-Aho, M., Saramäki, J., Kertész, J., Kaski, K.: Spatial snowdrift game with myopic agents. The European Physical Journal B 44(1), 129–135 (2005)
41. Szabó, G., Fáth, G.: Evolutionary games on graphs. Physics Reports 446, 97–216 (2007)
42. Vainstein, M.H., Silva, A.T.C., Arenzon, J.J.: Does mobility decrease cooperation? Journal of Theoretical Biology 244, 722–728 (2007)
43. Weidlich, W.: Sociodynamics: A Systematic Approach to Mathematical Modelling in the Social Sciences. Harwood Academic Publishers, Amsterdam (2000)

44. Yang, H.X., Wang, W.X., Wang, B.H.: Universal role of migration in the evolution of cooperation. physics.soc-ph, page arXiv:1005.5453v1 (2010)
45. Yang, H.-X., Wu, Z.-X., Wang, B.-H.: Role of aspiration-induced migration in cooperation. Physical Review E 81(6), 065101 (2010)
46. Yao, X., Darwen, P.: An experimental study of N-person iterated prisoner's dilemma games. Informatica 18(4), 435–450 (1994)
47. Zhang, J., Wang, W.-Y., Du, W.-B., Cao, X.-B.: Evolution of cooperation among mobile agents with heterogenous view radii. Physica A: Statistical Mechanics and its Applications 390, 2251–2257 (2011)
48. Zhang, J., Zhang, C., Chu, T.: The evolution of cooperation in spatial groups. Chaos, Solitons and Fractals 44, 131–136 (2011)

Improving the Reactivity of BDI Agent Programs

Hoa Khanh Dam, Tiancheng Zhang, and Aditya Ghose

School of Computer Science and Software Engineering
University of Wollongong
New South Wales 2522, Australia
{hoa,tz746,aditya}@uow.edu.au

Abstract. Intelligent agent technology has evolved rapidly over the past few years along with the growing number of agent applications in various domains. However, very little work has been dedicated to define quality metrics for the design of an agent-based system. Previous efforts mostly focus on adopting classical metrics such as coupling and cohesion to measure quality of an agent design. We argue that the time has come to work towards a set of software quality metrics that are specific to the distinct characteristics of agent-based systems. In this paper, we propose a method to measure the reactivity of an agent design which provides indications of how the agent system responds to changes in the environment in a timely fashion. The proposed metric is part of the framework which facilitates the restructuring of an Belief-Desire-Intention agent program to improve its reactivity. Our framework was developed into a prototype tool which is integrated with Jason, a well-known agent-oriented programming platform.

1 Introduction

Proactiveness and reactivity are arguably two important characteristics of an intelligent agent system which operates in a dynamic environment [30]. Agents should pursue their goals over time and they should be able to perceive their environment and respond in a timely fashion to changes that occur in it. A critical aspect in an agent's decision-making is balancing proactive and reactive aspects: we want the agent to achieve its goals by default while also taking changes in the environment into account. Practical Belief-Desire-Intention (BDI) [24] agent systems attempt to achieve an effective balance between goal-directed and reactive behaviour by constantly perceiving the environment and reasoning about how to act so as to achieve their goals in terms of selecting appropriate plans from their plan library. A crucial point in BDI systems is that execution occurs at each step and the particular choice of the specific plan to achieve a goal should be left for *as late as possible* so as to consider the *latest information in the environment* the agents might have.

In other words, the choice of plan for a goal which a BDI agent has should only be made when the agent is about to start acting upon it. The context of a

G. Boella et al. (Eds.): PRIMA 2013, LNAI 8291, pp. 85–100, 2013.

plan (or plan's preconditions) is used for checking the current situation in order to evaluate a particular plan among various alternative plans for the goal. For example, consider a goal to *be at the university without getting wet* with two plans: WalkPlan and BusPlan. WalkPlan has the context condition *weather is not raining* and involves walking to a friend's house to collect a book and then walking to the university. BusPlan has the context condition *weather is raining* and involves also walking to the friend's house to collect the book and then catching a bus to the university. According to the plans' definition, the context of each plan is evaluated (with respect to the latest information that the agent has about its environment) just before the agent is about to leave home and go to the university. If the weather is not raining when the agent is about to leave home, the agent would commit to its WalkPlan.

However, changes constantly occur in a dynamic environment and what have been true of the environment when the context of the chosen plan was evaluated may not still be true during the course of the agent executing the plan. In our earlier example, the weather was not raining when the agent was about to leave home but it may start raining while the agent is at the friend's house. If the agent continues executing the WalkPlan, it would get wet and fails to achieve its goal. The problem essentially resides in the way in which the two plans are written, resulting in the agent being not reactive to changes in the environment while pursuing its goal. The issue is that the agent is programmed to evaluate the situation quite early and thus makes an early commitment, which may eventually result in failures. Although there has been a range of work on addressing failure recovery in BDI (e.g. [26]), the issue illustrated in the above example can be dealt with by providing effective support for the software engineers in developing BDI plans that are more suitably reactive to changes in the environment. Unfortunately, this kind of support is rarely provided in the current proliferation of agent-oriented software engineering methodologies [12].

In this paper, we attempt to fill that gap by providing a framework which supports the software engineers in writting BDI agent plans. Specifically, we propose a design metric to measure how reactive a BDI agent is during the course of achieving its goals, i.e. measuring the reactivity of plans available to handle a given goal/event. We then present a methodology to increase the reactivity of an agent based on the effective use of subgoals as a device to postpone execution of actions until possibly more information is available about the context. More specifically, our framework facilitates the identification of actions that are dependent on both the plan's context and changes in the environment, and the grouping of those actions into subgoals. A distinct feature of our methodology is that it focusses only on restructuring the agent program without adding further capabilities to the agents. Our framework is implemented into a toolkit that works with Jason on the Eclipse platform.

The paper is structured as follows. In section 2, we discuss different factors that contribute to the reactivity of an agent program. An abstract programming environment is described in section 3. We then describe an reactivity measure in section 4 and a methodology to restructure an agent program to improve its reactivity in section 5. The prototype implementation of our framework is described in section 6. Finally, we discuss related work (section 7), and conclude and outline some future work (section 8).

2   Factors Contributing to Reactivity

One of the most well-established and widely-used agent models is the *Belief-Desire-Intention* (BDI) model [16]. BDI agents' behaviour is mostly determined in terms of their plans to handle events or achieve goals[1]. Each plan P is typically of the form $G : [C] \leftarrow B$, meaning that plan P is an applicable plan for achieving goal G when context condition C is believed true. A BDI agent also has a belief set which encodes what the agent perceives its environment. Mechanisms exist to check whether a plan's context condition hold with respect to the agent's beliefs, and to add and delete a ground basic belief to and from a belief base. The plan body[2] B (following abstract notations such as AgentSpeak(L) [24] or CAN [29]) typically contains a sequence of formulæ, each of which can be a domain action that is meant to be directly executed in the world (e.g. lifting an aircraft's flaps) or a subgoal (written as $!G$) (e.g. obtaining landing permission) to be resolved by further plans.

For example, the following two plans (design option 1) are to achieve goal g, one (P11) when condition c holds and the other (P12) when c does not hold. Both plans involves the execution of a sequence of basic actions (e.g. a_1, a_2, and a_3 in plan P11, and a_1, a_2', and a_3' in plan P12).

P11 $g : c \leftarrow a_1;\ a_2;\ a_3$ **Design Option 1**
P12 $g : \neg\, c \leftarrow a_1;\ a_2';\ a_3'$

Since agents are situated in dynamic environments, it is crucial that they are able to react to changes (that are relevant to the agents' interest) in the environment in a timely fashion. When designing an agent system, reactivity can be maximized in several ways. Firstly, the developers need to make sure that the agent's plan library has plans to cover all environmental possibilities that are significant to the agent's deliberation. For example, if changes in the weather are important, then a reactive agent should have a plan when the weather is fine and another plan when it is not fine. This is related to the completeness of the conjunction of all possible combinations of contextual data. For example, in the first design option above, the two plans completely cover two scenarios relating to the truth value of context condition c. This issue is known in agent-oriented software engineering as the concept of *coverage*, i.e. whether, for a given

---

[1] Goals can be declarative or procedural but this has no impact on the results of our approach.

[2] Note that different BDI languages provide different constructs for crafting plans. For example, Jason [5] differentiates between achievement goals and test goals, whereas 3APL [14] distinguishes actions into mental actions, communication actions, external actions, test actions and abstract plans.

goal, there will always be some applicable plan to achieve it. Recent work (e.g. [27]) has also refined this coverage concept and defined a numerical measure of the extent to which the set of plans for a goal cover the state space of the environment. In order to increase coverage, we may need to add further plans to an agent's capabilities. There are also other perspectives on agent reactivity, for example the ability of an agent to detect if the currently selected plan is not valid and possibly switch plans. These are however *not* the focus of our current work which we will illustrate in the following scenarios.

An agent's plans should be constructed in such a way that the agent it commits to a certain courses of action as late as possible in achieving its goals, i.e. to wait until the agent has the most updated information about the environment. Therefore, an alternative design for plans to achieve the same goal g is shown below. Note here the use of subgoals as a way to delay the evaluation for the current context.

P21 $g \leftarrow a_1; \, !sg$ **Design Option 2**
P22 $sg : c \leftarrow a_2; \, a_3$
P23 $sg : \neg \, c \leftarrow a_2'; \, a_3'$

Both design options would lead to the same ways of achieving goal g, i.e. by performing either $\langle a_1; \, a_2; \, a_3 \rangle$ or $\langle a_1; \, a_2'; \, a_3' \rangle$. However, in the second design option (i.e. plans P21, P22 and P23 with subgoal sg) the agent does not commit to do either $\langle a_2; \, a_3 \rangle$ or $\langle a_2'; \, a_3' \rangle$ until a_1 is completed. By contrast, with the first design option the agent makes this commitment earlier. This means in the case if there are any changes in the environment at the time after a_1 is completed (e.g. condition c no longer holds or vice versa), the agent fails to respond to this change (e.g. continues either doing $\langle a_2; \, a_3 \rangle$ or $\langle a_2'; \, a_3' \rangle$). Therefore, the second design option makes the agent more reactive than the first one does. This example indicates that the number of subgoals in the agent's plans has an impact on how reactive it is at run time.

The use of subgoals is also encouraged in agent design since it decouples a goal from its plan and makes it easy to add other plan choices later. However, just only turning basic actions into subgoals does not merely improve the reactivity of an agents. Let us consider the following design.

P31 $g : c \leftarrow a_1; \, !sg_2; \, a_3$ **Design Option 3**
P32 $g : \neg \, c \leftarrow a_1; \, !sg_2'; \, a_3'$
P33 $sg \leftarrow a_2$
P34 $sg' \leftarrow a_2'$

In this third design option, although there are two subgoals in the agent's plans, the actual behaviour of the agent in this example is identical to the one in the initial design. Therefore, only subgoals that have plans with non-empty context conditions affect the reactivity of an agent. However, simply counting the number of subgoals may not reveal the degree of reactivity of an agent programs. Let us consider the following design option.

P41 $g \leftarrow a_1; a_2; !sg$ **Design Option 4**
P42 $g \leftarrow a_1; a_2'; !sg$
P43 $sg : c \leftarrow a_3$
P44 $sg' : \neg c \leftarrow a_3'$

Both design options 2 and 4 are decomposed to the same sequence of actions and have the same number of subgoals with context conditions. The only difference here is how basic actions are grouped into subgoals. In order to differentiate those cases, we need to understand the semantic of the basic actions in terms of how the environment affects an action's executability and how it changes the current environmental context. In addition, we also need to assess whether subgoals occur at the appropriate places in the plan definitions. In the next section, we will describe an abstract BDI programming environment which supports the software engineers in reasoning about the reactivity of an agent program.

3   Abstract BDI Programming Environment

State-of-the-art BDI agent programming environment (e.g. Jason [5], JACK [6] or Jadex [23]) have only a partial and syntactical understanding of the BDI software system (while the meaning of the software is implicitly interpretable by human developers), and thus they provide limited support to understand and improve the reactivity of an agent program. We believe that in order to provide further value to the software engineers, a BDI programming environment should get a deeper, more semantic understanding of what each agent in the software does and how they operates in the environment. In order to achieve this, the semantics of agent actions and the environment states need to be explicitly specified in such a formal way that they can be automatically interpreted. Note that this information are already, albeit implicitly, available to the software engineers when they develop the agent system. We now define how such information can be formally defined and used for the purpose of improving the reactivity of an agent program.

Action Description Library
Agents are situated in an environment and thus must be able to act within that environment. As a result, each agent has a set of basic actions which are the basic means of the agent to change its environment. Basic actions define the capabilities that an agent can use to achieve its goals and should be made available to the software engineers when they develop the agent program. The software engineer refers to those basic actions in the program through their symbolic representation (e.g. predicates in AgentSpeak(L) [24]). For example, if the software engineer is programming a robot agent to collect garbages, they need to know the actions the agent is capable of doing (those its hardware allow it to do).

An agent's basic actions are defined and provided to the software engineer in the form of an *action description library*. Each action has an optional precondition[3] which is restricted to a conjunction of belief literals specifying the situation in which the action is executable. An action is executable if the belief literals in its precondition are in the agent's current belief. If the precondition of an action is not satisfied, the action is not executable and thus the plan to which it belongs fails. We have added this clarification to the paper. The description of an action in the action library also specifies the action's effects in terms of adding (i.e. $+b$) or deleting (i.e. $-b$) belief atoms. Some existing BDI programming languages such as the CAN (Conceptual Agent Notation) family of BDI languages [26], 3APL [14], or GOAL [18] also offer a similar STRIPS-like description of agents' actions. In this paper, we assume that all actions are deterministic and our future work will explore to include non-deterministic actions.

Table 1. An example of the action description library

Action	Precondition	Effect
collect(garbage)	at(robot, Place) $\land$ at(garbage, Place)	−at(garbage, Place)
moveTowards(NewPlace)	¬ weather(raining) $\land$ at(robot, OldPlace)	+at(robot, NewPlace) −at(robot, OldPlace)
notify(headquarter)	none	−sent(notification)
rainproof(self)	weather(raining)	+resistant(robot, water)

Table 1 shows an example of the action description library for a robot agent. As can be seen, there are four actions the robot can perform: collect a garbage, move to a new location, notify the headquarter agent and rainproof itself. Collecting a garbage, i.e. *collect(garbage)*, has a precondition that both the robot and the garbage are at the same *Place* and has the effect that the garbage is no longer at the *Place*, i.e. deleting *at(garbage, Place)* from the belief set. Moving towards a new place, i.e. *moveTowards(NewPlace)*, has a precondition that the weather is not raining and the robot is at the *OldPlace* (i.e. not at the *NewPlace*), and has the effect that the robot is at the *NewPlace*, i.e. deleting *at(robot, OldPlace)* and adding *at(robot, NewPlace)*. On the other hand, both *notify(headquarter)* and *rainproof(self)* are neutral actions since they do not change the environment, i.e. one sending a message to another agent while the other making itself rainproof. While the action *notify(headquarter)* has no precondition, the action *rainproof(self)* is executable only when the weather is raining.

Environmental State Model
Since an agent-based system is situated in an environment which it interacts with, an explicit modelling of the environment is very important to the development of an agent system [31]. Existing agent-oriented methodologies do not

---

[3] An omitted precondition is equivalent to *true*, i.e. the action can be executed in any situation.

address this aspect very well [12] and thus the software engineers may find it difficult when it comes to implementation. For example, Gaia [31] models the environment simply, in terms of variables (or tuples) that the agents can read and write (and consume). Prometheus' design [21] has an environment model capturing actors, percepts (inputs from the actor to the agent system) and actions (outputs from the system to actors), whereas INGENIAS' [22] environment viewpoint defines the entities (i.e. resources, other agents, and applications) with which an agent system interacts.

For the purpose of our current work in this paper, we are particularly interested in one important aspect of the environment: how the environment changes in responding to actions performed by agents in the system and other external events (caused by the actors of the system). Changes in the state of the environment may result in updating the agent's beliefs through perception of the environment. Thus, in an (abstract) environmental state model, we use the addition and deletion of belief atoms to describe changes in the sate of the environment. We represent the environment dynamics using a set of rules. In the left-hand side of a particular rule is an agent action (internal to the multi-agent system) or an external event, each of which is annotated with a source (i.e. the agent performing the action or the actor generating the event). In the right-hand side of the rule is a sequence of possible belief updates, reflecting perceived changes in the state of the environment due to the stimuli in the left-hand side. Rules that have external stimuli source (i.e. external events) denote that those environment-state changes can happen at any time regardless of whether the agent is executing any actions or not.

Table 2. An example of the environmental state model

rain[weather] $\rightarrow$ +weather(raining)
stop-rain[weather] $\rightarrow$ −weather(raining)
collect(garbage)[robot-agent] $\rightarrow$ −at(garbage,house)
moveTowards(NewPlace)[robot-agent] $\rightarrow$ +at(robot, NewPlace) ; −at(robot, OldPlace)

Table 2 shows an example of the environmental state model. The first two rules describe the environment changes from state *raining* to *not raining* or vice versa due to the external stimuli caused by an actor (i.e. the weather in this case). Those changes are non-deterministic which can happen at any time during the agent's execution. By contrast, the last two rules in Table 2 describe changes in the environment due to agent actions. They are extracted directly from the action description library. Note that only actions (e.g. *collect(garbage)* and *moveTowards(Place)*) which change the state of the environment are recorded here. The other two actions of the robot agent (i.e. *notify(headquarter)* and *rainproof(self)*) do not change the environment. The environment may also have static aspects, e.g. the location of the house, which are never changed and are not captured in the environmental state model.

4   Reactivity Measure

In this section, we define a measure of reactivity for a single plan or a set of plans (achieving the same goal) to capture the intuition that in the course of selecting and executing the plan(s), the agent takes into account the latest information from its environment to avoid potential plan failures. Our reactivity measure can be regarded as a static measure since it involves analysing source code, as opposed to dynamic measures which assess the characteristics of the software during execution [3].

Given goal G, let $\mathcal{PL}(G)$ be the set $\{P_1, P_2, ..., P_n\}$ of alternative plans for achieving G. The reactivity of goal G, denoting as $\mathcal{R}(G)$, is the product of the reactivity of each plan in $\mathcal{PL}(G)$. We take the product since any of the applicable plans may be selected to achieve the goal and each plan is independent of each other.

$$\mathcal{R}(G) = \prod_{P \in \mathcal{PL}(G)} \mathcal{R}(P)$$

The reactivity of a plan P, denoting as $\mathcal{R}(P)$, depends on two important factors: the number of *context dependent* actions in the plan and the reactivity of each subgoal in the plan (except the subgoals which are the same as the goal of the plan). An action A in plan P is said to be context dependent if the following conditions hold: (i) A is not the first formulæ appearing in the body of plan P; (ii) the precondition of A, denoting as $prec(A)$, intersects with the context condition of P; and (iii) the truth value of $prec(A)$ may change due to either an external stimuli or actions performed by another agent, or the actions preceding A in plan P. Note that this information can be gathered from the environmental state model and the action description library. For example, action $notify(headquarter)$ in plan $Pl1$ below is not a context dependent action since it does not satisfy condition (i). Action $moveTowards(house)$ is context dependent since it satisfied all the three conditions – one of its preconditions, $weather(raining)$, is part of the context condition of P, and the truth value of $weather(raining)$ changes over time as specified in the environment state model. By contrast, the truth value of the precondition of action $collect(garbage)$, which is $at(garbage, house)$, also changes over time but is not affected by either action $notify(headquarter)$ or action $moveTowards(house)$ or any external stimuli. Therefore, action $collect(garbage)$ is not a context dependent action. Overall, there is only one context dependent action in plan $Pl1$.

Formally, given a plan P, let $\mathcal{AC}(P)$ be the number of context dependent actions in plan P and $\mathcal{SG}(P)$ be the set of subgoals in P, the reactivity of plan P is defined as follows. Note that we again take the product since for a plan to succeed all the sub-goals must be accomplished, and we assume that the reactivity of each sub-goal is independent of each other's reactivity.

$$\mathcal{R}(P) = \frac{1}{1 + \mathcal{AC}(P)} \times \prod_{G \in \mathcal{SG}(P)} \mathcal{R}(G)$$

It can be easily seen that the reactivity of a goal or plan is the range of $(0, 1]$ where 1 represents the maximum reactivity. Let us illustrate how the reactivity measure is computed using the following example. The robot agent has a goal of possessing the garbage which is located at the house. To achieve this goal, it has two plans which are applicable when the weather is raining (plan $Pl1$) or not raining (plan $Pl2$) respectively. The robot is required to notify the headquarter before executing any plan. Plan $Pl1$ involves moving towards the house and collect the garbage, whereas plan $Pl2$ involves making the robot itself rainproof and continuing to try to achieve the goal.

Pl1 $+!has(robot, garbage) : \neg\, weather(raining) \wedge at(garbage, house)$
$$\leftarrow notify(headquarter);$$
$$moveTowards(house);$$
$$collect(garbage).$$

Pl2 $+!has(robot, garbage) : weather(raining) \wedge at(garbage, house)$
$$\leftarrow notify(headquarter);$$
$$rainproof(self);$$
$$!has(robot, garbage).$$

The above plans have some problems in responding to changes in the environment. If the weather is not raining, only plan $Pl1$ is applicable and the agent commits to execute this plan. However, after the first action of this plan is executed (i.e. $notifiy(headquarter)$), it starts raining and thus the agent cannot execute $moveTowards(house)$ since its precondition no longer holds. A similar problem is also found in plan $Pl2$ where the context is evaluated quite early (i.e. well before action $rainproof$ is executed), resulting in the agent being less reactive to changes in the environment. Those issues are correctly reflected in the reactivity measure that we have defined. More specifically, the reactivity of goal $+!has(robot, garbage)$ is the product of the reactivity measures of plans $Pl1$ and $Pl2$. As we have explained earlier, there is only one context dependent action, i.e. $moveTowards(house)$, and no subgoal in plan $Pl1$, and thus the reactivity of plan $Pl1$ is $1/2$ (i.e. 0.5). Plan $Pl2$ also has only one context dependent action, i.e. $rainproof(self)$, and its only subgoal, i.e. $has(robot, garbage)$, is the same as the plan's goal. Hence, the reactivity of plan $Pl2$ is also $1/2$. Therefore, the reactivity of goal $+!has(robot, garbage)$ is $\mathcal{R}(Pl1) \times \mathcal{R}(Pl2) = 0.25$. This value indicates that the set of plans to achieve goal $+!has(robot, garbage)$ are not strongly reactive. In the next section, we will describe a methodology of how they are restructured for reactivity improvement.

5   Restructuring for Reactivity Improvement

Note that the reactivity measure above does not include the coverage measure which has already specifically addressed in previous work [27]. To maximize the coverage, the software engineer may need to add additional plans (i.e. new capabilities) to cover as many situations in the environment as possible. By contrast, improving the reactivity measure (as defined in the previous section) only involves restructuring an existing body of an agent code (without adding any new capabilities) in order to improve the reactivity of a program. Although this is somewhat similar to the concept of refactoring in the mainstream software engineering, we avoid the use of that term here since refactoring would not change the software's behaviour, whereas restructuring for reactivity improvement may alter an agent's external behaviour (in terms of making it more reactive to environmental changes).

The definition of the reactivity measure indicates how an agent program can be restructured to improve its reactivity. More specifically, to improve reactivity of a goal, we need to improve the reactivity of each of its applicable plans. To improve the reactivity of a plan, we need to reduce the number of context dependent actions in the plan and increase the reactivity of its subgoals. One extreme method is making every action become a subgoal, which results in the agent unnecessarily making evaluation of the environment at every step of execution.

We can however restructure the program in a more systematic and elegant manner. Note that this restructuring process is done at design time and thus does not affect the run-time performance of an agent. The key is to find the context dependent actions in a plan and turn them into subgoals. The following steps are described as follows. Assume that plan P is written as $g : c \leftarrow b_1; b_2; ...; b_n$

1. Starting from b_2, we go through each formula*ae* b_i in the body of plan P and check the following.
2. If b_i is a subgoal and its reactivity measure is less than 1, then we identify the relevant plans for handling b_i and apply the same technique (steps 1 – 6) to restructure those plans.
3. If b_i is an action, we check whether b_i is a context dependent action using information in the action description library and the environmental state model. If b_i is a context dependent action, we do the following.
4. Create a subgoal sg and replace the remaining sequence of actions/subgoals $< b_i, b_{i+1}, ..., b_n >$ with subgoal sg in the plan body. Subgoal sg can be named after what it can achieve, and it has the same arguments as goal g. Plan P is now written as $g : c \leftarrow b_1; b_2; ...; b_{i-1}; !sg$.
5. Create a plan for handling the newly created subgoal sg with context condition c and the plan body containing the extracted sequence of actions/subgoals. The new plan P' is written as $sg : c \leftarrow b_i; b_{i+1}; ...; b_n$.
6. Continue restructuring plan P' following steps 1 – 5.

Let us illustrate how the above steps are applied to restructure the set of plans $\{Pl1, Pl2\}$ for achieving goal $has(robot, garbage)$ described in the previous section. For restructuring plan $Pl1$, we first identify that action $moveTowards(house)$ is context dependent. Therefore, we create a new subgoal $!sg1(rotbot, garbage)$ and extract the sequence $\langle moveTowards(house); collect(garbage) \rangle$ into a new plan $Pl12$ for handling this subgoal. We then continue trying to restructure plan $Pl12$ but $collect(garbage)$ is not an domain dependent action, and thus the restructuring process for plan $Pl1$ stops here, resulting into two new plans $Pl11$

and *Pl*12. We note that the capabilities of the agent still remain although its behaviour may change towards being more reactive during the course of achieving goal *has*(*robot, garbage*). The agent now makes an evaluation of the context when it is more appropriate to do so, i.e. before it performs the *moveTowards*(*house*) action (see plan *Pl*12).

Pl11   +!*has*(*robot, garbage*) : ¬ *weather*(*raining*) ∧ *at*(*garbage, house*)
                                    ← *notify*(*headquarter*);
                                    !*sg*1(*rotbot, garbage*).

Pl12   +!*sg*1(*rotbot, garbage*) : ¬ *weather*(*raining*) ∧ *at*(*garbage, house*)
                                    ← *moveTowards*(*house*);
                                    collect(*garbage*).

Since plan *Pl*11 no longer has any context-dependent action, its reactivity is equal to the reactivity of subgoal *sg*1, which is equal to the reactivity of plan *Pl*12. Plan *Pl*12 also does not have any context dependent action and thus its reactivity is 1. Similarly, plan *Pl*2 are restructured into two plans *Pl*21 and *Pl*22 as follows. The reactivity of both plans *Pl*21 and *Pl*22 are also 1 since they no longer have any context dependent action. Hence, the restructuring has improved the reactivity of achieving goal *has*(*robot, garbage*) from 0.25 to the maximum 1. In the restructured program, the agent make a choice of moving to collect the garbage or rainproofing itself later (i.e. after notifying the headquarter agent) to consider the latest weather information.

Pl21   +!*has*(*robot, garbage*) : *weather*(*raining*) ∧ *at*(*garbage, house*)
                                    ← *notify*(*headquarter*);
                                    !*sg*2(*rotbot, garbage*).

Pl22   +!*sg*2(*rotbot, garbage*) : *weather*(*raining*) ∧ *at*(*garbage, house*)
                                    ← *rainproof*(*self*);
                                    !*has*(*robot, garbage*).

Finally, since the two pairs of plans *Pl*11 and *Pl*21, and plans *Pl*12 and *Pl*22 are substantially similar, we can further restructure *Pl*11 and *Pl*21, into one plan by simply renaming goal *sg*2 to *sg*1.

6   Implementation

We have developed a prototype implementation of our framework. The tool was implemented as a plugin[4] on the Eclipse platform and thus can be run together with the Eclipse-based code editor of Jason[5], one of the most well-known platforms for developing agent applications in AgentSpeak. Figure 1 shows a

---

[4] The tool is available at https://code.google.com/p/agent-redesign.
[5] http://jason.sourceforge.net/Jason/

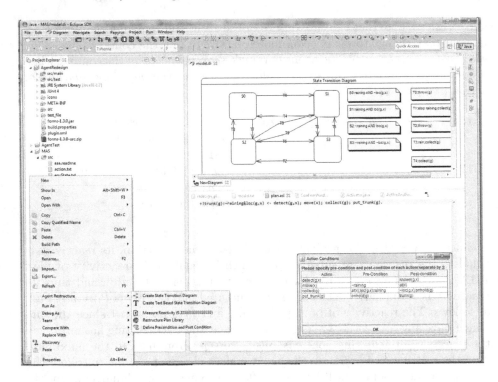

Fig. 1. A screenshot of our prototype tool

screenshot of the tool which is being used. The tool has all the features of the framework that we have proposed in this paper. These features are grouped under the "Agent Restructure" menu item when the user right-clicks on an agent project (see the right-hand-side part of Figure 1).

The tool provides a user interface which allows the user to establish an action description library in terms of defining actions and their preconditions and effects. In addition, the tool is able to parse an existing agent program and populate the library with actions. This feature is important since it allows for our tool to be used with existing agent programs. The tool allows the user to define an environmental state model as either text-based or graphical-based (UML state machine diagram). In addition, the tool is able to computes the reactivity measure of an agent program. Finally, the tool supports the user to interactively restructure the current program for reactivity improvement based on our methodology described in the previous section.

7   Related Work

During the past decade, there has been a proliferation of agent-oriented design methodologies [17] and programming languages [4] proposed in the literature. Some of them have become mature and been extensively used in both academic and industrial settings. Unfortunately, there have been however not many efforts in developing software metrics specifically for agent systems. Some early work by Barber and Martin [19] proposes an approach to measure an agent's autonomy in terms of the goals they pursue. Padgham and Winikoff [21] proposed the use of data coupling metric for the identification of agents, as part of Prometheus, an agent-oriented methodology. The work in [7] proposes an approach to evaluate how an agent-oriented methodology supports the pro-activeness of agents in the context of comparing a number of agent-oriented methodologies. Their measure is however coarse-grained and is not suitable for specific agent programs.

To the best our knowledge, there has been no work in measuring the reactivity of an agent program. Recent work by Alonso et. al. [1, 2] which proposes a set of metrics to measure the pro-activeness, autonomy and sociability of agent programs is perhaps the most closely related to ours. In particularly, one of the component in their pro-activeness metric is reaction, which is measured in terms of the number of requests from the environment that the agent can respond and the complexity of the agent operations. The former is similar to the ideas of the agent's ability to handle external events as in our reactivity metric. The latter is however not clearly defined in their work. One clear difference between their work and ours is that their metrics are applied to general-purpose agents while our work is specific to BDI agents (as we deal specifically with plans, events, and context conditions), the most well-known and popular agent types. More recently, Thangarajah et. al. [27] have proposed to measure plan coverage and overlap for BDI agents. Coverage indicates whether there will always be some plan with a matching context condition, whereas overlap refers to whether there is, in some situations, more than one plan that is applicable. Plan coverage are counted using model counting to measure the portion of the number of models in which a set of plans are applicable using their context conditions against the total number of models in the domain of concern. This is related to an agent's reactivity in terms of having plans to respond to different scenarios of the environment's changes. However, in order to increase the plan coverage, we may need to alter the existing context condition and/or adding further plans to the agent's capabilities. This is different from the methodology we have proposed in this paper. Some existing techniques that use planning to either generate new plans on the fly (e.g. [20]) or to perform lookahead of plan execution (e.g. [25]) are loosely related to our work. Unlike our approach, such techniques however require substantial changes and/or extensions made to the existing BDI programming languages and platforms.

Due to its maturity, the object-oriented software engineering literature has a substantial amount of work in software metrics. Such work (e.g. [8], [3]) target at defining metrics for classes and objects by examining their functions, attributes and the relationships between them. Although these concepts are specific to objects and cannot be applied directly to agents, our work is inspired and built up the notion and ideas from object-oriented software metrics. Our methodology of restructuring agent programs is also inspired by code reactoring [15] in mainstream software engineering and is part of the body of work that supports the maintenance and evolution of agent systems [9–11, 13]. Code refactoring refers to a set of techniques for restructuring an existing code to modify its internal structure without altering its external behaviour. Code refactoring is specifically for improving some of the nonfunctional attributes of the software including code readability, maintainability of the source code, and extensibility of the internal architecture. However, there has been very little work on refactoring for agent systems. The work in [28] identifies some common "bad smells" problems (e.g. duplicated behaviour structure and big plans) in multi-agent system design and proposes some refactoring patterns to eliminate those bad smells. Their work however only focuses on design models rather source code as in our work.

8   Conclusions

In this paper, we have argued that there are a number of factors that affect the reactivity of BDI agent systems, one of which is the ability to delay their commitment to a certain courses of action as late as possible (i.e. wait until the agent has the most updated information about the environment) by preferring subgoals over primitive actions. Based on this notion, we have developed a framework which facilitates the restructuring of a body of code of an BDI agent program in order to improve its reactivity. A novel aspect of the framework is a reactivity measure which reflects whether a particular choice of actions is left as late as possible so as to consider the latest information in the environment. The framework is built upon a programming environment where the semantic of agent actions and changes in the environment are explicitly defined. We also propose a methodology of how to improve the reactivity measure of an agent program. Although our approach is generally applicable to any BDI programming languages, we implemented a restructuring plug-in integrated with the Eclipse-based development environment of the well-known Jason platform.

In terms of future work, we plan to conduct an evaluation of our reactivity metric and methodology. In addition, we plan to investigate some dynamic measures for agents' reactivity, i.e. measure the reactivity of the agents during execution, and compare the reliability of both static and dynamic measures as well as explore how they can complement each other. We also plan to explore how to provide a more complex model of the environment. Our future work also involves implementing our approach and methodology to support other BDI programming languages, especially those that allow STRIPS-like specification of actions such as 3APL [14]. Finally, a long term plan of our work would involves proposing a metric suite for agent systems including not only reactivity but also other agent properties such as pro-activeness, autonomy and sociability, and developing a comprehensive set of discipline techniques to improve those quality aspects of an agent system.

References

1. Alonso, F., Fuertes, J.L., Martinez, L., Soza, H.: Towards a set of measures for evaluating software agent autonomy. In: Proceedings of the 2009 Eighth Mexican International Conference on Artificial Intelligence, MICAI 2009, pp. 73–78. IEEE Computer Society, Washington, DC (2009)
2. Alonso, F., Fuertes, J.L., Martinez, L., Soza, H.: Measuring the pro-activity of software agents. In: International Conference on Software Engineering Advances, pp. 319–324 (2010)
3. Barnes, G., Swim, B.: Inheriting software metrics. Journal of Object-Oriented Programming 6(7), 27–34 (1993)
4. Bordini, R.H., Dastani, M., Dix, J., El Fallah Seghrouchni, A. (eds.): Multi-Agent Programming: Languages, Platforms and Applications. Springer (2005)
5. Bordini, R.H., Hübner, J.F., Wooldridge, M.: Programming multi-agent systems in AgentSpeak using Jason. Wiley (2007) ISBN 0470029005
6. Busetta, P., Howden, N., Rönnquist, R., Hodgson, A.: Structuring BDI agents in functional clusters. In: Jennings, N.R. (ed.) ATAL 1999. LNCS, vol. 1757, pp. 277–289. Springer, Heidelberg (2000)
7. Cernuzzi, L., Rossi, G.: On the evaluation of agent oriented modeling methods. In: Proceedings of Agent Oriented Methodology Workshop, Seattle (2002)
8. Chidamber, S.R., Kemerer, C.F.: A metrics suite for object oriented design. IEEE Trans. Softw. Eng. 20, 476–493 (1994)
9. Dam, H.K., Ghose, A.: Automated change impact analysis for agent systems. In: Proceedings of the 27th IEEE International Conference on Software Maintenance, ICSM 2011, pp. 33–42. IEEE, Washington, DC (2011)
10. Dam, H.K., Ghose, A.: Supporting change impact analysis for intelligent agent systems. Science of Computer Programming 78(9), 1728–1750 (2013)
11. Dam, H.K., Winikoff, M.: An agent-oriented approach to change propagation in software maintenance. Journal of Autonomous Agents and Multi-Agent Systems 23(3), 384–452 (2011)
12. Dam, H.K., Winikoff, M.: Towards a next-generation AOSE methodology. Science of Computer Programming 78(6), 684–694 (2013)
13. Dam, K.H., Winikoff, M.: Cost-based BDI plan selection for change propagation. In: Padgham, Parkes, Müller, Parsons (eds.) Proceedings of the 7th International Conference on Autonomous Agents and Multiagent Systems (AAMAS 2008), Estoril, Portugal, pp. 217–224 (May 2008)
14. Dastani, M., Birna Riemsdijk, M., Meyer, J.-J.: Programming multi-agent systems in 3APL. In: Bordini, R., Dastani, M., Dix, J., Fallah Seghrouchni, A. (eds.) Multi-Agent Programming. Multiagent Systems, Artificial Societies, and Simulated Organizations, vol. 15, pp. 39–67. Springer US (2005)
15. Fowler, M., Beck, K.: Refactoring: improving the design of existing code. Addison-Wesley Longman Publishing Co., Inc., Boston (1999)
16. Georgeff, M., Rao, A.: Rational software agents: From theory to practice. In: Agent Technology: Foundations, Applications, and Markets, ch. 8, pp. 139–160 (1998)
17. Henderson-Sellers, B., Giorgini, P. (eds.): Agent-Oriented Methodologies. Idea Group Publishing (2005)
18. Hindriks, K.V., de Boer, F.S., van der Hoek, W., Meyer, J.-J.C.: Agent programming with declarative goals. In: Castelfranchi, C., Lespérance, Y. (eds.) ATAL 2000. LNCS (LNAI), vol. 1986, p. 228. Springer, Heidelberg (2001)

19. Martin, C.E., Barber, K.S., Barber, K.S.: Agent autonomy: Specification, measurement, and dynamic adjustment. In: Proceedings of the Autonomy Control Software Workshop, Agents 1999, pp. 8–15 (1999)
20. Meneguzzi, F., Luck, M.: Composing high-level plans for declarative agent programming. In: Baldoni, M., Son, T.C., van Riemsdijk, M.B., Winikoff, M. (eds.) DALT 2007. LNCS (LNAI), vol. 4897, pp. 69–85. Springer, Heidelberg (2008)
21. Padgham, L., Winikoff, M.: Developing intelligent agent systems: A practical guide. John Wiley & Sons, Chichester (2004) ISBN 0-470-86120-7
22. Pavon, J., Gomez-Sanz, J.J., Fuentes, R.: The INGENIAS methodology and tools. In: Henderson-Sellers, B., Giorgini, P. (eds.) Agent-Oriented Methodologies, ch. IX, pp. 236–276. Idea Group Publishing (2005)
23. Pokahr, A., Braubach, L., Lamersdorf, W.: Jadex: A BDI reasoning engine. In: Bordini, R., Dastani, M., Dix, J., El Fallah Seghrouchni, A. (eds.) Multi-Agent Programming, pp. 149–174. Springer Science+Business Media Inc., USA (2005)
24. Rao, A.S.: AgentSpeak(L): BDI agents speak out in a logical computable language. In: Van de Velde, W., Perrame, J. (eds.) MAAMAW 1996. LNCS (LNAI), vol. 1038, pp. 42–55. Springer, Heidelberg (1996)
25. Sardina, S., de Silva, L., Padgham, L.: Hierarchical planning in bdi agent programming languages: a formal approach. In: Proceedings of the Fifth International Joint Conference on Autonomous Agents and Multiagent Systems, AAMAS 2006, pp. 1001–1008 (2006)
26. Sardina, S., Padgham, L.: A BDI agent programming language with failure recovery, declarative goals, and planning. Autonomous Agents and Multi-Agent Systems 23(1), 18–70 (2011)
27. Thangarajah, J., Sardina, S., Padgham, L.: Measuring plan coverage and overlap for agent reasoning. In: Proceedings of the 11th International Joint Conference on Autonomous Agents and Multiagent Systems (AAMAS 2012), Valencia, Spain, pp. 1049–1056 (June 2012)
28. Tiryaki, A.M., Ekinci, E.E., Dikenelli, O.: Refactoring in multi agent system development. In: Bergmann, R., Lindemann, G., Kirn, S., Pěchouček, M. (eds.) MATES 2008. LNCS (LNAI), vol. 5244, pp. 183–194. Springer, Heidelberg (2008)
29. Winikoff, M., Padgham, L., Harland, J., Thangarajah, J.: Declarative & procedural goals in intelligent agent systems. In: Proceedings of the Eighth International Conference on Principles of Knowledge Representation and Reasoning (KR 2002), Toulouse, France, pp. 470–481 (2002)
30. Wooldridge, M.: An Introduction to MultiAgent Systems. John Wiley & Sons, Chichester (2002) ISBN 0 47149691X
31. Zambonelli, F., Jennings, N.R., Wooldridge, M.: Developing multiagent systems: The Gaia methodology. ACM Transactions on Software Engineering and Methodology 12(3), 317–370 (2003)

Higher-Order Theory of Mind in Negotiations under Incomplete Information

Harmen de Weerd[1], Rineke Verbrugge[1], and Bart Verheij[1,2]

[1] Institute of Artificial Intelligence, University of Groningen
[2] CodeX, Stanford University

Abstract. Theory of mind refers to the ability to reason explicitly about unobservable mental content such as beliefs, desires, and intentions of others. People are known to make use of theory of mind, and even reason about what other people believe about their beliefs. Although it is unknown why such a higher-order theory of mind evolved in humans, exposure to mixed-motive situations may have facilitated its emergence. In such mixed-motive situations, interacting parties have partially overlapping goals, so that both competition and cooperation play a role. In this paper, we consider negotiation using alternative offers in a particular mixed-motive situation known as Colored Trails, and determine to what extent higher-order theory of mind is beneficial to computational agents. Our results show limited effectiveness of first-order theory of mind, while second-order theory of mind turns out to benefit agents greatly by allowing them to reason about the way they communicate their interests.

1 Introduction

In everyday life, people regularly reason about what other people know and believe. People use this *theory of mind* [1] to understand why other people behave in a certain way, to predict their future behaviour, and to distinguish between intentional and accidental behaviour. People also take this ability one step further, and consider that others have a theory of mind as well. This second-order theory of mind allows people to consider and even expect that others will understand why they behave the way that they do. In this paper, we make use of agent-based computational models to explain why our ability to reason about mental content of others may have evolved.

Second-order theory of mind allows people to reason explicitly about belief attributions made by others. For example, in the sentence "Alice knows that Bob knows that Carol is throwing him a surprise party", a *second-order knowledge attribution* is made to Alice, in which she attributes knowledge to Bob. The human ability to make use of higher-order (i.e. at least second-order) theory of mind is well-established, both through tasks that require explicit reasoning about second-order belief attributions [2, 3], as well as in strategic games [4, 5]. However, the use of theory of mind of any kind by non-human species is a controversial matter [6–8]. These differences in the ability to make use of theory of mind raise the issue of the reason for the evolution of a system that allows

G. Boella et al. (Eds.): PRIMA 2013, LNAI 8291, pp. 101–116, 2013.
© Springer-Verlag Berlin Heidelberg 2013

humans to use higher-order theory of mind to reason about what other people understand about mental content, while other animals, including chimpanzees and other primates, do not appear to have this ability.

A possible explanation for the emergence of higher-order theory of mind is that it is needed in situations that involve mixed-motive interactions such as negotiations [9] or crisis management [10]. In these situations, interactions are partially cooperative in the sense that the interaction can lead to a mutually beneficial outcome, but also partially competitive in the sense that there is no outcome that is optimal for everyone involved. Mixed-motive situations can be understood as the task of sharing a pie [11]. When negotiating parties cooperate to find mutually beneficial solutions, they are searching for ways to enlarge the pie that they are trying to share. At the same time, negotiating parties compete to receive as large a portion of the pie as possible for themselves.

In this paper, we make use of agent-based computational models to investigate the advantages of making use of higher-order theory of mind in mixed-motive settings. Agent-based modeling has proven its usefulness as a research tool to investigate how behavioral patterns emerge from the interactions between individuals (cf. [12]), by allowing precise control and monitoring of the mental content of agents, including application of theory of mind. This approach differs from related work on prescriptive models of negotiation (see for example [13–15]) in that we simulate interactions between agents that differ in their theory of mind abilities to determine the extent to which higher-order theory of mind provides agents with an advantage over those that are more restricted in their use of theory of mind.

We have selected to investigate the effectiveness of higher-order theory of mind in the influential Colored Trails setting, introduced by Grosz, Kraus and colleagues [16–18], which provides a useful test-bed to study interactions in mixed-motive situations. In single-shot negotiations in Colored Trails, first-order theory of mind has been shown to benefit agents greatly, while the advantage of second-order theory of mind only appears when negotiations involve more than two players [19]. In the current paper, we change the Colored Trails setting to include incomplete information about the goals of the partner and to allow for multiple rounds of negotiation, where two agents alternate in making offers until an agreement is reached.

The remainder of the paper is structured as follows. Section 2 describes the details of the Colored Trails setting we investigate, after which Section 3 presents how theory of mind agents negotiate in this setting. To determine the effectiveness of theory of mind, we simulated negotiations between agents of different orders of theory of mind. The results of these can be found in Section 4. Finally, Section 5 provides discussion and gives directions for future research.

2   Colored Trails

To determine the effectiveness of higher orders of theory of mind in negotiations, we compare performance of computational agents in the setting of Colored Trails

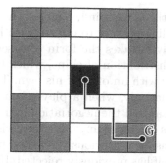

Fig. 1. The Colored Trails game is played on a 5 by 5 board. Players are initially placed on the black tile, and aim to approach their goal tile as closely as possible. To follow the black path from the initial tile to goal location G, a player would have to hand in two white chips and two gray chips.

(CT). Colored Trails is a board game designed as a research test-bed for investigating decision-making in groups of people and computer agents [17, 18]. Colored Trails is played by two or more players on a board of colored tiles. Each player starts the game at a given initial tile with a set of colored chips. The colors of the chips match those of the tiles of the board. A player can move to a tile adjacent to his current location by handing in a chip of the same color as the destination tile. Each player is also assigned a goal location, which the player has to approach as closely as possible. To achieve this goal, players are allowed to trade chips among each other. The Colored Trails setting represents a multi-issue bargaining situation, where each issue is represented by a color, while different paths towards the goal location represent different acceptable solutions.

We follow the scoring rules in [17] and award a player that reaches his goal tile 500 points. If a player is unable to reach the goal tile, he pays a penalty of 100 points for each tile in the shortest path from his current location to his goal location. Chips that have not been used to move on the board are worth 50 points. For each player, reaching the goal location is therefore the most valuable. Since a player generally needs a different set of chips to achieve his goal than his trading partner, there may be an opportunity for a trade that would allow both players to reach a higher score. But since unused chips increase a player's score as well, players compete to own as many chips as possible.

In our setting, the Colored Trails game is played by two players on a 5 by 5 board such as the one depicted in Figure 1. Both players start at the center of the board, indicated by the black square. This initial location is publicly announced to the players, so that each player knows the initial location of the other player. Each player also knows his own goal location, which has been randomly chosen from the 12 possible tiles that are at least three steps away from the goal location, indicated by the gray tiles in Figure 1. Although players know their own goal location, they do not know the goal location of their trading partner. This ensures that at the start of a game, players are uncertain about the bargaining position of their trading partner. That is, they do not know the score of their trading partner if negotiations should fail, or his preferences over chips. Through the use of theory of mind, agents can extract information from the offers made by the trading partner to try to learn his goal location.

Negotiation between players takes the form of a sequence of offers. Players take turns suggesting a redistribution of chips, which their trading partner can choose to accept or counter with an offer of his own. The game ends as soon as an offer is accepted. Alternatively, when a player believes that it is impossible to reach an agreement, he can end the negotiation and the initial distribution of chips becomes final. Players can make any offer they wish. For example, a player may repeat an offer that has been previously rejected by his trading partner, or make an offer that he himself has previously rejected. However, both players pay a 1 point penalty for each round of play. That is, when negotiations end after five offers, the final score of each player is reduced by five points.

In Colored Trails, players can achieve a higher score by trading chips in such a way that both players can move closer to their respective goal locations, thereby enlarging the pie they share. At the same time, players compete to obtain as large a piece of the pie as possible through trades that will increase their own score more than it will increase the score of their trading partner.

3   Theory of Mind Agents in Colored Trails

To investigate the effectiveness of theory of mind in mixed-motive settings, we constructed theory of mind agents that are able to play the game as outlined in Section 2. These agents are inspired by the theory of mind agents used by [20] to investigate the effectiveness of theory of mind in competitive settings. To focus our investigations to the effectiveness of theory of mind, we assume that agents make no mistakes in finding routes between locations and do not consider the possibility that mistakes could be made in finding these routes. In the following subsections, we describe how agents of different orders of theory of mind negotiate with their trading partner in the Colored Trails setting. [1]

3.1   Zero-Order Theory of Mind Agent

The zero-order theory of mind (ToM_0) agent is unable to attribute mental content to others. Instead, the ToM_0 agent forms zero-order beliefs about the likelihood of his trading partner accepting a certain offer. The ToM_0 agent uses these beliefs to calculate the expected value of making an offer, which takes into account the change in the score of the ToM_0 agent if his trading partner should accept his offer, as well as the cost of another round of negotiation. A negative expected value for some offer O means that the ToM_0 agent believes that it would be better to withdraw from negotiations rather than to make offer O.

The ToM_0 agent bases his zero-order beliefs on his observations of the behaviour of his trading partner. For example, if the trading partner rejects an offer made by the ToM_0 agent, the ToM_0 agent believes that his trading partner

---

[1] The formal model of theory of mind agents is available as an online appendix at http://www.ai.rug.nl/SocialCognition/Experiments/

will also reject any offer that assigns fewer chips to his trading partner and more to himself. Similarly, when the trading partner makes an offer that assigns many red chips to the trading partner, the ToM_0 agent concludes that it is unlikely that his trading partner is willing to accept an offer that assigns few red chips to the trading partner and adjusts his beliefs accordingly.

The degree to which the ToM_0 agent adjusts his beliefs based on the observed behaviour of his trading partner is represented by a learning speed parameter λ $(0 \leq \lambda \leq 1)$. A ToM_0 agent with zero learning speed does not adjust his beliefs over the course of negotiation. Such a ToM_0 agent rarely withdraws from negotiation, and keeps making the same offer until his trading partner either accepts or makes an acceptable counteroffer. Such a counteroffer made by the trading partner should increase of the score of the ToM_0 agent that is at least as much as the expected value the ToM_0 agent assigns to his own offer.

If the ToM_0 agent has the maximum learning speed $(\lambda = 1)$, he radically changes his beliefs based on the behaviour of his trading partner. For example, when his trading partner rejects an offer made by the ToM_0 agent, the ToM_0 agent considers it impossible that his trading partner would accept this offer at any future point in the negotiations. Similarly, when the trading partner makes an offer that assigns three red chips to the trading partner, a ToM_0 agent with learning speed $\lambda = 1$ believes that his trading partner will not accept any offer that assigns two or fewer red chips to the trading partner. With a learning speed $\lambda = 1$, a ToM_1 agent is therefore quick to end negotiations, either by accepting an offer made by his trading partner or by withdrawing from negotiation.

Example 1. Suppose two agents play the Colored Trails game as shown in Figure 2a, in which agent 1 is a ToM_0 agent who wants to move from the central square to the white square marked l_1. Each agent has an initial set of chips, which holds 3 gray chips and 1 black chip for agent 1, while agent 2 has 3 white chips and 1 gray chip. Figure 2a also shows that with the initial distribution, agent 1 can move two tiles towards his goal location, which results in a score of 0.

Suppose that agent 2 makes an offer to trade the black chip held by agent 1 for the gray chip held by agent 2. Since this offer assigns all black and white chips to agent 2, agent 1 decreases his belief that agent 2 will accept an offer in which agent 1 receives any of the black or white chips. After this belief update, agent 1 decides how to respond. Since accepting the offer would decrease the score of agent 1, agent 1 would rather withdraw from negotiation than accept the offer. However, agent 1 may still consider to make a counteroffer.

Agent 1 can reach his goal either with 1 gray chip, 1 black chip, and 1 white chip, or alternatively with 2 white chips and 1 gray chip. Both options would increase the score of agent 1 by 500. Agent 1 could also ask for more chips than he needs to reach his goal location. Each additional unused chip would increase the score of agent 1 by 50, but also decreases his belief that agent 2 will accept the offer. Depending on his exact beliefs, agent 1 decides whether there is any counteroffer that is worth risking the cost of rejection.

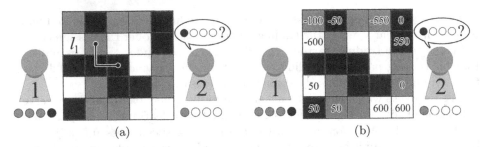

Fig. 2. Example of a negotiation setting in Colored Trails. Agent 1 wants to move from the central square to his goal location l_1. With his initial set of chips, agent 1 can move two tiles towards his goal location, as shown by the path in (a). When agent 1 is a ToM_1 agent, he tries to determine the goal location of agent 2 by calculating how accepting the offer an offer from agent 2 would change the score of agent 2, for all possible goal locations.

3.2   First-Order Theory of Mind Agent

The first-order theory of mind (ToM_1) agent considers the possibility that his trading partner has beliefs and goals, which determine whether or not his trading partner will accept an offer. The ToM_1 agent is able to consider his own offer from the perspective of his trading partner, and decide whether he would accept that offer if he were in the position of his trading partner. However, the ToM_1 agent does not know the actual goal location and zero-order beliefs of his trading partner, but forms beliefs about his trading partner's goal location and beliefs.

Unlike settings that have complete information like rock-paper-scissors [20], offers in Colored Trails can reveal information about a player's preferences. Using his first-order theory of mind, the ToM_1 agent can extract information about his trading partner's goal location from the offers he receives. By putting himself in the position of his trading partner, the ToM_1 agent knows that his trading partner would not make an offer that, if the ToM_1 agent were to accept it, would reduce the score of the trading partner. The ToM_1 agent therefore believes that locations for which this is the case cannot be the goal location of his trading partner. For other locations, the ToM_1 agent determines what offer he would have made if he were in the position of his trading partner. Those locations for which the ToM_1 agent would have made an offer similar to the one he received from his trading partner are assigned the highest likelihood.

To decide on the best offer to make, the ToM_1 agent explicitly considers how his trading partner will respond. This allows the ToM_1 agent to subtly manipulate his trading partner. While deciding what offer to make to his trading partner, the ToM_1 agent determines what counteroffer he believes his trading partner will be making, and whether he would be willing to accept that counteroffer. The ToM_1 agent may therefore decide to make an offer O that he believes will be rejected by his trading partner, but which he also expects to change the beliefs of the trading partner in such a way that the trading partner makes counteroffer

O', which the ToM_1 agent is willing to accept. However, to accurately predict the behaviour of the trading partner, the ToM_1 agent needs to know the goal location of the trading partner. Thus, first-order theory of mind has limited use for making the opening bid of a negotiation.

Although the ToM_1 agent forms explicit beliefs about goal location and beliefs of his trading partner, the ToM_1 agent makes no attempt to model the learning speed λ of his trading partner. Instead, the ToM_1 agent makes use of his own learning speed when he updates the beliefs he attributes to his trading partner, implicitly assuming that every agent has the same learning speed. This means that a ToM_1 agent with zero learning speed $\lambda = 0$ believes that the beliefs of his trading partner do not change in response to any offer he makes, while a ToM_1 agent with maximal learning speed $\lambda = 1$ believes that his trading partner will quickly withdraw from negotiations if he makes his trading partner offers that are too demanding. This implies that the ToM_1 agent will have an incorrect representation of the beliefs of his trading partner unless the ToM_1 agent and his trading partner have the same learning speed.

Example 2. We consider the game shown in Figure 2a, in which agent 1 is a ToM_1 agent. When agent 2 offers to trade the black chip held by agent 1 for the gray chip held by agent 2, agent 1 uses this to extract information about the goal location of agent 2. For each of the possible goal locations, Figure 2b shows the change in the score of agent 2 if agent 1 were to accept the offer. For example, if the goal location of agent 2 is the white square at the bottom right of the board, accepting the offer would increase the score of agent 2 by 600 points.

The ToM_1 agent 1 believes that the goal location of agent 2 cannot be any of the locations that have a negative or zero change in score, since in these cases, agent 2 would have been better off withdrawing from negotiation. Furthermore, by considering the game from the perspective of his trading partner, agent 1 believes that if the goal location of agent 2 had been any of the locations that show an increase by 50 points, agent 2 would have made a different offer. Agent 1 concludes that the offer made by agent 2 is most consistent with his goal location being one of the three remaining locations. If agent 1 were to accept the offer, agent 2 would be able to reach any one of these three locations.

After updating his goal location beliefs, ToM_1 agent 1 decides whether or not to make a counteroffer. Using his first-order theory of mind, agent 1 knows that agent 2 will only accept an offer that would increase his score. For two of the three most likely goal locations, agent 2 would be able to reach his goal location with 1 gray, 1 black, and 1 white chip, while agent 1 would be able to reach his goal location by using 2 white chips and 1 gray chip. The final possible goal location also allows both agents to reach their goal location, with agent 2 using 2 white chips and 2 gray chips, while agent 1 uses 1 black, 1 gray, and 1 white chip. However, there is no offer that is guaranteed to allow both agents to reach respective their goal locations given the information about the goal location of agent 2. The final decision depends on the beliefs of agent 1.

3.3 Higher Orders of Theory of Mind Agent

Agents that are able to use orders of theory of mind beyond the first can use this ability to attempt to manipulate the beliefs of lower orders of theory of mind to obtain an advantage. For example, a second-order theory of mind (ToM_2) agent models his trading partner as a ToM_1 agent, which means that the ToM_2 agent believes that his trading partner may be interpreting the offers he makes to find out what his goal location is. This allows the ToM_2 agent to construct an offer which will inform his trading partner about his goal location. This could speed up the process of finding a mutually beneficial offer.

Second-order theory of mind also allows the ToM_2 agent to deceive and manipulate his trading partner more effectively. By careful construction of the offers he makes, the ToM_2 agent can provide his trading partner with incomplete or ambiguous information about his goal location, or induce a false belief in his trading partner concerning his goal location. This may cause a ToM_1 trading partner to make an offer that is more generous towards the ToM_2 agent than the trading partner believes it to be.

For each additional order of theory of mind, agents also take an additional round of play into consideration. Where a ToM_0 agent only judges whether his trading partner is likely to accept an offer O, a ToM_1 agent believes that the way a ToM_0 trading partner reacts to an offer O depends on how likely the trading partner thinks it is that the ToM_1 agent will accept a possible alternative offer O'. A ToM_2 agent considers an additional round of play by realizing that the reaction of a ToM_1 trading partner to an offer O depends on what this trading partner believes to be the reaction of a ToM_0 agent to a possible alternative offer O', which in turn depends on how likely a ToM_0 agent considers it to be that his trading partner will accept a possible alternative offer O''.

Example 3. We consider the game shown in Figure 2a. Example 2 showed that if agent 1 is a ToM_1 agent, he believes that there are three possible goal locations for agent 2, and has to make a decision of what offer to make under this uncertainty of goal location. If agent 1 is a ToM_2 agent, he can decide to make an offer that is unlikely to be accepted, but may provide agent 2 with enough information to construct an offer that is acceptable to both agents. For example, ToM_2 agent 1 believes that if his offer assigns the black chip to agent 2, this provides agent 2 with information about his goal location. Agent 1 can make an offer that assigned 2 gray and 2 white chips to himself to signal that he does not assign a high value to the black chip. However, since the offer of agent 2 assigns the black chip to agent 2, this chip may be of high value for agent 2. By constructing an offer that assigns the black chip to himself, agent 1 can attempt to make agent 2 believe that the black chip is valuable to agent 1 as well. This may encourage agent 2 to give up more chips in exchange for the black chip.

4   Simulation Results

We performed simulations where the theory of mind agents described in Section 3 negotiated in the Colored Trails setting described in Section 2 according to an alternating offers protocol. Games were played by two agents on a 5 by 5 board of tiles, randomly colored with one of five possible colors. At the start of the game, each player received an initial set of four randomly colored chips, drawn from the same colors as those on the board. Since each player needs at most four chips to reach his or her goal location, it is sometimes possible that after a trade, both players can reach their respective goal location. However, this was not always the case. To ensure that both players have an incentive to negotiate to increase their score, game settings in which some player could reach his goal location with the initial set of chips without trading were excluded from analysis.

To determine the effectiveness of theory of mind, pairs of agents played 1,000 consecutive Colored Trails games. Although agents alternated in making offers, the literature suggests that the opening bid is influential [11, 21], because it serves as an anchor for the negotiation process. Because of this, we differentiate between *initiators*, who make the first offer in a game, and *responders*.

In our simulations, we determined the negotiation score of a ToM_i initiator playing Colored Trails with a ToM_j responder, for each combination of $i, j = 0, 1, 2$. The negotiation score is calculated as the average difference between the initiator's final score after negotiation ended and his initial score at the start of negotiation. A negative score therefore indicates that the initiator paid a higher cost for negotiation than he gained from the resulting trade. Agents started every game reasoning at their highest theory of mind ability. That is, a ToM_2 agent always started the game by taking into account the beliefs his trading partner might have about his own beliefs. Although negotiations could theoretically take infinitely long, games that continued for more than 100 rounds of offers made were considered to be unsuccessful. In this case, the initial situation became final, and both agents incurred the cost of 100 rounds of play. In our model, agents were unable to reason about this limit.

In the following subsections, we present competitive and cooperative aspects of negotiation in Colored Trails separately. In Section 4.1, we present the individual performance of agents, which shows how well agents compete. Section 4.2 focuses on the cooperative element of negotiation, and describes the effect of theory of mind on the combined score of the agents in the Colored Trails setting.

4.1   Individual Performance Results

In this section, we describe the individual performance of theory of mind agents when negotiating in Colored Trails. How large a piece of pie the agents end up with shows how theory of mind influences the competitive abilities of agents.

Figure 3a shows the average negotiation score of a ToM_0 initiator playing Colored Trails with a ToM_0 responder. The three-dimensional figure shows the negotiation score as a function of the learning speeds of both initiator and responder. Since most points in the figure are above the semi-transparent plane of zero negotiation score, the figure shows that ToM_0 agents are often able to increase their score through negotiation despite their inability to reason explicitly about the goals and desires of their trading partner.

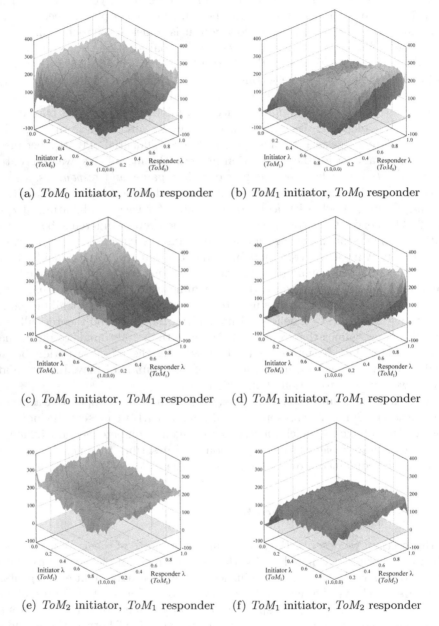

(a) ToM_0 initiator, ToM_0 responder   (b) ToM_1 initiator, ToM_0 responder

(c) ToM_0 initiator, ToM_1 responder   (d) ToM_1 initiator, ToM_1 responder

(e) ToM_2 initiator, ToM_1 responder   (f) ToM_1 initiator, ToM_2 responder

Fig. 3. Average negotiation score of theory of mind agents playing Colored Trails

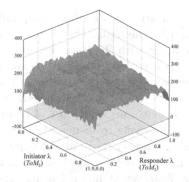

Fig. 4. Average negotiation score of a ToM_2 agent negotiating with a ToM_2 trading partner in Colored Trails

Figure 3a shows that the negotiation score of the ToM_0 initiator generally increases as his own learning speed decreases. An agent with a low learning speed changes his behaviour little in response to the offers his trading partner makes, and behaves as if he is unwilling to make concessions. An agent with zero learning speed ($\lambda = 0$) does not adjust his behaviour at all, but keeps repeating the same offer. When both agents follow this strategy, and neither is willing to accept the offer of ther trading partner, the agents will be unable to reach an agreement and only carry the burden of a failed negotiation. Summing up, there is an evolutionary pressure on ToM_0 agents to decrease their learning speed, which may result in the worst possible outcome in which negotiation fails.

Figure 3b shows that the score of a ToM_1 initiator negotiating with a ToM_0 responder is not always higher than that of a ToM_0 initiator in the same position. Although the ToM_1 obtains a higher score when both agents have a high learning speed, the ToM_1 initiator performs poorly when his learning speed is low. Moreover, a ToM_1 initiator with learning speed $\lambda = 0$ withdraws from negotiation before making his initial offer. The reason for this is that the ToM_1 agent attributes his own learning speed to his trading partner. A ToM_1 agent with zero learning speed predicts that his trading partner will keep repeating the same offer until the ToM_1 agent makes an acceptable offer. As a result, the ToM_1 agent believes that the only way to successfully complete negotiations is for him to give his trading partner what he wants. At the start of a game, however, the ToM_1 initiator does not know the goal location of the responder. As a result, there is no offer that the ToM_1 initiator believes to be successful, and the ToM_1 initiator chooses not to engage in negotiation.

Although the ToM_1 agent has an incentive to keep his learning speed high, Figure 3c shows that even in the presence of a ToM_1 responder, the ToM_0 initiator performs best when his learning speed is close to zero. Since a ToM_1 agent will adjust his offers to take into account the score of his trading partner, the trading partner has no incentive to make any concessions. That is, even though the presence of a ToM_1 agent prevents negotiation from failing, the ToM_0 agent benefits more from this outcome than the ToM_1 agent.

Figure 3d shows the negotiation score of a ToM_1 initiator playing Colored Trails with a ToM_1 responder. The figure shows a ridge along the line of equal learning speeds, where the agent with the lower learning speed generally obtains the higher score. A ToM_1 agent with a high learning speed attributes this learning speed to his trading partner and expects that his offers strongly influence the behaviour of his trading partner. Such a ToM_1 agent believes that his trading partner is quick to conclude that a negotiation will be unsuccessful. To prevent his trading partner from withdrawing from negotiations, the ToM_1 agent makes offers that benefit his trading partner more at the expense of his own score.

However, unlike ToM_0 agents, ToM_1 agents suffer when their learning speed becomes too low. When a ToM_1 agent has a learning speed below $\lambda = 0.2$, his performance does not increase as his learning speed goes down. Because of this, the evolutionary pressure on ToM_1 agents to have low learning speeds does not lead to a situation in which negotiation fails as it does for ToM_0 agents.

Figure 3e and Figure 3e show the performance of a ToM_1 and a ToM_2 agent negotiating in the Colored Trails setting. The figures show that the ToM_2 initiator is more effective in obtaining a large piece of the pie when negotiating with a ToM_1 responder than vice versa, irrespective of the learning speeds of the agents. Compared to results of lower orders of theory of mind, Figure 3e also shows a fairly flat surface, indicating that the score of the ToM_2 initiator is less dependent on learning speeds of the initiator and responder.

Figure 4 shows that when a ToM_2 initiator negotiates with a ToM_2 responder, his score is not influenced greatly by the learning speeds of either agent. Nonetheless, the ToM_2 initiator performs best when his learning speed is low, but greater than zero.

The results in this section show that although a ToM_1 agent succeeds in securing a larger pie when negotiating with a ToM_0 trading partner than a ToM_0 agent, the ToM_1 agent only obtains a small piece of this pie. The ToM_2 agent negotiates successfully with other theory of mind agents as well, but also ensures that he receives a large piece of pie for himself. In the next subsection, we take a closer look at the cooperative abilities of these theory of mind agents.

4.2   Social Welfare Results

In the previous section, we compared the individual competitive performance of agents of several orders of theory of mind negotiating in Colored Trails. In this section, we show how theory of mind affects the cooperative ability of agents. To this end, we take a closer look at the increase in social welfare that theory of mind agents achieve, where social welfare is measured by the sum of the scores of the initiator and the responder. Figure 5 and Figure 6 show the increase in social welfare for different combinations of theory of mind initiators and responders.

Figure 5a shows that ToM_0 agents can cooperate surprisingly well. However, cooperation between ToM_0 agents is not stable due to the competitive element of Colored Trails. The ToM_0 agents experience an evolutionary pressure towards zero learning speed, which can eventually lead to negotiation failure.

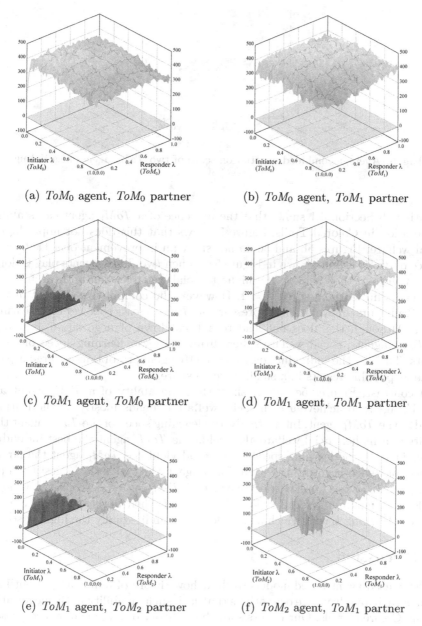

(a) ToM_0 agent, ToM_0 partner

(b) ToM_0 agent, ToM_1 partner

(c) ToM_1 agent, ToM_0 partner

(d) ToM_1 agent, ToM_1 partner

(e) ToM_1 agent, ToM_2 partner

(f) ToM_2 agent, ToM_1 partner

Fig. 5. Average combined negotiation score of theory of mind agents playing Colored Trails

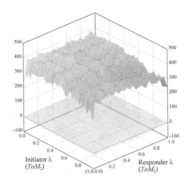

Fig. 6. Average combined negotiation score of two ToM_2 agents negotiating

Although Section 4.1 shows that the presence of a ToM_1 agent can stabilize cooperation in Colored Trails, Figure 5 shows that this does not imply higher social welfare. Figures 5b and 5c do not show an improvement over the performance of ToM_0 agents shown in Figure 5a. When two ToM_1 agents play Colored Trails together, they achieve the highest social welfare when both agents have the maximum learning speed $\lambda = 1$. However, the competitive element in Colored Trails puts an evolutionary pressure on ToM_1 agents to lower their learning speed. Although this does not lead to a breakdown of negotiation as it does for ToM_0 agents, social welfare suffers from the lower learning speed of ToM_1 agents. That is, the individual desire of ToM_1 agents to obtain as large a piece of pie as possible results in a smaller pie to share.

In contrast, Figures 5e and 5f show that the ability of a ToM_2 agent and a ToM_1 agent to achieve a high social welfare depends mostly on the learning speed of the ToM_1 agent. Interestingly, the learning speed of the ToM_1 agent that results in a higher social welfare also yields the ToM_1 agent the best individual score. That is, the learning speed that would yield the ToM_1 agent the largest piece of pie when negotiating with a ToM_2 agent also yields the largest total pie.

Figure 6 shows a similar effect when two ToM_2 agent negotiate in Colored Trails. The maximum social welfare is achieved when both agents have a low non-zero learning speed, which also yields them individually the highest score.

5   Discussion

We have used agent-based models to show how theory of mind can present individuals with an advantage over others that lack such an ability in the negotiation setting Colored Trails. Our results show how theory of mind can indeed present individuals with evolutionary advantages, by facilitating successful negotiation with others. Although agents without a theory of mind are very successful under optimal circumstances, zero-order theory of mind agents face a cooperative dilemma where agents can defect on cooperation by not making any concessions to their trading partner. When this strategy is adopted by all agents, these agents are unable to negotiate successfully. In terms of sharing a pie, the individual goals of agents to receive as large a piece of pie as possible increases competition until there no longer is any pie to share.

Agents negotiate more successfully when the ability to make use of theory of mind is introduced. By reasoning explicitly about the goals of their trading partner, first-order theory of mind agents can recognize the need for a mutually beneficial outcome. However, this does not solve the cooperative dilemma completely. The attempts of first-order theory of mind agents to obtain as large a piece as possible comes at the expense of the size of the pie as a whole.

Although first-order theory of mind has a limited effectiveness in the negotiation setting we describe, second-order theory of mind greatly benefits agents. When a second-order theory of mind agent negotiates with another agent capable of theory of mind, neither agent has an incentive to deviate from the outcome that maximizes social welfare. That is, agents that succeed in negotiating the largest possible pie could not have received a larger piece of pie for themselves by changing their behaviour. Moreover, second-order theory of mind also allows an agent to obtain a larger piece of the pie for himself. In future research, we aim to determine whether the extent to which theory of mind is effective in mixed-motive settings goes beyond second-order theory of mind.

The setting we investigate is similar to [16] in that we model bounded rational agents negotiating with incomplete information. However, the second-order theory of mind agents that we model also take into account that their trading partner has incomplete information concerning their own goals as well. In future work, these agents of [16] can be compared directly to theory of mind agents.

The effectiveness of theory of mind in our setup can be understood in terms of interest-based bargaining [11, 22]. Without theory of mind, agents can only negotiate in terms of positions, by making offers without regard for the interests of others. First-order theory of mind allows an agent to identify the interests of his trading partner, while a second-order theory of mind agent is able to communicate his interests through his choice of offers. That is, theory of mind allows agents to engage in interest-based bargaining, where agents reveal their interests to uncover mutually beneficial solutions.

Acknowledgments. This work was supported by the Netherlands Organisation for Scientific Research (NWO) Vici grant NWO 277-80-001, awarded to Rineke Verbrugge.

References

1. Premack, D., Woodruff, G.: Does the chimpanzee have a theory of mind? Behav. Brain Sci. 1(4), 515–526 (1978)
2. Apperly, I.: Mindreaders: The Cognitive Basis of "Theory of Mind". Psychology Press, Hove (2011)
3. Perner, J., Wimmer, H.: "John thinks that Mary thinks that..". Attribution of second-order beliefs by 5 to 10 year old children. J. Exp. Child Psychol. 39(3), 437–471 (1985)

 4. Hedden, T., Zhang, J.: What do you think I think you think?: Strategic reasoning in matrix games. Cognition 85(1), 1–36 (2002)
 5. Meijering, B., van Rijn, H., Taatgen, N.A., Verbrugge, R.: I do know what you think I think: Second-order theory of mind in strategic games is not that difficult. In: CogSci, Cognitive Science Society, pp. 2486–2491 (2011)
 6. Penn, D.C., Povinelli, D.J.: On the lack of evidence that non-human animals possess anything remotely resembling a 'theory of mind'. Philos. T. R. Soc. B 362(1480), 731–744 (2007)
 7. Tomasello, M.: Why we Cooperate. MIT Press, Cambridge (2009)
 8. van der Vaart, E., Verbrugge, R., Hemelrijk, C.K.: Corvid re-caching without 'theory of mind': A model. PLoS ONE 7(3), e32904 (2012)
 9. Verbrugge, R.: Logic and social cognition: The facts matter, and so do computational models. J. Philos. Logic 38, 649–680 (2009)
10. van Santen, W., Jonker, C., Wijngaards, N.: Crisis decision making through a shared integrative negotiation mental model. Int. J. Emerg. Manag. 6(3), 342–355 (2009)
11. Raiffa, H., Richardson, J., Metcalfe, D.: Negotiation Analysis: The Science and Art of Collaborative Decision Making. Belknap Press (2002)
12. Epstein, J.M.: Generative Social Science: Studies in Agent-based Computational Modeling. Princeton University Press, Princeton (2006)
13. Endriss, U., Pacuit, E.: Modal logics of negotiation and preference. In: Fisher, M., van der Hoek, W., Konev, B., Lisitsa, A. (eds.) JELIA 2006. LNCS (LNAI), vol. 4160, pp. 138–150. Springer, Heidelberg (2006)
14. Wooldridge, M., Parsons, S.: On the use of logic in negotiation. In: Proc. Workshop Agent Commun. Lang. (2000)
15. Fabregues, A., Sierra, C.: Hana: A human-aware negotiation architecture. Decision Support Systems (2013)
16. Lin, R., Kraus, S., Wilkenfeld, J., Barry, J.: Negotiating with bounded rational agents in environments with incomplete information using an automated agent. Artif. Intell. 172(6), 823–851 (2008)
17. Gal, Y., Grosz, B., Kraus, S., Pfeffer, A., Shieber, S.: Agent decision-making in open mixed networks. Artif. Intell. 174(18), 1460–1480 (2010)
18. van Wissen, A., Gal, Y., Kamphorst, B., Dignum, M.V.: Human–agent teamwork in dynamic environments. Computers Human Behav. 28, 23–33 (2012)
19. de Weerd, H., Verbrugge, R., Verheij, B.: Agent-based models for higher-order theory of mind. In: ESSA (in press, 2013)
20. de Weerd, H., Verbrugge, R., Verheij, B.: How much does it help to know what she knows you know? An agent-based simulation study. Artif. Intell. 199-200, 67–92 (2013)
21. Van Poucke, D., Buelens, M.: Predicting the outcome of a two-party price negotiation: Contribution of reservation price, aspiration price and opening offer. J. Econ. Psychol. 23(1), 67–76 (2002)
22. Rahwan, I., Sonenberg, L., Dignum, F.P.M.: On interest-based negotiation. In: Dignum, F. (ed.) ACL 2003. LNCS (LNAI), vol. 2922, pp. 383–401. Springer, Heidelberg (2004)

GAMA 1.6: Advancing the Art of Complex Agent-Based Modeling and Simulation

Arnaud Grignard[1], Patrick Taillandier[3], Benoit Gaudou[4], Duc An Vo[2],
Nghi Quang Huynh[5], and Alexis Drogoul[2]

[1] UMI 209 UMMISCO/MSI, UPMC, France
[2] UMI 209 UMMISCO/MSI, IRD, Vietnam
[3] UMR 6266 IDEES, CNRS/University of Rouen, France
[4] UMR 5505 IRIT, CNRS/University of Toulouse, France
[5] DREAM-CTU/IRD, CICT, Can Tho University, Vietnam

Abstract. Agent-based models tend to be more and more complex. In order to cope with this increase of complexity, powerful modeling and simulation tools are required. These last years have seen the development of several platforms dedicated to the development of agent-based models. While some of them are still limited to the development of simple models, others allow to develop rich and complex models. Among them, the GAMA modeling and simulation platform is aimed at supporting the design of spatialized, multiple-paradigms and multiple-scales models. Several papers have already introduced GAMA, notably in earlier PRIMA conferences, and we would like, in this paper, to introduce the new features provided by GAMA 1.6, the latest revision to date of the platform. In particular, we present its capabilities concerning the tight combination of 3D visualization, GIS data management, and multi-level modeling. In addition, we present some examples of real projects that rely on GAMA to develop complex models.

Keywords: Agent-based modeling, simulation, GIS, multi-level, ODE, platform, visualization, complex systems.

1 Introduction

The last years have seen an important increase in the use of agent-based modeling (ABM) in various scientific and application domains. Some of these applications, that rely on large sets of data, are more and more demanding in terms of representation, simulation and interpretation of complex models. While the classical KISS [10][3] approach appeared to be well suited in the early years of ABM, this recent trend, which for instance includes developments in serious games, participatory approaches or integrated models, requires the ability to design and manage more descriptive and detailed models.

The KISS-based approach has given birth to a plethora of small-size, mostly theoretical, toy models that, although they are well suited for training purposes, have had the paradoxical effect of establishing ABM as a mainstream approach to

G. Boella et al. (Eds.): PRIMA 2013, LNAI 8291, pp. 117–131, 2013.
© Springer-Verlag Berlin Heidelberg 2013

complex systems modeling while, at the same time, eliminating the reasons why people had wanted to adopt it in the first place. Building complex, incremental, data-driven modular models in NetLogo [28], for instance, is a difficult task. And it becomes even more difficult when different data sources, at different levels of representation, are to be used. Interpreting these models is also very tedious, given the lack of flexibility offered by the existing platforms in the visualization and parametrization of the models.

While some offers have tried to overcome these limitations (e.g. Repast [23], Mason [20]), they have failed until now to propose a credible alternative in terms of *modeling platforms*. Repast, for instance, is more a well designed *toolbox* than a *platform* as it requires modelers to be highly proficient in Java programming and Eclipse development, which is rarely the case in the scientific domains targeted by ABM. Similarly, these proposals also fall short in terms of *simulation platform*, as designing virtual experiments that combine easy parametrization and high-level interactive visualization is as complicated as building the model itself and requires the use of several external tools.

The GAMA[1] modeling and simulation platform [9] [26], developed since 2007 as an open-source project, aims at overcoming these lacks by providing modelers - which are not, most of the time, computer scientists - with tools to develop and experiment highly complex models through a well-thought integration of agent-based programming, geographical data management, flexible visualization tools and multi-level representation.

GAMA provides a complete modeling language (GAma Modeling Language) and an integrated development environment that allows modelers to build models as quickly and easily as in NetLogo while going beyond what Repast or Mason offer in terms of simulated experiments. It is currently applied in several projects in environmental decision-support systems, urban design, water management, biological invasions, climate change adaptation or disaster mitigation. This paper aims at presenting the new features developed in the latest version of GAMA. We will focus in particular on the following features: the evolution of the GAML language for specifying models using multiple paradigms (especially combinations of mathematical and computer approaches), the seamless integration of geographical data and other spatial data, the tools offered to support high-level visualization of simulations and the multi-level description of models.

2   GAMA Meta-Model

The concepts and the operational semantic of GAML are completely described in a meta-model (see Figure 1) from which every model written in the language derives. This meta-model supports the development of multi-level agent-based models by considering three main sets of abstract classes that represent, respectively, the *entities*, the *space* and the *time* of a model.

---

[1] http://gama-platform.googlecode.com

- The representation of *Entities* are described by two main classes:
  - **Agent** represents an individual entity of a simulation, which is conceptually similar to an object in an object-oriented language. It represents a simulated entity in the simulation.
  - **Population** represents a group of agents sharing the same structure and behavior in a simulation. The population is responsible for managing the agents it is composed of.
- The representation of the *space* of a model is tightly coupled with the previous set and supported by two main classes:
  - **Geometry** is, as its name implies, a geometrical shape (supported by the JTS library [2]) that represents the embodiment of an agent in its *environment*. It is strictly linked with one and only one agent.
  - **Topology** is meant to represent this *environment*. It provides a referential where geometries are located, an optional organization imposed to these geometries and a set of operations to support perception and movements of agents. A topology is linked with one population.
- The representation of *time* uses, similarly, a class linked with Agent and an another one linked with Population (**Scheduler** and **Scheduling Information**).

These three layers of representation (*entities*, *space* and *time*) are tied together by the last class of the meta-model: **Species**. A species, like a class in OOP, defines the attributes, geometries and behaviors common to all the agents of a population, but it also specifies the topology and scheduling of this population. More importantly, the *containment* relationships between species allow to describe hierarchical levels of agency in a very natural way, by considering nested species of a species S as prototypes for micro-agents of agents instance of S. This translates concretely into the possibility for these agents to be hosts of a set of populations, each of them being described by a micro-species of S.

GAMA entirely relies on this meta-model to create models. The first level of agency (the model itself) describes the global topology of the model, its basic scheduling, its parameters and global behaviors, and is the host of the populations of agents described by the species written by the modeler. Recursively, each agent can become the host of nested populations, as long as its species contains the (micro) species that describe them. All of these populations can be provided, through the definition of their species, with their own spatio-temporal scale, which are not necessarily constrained by the containment hierarchy (i.e. the topology of a population of micro-agents can for instance define boundaries larger than the one described in the population of its host). This definition of species also supports the description of shared contexts between macro and micro agents as a way to express the dynamic relationships and data transfer between levels. Additionally, the morphogenesis operation, not presented in the diagram of the Figure 1, allows agents to change species during the simulation, their current species and their target species are linked by a materialization relationship,

---

[2] http://sourceforge.net/projects/jts-topo-suite/

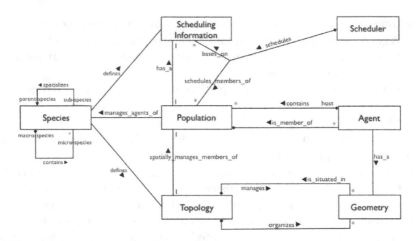

Fig. 1. GAMA meta-model

which effectively allows them to be represented at different levels of abstraction during a simulation.

3   GAMA Features

3.1   The GAML Modeling Language

In order to ease the work of modelers, GAMA provides a complete IDE (Integrated Development Environment) supporting the definition of models. In particular, the IDE, based on Eclipse and XText, provides modern features such as auto-compilation, auto-completion, quick fixes, text coloring, etc. Modelers define their models using the GAML language. The interest of providing a DSL (Domain Specific Language) to modelers is to ease the definition of models. Indeed, the GAML language is very simple to use, even by modelers that have low programming skills.

GAML is an agent-oriented language. Modelers define species of agents, i.e. archetype of agents, their characteristics, behaviors and aspects. It is a typed language, variables (static or dynamic) has to be typed. The behaviors of agents are defined through actions and reflexes. An action is a block of instructions executed when the action is called. A reflex is a block of instructions executed at each simulation step or when its optional attached condition is true. An aspect represents how an agent can be displayed. It is possible to define as many aspects as necessary. The richness of GAML comes from the numerous optimized operators concerning geometries, containers, statistics and graphs.

Figure 2 shows an example of a simple epidemiological SI model definition. In this model, a species of agents called *people* is defined. This species has the moving *skill* which provides some built-in variables (speed, direction, etc.) as well as some primitives(wander, goto, etc.). We redefine the variable *speed* in order to set its value to a random value between 5 and 10. The *people* species has another variable called *is_infected* that is a boolean initialized with true with a probability of 0.01. It has two reflexes: *move* and *infect*. The *move* reflex that is activated at each simulation cycle consists in a random movement: the agent uses the *wander* primitive of the moving skill to move to a random direction with a speed given by the value of the variable *speed*. The *infect* reflex is only activated when the agent is infected. It consists in trying to infect each people agent that is at distance lower or equals to 10m with a probability of 0.01. The *people* species has one aspect that will allow to display the *people* agents as a circle of radius 5m. The color will depend on the *is_infected* variable: if the agent is infected, its color will be red, green otherwise. At the initialization of the model, the world environment is initialized as a 500mx500m square and 1000 agents *people* are created (with a random location). The output of the *main_experiment* is a display called *map* where all the created agents can be visualized.

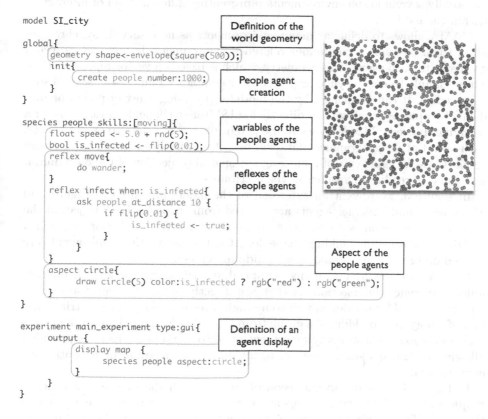

Fig. 2. Simple model definition in GAML and its display output

3.2 Geographic Information System Integration

Geographic information system integration (GIS) is the digital representation of landscapes captured by cameras, digitizers or scanners. This technology can be used for scientific investigation, resource management and development planning. With properties such as location, attributes and spatial relationship GIS vocabulary is really closed to the one used in agent-based modeling.

Many recent models rely on GIS data, allowing them to gain in realism. If most of modern simulation platforms allow to read/write GIS data, not so many allow to agentify vector geometries. Indeed, if Netlogo[28] or Cormas [18] provide some basic primitives to load and manipulate GIS data, they do not allow to create agents with a complex geometry from GIS data even with their GIS plugins. Another limitation of most of modern platforms is that they do not allow to define several environments with different topologies. Typically, for some complex models, its is necessary to define different environments such as a continuous one, to integrate vector data or several raster data with different resolutions and eventually several graph environments representing different level of interaction within the model.

GAMA allows to define as many environments as necessary. It synchronizes all of them by using a continuous reference environment. It provides as well a geometry to each agent. This geometry, which is based on vector representation, can be simple (point, polyline or polygon) or complex (composed of several sub-geometries). It can be defined by the modeler (by using a list of points or pre-defined graphical primitives) or directly loaded from a shapefile, a raster file or a mesh file. Indeed, GAMA allows to use geographic vector data to create agents, each object of the geographical data will be automatically used to instantiate an agent, GAMA taking care of managing the spatial projection of the data and, if necessary, of reading the values of the attributes.

In Figure 3, we present an extension of the model presented in Figure 2 in which *roads* and *buildings* agents are created from shapefile. Each object of the shapefile then becomes an agent: a *roads* agent for the road shapefile and a *buildings* agent for the building shapefile. At initialization, the *people* agents are located on one of the *building* agent randomly chosen.

GAMA provides as well many advanced spatial operators (spatial queries, union, difference, intersection....) that are directly usable through the GAML language. GAMA provides as well some high-level spatial operators : triangulation of a polygons, building of a graph from a set of points, polylines or polygons, skeletonization. At last, many movement operators and primitives are provided allowing to transparently move an agent on a grid, a graph or a continuous environment.

In Figure 4, we show an extension of the model of the Figure 3 in which a graph is created from the *roads* agents: each *roads* agent will become an edge of the graph. The *people* agents use this graph to move from building to building (a new target building is randomly chosen each time the people agent reaches the building).

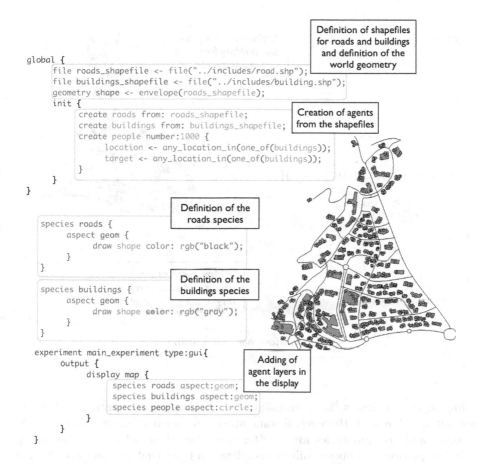

```
global {                                            Definition of shapefiles
    file roads_shapefile <- file("../includes/road.shp");   for roads and buildings
    file buildings_shapefile <- file("../includes/building.shp");   and definition of the
    geometry shape <- envelope(roads_shapefile);    world geometry
    init {
        create roads from: roads_shapefile;         Creation of agents
        create buildings from: buildings_shapefile;   from the shapefiles
        create people number:1000 {
            location <- any_location_in(one_of(buildings));
            target <- any_location_in(one_of(buildings));
        }
    }
}

species roads {                    Definition of the
    aspect geom {                   roads species
        draw shape color: rgb("black");
    }
}

species buildings {                Definition of the
    aspect geom {                   buildings species
        draw shape color: rgb("gray");
    }
}

experiment main_experiment type:gui{
    output {                        Adding of
        display map {               agent layers in
            species roads aspect:geom;   the display
            species buildings aspect:geom;
            species people aspect:circle;
        }
    }
}
```

Fig. 3. Agentification of *roads* and *buildings* from shapefiles

3.3 Visualization Tools

With the advancement in computer graphics and the availability of large scale data, ABM community has a big role to play in a better understanding of complex systems by using high-level representation [6]. For instance, in large-scale agent-based simulation systems where virtual agents are situated in a virtual city [2]. Techniques available for visualization of model execution enhance the capacity to interpret, understand and explore a model, in particular to extract abstract data or discover imperceptible dynamics. Visualization is, in many cases, the only way to understand and study model that can not be expressed thanks to equations.

In already existing popular platforms, languages and tools for visualization do exist [24] but most of them lack techniques for building, observing and interacting with models. Those platforms stay focused on the agent representation and do not propose any abstraction and multi-level representation or only by

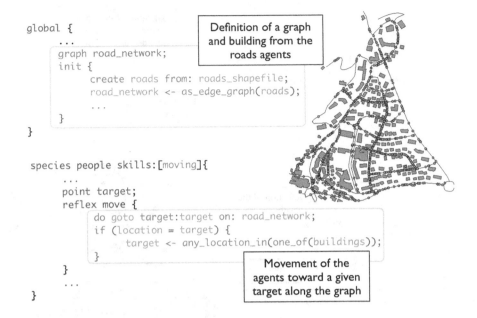

Fig. 4. Movement on a graph

using ad-hoc solutions, loose coupling or post-simulation treatment that are not yet standardized. However, if some standardization categorization of ABM emerges and give guidelines for a better agent-based model representation [7], only few platforms propose built-in visualization tools that run online and serve as feedback or indicator during the simulation (e.g using graph analysis or data clustering to build groups of agents [17]). Actually, the 3D integration in agent-based model can be only achieve in two ways. The first one consists in a loose coupling between an agent-based platform with a 3D visualization toolkit. The second one is to build an agent-based models in 3D animation and rendering packages[6] where the model is developed within a specific environment like game engine to import and handle 3D data and agent behavior is defined by using other programming languages.

In GAMA, 3D is fully integrated to agent based modeling paradigm with a dedicated language that handle high-level representation [14]. The 3D visualization library in GAMA 1.6 uses OpenGL via the Java Binding for the OpenGL (JOGL) API library. GAMA offers a generic framework to separate the visual representation of the model from the underlying model, allowing different visual representations at different levels of abstraction, and insures that the visualization of a simulation and the interaction on a simulation are independent processes that do not alter the reference model itself [13]. In this approach a view is seen as a model on which one can represent, abstract and interact without changing the definition of the observed model.

GAML language enables to define specific rich aspect by using operation such as repetition, modularity and recursion above the definition of graphical primitives. Agents are therefore associated with particular aspect and layers to determine its display location and representation. Agent can be displayed simultaneously in a variety of topologies (continuous, network, grid). GAMA allows the user to easily create a variety of geometric custom shapes, import and export scalable vector graphics-based geometry, images, GIS and 3D assets files. Geometrical operations can also be perform on the agent geometry to combined them by the the use of spatial operators (union, intersection, difference, scaling, rotation, etc.).

As mentioned in Section 3.2, GAMA allows a seamless integration of GIS data. Even with 2D GIS files, the handling of the third dimension is straightforward in GAMA where any depth can be assigned to a given shape. Thus, in Figure 5, we show a 3D rendering where a depth is added to the agent *buidlings* and where people agents are rendered as sphere instead of circle.

GAMA offers to modelers many tools to manipulate simulation displays. In particular, for each display, it provides a camera (Arcball and FreeFly) that can be used to reach any location of the model and therefore offers a more immersive experience. It also supports object selection, zooming, and panning. The new implementation of displays based on opengl has proven to be many times faster than the original Java2D approach when rendering large-scale simulations.

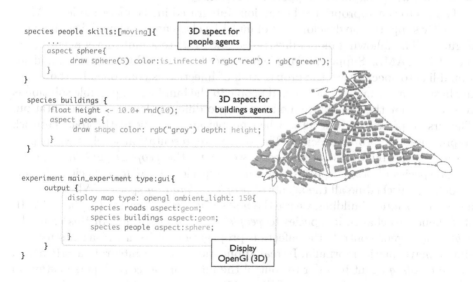

Fig. 5. Linking agents to places with geographic data. In GIS rendering, a depth is easily added to a shape file for a more realistic and accurate representation.

3.4   Multi-level Modeling

Multi-level agent-based modeling (ML-ABM) requires representing agents at different levels of representation in the same model with respect to time, space and behavior. Several reasons may justify the development of a multi-level agent-based. One reason may come from models that need to take into account entities at different spatial or organizational scales. For instance, models in biology may need to explicitly represent entities that belong to a hierarchy of containers, like molecules, cells and tissues. Another reason may be found in models in which the interactions between entities at one level make observables (usually called emergent structures [8]) appear, i.e. structures or patterns that are recognized as such by the modeler at another level of abstraction. In such a case, the modeler has the possibility to take into account and represent within agents, at the same time, the emergent structures and the agents that compose them. This problem of multi-level representation and articulation between agents at different levels is considered as one of the hardest issues to be tackled in the domain of complex systems modeling [29].

Recently, researchers of the community have begun to propose solutions to facilitate the development of multi-level agent-based models but existing approaches are still domain specific [25] [12] or only conceptual proposals without concrete implementation on established ABM platforms [21]. While current agent-based platforms (Repast [23], NetLogo [28]) still lack of appropriate abstractions, which explicitly support ML-ABM.

Thanks to the appropriate abstractions integrated in the meta-model, GAMA explicitly supports the development of multi-level agent-based model as shown in Figure 6. The following model illustrates how to write a multi-level agent-based model in GAML. Supposing that when people enter a building, the modeler would like to specify that the propagation of infection is controlled by the building basing on the number of infected people in the building. A possible solution is to specify that the people are modeled at two different levels of representation. The first representation level is when people are moving in the road network (represented by *people* species). The second representation level is when people are in the buildings. In this case, we define the *people_in_building* species (a sub-species of *people* species and a micro-species of *building* species). In this model, we unschedule all the agents of *people_in_building* species. When a *people* agent moves into a building, we use the *morphogenesis* operation (*capture* GAML statement), to change its species to *people_in_building* species. In this example, a *building* agent controls the infection propagation of its micro-agents using a simple mathematical formula. In real application, we can integrate a SIR model to the *building* agent in order to control the infection process. A person stays in a building for a certain amount of time. After that the *building* agent decides to release this person and the person continues to move in the road network. The modeler again uses the *morphogenesis* operation (*release* GAML statement), to change the representation level of people from *people_in_building* to *people*.

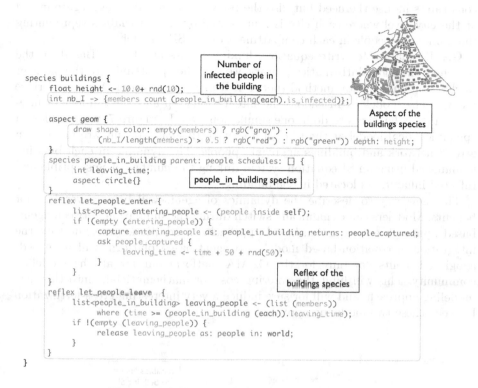

```
species buildings {
    float height <- 10.0+ rnd(10);
    int nb_I -> {members count (people_in_building(each).is_infected)};

    aspect geom {
        draw shape color: empty(members) ? rgb("gray") :
            (nb_I/length(members) > 0.5 ? rgb("red") : rgb("green")) depth: height;
    }
}
species people_in_building parent: people schedules: [] {
    int leaving_time;
    aspect circle{}
}
reflex let_people_enter {
    list<people> entering_people <- (people inside self);
    if !(empty (entering_people)) {
        capture entering_people as: people_in_building returns: people_captured;
        ask people_captured {
            leaving_time <- time + 50 + rnd(50);
        }
    }
}
reflex let_people_leave {
    list<people_in_building> leaving_people <- (list (members))
        where (time >= (people_in_building (each)).leaving_time);
    if !(empty (leaving_people)) {
        release leaving_people as: people in: world;
    }
}
}
```

Labels in figure: "Number of infected people in the building", "Aspect of the buildings species", "people_in_building species", "Reflex of the buildings species"

Fig. 6. Multi-level agent-based model in GAML

3.5 Equation-Based Modeling

Equation-based modeling (and in particular modeling using Ordinary Differential Equation, ODE) has been for a while the main modeling approach to represent dynamic systems. The most famous examples are the Lotka and Volterra [19] modeling of prey-predator dynamics or the Kermack and McKendrick [16] SIR model to represent epidemic dynamics.

Following the idea that we do not always need to represent every phenomenon at the individual level of details(as in the multi-level approach presented above) and the idea taken from meta-population trend in ecology [15], we have introduced in GAMA the possibility to describe the dynamics of agents variables using an ODE system and to integrate this system at each simulation step. A paradigmatic example of applications that would benefit from this new feature can take inspiration from Colizza et al. [5] or Meloni et al. [1] work. Let consider the network of main cities in the world connected by air flights. If a disease appears in a city it will quickly spread all around the world via these flights communication. In addition, in each city, the disease will also spread in the city population. In this case, we should consider thousands of millions of people. The observation level cannot be the individual one but rather the city one. These two constraints induce the need but also the relevance of using an aggregate model at the city level where each city is represented by three variables representing the number of people in each compartment of the SIR model.

GAML enables to write equations linking agents attributes. Based on the Apache Commons Mathematics Library, we give the opportunity to the modeler to choose its integration method (between Runge Kutta 4 and Dormand-Prince 8(5,3)). The modeler can choose the integration step and the number of integration steps he wants to do in one simulation step. In Figure 7, we consider an epidemiological model at the level of a city. In this case, people are moving on a road network and buildings aggregate people. The dynamic in each building is managed using an SI equation system linking the number of Susceptible and Infected inhabitants located in the building.

This new way to describe the dynamics of agents will bring several major benefits. Modelers can dynamically switch during the simulation between agent-based approach and equation-based approach. In addition, we argue that the integration of equation-based model into agent-based platform will have pedagogical benefits not only for the GAMA platform but for all the modeling community. This will limit the entering cost for mathematicians into this new modeling approach, and will for sure induce a very interesting cross-fertilization between these two modeling approaches.

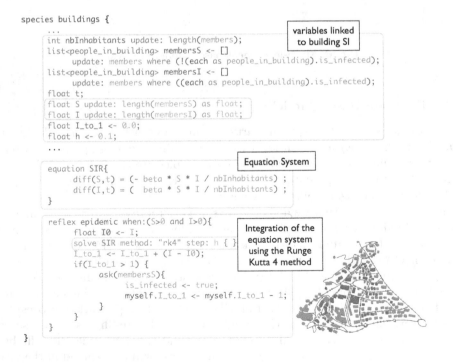

Fig. 7. Example of ODE-driven species

4   Conclusion

Since the beginning of its development in 2007, GAMA has been deeply enriched. In particular, the new 1.6 version provides many powerful features to manage GIS data, advanced visualization and multi-level models. Many others features that were not presented in this paper are also available: database management (SQL), connexion to R, a 3D-physics engine plug-in. This increase of functionalities has allowed to gain an ever growing number of new users. Nowadays, GAMA is used for many ambitious research projects dealing with a wide variety of domains.

The first one is MAELIA project, which consists in the development of a decision-support tool for natural resource management [27] [11]. This project aims at studying the social, economic and ecological impact of water management in the Adour-Garonne Basin (France) by the integration a huge amount of geographical data and models (from ecological models to human decision-making models). The second one is the MIRO project [4] which addresses the issue of sustainable cities. Therefore, improving urban accessibility merely results in increasing the traffic and its negative externalities, while reducing the accessibility of people to the city. Given real data the simulator is used to realize scenarios determined by geographers for quantifying service accessibility and identifying cities management strategies. This model makes use of high resolution GIS data and large number of individuals. Another project concerns the simulation of evacuation organization in case of a tsunami in Nha Trang (Vietnam). This model combines detailed GIS data of the city and the coupling of agent and equation-based modeling in order to upscale the number of inhabitants that can be simulated [22].

In term of performance, experimental results show that the platform can easily handle several thousands of agents in real time rendering and reasonably deal with million of agents for non real time simulation.

GAMA is an ever-evolving platform and many enhancements are already planned for the future versions: a complete refactoring of the batch parameter space exploration, a plug-in to allow users to develop models through a graphical interface to modify the model in a more intuitive way than with the code, the possibility to call R scripts, the distribution of operators on a GPU, the possibility to share simulation where a model could be played at runtime on or in a replay mode at different spatio-temporal scale on different devices using webGL to display simulation on a web browser. We did not mention it in this paper but we are also developing a 3D physics engine plug-in to obtain more realistic behavior in physical systems and primitives to access and interact with database management systems, in particular to store and retrieve spatial data.

References

1. Apolloni, A., Poletto, C., Colizza, V., et al.: Age-specific contacts and travel patterns in the spatial spread of 2009 h1n1 influenza pandemic. BMC Infectious Diseases 13(1), 1–18 (2013)
2. Araujo, F., Valente, J., Al-Zinati, M., Kuiper, D., Zalila-Wenkstern, R.: Divas 4.0: A framework for the development of situated multi-agent based simulation systems. In: Proceedings of the 2013 International Conference on Autonomous Agents and Multi-agent Systems, AAMAS 2013, pp. 1351–1352. International Foundation for Autonomous Agents and Multiagent Systems (2013)
3. Axelrod, R.M.: The complexity of cooperation: Agent-based models of competition and collaboration. Princeton University Press (1997)
4. Banos, A., Marilleau, N.: Improving individual accessibility to the city: An agent-based modelling approach. In: ECCS (2012)
5. Colizza, V., Vespignani, A.: Epidemic modeling in metapopulation systems with heterogeneous coupling pattern: Theory and simulations. Journal of Theoretical Biology 251(3), 450–467 (2008)
6. Crooks, A.T., Castle, C.J.E.: Agent-Based Models of Geographical Systems. Springer Netherlands, Dordrecht (2012)
7. Daniel Kornhauser, U.W., Rand, W.: Design Guidelines for Agent Based Model Visualization. Journal of Artificial Societies and Social Simulation 12(2) (2009)
8. De Wolf, T., Holvoet, T.: Emergence versus self-organisation: Different concepts but promising when combined. In: Brueckner, S.A., Di Marzo Serugendo, G., Karageorgos, A., Nagpal, R. (eds.) ESOA 2005. LNCS (LNAI), vol. 3464, pp. 1–15. Springer, Heidelberg (2005)
9. Drogoul, A., Amouroux, E., Caillou, P., Gaudou, B., Grignard, A., Marilleau, N., Taillandier, P., Vavasseur, M., Vo, D.A., Zucker, J.D.: Gama: multi-level and complex environment for agent-based models and simulations. In: AAMAS 2013, pp. 1361–1362. International Foundation for Autonomous Agents and Multiagent Systems (2013)
10. Edmonds, B., Moss, S.: From KISS to KIDS – an 'Anti-simplistic' modelling approach. In: Davidsson, P., Logan, B., Takadama, K. (eds.) MABS 2004. LNCS (LNAI), vol. 3415, pp. 130–144. Springer, Heidelberg (2005)
11. Gaudou, B., Sibertin-Blanc, C., Thérond, O., Amblard, F., Arcangeli, J.P., Balestrat, M., Charron-Moirez, M.H., Gondet, E., Hong, Y., Louail, T., Mayor, E., Panzoli, D., Sauvage, S., Sanchez-Perez, J., Taillandier, P., Nguyen, V.B., Vavasseur, M., Mazzega, P.: The MAELIA multi-agent platform for integrated assessment of low-water management issues (regular paper). In: International Workshop on Multi-Agent-Based Simulation (MABS), Saint-Paul, MN, USA. Springer (2013)
12. Gil-Quijano, J., Louail, T., Hutzler, G.: From biological to urban cells: lessons from three multilevel agent-based models. In: Desai, N., Liu, A., Winikoff, M. (eds.) PRIMA 2010. LNCS, vol. 7057, pp. 620–635. Springer, Heidelberg (2012)
13. Grignard, A., Drogoul, A., Zucker, J.D.: A model-view/controller approach to support visualization and online data analysis of agent-based simulation. In: Proceedings of 2013 IEEE RIVF (2013)
14. Grignard, A., Drogoul, A., Zucker, J.-D.: Online analysis and visualization of agent based models. In: Murgante, B., Misra, S., Carlini, M., Torre, C.M., Nguyen, H.-Q., Taniar, D., Apduhan, B.O., Gervasi, O. (eds.) ICCSA 2013, Part I. LNCS, vol. 7971, pp. 662–672. Springer, Heidelberg (2013)

15. Hanski, I.: Metapopulation Ecology. Oxford University Press (1999)
16. Kermack, W.O., McKendrick, A.G.: A contribution to the mathematical theory of epidemics. Proceedings of the Royal Society of London 115(772), 700–721 (1927)
17. Lamarche-Perrin, R., Demazeau, Y., Vincent, J.-M.: How to Build the Best Macroscopic Description of your Multi-agent System? In: Demazeau, Y., Ishida, T., Corchado, J.M., Bajo, J. (eds.) PAAMS 2013. LNCS, vol. 7879, pp. 157–169. Springer, Heidelberg (2013)
18. Le Page, C., Bousquet, F., Bakam, I., Bah, A., Baron, C.: Cormas: A multiagent simulation toolkit to model natural and social dynamics at multiple scales. In: Proceedings of Workshop "The Ecology of Scales", Wageningen, The Netherlands (2000)
19. Lotka, A.J.: Contribution to the theory of periodic reactions. The Journal of Physical Chemistry 14(3), 271–274 (1909)
20. Luke, S., Cioffi-Revilla, C., Panait, L., Sullivan, K., Balan, G.: Mason: A multiagent simulation environment. Simulation 81(7), 517–527 (2005)
21. Morvan, G.: Multi-level agent-based modeling-bibliography. arXiv preprint arXiv:1205.0561 (2013)
22. Nguyen, T.N.A., Zucker, J.D., Nguyen, H.D., Drogoul, A., Vo, D.A.: A hybrid macro-micro pedestrians evacuation model to speed up simulation in road networks. In: Dechesne, F., Hattori, H., ter Mors, A., Such, J.M., Weyns, D., Dignum, F. (eds.) AAMAS 2011 Workshops. LNCS, vol. 7068, pp. 371–383. Springer, Heidelberg (2012)
23. North, M.J., Collier, N.T., Ozik, J., Tatara, E.R., Macal, C.M., Bragen, M., Sydelko, P.: Complex adaptive systems modeling with repast simphony. Complex Adaptive Systems Modeling 1(1), 1–26 (2013)
24. Railsback, S.F., Lytinen, S.L., Jackson, S.K.: Agent-based Simulation Platforms: Review and Development Recommendations. Simulation, 609–623 (2006)
25. Servat, D., Perrier, E., Treuil, J.-P., Drogoul, A.: When agents emerge from agents: Introducing multi-scale viewpoints in multi-agent simulations. In: Sichman, J.S., Conte, R., Gilbert, N. (eds.) MABS 1998. LNCS (LNAI), vol. 1534, pp. 183–198. Springer, Heidelberg (1998)
26. Taillandier, P., Vo, D.-A., Amouroux, E., Drogoul, A.: GAMA: A simulation platform that integrates geographical information data, agent-based modeling and multi-scale control. In: Desai, N., Liu, A., Winikoff, M. (eds.) PRIMA 2010. LNCS, vol. 7057, pp. 242–258. Springer, Heidelberg (2012)
27. Taillandier, P., Thérond, O., Gaudou, B.: A new BDI agent architecture based on the belief theory. Application to the modelling of cropping plan decision-making (regular paper). In: International Environmental Modelling and Software Society (iEMSs), Leipzig, Germany, July 1-5 (2012)
28. Tisue, S., Wilensky, U.: Netlogo: A simple environment for modeling complexity. In: International Conference on Complex Systems, pp. 16–21 (2004)
29. Treuil, J.P., Drogoul, A., Zucker, J.D.: Modélisation et simulation à base d'agents: exemples commentés, outils informatiques et questions théoriques. Dunod (2008)

Defendable Security in Interaction Protocols

Wojciech Jamroga[1], Matthijs Melissen[1], and Henning Schnoor[2]

[1] Computer Science and Communication and Interdisciplinary Centre for Security, Reliability, and Trust, University of Luxembourg
{wojtek.jamroga, matthijs.melissen}@uni.lu
[2] Arbeitsgruppe Theoretische Informatik, University of Kiel
henning.schnoor@email.uni-kiel.de

Abstract. We study the security of interaction protocols when incentives of participants are taken into account. We begin by formally defining correctness of a protocol, given a notion of rationality and utilities of participating agents. Based on that, we propose how to assess security when the precise incentives are unknown. Then, the security level can be defined in terms of *defender sets*, i.e., sets of participants who can effectively "defend" the security property as long as they are in favor of the property. In terms of technical results, we present a theoretical characterization of defendable protocols under Nash equilibrium, and study the computational complexity of related decision problems.

1 Introduction

Interaction protocols are ubiquitous in multi-agent systems: As soon as two machines communicate, a protocol is required. Protocols can be modeled as games, since every participant in the protocol has several strategies that she can employ. From a game-theoretic perspective, protocols are an interesting class of games since they have a *goal*, i.e., a set of outcomes that are preferred by the designer of the protocol. A subclass of protocols are *security protocols* which use cryptography to enforce their goals against any possible behavior of participants. Such a protocol is deemed correct with respect to its goal if the goal is achieved in all runs where a predefined subset of players follows the protocol.

We point out that this definition of correctness can be too strong, since violation of the goal may be achievable only by irrational responses from the other players. On the other hand, the definition may also prove too weak when the goal can be only achieved by an irrational strategy of agents supporting the goal, in other words: one that they should never choose to play. To describe and predict rational behavior of agents, game theory has proposed a number of *solution concepts* [18]. Each solution concept captures some notion of rationality which may be more or less applicable in different contexts. We do not fix a particular solution concept, but consider it to be a parameter of the problem.

Our main contributions are the following. First, in Section 3.1, we define a parametrized notion of *rational correctness* for security protocols, where the parameter is a suitable solution concept. Secondly, based on this notion, we define

G. Boella et al. (Eds.): PRIMA 2013, LNAI 8291, pp. 132–148, 2013.

a concept of *defendability of security* in a protocol, where the security property is guaranteed under relatively weak assumptions (Section 3.3). Thirdly, we give complexity results for verification of rational protocol correctness and defendability (see Section 4). Fourthly, in Section 5, we propose a *characterization* of defendable security properties when rationality of participants is based on Nash equilibrium. Finally, we extend the results to mixed strategies in Section 6.

1.1 Related Work

There are several meeting points of security protocols and game theory. Some researchers have considered protocol execution as a game with the very pessimistic assumption that the only goal of the other participants ("adversaries") is to break the intended security property of the protocol. In this pessimistic analysis, a protocol is correct if the "honest" participants have a strategy such that, for all strategies of the other agents, the goal of the protocol is satisfied (cf. e.g. [14]). Recently, protocols have been analyzed with respect to some game theoretic notions of rationality [10,2] where preferences of participants are taken into account. An overview of connections between cryptography and game theory is given in [8]. Another survey [1,16] presents arguments suggesting that study of incentives in security applications is crucial.

Game theoretic concepts have been applied to analysis of specific security properties in a number of papers. Kremer and Raskin [15] used graph games to verify non-repudiation protocols. However, their method used neither a model of incentives nor of rationality. Buttyán, Hubaux and Čapkun [5] model games in a way similar to ours, and also use incentives to model the behavior of agents. However, they restrict their analysis to strongly Pareto-optimal Nash equilibria which is not necessarily a good solution concept for security protocols. First, it is unclear why agents would *individually* converge to a strongly Pareto-optimal play. Moreover, in many protocols it is unclear why agents would play a Nash equilibrium in the first place. Our method is more general, as we use the solution concept as a parameter to our analysis.

Asharov et al. (2011) [2] use game theory to study gradual-release fair exchange protocols, i.e., protocols in which at any round, the probability of any party to predict the item of the other player increases only by a negligible amount. They model this in a game-theoretical setting, where in every round, the player can either continue or abort. In every round, the item of the other player is predicted. The situation where the player predicts correctly and the other one does not has the highest utility, and the situation where the player predicts incorrectly and the other one predicts correctly the lowest. Then a protocol is said to be game-theoretically fair if the strategy that never aborts the protocol is a computational Nash-equilibrium (i.e., a configuration where no player can gain non-negligible advantage by polynomial-time computable unilateral deviations). They show that no protocol is both fair and effective, but fairness without effectiveness is achievable. They also show that their analysis allows for solutions that are not admitted by the traditional cryptographic definition.

Groce and Katz [12] show that if agents have a strict incentive to achieve fair exchange, then gradual-release fair exchange without trusted third party (TTP) is possible under the assumption that the other agents play rational. Chadha et. al [6] show that in any fair, optimistic, timely contract-signing protocol, there is a point where one player has a strategy to determine whether or not to complete the protocol and obtain a contract. Although they reason about strategies, they do not model incentives explicitly, and do not take different solution concepts into account. Syverson [19] presents a *rational exchange* protocol for which he shows that "enlightened, self-interested parties" have no reason to cheat.

Chatterjee & Raman [7] use assume-guarantee synthesis for synthesis of contract signing protocols. Finally, in [9], a logic for modeling coordination abilities between agents is presented, but incentives are not taken into account. [11] also studies coordination and applies iterated elimination of dominated strategies.

In summary, rationality-based correctness of protocols has been studied in a number of papers, but usually with a particular notion of rationality in mind. In contrast, we define a concept of correctness where a game-theoretic solution concept is a parameter of the problem. Even more importantly, our concept of *defendability* of a security property is completely novel. The same applies to our characterizations of defendable properties under Nash equilibrium.

2   Protocols and Games

We begin by recalling standard concepts used for modeling protocols on the one hand, and games on the other. We also point out where the two meet.

2.1   Security Protocols

A protocol is a specification of how agents should interact. Protocols can contain *choice points* where several actions are available to the agents. An agent is *honest* if he follows the protocol specification, and *dishonest* otherwise. In the latter case, the agent is only restricted by the physical and logical actions that are available in the environment. For instance, in a cryptographic protocol, dishonest agents can do anything that satisfies properties of the cryptographic primitives, assuming perfect cryptography (as in [15]). The protocol specification, together with a model of the environment of action, a subset of agents who are assumed to be honest, and the operational semantics of action execution, defines a multi-agent transition system that we call the *model* of the protocol. In the rest of the paper, we focus on protocol models, and abstract away from how they arise. We also do not treat the usual "network adversary" that can intercept, delay and forge messages, but essentially assume the existence of secure channels. The issue of the "network adversary" is of course highly relevant for the protocols we consider, but orthogonal to the aspects we discuss in this paper. A complete analysis of a protocol needs to take both aspects into account.

As a running example, we consider two-party contract signing protocols. Two agents, Alice and Bob, intend to sign a contract. The two main objectives in such

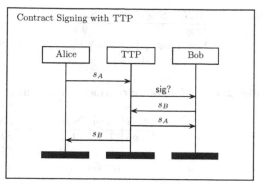

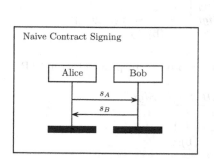

Fig. 1. Two contract-signing protocols

protocols are *fairness* and *effectivity*. Fairness requires that if one agent gets the signature of the other agent, the other agent will eventually get the signature of the first agent as well. A protocol run is *effective* if, at the end of the run, both agents have the signature of the other agent.

Example 1. Figure 1 displays two simple contract signing protocols. In the protocol on the left, Alice sends her signature to Bob, who responds with his signature. Alice and Bob can stop the protocol at any moment (thereby deviating from the protocol). Clearly, the run where Bob and Alice both send their signatures is fair. However, not all protocol runs are fair. In particular, if Bob is dishonest, he can stop the protocol right after receiving the signature of Alice.

The protocol on the right [4] uses a *trusted third party* (TTP) T, assumed to be honest. First, Alice sends her signature s_A to the TTP, then the TTP requests Bob's signature with the message **sig?**. Subsequently, Bob sends his signature s_B to the TTP. Finally, the TTP forwards the signatures to Bob and Alice. Again, each participant can stop executing the protocol at any point. Fairness is guaranteed as long as the TTP is honest.

2.2 Game Theoretic Models of Interaction

We use *normal-form games* as abstract models of interaction in a protocol.

Definition 1 (Frames and games). *A game frame is a tuple $\Gamma = (N, \Sigma, \Omega, o)$, where $N = \{A_1, \ldots, A_{|N|}\}$ is a finite set of agents, $\Sigma = \Sigma_{A_1} \times \cdots \times \Sigma_{A_{|N|}}$ is a set of strategy profiles, Ω is the set of outcomes, and $o : \Sigma \to \Omega$ is a function mapping each strategy profile to an outcome.*

A normal-form (NF) game is a game frame plus a utility profile $u = \{u_1, \ldots, u_{|N|}\}$ where $u_i : \Sigma \to \mathbb{R}$ is a utility function assigning utility values to strategy profiles.

Game theory uses *solution concepts* to define which strategy profiles capture rational interactions. Let $\mathcal{G}$ be a class of games with the same strategy profiles Σ.

$A\backslash B$	$Stop$	$Sign$
$Stop$	$\emptyset$	$\emptyset$
$Sign$	$\{\mathsf{sign}_B\}$	$\{\mathsf{sign}_A, \mathsf{sign}_B\}$

(a) Γ_1

$A\backslash B$	$Stop$	$Sign$
$Stop$	$\emptyset$	$\emptyset$
$Sign$	$\emptyset$	$\{\mathsf{sign}_A, \mathsf{sign}_B\}$

(b) Γ_2

Fig. 2. Game frames for contract signing: (a) naive protocol, (b) protocol with TTP

$A\backslash B$	$Stop$	$Sign$
$Stop$	1, 1	1, 1
$Sign$	0, 3	2, 2

(a) G_1

$A\backslash B$	$Stop$	$Sign$
$Stop$	1, 1	1, 1
$Sign$	1, 1	2, 2

(b) G_2

Fig. 3. NF games for contract signing: : (a) naive protocol, (b) protocol with TTP

Formally, a solution concept for $\mathcal{G}$ is a function $SC : \mathcal{G} \to \mathcal{P}(\Sigma)$ that, given a game, returns a set of *rational* strategy profiles. Well-known solution concepts include e.g. Nash equilibrium (NE), dominant and undominated strategies, Stackelberg equilibrium, Pareto optimality etc. For a detailed discussion, see [18].

2.3 Protocols as Games

Let P be a model of a protocol. We will investigate properties of P through the game frame $\Gamma(P)$ in which strategies are *conditional plans* in P, i.e., functions that specify for each choice point which action to take. A set of strategies, one for each agent, uniquely determines a *run* of the protocol, i.e., a sequence of actions that the agents will take. $\Gamma(P)$ takes runs to be the outcomes in the game, and hence maps strategy profiles to runs.

Example 2. Consider the protocols in Figure 1. Alice and Bob have the following strategies: *Stop* (stopping before sending the signature) and *Sign* (running the protocol honestly). The protocol can be modeled as game frame $\Gamma = (N, \Sigma, \Omega, o)$ with $N = \{A, B, T\}$, $\Sigma_T = \{-\}$ (the trusted third party T is deterministic), $\Sigma_A = \Sigma_B = \{Stop, Sign\}$, $\Omega = \mathcal{P}(\{\mathsf{sign}_A, \mathsf{sign}_B\})$, here sign_A (sign_B) denotes the event that Alice (Bob) gets a signed copy of the contract. For the protocol with TTP protocol we also have $o(\sigma) = \{\mathsf{sign}_A, \mathsf{sign}_B\}$ if $\sigma = (Sign, Sign, -)$, and $o(\sigma) = \emptyset$ otherwise. The game frame is displayed in Figure 2(b).

The "naive" protocol can be modeled in a similar way (Figure 2(a)). The available strategies are the same, but in this case $o(Sign, Stop, -) = \{\mathsf{sign}_B\}$.

We model agents' preferences with respect to outcomes by utility profiles.

Example 3. Assume the following utility function for A: $u_A(\{\mathsf{sign}_A\}) = 3$, $u_A(\{\mathsf{sign}_A, \mathsf{sign}_B\}) = 2$, $u_A(\emptyset) = 1$, $u_A(\{\mathsf{sign}_B\}) = 0$, and symmetrically for B. Thus, both agents prefer the exchange of signatures over no exchange; moreover, the most preferred option for an agent is to get the signature while the other agent does not, and the least preferred option is not to get the signatures while the other agent does. Combining this utility profile with the game frames from Figure 2 yields the normal-form games depicted in Figure 3.

Security protocols are designed to achieve one or more *security requirements* and/or *functionality requirements*. We only consider requirements that can be expressed in terms of individual runs having a certain property. We model this by a subset of outcomes, called the *objective of the protocol*.

Definition 2. *Given a game frame $\Gamma = (N, \Sigma, \Omega, o)$, an objective is a non-empty set $\gamma \subseteq \Omega$. We call γ nontrivial in Γ iff γ is neither impossible nor guaranteed in Γ, i.e., $\emptyset \neq \gamma \neq \Omega$.*

Example 4. Consider the following simple definition of fairness. A run is fair iff either both agents obtain the signature of the other agent, or none of them does. Moreover, the run is effective iff both agents obtain the other agent's signature. We can represent that by $\gamma_{\text{fair}} = \{\emptyset, \{\text{sign}_A, \text{sign}_B\}\}$ for the fairness objective, and $\gamma_{\text{eff}} = \{\{\text{sign}_A, \text{sign}_B\}\}$ for effectiveness.

3   Incentive-Based Security Analysis

In this section, we give a definition of correctness of security protocols that takes into account rational decisions of agents, based on their incentives. In NF games, it is often assumed that the mapping o is a bijection, i.e., every strategy profile determines a unique outcome. We therefore often identify Σ with Ω, and omit Ω and o from the representation of games to simplify notation.

3.1   Incentive-Based Correctness

As we have pointed out, the requirement that all strategy profiles satisfy the objective might be too strong. Instead, we will require that all *rational* runs satisfy the objective. In case there are no rational runs, all outcomes are equally rational; then, we adopt the usual pessimistic view and require that all outcomes must satisfy γ.

Definition 3. *A protocol model represented as game frame $\Gamma = (N, \Sigma)$ with utility profile u is correct with respect to objective γ under solution concept SC, written $(\Gamma, u) \models_{SC} \gamma$, iff:*

$$\begin{cases} SC(\Gamma, u) \subseteq \gamma & \text{if } SC(\Gamma, u) \neq \emptyset \\ \gamma = \Sigma & \text{otherwise.} \end{cases}$$

PROTOCOL VERIFICATION *is the following decision problem:*

- **Input:** *A protocol model P, a utility function u, an objective γ and a solution concept SC.*
- **Question:** *Does $(\Gamma(P), u) \models_{SC} \gamma$ hold?*

Example 5. Consider game G_1 from Figure 3(a) for the naive contract signing protocol. We saw that if Alice signs, Bob might stop the protocol, resulting in the worst possible utility for Alice. Therefore, Alice might consider it safer to never sign. This kind of reasoning can be captured by using Nash equilibrium as the solution concept, since $\text{NE}(G_1) = \{(Stop, Stop)\}$. For $\gamma_{\text{eff}} = \{(Sign, Sign)\}$, we have $\text{NE}(G_1) \not\subseteq \gamma_{\text{eff}}$, and thus G_1 is not effective under Nash equilibrium. On the other hand, for $\gamma_{\text{fair}} = \{(Stop, Stop), (Sign, Sign)\}$, we have $\text{NE}(G_1) \subseteq \gamma_{\text{fair}}$, so G_1 guarantees fairness under Nash equilibrium.

Moreover, if we think that the players are willing to take risks in order to obtain a better outcome, then using e.g. Halpern and Rong's maximal perfect collaborative equilibrium [13] as the solution concept is more appropriate. Since $MPCE(G_1) = \{(Sign, Sign)\} \subseteq \gamma_{\text{eff}} \subseteq \gamma_{\text{fair}}$, we have that the protocol is both fair and effective under $MPCE$.

The above example highlights that, for different situations, different solution concepts are appropriate.

3.2 Unknown Incentives

In the previous section, we studied correctness of a protocol when a utility profile is given. However, the exact utility profiles are often unknown. One way out is to require the protocol to be correct for *all possible* utility profiles.

Definition 4. *A protocol model represented by game frame Γ is valid with respect to objective γ under solution concept SC (written $\Gamma \models_{SC} \gamma$) iff $(\Gamma, u) \models_{SC} \gamma$ for all utility profiles u.*

PROTOCOL VALIDITY *is the following decision problem:*

- **Input:** *A protocol model P, an objective γ and a solution concept SC.*
- **Question:** *Does $\Gamma(P) \models_{SC} \gamma$ hold?*

It turns out that, under some reasonable assumptions, protocols are only valid for trivial objectives.

Definition 5. *Let $G = (N, \Sigma, (u_1, \ldots, u_n))$. Let $\pi = (\pi_1, \ldots, \pi_n)$, where for all $i \in N$, $\pi_i : \Sigma_i \to \Sigma_i$ is a permutation on Σ_i. We slightly abuse the notation by writing $\pi((s_1, \ldots, s_n))$ for $(\pi_1(s_1), \ldots, \pi_n(s_n))$. A solution concept is closed under permutation iff $s \in SC((N, \Sigma, (u'_1, \ldots, u'_n)))$ if and only if $\pi(s) \in SC((N, \Sigma, (u'_1 \circ \pi_1^{-1}, \ldots, u'_n \circ \pi_n^{-1})))$.*

Being closed under permutation is a very natural property. Essentially, it means that "renaming" of strategies does not have an effect on the output of the game. All solution concepts that we know of are closed under permutation.

Theorem 1. *If SC is closed under permutation, then $\Gamma \models_{SC} \gamma$ iff $\gamma = \Sigma$.*

Proof. Let Γ be a game frame, SC be a solution concept closed under permutation of utilities, and γ be an objective. Fix u such that $u_i(s) = 0$ for all $i \in N$

and $s \in \Sigma$. First, if $SC(\Gamma, u) = \emptyset$ then γ must be equal to Σ by Definition 3. On the other hand, suppose that $s \in SC(\Gamma, u)$, and consider any other $s' \in \Sigma$. It is easy to see that there is a permutation π such that $\pi(s) = s'$. Also, $(\Gamma, u \circ \pi)$ is the same game as (Γ, u) for this very special utility function u. By the closure property, $s' \in SC(\Gamma, u \circ \pi) = SC(\Gamma, u)$, which concludes the proof.

Thus, correctness for all distributions of incentives is equivalent to correctness in all possible runs. This characterization is natural: If we do not make any assumptions about the incentives of the participating agents, then no run can be regarded as "irrational," hence all runs need to be taken into account. Clearly, incentive-based analysis needs some assumptions about the incentives of the agents participating in a protocol.[1]

In the next section we look at the case where a subset of agents D, called the *defenders* of the protocol, have a genuine interest in achieving the objective of the protocol.

3.3   Defendability of Protocols

Typical analysis of a protocol implicitly assumes some participants to be aligned with its purpose. E.g., one usually assumes that communicating parties are interested in exchanging a secret without the eavesdropper getting hold of it, that a bank wants to prevent web banking fraud etc. In this section, we formalize this idea by assuming a subset of agents, called the *defenders* of the protocol, to be in favor of its objective. Our new definition of correctness says that a protocol is correct with respect to some objective γ if and only if it is correct with respect to every utility profile in which the preferences of all defenders comply with γ.

Definition 6. *A group of agents $D \in N$ supports the objective γ in game (N, Σ, u) iff for all $i \in D$, if $s \in \gamma$ and $s' \in \Sigma \setminus \gamma$ then $u_i(s) > u_i(s')$.*

A protocol model represented as game frame Γ is defended by agents D, written $\Gamma \models_{SC} [D]\gamma$, iff $(\Gamma, u) \models_{SC} \gamma$ for all utility profiles u such that D supports γ in game (Γ, u).

PROTOCOL DEFENDABILITY *is the following decision problem:*

- **Input:** *Protocol model P, objective γ, set of agents D, solution concept SC.*
- **Question:** *Does $\Gamma(P) \models_{SC} [D]\gamma$ hold?*

For example, it makes sense to assume that if Alice signs the contract then she prefers to get it also signed by Bob. In other words, Alice supports fairness for

---

[1]   An interesting special case of Theorem 1 appears in a study of rational secret sharing: Asharov and Lindell [3] proved that the *length* (number of rounds) of a protocol for rational secret sharing must depend on the utilities of the involved agents for the possible protocol outcomes. In particular, there can be no single protocol which works for every possible set of incentives of the agents. Their result even holds under some plausibility assumptions on the agents' incentives (i.e., agents prefer to learn the secret over not learning it, etc.).

herself. Note that the issue of support is different from that of honest execution of a protocol. The former is about preferences of a party; the latter about the actions that the party is bound to select. In particular, there might be protocols in which the objective can be only obtained by deviating from the protocol.[2] We do not go deeper into that, and focus only on defendability. We first note that $\Gamma(P) \models_{SC} [D]\gamma$ is *not* equivalent to D having a strategy to achieve γ: It is possible that such a strategy exists, but is not rational in the sense of the solution concept SC. We begin by investigating the borderline cases, where either none or all of the agents are defenders. Clearly, if there are no defenders, then defendability is equivalent to ordinary protocol validity.

Proposition 1. *If Γ is a game frame and SC is a solution concept, we have that $\Gamma \models_{SC} [\emptyset]\gamma$ iff $\Gamma \models_{SC} \gamma$.*

If all agents are defenders, any protocol is correct, as long as the solution concept does not select *strongly Pareto-dominated* strategy profiles.

Definition 7. *A solution concept is* weakly Pareto *iff it never selects a strongly Pareto dominated outcome (i.e., such that there exists another outcome strictly preferred by all the players). It is* efficient *iff it never returns the empty set.*

Theorem 2. *If Γ is a game frame and SC is an efficient weakly Pareto solution concept then $\Gamma \models_{SC} [N]\gamma$.*

Proof. Let Γ be a game frame, and let u be a utility function such that D supports γ in game (Γ, u). We have $SC(\Gamma, u) \neq \emptyset$ by assumption. Now we prove that $SC(\Gamma, u) \subseteq \gamma$. Assume $s \in SC(\Gamma, u)$ and $s \notin \gamma$. Let $s' \in \gamma$. Then $u_i(s') > u_i(s)$ for all $i \in N$. However, this implies that $s \notin SC(\Gamma, u)$, which is a contradiction.

Theorem 2 says that if our notion of rationality is efficient and weakly Pareto then designing a protocol for friendly agents is very easy. That is, rather unsurprisingly, if all players are defenders of the a goal γ then as long as there is *some* way of achieving the goal, the players will identify a working strategy. Many solution concepts are both efficient and weakly Pareto, for example: Stackelberg equilibrium, maximum-perfect cooperative equilibrium, backward induction and subgame-perfect Nash equilibrium in perfect information games. However, using such a solution concept is based on optimistic assumptions about both the players' goodwill and their ability to coordinate their strategies. In practice, other solution concepts are used, which in general do not satisfy the preconditions of Theorem 2. For example, Nash equilibrium is neither weakly Pareto nor efficient,[3] and equilibrium in dominant strategies is weakly Pareto but not necessarily efficient.

Given a protocol model, a solution concept and an objective, we can determine the smallest set of defenders for which the protocol is correct. Clearly, defendability of a protocol is monotonic with respect to the set of defenders.

---

[2] Arguably, that would mean that the protocol is badly designed.

[3] We will look closer at defendability under Nash equilibrium in Section 5.

Proposition 2. *For every $D \subseteq D' \subseteq N$, if $\Gamma \models_{SC} [D]\gamma$ then $\Gamma \models_{SC} [D']\gamma$.*

This justifies the following definition.

Definition 8. *The* game-theoretic security level *of protocol P is the antichain of minimal sets of defenders that make the protocol correct.*

Intuitively, the game-theoretic security level is the set of minimal coalitions $C \subseteq N$ such that if C supports the goal, then every rational play will fulfill it. Note that due to Proposition 2, the game-theoretic security level of a protocol is nonempty (i.e., the goal of the protocol can be defended) if and only if the "grand coalition" N of all players can defend the goal. We will concentrate on defendability by the grand coalition in Section 5.

4   Computational Complexity: General Case

In this section, we study the complexity of protocol verification, validity, and defendability for the general case when the solution concept is a parameter of the problem (and hence a part of the input). Algorithms for this case are useful to evaluate a protocol with respect to different solution concepts. Also, they give upper bounds for every specific subclass of the problem.[4] Since our definitions of correctness are parametrized by a solution concept and a security property, our results are relative to the complexity of verification for the two.

Theorem 3. *Let us measure the complexity w.r.t. the size of the NF game (i.e., the number of strategy profiles), and let $\mathfrak{SC}$, $\mathfrak{Obj}$ be the complexity of verification for the solution concept and the objective of the protocol, respectively. Then:*

1. *Protocol verification is in $\mathbf{P}^{\mathfrak{SC} \cup \mathfrak{Obj}}$ which is the class of decision problems that can be solved by a deterministic Turing machine running in polynomial time and making calls to an oracle for problems in $\mathfrak{SC} \cup \mathfrak{Obj}$;*
2. *Protocol validity is in $\mathbf{coNP}^{\mathfrak{SC} \cup \mathfrak{Obj}}$ (problems solvable by a TM for $\mathbf{coNP}$, calling an oracle for $\mathfrak{SC} \cup \mathfrak{Obj}$);*
3. *Protocol defendability is also in $\mathbf{coNP}^{\mathfrak{SC} \cup \mathfrak{Obj}}$.*

Proof. **Ad. 1.** For protocol verification, it suffices to check the outcome of every strategy profile whether it is not accepted by the solution concept or accepted by the objective. This can be done by a deterministic algorithm running in polynomial time (wrt to the number of strategy profiles) and making calls to oracles verifying the solution concept and the objective, respectively;

Ad. 2. We can reduce protocol validity to an instance of **coSAT** making calls to oracles for the solution concept and the objective. This is because every solution concept can be equivalently rephrased in terms of preference relations over outcomes rather than utility profiles. Since there are exponentially many such relations, they can be encoded by polynomially many binary variables. Then, a protocol is valid iff it is correct for *all possible valuations of the variables*;

Ad. 3. Protocol defendability reduces analogously.

---

[4]   In Section 5, we will give complexity results for the specific case when the notion of rationality is based on Nash equilibrium.

The next theorem proposes a lower bound.

Theorem 4. *Protocol validity and protocol defendability are* **coNP**-*hard.*

Proof. We prove hardness by a reduction of **coSAT** to protocol validity. Since protocol validity is a special case of defendability (Theorem 1), **coNP**-hardness for defendability follows as well.

Let $x_1, \ldots, x_n$ be Boolean variables and φ a formula in DNF. We construct an instance of protocol validity by simulating valuations of $x_1, \ldots, x_n$ by utility profiles, and formula φ by the solution concept. Formally, let Γ consist of $N = \{1, \ldots, n\}$ and $\Sigma = \{s^0, s^1\}$, and SC be defined as: $SC(\Gamma, u) = \{s^1\}$ if $\varphi((u_1(s^1) \geq u_1(s^0)), \ldots, (u_n(s^1) \geq u_n(s^0)))$ and $\{s^0\}$ otherwise. Finally, let $\gamma = \{s^1\}$. Note that membership in $SC(\Gamma, u)$ and γ can be verified in polynomial time. Now, **coSAT**$(x_1, \ldots, x_n, \varphi)$ iff $\Gamma \models_{SC} \gamma$.

In practice, a protocol model is rarely given as a normal form game, but rather as a sequence of transitions (cf. for example Figure 1). For this representation, the following theorem gives the complexity of protocol verification and validity:

Theorem 5. *Let* $\mathfrak{SC}, \mathfrak{Obj}$ *be as above. Protocol verification, protocol validity, and protocol defendability are in* **coNP**$^{\mathfrak{SC} \cup \mathfrak{Obj}}$ *wrt the number of possible transitions in the protocol model.*

Proof. We observe that a strategy profile in an extensive game can be encoded by an array of choices, one per agent and game position (i.e., protocol state in our case). Since the array has polynomial size wrt the size of the game tree, we obtain the result by analogous reasoning to the proof of Theorem 3.

We note that some natural solution concepts can be verified in deterministic polynomial time (e.g., Stackelberg equilibrium in NF games, subgame-perfect Nash equilibrium in EF games, etc.). Also, many objectives can be verified in polynomial time. Then, we obtain the following.

Theorem 6. *If the solution concept and the objective can be verified in polynomial time then:*

1. *Protocol verification is* **P**-*complete wrt to the size of the NF game and* **coNP**-*complete wrt the number of transitions in the protocol;*
2. *Protocol validity and protocol defendability are* **coNP**-*complete with respect to both types of input.*

5   Characterizing Defendability under Nash Equilibrium

In this section, we turn to properties that can be defended if agents' rationality is based on Nash equilibrium or Optimal Nash Equilibrium.

	t_1	t_2
s_1	hi, hi	$0, 0$
s_2	$0, 0$	lo, lo

(a)

	t_1	t_2	t_3
s_1	hi, lo	lo, hi	$0, 0$
s_2	lo, hi	hi, lo	$0, 0$
s_3	$0, 0$	$0, 0$	$0, 0$

(b)

Fig. 4. (a) HiLo game for 2 players; (b) Extended matching pennies. In both games, we assume that $hi > lo > 0$, e.g., $hi = 100$ and $lo = 1$

5.1 Defendability under Nash Equilibrium

From Theorem 1, we know that no protocol is valid under Nash equilibrium (NE) for any nontrivial objective, since NE is closed under permutation. Do things get better if we assume some agents to be in favor of the security objective? We now look at the extreme variant of the question, i.e., defendability by the grand coalition N. Note that, by Proposition 2, nondefendability by N implies that the objective is not defendable by any coalition at all.

Our first result in this respect is negative: we show that in every game frame there are nontrivial objectives that are not defendable under NE.

Theorem 7. *Let Γ be a game frame with at least two players and at least two strategies per player. Moreover, let γ be a singleton objective, i.e., $\gamma = \{\omega\}$ for some $\omega \in \Sigma$. Then, $\Gamma \not\models_{\mathrm{NE}} [N]\gamma$.*

Proof. Assume wlog that $N = 2$, $\Sigma_1 = \{s_1, s_2\}$, $\Sigma_2 = \{t_1, t_2\}$, and $\gamma = \{(s_1, t_1)\}$. Now, consider the utility function u^{hl} of the well known HiLo game (Figure 4(a)). Clearly, N support γ in u^{hl}. Moreover, $\mathrm{NE}(\Gamma, u^{hl}) \neq \emptyset$. On the other hand, $\mathrm{NE}(\Gamma, u^{hl}) = \{(s_1, t_1), (s_2, t_2)\} \not\subseteq \gamma$, which concludes the proof.

In particular, the construction from the above proof shows that, as mentioned before, there are cases where the "defending" coalition has a strategy to achieve a goal γ, but there are still rational plays in which the goal is not achieved.

To present the general result that characterizes defendability of security objectives under Nash equilibrium, we need to introduce additional concepts. In what follows, we use $s[t_i/i]$ to denote $(s_1, \ldots, s_{i-1}, t_i, s_{i+1}, \ldots, s_N)$, i.e., the strategy profile that is obtained from s when player i changes her strategy to t_i.

Definition 9. *Let γ be a set of outcomes (strategy profiles) in Γ. The* deviation closure *of γ is defined as $Cl(\gamma) = \{s \in \Sigma \mid \exists i \in N, t_i \in \Sigma_i \ . \ s[t_i/i] \in \gamma\}$.*

$Cl(\gamma)$ extends γ with the strategy profiles that are reachable by unilateral deviations from γ. Thus, $Cl(\gamma)$ can be seen as the closure of γ with the outcomes that are relevant for Nash equilibrium. Moreover, the following notion captures strategy profiles that can be used to construct sequences of unilateral deviations ending up in a cycle.

Definition 10. *A* strategic knot *in γ is a subset of strategy profiles $S \subseteq \gamma$ such that there is a permutation $(s^1, \ldots, s^k)$ of S where: (a) for all $1 \leq j < k$, $s^{j+1} = s^j[s_i^{j+1}/i]$ for some $i \in N$, and (b) $s^j = s^k[s_i^1/i]$ for some $i \in N, j < k$.*

Essentially, this means that every strategy s^{j+1} is obtained from s^j by a unilateral deviation of a single agent. If these deviations are rational (i.e., increase the utility of the deviating agent), then the knot represents a possible endless loop of rational, unilateral deviations which precludes a group of agents from reaching a stable joint strategy. We now state the main result of this section.

Theorem 8. *Let Γ be a finite game frame and γ a nontrivial objective in Γ. Then, $\Gamma \models_{\mathrm{NE}} [N]\gamma$ iff $Cl(\gamma) = \Sigma$ and there is a strategy profile in γ that belongs to no strategic knots in γ.*

Proof. "$\Rightarrow$" Let $\Gamma \models_{\mathrm{NE}} [N]\gamma$, and suppose that $Cl(\gamma) \neq \Sigma$. Thus, there exists $s_0 \in \Sigma$ which is not in $Cl(\gamma)$. Consider a HiLo-style utility function $u(s) = hi$ if $s \in \gamma$, lo if $s = s_0$, and 0 otherwise (for some values $hi > lo > 0$). Clearly, s_0 is a Nash equilibrium in (Γ, u), and thus $\mathrm{NE}(\Gamma, u) \neq \emptyset$ but also $\mathrm{NE}(\Gamma, u) \not\subseteq \gamma$, which is a contradiction.

Suppose now that $Cl(\gamma) = \Sigma$ but every $s \in \gamma$ belongs to a strategic knot. We construct the utility function akin to the extended matching pennies game (Figure 4(b)), i.e., for every node s in a strategic knot $u_i(s) = hi$ for the agent i who has just deviated, and lo for the other agents.[5] Moreover, $u_i(s) = 0$ for all $i \in N, s \notin \gamma$. Clearly, u_i is consistent with γ for every $i \in N$. On the other hand, no $s \in \Sigma$ is a Nash equilibrium: if s is outside of γ then there is a profitable unilateral deviation into γ, and every s inside γ lies on an infinite path of rational unilateral deviations. Thus, $\mathrm{NE}(\Gamma, u) = \emptyset$. Since γ is nontrivial, we have $\Gamma \not\models_{\mathrm{NE}} [N]\gamma$, a contradiction again.

"$\Leftarrow$" Assume $Cl(\gamma) = \Sigma$ and $s \in \gamma$ belongs to no strategic knot in γ. Let u be a utility function such that for every $i \in N, s \in \gamma, s' \in \Sigma \setminus \gamma$ it holds that $u_i(s) > u_i(s')$. Take any $\omega \notin \gamma$. Since $\omega \in Cl(\gamma)$, there is an agent i with a unilateral deviation to some $s \in \gamma$. Note that $u_i(\omega) < u_i(s)$, so $\omega \notin \mathrm{NE}(\Gamma, u)$. Thus, $\mathrm{NE}(\Gamma, u) \subseteq \gamma$. Moreover, s is a Nash equilibrium or there is a sequence of unilateral deviations leading from s to a Nash equilibrium (since Γ is finite and s does not lie on a knot). Thus, also $\mathrm{NE}(\Gamma, u) \neq \emptyset$, which concludes the proof.

Example 6. Consider contract signing with TTP, cf. Figure 1 (right). The properties of effectiveness and fairness can be defined as $\gamma_{\mathrm{eff}} = \{(Sign, Sign)\}$ and $\gamma_{\mathrm{fair}} = \{(Stop, Stop), (Sign, Sign)\}$. By Theorem 8, fairness in the protocol is N-defendable under Nash equilibrium. On the other hand, effectiveness is not.

It is important to note that the above result makes verification of defendability significantly easier than the general results from Section 4 suggest:

Theorem 9. *Let Γ be a finite game frame and γ a nontrivial objective in Γ. Then, checking $\Gamma \models_{\mathrm{NE}} [N]\gamma$ can be done in polynomial time wrt the size of γ.*

Proof (sketch). Checking if $Cl(\gamma) = \Sigma$: we look at every $s \notin \gamma$ and check if it can be "moved" to γ by a flip of an individual strategy.

---

[5] If a node lies on several knots, we need to assign several different hi values in a careful way; we omit the details here due to lack of space.

Checking strategic knots: (i) Take Θ to be the deviation grid for γ, i.e., the graph containing strategy profiles from γ as vertices and individually rational deviations as edges; (ii) Construct the minimal spanning graph $MSG(\Theta)$ (Kruskal or a similar algorithm); (iii) Let $Knotty = \emptyset$. For every edge (s, s') in $\Theta \setminus MSG(\Theta)$: add the vertices on the path from s to s' in $MSG(\Theta)$ to $Knotty$; (iv) For every $s \in \Theta \setminus Knotty$: add it to $Knotty$ iff there is a path in Θ between s and some $s' \in Knotty$. (v) The answer is "yes" iff $\Theta \setminus Knotty \neq \emptyset$.

5.2 Optimal Nash Equilibria

Nash equilibrium is a natural solution concept for a game played repeatedly until the behavior of all players converges to a stable point. For a one-shot game, NE possibly captures convergence of the process of deliberation. It can be argued that, among the available solutions, no player should contemplate those which are strictly worse for everybody when compared to another stable point. This gives rise to the following refinement of Nash equilibrium: $\mathrm{OptNE}(\Gamma, u)$ is the set of *optimal Nash equilibria* in game (Γ, u), defined as those equilibria *that are not strongly Pareto-dominated by another Nash equilibrium*. Defendability by the grand coalition under OptNE has the following simple characterization.

Theorem 10. *Let Γ be a finite game frame and γ a nontrivial objective in Γ. Then, $\Gamma \models_{\mathrm{OptNE}} [N]\gamma$ iff there is a strategy profile in γ that belongs to no strategic knots in γ.*

Proof. "$\Rightarrow$" If all $s \in \gamma$ lie on strategic knots in γ then there is u such that no $s \in \gamma$ is a Nash equilibrium in (Γ, u), cf. the proof of Theorem 8. Since $\mathrm{OptNE}(\Gamma, u) \subseteq \mathrm{NE}(\Gamma, u)$ and γ is nontrivial, this implies that $\Gamma \not\models_{\mathrm{OptNE}} [N]\gamma$.

"$\Leftarrow$" Let u be any utility profile. By analogous reasoning to Theorem 8, there must be a strategy profile $s \in \gamma$ in game (Γ, u) which is an optimal Nash equilibrium. Thus, $\mathrm{OptNE}(\Gamma, u) \neq \emptyset$. Suppose that there exists another optimal NE $s' \notin \gamma$. But then s' would be strictly Pareto-dominated, which cannot be the case. Thus, also $\mathrm{OptNE}(\Gamma, u) \subseteq \gamma$, and hence $\Gamma \models_{\mathrm{OptNE}} [N]\gamma$.

It is easy to see that checking N-defendability under OptNE is in **P**.

6 Defendability in Mixed Strategies

So far, we considered only deterministic (pure) strategies. It is well known that for many games and solution concepts, rational strategies exist only when taking mixed strategies into account. We now extend our definition of correctness to mixed strategies, i.e., randomized conditional plans represented by probability distributions over pure strategies from Σ_{A_i}. Let $dom(s)$ be the support (domain) of a mixed strategy profile s, i.e., the set of pure strategy profiles that have nonzero probability in s. We extend the notion to sets of mixed strategy profiles in the obvious way. By SC^m we denote the variant of SC in mixed strategy profiles. A protocol is correct in mixed strategies iff all the possible behaviors resulting from a rational (mixed) strategy profile satisfy the goal γ; formally: $\Gamma, u \models_{SC}^m \gamma$ iff $dom(SC^m(\Gamma, u)) \subseteq \gamma$ when $SC^m(\Gamma, u) \neq \emptyset$ and $\gamma = \Sigma_\Gamma$ otherwise. The definitions of protocol validity and defendability in mixed strategies ($\Gamma \models_{SC}^m \gamma$ and $\Gamma \models_{SC}^m [D]\gamma$) are analogous. For defendability in mixed strategies under Nash equilibrium, we have the following, rather pessimistic result.

Theorem 11. *Let Γ be a finite game frame, and γ an objective in it. Then, $\Gamma, u \models_{NE}^m [N]\gamma$ iff $\gamma = \Sigma$.*

Proof. "$\Leftarrow$" Straightforward. For "$\Rightarrow$", we observe the following:

(i) $Cl(\gamma) = \Sigma$ by the same reasoning as for pure strategies.

(ii) Let $Conv(\gamma)$ be the convex closure of γ, i.e., the set of strategy profiles obtained by combining individual strategies occurring in γ. Then, $Conv(\gamma) = \gamma$. (*Proof:* suppose that it is not the case, then there must be $s, s' \in \gamma$ such that one of their convex combinations s'' is not in γ. We play the Coordination game with 1 assigned to s, s', 0 to the other nodes in γ and -1 to the rest of nodes. The strategy profile $([s_{A_1}/0.5, s'_{A_1}/0.5], \ldots, [s_{A_{|N|}}/0.5, s'_{A_{|N|}}/0.5])$ is a mixed strategy Nash equilibrium, and clearly s'' is in its support. Since $\Gamma, u \models_{SC}^m [N]\gamma$, we have that $s'' \in \gamma$, which is a contradiction.)

(iii) By (i), every i's strategy must be a part of some strategy profile in γ. Thus, $Conv(\gamma) = \Sigma$, and hence $\gamma = \Sigma$.

On the other hand, it turns out that *optimal Nash equilibrium* yields a simple and appealing characteristics of N-defendable properties:

Theorem 12. *$\Gamma \models_{OptNE}^m [N]\gamma$ iff $\gamma = Conv(\gamma)$, i.e., γ is closed under convex combination of strategies.*

Proof (sketch). "$\Rightarrow$" Analogous to point (ii) in the proof of Theorem 11.

"$\Leftarrow$" Consider any utility profile u. By the result of Nash [17], (Γ, u) has a Nash equilibrium in mixed strategies. Moreover, $\gamma = Conv(\gamma)$ implies that all the Nash equilibria s such that $dom(s) \not\subseteq \gamma$ are strongly Pareto-dominated by a mixed NE in γ. Hence, $OptNE(\Gamma, u)$ is nonempty and entirely contained in γ.

Corollary 1. *$\Gamma \models_{OptNE}^m [N]\gamma$ iff there exist subsets of individual strategies $\chi_1 \subseteq \Sigma_1, \ldots, \chi_{|N|} \subseteq \Sigma_{|N|}$ such that $\gamma = \chi_1 \times \cdots \times \chi_{|N|}$.*

That is, security property γ is defendable by the grand coalition in Γ iff γ can be *decomposed into constraints on individual behavior of particular agents.*

7   Conclusions

We propose a framework for analyzing security protocols (and other interaction protocols), that takes into account the incentives of agents. In particular, we consider a novel notion of *defendability* that guarantees that all the runs of the protocol are correct as long as a given subset of the participants (the "defenders") is in favor of the security property. We have obtained some characterization results for defendability under Nash equilibria and optimal Nash equilibria. We also studied the computational complexity of the corresponding decision problems, both in the generic case and in some special cases based on Nash equilibrium. In the future, we plan to combine our framework with results for protocol verification using game logics (such as ATL), especially for those solution concepts that can be expressed in that kind of logics.

Acknowledgements. Wojciech Jamroga acknowledges support of the National Research Fund Luxembourg (FNR) under project GaLOT – INTER/DFG/12/06.

References

1. Anderson, R., Moore, T., Nagaraja, S., Ozment, A.: Incentives and information security. In: Algorithmic Game Theory (2007)
2. Asharov, G., Canetti, R., Hazay, C.: Towards a game theoretic view of secure computation. In: Paterson, K.G. (ed.) EUROCRYPT 2011. LNCS, vol. 6632, pp. 426–445. Springer, Heidelberg (2011)
3. Asharov, G., Lindell, Y.: Utility dependence in correct and fair rational secret sharing. In: Halevi, S. (ed.) CRYPTO 2009. LNCS, vol. 5677, pp. 559–576. Springer, Heidelberg (2009)
4. Ben-Or, M., Goldreich, O., Micali, S., Rivest, R.: A fair protocol for signing contracts. IEEE Transactions on Information Theory IT-36(1), 40–46 (1990)
5. Buttyán, L., Hubaux, J., Čapkun, S.: A formal model of rational exchange and its application to the analysis of Syverson's protocol. Journal of Computer Security 12(3,4), 551–587 (2004)
6. Chadha, R., Mitchell, J., Scedrov, A., Shmatikov, V.: Contract signing, optimism and advantage. Journal of Logic and Algebraic Programming 64(2), 189–218 (2005)
7. Chatterjee, K., Raman, V.: Assume-guarantee synthesis for digital contract signing. CoRR, abs/1004.2697 (2010)
8. Dodis, Y., Rabin, T.: Cryptography and game theory. In: Nisan, N., Roughgarden, T., Tardos, É., Vazirani, V.V. (eds.) Algorithmic Game Theory, ch. 8, pp. 181–208 (2007)
9. Finkbeiner, B., Schewe, S.: Coordination logic. In: Dawar, A., Veith, H. (eds.) CSL 2010. LNCS, vol. 6247, pp. 305–319. Springer, Heidelberg (2010)
10. Fuchsbauer, G., Katz, J., Naccache, D.: Efficient rational secret sharing in standard communication networks. In: Micciancio, D. (ed.) TCC 2010. LNCS, vol. 5978, pp. 419–436. Springer, Heidelberg (2010)
11. Ghaderi, H., Levesque, H., Lespérance, Y.: A logical theory of coordination and joint ability. ACM Press, New York (May 2007)
12. Groce, A., Katz, J.: Fair Computation with Rational Players. In: Pointcheval, D., Johansson, T. (eds.) EUROCRYPT 2012. LNCS, vol. 7237, pp. 81–98. Springer, Heidelberg (2012)
13. Halpern, J.Y., Rong, N.: Cooperative equilibrium (extended abstract). In: Proceedings of AAMAS 2010, pp. 1465–1466 (2010)
14. Kremer, S., Raskin, J.: Game analysis of abuse-free contract signing. In: Proceedings of the 15th IEEE Computer Security Foundations Workshop (CSFW 2002), pp. 206–220. IEEE Computer Society Press (2002)

15. Kremer, S., Raskin, J.: A game-based verification of non-repudiation and fair exchange protocols. Journal of Computer Security 11(3) (2003)
16. Moore, T., Anderson, R.: Economics and internet security: a survey of recent analytical, empirical and behavioral research. Technical Report TR-03-11, Computer Science Group, Harvard University (2011)
17. Nash, J.: Non-cooperative games. PhD thesis, Princeton (1950)
18. Osborne, M., Rubinstein, A.: A Course in Game Theory. MIT Press (1994)
19. Syverson, P.: Weakly secret bit commitment: Applications to lotteries and fair exchange. In: CSFW, pp. 2–13 (1998)

An Efficient Route Minimization Algorithm for the Vehicle Routing Problem with Time Windows Based on Agent Negotiation

Petr Kalina[1], Jiří Vokřínek[2], and Vladimír Mařík[3]

[1] Intelligent Systems Group, Czech Technical University in Prague, Czech Republic
[2] Agent Technology Center, Czech Technical University in Prague, Czech Republic
[3] Department of Cybernetics, Czech Technical University in Prague, Czech Republic
{petr.kalina,jiri.vokrinek,vladimir.marik}@fel.cvut.cz

Abstract. We present an efficient route minimization algorithm for the vehicle routing problem with time windows. The algorithm uses a generic agent decomposition of the problem featuring a clear separation between the local planning performed by the individual vehicles and the abstract global coordination achieved by negotiation — differentiating the presented algorithm from the traditional centralized algorithms. Novel negotiation semantics is introduced on the global coordination planning level allowing customers to be temporarily ejected from the emerging solution being constructed. This allows the algorithm to efficiently backtrack in situations when the currently processed customer cannot be feasibly allocated to the emerging solution. Over the relevant widely-used benchmarks the algorithm equals the best known solutions achieved by the centralized algorithms in 90.7% of the cases with an overall relative error of 0.3%, outperforming the previous comparable agent-based algorithms.

Keywords: multi-agent systems, logistics, optimization, VRPTW.

1 Introduction

The vehicle routing problem with time windows (VRPTW) is one of the most important and widely studied problems within the operations research (OR) domain featuring in many distribution and logistic systems. It is a problem of finding a set of routes starting and ending at a single depot serving a set of geographically scattered customers, each within a specific time-window and with a specific demand of goods to be delivered. The primary objective of the VRPTW is to find the minimal number of routes serving all customers.

Real world applications of VRPTW and routing problems in general are often very complex and semantically rich, featuring heterogenous fleets with varied operational costs [20], specific constraints e.g. loading constraints [29], driver shift times [26] reflecting also the typical real-world challenges e.g. traffic congestions, breakdowns, customers rescheduling etc.

G. Boella et al. (Eds.): PRIMA 2013, LNAI 8291, pp. 149–164, 2013.
© Springer-Verlag Berlin Heidelberg 2013

The multi-agent (MA) systems are an emerging architecture with respect to modeling new-generation systems based on smart actors and their intelligent coordination, promoting the autonomy of the individual actors. The outstanding attribute inherent to most MA planning techniques is thus the clear separation of local planning of the actors and the global coordination of their individual plans [2,15]. This enables for the problem specific constraints — such as the time-windows and capacity constraints inherent to VRPTW or those mentioned above — to be incorporated by developing fitting local planning strategies for the individual actors (vehicles). The global coordination mechanism, on the other hand, remains abstract and can be applied over a wide range of problems similar in nature e.g. general task allocation problems [28].

Within this work we present a significant extension to the global coordination framework extending the previous similar works [28,13]. The extension is based on introducing a specific backtracking strategy to the abstract allocation process based on the *ejection* principle [19], denoted here as *rotations*. The contribution is significant for two reasons: (i) it enables the resulting VRPTW algorithm to significantly outperform the previous comparable agent-based algorithms with a performance closely matching the established centralized algorithms and (ii) similar concepts within the coordination framework can be applied in a number of other similar problems — namely in highly constrained task allocation problems with scheduling/sequencing aspects e.g. general scheduling and temporal resource allocation problems and their extensions.

Thus a VRPTW algorithm is presented and the solving process is outlined in detail. The semantic of the negotiation based coordination process is analyzed and compared to the previous similar methods. In order to provide a relevant comparison of the presented algorithm to the best known centralized algorithms the experimental evaluation is based on the two most widely used benchmarks known from the OR literature. The comparison to the previous similar agent-based algorithms is provided as well.

As mentioned above, the presented algorithm differentiates itself from the traditional algorithms by featuring the clear separation between the problem specific agents' local decision making and the abstract global coordination, representing the core feature inherent to cooperative multi-agent planning [2,15]. On the other hand the finer details inherent to agency e.g. alternative agent behavioral patterns and commitment semantics [17], the complexity of the underlying network communication [6] or semantically rich problem extensions [10] are not discussed in detail, presenting further opportunities for future research.

2   Problem Statement and Notations

As mentioned above, the VRPTW consists of finding a set of routes starting and ending at a single depot serving a set of geographically scattered customers. The primary optimization criteria is to find a minimal set of such routes serving all the customers within the given time windows.

Let $\{1..N\}$ represent the set of customers with the depot denoted as 0. For each customer c_i let (e_i, l_i, s_i, d_i) denote the earliest/latest service start times (*time window*), service time and the demand. Let a sequence of customers $\langle c_0, c_1, ..c_m, c_{m+1} \rangle$ denote a single route with c_0 and c_{m+1} denoting the depot. Let D denote the vehicle capacity and let $t_{i,j}$ correspond to the travel time between customers c_i and c_j with all mutual travel times being known.

The objective of the VRPTW is finding a minimal set of routes serving all customers. For each route $\langle c_0, c_1, ..c_m, c_{m+1} \rangle$ the sum of corresponding customers' demands must be lower than the capacity of the vehicle serving the route $\sum_1^m d_i \leq D$ (capacity constraint) while the service at each customer c_i must begin within the interval given by (e_i, l_i) (time-windows constraints).

Given a route $\langle c_0, c_1, ..c_m, c_{m+1} \rangle$ let (E_i, L_i) correspond to the *earliest* and *latest possible service start* at customer c_i computed recursively according to:

$$E_1 = max\,(e_1, t_{0,1})$$
$$E_i = max\,(e_i, E_{i-1} + s_{i-1} + t_{i-1,i}) \tag{1}$$

and

$$L_m = l_m$$
$$L_i = min\,(l_i, L_{i+1} - t_{i,i+1} - s_i) \tag{2}$$

As shown in [5], the time window constraints are satisfied when $E_i \leq L_i$ for all $i \in 1..m$. The capacity constraint is satisfied when $\sum_1^m d_i \leq D$.

3   Related Work

The VRPTW has been extensively studied for for almost thirty years with the classical Solomon's [27] article dating back to 1987. The full review of relevant OR literature is outside the scope of this study, however we refer the reader to the excellent surveys of recent (up to 2005) literature provided by [3,4]. Instead we briefly introduce the state-of-the-art traditional algorithms and concentrate on the relevant agent-based studies. The performance of the individual algorithms is evaluated using the *cumulative number of vehicles* (CNV) metric used widely within OR field, corresponding to the total number of routes/vehicles over all problem instances across the whole corresponding set of problem instances.

3.1   Traditional Algorithms

As already mentioned, the majority of successful VRPTW algorithms combine several methods in a multi-phase solving approach. Thus within the initial *construction* phase a set of initial solutions is generated. The *route minimization* can be part of this phase (as it is with the presented algorithm) or it can be embedded as a separate phase - addressing the primary objective. The secondary objectives are typically addressed in an additional phase within which the number of routes remain constant [3,4,24,19,25]. The route minimization is also considered as being the computationally hardest phase of solving the VRPTW [3,4].

Thus developing efficient route minimization heuristics as a key initial step in providing efficient VRPTW algorithms.

The algorithm introduced in [19] is based on the *ejection pools* (EP) principle, performing very good potentially unfeasible insertions of customers to individual routes and subsequently recovering the feasibility by ejecting some other customers from the unfeasible routes. The insertion-ejection phase is interleaved with a local search procedure dynamically improving the solution throughout the solving process.

The algorithm presented by [25] is based on embedding a branch-and-price algorithm based on a modification of an exact algorithm presented in [9] into a large neighborhood search procedure based on series of destructive and recreative steps. Thus a subset of (routed or unrouted) customers is selected based on one of the four various operators introduced to provide means of search diversification and the identified customers are removed from the partial solution. The neighborhood corresponding to the partial solutions obtained by reinserting the removed customers is traversed using a branch-and-price algorithm in an effort to identify the next best partial solution and the process continues from there.

A memetic algorithm [22] achieving the contemporary best CNV of 405 and 10304 over the Solomon's and Homberger's benchmark respectively is presented in [24]. Initial feasible solutions are generated using an adaptation of the EP principle used by [19]. The EP mechanism is accompanied by a powerful feasible insertion method denoted as *squeeze* as well as a search diversification *perturb* procedure. The *squeeze* method also employs a specific adaptive local search procedure used to repair potentially unfeasible intermediate solutions using a heuristic carried over from [19]. The route minimization phase is followed by a travel time minimization phase combining an evolutionary algorithm used for traversing the more distant parts of the search space (the *exploration* phase) with a local search based improvement phase providing for traversing the immediate neighborhoods of the examined solutions (referred to as the *exploitation* phase). The exploration algorithm is based on adaptation of the known EAX operator [23], while the exploitation phase combines two alternative hill-climbing methods aimed at (i) reducing the level of unfeasibility within the intermediate emerging solution and (ii) reducing the travel time.

3.2   Agent-Based Algorithms

A number of approaches and systems have been proposed addressing a variety of routing and logistic problems relying on decentralized agent-based planning techniques. A survey of some of the most interesting works is provided for example by [7]. Also a number of studies was presented addressing the VRPTW in particular. However, as discussed in detail within the Section 5 there are some common deficiencies shared by most of these works, namely that (i) a relevant comparison of the presented algorithms to the established traditional algorithms is missing and (ii) where provided, it reveals a relatively weak performance of these algorithms. Thus within this work we present an agent-based VRPTW algorithm which boast a vastly improved performance and provide support for such a claim by pitting it against both the most relevant benchmarks known from the OR literature.

The algorithm presented in [10] is built around the concepts of Shipping Company Agents (SCA) representing individual shipping companies and their respective fleets of Truck Agents (TA). After registering a customer, the SCA negotiates with his fleet of TAs to estimate the price of serving the customer. The other SCAs are contacted as well and based on the corresponding cost estimates the SCA may assign the customer to one of its trucks or decide to cooperate with another company. The planning within each fleet is done dynamically and is based on the well known contract net protocol (CNP) [8] accompanied by a *simulated trading* improvement strategy based on finding the optimal customer exchanges by solving a modification of the maximal pairing problem on a graph representing the proposed exchanges originally presented in [1]. Both cooperative and competitive models are explored with respect to the cooperation of individual SCAs. Also a specific model for simulating traffic jams is presented.

The algorithm for the closely related pickup and delivery problem with time windows (PDPTW) presented by [14] is essentially a parallel insertion procedure with a subsequent improvement phase consisting of reallocating some randomly chosen tasks from each route. The used cost structure is based on the well known Solomon's I1 insertion heuristic [27].

The algorithm presented by [18] is based on agents representing individual customers, routes and a central planner agent. A sequential insertion procedure based on Solomon's I1 heuristic is followed by an improvement phase in which the agents propose moves gathered in a *move pool* with the most advantageous move being selected and performed. Additionally, a route elimination routine is periodically invoked — which is not well described in the text.

In [6] an algorithm is introduced based on Order agent — Scheduling agent — Vehicle agent hierarchy. The algorithm is based on a modified CNP insertion procedure limiting the negotiation to agents whose routes are in proximity of the customer being allocated in an effort to minimize the number of negotiations.

The algorithm presented in [12] features a similar agent architecture as the one used within this study inspired by the general agent architecture for task allocation problems presented in [28]. The negotiation process corresponds to a parallel customer insertion procedure with a specific *iterative* improvement method being periodically invoked after processing each customer. Also, an additional *final* improvement method is invoked at the end of the solving process after all customers have been allocated. Several alternative improvement methods are introduced based on relocating alternative sets of customers between the individual routes. The used local planning strategy corresponds to the well known *travel time savings* heuristics [27].

An improved version of the algorithm is presented in [13]. An alternative *slackness savings* based vehicles' local planning strategy is introduced based on [21] as well as the set of refined improvement methods to be used throughout the solving process. Also a specific parallel execution wrapper is introduced based on running in parallel the individual *algorithm instances* corresponding to the previously discussed algorithm differentiated by the order in which the customers are processed as well as the choice of the perticular improvement methods being used. The algorithm achieves a CNV of 10949 over the two mentioned benchmarks, corresponding to 2.2% relative error compared to [24], representing the best comparable result for an agent-based algorithm.

4   Agent-Based Algorithm for VRPTW with Rotations

Within this work we present an extension to the global coordination framework used by the previous similar works [28,13]. The main contributions is the introduction of a novel negotiation semantics allowing customers to be temporarily ejected from the emerging solution being constructed by means of *rotations*, providing for an efficient backtracking strategy. This enables the algorithm to proceed in situations where the semantic used by the previously presented algorithms got stuck and the negotiation process failed.

The underlying abstract negotiation framework is based on [28] and features the clear separation between the local planning of individual vehicles and the abstract global coordination achieved by negotiation — differentiating the presented algorithm from the traditional centralized algorithms. Thus, as already mentioned, the abstract coordination mechanism is generic and can be applied to a variety of problems that are similar in nature [28] — by developing a fitting local planning strategy to be used by individual vehicles (agents/resources in general). This enables for transparent inclusion of specific extensions such as heterogeneities within the fleet [20], loading or cargo organization strategies [29], driver-relevant constraints [26]. Alternatively the autonomic nature of the system can be exploited by introducing autonomous trajectory/path planning strategies or reflecting the non-cooperative or tactical aspects of the modeled system [16].

4.1   Abstract Global Coordination Framework

The abstract negotiation-based framework featuring at the global coordination level of the overall planning process is a modification of a similar framework presented in [13]. The underlying agent architecture is carried over featuring a top layer represented by a Task Agent, middle layer represented by an Allocation Agent and a fleet of Vehicle Agents present at the bottom level of the architecture.

Task Agent acts as an interface between the algorithm's computational core and the surrounding infrastructure. It is responsible for registering the cusotomers and submitting them to the underlying Allocation Agent.

Allocation Agent instruments the actual solving process by negotiating with the Vehicle Agents, corresponding to the global coordination phase of the overall planning process. The negotiation is conducted based upon the commitment/decommitment cost estimates provided by the Vehicle Agents.

Input: Stack of customers C, Fleet of empty vehicles — initial solution σ
Output: Solution σ — complete or partial based on success of the process

Procedure *negotiate*(C, σ)
```
 1:      Initialize rotation counters ∀c ∈ C, c.rts := 0;
 2:      while (C not empty and rotations < rotationLimit)
 3:          Pop c̄ ∈ C (LIFO strategy);
 4:          Cheapest := {v ∈ Feasible(σ, c̄), v.costCommit(c̄) is minimal};
 5:          if (Cheapest ≠ ∅) then
 6:              Randomly select v̄ ∈ Cheapest;
 7:              v̄.commit(c̄);
 8:              SHAKE(σ);
 9:          else
10:              SQUEEZE(c̄, σ);
11:          endif
12:          if (c̄ ∉ σ) then
13:              C_ej := ROTATE(c̄, σ);
14:              Push C_ej to top of C
15:              c̄.rts++;
16:              rotations++;
17:          endif
18:      enwhile
19:      return σ;
End
```

Fig. 1. The Abstract Global Coordination Process

Vehicle Agent represents an individual vehicle serving a route. It provides the Allocation Agent with the above mentioned inputs, computed based on the Vehicle Agent's local (private) planning strategy.

Figure 1 illustrates the modified coordination process instrumented by the Allocation Agent. In essence it consists of a series of *negotiation* interactions between the Allocation Agent and the vehicles represented by the Vehicle Agents, being part of the initially empty emerging solution σ. The process is abstract and is based solely on the cost estimates computed locally by the vehicles based upon the particular local planning strategy being used.

The process is started by resetting the *rotation counters* for all allocated customers (line 1). As discussed later, the counters are used for determining the best rotation within the ROTATE method (line 13) in an effort to diversify the search. Follows an attempt to feasibly allocate the customer to the emerging partial solution σ (lines 3 – 11). Initially the vehicles that can feasibly serve the customer (the set *Feasible*$(\sigma, \bar{c})$) at the lowest possible cost (the set *Cheapest* — a subset of *Feasible*$(\sigma, \bar{c})$) are identified based on the cost estimates provided by the individual Vehicle Agents (line 4). In case *Cheapest* $\neq \emptyset$ a random vehicle from the set is chosen and commits to serving the customer. In such a case an attempt follows to further improve the emerging solution within the SHAKE method (line 8). In the opposite case a further attempt is made to feasibly *squeeze* the customer into the emerging solution σ within the SQUEEZE method (line 10).

Both the SHAKE and the SQUEEZE methods are based on traversing the neighborhoods of the emerging solution σ in an effort to (i) improve the solution in a way that increases the chance for future customer allocations (the SHAKE method) and (ii) modify it in a way as to enable feasible insertion of $\bar{c}$ (the SQUEEZE method). The semantic of the corresponding negotiation is slightly different for the two methods and is discussed in detail in Section 4.2.

In case a feasible slot is not found for the customer $\bar{c}$ in any of the routes neither within the initial allocation effort nor within the SQUEEZE method the feasible allocation process has failed. Such a situation arises typically towards the end of the solving process as the individual routes get denser and all of the possible allocation slots are rendered unfeasible due to capacity or time-window constraints[1]. In such a situation an attempt is made to insert the customer to one of the routes at the expense of ejecting some other customers from that route. Thus, within the ROTATE method (line 13) each of the vehicles tries to identify a fitting set of customers in its schedule the ejection of which would enable the customer $\bar{c}$ to be feasibly inserted — an operation referred to as a *rotation* — and the most fitting rotation is identified and performed. As already mentioned the selection of the most fitting rotation is based on the values of the rotation counters with the cost of an ejection corresponding to $\sum_{i=1}^{k} c_{e_i}.rts$, with the $c_{e_i}, i = 1..k$ being the ejected customers. The criteria thus favors rotations that are (i) smaller and (ii) consist of customers that have caused the least number of rotations and thus are arguably easier to allocate feasibly. The ROATE method is discussed in detail within the Section 4.3.

The process continues with incrementing the rotation counter for the allocated customer $\bar{c}.rts$ and the global *rotations* counter. Thus either all customers are allocated or the *rotationLimit* is exceeded. In the latter case there still remain some unserved customers (solution σ is not complete). In such a case the process can be restarted with a different fleet size or an additional vehicle can be added to the fleet.

The initial size of the fleet — corresponding to the initial solution σ of empty vehicles — is thus a significant factor affecting the efficiency of the whole algorithm and should correspond to the theoretical lower bound on the number of vehicles for the solved problem instance. An estimate of this number can be computed based upon the total demand of all customers $d_t = \sum_{i=1}^{N} d_i$ and the

---

[1] The latter situation is actually much more frequent suggesting the temporal/schedulling aspects are the dominant constraining factor for the solved problem. However, we argue that this is also partly due to the fact that the problem instances from the used benchmarks present a rather simple variant of the underlying multiple bin-packing problem. Individual customer demands are rather small and distributed only across several specific values (e.g. 10, 20, 30 with the vehicle capacity being 200) — an observation that might prove to be interesting from the point of view of the OR community where the used benchmarks are widely used and considered de-facto standard.

vehicle capacity D as d_t/D. An alternative estimate uses the temporal mutual incompatibilities between the customers. Two customers are temporally incompatible if it's not possible to start the service in either of them at the earliest possible moment and then reach the other customer in time, given the corresponding time windows. Considering a graph with nodes corresponding to the customers and edges to their temporal incompatibilities, the minimal size of the fleet is given by the size of the maximal clique within this graph [21]. Thus the overall theoretical lower bound on the size of the fleet is the bigger of these two numbers. As the max-clique problem is a NP-hard problem in its own right, the latter number is computed using a well known $O(N^3)$ polynomial approximate algorithm presented in [21].

4.2 The SHAKE and the SQUEEZE Methods

As already mentioned, the two methods are based on traversing the closer neighborhoods of the emerging solution σ. With the SHAKE method an effort is made to improve the solution by performing *improving* relocations of customers within and between the routes. The term improving reflects the fact that only moves that increase the utility from the point of view of the cost structure provided by the used local planning strategy are executed. In case of the used travel time savings (TTS) strategy [13] this corresponds to *shaking* the customers in a way as to reduce the traveled distances (with vehicle speed being constant for all the vehicles, the travel times are proportional to traveled distances). Thus only relocations that result in decrease in the overall traveled distance of the whole solution are performed.

The SQUEEZE method uses a similar semantics, however with some key extensions reflecting the effort to allocate the customer $\bar{c}$ that has previously failed to be feasibly allocated. Each relocation effectively consists of removing a customer (denoted as c_r) from the original route v and then requiring all the vehicles to estimate the feasibility and cost of a possible insertion of c_r to their schedules. Within the SQUEEZE method, after the relocated customer c_r was removed from the underlying route the feasibility of inserting the customer $\bar{c}$ is within this route is examined. In case the insertion of $\bar{c}$ to v is feasible, it is performed and an effort is made to feasibly allocate the c_r to the thus modified solution. In case the attempt is successful, the $\bar{c}$ has been successfully squeezed within the merging solution σ. In the opposite case the $\bar{c}$ is removed and the relocation proceeds by reinserting c_r back to v (to either the original or a different slot within the schedule).

The importance of the SQUEEZE method is twofold. On one hand it presents an opportunity to examine some simple yet helpful moves during the phase where the emerging solution σ is improved, potentially avoiding the need to perform a full fledged rotation. On the other hand it marks the place within the algorithm where there is arguably the biggest potential for further improvement in terms of performance. The contemporary VRPTW algorithms e.g. [19,24] present strategies enabling to repair the unfeasible intermediate solutions within a specific local search procedure guided by an utility function corresponding to the level of unfeasibility of the solution. As will be discussed later within the Section 5.2 we believe such an approach could significantly improve the convergence and efficiency of the algorithm.

4.3 The ROTATE Method

As already mentioned above, the ROTATE method enables the algorithm to proceed even when it is not possible to feasibly allocate the currently processed customer $\bar{c}$. In previous similar algorithms [12,13] such a situation caused the whole allocation process to fail, requiring another vehicle to be added to the fleet. The situation typically occurs towards the end of the solving process as the solution gets denser and the schedules of individual routes tighter. Based on previous findings [13], given the customers are processed in an unfitting order the situation is even likelier to occur. The resulting algorithms are therefore very sensitive to the initial customer ordering.

A single *rotation* thus consists of identifying a specific set of customers to be ejected from one of the routes such that it is possible to subsequently feasibly insert the currently processed customer $\bar{c}$ to the route. In order to identify the best possible rotation two criteria can be considered — the effects the ejecting of the specific identified set of customers will have on the solving process and also the fittingness of the subsequent insertion of $\bar{c}$ made possible by the ejection. Considering the first criterion, it is especially important to prevent the rotation mechanism from cycling by appropriately diversifying the ejections.

Within this work thus an approach is used that is an adaptation of the insertion-ejection mechanism presented in [23]. For each route the possible ejections are traversed in a specific way corresponding to the lexicographic ordering. Let $\langle c_{e_1}, c_{e_2}, .., c_{e_k} \rangle$ denote an ejection of size k from the route $\langle c_0, c_1, ..c_m, c_{m+1} \rangle$ with $e_i \in 1..m$. The maximal rotation size is bounded by the k_{max} parameter. Thus for example given $k_{max} = 3$ the rotations are traversed in the following order: $\langle c_1 \rangle$, $\langle c_1, c_2 \rangle$, $\langle c_1, c_2, c_3 \rangle$, $\langle c_1, c_2, c_4 \rangle$ ... $\langle c_1, c_2, c_m \rangle$, $\langle c_1, c_3, c_4 \rangle$ ... $\langle c_1, c_{m-1}, c_m \rangle$, $\langle c_1, c_m \rangle$, $\langle c_2 \rangle$, $\langle c_2, c_3 \rangle$ etc. The cost of an ejection is determined based on the values of the rotation counters as $\sum_{i=1}^{k} c_{e_i}.rts$ and the ejection with the minimal cost is chosen. In case of equality the following criteria is used (in following hierarchical order): (i) minimization of the size of the ejection and (ii) minimization of the travel time increase for the corresponding route after $\bar{c}$ has been inserted. These criteria have proved to be the most efficient based on our computational tests being out of scope of this study.

The ejected customers are then added to the set (stack) C using a LIFO strategy. This means that prior to proceeding to the customer following $\bar{c}$ in the original customer ordering, the $\bar{c}$ and all the ejected customers from the corresponding chain of rotations have to be feasibly allocated. Such an approach corresponds to the fact that if any of the customers cannot be feasibly allocated to the partial solution σ at this point, it is very unlikely it could be allocated later within the solving process as the solution becomes even more constrained. It is also supported by our computational experiments not being presented in detail within this study. Thus in effect the solution is *rotated* until $\bar{c}$ can be

Table 1. Results for alternative settings of the *rotationLimit* parameter

Set	CNV	Absolute (relative) error for alternative *rotationLimit* values			
	Nagata [24]	*Presented Algorithm*			
		2,000	5,000	20,000	1,000×N/5
100	405	5 (1.2%)	4 (1.0%)	3 (0.7%)	3 (0.7%)
200	694	5 (0.7%)	4 (0.6%)	2 (0.3%)	0 (0.0%)
400	1,381	18 (1.3%)	13 (0.9%)	12 (0.9%)	4 (0.3%)
600	2,067	35 (1.7%)	23 (1.1%)	11 (0.5%)	4 (0.2%)
800	2,738	63 (2.3%)	43 (1.6%)	16 (0.6%)	8 (0.3%)
1000	3,424	83 (2.4%)	49 (1.4%)	18 (0.5%)	8 (0.2%)
All	10,709	206 (1.9%)	134 (1.3%)	55 (0.5%)	27 (0.3%)

feasibly allocated, corresponding to an efficient backtracking strategy based on the introduced search diversification heuristic guiding the ejections.

The number of potential ejections is huge. Also testing the feasibility of insertion of $\bar{c}$ for a particular ejection requires the E_i, L_i values (see Equations 1 and 2) to be recomputed along the route [5]. Therefore in order to speed up the process several pruning strategies have been developed. The first strategy is trivial - by storing the contemporary best cost ejection all the ejections with costs higher than this ejection can be ignored. The second strategy is based on two trivial observations: (i) if a rotation is a subset of an unfeasible rotation (in terms of allowing $\bar{c}$ to be inserted after the ejection) it is also unfeasible and (ii) if a rotation is a superset of a feasible rotation it is feasible and has higher cost than that rotation. In both of these cases thus the corresponding rotations can be pruned. The mentioned strategies provide a significant speedup of the rotation process. However we argue that significant saving could be achieved by introducing concepts of interesting temporal/spatial neighborhoods to the overall negotiation process that would enable to limit the number of considered routes and insertion slots within this and also the other phases of the negotiation process to only the heuristically identified interesting neighborhoods.

5   Experimental Validation

The experiments were carried out using the two well known benchmarks of Homberger and Solomon [27,11]. The Solomon's set consists of 56 problem instances with 100 customers each, while the extended Homberger's provides for additional 5 sets of 60 instances with 200, 400, 600, 800 and 1000 customers respectively sharing otherwise the same basic attributes as the Solomon's problems. Thus for each instance size there are 6 instance types provided — the R1, R2, RC1, RC2, C1, and C2 type, each with a slightly different topology and time windows properties. For C1 and C2 types the customer locations are grouped in clusters, unlike the R1 and R2 classes where the customers are randomly placed.

Table 2. Comparison with previous agent-based VRPTW algorithms

Set	CNV		Absolute (relative) error			
	Nagata			*Agents*		
	[24]	*Fisher* [10]	*Leong* [18]	*Kalina* [12]	*Kalina* [13]	*Presented*
100	405	31 (7.7%)			25 (6.2%)	3 (0.7%)
100-R1	143		30 (21.0%)		11 (7.7%)	2 (1.4%)
200-1000	10,304			573 (5.6%)	331 (3.2%)	24 (0.2%)
All	10,709				240 (2.2%)	27 (0.3%)

The RC1 and RC2 instance types combine the previous two types with a mix of both random and clustered locations. The C1, R1 and RC1 also differ from C2, R2 and RC2 in terms of the scheduling horizon, the former having a shorter horizon resulting in routes of about 10 customers on the average, the latter having a longer horizon providing for routes of around 50 customers.

The presented results correspond to the Travel Time Savings [13] local planning strategy being used by the individual vehicles and a $k_{max} = 3$ setting for the maximal rotation size.

5.1   Overall Solution Quality Analysis

The performance of the algorithm in terms of the primary optimization criteria is illustrated by Table 1. The results are listed for alternative subsets from the experimental data identified by the first column, expressed using the previously discussed cumulative number of vehicles (CNV) metric. The "100" subset corresponds to the Solomon's benchmark while the "200–1000" rows denote alternative sizes within the Homberger's benchmark. The "All" row lists the overall result over both benchmarks. The second column lists the CNV achieved by [24] representing the currently best known overall results. The rest of the columns correspond to the absolute and relative errors in terms of CNV for various settings for the *rotationLimit* parameter, with the N denoting the size of the instance for the setting within the last column.

The Table 2 further presents the comparison of the algorithm to the previous comparable agent-based algorithms. The notation is similar as with the previous table with "100-R1" corresponding to the R1-type problems from the Solomon's benchmark and the 200–1000 row denoting the complete Homberger's benchmark. Note that to our knowledge these are the only comparable results presented by the previous agent-based VRPTW studies addressing at least specific subsets of problems from the two benchmarks otherwise widely used within the OR community.

In the most complex setting the algorithm was able to match the best known solutions in 90.7% of all tested problem instances, resulting in an overall relative error of 0.3%. Also importantly, the algorithm significantly outperforms the

Table 3. Average runtimes for individual instance sizes

Size	Lim [19]	Prescott-Gagnon [25]	Nagata [24]	*Presented*
100	39 min	192.5 min	25 min	9 min
200	93 min	265 min	20.5 min	67 min
400	296 min	445 min	81 min	345 min
600	647 min	525 min	80.4 min	615 min
800	1269 min	645 min	138 min	1253 min
1000	1865 min	810 min	186 min	1765 min
CPU	P4-2.8G	OPT-2.4G	OPT-2.4G	K8-2.3G

comparable previously presented agent-based algorithms over the comparable problem subsets.

The effect of the proposed ejection based ROTATE method is clearly illustrated. The method is based on a powerful search diversification criteria using the rotation counters $c.rts, c \in C$ to express the measure of difficulty of feasibly allocating individual customers. Considering the most complex setting with the *rotationLimit* parameter being linearly proportional to the size of the problem instance the performance of the algorithm is consistent across alternative instance sizes. This further supports the efficiency of the proposed method with respect to the existing traditional centralized algorithms. The difference in performance over the Solomon's 100 customer instances is arguably due to the fact that over the smaller benchmark the competing algorithms (that are typically not computationally bound) often use a non-proportionally long running times, as also illustrated by Table 3.

5.2   Runtime and Convergence Analysis

The comparison in terms of runtime with the traditional VRPTW algorithms is presented by Table 3. The listed values correspond to the average runtime for individual instance sizes. The abbreviations in the "CPU" row correspond to AMD Opteron 2.4GHz, Pentium 4 2.8GHz and AMD K8 2.4GHz processors.

The results show that the convergence of the presented algorithm is significantly worse than in case of the best compared traditional algorithm [24] as outlined by the increasing gap between the runtimes for bigger instance sizes. Note also, that the runtimes listed for the compared algorithm include addressing also the secondary travel time optimization criteria.

As already mentioned, we argue that this is primarily due to the fact that the negotiation semantic adopted by the SQUEEZE and SHAKE methods is very simple. When the currently processed customer $\bar{c}$ cannot be feasible allocated to the emergent solution σ the solution is *rotated* until all affected customers can be *squeezed* in. The SQUEEZE method is based on performing simple customer relocations between the routes. However, at this stage of the solving process, the solution σ is already tightly constrained and the chance of modifying it significantly using the simple negotiation semantic is correspondingly as most possible relocations are rendered unfeasible due the time-window or capacity constraints. Thus the number of necessary rotations grows dramatically.

In comparison, the *sqeeze* method employed by the compared traditional centralized algorithm [24] corresponds to a much more sophisticated local search procedure. Apart from customer relocations several other moves are considered. Most significantly, also the unfeasible moves are considered and a specific cost function is introduced driving the search process corresponding to the *level of unfeasibility* of the underlying intermediate solution. Thus the chance of allocating the customers affected by the individual rotations into the tightly constrained solution is higher, resulting in significantly less rotations being performed.

6   Conclusion

Within this paper we introduce an efficient agent-based algorithm for the VRPTW. The algorithm is based on coordinating the fleet of autonomously planning vehicles within an abstract global coordination framework based on agent negotiation. The main contribution of the paper is the extension of the used negotiation semantic. Core to the novel semantic is the introduction of the ROTATE and SQUEEZE methods, enabling the algorithm to efficiently backtrack in situations where the previous algorithms failed. Due to the clear separation between the local planning and the global coordination the presented framework can be easily adopted to (i) incorporate typical real-word extensions of the problem and to (ii) solve a variety of task allocation and scheduling problems in general, further supporting the significance of this study.

The performance of the resulting algorithm is evaluated using the relevant widely-used benchmarks known from the OR literature. A comparison the traditional centralized algorithms is presented in terms of algorithm's performance and convergence. The algorithm equals the best-known solutions in 90.7% of all considered problem instances with an average relative error of 0.3%. Also, a comparison to the previous comparable agent-based algorithms is presented revealing that the algorithm significantly outperforms these algorithms.

The coordination solving process is discussed in detail. Promising research opportunities were identified in: (i) introducing more complex negotiation semantics within the SQUEEZE method enabling for recovering feasibility of intermediate infeasible solutions and (ii) exploiting the potential of the algorithm by adapting it to complex problem variants by introducing real-world relevant constraints to the local planning strategy — or pitting it against different task allocation and scheduling problems.

Acknowledgements. This effort was supported by the Grant Agency of the CTU in Prague, grant No. SGS12/188/OHK3/3T/13, the Ministry of Education, Youth and Sports of the Czech Republic, grant No. LD12044 and the Centre of Applied Cybernetics III, Competence Centre funded by TACR, grant No. TE01020197.

References

1. Bachem, A., Hochstättler, W., Malich, M.: The simulated trading heuristic for solving vehicle routing problems. Technical report, Discrete Applied Mathenatics (1996)
2. Brafman, R.I., Domshlak, C.: From one to many: Planning for loosely coupled multi-agent systems. In: Proceedings of the International Conference on Automated Planning and Scheduling (ICAPS), pp. 28–35 (2008)
3. Bräysy, O., Gendreau, M.: Vehicle routing problem with time windows, part I route construction and local search algorithms. Transportation Science 39(1), 104–118 (2005)
4. Bräysy, O., Gendreau, M.: Vehicle routing problem with time windows, part II metaheuristics. Transportation Science 39(1), 119–139 (2005)
5. Campbell, A.M., Savelsbergh, M.: Efficient insertion heuristics for vehicle routing and scheduling problems. Transportation Science 38, 369–378 (2004)
6. Dan, Z., Cai, L., Zheng, L.: Improved multi-agent system for the vehicle routing problem with time windows. Tsinghua Science Technology 14(3), 407–412 (2009)
7. Davidsson, P., Henesey, L., Ramstedt, L., Törnquist, J., Wernstedt, F.: An analysis of agent-based approaches to transport logistics. Transportation Research Part C: Emerging Technologies 13(4), 255–271 (2005)
8. Davis, R., Smith, R.G.: Negotiation as a metaphor for distributed problem solving. Artificial Intelligence 20, 63–109 (1983)
9. Desaulniers, G., Lessard, F., Hadjar, A.: Tabu search, partial elementarity, and generalized k-path inequalities for the vehicle routing problem with time windows. Transportation Science 42(3), 387–404 (2008)
10. Fischer, K., Müller, J.P., Pischel, M.: Cooperative transportation scheduling: an application domain for dai. Journal of Applied Artificial Intelligence 10, 1–33 (1995)
11. Gehring, H., Homberger, J.: A two-phase hybrid metaheuristic for the vehicle routing problem with time windows. European Journal of Operational Research 162(1), 220–238 (2005)
12. Kalina, P., Vokřínek, J.: Parallel solver for vehicle routing and pickup and delivery problems with time windows based on agent negotiation. In: 2012 IEEE Conference on Systems, Man, and Cybernetics (SMC), pp. 1558–1563 (2012)
13. Kalina, P., Vokřínek, J., Mařík, V.: The art of negotiation: Developing efficient agent-based algorithms for solving vehicle routing problem with time windows. In: Mařík, V., Lastra, J.L.M., Skobelev, P. (eds.) HoloMAS 2013. LNCS, vol. 8062, pp. 187–198. Springer, Heidelberg (2013)
14. Kohout, R., Erol, K.: In-time agent-based vehicle routing with a stochastic improvement heuristic. In: 11th Conference on Innovative Applications of Artificial Intelligence. AAAI/MIT Press (1999)
15. Komenda, A., Novák, P., Pěchouček, M.: Domain-independent multi-agent plan repair. Journal of Network and Computer Applications (in print, 2013)
16. Komenda, A., Vokrinek, J., Cap, M., Pechoucek, M.: Developing multiagent algorithms for tactical missions using simulation. IEEE Intelligent Systems 28(1), 42–49 (2013)
17. Komenda, A., Vokřínek, J., Pěchouček, M.: Plan representation and execution in multi-actor scenarios by means of social commitments. Web Intelligence and Agent Systems 9(2), 123–133 (2011)
18. Leong, H.W., Liu, M.: A multi-agent algorithm for vehicle routing problem with time window. In: Proceedings of the 2006 ACM Symposium on Applied Computing, SAC 2006, pp. 106–111. ACM, New York (2006)

19. Lim, A., Zhang, X.: A two-stage heuristic with ejection pools and generalized ejection chains for the vehicle routing problem with time windows. INFORMS Journal on Computing 19(3), 443–457 (2007)
20. Liu, F.-H., Shen, S.-Y.: The fleet size and mix vehicle routing problem with time windows. Operational Research Society 50, 721–732 (1999)
21. Lu, Q., Dessouky, M.M.: A new insertion-based construction heuristic for solving the pickup and delivery problem with hard time windows. European Journal of Operational Research 175, 672–687 (2005)
22. Moscato, P.: On evolution, search, optimization, genetic algorithms and martial arts: Towards memetic algorithms. Technical Report C3P Report 826, California Institute of Technology (1989)
23. Nagata, Y.: Edge assembly crossover for the capacitated vehicle routing problem. In: Cotta, C., van Hemert, J. (eds.) EvoCOP 2007. LNCS, vol. 4446, pp. 142–153. Springer, Heidelberg (2007)
24. Nagata, Y., Bräysy, O., Dullaert, W.: A penalty-based edge assembly memetic algorithm for the vehicle routing problem with time windows. Comput. Oper. Res. 37(4), 724–737 (2010)
25. Prescott-Gagnon, E., Desaulniers, G., Rousseau, L.-M.: A branch-and-price-based large neighborhood search algorithm for the vehicle routing problem with time windows. Netw. 54(4), 190–204 (2009)
26. Ren, Y., Dessouky, M., Ordóñez, F.: The multi-shift vehicle routing problem with overtime. Comput. Oper. Res. 37(11), 1987–1998 (2010)
27. Solomon, M.M.: Algorithms for the vehicle routing and scheduling problems with time window constraints. Operations Research 35, 254–265 (1987)
28. Vokřínek, J., Komenda, A., Pěchouček, M.: Abstract architecture for task-oriented multi-agent problem solving. IEEE Transactions on Systems, Man, and Cybernetics, Part C: Applications and Reviews 41(1), 31–40 (2011)
29. Wang, F., Tao, Y., Shi, N.: A survey on vehicle routing problem with loading constraints. In: Proceedings of the 2009 International Joint Conference on Computational Sciences and Optimization, CSO 2009, vol. 2, pp. 602–606. IEEE Computer Society, Washington, DC (2009)

Designing a Multiagent System
for Course-Offering Determination

Fuhua Lin[1] and Wu Chen[2]

[1] School of Computing and Information System, Athabasca University
Alberta, Canada
oscarl@athabascau.ca
[2] Long View Systems, Alberta, Canada
william.chen@lvs1.com

Abstract. This paper describes the design of a multiagent system that facilitates course-offering decision making for a program in an institution. We model course-offering determination for upcoming semesters as a multi-winner election with exogenous constraints that is a problem of computational social choice in multiagent systems, which has rarely been considered. We propose a practical and effective approach to solving the problem, which is based on Contract-Net Protocol, Single Transferable Voting, and Monotonic Concession Protocol. We describe the goal model, agent behavior models, and the interaction protocols of the system through using the Gaia role model methodology, Tropos strategic actor diagram, Pseudo-code algorithms, and Agent Unified Modeling Language sequence diagram. The effectiveness of the approach and the implemented system has been showed with the initial experimental results.

Keywords: multiagent systems, agent-oriented software engineering, course-offering determination, and voting.

1   Introduction

Course offering determination (COD) can be defined as deciding on what courses of an academic program in an institution will be offering for the upcoming one or more semesters. There are many factors like the historic data in enrollments, budget and staffing constraints, which the university administration needs to take into account in order to provide a list of offering courses. A poorly designed course offering schedule could lead to a low enrollment to the program, delayed graduation, and unsatisfied students. Students in degree programs have various course selection preferences and priorities. A department of an academic institution may not be able to offer all courses in a program every semester, especially under contemporary fiscal and staffing constraints. Some courses could be only arranged every other semester or even less frequently. In the current course offering workflow, after a course delivery schedule for a new semester becomes available as the registration period is approaching, the student can select courses to be taken in the coming semester. The competing or even

G. Boella et al. (Eds.): PRIMA 2013, LNAI 8291, pp. 165–180, 2013.

adversarial goals of students and the department as well as the mutability of those goals indicate that COD is a complex constraint-satisfaction problem. Effective COD permits the efficient assignment of limited resources like faculty, labs, and classrooms while satisfying the desires of most students.

The multiagent system (MAS) approach [1] allows the representation of every principal in the system as a single autonomous agent with unique goals and permits decision-making based on the preferences of multiple agents [2]. The MAS approach is used to solve the COD problem because it has the following characteristics: (1) its optimal solution can change during calculation; (2) The relation between a user and the scheduling system lasts for a long period of time, which features a high degree of repetition, and may count for the possibility of learning by feedback; (3) The course scheduling is time consuming; (4) The process of scheduling for course-offering involves different parties, e.g. program administrators and students; (5). Program administrators consider job markets and the unpredictable nature of preferences students, which generate the need in course scheduling to adapt fast and flexibly to environmental variables and their changes.

Since the goals of the students and program administrators are different, therefore there are conflicts of interests between them, these conflicts should be resolved in a fair cooperative decision making manner. The main question of COD is:

What course offering determination strategy of a program in an institution maximizes the satisfaction of the students and the enrollment of the courses within budget?

In this research, we model the COD problem as a *multi-agent constraint resource allocation problem* and design a mechanism to identify optimal solutions through using voting and agent negotiation. The system is expected to solve the problem in optimization and flexibility in a fair and rational way, balancing the competing needs of academic requirements, economics and student preferences, and considering the usability issues for all participants. This paper formally describes the design of the system for COD using Agent-Oriented Analysis and Design [3] and Agent-Oriented Software Engineering (AOSE)[4].

This paper is organized as follows. Following a brief survey of relevant published research, Section 3 will describe the goal model, scenarios, and interfaces between the system and its environment. This is followed by a session (Section 4) detailing the system architecture, particularly the various software agents and their roles and responsibilities. Section 5 describes with a detailed discussion of the voting and negotiating protocols used by the agents in solving the course-offering determination problem. Section 6 presents the implementation and initial experimental results. The paper ends with the conclusion and future work.

2   Literature Review

The majority of Artificial Intelligence applications to education address pedagogical tasks related to tutoring and personalized instruction, such as [5-6]. Significantly fewer publications are related to the decision-making or administrative tasks in education such as school choice [7], academic advising [8], and course timetable scheduling [9]. The MAS approach has proven an important and effective framework for intelligent educational systems, for example iHelp [10], program planning [11], time table scheduling [12], and personalized study planning [13]. To the best knowledge of the authors, there is no significant extant work on solving the COD problem.

Voting procedures focus on the aggregation of individuals' preferences to produce collective decisions. There are many different voting rules; many of which are defined in the survey paper by Brams and Fishburn (2002) [14]. Lang (2007) considered voting and aggregation rules in the case where voters' preferences have a common preferential independence structure, and addressed the issue of decomposing a voting rule or an aggregation function following a linear order over variables [15]. Conitzer (2010) explained voting rules in more detail [16]. Plurality voting is one of the most common rules. In this scheme, the alternative with the greatest number of "first place votes" wins. Plurality voting does not require that voters provide rankings. This feature seems to be an advantage; however, this "elicitation advantage" means that it fails to account for relative voter preferences for any alternative other than its top choice. Other schemes produce winners that are more sensitive to relative preferences, among them are Positional scoring rules, Maxmin fairness, Copeland, Maximin, and Bucklin [17]. An obstacle to the widespread use of voting schemes that require full rankings is the informational and cognitive burden imposed on voters, and concomitant ballot complexity.

In this paper, we first model COD decision settings, e.g. modeling students as a group of self-interested agents, expressing their preferences [18] and then use a group decision-making protocol --- voting theory [19] to aggregate the preferences of the different participants toward a single joint decision. Single Transferable Vote (STV) is a staged procedure [19]. In practice, voters need not be required to rank all candidates. It has been shown that STV, in comparison with other voting schemes in actual use, is computationally resistant to manipulation [20]. The use of multiple fractional votes also provides another advantage – it makes the systems sufficiently computationally complex that it is resistant to manipulation [20] in the way that whole vote plurality systems might be [21].

Finally, we show how the negotiation techniques [22] is used to generate a set of course offerings for the next term that reflects those preferences, academic requirements, and economic necessities to mutual benefit between the department and the students.

COD is a multiagent resource allocation issue [23]. Thus it is needed to devise a protocol for it. There are two approaches for it: centralized such as combinatorial auctions [24] and distributed, e.g. Contract-Net Protocol (CNP) [25]. We can not directly implement COD system using auction-based resource allocation mechanism as the winner determination mechanism between auction based resource allocation and what we expect in the COD system is different. Auction based resource allocation is seeking for the highest price bid to win the resource. The winner is a buyer with the highest price bidding. In the COD system, however, the winner is a course (a resource from the seller) that has the most preferred enrolment from the students (buyers). CNP is mainly for solving the problem of distributing tasks to appropriate agents to execute the tasks for efficiency in general. It includes a negotiation protocol for interaction between agents like immediate response, direct contracts, request and information message, and node available messages. It can be used to form a team through mutual selection, exchange information in a structured way to converge on assignments. In this research, we use it as a viable and flexible coordination mechanism for planning and enacting the collective course-offering decision making tasks.

3   Requirement Analysis

COD is concerned with the optimal assignment of the courses for a specific academic semester by program administration to meet the needs of students within budget and other resource constraints. Students in degree programs frequently have to balance personal career objectives, preferences, and financial and temporal constraints against degree requirements, course availability, and course inter-relationships. These and other constraints make the COD problem a complex one. The problem is made more complex by the fact that the constraints within which course offering determination is performed are fluid: students change their goals or are unsuccessful in completing prerequisite courses; faculty go on leave or modify research priorities; funding is awarded or withdrawn; other programs or institutions reserve or release facilities for instructional use. The fundamental business need of the research is for a program to identify those courses with sufficient interest to support the economics of offering them. To offer an optimal course list, information on learner needs, constraints, and preferences must be considered. To facilitate collaboration among learners, it can be desirable to allow students to share personal preferences and goals as well as create various learning communities/social networks during program study.

3.1   Goal Model

Students and program administrators have different goals. From the perspective of the student, course selection and planning is important in current educational environments. Selection of the 'right' course(s) can be a high-risk decision-making process because the cumulative effect of a series of choices made on successive semesters or quarters may impact their college major selection, their ability to take additional course work, their graduation date or even their career direction and future employment opportunities. From the perspective of educational providers, effective course offering determination permits the efficient assignment of limited resources like faculty, laboratories, and classrooms while at the same time satisfying the needs and desires of most students. Consequently, there is an inherent tension between the needs of the student body and the available resources of the educational provider. Fig. 1 illustrates the goal model of the system proposed consisting of Students and Program Administrator. The goal of a program student is to "complete a program" while the goal of a program administrator is to "determine a course-offering schedule". The goal "complete a program" is associated with a quality goal "study desirable courses and complete a program efficiently". The goal "determine course offering schedule" is associated with "offer courses cost-effectively." The goal "complete a program" has the subgoals "select preferred courses" and "express preferences." The goal "determine course offering schedule" has the subgoals "aggregate students preferences", "calculate cost and revenue", and "decide courses to be offered".

The competing goals between students and resource providers mean that COD is a complex dynamic constraint-optimization problem where the optimal solution can change during calculation. Consequently, the use of a multi-agent system that continually re-evaluates the current constraint state as reported by constituent agents in order to maintain an appropriate solution plan as the environment changes.

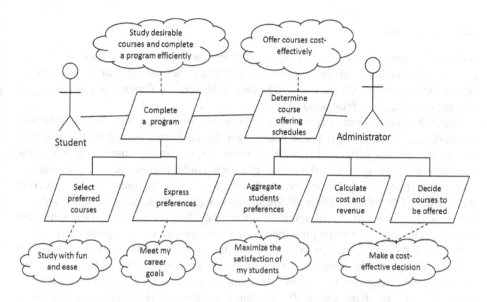

Fig. 1. The goal model for a course-offering decision support system

3.2   Agents

We designed a MAS system that consists of an administrator (AD) agent, a group of student (SA) agents, and a student representative (SR) agent. This correlates with an academic program, where a course scheduling process is initiated by having the program administrator determine the priority of courses available in the program, based on expressed student needs, preferences, and goals. The agents have distinct areas of concern and intent, but collectively interact to generate a set of recommendations for courses to be offered that will be satisfactory to most students while fitting within the operational limitations of the offering program. A SA agent has three major responsibilities: (1) representing the student principal's interest in interactions with other agents; (2) generating plans for their principals; and (3) generating course selection requests for their principals. A SR agent is instantiated for any identifiable student group with shared interests and resources. Typically, this would be one per academic program. The SR agent has the following major responsibilities: (1) Managing voting among student agents, ensuring fairness. (2) Representing the student body to other agents, particularly the AD agent. The AD agent is the representative of the program administrations calculating the needs of the academic department as determined by factors such as course delivery policies, budget, and resource availability. It is responsible to: (1) Provide executive control and oversight for the system; (2) Enforce resource and other course availability constraints; (3) Inform other agents of those constraints; (4) Negotiate with the SR agent to provide an optimal set of course offering recommendations to the offering academic program.

3.3   Scenarios

Within this system, for each semester, before the course registration starts, the program administrator of the department delegates the task of initial selection to his/her AD agent, which performs this task using course dependency graphs, past offerings, and departmental obligations.

The AD agent collects requirement information from the program administrator, which determines a set of required courses for the next term as well as the proposed budget for course delivery in the next term. At the same time, each SA agent generates a study plan based on the program study preferences of the student, identifies *"ready-to-take"* courses of the student, and captures course selection preferences of the student. Once all SA agents complete the actions mentioned above, they send their votes to the SR agent. And then the SR agent aggregates the votes and generates the set of all ranked preference ordering over courses as a group decision.

Once the AD agent has this information, it initiates a one-to-one agent negotiation with the SR agent. The negotiation then proceeds iteratively between the two agents, the AD agent attempting to maximize the course enrolments and minimize delivery overhead, and to maximize staff efficiency of the offering, and the SR agent attempting to maximize the availability of courses desired or needed by students to complete their programs.

4   Architectural Design

In the current model, there are three roles coming into play in COD system –SA agents, SR agent, and AD agent. As shown in the Table 1 below, the main activities of SA Agent is to present students' interest, generate a study plan, and select course they want for vote. They read the interests from the students and select courses based on the student's interest and offering course list. The sequence of activities of SA agent is the more than one time of repeat on PresentInterest, GeneratePlan, CourseSelection, GenerateVotes, and CalculateDisutilitySA. The constraint on these actions is the number of selected course must be less than or equal the total number of interest presented courses.

Please note that unlike obligations in normative framework refer to the consequence of some action, responsibilities in Gaia methodology [3] we use in this paper is one of attributes of a role and they determine functionality of an agent. Responsibilities include liveness properties and safety properties. In order to realize responsibilities, a role has a set of permissions. In Gaia, resources are thought of as relating to the information or knowledge the agent has. That is, in order to carry out a role, an agent will typically be able to 'access', 'modify' or 'generate' certain information. This specification defines two types of permissions for SA agent: read, change, and generate. It says that the agent carrying out the role has permission to *access* the value Presentinterests, and has permission to both *change* (*read and modify*) the value CourseSelection. Also, the role is the producer of Plan, Votes, and Disutility.

Table 1. SA Agent role model

Role Schema	SA Agent
Description	SA Agent represents the student principal's interest, generates plans, and requests course selection for their principals.
Protocols & Activities	PresentInterest, GeneratePlan, CourseSelection CalculateDisutilitySA(), GenerateVotes()
Permissions	Reads Presentinterests // all interested courses presented GeneratePlan // retrieve info from the student study plan Changes CourseSelection //select courses from the list GenerateVotes() // generate vote count on the course CalculateDisutilitySA() // Calculate the SA agent Disutility
Responsibilities	Liveness: SA Agent = (PresentInterest.GeneratePlan.CourseSelection. Safety: GenerateVotes. CalculateDisutilitySA)+ Number_of_SelectedCourse <= Number_of_InterestPresente.

The role schemas of AD agent and SR agent are similar to the SA agent role model.

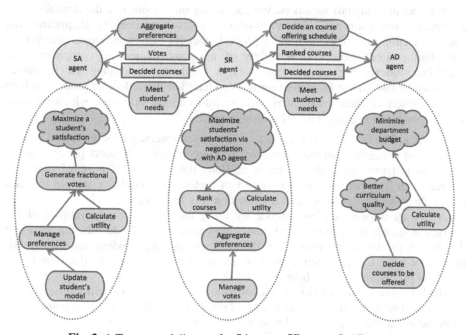

Fig. 2. A Tropos goal diagram for SA agent, SR agent, & AD agent

Three actors are identified: SA agent, SR agent, and AD agent. Fig. 2 illustrates a Tropos (http://www.troposproject.org/) goal diagram for three types of agents in the system proposed. Two dependencies are modeled as goal dependencies: **Aggregate preferences** and **Decide an course offering schedule**. In a goal dependency, one actor depends on another actor for achieving a goal. Four dependencies are modeled as resource dependencies: vote, decided courses, ranked courses, and decided courses. The goals of the three types of agents are decomposed into some subgoals. Soft goals like **Maximize a student's satisfaction**, **Better curriculum quality** are considered, which may contribute to the achievement of a goal or prevent its achievement. The soft goals are represented as clouds in the figure.

5   Detailed Design

In order to design and implement a system that provides support for COD, there are a number of critical pieces that must be assembled into an integrated whole: (1) An effective way of collecting and representing student preferences with regard to their current and future studies as well as their plans following graduation; (2) A means of modeling relationships and interdependencies amongst courses, programs of study and learning objectives; (3) An efficient and fair means for balancing the competing desires and needs of students; and (4) A fair means of apportioning the available faculty, facility and funding resources of the program, faculty or school providing education.

5.1   Preference Models of Student Agent

Our initial investigation was through interviews and anecdotal discussions with current students and staff members. We had strong indications that the desirability of a particular course was not independent of other course's availability. It appeared that course selection preferences are more properly thought of as conditional preferences [18]. Furthermore, there were a variety of ways and degrees of complexity that individual students might express the way in which they determine which courses they want to take in the upcoming term. We identified three distinct models of how students described their preferences with regard to course offerings, which we have termed: *precedence*, *grouping*, and *progression* [25].

Precedence. The first model, precedence, simply referenced a most-preferred course, a next-most preferred, and etc. However, after a comparatively short list of courses, the students lapse into a don't-care state along the lines of "if none of those are offered, then it doesn't matter". This sort of preference model is common in cases where the student only plans on taking one or a very few courses.

A SA agent generates precedence by using the degrees of desirability of the courses in his/her study plan prior to the voting process [8]. To do this, the SA agent determines the list of all courses in the program that that student can legally and preferably take, C_{ready}, which consist of all incomplete courses of the student for which all pre-requisites have been completed.

The SA agent receives a list of courses from the AD agent that will not be offered, $C_{not\_to\_offer}$. The SA agent receives a list of courses that will already be recommended from the AD agent, $C_{recommended}$. These are similarly removed from the "legal" course set –but are treated as though they will be offered for purposes of other decisions.

Thus, the SA agent automatically generates $C_{precedence}$ by removing $C_{not\_to\_offer}$ and $C_{recommened}$: $C_{precedence} = C_{ready} - C_{not\_to\_offer} - C_{recommended}$ and then the elements in $C_{precedence}$ are ranked by the degrees of *desirability* and shown in the *precedence* interface so that the student can modify them if wish. It is represented as

$$C_{prededence} = \{(C_i, w_i): w_1 \geq w_2 \geq ... \geq w_n, c_i \in C\}.$$

here, $c_1 \succ c_2 \succ ... \succ c_n$. Here C is the set of all courses in the system. Integer n is the number of all elements in $C_{precedence}$.

Grouping. This model was more common amongst students planning on taking several courses. With it, students express their desires in terms of sets - a group of courses is desired en masse, and if not all courses are available, and then the remainder are less desirable. *Grouping* = $\{G_i \subset C, 1 \leq i \leq l\} (l \geq 0)$. We use an array to represent the grouping preference: $A_{grouping} = \{ (g_{ij})_{nxn}: g_{ij} = 1$, if c_i and c_j are in the same group, otherwise 0; $g_{ii} = 0\}$.

Progressions. Finally, there is the case of those students that plan their program *progressions* sequentially – their desire is to complete some set of courses, then progress to another set, etc, which we have termed the progression model. This sort of preference closely approximates the way in which academic departments model academic progression and is common in the case where students are in a full-time degree program or wish to systematically complete a program. This progression model is also most similar to that expressed in the CP-net [18].

We use a directed acyclic graph (DAG), $P = (C, A)$, to represent the progression model. Set C represents all courses in the program. Set A consists of arcs. An arc $e = (c_1, c_2)$ is considered to be directed from c_1 to c_2; c_2 is called the *head* and c_1 is called the *tail* of the arc; c_2 is said to be a *direct successor* of c_1, and c_1 is said to be a *direct predecessor* of c_2. If a path made up of one or more successive arcs leads from c_1 to c_2, then c_2 is said to be a *successor* of c_1, and c_1 is said to be a *predecessor* of c_2.

For implementation, we use an array to represent P:

$$A_{progression} = (p_{ij})_{nxn}. \quad p_{ij} = 1, \text{ if } (c_i, c_j) \in A, \text{ otherwise } p_{ij} = 0.$$

Let $\vec{T}_{taken} = (t_1, t_2, ..., t_n)$ represent the status of the courses about whether or not the student has completed. $t_i = 0$ means that c_i has not been taken while $t_i = 1$ means that c_i has been taken and completed by the student. Then $\vec{T}_{taken} \in A_{progression}$ represents the readiness of the courses in terms of the progression preference of the student. That is, if $r_j \triangleq \sum_{i=1}^{n} t_i \times p_{ij} \geq 1$ then c_j is ready to take according to student's progression preference.

5.2   Generating Fractional Votes by Student Agents

Based on the preferences expressed by the principal on one or more of our preference models, the SA agent automatically generates a set of fractional votes for each round of an election. From the precedence set, the highest *ranked* course that can be preferably and legally taken is added. From the *grouping* interface, all courses from groups in which all member courses can legally be taken are added to the list.

From the *progression* interface, all legal courses that are either in the first block of a progression or whose predecessor block contains only courses that have already been taken are added to the list. Each of the courses on the list then gets a relative fraction of the agent's single vote for that round, with repeat courses getting a proportionately higher portion of the vote. The vote is recalculated for each round, and can be affected by the results of previous votes.

For the sake of illustration, let's consider a real case. Suppose $C = \{c_i\}_1^{10}$. Let us assume that a student has previously completed c_1 and c_2. According to curriculum checking, could legally take c_3, c_4, c_5, not including c_7. For the coming semester, the student expressed the following preference: *Precedence:* $\{(c_3, .88), (c_4, .56), (c_5, .55)\}$; *Grouping:* $\{c_3, c_4\}, \{c_5, c_7, c_9\}$; *Progression:* $\{c_1\} \rightarrow \{c_2\} \rightarrow \{c_3, c_7\}$. From the precedence expressed, c_3 would be added with a weight 0.88, c_4 with a weight 0.56, c_5 with a weight 0.55 to that student's vote list. From the groups identified, c_3 and c_4 would be added to the vote list, as the first group can be fulfilled. However, no entries from the second group would be added, as c_7 is not legal (in this case, the status of c_9 is irrelevant). Finally, from the progression, c_3 would be added to the vote list, however c_7 would not be added until it is legal later. Each of the courses on the list then gets a *relative* fraction of the agent's single vote for that round, with repeat courses getting a proportionately higher portion of the vote. The total vote set for our fictitious student is thus: $\{(c_3, 1), (c_3, 1), (c_4, 1), (c_3, .88), (c_4, .56), (c_5, .55)\}$. *Let* v_i represent the fractional vote on course c_i. The student's vote is then rationalized into the votes as follows: $v_3 = (1+1+0.88)/(1+1+1+0.88+0.56+0.55) = 0.58$; $c_4 = 0.31$, $c_5 = 0.11$. The algorithm for generating fractional votes is listed as follows:

```
ALGORITHM: Generate Fractional Votes
input:    C, C_precedence , A_grouping  A_progression
T_taken = (t_1, t_2, ..., t_n), course completion status vector
R = (r_1, r_2, ..., r_n), course progression readiness vector
Returns: V = {v_i: 1 ≤ i ≤ n}
begin
generate C_precedence;
retrieve A_grouping and A_progression
    for  i = 1 to n do // consider "Precedence Model"
          if c_i in C_precedence then   v_i ← w_i ; end if
    end for
    for i = 1 to n do   // consider "Grouping model"
          if not(c_i in C_precedence) then
                for j = 1 to n do  g_ij ← 0; g_ji ← 0; end for
          for i = 1 to n do
                for j = 1 to n do
                if g_ij = 1 then v_i ← v_i +1; end if
            end for     end for
        for   j = 1 to n do// consider "Progression Model"
                for i = 1 to n do   r_j ← t_i•p_ij + r_j; end for
                if (t_j = 0) and (t_j = 1) then v_j ← v_j + 1 end if;
    end for
end
```

5.3   Interaction Protocols

We use an Agent Unified Modeling Language (AUML) (www.auml.org) sequence diagram (see Fig. 3) to depict the interaction protocols for coordination, voting, and agent negotiation.

Determining Negotiable Courses: First, AD agent starts the process by sending a message to the administrator once the registration period is approaching to acquire the must-to-offer list C_0, the must-no-to-offer list C_{-1}, and maximum number of courses that can be offered n_0. The administrator determines them through using the past experience, the course dependency, and the department obligations.

At the same time, the students then will develop their study plans according to the initial course lists, study preferences, ready-to-take courses, and course selection preferences.

The AD agent determines a list of negotiable courses C'' as the first proposal. And then AD agent will send $C'' = C_0/C_{-1}$ to all SA agents. And then the student agents will notify all students to register courses from the initial course offering list $C_f \leftarrow C''$.

The AD agent computes the initial disutility U_{AD} based on the registration. It means the difference between the actual operating cost $Cost$ and the targeted budget $Cost_{ideal}$, and determine a list of negotiable courses $C' = C/(C_0 \sqcup C_{-1})$.

Voting: SR agent uses CNP to work with all SA agents to coordinate the voting and election process. The study plan of each student is passed to his/her SA agent and is used to generate precedence relation and be combined with other preferences to be turned into a fractional vote to their SR agent. SR agent aggregates the fractional votes from all SA agents and generates a set of all ranked preference ordering over the course set C', denoted as *STV-k*, through using an algorithm based on STV [19] and the number of the slots to fill, i.e. $k = n_0 - |C'|$. And then it sends the to AD agent. This allows the protocol to converge more rapidly on an acceptable solution by initially jumping by several courses before dropping down ultimately to one course at a time for the final negotiations. It also allows us to use STV more optimally, as its value is more readily apparent in elections where several candidates will be elected. AD agent sends STV-k to the administrator.

Based on a monotonic concession protocol (MCP) [22], a negotiation protocol between AD agent and SR agent to determine an optimal offering course list is developed.

For each round of agent negotiation r, AD agent proposes δA (the first round its value is $C'' \sqcup \Phi$) with its utility $U_{AD}(\delta A, r)$ while SR agent proposes $\delta S = C'' \sqcup$ *STV-k'* and computes disutility $U_{SR}(\delta A, r)$ and $U_{SR}(\delta S, r)$. The algorithm for computing U_{SR} is listed in Appendix A.

SR agent determines if $U_{SR}(\delta A, r) < U_{SR}(\delta S, r)$, which means that for SR agent offering more courses will not decrease the dissatisfaction of the students and thus does not need to add more courses. The negotiation ends. Otherwise, AD concedes and selects the first course in *STV-k*, c, and adds c to the new proposal δA, the course offering C_f list is updated. And then the student agents will notify the students to register courses from the current course offering δA. It is worthy to mention that for AD agent, due to the fact that we can not compute $U_{AD}(\delta S, r)$ without knowing the registration, we can not check if $U_{AD}(\delta A, r) > U_{AD}(\delta S, r)$ to apply standard MCP. Our approach is that if there is a need to increase some courses, we select the first course in *STV-k* and add it to new proposal δA and get the enrollments for the courses.

The AD agent computes the initial utility $U_{AD}(\delta A, r)$ based on the registration and the budget, and updates ranked negotiable courses *STV-k* with *STV-k* /{c}. The negotiation goes to the next round. For each round of the agent negotiation, AD agent needs to check if *STK-k* is empty, or $U_{AD}(\delta A, r)$ still meets a satisfied predicate AD_{sat}. $AD_{sat} = (U_{AD} <= \Delta U_{AD})$. ΔU_{AD} is a pre-set threshold. If AD_{sat} is true, the AD agent is satisfied with the current offering. Also, SR agent checks a satisfied predicate, SR_{sat} which indicates whether the aggregate disutility is less than the permitted variance $SR_{sat} = (U_{SR} <= \Delta U_{SR})$. ΔU_{SR} is a pre-set threshold. If SR_{sat} is true, the SR agent is satisfied with the current offering.

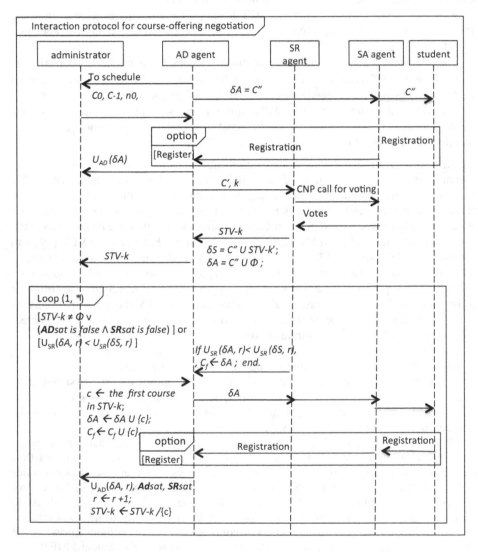

Fig. 3. AUML sequence diagram for interaction protocol of the negotiation

If A_{sat} is true and the SR agent has indicated that the last round satisfied it, the negotiation is concluded and the AD agent records the final offering list and sends it to the SA agents. If the A_{sat} is false, the negotiation will always continue. If the AD agent is satisfied, but the SR agent is unsatisfied, the negotiation will continue until the count of courses in a proposal reaches zero. In this way, the negotiation converges fairly rapidly to a set that is near the budgeted amount for the department, while trying to add courses most likely to fit into the plans of the majority of students.

6   Implementation

To evaluate the proposed approach, a prototype was implemented with JADE (http://jade.tilab.com) and Jason (http://jason.sourceforge.net/wp/), which allows simulating different scenarios by varying several parameters, such as the course number of the program, the divergence of preferences for course selection, or the must-offer courses due to emergence cases. We simulated a collection of master program students consisting of from 30 to 90 MSc in Information Systems students of Athabasca University in Canada. Fig. 4 shows a screen shot of entering student course selection preferences. Fig. 5 is an example of voting result generated from one of the experiments.

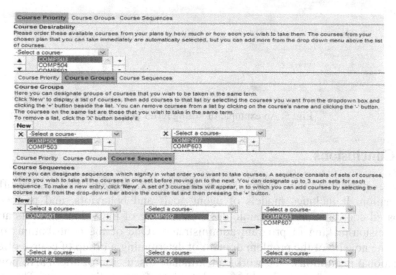

Fig. 4. A screen shot of student course selection preferences

Given that a course set $C = \{c_i\}_{i=1}^{n_c}$ to be offered in a semester in the program, the actual cost to be paid for the course offering is calculated as follows:

$$U_{AD} = |Cost(C) - Cost_{ideal}|, \quad Cost(C) = b(n_c) + r\sum_{i=1}^{n_c} h_i$$, where b is the base salary for one

course to be paid to the instructor for the course, e.g., $b = \$5000$; r is the amount of money to pay to the instructor for one student minus the course fee, e.g. $r = \$500$; h_i is the number of the students who will take course c_i for $1 \leq i \leq n_c$, and $C_{ideal} = \$75,000$.; n_c = 30, 50, 90; $C_0 = \{c_{501}, c_{503}, c_{504}, c_{601}, c_{695}\}$; $C_{-1} = \{c_{602}, c_{604}, c_{617}, c_{636}, c_{637}, c_{682}\}$; $\Delta U_{AD} = \$100$; $\Delta U_{SR} = 3$.

In Round 1: $C_1 = C_0 \cup \{c_{602}, c_{605}, c_{607}, c_{610}, c_{648}, c_{660}, c_{667}, c_{689}, c_{691}\}$. Getting h_i, $U_{AD}(C_1) = \$11500.0$. In Round 2: c_{691} is chosen in this round, with a voting result of 60. Getting $h_{691} = 64$ since it is the first course chosen, and many students have it as their first pick due to it being on many plans and not having many prerequisites. $U_{AD}(C_1) = \$15000.0$. Comparing C_{ideal}, the Administrator is still not satisfied with required courses. The SR agent is also unsatisfied with course offering as SR Weight: 10.31. After Round 3 and Round 4, in Round 5, the required 9 courses are: $c_{691}, c_{605}, c_{648}$, and c_{667}. c_{689} is chosen in this round, with a result of 2.0. $U_{AD} = \$48,000$. So the AD agent is still unsatisfied with the list. The SR agent is now satisfied with course offering. The SR agent's weight is 0.86. Negotiation concluded with a list: $C_1 = C_0 \cup \{c_{691}, c_{605}, c_{648}, c_{667}\}$. The size limit of a class is not considered.

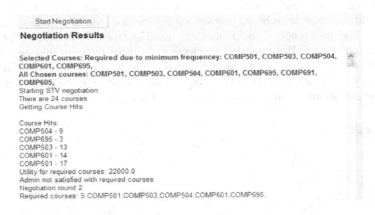

Fig. 5. An example of voting result generated

7   Conclusions

We have presented the design of a multiagent system for course-offering determination. It includes models of agent goals and behaviors, and protocols of agent-based coordination in dynamic decision making of individual students and the group decision-making of program administrators. One of the contributions of this paper is the novelty of the problem domain of determining a group of course offerings in educational institutions. The work can stimulate discussion of alternative points of view for how to solve the problem and lead to further discoveries. The second contribution of this research is the multi-agent system architecture proposed and the algorithm for the reasoning capability of the student agent, preference elicitation and inference algorithm. Finally, there is significant value to the mechanism design — the administrative agent's coordination capability to recommend suitable course offerings to departments in academic terms; in which multiple student preferences are aggregated using STV for the aggregation of multiple student preferences, the course budget of the department, and the derived cost of the courses offered. Each student's preferences are translated into fractional votes that inform a negotiation process bounded by academic and resource constraints. The future work includes more testing and deploying the system to turn it into a practical application. We will study multi-winner election problem with exogenous constraints in other application domains.

Acknowledgement. We thank anonymous reviewers for their constructive feedback, NSERC for the financial support to the research, and AJ Armstrong and Alex Newcomb for their help.

References

1. Weiss, G. (ed.): Multiagent Systems, A modern approach to distributed artificial intelligence. MIT Press (1999) ISBN 0-262-23203-0
2. Conitzer, V.: Making decisions based on the preferences of multiple agents. Comm. ACM 53(3), 84–94 (2010)
3. Wooldridge, M., Jennings, N.R., Kinny, D.: The Gaia Methodology for Agent-Oriented Analysis and Design. Journal of Autonomous Agents & Multi-Agent Systems 3, 285–312 (2000)
4. Winikoff, M., Padgham, L.: Agent-Oriented Software Engineering. In: Weiss, G. (ed.) Multiagent Systems, 2nd edn., ch. 15. MIT Press (2013)
5. Graesser, A., Chipman, P., Haynes, B., Olney, A.: AutoTutor: an intelligent tutoring system with mixed-initiative dialogue. IEEE Trans. on Education 48(4), 612–618 (2005)
6. Mitrovic, A., Ohlsson, S.: Evaluation of a constraint-based tutor for a database language. International Journal on Artificial Intelligence 10, 238–256 (1999)
7. Wilson, D.C., Leland, S., Godwin, K., Baxter, A., Levy, A., Smart, J., Najjar, N., Andaparambil, J.: SmartChoice: An Online Recommender System to Support Low-Income Families in Public School Choice. AI Magazine 30(2), 46–58 (2009)
8. Lin, F., Leung, S., Wen, D., Zhang, F., Kinshuk, McGreal, R.: e-Advisor: A Multi-agent System for Academic Advising. In: Workshop on Agent-Based Systems for Human Learning and Entertainment (ABSHLE) at Autonomous Agents and Multi-Agent Systems (AAMAS), Honolulu, Hawaii, USA (2007)
9. Oprea, M.: MAS UP-UCT: A multi-agent system for university course timetable scheduling. Inter. J. of Computers, Communications & Control II(1), 1024–1020 (2007)
10. Vassileva, J., McCalla, G., Greer, J.: Multi-Agent Multi-User Modeling In I-Help, User Model. User-Adapt. Interact., 179–210 (2003)
11. Hamdi, M.S.: MASACAD: A Multiagent-Based Approach to Information Customization. IEEE Intelligent Systems 21(1), 60–67 (2006)
12. Tariq, M., Mirza, M., Akbar, R.: Multi-agent Based University Time Table Scheduling System (MUTSS). Inter. J. of Multidisciplinary Sci. and Engg. 1(1), 33–39 (2010)
13. Vainio, A., Salmenjoki, K.: Improving Study Planning with an Agent-based System. Informatica 29, 453–459 (2005)
14. Brams, S.J., Fishburn, P.C.: Voting Procedures. In: Arrow, K.J., et al. (eds.) Handbook of Social Choice and Welfare, pp. 173–236. Elsevier (2002)
15. Lang, J.: Vote and aggregation in combinatorial domains with structured preferences. In: Proc. of the 20th Inter. Joint Conf. on AAAI, pp. 1366–1371 (2007)
16. Conitzer, V.: Making decisions based on the preferences of multiple agents. Comm. ACM 53(3), 84–94 (2010)
17. Lu, T., Boutilier, C.: Robust Approximation and Incremental Elicitation in Voting Protocols. In: Proceedings of the Twenty-Second International Joint Conference on Artificial Intelligence, IJCAI 2011, vol. 1, pp. 287–293 (2011)
18. Boutilier, C., Brafman, R.I., Domshlak, C., Hoos, H.H., Poole, D.: CP-nets: A tool for representing and reasoning with conditional ceteris paribus preference statements. J. Artificial Intelligence Research (JAIR) 21, 135–191 (2004)

19. Bartholdi, J.J., Orlin, J.B.: Single Transferable Vote Resists Strategic Voting. Social Choice and Welfare 8, 341–354 (1991)
20. Walsh, T.: An Empirical Study of the Manipulability of Single Transferable Voting. In: Proceedings of the 2010 Conference on ECAI, pp. 257–262 (2010)
21. Sandholm, T.: Vote elicitation: Complexity and strategy-proofness. In: AAAI 2002 Proceedings, pp. 392–397 (2002)
22. Rosenschein, J.S., Zlotkin, G.: Rules of Encounter: Designing Conventions for Automated Negotiation among Computers. MIT Press (1994)
23. Lin, F., Armstrong, A.J., Newcomb, A.: A MAS Approach to Course Offering Determination. In: 2012 IEEE/WIC/ACM International Conferences on Web Intelligence and Intelligent Agent Technology (WI-IAT), vol. 3, pp. 331–336 (2012)
24. Cramton, P., Shoham, Y., Steinberg, R. (eds.): Combinatorial Auctions. MIT Press (2006)
25. Smith, R.G.: The contract net protocol: High-level communication and control in a distributed problem solver. IEEE Trans. on Computers C-29(12), 1104–1113 (1980)

Appendix A

ALGORITHM CalculateDisutilitySA(C_{offer}, U_{SA})

input: C_{offer};   //current *offering list*
      $C_{student}$;//*course set that the student plans to take in the* upcoming term *in the precedence preference model.*
variables:
output: U_{SA}
$U_{SA} \leftarrow 0$;
for each course c in $C_{student}$
  if $c \in C_{offer}$ **then**
    $U_{SA} \leftarrow U_{SA} + 0$; // *The smaller is the value R, the happier is the student.*
    else $U_{SA} \leftarrow U_{SA} + 1$; **end if**
return U_{SA};

ALGORITHM CalcuateDisutilitySR(l_1, l_2, U_{SA}) // *Calculate* U_{SR} *- Collective Disutility of SR agent.*
input: $\{U_{SAi}\}$
variables: $\bar{x}$: *arithmetic mean; the average of* U_{SA}.
σ : *standard deviation of the reported* U_{SAi}. l_1, l_2 : *weights for* $\bar{x}$ *, and* σ *used to tune the contribution of each component.* $l_1 + l_2 =1$. Initially, they both are set to 0.5, which can be optimized through a machine-learning algorithm like the genetic algorithm.
for each SA_i **CalculateDisutilitySA**(C_{offer}, U_{SAi})   **end for**
$\bar{x} \leftarrow$ the average value of U_{SAi};
$\sigma \leftarrow$ *The deviation sigma* σ;
$U_{SR} \leftarrow l_1\bar{x} + l_2\sigma$;
return U_{SA} ;

A Human-Inspired Collision Avoidance Method for Multi-robot and Mobile Autonomous Robots

Fan Liu and Ajit Narayanan

Auckland University of Technology
School of Computing and Mathematical Sciences
{rliu,ajnaraya}@aut.ac.nz
http://www.aut.ac.nz

Abstract. In this paper a novel and dynamic rectangular roundabout ('rectabout') collision avoidance method based on human behaviour is presented for multiple, homogeneous, autonomous and mobile robots. The approach does not depend on priority schemes and instead involves only local views. There is therefore no need for inter-robot communication. The decentralized collision avoidance maneuver employs a virtual rectabout that allows each robot to re-plan its path. This maneuver is calculated independently by each robot involved in the possible collision. The virtual rectabout lies in the intersecting and conflicting position of two robot routes. Experimental simulations involving multi-robot systems indicate that virtual rectabouts ensure that all robots remain free of collision while attempting to follow their goal direction. Comparisons with a centralized collision detection and avoidance approach demonstrate no additional move costs. However, the advantages of rectabouts are that no inter-robot communication or centralized coordination is required, thereby cutting down significantly on communication and coordination overheads.

Keywords: Rectangular Roundabout, Decentralized Collision Avoidance, Minimum Enclosing Rectangle.

1 Introduction

Collision between multiple, autonomous robots is one of the main problems in decentralized, distributed task cooperation. The collision avoidance problem arises when the environment is dynamic and robots need to use paths to reach their destination that conflict with other robots' paths on specific moves. Decentralized collision avoidance in these situations is more challenging than centralized approaches since autonomous robots must manage their moves independently and may have only a limited capability to detect the potential risk of collision. Moreover, another problem is no communication while avoiding collisions since the true autonomy is no central coordinator and no communication between robots. A secondary problem is how to ensure that robots resume their paths after collision avoidance to still reach their goals effectively and efficiently.

G. Boella et al. (Eds.): PRIMA 2013, LNAI 8291, pp. 181–196, 2013.
© Springer-Verlag Berlin Heidelberg 2013

In this study, collision detection is inspired by studies on how human pedestrians detect possible collision, and collision avoidance is inspired by the use of roundabouts for resolving potential vehicle collisions at road intersections. When a vehicle approaches a roundabout, drivers adopt a specific set of autonomous but shared procedures for negotiating the roundabout to continue on their routes while avoiding collision with other vehicles already on the roundabout. Drivers do not require a central command and control structure or communication with each other to avoid collision. While roundabouts are concrete in the real traffic world, the temporary roundabouts used here by robots are virtual: they do not actually exist in the configuration space but do exist temporarily on the paths of each robot involved in a possible collision before disappearing from each robot's paths once collision is avoided. No other robot sees this roundabout. Because the configuration space used in our experiments can be regarded as consisting of rectangular grids, the virtual roundabout necessarily becomes straight-lined and rectangular, hence 'rectabout'. Moreover, real roundabouts can vary in size depending on various parameters such as approach speed, one-lane or multi-lane, number of roads leading to that intersection, etc. In our experiments below, all robots move at the same speed and the size of their local views will determine the size of the roundabout. The larger the local view, the further ahead the robots can plan and therefore the larger the roundabout can be to ensure a smooth deviation from a planned straight line for collision avoidance. However, for the experiments below, the local view is fixed for all robots and therefore the roundabouts are of fixed size.

A desirable roundabout collision avoidance system has to satisfy the following principles. (1) Flexibility in size: since the degree of collision risk depends on the distance between the two robots, the system should have the ability to shift its scale according to the distance of the nearby robots. As noted above, our experiments below assume fixed size roundabouts for demonstration of feasibility and further work will be required to evaluate flexibility in roundabout size. (2) Orientation: The topology of the roundabout must be such that it is correctly oriented to deal with the conflict. That is, the location and orientation of the roundabout must be able to deal with two robots approaching each other from any angle and not assume a fixed entry and/or fixed exit points. (3) System adaptability: the system can be used for resolving any type of possible collisions for multi-robot systems. (4) System independence: the system should not be restricted to deal with a predetermined number of robots, or a predetermined and fixed configuration space.

In this paper we use Minimum Enclosing Rectangle (MER) to support these principles. According to Das et al. [1], given a set of points $P = \{p_1, p_2, ..., p_k\}$ with $p_k \in \Re^2$, the minimum enclosing square (or rectangle) of P is the smallest square (or rectangle) that contains all points of P. For the purposes of this paper, the smallest square or rectangle is defined to be the smallest rectangle that contains a given number k such that $\frac{n}{2} < k \leq n$ of x-consecutive points in a set of n point in the plane. The problem of computing k-square and k-rectangle has been investigated since 1991 (for a review, see [2–4, 1, 5]). MER has been applied in various areas, such as pattern recognition [6], facility location [7], similarity search [8, 9] and collision detection [10]. In order to classify the *k-square* with respect to the number of points η present on its boundary, Das et al. [1] investigated all different possibilities of *k-squares*. As a result, no *k-square* is possible with $\eta = 0$ or 1. The only possibility with $\eta = 2$ is that the two points appear at the two diagonally opposite corners of the corresponding *k-squares*. In this study, $k = \eta = 2$ is the MER or MES that the robots are searching for, as shown in Figure 1.

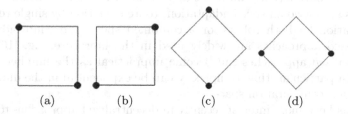

(a)   (b)   (c)   (d)

Fig. 1. MER of $\eta = 2$, with dots representing the position of the two robots. The orientation of the rectabout can differ according to the local view.

The proposed method builds on an implicit assumption that other robots make similar collision avoidance reasoning via MER. That is, knowledge of MER is shared by all robots. It consists of two components: Minimal Predicted Distance (MPD) detection and MER rectabout collision avoidance algorithm. The MPD is a metric inspired by real human pedestrian collision avoidance behaviour (for a review, see [11, 12] and more details below). As far as we are aware, this is the first time that MPD has been used for addressing collision problems in multi-robot systems. The MER-based rectabout collision avoidance algorithm is a pairwise approach which computes and re-plans robots' moving direction by following a 'keep left' rule at the rectabout. This rule can be changed if necessary to keep right. The proposed collision avoidance method is demonstrated for multi-robot systems using different types of collision investigated in [13]. So far, our simulations indicate that our approach generates collision-free motions.

We envisage our approach being of use in autonomous cars [14], such as Google's driverless car [15]. If in the future all cars are autonomous (to compress more traffic onto increasingly busy roads), our approach may be of use in automatic traffic control systems that are fully decentralized and distributed (e.g. traffic-light free roads). As the need for unmanned vehicles grows and their speeds increase, fully decentralized traffic control systems may be the only way to ensure speedy response to possible collisions without the need to communicate with a centralized controller and the delays involved in such communication. Even if there is an efficient centralized controller, autonomous vehicles will still need some independent emergency systems to overcome central control failure.

The rest of this paper is organized as follows. Section 2 provides an overview of prior work on collision avoidance. Section 3 provides a brief summary of minimal predicted distance and definition of conflict and collision in our approach. In section 4 we describe the rectabout collision avoidance maneuver for multiple mobile robots. Section 5 presents the experimental (simulation) results of the obtained collision avoidance maneuver. Finally, section 6 gives the conclusion of this work and some further research directions.

2   Previous Work

Historically, collision avoidance approaches have been focused on robotic applications and only recently on robot applications. Previous collision avoidance approaches are based on speed adaptation, route deviation by single robot only, route deviation by both robots, or a combined speed and route adjustment. Priority-based approaches are widely used in the literature, e.g. [16–18], but these centralized approaches can become impractical as the number of robots increases. In particular, time complexity can be exponential in the dimension of the composite configuration space.

There has been more interest recently in decentralized approaches to collision avoidance that involve no priority. Distributed reactive collision avoidance [19] is a global deconfliction maneuver which mimics a 'rules of the road' approach such as roundabout passing behaviour. In this approach all vehicles turn the same way until a conflict-free state is reached for the whole system. The approach is 'global' because the positions of all vehicles are required by a deconfliction maintenance controller even if they are not involved in collision, and 'distributed' because collision avoidance computation is distributed among a group of robots. The approach is therefore not autonomous. A collision avoidance approach based on Bernstein-Bézier curves [20] is a cooperative method, where reference-tracking control is used to direct the robots by minimizing the difference in a future trajectory and using the deviation of a robot from its reference path. In this case all robots have a global view and change their paths cooperatively to achieve their individual goals. The limitation of these two approaches is that all-to-all information is needed, where one robot has to consider all other robots' information. Although decentralized in terms of control, these two approaches require a constantly updated global data structure or map for each robot containing the positions of all other robots. Reciprocal velocity obstacle [21] is a velocity-based collision avoidance approach that lets a robot take just half the responsibility for avoiding collision, while assuming the other robot reciprocates by taking care of the other half. However, the reciprocal velocity obstacle approach can cause robots to select oscillating velocities as a result of not reaching agreement on which sides to pass each other. The latest work (hybrid reciprocal velocity obstacle [22]) reduces the possibility of oscillations but introduces priority. In addition, Toll et al. [23] proposed a multi-layered path planning algorithm for collision avoidance at an airport or a multi-storey building, but again the algorithm is based on global information being available to each robot. Kato et al. [24] outline a traffic rule system for collision avoidance between multiple mobile robots. However, their approach is restricted to route networks, where traffic follows predictable connections between nodes. It is not certain how their approach can be generalized to a complex and large configuration space, where the number of connections can grow exponentially with size. The approach closest to the one adopted here is [25], where a fully flyable tangential roundabout (FFTR) maneuver is used to prevent collision between two aircraft. However, FFTR requires communication between the two aircraft to agree on the roundabout center and assumes fixed entry and exit points.

Previous work in collision avoidance also does not always take obstacles into account. Obstacles can be fixed (blockages on a straight-line path to a goal) or dynamic (a moving robot getting in the way of another moving robot is an obstacle, and vice versa). Our approach takes both sets of potential obstacle into account. Nature-inspired computing can be a major source of inspiration for improving the designs of autonomous robots and robotics. The approach described below is nature-inspired as it applies metrics and processes taken from the area of human kinematics science (for a review, see [11, 12]) to address collisions between autonomous robots. This research aims to develop and implement a human-like autonomous collision avoidance approach for multi-robot system using non-priority, local views and a configuration space where a robot can make any move it likes as long as there is no obstacle (fixed or dynamic) in the way. In such a configuration space there are no predetermined routes. Every space in the configuration space is reachable from every neighbouring space provided there is no obstacle.

3 Preliminaries

3.1 Collision Avoidance through Minimal Predicted Distance

Olivier et al. [11, 12] proposed a new minimal predicted distance metric to investigate collision avoidance between two pedestrians. Given two persons with positions p_i and p_j, for $i, j = 1, 2, i \neq j$, each person is considered as a moving obstacle for the other. At each instant t, $MPD(t)$ represents the distance at which a person would meet the other if they did not perform motion adaptation after instant t. According to the model of MPD [11], the future trajectory for each person is modeled as follows:

$$p'(t, u) = p(t) + (u - t)v(t), \tag{1}$$

where u is a future time instant with $u, t > 0$ and $u > t$, $p(t)$ and $v(t)$ are the position and velocity at time instant t, respectively. Their experimental studies showed that MPD is constant and that walkers adapt their motion only when MPD is small. Therefore, we can predict potential collisions by computing the absolute distance between p_i and p_j at each time instant t:

$$MPD(t) = \arg\min_u \left\| p'_i(t, u) - p'_j(t, u) \right\|. \tag{2}$$

MPD is a strategy adopted by each robot for predicting potential collision risk. It is also a strategy that attempts to explain how individual humans implicitly adapt their motion and proposes implicit rules that humans naturally

and intuitively follow for this adaptation. We further develop this strategy to
devise a computational, geometric approach to compute a conflict-free solution
for each robot separately and autonomously.

Physical robots will typically calculate paths that suit their own needs. The
moves of two or more robots will need to be separated by a minimal safety
distance Ω, to ensure no collisions. If two moves along planned paths never take
robots within Ω of one another, we say they are conflict-free. That is, paths
can intersect but moves along these paths cannot. Put differently, paths can be
time-independent but moves along these paths cannot. Formally, moves along
paths are conflict-free if and only if

$$\forall t, \forall p_i, p_j, i \neq j, MPD(p_i(v_i, t), p_j(v_j, t)) > \Omega, \tag{3}$$

where $MPD(p_i(v_i, t), p_j(v_j, t))$ is the Euclidean distance between two positions
at each time step, and Ω is here the grid size dynamically adapted to the configuration space to compute the minimal safety distance.

3.2   Collision and Conflict Definition

The robots considered here are modeled as point masses. However, physical
robots have actual size constraints and we need to take physical size into account in the theoretical model. Liu and Narayanan [13] investigated all possible
collision types between two moving robots in a configuration grid space, where
the collision avoidance condition is to not occupy the same position during the
same time-step when following paths, but rather to keep moving within a minimal safety distance at all times. This minimal safety distance has been studied
in [11, 12] and is considered a useful metric for minimal predicted distance.
Collision can be defined as follows:

Definition 1 (Collision State). A collision occurs between robots A_i and A_j
when

$$\mathcal{C}_{ij} \Leftrightarrow \|p_i - p_j\| < \Omega(A_i, A_j), \tag{4}$$

where $\mathcal{C}_{ij}$ represents the collision between two robots A_i and A_j, Ω is a distance
threshold for the minimal safety distance, which in turn is the absolute distance
between the robots' geometric centers. Thus, we have the non-collision state
description as follow:

Definition 2 (Non-Collision State).

$$\mathcal{S}_{ij} \Leftrightarrow \|p_i - p_j\| \geq \Omega(A_i, A_j), \tag{5}$$

where $\mathcal{S}_{ij}$ represents the non-collision state of the two robots corresponding to
$\mathcal{C}_{ij}$ condition.

Definition 3 (Conflict State). Another situation that must be accounted for
is when collision would occur if two robots do not perform motion adaptation

at a future time instant t. According to Equation 2, a conflict occurs between robots A_i and A_j if the robots are not currently in a collision situation but will enter a collision situation at time u if they do not perform motion adaptation. Equation 6 gives the definition of this conflict:

$$\mathcal{H}_{ij}(t) \Leftrightarrow \mathcal{S}_{ij}(t) \wedge MPD(u) < \Omega(A_i, A_j), \tag{6}$$

where $\mathcal{H}_{ij}(t)$ represents conflict between two robots A_i and A_j at time instant t taking into account the future time u (Equation 2). $\wedge$ is the conjunction operator.

4 Deconflict through MER Roundabout Method

Our MER roundabout method is a pairwise collision avoidance maneuver and includes two phases – a conflict detection phase and a deconflict phase.

4.1 Local View Definition

We define a local view LV in front of the current position of a robot and only take into account the robots and any other obstacles inside this local view. The local view has to be of a minimum size to ensure satisfactory conflict detection. If the configuration space is considered as consisting of a grid of squares or rectangles, the size of which is equal to the size of the robot, each robot has 8 moving directions at each time step, as shown in Figure 2(a) and a wait action, plus front local view, as shown in Figure 2(b) and (c). All robots have a constant speed for simplicity. Our approach requires each robot to consider its moves within its front local view at each time step, so each robot potentially has 9 legal actions. Each of these legal actions is a solution to the constraint satisfaction problem in which each robot must determine a move from $\{E,S,W,N,NE,SE,SW,NW,wait\}$, as shown in Figure 2(a), provided that the chosen move does not lead to collision with another robot.

The front local view will be restricted to the region that the robot can actually see, given the direction of motion of the robot, its view angle, and the position of any static obstacles (and perhaps other robots). The LV needs to be updated once the new velocity v is computed. Fixed and dynamic obstacles will be presented in the LV of each robot, not in a global data structure to be shared by all robots.

4.2 Deconflict Maneuver

Given a robot A_i and n number of neighbour robots $A = \{A_1, A_2, ..., A_n\}$ with $1 \leq j \leq n$ in LV, if two robots' moves conflict $\mathcal{H}_{ij}$, a virtual rectangular roundabout can be computed by calculating a minimum enclosing rectangle,

$$R^{ij} = MER(p_i, p_j), \tag{7}$$

where $p_i, p_j \in R^{ij}, \eta \equiv 2$. That is, the boundary of the rectangle is also included in the rectangle. Then, a new velocity is calculated over R^{ij}.

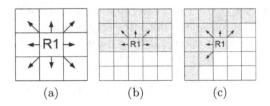

(a)   (b)   (c)

Fig. 2. (a) 8 possible moving directions. (b) and (c) The front local view (LV) of the robot.

To calculate the new velocity v over R^{ij} for deconfliction between A_i and A_j, we calculate the other two diagonal opposite corner points p'_i and p'_j, and we have

$$p' = \begin{cases} q_1 & \min\{x_i, x_j\} \ and \ \min\{y_i, y_j\}, \\ q_2 & \min\{x_i, x_j\} \ and \ \max\{y_i, y_j\}, \\ q_3 & \max\{x_i, x_j\} \ and \ \min\{y_i, y_j\}, \\ q_4 & \max\{x_i, x_j\} \ and \ \max\{y_i, y_j\}. \end{cases} \tag{8}$$

Here, p_i, p_j correspond to two distinct elements of p'. Then we have another two points p'_i and p'_j

$$\{p'_i, p'_j\} = p' \cap \neg\{p_i, p_j\}. \tag{9}$$

Some elementary properties of rectabout maneuver is introduced as follows that we will use in this paper:

Lemma 1 (Symmetry).
$v_i \in MER(p_i, p_j) \Leftrightarrow v_j \in MER(p_j, p_i),$

Symmetry property follows from Figure 1. The velocities v_i and v_j belong to the boundary of the rectabout (see Figure 3).

Lemma 2 (Keep Left Traffic Rule).
$p'_i \in MER(p_i, p_j) \wedge p'_j \in MER(p_j, p_i) \Leftrightarrow \Delta p_i p_j p'_i > 0 \wedge \Delta p_i p_j p'_j < 0.$

Proof. Construct three vertices p_i, p_j, p'_i and p_i, p_j, p'_j to form two triangles. According to the vector cross product theory [26], the area of a triangle Δ can be calculated using the cross product to keep track of the signs of each angle, i.e., by the sign of the expression

$$\Delta = \begin{cases} \frac{1}{2}((x_i - x'_i)(y_j - y'_i) - (y_i - y'_i)(x_j - x'_i)), \\ \frac{1}{2}((x_i - x'_j)(y_j - y'_j) - (y_i - y'_j)(x_j - x'_j)). \end{cases} \tag{10}$$

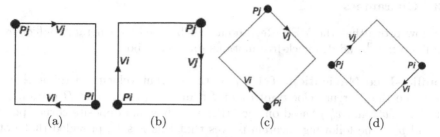

Fig. 3. The symmetry property of the rectabout maneuver for collision avoidance. The velocities v_i and v_j are the new velocities after deconfliction by MER rectabout.

Since the 'keep left' traffic rule is used in this work, we always select an anticlockwise point as a solution from the two diagonal opposite corner points p'_i and p'_j. Clockwise motion is represented by a negative value and anticlockwise by a positive value. Therefore:

$$\mathbf{p}' = \begin{cases} p'_i & \Delta > 0 \quad \text{anticlockwise - keep left traffic rule,} \\ p'_j & \Delta < 0 \quad \text{clockwise - keep right traffic rule.} \end{cases} \tag{11}$$

The new velocity v'_i can be calculated as

$$p'_i - p_i = (x'_i - x_i) \wedge (y'_i - y_i). \tag{12}$$

For $x < 0$,

$$v'_i = \begin{cases} (-1, -1) & \text{if } y < 0, \\ (-1, 0) & \text{if } y = 0, \\ (-1, 1) & \text{if } y > 0. \end{cases}$$

For $x = 0$,

$$v'_i = \begin{cases} (0, -1) & \text{if } y < 0, \\ (0, 1) & \text{if } y > 0. \end{cases}$$

For $x > 0$,

$$v'_i = \begin{cases} (1, -1) & \text{if } y < 0, \\ (1, 0) & \text{if } y = 0, \\ (1, 1) & \text{if } y > 0. \end{cases}$$

Assuming the system consists of n neighbour robots, this algorithm's computation time on each robot scales as $O(n)$, since it only requires the computation of each robot's move to detect conflict and then compute the MER for deconfliction. Formally, $O(n^2)$ MER computations occur in the worst case, but since these computations are independent of each other, they are calculated in parallel in a distributed fashion, so only the per-robot scaling matters. However, to calculate the performance of a system of multiple robots for comparison with other approaches we need to assume a centralized control strategy version of this distributed conflict detection and deconfliction strategy (Results, below).

4.3   Guarantees

We now prove that the MER Rectabout can be used to generate conflict-free, deadloop-free [1] and deadlock-free motions for each robot.

Conflict-Free Navigation. Let v_A be the current velocity of robot A, and let v_B be the current velocity of robot B, and let both A and B choose new velocities (v'_A and v'_B) based on the other two diagonal opposite corner points p'_A and p'_B. The following theorem proves that this is safe, provided that both robots choose the same side (keep left) to pass each other:

Theorem 1 (Conflict-Free).
$$v'_A \in MER(p_A, p_B) \wedge v'_B \in MER(p_B, p_A) \Rightarrow v'_A \times v'_B = 0$$

Proof.
$MER(p_A, p_B) \wedge MER(p_B, p_A)$
$\Rightarrow$ {Equation 7 and Equation 9}
$p'_A \in MER(p_A, p_B) \wedge p'_B \in MER(p_B, p_A)$
$\Leftrightarrow$ {Equation 12 and Lemma 2}
$v'_A \in MER(p_A, p_B) \wedge v'_B \in MER(p_B, p_A)$
$\Rightarrow$ {Lemma 2}
$v'_A \times v'_B = 0$
$\Leftrightarrow$ {Equation 3 and Definition 3}
$MPD(p_A(v'_A, t), p_B(v'_B, t)) > \Omega(A, B)$

Deadloop-Free Navigation. If all robots follow the same 'keep left' rule, this guarantees deadloop-free navigation. This is proven by the following theorem:

Theorem 2 (Deadloop-Free).
$$v'_A \in MER(p_A, p_B) \Leftrightarrow \Delta p_A p_B p'_A > 0 \wedge v'_B \in MER(p_B, p_A) \Leftrightarrow \Delta p_B p_A p'_B > 0$$

Proof.
$v'_A \in MER(p_A, p_B) \wedge v'_B \in MER(p_B, p_A)$
$\Leftrightarrow$ {Equation 12}
$p'_A \in MER(p_A, p_B) \wedge p'_B \in MER(p_B, p_A)$
$\Leftrightarrow$ {Theorem 1}
$v'_A \times v'_B = 0$
$\Leftrightarrow$ {Lemma 2}
$\Delta p_A p_B p'_A > 0 \wedge \Delta p_B p_A p'_B > 0$

Deadlock-Free Navigation. Let the conflict group, $\mathcal{S}_\mathcal{H}$, contains n constant-speed robots that are in conflict and deadlock. Let m robots be in deadlock in $\mathcal{S}_\mathcal{H}$ where no solution is found and choose the 'wait' action, $m, n \in \Re, n > m$. We guarantee deadlock-free navigation if and only if $n > m$. This is the case even

---

[1] Deadloop problem is defined in [13]. Oscillation problem [27] is similar to the dead-loop and is considered as deadloop in this work.

though these conflicts can be daisy-chained such that, if each robot is in conflict with another, this analysis still guarantees that at least one robot in the group can find a move solution. Hence, some robots must eventually attain their goal and allow another to progress, thereby breaking the deadlock. This is proven by the following theorem:

Definition 4 (Deadlock State). We consider that the deadlock state if the new velocity belong to a set of conflict velocities for the current robot A_i:
$$v'_i \in \mathcal{S}_{\mathcal{H}}(A_i, A_j),$$
where $\mathcal{S}_{\mathcal{H}}(A_i, A_j)$ is a set of conflict velocities for the current robot A_i with neighbour robots A_j, denoted as $\mathcal{S}_{\mathcal{H}}(A_i, A_j) = \{v_i | v_i \in MER(p_i, p_j)\}, i \neq j, j \in n$. The $\mathcal{S}_{\mathcal{H}}$ is always updated once the new velocity v' is computed for each robot.

Theorem 3 (Deadlock-Free).
A_i, A_j are in conflict, $v_i, v_j \in \mathcal{S}_{\mathcal{H}}, i \in m, j \in n, n > m \Rightarrow \|v'_i\| \neq 0$.

Proof.
A_i, A_j are in conflict
$\Rightarrow \{\text{Definition 6}\}$
$\mathcal{H}_{ij}(t)$
$\Rightarrow \{\text{Equation 7}\}$
$p'_i \in MER(p_i, p_j) \wedge p'_j \in MER(p_j, p_i)$
$\Leftrightarrow \{\text{Lemma 1}\}$
$v'_i \in MER(p_i, p_j) \wedge v'_j \in MER(p_j, p_i)$
$\Rightarrow \{\text{Theorem 1 and Definition 4}\}$
$\|v'_i\| = 0 \wedge \|v'_j\| \neq 0$ at time instant t
$\Rightarrow \{\text{Theorem 1 and Definition 4}\}$
$\|v'_i\| \neq 0$ at time instant $t + 1$

4.4 Rectabout Algorithm

Given $n > 0$, the rectabout is calculated as the following at each time step:

1. Estimate the motion state pairwise for robot A_i with neighbour robots A_j in LV of velocity v by $MPD(A_i, A_j)$ where $i, j \in n$, $i \neq j$,
2. Repeat until there is no conflict: If there is conflict, then compute R^{ij} by $MER(p_i, p_j)$. If no solution is found, then execute the wait action and terminate, otherwise
3. Find the other two diagonally opposite corner positions p'_i and p'_j,
4. Calculate the new velocity v'_i using the two points p_i and p'_i.
5. Update the information of neighbour robots and static obstacles in LV of new velocity v'.

This procedure is repeated until the deconfliction motion is found (including a wait action) for all the neighbour robots. Figure 4 illustrates robot 1 (R1) computing pairwise virtual rectabouts to avoid collisions with two other robots

R2 and R3 (a). First, R1 calculates a rectabout to avoid R2 and plans a move NW (b). However, R3 is also in conflict (c), so R1 calculates another rectabout and planned move W to avoid R3 (d). Similarly, other two robots use the same procedure to deconflict.

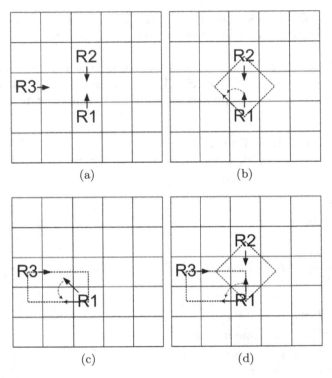

Fig. 4. Illustration of how rectabouts resolve conflicts between three robots. Robot 1 computes virtual rectabouts by pairwise based on MER for deconfliction.

5   Experimental Results

We performed both small-scale simulations to test local behaviour and large-scale simulations to analyze performance scaling. We also compared our approach to a centralized approach. The simulations model mobile robots of constant size and speed, where the task is to move from their current position towards a goal position. Each robot has its own random current and goal positions. Paths calculated by robots can intersect and in certain move situations lead to conflict. The aim is to minimize stop and wait states so that robots can reach their goal in the minimum time while avoiding collision.

Local Behavioural Results: We show two scenarios which demonstrate how robots smoothly avoid collisions with each other at the local level. In the first scenario shown in Figure 5(a), two robots are moving towards each other. Each robot is able to detect conflict with the other and computes a virtual rectabout based on MER ($MER(p_1, p_2)$). A new velocity is planned along the path of MER and the robots follow a shared 'keep left' traffic rule to resolve the conflict independently. The virtual rectabout is removed after one time-step, after which each robot needs to independently operate the process again, since the information around the robot always changes with every time step. However, robots always attempt to move towards their own goal position at every time-step. The second scenario involves 16 robots where all robots are densely located in the center of the environment, shown in Figure 5(b). In this worst-case scenario, using rectabouts may cause deadlock and the wait action (one timestep) is used for the robots involved in deadlock. Robots will follow their goal-direction again after one time step. A robot takes avoiding action irrespective of whether an obstacle in its LV is fixed (non-moving robot) or dynamic (moving robot). Videos of these scenarios can be found at http://youtu.be/GSH_i98Ju6w.

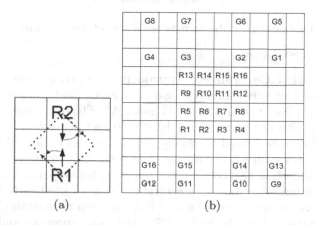

(a)   (b)

Fig. 5. Two small behavioural simulations. R and G represent Robot and Goal for each robot, respectively. (a) Solid arrow line is the intended trajectory. Dotted arrow line is the deconfliction trajectory. The central dotted rectangle is a virtual rectabout enclosing two robots R1 and R2. (b) The 16 robots are densely located in a 10x10 grid environment. Each robot moves to its antipodal position in the environment, leading to maximum possible conflict and possible deadlock.

Large Scale Simulation Results: In order to test the performance of our method we varied the number of robots in different configuration space (200x200 grid, 300x300 grid and 400x400 grid) to see how our approach scales when the number of robots increases. We performed our experiments on an Intel Core(TM) i5 processor 3.20 GHz with 4GByte of memory. Each scenario was repeated 10 times and results were averaged. All start and goal positions were generated randomly. Figure 6 shows the total running time for various numbers of robots. We note that the total running time of our method scales nearly linearly with the number of robots. Furthermore, the computation time increases as the density of robots increases, as would be expected given that deadlock is more frequent with high density.

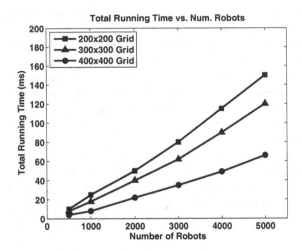

Fig. 6. The total running can be seen to scale almost linearly with the number of robots

Comparison with Centralized Approach: The performance of the MER rectabout maneuver was compared against a centralized priority-based algorithm by Liu and Narayanan [13], called Super A*. The test configuration space was based on a 50x50 grid involving 10, 20, 50 and 100 robots. All start and goal positions were generated randomly. The result was evaluated by the total number of moves for all robots moving from their start positions to their goal positions. To undertake this comparison, our decentralized approach was represented as a centralized approach (a central coordinator needing to calculate all LVs for every robot and all collision and collision avoidance strategies). Table 1 presents the statistical results for the MER rectabout approach and shows that it is comparable to a centralized approach. The big difference, however, is that Super A* (and other centralized approaches) has costly overheads in terms of communication and global map updates.

Table 1. MER rectabout comparing with a centralized priority-based approach. Performance evaluation on the total number of moves for 10, 20, 50 and 100 robots by 50x50 grid configuration space.

Number of Robots	10	20	50	100
Super A*	194	543	1318	2554
MER rectabout	194	552	1341	2568

6 Conclusion and Future Work

A novel non-priority and non-global view rectabout approach based on MER for collision avoidance is proposed in this paper. The kinematic research on minimal predicted distance between two human walkers is applied for the first time to deal with robot collision problems in conjunction with a rectabout maneuver. We use MPD to detect the possible collisions along robot paths and trajectories. The robots involved in conflict will compute a rectabout and re-plan a new velocity when MPD is below the threshold. This process is repeated until all robots reaching their goals. Our approach also takes into account obstacles and sudden changes of direction by robots.

While this paper presents a significant advance, there are several issues which require further work. One key area for future work is the effect on MPD and MER of variable sized local views. The second is the need for dealing with variable speed robots. Also, while the aim of this paper is to remove the need for any communication between agents, there may be occasions (e.g. deadlocks, cooperative behaviour) where some form of communication is required or desired.

Finally, while the paper has focused on collision detection and avoidance among robots and has presented simulations involving robots of fixed size and speed, the research needs extending to problem solving by a number of robots needing to search a complex space cooperatively as well as autonomously. In particular, it is not clear how generalizable the use of rectangles will be in more complex spaces. Nevertheless, it could be argued that the most important aspect of any mobile multi-robot system is how to prevent robots from getting in each other's way. Such collision avoidance is often overlooked or ignored in mobile multi-robot and swarm-based approaches and simulations. Swarm simulations frequently assume that swarm members can fly through each other.

References

1. Das, S., Goswami, P.P., Nandy, S.C.: Smallest k-point enclosing rectangle and square of arbitrary orientation. Information Processing Letters 94(6), 259–266 (2005)
2. Aggarwal, A., Imai, H., Katoh, N., Suri, S.: Finding k points with minimum diameter and related problems. Journal of Algorithms 12(1), 38–56 (1991)
3. Eppstein, D., Erickson, J.: Iterated nearest neighbors and finding minimal polytopes. Discrete & Computational Geometry 11(1), 321–350 (1994)
4. Segal, M., Kedem, K.: Enclosing k points in the smallest axis parallel rectangle. Information Processing Letters 65(2), 95–99 (1998)
5. Mahapatra, P.R.S., Karmakar, A., Das, S., Goswami, P.P.: k-enclosing axis-parallel square. In: Murgante, B., Gervasi, O., Iglesias, A., Taniar, D., Apduhan, B.O. (eds.) ICCSA 2011, Part III. LNCS, vol. 6784, pp. 84–93. Springer, Heidelberg (2011)
6. Pang, S., Liu, F., Kadobayashi, Y., Ban, T., Inoue, D.: Training minimum enclosing balls for cross tasks knowledge transfer. In: Huang, T., Zeng, Z., Li, C., Leung, C.S. (eds.) ICONIP 2012, Part I. LNCS, vol. 7663, pp. 375–382. Springer, Heidelberg (2012)
7. Drezner, Z., Hamacher, H.W.: Facility Location: Applications and Theory. Springer, Berlin (2002)
8. Nandy, S.C., Bhattacharya, B.B.: A unified algorithm for finding maximum and minimum object enclosing rectangles and cuboids. Computers & Mathematics with Applications 29(8), 45–61 (1995)

9. De, M., Maheshwari, A., Nandy, S.C., Smid, M.H.M.: An in-place min-max priority search tree. Computational Geometry 46(3), 310–327 (2013)
10. Liu, F., Narayanan, A.: Roundabout collision avoidance for multiple robots based on minimum enclosing rectangle (demonstration). In: AAMAS, pp. 1375–1376 (May 2013)
11. Olivier, A.H., Marin, A., Grétual, A., Pettré, J.: Minimal predicted distance: A common metric for collision avoidance during pairwise interactions between walkers. Gait & Posture 36(3), 399–404 (2012)
12. Olivier, A.H., Marin, A., Grétual, A., Pettré, J.: Minimal predicted distance: A kinematic cue to investigate collision avoidance between walkers. Computer Methods in Biomechanics and Biomedical Engineering 15(1), 240–242 (2012)
13. Liu, F., Narayanan, A., Bai, Q.: Effective methods for generating collision free paths for multiple robots based on collision type (demonstration). In: AAMAS, pp. 1459–1460 (June 2012)
14. Wikipedia: Autonomous car (May 2013)
15. Spectrum, I.: How google's self-driving car works (October 2011)
16. Bennewitz, M., Burgard, W., Thrun, S.: Finding and optimizing solvable priority schemes for decoupled path planning techniques for teams of mobile robots. Robotics and Autonomous Systems 41(2-3), 89–99 (2002)
17. van den Berg, J., Snoeyink, J., Lin, M., Manocha, D.: Centralized path planning for multiple robots: Optimal decoupling into sequential plans. In: RSS (July 2009)
18. Sharon, G., Stern, R., Felner, A., Sturtevant, N.: Conflict-based search for optimal multi-agent path finding. In: AAAI, pp. 563–569 (June 2012)
19. Lalish, E., Morgansen, K.A.: Distributed reactive collision avoidance. Autonomous Robots 32(3), 207–226 (2012)
20. Škrjanc, I., Klančar, G.: Optimal cooperative collision avoidance between multiple robots based on bernstein-bézier curves. Robotics and Autonomous Systems 58(1), 1–9 (2010)
21. van den Berg, J., Guy, S.J., Lin, M.C., Manocha, D.: Reciprocal n-body collision avoidance. In: ISRR, pp. 3–19 (August 2009)
22. Snape, J., van den Berg, J., Guy, S.J., Manocha, D.: The hybrid reciprocal velocity obstacle. IEEE Transactions on Robotics 27(4), 696–706 (2011)
23. van Toll, W., Cook IV, A.F., Geraerts, R.: Navigation meshes for realistic multi-layered environments. In: IROS, pp. 3526–3532 (September 2011)
24. Kato, S., Nishiyama, S., Takeno, J.: Coordinating mobile robots by applying traffic rules. In: IROS, pp. 1535–1541 (July 1992)
25. Platzer, A., Clarke, E.M.: Formal verification of curved flight collision avoidance maneuvers: A case study. In: Cavalcanti, A., Dams, D.R. (eds.) FM 2009. LNCS, vol. 5850, pp. 547–562. Springer, Heidelberg (2009)
26. Massey, W.S.: Cross products of vectors in higher dimensional euclidean spaces. The American Mathematical Monthly 90(10), 697–701 (1983)
27. van den Berg, J., Lin, M., Manocha, D.: Reciprocal velocity obstacles for real-time multi-agent navigation. In: ICRA, pp. 1928–1935 (May 2008)

Embedding Preference Ordering
for Symmetric DCOP Solvers on Spanning Trees

Toshihiro Matsui[1], Marius Silaghi[2], Katsutoshi Hirayama[3], Makoto Yokoo[4],
and Hiroshi Matsuo[1]

[1] Nagoya Institute of Technology, Gokiso-cho Showa-ku Nagoya 466-8555, Japan
{matsui.t,matsuo}@nitech.ac.jp
[2] Florida Institute of Technology, Melbourne FL 32901, United States of America
msilaghi@fit.edu
[3] Kobe University, 5-1-1 Fukaeminami-machi Higashinada-ku Kobe 658-0022, Japan
hirayama@maritime.kobe-u.ac.jp
[4] Kyushu University, 744 Motooka Nishi-ku Fukuoka 819-0395, Japan
yokoo@is.kyushu-u.ac.jp

Abstract. The Max-Sum algorithm is a solution method for the Distributed Constraint Optimization Problem (DCOP) which is a fundamental problem in multi-agent cooperation. Particularly, we focus on the case of Max-Sum on a spanning tree, where the algorithm is an exact solution method. In this case, all agents simultaneously compute globally optimal objective values as erootf nodes of the tree that represents the problem. On the other hand, a tiebreak is generally necessary in order to determine a unique optimal solution among the agents. While top-down post-processing is a well-known solution, one can prefer to design the solver as a bottom-up computation that is simply integrated to pre-processing. To address this issue, we investigate a technique that employs a preference ordering based on spanning trees for the optimization algorithms. With this technique, top-down processing to choose a unique optimal solution can be embedded into bottom-up optimization via small weight values for the preference ordering. We also evaluate an integrated algorithm that maintains both tree structures and quasi-optimal solutions using the bottom-up approaches.

Keywords: Distributed Constraint Optimization, multi-agent, cooperation, tiebreak.

1 Introduction

Distributed Constraint Optimization Problems (DCOPs) [3,7,9,10,13] have been studied as fundamental building blocks in multi-agent cooperation. With DCOPs, the multi-agent optimization is represented as a constraint optimization problem that consists of variables, constraints and objective functions which represent valuations of the constraints.

Several cooperative problems including distributed resource scheduling, sensor networks and smart grids are represented as DCOPs [6,8,13].

The Max-Sum algorithm [3] is a solution method for DCOPs. Important characteristics of the algorithm are introduced by the utilization of factor graphs and a kind

G. Boella et al. (Eds.): PRIMA 2013, LNAI 8291, pp. 197–212, 2013.
© Springer-Verlag Berlin Heidelberg 2013

of 'symmetric' computation. In contrast to a traditional constraint network, the factor graph directory represents n-ary objective functions because the graph consists of nodes for variables and nodes for functions. The computation of the Max-Sum basically resembles DPOP [10], which is based on dynamic programming in the pseudo-tree of the constraint network. However, in the case that the factor graph is cyclic, the Max-Sum is an inexact method. Therefore several studies apply Max-Sum only for trees. In bounded Max-Sum [11], a graph is approximated to a minimum (maximum) spanning tree using prepressing that eliminates the cycles. In this paper, we focus on the case of Max-Sum on a spanning tree, where the algorithm is an exact solution method. While DPOP is basically performed on a rooted spanning tree, Max-Sum is performed on multiple rooted spanning trees. The computation of the multiple trees is partially integrated.

Max-Sum on a spanning tree consists of a set of bottom-up computations that are symmetrically and simultaneously performed for different root nodes. Here we call this approach 'symmetric' processing. On the other hand, tiebreak among multiple root nodes is generally necessary in order to determine a unique optimal solution. One such method consists of an additional post-processing that is conducted by a root agent of a spanning tree in a top-down manner [11]. However, such asymmetric processing is separated in time from the original symmetric optimization method as a second stage. It is often preferred to employ a bottom-up computation that is simply integrated to pre-processing in a single homogeneous stage. Such bottom-up approaches generally emphasize the autonomy of each agent. An alternative method employs additional small weight values to break ties. While previous studies use random weight values, such values are theoretically inexact. On the other hand, in the general case, the exact weight values need a large domain that grows with the number of variables.

We study a technique that employs a preference ordering based on spanning trees for the optimization algorithms. With this technique, top-down processing for breaking ties can be embedded into bottom-up optimization via small weight values of the preference ordering. While the size of the domain of the weight values is the same as that of the domain of original variables, there is a computational tradeoff for a sort processing to re-map the weight values in each agent. In addition, the proposed method also gives an analysis about the amount of information to break ties. Note that our main motivation is not concerned with reducing message sizes, but with achieving a simple (and exact) protocol for the tiebreak. Since the symmetric processing of Max-Sum has a redundant computation, it will be robust in dynamic environments where single-phase solution methods that can be easily integrated to the maintenance of graphs are practical. We also evaluate an integrated algorithm that maintains both tree structures and quasi-optimal solutions using the bottom-up approaches.

The rest of the paper is organized as follows. In Section 2, we address the backgrounds of the study. We introduce weight values to break ties in Section 3. Then, an integrated self-stabilizing algorithm is shown in Sections 4. The proposed methods are experimentally investigated in Section 5. In Section 6, several related works and discussions are presented, and we conclude our study in Section 7.

2 Backgrounds

2.1 Distributed Constraint Optimization Problem

DCOP A distributed constraint optimization problem is defined as follows.

Definition 1 (DCOP). *A DCOP is defined by* (A, X, D, F) *where A is a set of agents, X is a set of variables, D is a set of domains of variables, and F is a set of objective functions. A variable $x_n \in X$ takes values from its domain defined by the discrete finite set $D_n \in D$. A function $f_m \in F$ is an objective function defining valuations of a constraint among several variables. Here, f_m represents utility values that are maximized. $X_m \subset X$ defines a set of variables that are included in the scope of f_m. $F_n \subset F$ similarly defines a set of functions that include x_n in its scope. f_m is formally defined as $f_m(d_i, \cdots, d_k) : D_i \times \cdots \times D_k \to \mathbb{N}_0$ where $\{x_i, \cdots, x_k\} = X_m$. $f_m(d_i, \cdots, d_k)$ is also simply denoted by $f_m(x_i, \cdots, x_k)$ or $f_m(X_m)$. The aggregation $F(X)$ of all the objective functions is defined as follows: $F(X) = \sum_{m \ s.t. \ f_m \in F, X_m \subseteq X} f_m(X_m)$. The goal is to find a globally optimal assignment that maximizes the value of $F(X)$.*

The variables and functions are distributed among the agents in A. An agent constrains variables in X that represent its decision.

Each agent locally knows the set of variables and the set of functions in the initial state. A distributed optimization algorithm is performed in order to compute the globally optimal solution.

Factor Graph. The factor graph is a representation of a DCOP. The factor graph consists of nodes for variables (called *variable nodes*), function nodes and edges. An edge represents a relationship between a variable and function. Figure 1 shows examples of acyclic factor graphs. As shown below, cyclic factor graphs are modified to acyclic graphs in preprocessing. The Max-Sum algorithm is based on the factor graph. Agents therefore at least either know a function node or are involved in decisions on a variable node. In the following, we simply use a model in which a node corresponds to an agent.

2.2 Symmetric Solution Method

Max-Sum Algorithm. The Max-Sum algorithm is a solution method based on dynamic programming. The computation of the method is performed on a factor graph. Each node of the factor graph corresponds to an agent that is also called a variable node or function node. Each node communicates with neighborhood nodes using messages and computes globally optimal solutions.

The information of a message is an evaluation function for a variable. The function is represented as a table of evaluation values for the variable's values. A node computes a table for each variable that corresponds to each neighborhood node. The table is then sent to the corresponding neighborhood node. Therefore, a node knows evaluation functions for all neighborhood nodes. The evaluation function that is sent from variable node x_n to function node f_m is denoted by $q_{x_n \to f_m}(x_n)$. Similarly, $r_{f_m \to x_n}(x_n)$ denotes the evaluation function sent from function node f_m to variable node x_n. An

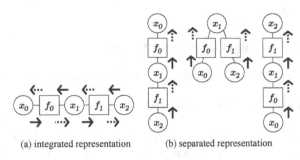

(a) integrated representation   (b) separated representation

Fig. 1. Symmetric computation on factor graph

evaluation function $q_{x_n \to f_m}(x_n)$ that is sent from variable node x_n to function node f_m is represented as follows.

$$q_{x_n \to f_m}(x_n) = 0 + \sum_{m' \text{ s.t. } f_{m'} \in F_n \setminus \{f_m\}} r_{f_{m'} \to x_n}(x_n) \tag{1}$$

Here F_n denotes the set of neighborhood function nodes of variable node x_n.

An evaluation function $r_{f_m \to x_n}(x_n)$ that is sent function node f_m to variable node x_n is represented as:

$$r_{f_m \to x_n}(x_n) = \max_{X_m \setminus \{x_n\}} \left(f_m(X_m) + \sum_{n' \text{ s.t. } x_{n'} \in X_m \setminus \{x_n\}} q_{x_{n'} \to f_m}(x_{n'}) \right) \tag{2}$$

Here X_m denotes the set of neighborhood variable nodes of function node f_m. $\max_{X_m \setminus \{x_n\}}$ denotes the maximization for all assignments of variables in $X_m \setminus \{x_n\}$.

A variable node x_n computes a marginal function that is an evaluation function of x_n. The marginal function $z_n(x_n)$ is represented as follows.

$$z_n(x_n) = \sum_{m \text{ s.t. } f_m \in F_n} r_{f_m \to x_n}(x_n) \tag{3}$$

$z_n(x_n)$ corresponds to global objective values for variable x_n. The value of x_n that maximizes $z_n(x_n)$ is therefore the globally optimal assignment. Each variable node chooses such assignment as the optimal solution.

In the case that the factor graph is a tree, values of all evaluation functions converge to optimal values. In bounded Max-Sum [11], a graph is approximated to a minimum (maximum) spanning tree to eliminate the cycles.

Symmetric Computation. The computation of Max-Sum on a spanning tree is considered a set of bottom-up computations that are symmetrically and simultaneously performed for different root nodes. The root node of each computation is a variable node. In each computation, dynamic programming is performed from leaf nodes to the root node. For instance, the computation shown in Figure 1(a) is actually decomposed into the computations shown in Figure 1(b). There are three trees rooted at variable nodes. While all variable nodes individually compute the global optimal objective value, several nodes share the common computation and communication.

This characteristic of Max-Sum is interesting because each variable node has an authority to determine its optimal assignment based on its knowledge of the global objective value. In contrast to Max-Sum, several distributed reasoning processes based on dynamic programming employ a single tree to compute the globally optimal cost. The optimal assignments are therefore separately determined in a top-down manner based on the tree.

2.3 Issue of Multiple Optimal Solutions

As shown above, in Max-Sum, a variable node knows globally optimal objective functions. The variable nodes individually perform as 'root nodes'. On the other hand, there is insufficient information for coordination between root nodes. The variable nodes therefore have to break the tie when there are multiple optimal solutions.

For example, in the case of traditional graph coloring problems, the root node x_n of a tree computes $z_n(x_n)$ that takes the same value for all values in D_n. Namely, the agent can choose any value from D_n as the optimal assignment. The situation is the same in all variable nodes.

To determine a unique optimal solution, tiebreak is generally necessary. One such method consists of an additional post-processing that is conducted by a root agent of a spanning tree in a top-down manner [11]. However, such asymmetric processing is separated from the original symmetric optimization method. The algorithm complexity is increased by the need to manage the timings of the top-down computation.

Another method employs additional small random weight values to break ties [3]. On the other hand, the random number may not sufficiently well represent the solution ordering. One can introduce the exact weight values that represent a lexicographic solution ordering. However, the exact weight values need a large domain that grows with the number of variables and with the size of the domain of variables.

3   Embedding Ordering into Optimization

3.1   Basic Ideas

In this study, we investigate exact weight values that give a kind of lexicographic solution ordering. To improve on the simple ordering, we devise a procedure described by the following points: (1) The ordering is defined based on a spanning tree rooted at the 'top priority' node. (2) In the computation of Max-Sum, the weight values are inserted in the opposite direction of the top priority node, if the objective function is computed for neighborhood nodes. (3) An ordering of subtrees in the spanning tree is defined, ensuring a total ordering on solutions. (4) The weight values are re-mapped into other values to avoid an increase of the domain size.

As shown above, we employ a spanning tree to define the solution ordering. There are assumptions for the spanning tree. A spanning tree for the solution ordering is the same as the tree of Max-Sum. There is a top priority node in the spanning tree. Each node knows which adjacent edge is connected to the top priority node.

Based on the spanning tree, weight values are determined. The weight value is defined as follows. A weight value represents the priority of a solution. A weight value is sufficiently smaller than objective values. The summation of weight values is always less than the objective values. The weight value is combined with an objective value. The objective values are therefore extended to a pair of an objective value and a weight value. In the optimization, a pair of the values is compared with another pair. In the comparison, the comparison between objective values is more significant than the comparison between weight values. There is hierarchy between any objective values and any weight values. The weight values only give a priority between the same objective values.

To construct a weight value, the value ordering of the variable is considered. In addition, the variable ordering is considered. For each value a of each variable x_i, a weight value $w_{i,a}$ is defined. For any pair of different values a and b of x_i, $w_{i,a} > w_{i,b}$ iff a is more preferred than b. For any pair of different variables x_i and x_j, iff x_i has higher priority than x_j, the following holds: $\min_{a \in D_i} w_{i,a} > \sum_{b \in D_j} w_{j,b}$.

An example of the weight values is shown in Figure 2(a). In this example, x_0 is the top priority node. The objective values of functions f_0 and f_1 are the most significant. The weight values are defined to satisfy the hierarchical relations.

3.2 Inserting Weight Values

The weight values are inserted into the original objective values. Basically, the weight values are inserted at the variable nodes. Note that this modification is out of the factor graph. Formally, such weight value can be represented as a unary function node. However, we prefer the special extension of the Max-Sum here.

As addressed above, Max-Sum can be considered as individual bottom-up computations. We therefore focus on each tree rooted at a variable node. While the weight values can be inserted in all variable nodes, such insertion is redundant in several cases.

In the case of Figure 2(b), the ordering of the nodes is the same as that of variable ordering in Figure 2(a). Therefore, the root node x_0 has higher priority than other nodes. Namely, decision of x_0 dominates other nodes. By this observation, we can conclude that only the weight values of x_0 are necessary to choose a unique optimal solution.

In the case of Figure 2(c), the ordering of the nodes is completely opposite. The root node x_2 has lower priority than other nodes. Namely, decision of x_2 is dominated by other nodes. We therefore conclude that all weight values are necessary to break ties of optimal solutions.

Figure 3(a) shows the case of graph coloring problems with binary variables. A small node in the graph represents a value of a variable. This problem contains binary variables. An edge denotes a pair of the values of two variables. Its label shows the corresponding objective value. The right side of the figure shows the process of the computation. $r_{f_m \to x_n}$ and related weight values w_n are computed in a bottom-up manner. In this example, for variable x_n, weight values w_n ($w_{n,0} = 1$ for $x_n = 0$, and $w_{n,1} = 0$ for $x_n = 1$) are inserted. For variable x_0, the weight values are simply applied. For variable x_1, the maximizing operation is performed for each values of x_1 considering combination of function and weight values. In the case of $x_1 = 0$, $(x_1, x_0) = (0, 1)$ corresponds to $(r_{f_0 \to x_1}, w1, w0) = (1, 1, 0)$. Another combination $(x_1, x_0) = (0, 0)$ corresponds to $(r_{f_0 \to x_1}, w1, w0) = (0, 1, 1)$. The first combination is preferred since its value of $r_{f_0 \to x_1}$ is greater than another one. Other values are similarly computed. In the case of $x_2 = 0$, $(x_2, x_1) = (0, 1)$ corresponds to $(r_{f_1 \to x_2}, w2, w1, w0) = (2, 1, 0, 1)$ and this combination is preferred. Here, values $(r_{f_0 \to x_1}, w1, w0) = (1, 0, 1)$ for $x_1 = 1$

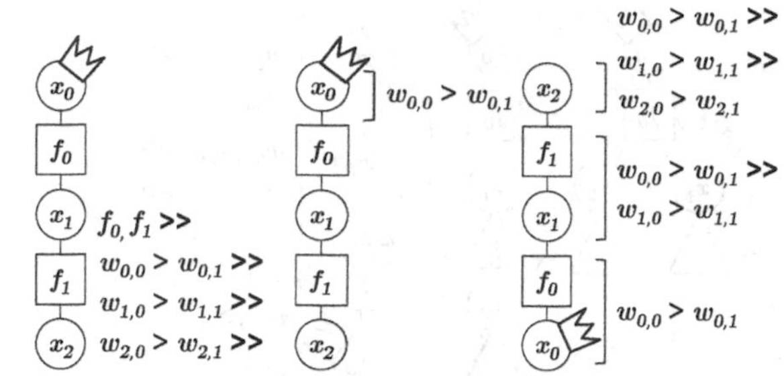

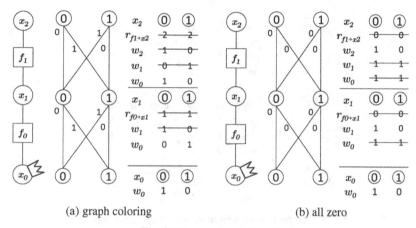

Fig. 2. Insertion of weight values

Fig. 3. Effects of weight values

are aggregated to values of f_1 and w_2. Note that several weight values have no effect in aggregated weight values because those take the same value or values of higher priority exist. In the figure, horizontal lines erase such values. The root node x_2 is affected by weight values w_0 of the top priority node x_0.

Figure 3(b) shows the case that all objective values are zero. Several weight values also have no effect in aggregated weight values. As a result, the root node x_2 is only affected by its own weight values w_2. That is intuitively reasonable because there are no actual objectives. Thus, this computation reveals that the importance of each weight value depends on problems.

The case where x_1 is the root node requires more discussions and revisions of the idea.

3.3 Serialization of Subtrees

In the previous subsection, we omitted the case in which there are multiple subtrees. The subtrees are useful because they introduce parallelism of the computation of Max-Sum. However, a tree only defines a partial ordering of the variables. On the other hand, we need a total ordering to define a solution ordering.

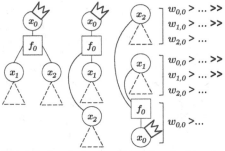

(a) serialization of subtrees   (b) insertion of weight values

Fig. 4. Serialization of subtrees

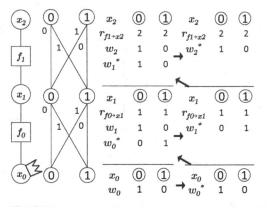

Fig. 5. Compaction of weight values (graph coloring)

To address this issue, we serialize subtrees. When a node has multiple subtrees, the ordering on its neighborhood nodes is defined. The neighborhood node in the direction of top priority node has the highest order. Other nodes are sorted using an appropriate method. Then weight values are inserted for each variable for the neighbor nodes.

Note that there are no assignments of weight value from lower nodes in the variable ordering tree. In addition, the interface of each subtree is the values of the neighboring variables. Therefore, that weight values can isolate each subtree without contradictions. Now 'higher' nodes set weight values for each value of variables. Variable nodes do not need to insert its own weight values.

Figure 4 shows an example of the serialization. In function node f_0, the weight values are inserted for each subtree. An important point is that both subtrees rooted at x_1 and x_2 are affected by the weight values $w_{1,}$ and $w_{2,}$ for x_1 and x_2. That is necessary to evaluate the influence of other subtrees in all nodes in each subtree.

3.4   Compaction of Weight Values

The weight values are inserted based on the tree of the variable ordering. However, the number of the inserted weight values linearly increase with the depth of the tree. Moreover, the serialization of subtrees needs extra weight values.

On the other hand, in the optimization, the number of weight values is the same as the number of the assignments. Based on the property, we re-map the weight values into the domain whose size is the same as that of a variable. After a table of a function is computed, the weight values are sorted. The weight values are then replaced by new values considering the ordering. Here we assume that the overhead of sorting is allowed for relatively small domains of variables. The compaction of the weight values also can be performed in the limited number of nodes to reduce the total computation.

Figure 5 shows an example of the compaction. Notations of the figure resemble Figure 3. The computation is performed in a bottom-up manner using aggregation and maximization on the combinations of objective/weight values. In addition, combinations of weight values in the left table are re-mapped to single weight value in the right table. The re-mapped weights w_1^* and w_2^* only require small domain sizes. In the case of x_1, the combination $(w_1, w_0^*) = (1, 0)$ is less preferred than $(w_1, w_0^*) = (0, 1)$. Therefore, those combinations are mapped into $w_1^* = 0$ and $w_1^* = 1$, respectively.

3.5 Correctness and Complexity

The proposed method inserts weight values that correctly break ties among solutions. The weight values define a solution ordering that does not conflicts between any two solutions. The weight values are hierarchically defined for any variables in any top-down path from the top priority node to other nodes. In addition, subtrees are serialized and isolated from each other. In the propagation of weight values, any non-zero weight values are not sent in the direction of the top priority node. Therefore, each weight value in each node is greater than the summation of all weight values of the lower nodes in the top-down path. As a result, the decisions of each node dominate the decisions of lower nodes.

The number of the weight values is the same as that of original objective values in Max-Sum. The size of a weight value linearly grows with the number of inserted weight values. The complexity of the additional computation linearly grows with the number of inserted weight values. It depends on the depth of trees and the degree of each node.

On the other hand, with the compaction of weight values, the size for the domain is the same as the size of domain of variables. Actually, at most, unique weight values are independently necessary for each variable. Therefore, its computation is linear in the size of the domain of the variable. For the compaction of weight values, we can employ various sort algorithms. The complexity mainly depends on the sort algorithms. Other computations mainly depend on the degree of each node, similar to that of Max-Sum on spanning trees. The weight values eliminate the top-down computation.

4 An Integrated Algorithm

The weight values shown in Section 3 enable a single-phase optimization processing in a bottom-up manner. Therefore, the optimization processing is simply integrated to pre-processing that generates tree structures. As a result, an integrated algorithm based on those processing is constructed. Here we study an example of the integrated algorithm that maintains both tree structures and optimal solutions.

```
1   Inititalize:
2   prn_i ← ∅: parent of i. lbl_i ← ∅: list of nodes from i's root to i.
3   chl_i ← ∅: child nodes of i.
4   mwe_i ← unknown: minimum (maximum) weight outgoing edge known by i.
5   rce_i ← unknown: internal edge of the tree known by i.
6   ror_i ← false: flag of reorientation from i to one of neighbor nodes.
7   for each k ∈ nbr_i, q_{i→k}(x_i) or r_{i→k}(x_k) ← ∅: message of Max−Sum (sent to k).

9   Main procedure:
10  repeat{
11    Send status of i to all k ∈ nbr_i. Receive status from all k ∈ nbr_i.
12    if(ror_i ∧ (∃k ∈ nbr_i, prn_i = k ∧ prn_k ≠ i)){ ror_i ← false. }
13    if(prn_i = ∅){ lbl_i ← {i}. }
14    else if(∃k ∈ nbr_i, prn_i = k){
15      if(prn_k = i){ if(ror_k){ prn_i ← ∅. lbl_i ← {i}. }}
16      else{ if(lbl_k ≠ unknown){ lbl_i ← lbl_k. append i to lbl_i. }}
17    }
18    chl_i ← {k|prn_k = i ∧ k ≠ prn_i}.
19    if(lbl_i ≠ unknown ∧ (∀k ∈ chl_i, (lbl_i and lbl_k are consistent)∧ mwe_k ≠ unknown)∧
20      (∀k ∈ (nbr_i\{prn_i}\chl_i), lbl_k ≠ unknown)){
21      mwe_i ← edge e of minimum weight s.t.
22      (e = (k,i), k ∈ (nbr_i\{prn_i}\chl_i)∧ (lbl_k and lbl_i show different trees) ) ∨
23      (e = mwe_k, k ∈ chld_i) if such e exists. Otherwise, mwe_i ← ∅. }
24    if(mwe_i ≠ unknown ∨ mwe_i ≠ ∅){
25      if(prn_i = ∅){
26        if(∃k ∈ nbr_i, (k,i) = mwe_i){
27          if(i is prior to k){ if(prn_k = i){ set unknown to mwe_i, rce_i.}}
28          else{ prn_i ← k. set unknown to lbl_i, mwe_i, rce_i. }}
29        else{ choose k s.t. (k ∈ chl_i ∧ mwe_k = mwe_i).
30          prn_i ← k. ror_i ← true. set unknown to lbl_i, mwe_i, rce_i.}}}
31    if(mwe_i = ∅){
32      if(rce_i ≠ ∅){
33        Propagate an internal non−tree edge (recovery edge) in a bottom−up manner.
34        Store the recovery edge into rce_i. }
35      else{
36        if(rce_i ≠ unknown ∧ (its weight is greater than edge (prnt_i, i)) ){
37          prn_i ← ∅. set unknown to lbl_i, mwe_i, rce_i. }
38        Propagate next recovery edge if it exists. }}
39    for each k ∈ {prn_i} ∪ chl_i update q_{i→k}(x_i) or r_{i→k}(x_k) based on related status.
40  } // end of repeat
```

Fig. 6. Integrated algorithm (processing in node i)

Similar to bounded Max-Sum [11], we employ minimum (maximum) spanning trees (MSTs) on factor graphs that are generally constructed using GHS algorithms [4]. Here, weight values of MST are defined by 'impact' on the edges (i.e. difference of maximum and minimum objective values). Especially, we choose a self-stabilizing GHS [2] to employ its bottom-up nature. The GHS algorithm starts from fragments of spanning trees. The nodes in each fragment compute the minimum (maximum) weight outgoing edge (MWE). Then two fragments are connected using the MWE. Eventually, a single minimum (maximum) spanning tree is constructed. Moreover, a part of the graph can be modified. In that case, new fragments are firstly added. Then, if the spanning tree contains incorrect edges that do not compose MST, several edges of the spanning tree are cut to reconstruct MST. To this end, each node reports internal non-tree edges (recovery edges) to higher nodes in the tree. Here 'internal' means that two end nodes of a recovery edge are contained in the same fragment.

Max-Sum algorithm is performed on the spanning tree. Using preference weight values, the processing is performed in a single-phase. The Max-Sum immediately responds to status of neighborhood nodes even if there are fragments of the spanning-tree.

The pseudo code of the algorithm is shown in Figure 6. We use a minimal version of the algorithm for explanation. Please see [2] for the details. For the sake of simplicity, each node i communicates with all neighborhood nodes nbr_i in the factor graph. The following states of neighborhood node k are received from k and stored. edg_k: information of edge (weight value and pair of nodes) to k. prn_k: parent node of k. lbl_k: list of nodes from k's root to k. mwe_k: minimum (maximum) weight outgoing edge known by k. rce_k: internal edge of the tree known by k. ror_k: flag of reorientation from k to i. $q_{k \to i}(x_k)$ or $r_{k \to i}(x_i)$: message of Max-Sum (received from k).

Important points of the algorithm are as follows. Each nodes are initialized as a fragment of MST (lines 1-7). Then main loop is repeated (lines 10-40). The neighboring nodes exchange their status (line 11). Based on the status of own node and neighborhood nodes, information of parent, child, and ancestor nodes are updated (lines 13-18). When a fragment is converged, the MWE is computed in a bottom-up manner (lines 19-23). If the MWE exists, the fragment intends to integrate it with another fragment (line 24-30). The integration is always performed at root nodes of two fragments. Namely, the root nodes must be connected to the MWE. Otherwise, the root node 'moves' to the node of the MWE using a processing called 'reorientation' (line 12, 15, 29 and 30). In the integration, one of the root nodes dominates another one (line 27). If the MWE does not exist, the fragment propagates recovery edges (line 33). If the weight value of a tree edge exceeds the weight value of a recovery edge, such tree edge is eliminated and the spanning tree will be reconstructed (lines 36, 37). The Max-Sum algorithm very simply performs beside the GHS (line 39).

This algorithm eventually converges to an approximate solution. It also adapts the dynamic change of problems. In the following section, we will show several evaluations of the algorithm.

5 Evaluation

We experimentally evaluated the proposed method. Our aim is to clarify several characteristics of the preference weight values. We composed the following two experiments. In the first experiment, the proposed methods shown in Section 3 are evaluated. The second one evaluates an integrated solution method in Section 4.

5.1 Effects of Weight Values

In the first experiment, we evaluate the size of the domains of weight values. The highest digit of each weight value in binary notation defines the size of weight values. In other words, the size is the bit precision to represent the weight values. Since the proposed

Table 1. Size of weight values [bits]

problem	#v=21,#f=10						#v=61,#f=30						#v=181,#f=90					
	internal			message			internal			message			internal			message		
algorithm	min.	max.	ave.	min.	max.	ave.	min.	max.	ave.	min.	max.	ave.	min.	max.	ave.	min.	max.	ave.
										gcl								
total	1	49	35	1	49	33	1	142	105	1	142	97	1	421	317	1	421	292
tree	1	45	12	1	45	10	1	77	19	1	77	15	1	119	28	1	119	23
tree+cmpct	1	14	3	1	3	1	1	17	4	1	3	1	1	21	4	1	3	1
										random dcop								
total	1	49	35	1	49	32	1	142	104	1	142	96	1	421	316	1	421	291
tree	1	45	11	1	45	9	1	77	18	1	77	15	1	119	28	1	119	23
tree+cmpct	1	14	3	1	3	1	1	17	3	1	3	1	1	21	3	1	3	1

Table 2. Number of incorrect results in the case of random weight values

problem	#v=21,#f=10		#v=61,#f=30		#v=181,#f=90	
precision [bits]		(ratio)		(ratio)		(ratio)
			gcl			
4	15	(0.30)	46	(0.92)	50	(1.00)
8	1	(0.02)	2	(0.04)	6	(0.12)
16	0		0		0	
			random dcop			
4	7	(0.14)	22	(0.44)	40	(0.80)
8	0		0		5	(0.10)
16	0		0		0	

method is an additional processing, the size of weight values is the main issue. As shown below, the size reveals the amount of information that is necessary to break ties among decisions of agents.

For the benchmark problems, acyclic factor graphs are randomly generated as follows. First, a connected component of three variables and one ternary function is generated. Then additional units of ternary functions (i.e. units of two variables and one function) are incrementally appended to a variable node in the existing component. The graph consists of #v variables and #f ternary functions. The size of domain of each variable is five. Therefore, each objective function defines 125 objective values.

We evaluated the different types of objective functions and found very similar results. Here, we show the following two cases. **gcl:** graph coloring problems. The objective values of a function are zero if all corresponding variables take the same value. Otherwise, the objective value is 1. **random dcop:** optimization problems with random objective values. The objective values are integer values between 0 and 10 with a uniform distribution.

To analyze the partial effects of the proposed method, we compared the following three methods. **total:** this method employs weight values that represent the total solution ordering for all values and all variables. **tree:** the solution ordering is defined based on a tree as shown in Section 3. However, the compaction of the weight values is not employed. **tree+cmpct:** The compaction of the weight values is applied to 'tree'. The variables for weight values are implemented as multiple precision variables to avoid overflow. The results are averaged for 50 instances.

Table 1 shows the size of weight values. The unit of the size is 'bit'. There, 'internal' denotes the size of weight values in the nodes including marginal functions, and 'message' denotes the size of weight values that are transferred in messages. Note that the size of 'message' affects that of 'internal' because the received functions are aggregated into internal weight values. While 'total' needs 421 bits in the largest case, 'tree+cmpct' needs 3 bits in the messages. In the same case, 'tree+cmpct' needs 21 bits for the internal computation. The size of 'internal' and that of 'message' are different in 'tree+cmpct'. That shows the effect of the compaction of weight values. Moreover, the important characteristic is that the size of weight value is similarly reduced in the case of large problems. In the comparison between 'gcl' and 'random dcop', the results are almost the same. It is considered that the proposed method well fits in both cases.

An important observation from the results is that, with 'tree+cmpct', few bits of weight values are necessary to be transferred to break ties. The number of bits can be considered as the amount of information. While we only applied the compaction of weight values to messages, it is also possible to compress weight values of internal tables. That will reveal more accurate amount of information in internal tables. Hence, the proposed method also gives an analysis about the amount of information to break ties.

From these results, it is considered that a reason of relatively good effects of conventional random weight values is that tiebreak needs not so much information. We applied random weight values to the same set of problems. Here, the precision of random values is k bits and the weight values take integer values between 0 and $(2^k - 1)/\#v - 1$. Table 2 shows the number of incorrect results in the case of random weight values. The incorrect result is the case that assignments are not optimal due to wrong tiebreak. In the comparison between 'gcl' and 'random dcop', 'gcl' needs slightly many bits in several cases. It is considered that 'gcl' contains many symmetrical solutions than 'random dcop'. Compared with 'tree+cmpct' in Table 1, in most cases of problems, the sufficient precision (i.e. the number of incorrect results is zero) are within the maximum size of 'internal' weight values. There is possibility to estimate the sufficient precision of random weights using the proposed method. On the other hand, the random weight values are not theoretically exact.

5.2 Integrated Algorithm on Dynamic Problems

In the next experiment, we evaluated the integrated algorithm shown in Section 4. For this experiment, cyclic factor graphs are randomly generated so that the degree of each variable is 3. The size of domain of each variable is 5 and the objective function is 'random dcop'. For each problem, a tree is generated and the problem is solved simultaneously. To evaluate effects on dynamic problems, the problems are modified after a number of iterations of message passing. In the second problem, we added new variable nodes and edges from the new variable nodes to existing function nodes. The degree of new variables is the same as for original variables. The modification causes a new fragment. Also, existing tree edges possibly change to wrong edges that will be removed.

Clearly, the conventional algorithm that employs top-down messages only determines the optimal solution when the tree is completely constructed. On the other hand, our interest is the behavior of the solution methods during the construction. Namely, the proposed method computes objective values and assignments of variables when fragments of trees are available.

Here, we compared the following three methods. **prefwgt:** the algorithm shown in Section 4. **prefwgt+sync:** a synchronization processing is added to 'prefwgt'. We introduced, a global clock, a timestamp for each message, and a message buffer for

Table 3. Results of integrated method (random dcops, until convergence)

problem	first			second					
				add 1var. with 3 edgs.			add 2vars. with 2 edgs.		
algorithm	iter.	util.	#chg.	iter.	util.	#chg.	iter.	util.	#chg.
#v=10,#f=10									
prefwgt	454	28.64	65	125	37.79	20	215	36.84	37
prefwgt+sync	454	28.21	57	125	37.05	18	215	36.27	31
topdown	454	28.66	43	125	37.79	19	215	36.88	28
#v=20,#f=20									
prefwgt	1723	63.45	238	257	86.85	37	442	85.59	68
prefwgt+sync	1723	62.97	198	257	86.31	28	442	85.05	48
topdown	1723	63.57	143	257	86.97	24	442	85.67	50

Table 4. Results of integrated method (random dcops, 25% of iterations)

problem	first			second					
				add 1var. with 3 edgs.			add 2vars. with 2 edgs.		
algorithm	iter.	util.	#chg.	iter.	util.	#chg.	iter.	util.	#chg.
#v=10,#f=10									
prefwgt	113	17.49	22	31	19.79	8	53	19.00	12
prefwgt+sync	113	17.15	22	31	19.06	7	53	18.38	10
topdown	113	17.40	13	31	19.73	5	53	18.92	9
#v=20,#f=20									
prefwgt	430	42.82	70	64	48.08	11	110	46.10	19
prefwgt+sync	430	42.44	65	64	47.40	10	110	45.60	16
topdown	430	42.87	36	64	48.09	8	110	46.13	14

each node. Only 'leaf' nodes (i.e. nodes that have one neighborhood nodes) attach time stamps to messages based on the global clock. Using the time stamps, non-leaf nodes synchronize the messages of the same clock from different leaf nodes. During waiting the other messages, received messages are stored into the message buffer. In addition, each node synchronically updates the value of its variable considering the delay of messages to other nodes. Thus, the computation is performed for the same global clock as possible. Several messages are purged without the processing due to dynamics of tree generation. **topdown:** this method employ top-down messages instead of preference weight values. However, each node always sends the top-down messages if the information of neighborhood nodes is (locally) consistent. Therefore, it resembles 'prefwgt' except that it employs both bottom-up and top-down processing. Those methods are performed on the same self-stabilizing GHS algorithm.

Table 3 shows the results in the case that the problem changes after the convergence of solution methods. Here, 'iter.' denotes the number of iterations. In each iteration, all node exchange messages with all neighborhood nodes. The result shows that the second problem needs less number of iterations than the first problem because the previous result is available.

'util.' denotes the global utility (i.e. total objective value) which is averaged for all iterations. The global utility values resemble for all methods. Actually, at the convergence, all methods compute the same quality of solutions. On the other hand, there are minor differences due to different updates of assignments during executions. While the discussion of those behaviors (that depend on several factors including the behavior of GHS) is not easy, we can see the following points. 1) In several cases, 'prefwgt' computes solutions of slightly less utility values than 'topdown'. Because 'prefwgt' does not employ top-down messages, it is more sensitive to the changes of trees. The total number of changes of assignments ('#chg.') shows this behavior. It is considered as a trade-off between the simple bottom-up protocol 'prefwgt' and the complex top-down/bottom-up protocol 'topdown'. However, such reactivity often gives better response. There are possibilities to improve the proposed methods. 2) The utility value of 'prefwgt' is better than 'prefwgt+sync'. The result shows that the global synchronization causes slightly poor response due to its delay.

Table 4 shows the results in the case that the problem changes at 25% of the average number of iterations in Table 3. While the solution methods are not completed in several problems, the results resemble Table 3.

6 Related Works and Discussions

As mentioned above, a method proposed in [3] for breaking symmetry consists in adding small weight values to objective functions. Our method builds on this approach. One improvement we add consists in computing the exact weight values needed for efficient processing. While the size of exact weight values increases with the number of related variables and domains, this size can be reduced dynamically during computation. We are aware that random weight values may also break the symmetries. On the other hand, one of our interests is investigation of an optimal method that computes exact weight values. In [11], a top-down processing that is conducted by the root node of the spanning tree, is applied as the final phase of the solver. In the case of Max-Sum, there are multiple bottom-up computations based on different spanning trees. The single top-down computation therefore is the only element that breaks the homogeneity of the process. The timing for starting the top-down processing is an additional overhead that we remove. As a conclusion, our method is a top-down processing that is embedded into Max-Sum via weight values. The proposed solution can be described as phase-less.

In [5], a bounded Max-Sum is employed with an inexact GHS that partially updates MST. The study mainly focuses on small modification of spanning trees. They employ a sequence of multiple separated distributed processes. Our study is not directly comparable since we focus on bottom-up frameworks with any-time response. However, we believe that our framework can be modified with another (inexact) self-stabilizing GHS that is partially maintained by multiple root nodes. As a limitation, we mention that bottom-up processing introduces a certain computational overhead. However, we consider that this overhead is not significant for the agents we envision. Rather, agents can now benefit of an awareness concerning their state during the whole processing. Another issue consists in the lack of commitment to solutions. For that issue, a safeguard should be designed if necessary.

This approach will be applied to other new solution methods based on GDL [1,12] (e.g. a symmetric version of DPOP [10] on spanning trees, similar to Bounded Max-Sum [11]). While the proposed method is designed for spanning trees, there are opportunities of similar approaches on other types of graphs including DAGs.

7 Conclusions

In this work, we studied a technique that employs a preference ordering based on spanning trees for symmetric optimization algorithms. With this technique, top-down processing for tiebreak on solutions can be embedded into bottom-up optimization via small weight values of the preference ordering. With a computational tradeoff for a sort processing to re-map the weight values in each agent, the size of the domain of the weight values is the same as that of the domain of original variables. Based on the weight values, a technique composed of a single homogeneous phase is obtained by integrating a single-phase optimization algorithm with the pre-processing that maintains tree-structures. The obtained framework achieves a bottom-up cooperation among agents that can immediately adopt changes in the graph structure.

The integrated algorithm can be further improved with more efficient mechanisms for maintaining dynamic spanning trees. Future work will also address more detailed analysis of the effects of the weight values and safeguards that inhibit undesirable anytime solutions.

Acknowledgments. This work was supported in part by KAKENHI, a Grant-in-Aid for Scientific Research (B), 23300060.

References

1. Aji, S.M., McEliece, R.J.: The generalized distributive law. IEEE Transactions on Information Theory 46(2), 325–343 (2000)
2. Blin, L., Dolev, S., Potop-Butucaru, M.G., Rovedakis, S.: Fast self-stabilizing minimum spanning tree construction - using compact nearest common ancestor labeling scheme. In: Lynch, N.A., Shvartsman, A.A. (eds.) DISC 2010. LNCS, vol. 6343, pp. 480–494. Springer, Heidelberg (2010)
3. Farinelli, A., Rogers, A., Petcu, A., Jennings, N.R.: Decentralised coordination of low-power embedded devices using the max-sum algorithm. In: AAMAS 2008, pp. 639–646 (2008)
4. Gallager, R.G., Humblet, P.A., Spira, P.M.: A distributed algorithm for minimum-weight spanning trees. ACM Trans. Program. Lang. Syst. 5(1), 66–77 (1983)
5. Macarthur, K., Farinelli, A., Ramchurn, S., Jennings, N.: Efficient, superstabilizing decentralised optimisation for dynamic task allocation environments. In: OPTMAS 2010, pp. 25–32 (2010)
6. Maheswaran, R.T., Tambe, M., Bowring, E., Pearce, J.P., Varakantham, P.: Taking dcop to the real world: Efficient complete solutions for distributed multi-event scheduling. In: AAMAS 2004, pp. 310–317 (2004)
7. Mailler, R., Lesser, V.: Solving distributed constraint optimization problems using cooperative mediation. In: AAMAS 2004, pp. 438–445 (2004)
8. Miller, S., Ramchurn, S.D., Rogers, A.: Optimal decentralised dispatch of embedded generation in the smart grid. In: 11th International Conference on Autonomous Agents and Multiagent Systems, vol. 1, pp. 281–288 (2012)
9. Modi, P.J., Shen, W., Tambe, M., Yokoo, M.: Adopt: Asynchronous distributed constraint optimization with quality guarantees. Artificial Intelligence 161(1-2), 149–180 (2005)
10. Petcu, A., Faltings, B.: A scalable method for multiagent constraint optimization. In: IJCAI 2005, pp. 266–271 (2005)
11. Rogers, A., Farinelli, A., Stranders, R., Jennings, N.R.: Bounded approximate decentralised coordination via the Max-Sum algorithm. Artificial Intelligence 175(2), 730–759 (2011)
12. Vinyals, M., Rodriguez-Aguilar, J.A., Cerquides, J.: Constructing a unifying theory of dynamic programming dcop algorithms via the generalized distributive law. Autonomous Agents and Multi-Agent Systems 22(3), 439–464 (2011)
13. Zhang, W., Wang, G., Xing, Z., Wittenburg, L.: Distributed stochastic search and distributed breakout: properties, comparison and applications to constraint optimization problems in sensor networks. Artificial Intelligence 161(1-2), 55–87 (2005)

Compliant Business Process Design by Declarative Specifications

Francesco Olivieri[1,2,3], Guido Governatori[1,2],
Simone Scannapieco[1,2,3], and Matteo Cristani[3]

[1] NICTA, Queensland Research Laboratory, Australia*
[2] Institute for Integrated and Intelligent Systems, Griffith University, Australia
[3] Department of Computer Science, University of Verona, Italy

Abstract. We propose algorithms to synthesise the specifications modelling the capabilities of an agent, the environment she acts in, and the governing norms, into a process graph. This process graph corresponds to a collection of courses of action and represents all the licit alternatives the agent may choose to meet her outcomes. The starting point is a compliant situation, i.e., a situation where an agent is capable of reaching all her outcomes without violating the norms. In this case, the resulting process will be *compliant by design*.

Keywords: Rules, agents, and norms, Defeasible Logic, BDI paradigm.

1 Introduction

Frodo, the Ring bearer, must leave Rivendell to destroy the Ring of Power in Mount Doom. Since he fears orcs, he would prefer to cross the Misty Mountains by either climbing them, or passing south of them. As a last option, he may pass through Moria. The Fellowship tries to climb the mountains, but fails due to some very unlucky weather conditions. Then, Gandalf tells Frodo not to go south since Saruman would imprison him and take the Ring for himself. Finally, Frodo may not choose to keep the Ring for himself, because he will eventually be subjugated by Sauron's will if he does.

The previous example reveals a very (un)common situation: an agent operates in an environment to reach some objectives. Such an environment is represented by the description of the world, the norms governing it, and the agent's objectives. The agent may have her own desires or intentions, and the combination of such mental attitudes with the factuality of the world defines her deliberative process, i.e., the objectives she decides to pursue. The agent may give up some of them to comply with the norms, if required. Many contexts (as the scenario of Frodo and the Ring) prevent the agent from achieving all her objectives; the agent must then understand which objectives are mutually compatible with each other and choose which objectives to attain the least of in given situations by ranking them in a preference ordering.

In this paper we study the following two problems: (1) determining whether an agent is able to reach her objectives without violating the norms, and (2) if this is possible, identifying what are the (alternative) courses of action to fulfil the objectives.

---

* NICTA is funded by the Australian Government as represented by the Department of Broadband, Communications and the Digital Economy and the Australian Research Council through the ICT Centre of Excellence program.

G. Boella et al. (Eds.): PRIMA 2013, LNAI 8291, pp. 213–228, 2013.

We can distinguish three phases an agent must pass through to bring about certain states of affairs: understanding the environment she acts in, deploying such information to deliberate which objectives to pursue, and how to act to reach them.

In the first phase, the agent gives a formal declarative description of the environment (in our case, a rule-based formalism). Rules allow the agent to represent relationships between pre-conditions and actions, actions and their effects (post-conditions), relationships among actions, which conditions trigger new obligations to come in force, and in which contexts the agent is allowed to pursue new objectives. In the second stage, the agent combines the formal description with an input describing a particular state of affairs of the environment, and determines which norms are actually in force, which objectives she decides to commit to and to which degree. The agent's decision is based on logical derivations. Since the agent's knowledge is represented by rules, during the last phase, the agent exploits information from derivation to select the activities to carry out in order to achieve the objectives. Here, it is important to notice that a derivation can be understood as a virtual simulation of the various activities involved.

In [1], authors developed a framework based on a modal variant of Defeasible Logic (DL) [2] that models agents by distinguishing three kind of knowledge: the internal constraints guiding the agent (mental attitudes), the external constraints regulating the setting (norms), and how the agent perceives the world (beliefs). Modelling rational agents in this fashion was first proposed by Bratman in [3].

Mental attitudes identified in [1] have strong similarities with those of classical BDI architecture [4,5,6], while the proposed framework considers desires, goals and intentions as facets of the same phenomenon: the notion of *outcome*, which is simply something an agent would like to achieve. As a result, mental attitudes were modelled through a single type of rule (*outcome rule*) by adopting the methodology of *reparative chains* to model *contrary-to-duties* (CTDs). Reparative chains were first introduced in [7] to formalise reparations of previously violated norms. Given the rule $r : \Gamma \Rightarrow o_1 \otimes o_2 \otimes \cdots \otimes o_n$, if the context described by Γ holds, then the obligation in force is o_1; in case o_1 is violated then the new obligation in force is o_2, and so on.

Using reparative chains to model outcomes reflects the natural way for an agent to give a fixed ordering in objective selection. This is natural in real-life situations when the agent gives alternatives to more preferred objectives. When settled in a given context, an agent combines preferences expressed by outcome rules with her beliefs and the norms to filter out which objectives are feasible for her, and which ones she commits to.

We make a step further in our investigation by addressing two main sequential issues. The former is to adapt the notion of *norm* and *goal compliance* presented in [8] to the (more expressive) logic proposed in [1]. This will result in determining not just whether an agent is capable of reaching a (sub)set of these outcomes without violating the norms, but also her level of commitment to them (i.e., which mental attitude the agent decides to comply with). Accordingly, the agent's mental attitudes are the result of a filtering mechanism through beliefs and norms. This allows us to pass from the (more specific) concept of goal compliance to the (more general) one of *outcome compliance*, which can be varied to suit a particular application.

The latter, and main problem, being to determine the agent's courses of action after both compliances have been established. To this end, we take inspiration from *Business*

Process Modelling. A *business process* is a collection of related, structured tasks that produce a specific service, where a *task* is an activity that needs to be accomplished within a defined period of time [9]. A business process can be understood as the set of all its possible execution traces, i.e., all the possible ways in which the process can be executed, where a *trace* is just a linear sequence of tasks/actions (notice that a trace is equivalent to a classical AI plan [10]).

A derivation of a given (outcome) literal corresponds to a specific course of action which reaches that particular outcome, the reason being the information encoded in the agent's knowledge base. Thus, we can consider such a derivation a trace. One of the reasons to use business processes is because it is possible to have multiple ways in which the agent reaches her outcomes and still remains norm compliant. If this is the case, it is pointless for the agent to perform all the alternatives to bring about the same state of affairs. Instead, the agent should be equipped with a *process graph* showing her all such alternatives and allowing her to carry out the best strategy. Choosing the best strategy relies on external information that does not affect the construction of the process graph, such as risks, task cost, execution time, minimum number of task to perform, and so on.

The paper is presented as follows. Section 2 illustrates the logical formalism. In particular, in Subsection 2.3 we discuss norm and outcome compliance. Section 3 shows the algorithms used to compute a process graph starting by the declarative specifications; such processes are compliant by design with the norms and meet the objectives selected by the agent. We summarise and comment some related works in Section 4.

2   Logic

The logic exploited in this work was proposed in [1], where four different types of mental attitudes were identified: desires, goals, intentions, and social intentions.

Desires as acceptable outcomes. Consider an agent equipped with the *outcome rules*

$$r : a_1, \ldots, a_n \Rightarrow_U b_1 \odot \cdots \odot b_m \qquad s : a'_1, \ldots, a'_n \Rightarrow_U b'_1 \odot \cdots \odot b'_k$$

where the notation $\Rightarrow_U$ denotes a rule introducing outcomes and that the situation described by $a_1, \ldots, a_n$ and $a'_1, \ldots, a'_n$ are mutually compatible but b_1 and b'_1 are not, namely $b_1 = \neg b'_1$. In this case $b_1, \ldots, b_m, b'_1, \ldots, b'_k$ are anyway all *acceptable outcomes*, including b_1 and b'_1. *Desires* are expected or acceptable outcomes, independently of whether they are compatible with other expected or acceptable outcomes.

Goals as preferred outcomes. For rule r alone the preferred outcome is b_1, and for rule s alone it is b'_1. But if both rules are applicable, then the agent would not be rational if she considers both b_1 and $\neg b_1$ as her preferred outcomes. Hence, the agent has to decide if she prefers a state where b_1 holds to one where b'_1 (i.e., $\neg b_1$) holds, or *vice versa*. If the agent has no way to decide which is the most suitable option for her, then neither the chain of r nor that of s can produce preferred outcomes. Suppose that the agent opts for b'_1; this can be done if she establishes that the second rule overrides the first one, i.e., $s > r$. Accordingly, the preferred outcome is b'_1 for the chain of outcomes defined by s, and b_2 is the preferred outcome of r. b_2 is the second best alternative according to rule r: in fact b_1 has been discarded as an acceptable outcome given that s prevails over r.

Two degrees of commitment: intentions and social intentions. We now clarify which are the outcomes for an agent to commit to. Naturally, if the agent values some outcomes more than others, she should strive for the best, i.e., for the most preferred outcomes.

We first consider the case where only rule r applies. Here, the agent should commit to the outcome she values the most, i.e., b_1. But what if the agent *believes* that b_1 cannot be achieved in the environment, or she knows that $\neg b_1$ holds? Committing to b_1 would result in a waste of agent's resources; rationally, she should target the next best outcome, in this case b_2. Accordingly, the agent would derive the *intention* of b_2.

Suppose, now, that b_2 is *forbidden*, and the agent is social (an agent is social if the agent would not knowingly commit to anything that is forbidden [11]). Once again, in this situation the agent has to lower her expectation and settle for b_3 (the agent would obtain the *social intention* of b_3).

To complete the analysis, consider the situation where both rules r and s apply and the agent prefers s to r. As we have seen before, $\neg b_1$ (b_1') and b_2 are the preferred outcomes since the agent stated $s > r$. Assume that, this time, the agent knows she cannot achieve $\neg b_1$ (or equivalently, b_1 holds). If the agent is rational, she cannot commit to $\neg b_1$. Thus, the best option for her is to commit to b_2' and b_1, where she is guaranteed to be successful. In this scenario, the best course of action for the agent is where she commits herself to some outcomes that are not her preferred ones, or even that she would consider not acceptable based only on her preferences, but such that they influence her decision process given that they represent relevant external factors (either her beliefs or the norms that apply to her). The agent would have the (social) intentions of b_1 and b_2'.

2.1 Language

Let PROP be a set of propositional atoms, $\text{MOD} = \{\text{B}, \text{O}, \text{D}, \text{G}, \text{I}, \text{SI}\}$ the set of modal operators, whose reading is B for *belief*, O for *obligation*, D for *desire*, G for *goal*, I for *intention* and SI for *social intention*. Let Lbl be a set of arbitrary labels. The set $\text{Lit} = \text{PROP} \cup \{\neg p | p \in \text{PROP}\}$ denotes the set of *literals*. The *complementary* of a literal q is denoted by $\sim q$; if q is a positive literal p, then $\sim q$ is $\neg p$, and if q is a negative literal $\neg p$ then $\sim q$ is p. The set of *modal literals* is $\text{ModLit} = \{\Box l, \neg \Box l | l \in \text{Lit}, \Box \in \{\text{O}, \text{D}, \text{G}, \text{I}, \text{SI}\}\}$. We assume that the "$\Box$" modal operator for belief B is the empty modal operator, thus a modal literal Bl is equivalent to literal l. Accordingly, the complementary of B$\sim l$ and $\neg$Bl is $\sim l$.

We define a *defeasible theory D* as a structure $(F, R, >)$, where (i) $F \subseteq \text{Lit} \cup \text{ModLit}$ is a finite set of *facts* or indisputable statements, (ii) R contains three finite sets of *rules*: for beliefs, obligations, and outcomes and (iii) $> \subseteq R \times R$ is a *superiority relation* to determine the relative strength of conflicting rules. *Belief rules* are used to relate the factual knowledge of an agent (her vision of the environment), and defines the relationships between states of the world. As such, provability for beliefs does not generate modal literals. *Obligation rules* determine when and which obligations are in force. The conclusions generated by obligation rules are modalised with obligation. *Outcome rules* establish the possible outcomes of an agent depending on the particular context. Apart from obligation rules, outcome rules derive conclusions for all modes representing possible types of outcomes: desires, goals, intentions, and social intentions.

Following ideas given in [7], rules can gain more expressiveness when a *preference operator* $\odot$ is used: an expression like $a \odot b$ means that if a is possible, then a is the first choice and b is the second one; if $\neg a$ holds, then the first choice is not attainable and b is the actual choice. This operator is used to build chains of preferences, called $\odot$-*expressions*. The formation rules for $\odot$-expressions are: (i.) every literal is an $\odot$-expression, (ii.) if A is an $\odot$-expression and b is a literal then $A \odot b$ is an $\odot$-expression.

In this paper we exploit the classical definition of *defeasible rule* in DL [2]. A defeasible rule is an expression $r : A(r) \Rightarrow_\square C(r)$, where

1. $r \in \text{Lbl}$ is the name of the rule;
2. $A(r) = \{a_1, \ldots, a_n\}$ with $a_i \in \text{Lit} \cup \text{ModLit}$ is the set of the premises (or the *antecedent*) of the rule;
3. $\square \in \{B, O, U\}$ represents the *mode* of the rule (from now on, we omit the subscript B in rules for beliefs, i.e., $\Rightarrow$ is used as a shortcut for $\Rightarrow_B$);
4. $C(r)$ is the *consequent* (or *head*) of the rule, which is a single literal if $\square = B$, or an $\odot$-expression otherwise. It is worth noting that modal literals can occur only in the antecedent of rules: the reason is that the rules are used to derive modal conclusions and we do not conceptually need to iterate modalities The motivation of a single literal as a consequent for belief rules is dictated by the intended reading of the belief rules, where these rules are used to describe the environment.

We use the following abbreviations on sets of rules: $R^\square$ ($R^\square[q]$) denotes all rules of mode $\square$ (with consequent q), and $R[q] = \bigcup_{\square \in \{B,O,U\}} R^\square[q]$. $R[q,i]$ denotes the set of rules whose head is $\odot_{j=1}^n c_j$ and $c_i = q$, with $1 \leq i \leq n$.

Notice that labelling the rules of DL produces nothing more but a simple treatment of the modalities, thus two interaction strategies between modal operators are analysed.

Rule conversions and conflict-detection/resolution. It is sometimes meaningful to use rules for a modality $\square$ as they were for another modality $\blacksquare$, i.e., to convert one type of conclusions into a different one. Formally, given rule $r : a_1, \ldots, a_n \Rightarrow_\square b$ and the situation where $\blacksquare a_1, \ldots, \blacksquare a_n$ hold, the (asymmetric binary relation) Convert($\square, \blacksquare$) permits to derive $\blacksquare b$. In our framework, we consider Convert($B, \square$) with $\square \in \{O, D, G, I, SI\}$. Accordingly, we enrich the notation with $R^{B,\square}$, denoting the set of belief rules that can be used for a conversion to mode $\square$. The antecedent of all such rules is not empty, and does not contain any modal literal.

Moreover, it is crucial to identify criteria for detecting and solving conflicts between different modalities. Formally, we define an asymmetric binary relation Conflict $\subseteq$ MOD $\times$ MOD such that Conflict($\square, \blacksquare$) means 'modes $\square$ and $\blacksquare$ are in conflict and mode $\square$ prevails over $\blacksquare$'. In our framework, we consider: (i.) Conflict(B, I), Conflict(B, SI) defining the realistic attitude of the agents (cf. [12]), and (ii.) Conflict(O, SI) defining the social attitude of the agents (cf. [11]).

Notice that there are two applications of the *superiority relation*: the first considers rules of the same mode; the second when we have two rules of different mode, with complementary literals and two modes are related by the convert relation.

2.2 Inferential Mechanism

A *proof P* of *length n* is a finite sequence $P(1), \ldots, P(n)$ of *tagged literals* of the type $+\partial_X q$ and $-\partial_\square q$, where $\square \in$ MOD. As a conventional notation, $P(1..i)$ denotes the initial part of the sequence P of length i. Given a defeasible theory D, $+\partial_\square q$ means that q is defeasibly provable in D with the mode $\square$, and $-\partial_\square q$ that it has been proved in D

that q is not defeasibly provable in D with the mode $\square$. From now on, the term *refuted* is a synonym of *not provable* and we use $D \vdash \pm\partial_\square l$ iff there is a proof P in D such that $P(n) = \pm\partial_\square l$ for an index n.

To characterise the notions of provability for all modalities, it is essential to define when a rule is *applicable* or *discarded*. To this end, the preliminary notion of when a rule is *body-applicable/discarded* is needed, stating that each literal in the body of the rule must be proved/refuted with the suitable mode.

Definition 1. *Let P be a proof and $\square \in \{O, D, G, I, SI\}$. A rule $r \in R$ is* body-applicable *(at step $n+1$) iff for all $a_i \in A(r)$:*

1. *if $a_i = \square l$ then $+\partial_\square l \in P(1..n)$,*
2. *if $a_i = \neg\square l$ then $-\partial_\square l \in P(1..n)$,*
3. *if $a_i = l \in$ Lit then $+\partial l \in P(1..n)$.*

Conditions to establish that a rule is *body–discarded* correspond to the constructive failure to prove that the same rule is body–applicable, and follow the principle of *strong negation*. The strong negation principle is related to the function that simplifies a formula by moving all negations to an inner most position in the resulting formula, and replaces the positive tags with the respective negative tags, and the other way around [13].

As already stated, belief rules allow us to derive literals with different modes. The applicability mechanism must take into account this constraint.

Definition 2. *Let P be a proof. A rule $r \in R$ is 1.* Conv-applicable, *2.* Conv-discarded *(at step $n+1$) for $\square$ iff*

1. *$r \in R^B$, $A(r) \neq \emptyset$ and for all $a \in A(r)$, $+\partial_\square a \in P(1..n)$;*
2. *$r \notin R^B$ or $A(r) = \emptyset$ or $\exists a \in A(r)$, $-\partial_\square a \in P(1..n)$.*

As an example, consider theory $D = (\{a, b, Oc\}, \{r_1 : a \Rightarrow_O b, r_2 : b, c \Rightarrow d\}, \emptyset)$. Rule r_1 is applicable, while r_2 is not since c is not proved as a belief. Instead, r_2 is Conv-applicable for O, since Oc is a fact and r_1 proves Ob.

The notion of applicability gives guidelines on how to consider the next element in a given chain. Since a rule for belief cannot generate reparative chains but only single literals, we can conclude that the applicability condition for belief collapses into body-applicability. The same happens to desires, where we also consider the Convert relation. For obligations, each element before the current one must be a violated obligation. A literal is a candidate to be a goal only if none of the previous elements in the chain have been proved as a goal. For intentions, the elements of the chain must pass the wishful thinking filter, while social intentions are also constrained not to violate any norm.

Definition 3. *Given a proof P, $r \in R[q, i]$ is applicable (at index i and step $n+1$) for*

1. *B iff $r \in R^B$ and is body-applicable.*
2. *O iff either: (2.1.1) $r \in R^O$ and is body-applicable, (2.1.2) $\forall c_k \in C(r)$, $k < i$, $+\partial_O c_k \in P(1..n)$ and $-\partial c_k \in P(1..n)$, or (2.2) r is Conv-applicable.*
3. *D iff either: (3.1) $r \in R^U$ and is body-applicable, or (3.2) Conv-applicable.*

4. $\Box \in \{G, I, SI\}$ *iff either: (4.1.1)* $r \in R^U$ *and is body-applicable, (4.1.2)* $\forall c_k \in C(r)$, $k <$
i, $+\partial_{\blacksquare} \sim c_k \in P(1..n)$ *for some* ■ *such that* $\mathrm{Conflict}(\blacksquare, \Box)$ *and* $-\partial_{\Box} c_k \in P(1..n)$ *or*
(4.2) r is Conv-applicable.
For G *there are no conflicts; for* I *we have* $\mathrm{Conflict}(B, I)$, *and for* SI *we have*
$\mathrm{Conflict}(B, SI)$ *and* $\mathrm{Conflict}(O, SI)$.

Again, conditions to establish that a rule is discarded follow the principle of strong
negation. We now describe the proof conditions for the various modal operators; we
start with those for desires:

$+\partial_D$: If $P(n+1) = +\partial_D q$ then
(1) $Dq \in F$ or
(2) (2.1) $\neg Dq \notin F$ and
    (2.2) $\exists r \in R[q, i]$: r is applicable for D and
    (2.3) $\forall s \in R[\sim q, j]$ either (2.3.1) s is discarded for D, or (2.3.2) $s \not\succ r$.

We say that a *desire* is each element in a chain of an outcome rule for which there
is no stronger argument for the opposite desire. The proof conditions for $+\partial_{\Box}$, with
$\Box \in \{B, O, G, I, SI\}$ are as follows:

$+\partial_{\Box}$: If $P(n+1) = +\partial_{\Box} q$ then
(1) $\Box q \in F$ or
(2) (2.1) $\neg \blacksquare q \notin F$ for ■ $= \Box$ or $\mathrm{Convert}(\blacksquare, \Box)$ and
    (2.2) $\exists r \in R[q, i]$: r is applicable for $\Box$ and
    (2.3) $\forall s \in R^{\blacksquare}[\sim q, j]$ either
        (2.3.1) s is discarded for ■, or
        (2.3.2) $\exists t \in R^{\Diamond}[q, k]$: t is applicable for $\Diamond$ and either
            (2.3.2.1) $t > s$ if ■ $= \Diamond$, $\mathrm{Convert}(\blacksquare, \Diamond)$, or $\mathrm{Convert}(\Diamond, \blacksquare)$; or
            (2.3.2.2) $\mathrm{Conflict}(\Diamond, \blacksquare)$.

To show that a literal q is defeasibly provable with modality $\Box$ we have two choices:
(1) modal literal $\Box q$ is a fact; or (2) we need to argue using the defeasible part of D.
In this case, we require that a complementary literal (of the same modality, or of a
conflictual modality) does not appear in the set of facts (2.1), and that there must be an
applicable rule for q for mode $\Box$ (2.2). Moreover, each possible attack brought by a rule
s for $\sim q$ has to be either discarded (3.1), or successfully counterattacked by another
stronger rule t for q (2.3.2). We recall that the superiority relation combines rules of the
same mode, rules with different modes that produce complementary conclusion of the
same mode through conversion (both considered in clause (2.3.2.1)), and conflictual
modalities (clause 2.3.2.2). Obviously, if $\Box = B$, then the proof conditions reduce to
those of classical defeasible logic [2].

Again, the negative counterparts ($-\partial_D$ and $-\partial_{\Box}$) are derived by strong negation applied to conditions for $+\partial_D$ and $+\partial_{\Box}$, respectively.

Let us consider the theory $D = (\{\neg b_1, O\neg b_2, SI b_4\}, \{r: \Rightarrow_U b_1 \odot b_2 \odot b_3 \odot b_4\}, \emptyset)$.
Then r is trivially applicable for D and $+\partial_D b_i$ holds, for $1 \leq i \leq 4$. Moreover, we have
$+\partial_G b_1$ and r is discarded for G after b_1. Since $+\partial \neg b_1$ and $\mathrm{Conflict}(B, I)$, $-\partial_I b_1$ holds
(as well as $-\partial_{SI} b_1$); the rule is applicable for I and b_2, and we are able to prove $+\partial_I b_2$,
thus the rule becomes discarded for I after b_2. Given that $O\neg b_2$ is a fact, r is discarded
for SI and b_2 and $-\partial_{SI} b_2$ is proved, which in turn makes the rule applicable for SI at b_3,
proving $+\partial_{SI} b_3$. As we have argued before, this would make the rule discarded for b_4.

Nevertheless, b_4 is still provable with modality SI (in this case because it is a fact, but in other theories there could be more rules with b_4 in their head).

In [1], authors showed coherency and consistency of the logical apparatus.

2.3   Norm and Outcome Compliance

Our logic is able to model in a natural way the concept of being compliant with respect to norms and outcomes. We introduce the literal $\perp$ whose interpretation is an un-compliant situation, and we exploit the modal derivations of $\perp$ to formally characterise norm compliant $(-\partial_O \perp)$ and goal compliant $(-\partial_\Box \perp, \Box \in \{G, I, SI\})$ situations.

$-\partial_O \perp$: If $P(n+1) = -\partial_O \perp$ then
(1) $\forall r \in R^O \cup R^{B,O}$ either r is discarded, or either
    (2.1) $\forall c_i \in C(r). -\partial_O c_i$ or
    (2.2) $\exists c_i \in C(r)$ such that $+\partial_O c_i \in P(1..n)$ and $+\partial c_i \in P(1..n)$.

To be norm compliant, all applicable rules producing an obligation are such that either all elements in the consequent are not actually active obligations (condition (2.1)), or one element c_i is an obligation in force which is fulfilled, i.e., we prove it as a belief (condition (2.2)). The situation is slightly different when addressing outcome compliance.

$-\partial_\Box \perp$: If $P(n+1) = -\partial_\Box \perp$ ($\Box \in \{D, G, I, SI\}$) then
(1) $\forall r \in R^U \cup R^{B,\Box}$, Conflict($\blacksquare, \Box$), either r is discarded or
(2) $\exists c_i \in C(r)$ such that $+\partial_\Box c_i, \forall c_j \in C(r), j < i, -\partial_\Box c_j, \exists c_k, k \geq i: +\partial c_k$ and $-\partial_\Box \sim c_k$.

First, the agent chooses her level of commitment, that is the mode $\Box$ among D, G, I, or SI to comply with. Then, we select the first element proved with mode $\Box$ in the consequent of any applicable rule (e.g., element c_i in rule r). We are outcome compliant with respect to r if a following element c_k has been proved as a belief, and its opposite has not been chosen as an outcome to achieve (in this case r is an *outcome-compliant* rule).

3   Algorithmic Results

We now show how to model a process graph starting from a compliant situation. Accordingly, the process graph resulting by the execution of Algorithm 1 COMPLIANCE-BYDESIGN will be compliant by design. Here, we choose intention as the mental attitude the agent has to comply with, thus theory describing the agent capabilities derives $-\partial_O \perp$ as well as $-\partial_I \perp$. The algorithm can be easily modified to treat outcome compliance with respect to the other mental attitudes.

The intuitive idea of the approach is the following. First, for each outcome-compliant rule we select the first element in the corresponding chain proved as an intention (u_i in the algorithm). Elements in such chains are ranked in a preference order and each represents an acceptable outcome for the agent. Thus, we create an X–OR SPLIT/JOIN pattern among u_i and all the elements in the chain following it that are desires with a factual derivation. We propose the exclusive choice pattern among elements since achieving any one of these elements implies the outcome compliance of the entire chain.

As a second step, we navigate backwards the derivation tree, rule by rule, until the facts of the theory are met. We create a node for every l proved within the theory, and we collect all the rules proving it. All rules deriving such a literal correspond to the different ways in which the agent can bring about the state of affairs described by l. These multiple choices can be naturally represented by an OR JOIN pattern. Moreover, we recall that a rule consists of a conclusion and a set of premises: each premise must be proved individually for the rule to be applicable. Again, this property has a natural counterpart in the AND JOIN pattern among the premises. This reasoning is iterated for each antecedent of each rule for l and is processed by Algorithm 2 BACKTRACK.

Once this backwards procedure ends, we are ready to synthesise the process graph in three subsequent steps.

First, we identify the co-occurrence of literals. We say that a set $S \subseteq (\text{Lit} \cup \text{ModLit})$ *co-occurs* iff whenever one of its element is in the antecedent $A(r)$ of a rule, then all the other elements of S are in $A(r)$ as well. The idea is to represent literals in S as a separate building block able to interact with the other parts of the graph.

Second, based on the idea that a trace is a sequence of only tasks, we remove nodes for conditions and modal literals which become labels of annotated edges.

Third, we recognise SPLIT patterns (Algorithm 3 SPLITPATTERN). This step is needed because literals may occur together in more than one antecedent but not co-occur. One can be tempted to solve the problem by a simple incremental approach, that is by identifying those literals which appear together with more frequency, grouping them and iterating the step. For instance, given the rules $r_1 : a,b \Rightarrow u_1, r_2 : a,b,c \Rightarrow u_2, r_3 : a,b,c,d \Rightarrow u_3$ the process described above is depicted in Figure 1(a). However, it can be shown that this method fails for certain configurations. For example, if we consider the sets of antecedents $r_4 : e,f,g \Rightarrow u_4, r_5 : e,f,h \Rightarrow u_5, r_6 : f,g,i \Rightarrow u_6$, the approach would produce the graph reported in Figure 1(b) which is incorrect since it represents two ways to achieve u_4 and not one, namely r_4. Therefore, given a set of antecedents and a pivot literal (resp., sL and l in the algorithms), the proposed solution is to identify a set S such that: (i) the intersection between sets in sL is either l or S, and (ii) S is minimal.

At this level of analysis we make no distinction between OR SPLIT and AND SPLIT, and we consider them in the graph simply as OR SPLIT (OR-S).

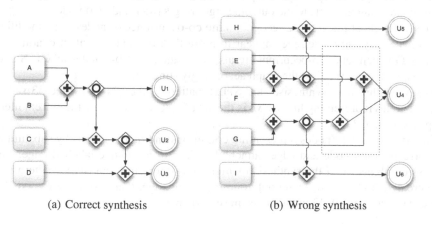

(a) Correct synthesis   (b) Wrong synthesis

Fig. 1. Two instances of SPLIT pattern recognition

Algorithm Notation. As already pointed out, we model the collection of possible alternative courses of action as a process graph $G = (V, E)$, namely *ComplianceGraph* in the algorithms, where V is a set of *nodes* and E a set of *edges*. Nodes represent relevant tasks, while (possibly labelled) edges represent logical dependency among literals, based on rules in the initial theory. Each literal $l \in$ Lit has a unique counterpart in the graph, namely a node labelled with L. This will ease the definition of the formal properties and operations in the algorithms since we can talk about a given node and then refer to the corresponding literal in the theory (and the other way around) without formally bind them every time. For any $X \in V$, we define $in_V(X) = \{Y \in V | (Y, X) \in E\}$ and $out_V(X) = \{Y \in V | (X, Y) \in E\}$.

We are using a semi-formalised language, a pseudocode, that makes use of reserved words. In particular we use the word *procedure* to refer to any kind of subprogram in the code. Moreover, we use the two reserved words **Exit** and **Break** with the following semantics. The first command ends the actual run of the algorithm, while the latter ends the computation of the loop construct.

Here follows a detailed description of the above mentioned algorithms. We begin with Algorithm 1 COMPLIANCEBYDESIGN, the startup of the entire computation.

Algorithm 1 COMPLIANCEBYDESIGN starts by selecting the set of *active* rules (lines 1–3). An *active rule* is an applicable rule which (i) contributes to derive a literal in the positive extension, and (ii) is not defeated by an applicable rule for the opposite. We recall that a modal literal $\Box l$ can be derived in two ways: either directly through a rule $r \in R^\Box$, or by exploiting the Convert relation through a belief rule $r \in R^{B,\Box}$.

The **for** cycle at lines 5–23 models the backtrack procedure briefly described above. Line 6 selects the compliant choices for each active outcome rule. If the step picks more than one element (**if** condition at line 7), then we represent them with an X-OR pattern (**then** branch at lines 8–14), otherwise no additional construct is needed (lines 19–20).

Depending on the number of outcomes selected by line 7, Algorithm 2 BACKTRACK is invoked with a different node as second parameter (lines 16 and 21). In both cases, the computation only considers the factual part of the rules leading to the current outcome u_j. Figure 2(a) shows the graph resulting from the execution of Algorithm 2 BACKTRACK with input theory D of Example 1. In the figures we consider only the subprocesses connecting the facts to the outcomes ignoring START and END nodes.

The **for** cycle at lines 24–32 recognises the co-occurrence of nodes. This modification is necessary only when they appear in more than one antecedent (**if** condition at line 27). For each set of co-occurrent literals, we create an AND-J node and OR-S node (line 28), and then we adjust the graph accordingly (line 29).

The algorithm now synthesises the SPLIT patterns (lines 34–38). Line 33 selects only the nodes representing literals; sL is the set of antecedents where the current literal l appears in (line 35).

Finally, we remove nodes representing conditions and modal literals by substituting the corresponding node and edges attached to it with an unique labelled edge. This process combined with the synthesis of literal co-occurrence and SPLIT pattern may have created AND–J nodes with only one incoming edge, that have to be erased. The **while** cycle at lines 39–43 implements these two operations.

Algorithm 1. COMPLIANCEBYDESIGN

Require: A modal defeasible theory D and its extension $E(D)$
Ensure: A process graph G
1: $R_{ACT} \leftarrow \{r \in R^{\square} \cup R^{B,\square} : C(r) \in +\partial_{\square}\}$ with $\square \in MOD \setminus \{B\}$
2: $R_{ACT} \leftarrow R_{ACT} \setminus \{r \in R_{ACT} : \exists \blacksquare a \in A(r)$ such that $a \in -\partial_{\blacksquare}\}$
                             $\triangleright$ if $r \in R^{B,\square}$ then $\blacksquare = \square$ and $\exists a \in A(r)$ such that $a \in -\partial_{\blacksquare}$
3: $R_{ACT} \leftarrow R_{ACT} \setminus \{r \in R_{ACT} : s > r, s \in R_{ACT}\}$
4: $ComplianceGraph = (V = \{START, END\}, E = \emptyset)$
5: **for** $r \in R^{U} \cap R_{ACT}$ such that $\exists u_i \in C(r)$ such that $u_i \in +\partial_l$ and $\forall u_j, j < i, u_j \notin +\partial_l$ **do**
6:     $goals \leftarrow \{u_j \in C(r) | j \geq i, u_j \in +\partial_D, $ and $u_j \in +\partial_B\}$
7:     **if** $|goals| \geq 2$ **then**
8:        $V \leftarrow V \cup \{XOR\text{-}S_r\} \cup \{XOR\text{-}J_r\}$
9:        $E \leftarrow E \cup \{(XOR\text{-}J_r, END)\}$
10:        **for** $u_j \in goals$ **do**
11:           $V \leftarrow V \cup \{U_j\}$
12:           $E \leftarrow E \cup \{(XOR\text{-}S_r, U_j)\}$
13:           $E \leftarrow E \cup \{(U_j, XOR\text{-}J_r)\}$
14:        **end for**
15:        **for** $u_j \in goals$ **do**
16:           BACKTRACK(u_j, XOR-S_r, $\{r \in R_{ACT} \cap R^B | r$ proves $u_j\}$)
17:        **end for**
18:     **else**
19:        $V \leftarrow V \cup \{U_i\}$
20:        $E \leftarrow E \cup \{(U_i, END)\}$
21:        BACKTRACK(u_i, U_i, $\{r \in R_{ACT} \cap R^B | r$ proves $u_i\}$)
22:     **end if**
23: **end for**
24: $V' \leftarrow V$
25: **for** $L \in V'$ **do** $\triangleright$ Co-occurrence
26:     $cO \leftarrow \{M \in V' | out_V(L) = out_V(M)$ and $m \neq l\}$
27:     **if** $|out_V(L)| \geq 2$ and $|cO| \geq 2$ **then**
28:        $V \leftarrow V \cup \{AND\text{-}J_{cO}\} \cup \{OR\text{-}S_{cO}\}$
29:        $E \leftarrow E \cup \{(M, AND\text{-}J_{cO}) | M \in cO)\} \cup \{(AND\text{-}J_{cO}, OR\text{-}S_{cO})\} \cup \{(OR\text{-}S_{cO}, N) | N \in out_V(L)\}$
                 $\setminus \{(M, N) | M \in cO$ and $N \in out_V(L)\}$
30:     **end if**
31:     $V' \leftarrow V' \setminus cO$
32: **end for**
33: Let $Vlist$ be the list of nodes representing literals
34: **for** $L \in Vlist$ **do** $\triangleright$ SPLIT pattern
35:     $sL \leftarrow \{A(r) | r \in R_{ACT}$ and $l \in A(r)\}$
36:     SPLITPATTERN(l, sL, $null$)
37:     Remove L from $Vlist$
38: **end for**
39: **while** $\exists L \in V$ such that: i. L is an AND-J node and $|in_V(L)| = 1$, ii. l is a condition, or iii. $l = \square m$, with
    $\square \in MOD \setminus \{B\}$ **do** $\triangleright$ Contraction
40:     $E \leftarrow E \cup \{e = (X, Y) | (X, L) \in E$ and $(L, Y) \in E\} \setminus \{(X, Y) |$ either $X = L$, or $Y = L\}$
41:     $label(e) \leftarrow \{l\} \cup label((X, Y))$ with $X = L$ or $Y = L$
42:     $V \leftarrow V \setminus \{L\}$
43: **end while**
44: **return** G

Figure 2(b) shows the final process graph for theory D presented in Example 1 (notice that here Algorithm 3 SPLITPATTERN keeps the graph unchanged). Figure 3 shows the execution of Algorithm 1 COMPLIANCEBYDESIGN on theory D' of Example 2, where Algorithm 3 SPLITPATTERN effectively modifies the graph.

Example 1. Let $D = (\{\Gamma, \Delta, t_1, \ldots, t_5, c_1\}, R, \emptyset)$ be a theory such that

$$R = \{r_1 : \Gamma \Rightarrow_U u_1 \odot u_2 \odot u_3 \qquad r_2 : \Delta \Rightarrow_U \neg u_2$$
$$r_3 : t_1, t_2, t_3 \Rightarrow u_1 \qquad r_4 : t_4, c_1 \Rightarrow u_1$$
$$r_5 : t_1, t_2, O o_1 \Rightarrow u_3 \qquad r_6 : t_4, t_5 \Rightarrow_O o_1\}.$$

Labels of the edges for c_1 and $O o_1$ are highlighted by *dotted* squares; the co-occurrence of tasks T_1 and T_2 is highlighted by a *dashed* square.

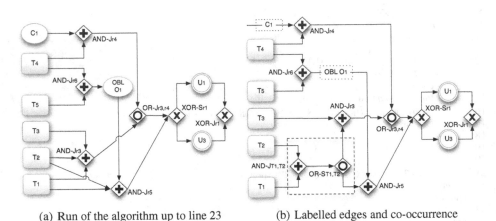

(a) Run of the algorithm up to line 23   (b) Labelled edges and co-occurrence

Fig. 2. Process graph of theory D resulting from Algorithm 1 COMPLIANCEBYDESIGN

Algorithm 2 BACKTRACK performs the backwards construction of the process graph. It receives as input the last processed literal, the set of active rules to be considered (R^{bT}), and the node (N) that will be attached to the edges introduced by the current run of the algorithm. Such a node is either the literal l itself, or the XOR–S whenever l is in the chain of an outcome rule.

The algorithm performs different operations depending on: (i) how many rules prove l, and (ii) the number of elements in the antecedent. If l is a fact (lines 3–6), then we link N to START. Otherwise, we create a node for each element in the antecedent not already in V. If the antecedent contains more than one element, we add an AND–J node between the nodes representing the antecedent and L (**if** condition at line 13, **else** at line 31). Furthermore, if l is derived by more than one rule, the algorithm adds an OR–S node and links it to the suitable nodes (**if** condition at line 23). The algorithm invokes itself on every antecedent of every rule found (lines 10, 19, 30, and 37).

Algorithm 3 SPLITPATTERN takes three input parameters. The third one distinguishes if the algorithm was invoked either (1) by the **while** loop at lines 2–25, or (2.1) by the **while** loop at lines 26–32 or (2.2) by Algorithm 1 COMPLIANCEBYDESIGN at line 36; moreover, the AND–J node created at line 5 will be linked to it.

First, the set S is computed based on the constraints previously discussed (line 2). Notice that condition a) prevents S to contain only l when the algorithm is invoked at line 28 or by Algorithm 1 COMPLIANCEBYDESIGN. The algorithm links each element in S with a new AND–J node, unique for each distinct S (lines 10–12), which is in turn

Algorithm 2. BACKTRACK

```
 1: procedure BACKTRACK(literal l, node N, set of rules R^bT)
 2:     R_ACT ← R_ACT \ R^bT
 3:     if l ∈ F then
 4:         E ← E ∪ {(START, N)}
 5:         Exit
 6:     end if
 7:     if R^bT = {r} and A(r) = {a} then
 8:         V ← V ∪ {A}
 9:         E ← E ∪ {(A, N)}
10:         BACKTRACK(a, A, {r ∈ R_ACT ∩ (R^□ ∪ R^{B,□}) | a ∈ C(r)})
                                    ▷ □ = O if a = Ob, □ = U if a = ■b with ■ = {D, G, I, SI}
11:         Exit
12:     end if
13:     if R^bT = {r} and |A(r)| > 1 then
14:         V ← V ∪ {AND–J_r}
15:         E ← E ∪ {(AND–J_r, N)}
16:         for a ∈ A(r) do
17:             V ← V ∪ {A}
18:             E ← E ∪ {(A, AND–J_r)}
19:             BACKTRACK(a, A, {r ∈ R_ACT ∩ (R^□ ∪ R^{B,□}) | r proves a})
20:         end for
21:         Exit
22:     end if
23:     if |R^bT| > 1 then
24:         V ← V ∪ {OR–J_N}
25:         E ← E ∪ {(OR–J_N, N)}
26:         for r ∈ R^bT do
27:             if A(r) = {a} then
28:                 V ← V ∪ {A}
29:                 E ← E ∪ {(A, OR–J_N)}
30:                 BACKTRACK(a, A, {r ∈ R_ACT ∩ (R^□ ∪ R^{B,□}) | r proves a})
31:             else
32:                 V ← V ∪ {AND–J_r}
33:                 E ← E ∪ {(AND–J_r, OR–J_N)}
34:                 for a ∈ A(r) do
35:                     V ← V ∪ {A}
36:                     E ← E ∪ {(A, AND–J_r)}
37:                     BACKTRACK(a, A, {r ∈ R_ACT ∩ (R^□ ∪ R^{B,□}) | r proves a})
38:                 end for
39:             end if
40:         end for
41:         Exit
42:     end if
43: end procedure
```

attached to an OR–S node (line 6). This operation removes only the edges (N, X), with $n \in S$, such that L is linked to X (i.e., $(L, X) \in E$).

Sets in S can be grouped based on whether they contain another subset $S' \neq S$ joining properties in line 2, or not (resp., *sLrest* in line 18 and *onlyS* in line 14). Thus, for the sets of antecedents in *onlyS*, we just link the OR–S_S to the AND–J_r which was added by Algorithm 2 BACKTRACK (**for** loop at lines 15–17). If *sLrest* is not empty, we choose a new pivot element (m in line 22) and we invoke Algorithm 3 SPLITPATTERN (line 23).

Once the **while** loop at lines 2–25 ends, the remaining sets in *sL* suffer the issue shown in Figure 1(b). This means that no set S satisfying condition c) of line 2 exists. The **while** loop at lines 26–32 solves this problem. By selecting a set of antecedents

---

Algorithm 3. SPLITPATTERN

1: **procedure** SPLITPATTERN(literal l, set sL, node OR-NODE)
2:     **while** $\exists S \subseteq \bigcup_{A(r) \in sL} A(r)$ such that
                    a) if OR-NODE $= null$, then $S \neq \{l\}$
                    b) $\exists T, U \in sL$ such that $T \neq U$ and $S \subseteq T, S \subseteq U$
                    c) $\forall X, Y \in sL$. either $X \cap Y = \{l\}$, or $S \subseteq X \cap Y$
                    d) $\forall X \in \bigcup_{M \in sL}$ if $X \subseteq S$, then $X = S$ **do**
3:         $supp_{sL} \leftarrow \{A(r) \in sL | S \subseteq A(r)\}$
4:         $sL \leftarrow sL \setminus supp_{sL}$
5:         $V \leftarrow V \cup \{\text{AND-J}_S\} \cup \{\text{OR-S}_S\}$
6:         $E \leftarrow E \cup \{(\text{AND-J}_S, \text{OR-S}_S)\}$
7:         **if** OR-NODE $\neq null$ **then**
8:             $E \leftarrow E \cup \{(\text{OR-NODE}, \text{AND-J}_S)\}$
9:         **end if**
10:        **for** $n \in S$ **do**
11:           $E \leftarrow E \setminus \{(\text{N}, \text{X}) | \text{X} \in out_V(\text{L}) \cap out_V(\text{N})\} \cup \{(\text{N}, \text{AND-J}_S)\}$
12:        **end for**
13:        $supp_{sL} \leftarrow \{A(r) \setminus S | A(r) \in supp_{sL}\}$
14:        $onlyS \leftarrow \{A(r) \in supp_{sL} | (\bigcup_{A(t) \in supp_{sL}, r \neq t} A(t)) \cap A(r) = \emptyset\}$
15:        **for** $A(r) \in onlyS$ **do**
16:           $E \leftarrow E \cup \{(\text{OR-S}_S, \text{AND-J}_r)\}$
17:        **end for**
18:        $sLrest \leftarrow supp_{sL} \setminus onlyS$
19:        **if** $sLrest = \emptyset$ **then**
20:           **Break**
21:        **else**
22:           choose $m \in \bigcap_{A(r) \in sLrest} A(r)$
23:           SPLITPATTERN($m, sLrest, \text{OR-S}_S$)
24:        **end if**
25:     **end while**
26:     **while** $\exists W \subseteq \bigcup_{A(r) \in sL} A(r)$ such that satisfies *b*) and *d*) **do**
27:         $supp_W \leftarrow \{A(r) \in sL | W \subseteq A(r)\}$
28:         SPLITPATTERN($l, supp_W, null$)
29:         $sL \leftarrow sL \setminus supp_W$
30:         $intersec_W \leftarrow (\bigcup_{A(r) \in supp_W} A(r) \cap \bigcup_{A(t) \in sL} A(t)) \setminus \{l\}$
31:         $sL \leftarrow \{A(r) \setminus intersec_W | A(r) \in sL\}$
32:     **end while**
33: **end procedure**

---

satisfying conditions *b*) and *d*) ($supp_W$ in line 28), we exclude those sets for which condition *c*) would fail ($A(r_3)$, $A(r_4)$, and $A(r_5)$ in Example 2). Accordingly, if we now run Algorithm 3 SPLITPATTERN on $supp_W$, a new S will be found.

Example 2. Let $D' = (\{t_1, \ldots, t_7, lu_1, \ldots, lu_5\}, R, \emptyset)$ be a theory such that

$$R = \{r_1 : t_1, t_2 \Rightarrow u_1 \qquad\qquad r_2 : t_1, t_2, t_3 \Rightarrow u_2$$
$$r_3 : t_1, t_4, t_5 \Rightarrow u_3 \qquad\qquad r_4 : t_1, t_4, t_6 \Rightarrow u_4$$
$$r_5 : t_1, t_5, t_7 \Rightarrow u_5\}.$$

S is initially $\{t_1, t_2\}$, thus the algorithm creates AND-J_{T_1, T_2} and OR-S_{T_1, T_2} at lines 26–32. Then, the algorithm enters the **while** guard at line 26 with $sL = \{A(r_3), A(r_4), A(r_5)\}$. There are two Ws which satisfy conditions *b*) and *d*), that is $\{t_1, t_4\}$ and $\{t_1, t_5\}$. In this example, the algorithm chooses the former set and invokes itself by passing $l = t_1$ and $supp_W = \{A(r_3), A(r_4)\}$.

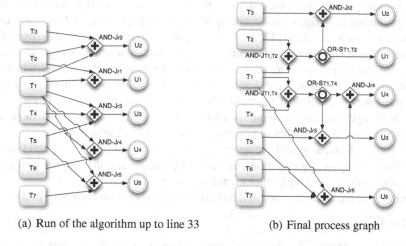

(a) Run of the algorithm up to line 33   (b) Final process graph

Fig. 3. Process graph of theory D' resulting from Algorithm 1 COMPLIANCEBYDESIGN

Computational results. For space reason, we only present a sketch of proof for termination and soundness of the algorithms. Termination of Algorithm 1 COMPLIANCEBY-DESIGN depends on termination of its sub-routines, being the set of literals and rules of theory finite. Algorithm 2 BACKTRACK terminates since: (1) literals and rules of the theory are finite, and (2) each rule is considered exactly once. Algorithm 3 SPLIT-PATTERN terminates since: (1) set sL is finite and this implies that the set possible candidates S is finite as well; (2) rules of the theory in sL are considered once, (3) each operation from line 3 to 18 operates on finite sets, (4) recursive invocation at line 23 takes as input set $sLrest$ which is a subset of sL and contains only (antecedents of) rules not yet handled. The same reasoning applies for operations at lines 26–32.

The soundness of the algorithms is ensured if (1) all the traces generated by the algorithms are compliant and (2) the operations preserve the structure of the theory, i.e. if rule r is $a \Rightarrow b$, in the graph node B does not occur before node A. (1) is guaranteed since R_{ACT} contains only (not defeated) rules with both antecedents and conclusion(s) in the positive extensions. (2) is ensured by Algorithm 2 BACKTRACK which, given a rule $r : a_1, \ldots, a_n \Rightarrow c$, establishes an equivalence between (i) the causality among $a_1, \ldots, a_n$ and c, and (ii) the sequentiality of nodes representing $a_1, \ldots, a_n$ with respect to c. Algorithm 3 preserves these properties. Specifically, causality is guaranteed by conditions $b)$ and $c)$ being T, U, X and Y subsets of sL, and since the AND-J$_S$ and OR-S$_S$ gates generated at line 5 are always placed between the elements in S and the nodes representing conclusions of rules where such elements appear as antecedents.

4 Conclusions and Related Work

The contribution of this paper is twofold: (1) we extended the definition of compliance provided in [8] to accommodate the notion of outcome, and, as the main contribution of the paper, (2) we presented algorithms to generate outcome and norm compliant business processes starting from the description of the environment, norms and the agent's capabilities.

The approach we have presented departs from the standard BDI architecture and agent programming languages implementing it (e.g., 2APL [14], Jason [15]), and extensions with norms (e.g., BOID [12], and see [16] for an overview) in several respects. First, the use of reparation chains allows us to use the same deductive process to compute what are the norms in force, the outcomes the agent subscribe to, and whether agents are outcome and norm compliant. Second, while in the above mentioned approaches the agent has to select (partially) predefined plans from a plan library, we propose that the agent generates on the fly a business process (corresponding to a set of plans) to meet the objectives without violating the norms she is subject to.

There are agent frameworks where agents generate plans (e.g., KPG [17] and Golog [18]), but these are typically based on classical AI planning and they do not consider norms and their interactions with other mental attitudes.

As future research, we will prove that our algorithms work in polynomial time.

References

1. Governatori, G., Olivieri, F., Rotolo, A., Scannapieco, S., Cristani, M.: Picking up the best goal: An analytical study in defeasible logic. In: Morgenstern, L., Stefaneas, P., Lévy, F., Wyner, A., Paschke, A. (eds.) RuleML 2013. LNCS, vol. 8035, pp. 99–113. Springer, Heidelberg (2013)
2. Antoniou, G., Billington, D., Governatori, G., Maher, M.J.: Representation results for defeasible logic. ACM Transactions on Computational Logic 2(2), 255–287 (2001)
3. Bratman, M.E.: Intentions, Plans and Practical Reason. Harvard University Press (1987)
4. Cohen, P.R., Levesque, H.J.: Intention is choice with commitment. Artificial Intelligence 42(2-3), 213–261 (1990)
5. Rao, A.S., Georgeff, M.P.: Modeling rational agents within a BDI-architecture. In: Allen, J.F., Fikes, R., Sandewall, E. (eds.) KR, pp. 473–484. Morgan Kaufmann (1991)
6. Rao, A.S., Georgeff, M.P.: Decision procedures for bdi logics. JLC 8(3), 293–342 (1998)
7. Governatori, G., Rotolo, A.: Logic of violations: A gentzen system for reasoning with contrary-to-duty obligations. Australasian Journal of Logic 4, 193–215 (2006)
8. Governatori, G., Olivieri, F., Scannapieco, S., Cristani, M.: Designing for compliance: Norms and goals. In: Olken, F., Palmirani, M., Sottara, D. (eds.) RuleML - America 2011. LNCS, vol. 7018, pp. 282–297. Springer, Heidelberg (2011)
9. Davenport, T.H.: Process innovation: reengineering work through information technology. Harvard Business School Press (1993)
10. Ghallab, M., Nau, D., Traverso, P.: Automated planning - theory and practice. Elsevier (2004)
11. Governatori, G., Rotolo, A.: BIO logical agents: Norms, beliefs, intentions in defeasible logic. Journal of Autonomous Agents and Multi-Agent Systems 17(1), 36–69 (2008)
12. Broersen, J., Dastani, M., Hulstijn, J., van der Torre, L.: Goal generation in the BOID architecture. Cognitive Science Quarterly 2(3-4), 428–447 (2002)
13. Antoniou, G., Billington, D., Governatori, G., Maher, M.J., Rock, A.: A family of defeasible reasoning logics and its implementation. In: ECAI 2000, pp. 459–463 (2000)
14. Dastani, M.: 2APL: A practical agent programming language. AAMAS 16(3), 214–248 (2008)
15. Bordini, R.H., Wooldridge, M., Hübner, J.: Programming multi-agent systems in agentspeak using Jason. John Wiley & Sons (2007)
16. Alechina, N., Bassiliades, N., Dastani, M., De Vos, M., Logan, B., Mera, S., Morris-Martin, A., Schapachnik, F.: Computational models for normative multi-agent systems. In: Normative Multi-Agent Systems, pp. 71–92 (2013)
17. Kakas, A., Mancarella, P., Sadri, F., Stathis, K., Toni, F.: The kgp model of agency. In: ECAI, pp. 33–37 (2004)
18. Gabaldon, A.: Making golog norm compliant. In: Leite, J., Torroni, P., Ågotnes, T., Boella, G., van der Torre, L. (eds.) CLIMA XII 2011. LNCS, vol. 6814, pp. 275–292. Springer, Heidelberg (2011)

Non-standard Uses of PIRIKA: Pilot of the Right Knowledge and Argument

Yutaka Oomidou[1], Hajime Sawamura[2], Takeshi Hagiwara[2], and Jacques Riche[3]

[1] Graduate School of Science and Technology, Niigata University
8050, 2-cho, Ikarashi, Niigata, 950-2181 Japan
y-oomidou@cs.ie.niigata-u.ac.jp
[2] Institute of Science and Technology, Niigata University
8050, 2-cho, Ikarashi, Niigata, 950-2181 Japan
{sawamura,hagiwara}@ie.niigata-u.ac.jp
[3] Department of Computer Science, Katholieke Universiteit Leuven
Celestijnenlaan 200A, 3001 Heverlee, Leuven, Belgium
riche@cs.kuleuven.ac.be

Abstract. Argumentation is a dialectical process of knowing things (inquiry) and justifying them (advocacy) in general. Computational argumentation has been recognized as a social computing mechanism or paradigm in the multi-agent systems community. We have developed a computational argumentation framework that basically consists of EALP (Extended Annotated Logic Programming) and LMA (Logic of Multiple-valued Argumentation) constructed on top of EALP. In this paper, we describe some non-standard uses of the implemented argumentation system: PIRIKA (Pilot of the Right Knowledge and Argument) based on EALP and LMA, which is now opened to the public as open source software, and show that those uses can extend further the usefulness and usability of PIRIKA together with the standard use of PIRIKA. PIRIKA allows to us to put forward indefinite agendas (partially unspecified ones) with variables, to represent formal literals as semi-natural language sentences, and to use semi-lattice for annotations of truth-values particularly for the Eastern argumentation.

1 Introduction

Argumentation is a dialectical process of knowing things (inquiry) and justifying them (advocacy) in general. In the last years, argumentation has been accepted as a promising social computing mechanism or paradigm in the multi-agent systems community [1]. It has proven to be particularly suitable for dealing with reasoning under incomplete or contradictory information in a dynamically changing and networked distributed environment.

We have developed a computational argumentation framework that basically consists of EALP and LMA [2]. EALP (Extended Annotated Logic Programming) is an expressive logic programming language we formalized for argumentation. The basic language constituents are literals associated with annotations as truth-values or epistemic states of agents. LMA is a Logic of Multiple-valued Argumentation constructed on top of EALP. It has three notions of negation to yield a momentum or driving force for argumentation. LMA is a generic logic of multiple-valued argumentation that allows us

G. Boella et al. (Eds.): PRIMA 2013, LNAI 8291, pp. 229–244, 2013.

to specify various types of truth values depending on application domains, and to deal with uncertain arguments. Such a feature brings us the extensive applicability of LMA that is considered the most advantageous point in comparison to other approaches to argumentation [1].

In this paper, we describe some non-standard uses of the implemented argumentation system: PIRIKA (Pilot of the Right Knowledge and Argument) based on EALP and LMA, which is now opened to the public as open source software, and show that those uses can extend further the usefulness and usability of PIRIKA together with the standard use of PIRIKA. Standard argumentation systems developed so far allow only for determining whether the given definite issues are justified or not. PIRIKA, on the other hand, allows us to put forward indefinite agendas (partially unspecified ones) with variables. It also allows to represent formal literals of EALP as semi-natural language sentences which are composed of simple natural language sentences and annotations as truth-values which can be viewed as qualification of the sentences. The last non-standard use of PIRIKA is one in which we can use upper semi-lattice for annotations of truth-values instead of the underlying standard lattice of EALP and LMA. This is useful particularly for dealing with the Eastern argumentation, and exemplified by applying PIRIKA to arguments concerned with the Jaina seven-valued logic whose truth values is assumed to have an upper semi-lattice structure.

The paper is organized as follows. In Section 2 and 3, we overview EALP and LMA as background of the paper. In Section 4, we present an overall picture of PIRIKA which provides the basic features and various auxiliary ones for standard uses. Section 5 is concerned with non-standard uses of PIRIKA, where we describe (i) argument about issues with variables, (ii) semi-natural language arguments, and (iii) use of upper semi-lattice as truth-values for Eastern argumentation based on Indian logic, together with illustrative examples. The final section includes concluding remarks and future work.

2   Overview of EALP

EALP is an underlying knowledge representation language that we formalized for our logic of multiple-valued argumentation LMA. EALP has two kinds of explicit negation: epistemic explicit negation '$\neg$' and ontological explicit negation '$\sim$', and the default negation 'not'. They are supposed to yield a momentum or driving force for argumentation or dialogue in LMA. In what follows, we describe an outline of EALP.

2.1   Language

Definition 1. (Annotation and annotated atoms[3]). *We assume a complete lattice* $(\mathcal{T}, \leq)$ *of truth values, and denote its least and greatest element by* $\perp$ *and* $\top$ *respectively. The least upper bound operator is denoted by* $\sqcup$. *An annotation is either an element of* $\mathcal{T}$ *(constant annotation), or an annotation variable on* $\mathcal{T}$. *If A is an atomic formula and* μ *is an annotation, then* $A : \mu$ *is an annotated atom. We assume an annotation function* $\neg : \mathcal{T} \to \mathcal{T}$, *and define that* $\neg(A : \mu) = A : (\neg\mu)$. $\neg A : \mu$ *is called the epistemic explicit negation(e-explicit negation) of* $A : \mu$.

Definition 2. (Annotated literals). *Let $A : \mu$ be an annotated atom. Then $\sim (A : \mu)$ is the ontological explicit negation (o-explicit negation) of $A : \mu$. An annotated objective literal is either $\sim A : \mu$ or $A : \mu$. The symbol $\sim$ is also used to denote complementary annotated objective literals. Thus $\sim\sim A : \mu = A : \mu$. If L is an annotated objective literal, then* **not** L *is a default negation of L, and called an annotated default literal. An annotated literal is either of the form* **not** L *or L.*

Definition 3. (Extended Annotated Logic Programs (EALP)). *An extended annotated logic program (EALP) is a set of annotated rules of the form: $H \leftarrow L_1 \& \ldots \& L_n$, where H is an annotated objective literal, and L_i $(1 \le i \le n)$ are annotated literals.*

For simplicity, we assume that a rule with annotation variables or objective variables represents every ground instance of it. We identify a distributed EALP with an *agent*, and treat a set of EALPs as a *multi-agent system*.

2.2 Interpretation

Definition 4. (Extended annotated Herbrand base). *The set of all annotated literals constructed from an EALP P on a complete lattice $\mathcal{T}$ of truth values is called the extended annotated Herbrand base $H_P^{\mathcal{T}}$.*

Definition 5. (Interpretation). *Let $\mathcal{T}$ be a complete lattice of truth values, and P be an EALP. Then, the interpretation on P is the subset $I \subseteq H_P^{\mathcal{T}}$ of the extended annotated Herbrand base $H_P^{\mathcal{T}}$ of P such that for any annotated atom A,*

1. *If $A : \mu \in I$ and $\rho \le \mu$, then $A : \rho \in I$ (downward heredity);*
2. *If $A : \mu \in I$ and $A : \rho \in I$, then $A : (\mu \sqcup \rho) \in I$ (tolerance of difference);*
3. *If $\sim A : \mu \in I$ and $\rho \ge \mu$, then $\sim A : \rho \in I$ (upward heredity).*

The conditions 1 and 2 of Definition 5 reflect the definition of the ideal of a complete lattice of truth values. The ideals-based semantics was first introduced for the interpretation of GAP by Kifer and Subrahmanian [3]. Our EALP for argumentation also employs this since it was shown that the general semantics with ideals is more adequate than the restricted one simply with a complete lattice of truth values [2]. We define three notions of inconsistencies corresponding to three concepts of negation in EALP.

Definition 6. (Inconsistency). *Let I be an interpretation. Then,*

1. *$A : \mu \in I$ and $\neg A : \mu \in I \Leftrightarrow I$ is epistemologically inconsistent (e-inconsistent).*
2. *$A : \mu \in I$ and $\sim A : \mu \in I \Leftrightarrow I$ is ontologically inconsistent (o-inconsistent).*
3. *$A : \mu \in I$ and* **not** $A : \mu \in I$, *or $\sim A : \mu \in I$ and* **not** $\sim A : \mu \in I \Leftrightarrow I$ *is inconsistent in default (d-inconsistent).*

When an interpretation I is o-inconsistent or d-inconsistent, we simply say I is *inconsistent*. We do not see the e-inconsistency as a problematic inconsistency since by the condition 2 of Definition 5, $A : \mu \in I$ and $\neg A : \mu = A : \neg\mu \in I$ imply $A : (\mu \sqcup \neg\mu) \in I$ and we think $A : \mu$ and $\neg A : \mu$ are an acceptable differential. Let I be an interpretation such that $\sim A : \mu \in I$. By the condition 1 of Definition 5, for any ρ such that $\rho \ge \mu$, if $A : \rho \in I$ then I is o-inconsistent. In other words, $\sim A : \mu$ rejects all recognitions ρ such that $\rho \geq \mu$ about A. This is the underlying reason for adopting the condition 3 of Definition 5. These notions of inconsistency yield a logical basis of attack relations described in the multiple-valued argumentation of Section 3.

Definition 7. (Satisfaction). *Let I be an interpretation. For any annotated objective literal H and annotated literal L and L_i, we define the satisfaction relation denoted by '$\models$' as follows.*

- $I \models L \Leftrightarrow L \in I$
- $I \models L_1 \& \cdots \& L_n \Leftrightarrow I \models L_1, \ldots, I \models L_n$
- $I \models H \leftarrow L_1 \& \cdots \& L_n \Leftrightarrow I \models H$ *or* $I \not\models L_1 \& \cdots \& L_n$

3   Overview of LMA

In formalizing logic of argumentation, the most primary concern is the rebuttal relation among arguments since it yields a cause or a momentum of argumentation. The rebuttal relation for two-valued argument models is most simple, so that it merely appears between the contradictory propositions of the form A and $\neg A$. In case of multiple-valued argumentation based on EALP, much complication is to be involved into the rebuttal relation under the different concepts of negation. One of the questions arising from multiple-valuedness is, for example, how a literal with truth-value ρ confronts with a literal with truth-value μ in the involvement with negation. In the next subsection, we outline important notions proper to logic of the multiple-valued argumentation LMA in which the above question is reasonably solved.

3.1   Annotated Arguments

Definition 8. (Reductant and Minimal reductant)
Suppose P is an EALP, and C_i $(1 \leq i \leq k)$ are annotated rules in P of the form: $A : \rho_i \leftarrow L_1^i \& \ldots \& L_{n_i}^i$, in which A is an atom. Let $\rho = \sqcup \{\rho_1, \ldots, \rho_k\}$. Then the following annotated rule is a reductant of P.
$A : \rho \leftarrow L_1^1 \& \ldots \& L_{n_1}^1 \& \ldots \& L_1^k \& \ldots \& L_{n_k}^k$.
A reductant is called a minimal reductant when there does not exist non-empty proper subset $S \subset \{\rho_1, \ldots, \rho_k\}$ such that $\rho = \sqcup S$

Definition 9. (Annotated arguments). *Let P be an EALP. An annotated argument in P is a finite sequence $Arg = [r_1, \ldots, r_n]$ of rules in P such that for every i $(1 \leq i \leq n)$,*

1. *r_i is either a rule in P or a minimal reductant in P.*
2. *For every annotated atom $A : \mu$ in the body of r_i, there exists a r_k $(n \geq k > i)$ such that $A : \rho$ $(\rho \geq \mu)$ is head of r_k.*
3. *For every o-explicit negation $\sim A : \mu$ in the body of r_i, there exists a r_k $(n \geq k > i)$ such that $\sim A : \rho$ $(\rho \leq \mu)$ is head of r_k.*
4. *There exists no proper subsequence of $[r_1, \ldots, r_n]$ which meets from the first to the third conditions, and includes r_1.*

In the subsection 5.4 below, readers will see an argument with reductants.

We denote the set of all arguments in P by $Args_P$, and define the set of all arguments in a set of EALPs $MAS = \{KB_1, \ldots, KB_n\}$ by $Args_{MAS} = Args_{KB_1} \cup \cdots \cup Args_{KB_n}$ ($\subseteq Args_{KB_1 \cup \cdots \cup KB_n}$). This means that each agent has its own knowledge base and do not know other agent's ones before starting arguments. This is a natural assumption for argument settings, differently from other argumentation models [1].

3.2 Attack Relation

Definition 10. (Rebut). *Arg_1 rebuts $Arg_2 \Leftrightarrow$ there exists $A:\mu_1 \in concl(Arg_1)$ and $\sim A:\mu_2 \in concl(Arg_2)$ such that $\mu_1 \geq \mu_2$, or exists $\sim A:\mu_1 \in concl(Arg_1)$ and $A:\mu_2 \in concl(Arg_2)$ such that $\mu_1 \leq \mu_2$.*

Definition 11. (Undercut). *Arg_1 undercuts $Arg_2 \Leftrightarrow$ there exists $A:\mu_1 \in concl(Arg_1)$ and not $A:\mu_2 \in assm(Arg_2)$ such that $\mu_1 \geq \mu_2$, or exists $\sim A:\mu_1 \in concl(Arg_1)$ and not $\sim A:\mu_2 \in assm(Arg_2)$ such that $\mu_1 \leq \mu_2$.*

Definition 12.   (Strictly undercut). *Arg_1 strictly undercuts $Arg_2 \Leftrightarrow Arg_1$ undercuts Arg_2 and Arg_2 does not undercut Arg_1.*

Definition 13.   (Defeat). *Arg_1 defeats $Arg_2 \Leftrightarrow Arg_1$ undercuts Arg_2, or Arg_1 rebuts Arg_2 and Arg_2 does not undercut Arg_1.*

When an argument defeats itself, such an argument is called a *self-defeating argument*. For example, $[p:\mathbf{t} \leftarrow \mathbf{not}\ p:\mathbf{t}]$ and $[q:\mathbf{f} \leftarrow \sim q:\mathbf{f},\ \sim q:\mathbf{f}]$ are all self-defeating. In this paper, however, we rule out self-defeating arguments from argument sets since they are in a sense abnormal, and not entitled to participate in argumentation or dialogue. In this paper, we employ defeat and strictly undercut to specify the set of justified arguments where d stands for defeat and su for strictly undercut.

Definition 14. (acceptable and justified argument [4]**).** *Suppose $Arg_1 \in Args$ and $S \subseteq Args$. Then Arg_1 is acceptable wrt. S if for every $Arg_2 \in Args$ such that $(Arg_2, Arg_1) \in d$ there exists $Arg_3 \in S$ such that $(Arg_3, Arg_2) \in su$. The function $F_{Args,d/su}$ mapping from $\mathcal{P}(Args)$ to $\mathcal{P}(Args)$ is defined by $F_{Args,d/su}(S) = \{Arg \in Args \mid Arg$ is acceptable wrt. $S\}$. We denote a least fixpoint of $F_{Args,d/su}$ by $J_{Args,d/su}$. An argument Arg is justified if $Arg \in J_{d/su}$; an argument is overruled if it is attacked by a justified argument; and an argument is defensible if it is neither justified nor overruled.*

Since $F_{x/y}$ is monotonic, it has a least fixpoint, and can be constructed by the iterative method [4]. Justified arguments can be dialectically determined from a set of arguments by the dialectical proof theory.

Definition 15. (dialogue [5]**)**
A dialogue is a finite nonempty sequence of moves $move_i = (Player_i, Arg_i)$, $(i \geq 1)$ such that

1. $Player_i = P$ (Proponent) $\Leftrightarrow i$ is odd;
   and $Player_i = O$ (Opponent) $\Leftrightarrow i$ is even.

2. *If $Player_i = Player_j = P$ $(i \neq j)$ then $Arg_i \neq Arg_j$.*
3. *If $Player_i = P$ $(i \geq 3)$ then $(Arg_i, Arg_{i-1}) \in su$; and if $Player_i = O$ $(i \geq 2)$ then $(Arg_i, Arg_{i-1}) \in d$.*

In this definition, it is permitted that $P = O$, that is a dialogue is done by only one agent. Then, we say such an argument is a self-argument.

Definition 16. (dialogue tree [5]). *A dialogue tree is a tree of moves such that every branch is a dialogue, and for all moves $move_i = (P, Arg_i)$, the children of $move_i$ are all those moves (O, Arg_j) $(j \geq 1)$ such that $(Arg_j, Arg_i) \in d$.*

Definition 17. (Provably x/y-justified). *Let x be d(efeat) and y su(strictly undercut). An x/y-dialogue D is a winning x/y-dialogue $\Leftrightarrow$ the termination of D is a move of proponent. An x/y-dialogue tree T is a winning x/y-dialogue tree $\Leftrightarrow$ every branch of T is a winning x/y-dialogue. An argument Arg is a provably x/y-justified argument $\Leftrightarrow$ there exists a winning x/y-dialogue tree with Arg as its root.*

We have the sound and complete dialectical proof theory for the argumentation semantics $J_{Args,x/y}$ [2]:

4 Standard Uses of PIRIKA

PIRIKA [1] is an implemented system of EALP/LMA [6]. The argumentation scenario of PIRIKA basically consists of the following phases that constitute the standard use of PIRIKA:

- Registering agents (as avatars of humans) with the argument server so that they can commit to argumentation
- Preparing a lattice of truth values for dealing with uncertainty, depending on application domains
- Designing knowledge bases under the specified truth values in terms of EALP
- Starting argumentation on submitted issues/claims in LMA
- Visualizing the live argumentation process and diagramming arguments
- Determining the status of an argument
- Storing arguments and their results in the argument repository for the future reuse

In addition, many other unique features proper to the logic of multiple-valued argumentation are integrated with the core part of PIRIKA. They are,

- Neural network argumentation to compute Dungean semantics [7]
- Pluralistic argumentation (Western and Eastern arguments) [8]
- Syncretic argumentation [9]
- Frequent sub-argument mining [10]
- Argument animation [11]

---

[1] An acronym for PIlot for the RIght Knowledge and Argument. It is now open to the public as downloadable OSS together with video clips and operation's and users' manual.
http://www.cs.ie.niigata-u.ac.jp/Research/PIRIKA/PIRIKA.html

The overall system architecture of PIRIKA is shown in Figure 1, where the flow in the left side represents a main stream of the argument process, and the right side represents the argument supporting features.

The standard use of PIRIKA is to compute an outcome of argumentation and display it, under the prepared knowledge bases for argumentation in terms of EALP, given a definite issue of the grounded form without variables, as in many argumentation system developed so far [1].

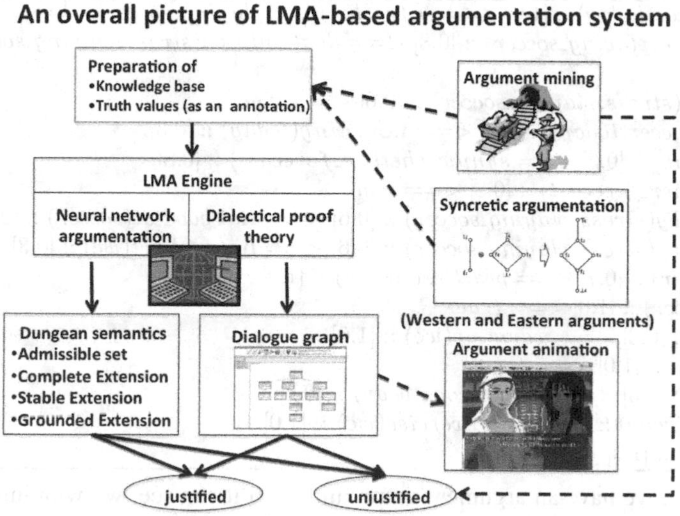

An overall picture of LMA-based argumentation system

Fig. 1. Architecture of PIRIKA

5 Non-standard Uses of PIRIKA

In this section, we present three non-standard uses of PIRIKA, which are helpful for users in one way or another, but can not be seen in argumentation systems developed so far [1].

5.1 Arguing about Issues with Variables

Standard argumentation systems developed so far allow only for determining the argumentation status of definite issues, such as 'human(Socrates)', 'unsafe(nuke)' and so on, under the given knowledge bases. However, we often wish to argue about indefinite issues such as questions or problems satisfying certain conditions. In terms of our EALP, they are annotated literals typically of the following form: $p(X) : 0.8$, $p(a) : Y$, and $p(Y) : W$, where p is a predicate, and X, Y, Z, and W are variables. It should be noted that those questions are of the type 'deliberative', and individual questions of the form [Hx?], read 'Which things satisfy H?', borrowing the terms from the specific area of the logic of question and answer [12].

Furthermore, the argument on the form of $p(a) : Y$ is concerned with 'To what extent the issue $p(a)$ is justified' or 'With how much truthhood the issue $p(a)$ is justified'. We then know the value of Y in the process of argumentation.

Example 1. Let us consider the following knowledge base (we also have the knowledge base on karaoke and game for alternative choices, but omitted) in the EALP notation and an issue be 'What sort of a pastime should we take today?', which is represented as $play(we, X, today) :: [1.0]$.

$play(we, soccer, today) :: [1.0] \mathrel{<==} refresh\_by(we, playing\_soccer) :: [0.8]$.

$refresh\_by(we, playing\_soccer) :: [0.8] \mathrel{<==} deal\_with\_by(stress, playing\_soccer)$
      $:: [0.6]$.

$deal\_with\_by(stress, playing\_soccer) :: [0.6] \mathrel{<==} true$.

$\sim play(we, soccer, today) :: [1.0] \mathrel{<==} \mathbf{not}\, rainy(today) :: [0.5]$.

$\sim rainy(today) :: [0.5] \mathrel{<==} sunny(whether\_forecast) :: [0.8]$.

$sunny(whether\_forecast) :: [0.8] \mathrel{<==} true$.

$\sim deal\_with\_by(stress, playing\_soccer) :: [0.6] \mathrel{<==} \mathbf{not}\, good\_at(soccer) :: [0.7]$.

$\sim deal\_with\_by(stress, playing\_soccer) :: [0.6] \mathrel{<==} \mathbf{not} \sim hurt(we) :: [0.3]$.

$good\_at(soccer) :: [0.7] \mathrel{<==} practice(soccer) :: [1.0]$.

$practice(soccer) :: [1.0] \mathrel{<==} true$.

$\sim hurt(we) :: [0.3] \mathrel{<==} warm\_up(we) :: [1.0]$.

$warm\_up(we) :: [1.0] \mathrel{<==} true$.

$\sim hurt(we) :: [0.3] \mathrel{<==} have(strong\_body) :: [0.9]$.

$have(strong\_body) :: [0.9] \mathrel{<==} exercise(we) :: [1.0]$.

$exercise(we) :: [1.0] \mathrel{<==} true$.

In Figure 2, we have an argument graph and from it can see two winning dialogue trees on the issue $play(we, soccer, today) :: [1.0]$ in which the term *soccer* is substituted to the variable X of the given original issue, $play(we, X, today) :: [1.0]$ from the knowledge base. The existence of two winning dialogue trees can be seen in the leftmost pane of Figure 2.

5.2   Semi-natural Language Arguments

General users may prefer specifying knowledge for argumentation in natural language as much as possible to in logical one. PIRIKA allows to represent formal literals of EALP as semi-natural language sentences which are composed of simple natural language sentences and annotations as truth-values which can be viewed as qualification of the sentences. In EALP, such an uncertain locution as 'the weather will be good as the sky is dyed red by the sunset' can be represented in terms of semi-natural language representation with non-assertive tone as '$weather\_will\_be\_good : 0.7 \leftarrow sky\_is\_dyed\_red\_by\_sunset : 0.8$', for instance. ELP (Extended Logic Programming), on the other hand, forces us to speak even uncertain locutions in an assertive tone: $weather\_will\_be\_good \leftarrow sky\_is\_dyed\_red\_by\_sunset$. This obviously sounds uneasy and we want to say something uncertain as it is like in EALP.

Example 2. The following EALP expressions are written in semi-natural language with definite annotations on the real numbers. Figure 3 displays its resulting dialogue

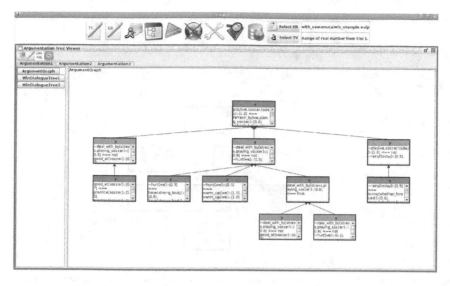

Fig. 2. Argument graph which includes two winning dialogue trees about an issue with variables

process, which is obviously more readable than formal dialogues only even in such a semi-natural language. The existence of one winning dialogue tree can be seen in the leftmost pane of Figure 3.

$we\_play\_soccer :: [1.0] <== we\_can\_refresh :: [0.8] \& we\_can\_go\_out :: [0.9].$

$we\_can\_refresh :: [0.8] <== deal\_with\_stress :: [0.6].$

$deal\_with\_stress :: [0.6] <== true.$

$\sim we\_play\_soccer :: [1.0] <== \textbf{not} \sim rainy :: [0.5].$

$\sim rainy :: [0.5] <== sunny :: [0.7].$

$we\_can\_go\_out :: [0.9] <== sunny :: [0.7].$

$sunny :: [0.7] <== true.$

$\sim we\_deal\_with\_stress :: [0.4] <== \textbf{not}\ i\_good\_at\_soccer :: [0.8].$

$i\_good\_at\_soccer :: [0.8] <== i\_practice\_soccer :: [1.0].$

$i\_practice\_soccer :: [1.0] <== true.$

$\sim i\_good\_at\_soccer :: [0.8] <== i\_have\_no\_sense :: [0.5].$

$i\_have\_no\_sense :: [0.5] <== true.$

$\sim we\_can\_refresh :: [0.8] <== \textbf{not} \sim we\_hurt :: [0.3].$

$\sim we\_hurt :: [0.3] <== we\_warm\_up\_enough :: [0.7].$

$we\_warm\_up\_enough :: [0.7] <== true.$

With this representation, we can obtain an unexpected advantage. PIRIKA can be viewed as a scenario writer since it produces an argumentative dialogue among agents, based on the dialectical proof theory or grounded semantics of PIRIKA. We have been further promoting this observation to argument animation [11]. The way to this consists of three phases.

1. Producing a dialogue process in logical formulas by PIRIKA
2. Translating it to a natural language dialogue by a simple language translation
3. Generating an animation script from it with the help of humans.

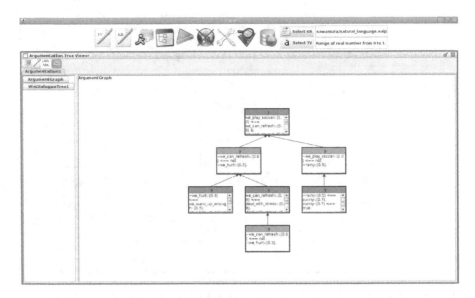

Fig. 3. Dialogue graph with semi-natural language arguments

For example, the following unscientific and empirical but persuasive phrase in EALP, $weather\_is\_good : 0.7 \leftarrow sky\_is\_dyed\_red\_by\_sunset : 0.8$, is almost directly translated to *If the sky is considerably dyed red by sunset, the weather is surely good* in the preparation of a corresponding list of annotations and adverbs or adjectives, without relying on a full-fledged machine translation. In this translation, 0.7 translates to *surely*, and 0.8 *considerably*. The third phrase can be semi-automatically accomplished by using an animation generation software that usually has a script language proper to animation generation. The argument animation allows for enhancing an easy and quick understanding of symbolically generated argumentative dialogues. We refer readers to [13] for extracting argumentative dialogues from the other Dungeon semantics by the neural network.

5.3 Upper Semi-lattice as Truth-Values

In this subsection, we deal with Jaina seven-valued logic [14][15], which is to be captured within an upper semi-lattice. It is a substructure of the lattice assumed in the EALP/LMA framework.

The Jaina logic is said to be an intellectual ahimsa in a word [14], and its doctrines consist of Anekāntavāda, Syādvāda and Nayavāda [16]. Anekāntavāda is one of the most important and fundamental doctrines of Jainism. It refers to the principles of pluralism and multiplicity of viewpoints, the notion that truth and reality are perceived differently from diverse points of view, and that no single point of view is the complete truth.

Syādvāda is the theory of conditioned predication, which provides an expression to anekānta by recommending that the epithet Syād be prefixed to every phrase or expression, and Nayavāda is the theory of partial standpoints. Syād means 'in some ways', 'from a perspective', 'in some aspect', 'somehow', 'maybe', etc. As reality is complex, no single proposition can express the nature of reality fully. Thus the term 'syāt'(in composition 'syād') should be prefixed before each proposition giving it a conditional point of view and thus removing any dogmatism in the statement. Since it ensures that each statement is expressed from seven different conditional and relative viewpoints or propositions, syādvāda is known as the theory of seven conditioned predications. These seven propositions are:

1. syād-astiin some ways, it is.
2. syād-nāstiin some ways, it is not.
3. syād-avaktavyahin some ways, it is indescribable.
4. syād-asti-nāstiin some ways, it is, and it is not.
5. syād-asti-avaktavyahin some ways, it is, and it is indescribable.
6. syād-nāsti-avaktavyahin some ways, it is not, and it is indescribable.
7. syād-asti-nāsti-avaktavyahin some ways, it is, it is not, and it is indescribable.

Each of these seven propositions examines the complex and multifaceted nature of reality from a relative point of view of time, space, substance and mode. To ignore the complexity of reality is to commit the fallacy of dogmatism [16].

The two-valued (Aristotelian or Boolean) logic is based on the 'Laws of Thought.' The Jain theory of modes of truth (saptabhangivada, 'seven-division-ism,' perfected by the sixth-century Samantabhadra) recognizes seven truth-values [14].

We relate those seven propositions (or the seven modes of truth) to the seven truth-values : t, f, i, tf, ti, fi, tfi respectively. Then, we can well capture the structure of the seven truth-values of Jaina logic as the upper semi-lattice as seen in Figure 4, that is,

$$\mathcal{JAINA} = \langle \{t, f, i, tf, ti, fi, tfi\}, \leq \rangle.$$

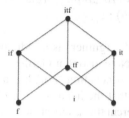

Fig. 4. The upper semi-lattice of seven truth-values in Jaina logic

In what follows, we present argument examples in which intriguing language and logic phenomena can be captured on the basis of the Jaina seven-valued logic.

5.4 Illustrative Argument Examples

We illustrate two arguments in which the principles of pluralism and multiplicity of viewpoints in Jainism deeply get involved, using the upper semi-lattice $\mathcal{JAINA}$ in Figure 4.

Example 3 (Pluralistic or multicultural argument example). Let us consider the Western (Arstotle, Galileo), Eastern and Modern scientist's arguments on free fall. Aristotle believed that the heavier a body is, the faster it falls to the ground. We simply represent this as

[Aristotle's belief]
$aristotle\_hyp : \mathsf{t} \leftarrow not \sim empirically\_factual : \mathsf{t}.$

Galileo's logical argument against this proceeds verbally as follows: "Suppose that we have two bodies, a heavy one called H and a light one called L. Under Aristotle's assumption, H will fall faster than L. Now suppose that H and L are joined together. Now what happens? Well, L plus H is heavier than H so by the initial assumption it should fall faster than H alone. But in the joined body, L is lighter and will act as a 'brake' on H, and L plus H will fall slower than H alone. Hence it follows from the initial assumption that L plus H will both faster and slower than H alone. Since this is absurd, the initial assumption must be false." On the other hand, Easterners prefer a more holistic or dialectical argument like this: 'Aristotle is based on a belief that the physical object is free from any influences of other contextual factors, which is impossible in reality." [17]

These are well translated into EALP as follows:
[Galileo's knowledge]
$\sim aristotle\_hyp : \mathsf{t} \leftarrow faster(l+h, h) : \mathsf{tf}$
$faster(l+h, h) : \mathsf{t} \leftarrow not\ aristotle\_hyp : \mathsf{f}$
$faster(l+h, h) : \mathsf{f} \leftarrow slower(l+h, h) : \mathsf{t}$
$slower(l+h, h) : \mathsf{t} \leftarrow brake(l, h) : \mathsf{t}$
$brake(l, h) : \mathsf{t}$

With this knowledge, Galileo can put forward the following argument
$\sim aristotle\_hyp : \mathsf{t} \leftarrow faster(l+h, h) : \mathsf{tf}$
$faster(l+h, h) : \mathsf{tf} \leftarrow not\ aristotle\_hyp : \mathsf{f}, slower(l+h, h) : \mathsf{t}$
$slower(l+h, h) : \mathsf{t} \leftarrow brake(l, h) : \mathsf{t}$
$brake(l, h) : \mathsf{t},$

where the second rule in Galileo's argument is a reductant (Definition 8 in Section 3) made from his knowledge base. Note also that Galileo made his argument by reductio ad absurdum for which the default negation 'not' has a crucial role in the rule representation. Furthermore, we note that the head $\sim aristotle\_hyp : \mathsf{t}$ in the first rule of Galileo's argument does not undercut the assumption $\sim aristotle\_hyp : \mathsf{f}$ of the second rule, that is, Galileo's argument is coherent or not self-defeating.
[Eastern agent's knowledge]
$\sim aristotle\_hyp : \mathsf{t} \leftarrow distrust\_decontextualization : \mathsf{t}$
$distrust\_decontextualization : \mathsf{t}$

The modern scientist has the following firm belief on verificationism.
[Modern scientist's knowledge]
$\sim empirically\_factual : \mathsf{t} \leftarrow not\ scientifically\_verified : \mathsf{t}.$

Then, under this setting, Galileo's argument is justified as depicted in Figure 5, which is accomplished using PIRIKA on top of iPad.

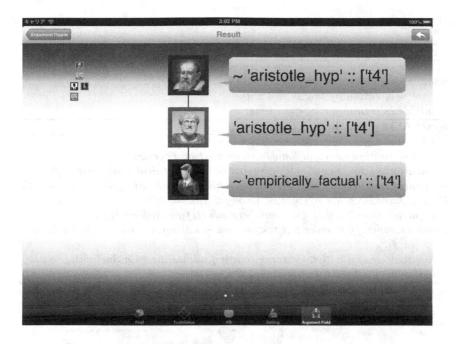

Fig. 5. Galileo's argument justified using PIRIKA on top of iPad

Example 4 (Ethical argument example). We next take up an ethical question 'Is homicide evil?' The knowledge bases of two agents: $A1$ and $CA1$ for the argument are shown in Table 1 in the semi-natural language representation. Agent $A1$ says '*homicide_is_evil* :: $[t\_i]$' with the ground '*when_we_say_no_we_mean_no* :: $[i]$'. Then $[t\_i]$ means 'we cannot explain it, but it is so'. He also believes '*homicide_is_evil* :: $[t]$' with the definite ground. However, both of the assertions turn out to be defeated by the other Agent $CA1$. Agent $CA1$ has a wealth of knowledge compared with $A1$, quoting the famous words of Charlie Chaplin and Georg Jellinek, and exploiting that there is a scene where homicide is permitted. Furthermore, he also has such a unique assertion that '*millions_murder_makes_a_hero* :: $[i\_t\_f]$'. $[i\_t\_f]$ means that if it is stated from a viewpoint of the meaning of the word, it is so, but if it is stated from a viewpoint of one homicide, it is not so, and if it is stated from a viewpoint of a hero's definition, it is indescribable. Actually it is a statement that gets involved in three perspectives.

The arguments on the issue '$\sim$ *homicide_is_evil* :: $[t]$' is justified since they are defeated (rebut) from $A1$, but $A1$'s ground are defeated (undercut) too. We can see the winning dialogue tree in the rightmost branch of the dialogue tree in Figure 6.

PIRIKA usually yields argument results based on the grounded semantics (dialectical proof theory). However, its neural network argumentation engine also provides the other Dungeon semantics such as the admissible extension, stable extension and complete extension as well as the grounded extension [4] as well [7].

Table 1. Knowledge base for seven-valued argumentation in terms of semi-natural language

agent A1 knowledge base : KB_{A1}
$homicide\_is\_evil :: [i\_t] <== not \sim when\_we\_say\_no\_we\_mean\_no :: [i]$.
$homicide\_is\_evil :: [t] <== homicide\_is\_criminal :: [t]$ &
$not \sim violation\_of\_law\_is\_evil :: [t]$.
$homicide\_is\_criminal :: [t] <== true$.
agent CA1 knowledge base : KB_{CA1}
$\sim when\_we\_say\_no\_we\_mean\_no :: [i] <==$
$not \sim anything\_are\_pardonable\_in\_case\_of\_emergency :: [t]$.
$\sim violation\_of\_law\_is\_evil :: [t] <== not \sim law\_is\_ethical\_minimum :: [t]$.
$\sim violation\_of\_law\_is\_evil :: [t] <== law\_has\_no\_sense\_of\_right\_or\_wrong :: [t]$.
$the\_law\_have\_no\_sense\_of\_right\_or\_wrong :: [t] <== true$.
$\sim homicide\_is\_evil :: [i\_t] <== numbers\_sanctify\_murder :: [i\_t]$.
$numbers\_sanctify\_murder :: [i\_t] <== not \sim killing\_millions\_makes\_a\_hero$
$:: [i\_t\_f]$.
$\sim homicide\_is\_evil :: [t] <== some\_country\_allows\_die\_in\_a\_duel :: [t]$.
$some\_country\_allows\_die\_in\_a\_duel :: [t] <== true$.

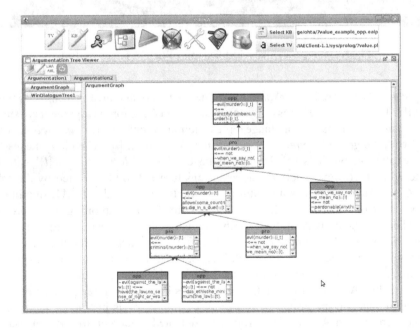

Fig. 6. $\sim murder\_is\_evil : ti \ is \ justified$

6   Related Work

Recently, the importance of multi-valudness in argumentation has been emphasized in one way or another. Here, however, we focus only on the argumentation research with the nature of generality in argumentation, due to the limitation of pagination. There have been a number of proposals for extending Dung's abstract argumentation framework by incorporating preferences or weights on attacks between arguments or on argument themselves. Bistarelli and Santini proposed semiring-based argumentation framework which is a single general one for considering such a range of proposals [18]. He showed that different choices of the semiring represent those different argumentation frameworks. PIRIKA, on the other hand, is a generic argumentation system in the sense that it allows for dealing with various uncertain arguments by choosing appropriate lattices of truth-values according to uncertainty under consideration. Bistarelli and Santini and we have been dealing with different aspects of generality of argumentation system.

7 Concluding Remarks and Future Work

EALP is a very generic knowledge representation language for uncertain arguments, and LMA built on top of it also yields a generic argumentation framework so that it allows agents to construct uncertain arguments under truth values specified depending on application domains. PIRIKA is the only argumentation system that allows uncertainty in computational argument system in a full-fledged manner, and is integrated with such unique features as neural network argumentation, syncretic argumentation, argument mining, and argument animation.

In this paper we manifested the non-standard uses of PIRIKA, an implemented system of EALP/LMA, and revealed their potential usefulness in many application domains. The non-standard uses does not mean deviant uses. By the term non-standard uses, we rather mean that they are ones proper to PIRIKA and have not been attained by other argumentation systems developed so far. Together with the standard use of PIRIKA, those non-standard uses help to lead to practical usefulness from potential one.

We have just started porting PIRIKA on Linux, Windows and Mac OX to pervasive personal tools such as iPhone and iPad. Those tools with argument capability would allow arguing agents to commit and decide whenever convenient for one in a way different from email systems. Here is an interesting and promising scenario of use. Suppose people have their own ideas or opinions on the issue concerned. Then we might want to know what sort of consensus or tendency of the times can be seen for now. We may get it through those tools with argument capability if we foster an avatar or electronic secretary in our own PDAs on a regular basis so that our knowledge and wisdom are reflected to it. It is expected that such an attempt will open up a new horizon for computational argumentation research as well as for the social network service in the future.

Acknowledgments. Dedicated to the memory of Pirika.

References

1. Rahwan, I., Simari, G.R.E.: Argumentation in Artificial Intelligence. Springer (2009)
2. Takahashi, T., Sawamura, H.: A logic of multiple-valued argumentation. In: Proceedings of the Third International Joint Conference on Autonomous Agents and Multi Agent Systems (AAMAS), pp. 800–807. ACM (2004)

3. Kifer, M., Subrahmanian, V.S.: Theory of generalized annotated logic programming and its applications. J. of Logic Programming 12, 335–397 (1992)
4. Dung, P.: On the acceptability of arguments and its fundamental role in nonmonotonic reasoning, logics programming and n-person games. Artificial Intelligence 77, 321–357 (1995)
5. Prakken, H., Sartor, G.: Argument-based extended logic programming with defeasible priorities. J. of Applied Non-Classical Logics 7(1), 25–75 (1997)
6. Tannai, S., Ohta, S., Hagiwara, T., Sawamura, H., Riche, J.: The state of the art in the development of a versatile argumentation system based on the logic of multiple-valued argumentation. In: Proc. of International Conference on Agents and Artificial Intelligence (ICAART 2013), pp. 217–224. INSTICC (2013)
7. Goto, Y., Hagiwara, T., Sawamura, H.: Neural networks computing the dungean semantics of argumentation. In: Madani, K., Kacprzyk, J., Filipe, J. (eds.) IJCCI (NCTA), pp. 5–14. SciTePress (2011)
8. Sawamura, H., Takahashi, T., Matsunaga, K.: An eastern specialization of logic of multiple-valued argumentation to tetralemma originated in india. In: Prasad, B. (ed.) Proceedings of the 2nd Indian International Conference on Artificial Intelligence (IICAI 2005), pp. 1274–1291 (2005)
9. Maruyama, Y., Hasegawa, T., Hagiwara, T., Sawamura, H.: Syncretic argumentation for multi-agents by lattice homomorphism, fusion and sum. In: McBurney, P., Parsons, S., Rahwan, I. (eds.) ArgMAS 2011. LNCS, vol. 7543, pp. 46–65. Springer, Heidelberg (2012)
10. Seino, Y., Sawamura, H., Hagiwara, T.: Towards argument mining. In: Proceedings of 2011 International Conference on Data Engineering and Internet Technology (DEIT 2011), pp. 27–34. IEEE (2011)
11. Narita, T., Sawamura, H.: An attempt to argument metamorphosis from symbols to moving images. In: Proceedings of 2008 Joint Agent Symposium, JAWS 2008 (2008)
12. Harrah, D.: The logic of questions. In: Gabbay, D., Guenthner, F. (eds.) Handbook of Philosophical Logic, vol. II, pp. 715–764. D. Reidel Publishing Company (1984)
13. Goto, Y., Hagiwara, T., Sawamura, H.: Extracting argumentative dialogues from the neural network that computes the dungean argumentation semantics. In: 7th International Workshop on Neural-Symbolic Learning and Reasoning (NESY 2011), pp. 28–33. IEEE (2011)
14. Burch, G.B.: Seven-valued logic in Jain philosophy. International Philosophical Quarterly: An Intercultural Forum 4(1), 68–93 (1964)
15. Ganeri, J.: Jaina logic and the philosophical basis of pluralism. History and Philosophy of Logic 23, 267–281 (2002)
16. Wikipedia: Jainism (2013), http://en.wikipedia.org/wiki/Jainism
17. Nisbett, R.E.: The Geography of Thought: How Asians and Westerners Think Differently... and Why. The Free Press (2003)
18. Bistarelli, S., Santini, F.: A common computational framework for semiring-based argumentation systems. In: Coelho, H., Studer, R., Wooldridge, M. (eds.) ECAI. Frontiers in Artificial Intelligence and Applications, vol. 215, pp. 131–136. IOS Press (2010)

Agents Homogeneous: A Procedurally Anonymous Semantics Characterizing the Homogeneous Fragment of ATL

Truls Pedersen[1] and Sjur Kristoffer Dyrkolbotn[2]

[1] Department of Information Science and Media Studies, University of Bergen, Norway
truls.pedersen@uib.no
[2] Durham Law School, Durham University, UK
s.k.dyrkolbotn@durham.ac.uk

Abstract. In many multi-agent scenarios we encounter *homogeneous* groups of agents; agents that have the same actions available, and for which the system does not care who performs a given action, but only cares about how many agents perform it. Sometimes homogeneity is a descriptive fact, arising from a lack of interest in agents' identity, or the fact that we are simply unable to distinguish between them. Other times, it is a normative requirement, for instance in the context of voting, where we do not want the outcome to depend on who voted for what, only on how many votes each candidate receives. Another important notion is anonymity, which also often arise in multi-agent scenarios, either because we do not know an agent's identity, or else because the systems comes with an explicit commitment to ensure that this information is kept secret. Clearly, the two notions are closely related, and in this paper we explore the relationship that exists between them within the framework of Alternating-time Temporal Logic. We add an homogeneity axiom to this logic, and proceed to show that the resulting logic, which we dub HATL, is sound and complete with respect to a class of structures that are both homogeneous and *procedurally anonymous*, meaning that no information whatsoever needs to be maintained about the actions of individual agents.

1 Introduction

We introduce HATL, a temporal multi-agent logic for studying the strategic ability of coalitions of *procedurally anonymous, homogeneous* agents. The language of HATL is the language of Alternating-time Temporal Logic (ATL), introduced in [1,2], while the semantics is defined using the *role-based* models for ATL introduced in [12], by restricting attention to models with a single role. The resulting structures assume homogeneity among agents and they satisfy a very strong anonymity requirement; not even the modeler needs to know what agents perform what actions. This follows since all that is relevant in our models – and all that is explicitly maintained by them – is information about how *many* agents

G. Boella et al. (Eds.): PRIMA 2013, LNAI 8291, pp. 245–259, 2013.

perform a given action. No information is needed, or maintained, concerning who does what.

It follows from this that the language of ATL, which is built from coalition modalities of the form $\langle\langle A \rangle\rangle X\phi$, for A a set of agents and X a temporal operator[1], can be equivalently replaced by coalition modalities of the form $\langle\langle k \rangle\rangle X\phi$, where k is a natural number. Moreover, it turns out that ensuring faithfulness of this transformation, for the next-time fragment of ATL, is enough to *axiomatize* HATL in terms of the standard ATL-language. This can be done by adding the following *homogeneity* axiom to the standard axiomatization of ATL given in [8].

$$\langle\langle A \rangle\rangle \bigcirc \phi \leftrightarrow \langle\langle B \rangle\rangle \bigcirc \phi \quad \text{iff } |A| = |B| \qquad \textbf{(HOM)}$$

The main result of the paper is that the logic HATL, which is the logic we obtain by adding the homogeneity axiom (**HOM**) to ATL is a sound and complete system with respect to the class of all role-based ATL models with a single role. This result is computationally significant, since it follows by a simple extension of the work done in [12] that model checking HATL is polynomial in the *number of agents*. This is not the case for ATL, and has been regarded as a shortcoming of this logic, especially with respect to applications [10].

The lesson, we believe, is that scenarios which satisfy the homogeneity axiom should *not* be modeled by structures that explicitly maintain a link between agents and the actions they perform (as in the standard CGS-semantics for ATL). Rather, our result shows that a computationally more efficient class of models can be relied on instead. Moreover, we note that this class also accommodates procedural anonymity, in the sense that it suggests implementations that preserve secrecy about which agent perform what actions (trivially so, since this information is not recorded in our models). This, we believe, is a further argument suggesting its appropriateness in applications.

While it is a technically trivial consequence of our axiomatization, we are particularly interested in this latter aspect, and we think of our result as a first step in a more general investigation into the relationship between homogeneity and anonymity. We believe, in particular, that it is a highly relevant aspect of the development of multi-agent systems, and that it has so far been overlooked, particularly in developments that rely on formal logic.

The structure of the paper is as follows. In Section 2 we offer a conceptual discussion on the notions of homogeneity and procedural anonymity. We argue that the mutual dependence and tension between these two notions should be explored further, and that identifying necessary and sufficient conditions for homogeneity in multi-agent formalisms is a worthwhile research challenge. Then, in Section 3 we present our own contribution in this regard, defining HATL directly in terms of homogeneous role-based structures. The main result follows in Section 4, which contains a construction demonstrating that our axiomatization of HATL in terms of ATL is indeed correct.

---

[1] By X here, we mean some arbitrary temporal connective. We use a sufficient set of connectives $\{\bigcirc, \square, \mathcal{U}\}$ and mean by $X\phi$ any formula of the form $\bigcirc\phi$, $\square\phi$, or $\phi\,\mathcal{U}\psi$.

2   Procedural Anonymity and Homogeneity in Multi-agent Systems

In many real-life scenarios involving multi-agent interaction, an important over-riding constraint is that the *identity* of the agents should not be possible to infer by watching how the scenario evolves. We do not want agents to be able to in-fer, by watching the result of each others' actions, who it was that performed a specific action. We want, in particular, to preserve the *anonymity* of those who participate. How can we do this, while at the same time allowing agents to make meaningful individual and/or collective decisions that change the properties of the system? As pointed out in [9,14], this question, which seems like a crucial as-pect to many applications of multi-agent systems, deserves further investigation from a logical point of view.

While the anonymity requirement is intuitively meaningful, it is hard to for-malize, as evidenced for instance by the discussion and various notions considered in [9]. What, in particular, does it mean that it should *not be possible to infer*, by observing how the system develops, which agents made what choices? In some cases this is clearly an impossible requirement, for instance if there is only one agent present, or if there are two agents, and we are referring to the fact that the second agent can infer what the first one did, which indeed he always can (we assume here that the system specification itself is common knowledge, i.e., that any observer knows the set of available actions and by which rules the system develops as a response to agents' actions).

Looking to cryptography, however, we note that it is common to talk of *un-conditional* anonymity in communication when it is not possible to infer who was the sender and who was the receiver of a particular message. As long as there are at least three agents present, a protocol that achieves this is Chaum's protocol [6], a simple suggestion that has proved highly influential. In the con-text of a multi-agent system it achieves what we will refer to here as *procedural anonymity*; by adopting the protocol it is not possible to infer, by observing the *actual data transmitted* between agents, what action is being taken (what mes-sage is being sent) by the individual agents. This, in particular, allows agents to interact without making their actions *visible*. In this way, the protocol allows us to implement, in a procedurally anonymous manner, such multi-agent systems that can be modeled *without making reference* to which agent performs what actions. That is, we can use procedurally anonymous structures to model sys-tems where the effects of actions on the system depends only on *what* actions are taken, not on *who* it was that performed them. We will call systems that satisfies this property *homogeneous*.

Interestingly, as we show in this paper, many systems modeled using het-erogeneous means, where we keep track of what individual agents do, can be equivalently modeled by a homogeneous model, where this information is *not stored*. This can give rise to computational benefits – allowing us to traverse more compact data structures when performing algorithmic tasks – but it also ensures procedural anonymity in the strongest possible sense; inferring what agent did what action is impossible for the simple reason that the model does not record this information. Moreover, this is possible precisely because the system is homogeneous in the sense that it does not in any way depend on such information having been recorded.

In such cases it seems to us that modeling *should* take advantage of this fact, and avoid explicit representation of individual agency. After all, Chaum's protocol means that even when deployed, it is possible to ensure, for such a system, that procedural anonymity is always guaranteed.

We also note, conversely, that while procedural anonymity can certainly be ensured at a lower level of abstraction irrespectively of the high-level design, and also irrespectively of the degree of homogeneity in the system, this will, in many cases, give rise to a superficial notion of anonymity which is often inadequate. As an example, let us consider the motivating scenario used by Chaum himself: There are three cryptographers, they are having dinner and they are informed that the bill has been paid. They want to know if it was *one of them* who paid it, and they want to answer this without making it known *who* it was that paid the bill. The protocol that Chaum describes enables us to do this, but only under the assumption that *nothing else is known* about the cryptographers. If, for instance, it happens to be known that two of them do not have their wallets, then, even if the third person can secretly communicate that he paid the bill, his identity would immediately be possible to infer for everyone with this crucial bit of background information.

The problem, in particular, is that while procedural anonymity ensures that actions can be made invisibly, it does not ensure that it is not possible to infer, from *observing the effect* of that action on the system, who it was that carried it out. In order to ensure that this is also unconditionally impossible, we *need* homogeneity among agents. We must stipulate, in particular, that all the actions are shared among the agents and that, moreover, the outcome of an action does not depend on who it was that performed it.

We remark that this strong form of anonymity, invariance under permutation of players, have recently received interest from the algorithmic game theory community as part of the search for compact, tractable representations of games with a large number of agents, useful for modeling large scale systems such as those studied in internet economics. See for instance [4,3,7].

This notion of homogeneity corresponds to the notion of anonymity studied in social choice theory, stating that the choice aggregated from agents' preferences should not change under renaming of agents, see for instance [5] which also studies some more refined notions. Indeed, anonymity is intuitively reasonable to require from a social choice procedure, as it seems to capture an important notion of *fairness* in this context. Notice that there is no logical implication between procedural anonymity and homogeneity (anonymity in the social choice/game theoretic sense). For instance, it is easy to implement an anonymous voting procedure in a way that is not procedurally anonymous: consider a protocol that demands everyone to cast their vote in full view of all the other agents, for instance by raising their hands. In the sense of voting theory, we could still apply a procedure that gave an "anonymous" outcome. However, in most cases it must be expected that the *actual* outcome of such a protocol will be quite different than it would have been if we had allowed people to vote in secret. This also illustrates our reason for referring to this non-procedural form of anonymity as homogeneity, to stress that it captures a property of how the system regards agents, not a property of how visible agents are to an observer.

To further motivate our work, let us briefly consider multi-agent systems more generally, taking into account the social software paradigm, which argues that multi-agent formalisms can be used as tools for modeling social phenomena [11]. It seems clear that homogeneity is often naturally satisfied, for instance because the systems we design are specifically intended to be such that it can be deployed in settings where it cannot be predicted who the participating agents will be. In even more cases, however, the constraint is *normative*; we want to ensure equality before the law, say, or we aim to facilitate private communication on the web, and worry that procedural anonymity is not sufficient in light of all the background information that the spies have already gathered.

In fact, it seems that even after a superficial look at the range of applications of multi-agent systems, we can conclude that it is of great importance to know when a system displays homogeneous properties. We note that some logical work has been devoted to procedural anonymity, for instance [9,14], where notions of anonymity are investigated from the point of view of epistemic logic, and where the focus is on giving a logical account of circumstances for which it can be ensured that agents do not *know* who does what in a given multi-agent scenario. This is certainly interesting, but it focuses on *internalizing* anonymity as an epistemic notion, allowing us to model anonymity constraints of various kinds. This, in turn, facilitates the study of the effect of requiring such constraints to hold *within* the system, and it facilitates the use of logical tools to verify that these constraints are met.

In this paper, we take a different route, by studying homogeneity and procedural anonymity *semantically*, focusing on studying semantic structures that can be represented in such a way as to satisfy both these constraints unconditionally. In effect, we study a class of models that can be made anonymous in the strongest possible kind: with respect to the modeler himself. As mentioned in the introduction, our starting point is the logic ATL [2], and we build on [12], where an equivalent semantics for ATL was provided using *roles*. There, each role is conceived of as a homogeneous and procedurally anonymous group of agents, and it was shown that this gave rise to more compact models, and hence more efficient model checking. In this paper, we focus instead on the *axiomatic characterization* of *absolute homogeneity*, the case we obtains when there is only one role.

The structures of this kind are shown to provide an equivalent, procedurally anonymous representation of all ATL-models that satisfy the homogeneity axiom introduced in the introduction. This is the main result of the paper, and while it seems satisfying in its own right, it also formalizes the intuition that the *distinction* between homogeneity and procedural anonymity cannot be expressed in ATL. This, we believe, suggests further work where we extend the language of ATL such that we can express properties relating to the interaction between these two notions. The eventual goal of this work should, in our opinion, be to provide an *epistemic* account of anonymity and homogeneity properties of ATL-structures, building on the work done in [9,14].

3   Homogeneous ATL

Let Π and $\mathcal{A}$ be fixed sets of propositional symbols and agents respectively. The standard semantics of ATL can be given in terms of *concurrent game structures*, which are temporal Kripke structures where edges are labeled by sets of action-tuples, specifying how given combinations of actions performed by the agents lead to new states (for a full technical definition, we refer the reader to, e.g., [8]). The language of ATL is defined as follows.

$$\phi ::= p \mid \neg\phi \mid \phi \wedge \phi \mid \langle\!\langle A \rangle\!\rangle \bigcirc \phi \mid \langle\!\langle A \rangle\!\rangle \Box \phi \mid \langle\!\langle A \rangle\!\rangle \phi \mathcal{U} \phi$$

where p is propositional letter, and $A \subseteq \mathcal{A}$ is a coalition of agents. So the language relies on temporal operators indexed by coalitions, where the modality $\langle\!\langle A \rangle\!\rangle X\phi$ should intuitively be understood as saying that the coalition $A \subseteq \mathcal{A}$ can enforce the temporal formula $X\phi$. We follow standard abbreviations (e.g. $\langle\!\langle \ \rangle\!\rangle$ for $\langle\!\langle \emptyset \rangle\!\rangle$) and skip connectives that are derivable.

We will often refer to sets of natural numbers from 1 to some number $n \geq 1$. To simplify the reference to such sets we introduce the notation $[n] = \{1, \ldots, n\}$. Furthermore we will let A^B denote the set of functions from B to A. We will often also work with tuples $v = \langle v_1, \ldots, v_n \rangle$ and view v as a function with domain $[n]$ and write $v(i)$ for v_i. Given a function $f : A \times B \rightarrow C$ and $a \in A$, we will use f_a to denote the function $B \rightarrow C$ defined by $f_a(b) = f(a, b)$ for all $b \in B$.

The semantic structures we will use are defined as follows, following [12].

Definition 3.1. *A* 1RCGS *is a tuple* $H = \langle n, Q, \Pi, \pi, \mathbb{A}, \delta \rangle$ *where:*

- *n is the number of agents,*
- *Q is the non-empty set of states,*
- *Π is a set of propositional letters and $\pi : Q \rightarrow \wp(\Pi)$ maps each state to the set of propositions true in it.*
- *$\mathbb{A} : Q \rightarrow \mathbb{N}^+$ is the number[2] of available actions in a given state.*
- *For every state q we have a set of vectors $P_q = \{F \in [n]^{\mathbb{A}_q} \mid \sum_{i \leq \mathbb{A}_q} F_i = n\}$. We will refer to the elements of P_q as the* profiles *at q. For every such profile $F \in P_q$ we have a successor state $\delta(q, F) = q'$.*

The profiles assigns a natural number to each action such that the sum of these numbers (over all actions) sums up to the number of agents n. The intended meaning of this is that the profile describes how many agents perform each action.

---

[2] We could have included a set of *actions* in the model, but for simplicity index all actions per state and refer only to these indexes in the model.

Definition 3.2. *Given a model and a state q a* partial profile *for $k \leq n$ agents is a vector of numbers, similar to the profiles defined above, summing up to k*

$$P_q(k) := \left\{ F \in [n]^{\mathbb{A}_q} \;\middle|\; \sum_{i \leq \mathbb{A}_q} F_i = k \right\}$$

A (partial) profile $F \in P_q \cup \bigcup_{l \leq n} P_q(l)$ extends *a (partial) profile $G \in P_q \cup \bigcup_{l \leq n} P_q(l)$ iff for every $i \leq \mathbb{A}_q$ we have $G_i \leq F_i$.*

Given two states $q, q' \in Q$, we say that q' is a *successor* of q if there is some $F \in P(q)$ such that $\delta(q, F) = q'$. A *computation* is an infinite sequence $\lambda = q_0 q_1 \dots$ of states such that for all positions $i \geq 0$, q_{i+1} is a successor of q_i. We follow standard abbreviations, hence a q-computation denotes a computation starting at q, and $\lambda[i]$, $\lambda[0, i]$ and $\lambda[i, \infty]$ denote the i-th state, the finite prefix $q_0 q_1 \dots q_i$ and the infinite suffix $q_i q_{i+1} \dots$ of λ for any computation λ and its position $i \geq 0$, respectively.

Definition 3.3. *A* k-strategy *is a map $s_k : Q \to \bigcup_{q \in Q} P(q, k)$ which assigns a k-profile to each state. That is for any $1 \leq k \leq n$, s_k is a k-strategy if, and only if,*

$$s_k(q) \in P(q, k) \text{ for each } q \in Q$$

The set of all k-strategies is denoted by $strat(k)$.

If s is an n-strategy and we apply δ_q to $s(q)$, we obtain a unique new state $q' = \delta_q(s(q))$. Iterating, we get the *induced* computation $\lambda_{s,q} = q_0 q_1 \dots$ such that $q = q_0$ and $\forall i \geq 0 : \delta_{q_i}(s(q_i)) = q_{i+1}$. Given two strategies s and s', we say that $s \leq s'$ iff $\forall q \in Q : s(q) \leq s'(q)$. Given a k-strategy s_k and a state q we get an associated *set* of computations $out(s_k, q)$. This is the set of all computations that can result when at any state, the k of the agents are acting in the way specified by s_k, that is

$$out(s_k, q) := \{\lambda_{s,q} \mid s \text{ is an } n\text{-strategy and } s_k \leq s\}.$$

It is also useful to refer to set of successor states that can result when k agents act according to s_k

$$succ(s_k, q) := \{q' \in Q \mid \text{ there is a profile } F \text{ s.t. } \delta(F, q) = q' \text{ and } s_k(q) \leq F\}$$

Example 3.1 (Deciding on dinner). Imagine n agents trying to decide what to have for dinner. Their protocol is to first decide between a vegetarian and a non-vegetarian option, and then to decide on the meal. They have narrowed the choice down to either couscous or tofu in the vegetarian case, and either sirloin or sea-bass if they decide to go non-vegetarian. The reason why they use a two step protocol is because they are considerate and want to go vegetarian whenever there is a vegetarian among them. As soon as this has been made clear, they wish to let the majority decide. Figure 1 depicts a 1RCGS which models this

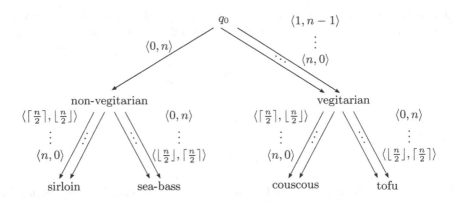

Fig. 1. Example 1RCGS: n agents deciding on dinner

scenario. The names of the states also convey what atoms are true there, and the transitions are labeled by the profiles that trigger them under δ.

Satisfaction of ATL formulas on 1RCGS's is defined as follows.

Definition 3.4. *Given a 1RCGS H and a state q, the satisfaction relation $\models$ is defined inductively:*

- $H, q \models p$ *iff* $p \in \pi(q)$.
- $H, q \models \neg\phi$ *iff not* $H, q \models \phi$.
- $H, q \models \phi \wedge \phi'$ *iff* $H, q \models \phi$ *and* $H, q \models \phi'$.
- $H, q \models \langle\langle A \rangle\rangle \bigcirc \phi$ *iff there is* $s_{|A|} \in strat(|A|)$ *such that for all* $\lambda \in out(s_{|A|}, q)$, *we have* $H, \lambda[1] \models \phi$.
- $H, q \models \langle\langle A \rangle\rangle \square \phi$ *iff there is* $s_{|A|} \in strat(|A|)$ *such that for all* $\lambda \in out(s_{|A|}, q)$ *we have* $S, \lambda[i] \models \phi$ *for all* $i \geq 0$
- $H, q \models \langle\langle A \rangle\rangle \phi \mathcal{U} \phi'$ *iff there is* $s_{|A|} \in strat(|A|)$ *such that for all* $\lambda \in out(s_{|A|}, q)$ *we have* $H, \lambda[i] \models \phi'$ *and* $H, \lambda[j] \models \phi$ *for some* $i \geq 0$ *and for all* $0 \leq j < i$.

One benefit of interpreting ATL-formulas over 1RCGS's is the fact that it gives rise to model checking that has *polynomial* complexity, not only in the size of the model, as for general ATL, but also in the number of players. This was shown and elaborated on in [12], for the case of an arbitrary number of roles (when the exponential dependency attaches to the number of roles, nor the number of agents). The remainder of the present paper is devoted to providing an axiomatization of 1RCGS's. We will show, in particular, that the logic HATL, defined as the following system of axioms and rules, suffice for this purpose. It is obtained by adding the homogeneity axiom (**HOM**) to the sound and complete axiomatization of ATL provided in [8].

Axioms (for any $A \subseteq \mathcal{A}$)

(**TAUT**) Propositional tautologies.

($\bot$) $\neg \langle\!\langle A \rangle\!\rangle \bigcirc \bot$.

($\top$) $\langle\!\langle A \rangle\!\rangle \bigcirc \top$.

(n) $\neg \langle\!\langle \emptyset \rangle\!\rangle \bigcirc \neg \phi \rightarrow \langle\!\langle \mathcal{A} \rangle\!\rangle \bigcirc \phi$.

(**S**) $\langle\!\langle A \rangle\!\rangle \bigcirc \phi_1 \wedge \langle\!\langle B \rangle\!\rangle \bigcirc \phi_2 \rightarrow \langle\!\langle A \cup B \rangle\!\rangle \bigcirc (\phi_1 \wedge \phi_2)$ whenever $A \cap B = \emptyset$.

((**HOM**)) $\langle\!\langle A \rangle\!\rangle \bigcirc \phi \leftrightarrow \langle\!\langle B \rangle\!\rangle \bigcirc \phi$ for all coalitions A, B s.t. $|A| = |B|$

(**FP$_\square$**) $\langle\!\langle A \rangle\!\rangle \square \phi \leftrightarrow \phi \wedge \langle\!\langle A \rangle\!\rangle \bigcirc \langle\!\langle A \rangle\!\rangle \square \phi$.

(**GFP$_\square$**) $\langle\!\langle \emptyset \rangle\!\rangle \square (\theta \rightarrow (\phi \wedge \langle\!\langle A \rangle\!\rangle \bigcirc \theta)) \rightarrow \langle\!\langle \emptyset \rangle\!\rangle \square (\theta \rightarrow \langle\!\langle A \rangle\!\rangle \square \phi)$.

(**FP$_\mathcal{U}$**) $\langle\!\langle A \rangle\!\rangle \phi_1 \mathcal{U} \phi_2 \leftrightarrow \phi_2 \vee (\phi_1 \wedge \langle\!\langle A \rangle\!\rangle \bigcirc \langle\!\langle A \rangle\!\rangle \phi_1 \mathcal{U} \phi_2)$.

(**LFP$_\mathcal{U}$**) $\langle\!\langle \emptyset \rangle\!\rangle \square ((\phi_2 \vee (\phi_1 \wedge \langle\!\langle A \rangle\!\rangle \bigcirc \theta)) \rightarrow \theta) \rightarrow \langle\!\langle \emptyset \rangle\!\rangle \square (\langle\!\langle A \rangle\!\rangle \phi_1 \mathcal{U} \phi_2 \rightarrow \theta)$.

Inference rules (for every $A \subseteq \mathcal{A}$)

(**MP**)

$$\frac{\phi_1 \; ; \; \phi_1 \rightarrow \phi_2}{\phi_2}$$

($\langle\!\langle k \rangle\!\rangle \bigcirc$-**monotonicity**)

$$\frac{\phi_1 \rightarrow \phi_2}{\langle\!\langle A \rangle\!\rangle \bigcirc \phi_1 \rightarrow \langle\!\langle A \rangle\!\rangle \bigcirc \phi_2}$$

($\langle\!\langle \emptyset \rangle\!\rangle \square$-**necessitation**)

$$\frac{\phi}{\langle\!\langle \emptyset \rangle\!\rangle \square \phi}$$

As we have already mentioned in Section 2, it seems to us that in many real-world scenarios, the names of the agents are either irrelevant, unknown, or meant to be kept secret. Either way, homogeneity is by necessity a feature of such a scenario, and we think it is appropriate to recognize this also at the level of the logical model. In distributed computer systems, for example, we do not necessarily know (or care about) the identity/names of the computers performing tasks, rather, what is interesting is *how many* computers are working towards some goal. Other scenarios include any group of agents that we refer to *collectively*, such as "users", "consumers", "voters" and so on. Importantly, as we also discussed in Section 2, when we are reasoning about a homogeneous situation we do not need to name the agents explicitly, and for any coalition who's power we wish to study, keeping note of its size will do. This reflects the procedural anonymity of our semantics structures, and it also warrants the following abbreviation for ATL-formulas, where we replace explicit coalitions with some number $0 \leq k \leq n$:

$$\langle\!\langle k \rangle\!\rangle \phi \; \in \; \{ \; \langle\!\langle A \rangle\!\rangle \phi \mid |A| = k \; \}$$

where $\langle\!\langle k \rangle\!\rangle \phi$ is any arbitrary element of the specified set. Because of (**HOM**), we know that which formula is picked out is irrelevant.

We omit the proof of soundness, which is straightforward, and focus on completeness, which is not. The construction is a non-trivial adaptation of the proof in [8], as presented in the next section.

4   Proving Completeness

We follow the same approach as used in [8], and we will use the normal form introduced there, defined as follows.

- $p, \neg p$ for $p \in \Pi$,
- $\phi_1 \vee \phi_2, \phi_1 \wedge \phi_2$ where ϕ_1, ϕ_2 are normal form ATL-formulas,
- $\langle\!\langle k \rangle\!\rangle \bigcirc \phi, \neg\langle\!\langle k \rangle\!\rangle \bigcirc \phi, \langle\!\langle k \rangle\!\rangle \phi_1 \mathcal{U} \phi_2, \neg\langle\!\langle k \rangle\!\rangle \phi_1 \mathcal{U} \phi_2, \langle\!\langle A \rangle\!\rangle \square \phi, \neg\langle\!\langle A \rangle\!\rangle \square \phi$ where $k \in [n]$ and ϕ, ϕ_1, ϕ_2 are normal form ATL-formulas.

We will also use the *extended closure* of a normal form ATL-formula, denoted $ecl(\phi)$, as defined by Definitions 23 and 24 in [8]. The extended closure is based on a standard closure (taking sub-formulas), but includes some additional elements that concerns eventuality-realization (satisfiability of $\mathcal{U}, \square$-formulas). This aspect of the proof given in [8] can be carried over to HATL with no modification, so we omit going into detail on this point. Rather, we focus on the structure of the proof, pointing out what is different when we restrict attention to 1RCGS's.

The approach of [8] is to construct, for any consistent formula Ψ, a CGS model S^{Ψ} for which there is a state q such that $S^{\Psi}, q \models \Psi$. In doing so, the authors make use of the following.

- Θ-*labeled trees*: a pair $\langle T, V \rangle$ where $T \subseteq \mathbb{N}^*$ is a prefixed closed set of natural numbers and $V : T \to \Theta$.
- ε (the empty string): the root of $\langle T, V \rangle$.
- *Simple trees*: a (labeled) tree which consists of only the root ε and its successors.

In outline, the proof proceeds as follows:

1. Show that a labeled tree corresponds to a CGS.
2. Construct a tree $\langle T, V \rangle$ where the nodes are labeled by maximal consistent sets of formulas from ecl(Ψ).
3. For this tree, show that a formula ϕ from ecl(Ψ) is true at q if, and only if, $\phi \in V(q)$, thereby showing that the tree corresponds to S^{Ψ}.

To build the desired labeled tree, the construction proceeds by putting together simple trees, $\langle T, V \rangle$, labeled with formulas, that are *locally consistent* in the sense that:

1. if $\langle\!\langle A \rangle\!\rangle \bigcirc \phi \in V(\varepsilon)$, then there is a $|A|$-strategy, $s_{|A|}$, s.t. for each $q \in succ(s_{|A|}, t)$, $\phi \in q$, and
2. if $\neg\langle\!\langle A \rangle\!\rangle\bigcirc\eta \in V(t)$, then, for all $|A|$-strategies, $s_{|A|}$, there is a $q \in succ(s_{|A|}, t)$ with $\neg\eta \in q$.

It follows from this that we can show completeness of HATL with respect to 1RCGS's by showing how to use axiom (**HOM**) in such a way that the method in [8] actually gives rise to a 1RCGS. Now, it is easy to see that the CGS that is constructed in [8] will correspond to a 1RCGS if and only if all the simple trees used in the construction corresponds to such models. In the following, we show that when (**HOM**) holds, such simple trees can indeed be constructed. This part of the construction is novel, however; the simple trees from [8] can not be relied on here.

4.1   The Construction

We have some consistent set of formulas Φ for which we will construct a collection of simple trees corresponding to 1RCGS structures where this formula is true. We will assume that Φ does not contain any formulas of the form $\neg\langle\langle n\rangle\rangle \bigcirc \eta$. If it contains such a formula, we replace it with the provably equivalent formula $\langle\langle 0\rangle\rangle \bigcirc \neg\eta$. We will also add the axiom $\langle\langle 0\rangle\rangle \bigcirc \top$ to Φ.

First we define two subsets of $\Phi \subseteq \mathrm{ecl}(\Psi)$, the second of which we'll partition into further sets:

- The *positive* $\bigcirc$-formulas:

$$\Phi^{\oplus} \quad := \bigcup_{\{\ \langle\langle k_i\rangle\rangle \bigcirc \phi_i \in \Phi\ \}} \{\langle\langle k_i\rangle\rangle \bigcirc \phi_i\}$$

We order $\Phi^{\oplus}$ arbitrarily and refer to the i-th formula ($\langle\langle k_i\rangle\rangle \bigcirc \phi_i$) as $\Phi_i^{\oplus}$.
- The *negative* $\bigcirc$-formulas:

$$\Phi^{\ominus} \quad := \bigcup_{\{\ \neg\langle\langle k_i\rangle\rangle \bigcirc \phi_i \in \Phi\ \}} \{\neg\langle\langle k_i\rangle\rangle \bigcirc \phi_i\}$$

We order $\Phi^{\ominus}$ arbitrarily such that the numbers k_i are decreasing and we partition them into segments[3], one for each $0 \le k \le n$, such that if $k_j = k_l$, both corresponding formulas belong to the $(n - k_j)$-th segment. We let $S(\Phi^{\ominus}, k)$ denote the k-th segment, and we let $I(k, i)$ denote the i-th formula of the k-th segment of $\Phi^{\ominus}$.

We define a constant l to be the size of the largest segment of $\Phi^{\ominus}$:

$$l \quad := \quad \max_{k<n}\{\ |S(\Phi^{\ominus}, k)|\ \}$$

We let the actions available to the agents be triples, so that each agent gets to choose three numbers (a, b, c) where a will contribute towards satisfaction of positive formulas and b and c will go towards ensuring satisfaction of negative formulas. We describe the details in what follows, beginning with defining the set of all available triples (actions) in the following set:

$$\mathbb{A} \quad := \quad \{(a, b, c) \in \mathbb{N}^3 \mid a \in [|\Phi^{\oplus}|], b \in [l], \text{ and } c \in [n]\}$$

Complete action vectors are functions of the form $v : \mathbb{A} \to [n]$, telling how many agents have done each action. We will denote the set of complete action vectors as V, and individual action vectors as v. By $v(a, b, c)$ we denote the number of agents performing the action (a, b, c) in v. By $v(*, b, c)$ we denote the sum of $v(a, b, c)$ for all possible a, and similarly for $v(*, *, c)$ and other variants.

Each complete action vector v will correspond to one arrow in the simple tree we construct. We will abuse notation slightly and denote by v^M the endpoint

---

[3] We include a 0-th segment which will always be empty for book-keeping purposes.

of this arrow, i.e., the state that results when agents vote as detailed in v. Remember that points in our model are sets of formula, and we will now describe which formulas we include in the point v^M.

We first give three functions on complete action profiles. We will then use these to define, for each complete action profile, which formulas should be a member of the resulting state.

1. α, which gives all the positive formulas we include in v^M:

$$\alpha(v) \quad := \quad \{ \langle\!\langle k_i \rangle\!\rangle \bigcirc \phi_i \mid \langle\!\langle k_i \rangle\!\rangle \bigcirc \phi_i \in \Phi^{\oplus} \text{ and } k_i \leq v(i, *, *) \}$$

Two refinements of this set of formulas will be useful to us. One is the sum of numbers mentioned in the formulas in $\alpha(v)$, and the other is the set of "activated formulas".

$$\alpha^{\Sigma}(v) \quad := \quad \sum \{ k \mid \langle\!\langle k \rangle\!\rangle \bigcirc \phi \in \alpha(v) \}$$
$$\alpha^{\rightarrow}(v) \quad := \quad \{ \phi \mid \langle\!\langle k \rangle\!\rangle \bigcirc \phi \in \alpha(v) \}$$

2. χ, which gives the least c such that $v(*, *, c)$ is even:

$$\chi(v) = \begin{cases} \text{The least } c \leq n \text{ s.t. } (v(*, *, c) \mod 2) = 0 & \text{if one such } c \text{ exist} \\ \star & \text{otherwise} \end{cases}$$

Note that given a partial action profile v' for $n - k$ agents, the remaining k agents can respond in such a way as to ensure $\chi(v) = k$. Notice the special case of $k = n$ where our construction works because we look for the least segment-index which received an *even* number of votes, and all segments $0 \leq i < n$ can receive one vote each leaving the n-th segment with 0 votes (an even number)[4].

3. β, which picks out a negative formula for possible inclusion in v^M

$$\beta(v) \quad := \quad \begin{cases} \Phi^{\ominus}_{(I(\chi(v), \ \sum_{b \in [l]} b \times v(*, b, *)) \mod |\Phi^{\ominus}_{\chi(v)}|)} & \text{when } \Phi^{\ominus}_{\chi(v)} \neq \emptyset \\ \text{undefined} & \text{otherwise} \end{cases}$$

It is the i-th formula in the $\chi(v)$-th segment, where i is a weighted sum constructed in a way such that we can, by increasing a single element by one, increase the index by any number up to $|\Phi^{\ominus}_{\chi(v)}|$. This will ensure that any formula from the selected section $\Phi^{\ominus}_{\chi(v)}$ can be chosen by increasing a single $v(a, b, c)$ by 1. That is, for all segments, no coalition except the grand coalition can exclude *any* formula from this segment. Equivalently, if we fix some agent and a formula from a segment, the agent always has the power to respond to the votes of the other agents in such a way that his formula gets chosen. This is safe since the choice of segment k, which is the choice

---

[4] This explains why we included the 0-th segment in the construction, even though it is always empty.

of attempting to satisfy *some* formula of the form $\neg\langle\langle n - k\rangle\rangle \bigcirc \phi$, already requires k spoiler agents. However, it is also necessary, since in order to correctly handle the case of $k = 1$, any agent should be able to spoil ϕ all on his own.

We have the following technical lemma, which is significant because it will ensure consistency of the construction of v^M that is to follow.

Lemma 4.1. *If $\beta(v) = \neg\langle\langle n-k\rangle\rangle\bigcirc\eta$ and $\alpha^\Sigma(v)+k \leq n$, then $\alpha^\rightarrow(v)\cup\{\neg\eta\} \nvdash \bot$.*

Proof. (Sketch) Assume to the contrary that $\alpha^\rightarrow(v)\cup\{\neg\eta\}\vdash \bot$. By assumption and definition of $a(v)$ from (1), this means that there are formulas $\langle\langle k_1\rangle\rangle \bigcirc$ $\phi_1,\dots,\langle\langle k_m\rangle\rangle\bigcirc\phi_m$ and $\neg\langle\langle k\rangle\rangle\bigcirc\eta$ such that $\Sigma_{1\leq i\leq m}k_i \leq n-k$. Remember that $\langle\langle k\rangle\rangle\bigcirc\phi$ just denotes some arbitrary member of $\{\langle\langle A\rangle\rangle\bigcirc\phi \mid |A| = k\}$, all of these being equivalent by axiom (**HOM**). Then, what $\Sigma_{1\leq i\leq m}k_i \leq n - k$ means is that we can choose the actual coalitions involved in the positive formulas such that they are all disjoint and such that their union contains the coalition involved in $\neg\langle\langle k\rangle\rangle\bigcirc\eta$. Then we obtain this is a collection of formulas that satisfy the conditions of Lemma 31 in [8]. This is a contradiction, since this lemma is proved syntactically by rules we also have in our system. $\quad\square$

Inclusion in v^M: We now define the set v^M as the least set satisfying the following two conditions.

1. $\alpha^\rightarrow(v) \subseteq v^M$ (all the positive formulas).
2. If $\beta(v) = \neg\langle\langle n - k\rangle\rangle\bigcirc\eta$ and $k + \alpha^\Sigma(v) \leq n$ (which is equivalent to $\alpha^\Sigma(v) \leq n-k$), then $\neg\eta \in v^M$ (add the negative candidate, provided this can be done consistently)

Lemma 4.2 (Existence Lemma). *Let Φ be a finite set of HATL-consistent formulas (which we assume are in normal form, see [8]). We denote by $\Phi^\oplus$ the set of formulas of the form $\langle\langle A\rangle\rangle\bigcirc\phi$ and by $\Phi^\ominus$ the set of formulas of the form $\neg\langle\langle A\rangle\rangle\bigcirc\eta$. Then there is a locally consistent simple labeled tree $\langle T, V\rangle$, labeled with HATL-consistent sets of formulas, having branching degree $\mathcal{O}(|\Phi^\oplus||\Phi^\ominus|)$ such that $V(\varepsilon) = \Phi$.*

Proof. (Sketch) In light of the corresponding Lemma 33 in [8], it is clearly sufficient to show that all formulas in $\Phi^\ominus \cup \phi^\oplus$ are included in $V(\varepsilon)$. The claim for an arbitrary positive formula $\langle\langle A\rangle\rangle\bigcirc\phi$ follows easily from definition of α which ensures that any coalition of size $|A|$ can choose their actions such that ϕ is in the next state. The claim for an arbitrary negative formula $\neg\langle\langle A\rangle\rangle\bigcirc\phi$ is equally straightforward, but results from the more complex definitions of χ and β, and the consistency check that we proved to be sound in Lemma 4.1 above. To see how it all fits together, first remember that when defining χ, we ensured that any coalition of $n \setminus |A|$ agents can, as a response to any joint action taken by A, trigger the segment containing (a formula equivalent to) $\neg\langle\langle A\rangle\rangle\bigcirc\phi$. Then, by our definition of β, we ensure that keeping the actions of all other agents fixed, *any* agent can choose which formula in this segment will be included in the next state. So, as a whole, when $|A| \leq n - 1$, any coalition $\mathcal{A} \setminus A$, has, for every action taken by A, a counter-action that ensures $\neg \phi$. Moreover, if $n \setminus |A|$ agents are truly committed to this, and wants to play the role of spoiler, they can choose $\langle\langle \emptyset \rangle\rangle \bigcirc \top$ as their positive formula in the a-coordinate (remember that it was added to Φ). Then, in particular, they do not contribute to filling up $\alpha^{\Sigma}(v)$, so they also ensure that we pass the consistency check, proved to be sufficient in Lemma 4.1. It follows, in particular, that whatever A does, whenever the complement of A responds by doing all this, we get to a state with $\neg \phi$, witnessing to the satisfiability of $\neg\langle\langle A \rangle\rangle\phi$ as desired.   □

In light of this lemma the desired result follows upon noting that all other parts of the proof in [8] can be carried out in the same way for HATL.

Theorem 4.1. *The logic* HATL *is sound and complete with respect to the class of all* 1RCGS *structures*

5   Conclusion

We added a homogeneity axiom to ATL, and studied the resulting logic HATL. We introduced two conceptual notions of procedural anonymity and homogeneity, with the former being derived from the notion of unconditional intractability in cryptography, and the latter deriving from the anonymity requirement in social choice theory. Then we showed that the logic HATL is sound and complete for a class of models that satisfies both these properties trivially, noting also that these models are more compact, and lead to more efficient model checking than the standard semantics for ATL. We argued, moreover, that the search for characterizations of homogeneity in multi-agent systems is worthwhile more generally.

For future work we would like to explore the link between anonymity and homogeneity further, by considering extensions of the language of ATL that allows us to express the difference between these two notion in the object language. Following this, we would also like to consider epistemic connections, allowing us to *internalize* the analysis, along the lines of the work done in [9,14]. Eventually, we would like to move on in order to explore the relationship between homogeneity and anonymity in other logical formalisms for modeling agent interaction, such as Dynamic Epistemic Logic [13].

References

1. Alur, R., Henzinger, T.A., Kupferman, O.: Alternating-time temporal logic. In: de Roever, W.-P., Langmaack, H., Pnueli, A. (eds.) COMPOS 1997. LNCS, vol. 1536, p. 23. Springer, Heidelberg (1998)
2. Alur, R., Henzinger, T., Kupferman, O.: Alternating-time temporal logic. Journal of the ACM (JACM) 49(5), 672–713 (2002)
3. Blonski, M.: Characterization of pure strategy equilibria in finite anonymous games. Journal of Mathematical Economics 34, 225–233 (2000)

4. Brandt, F., Fischer, F., Holzer, M.: Symmetries and the complexity of pure nash equilibrium. Journal of Computer and System Sciences 75(3), 163–177 (2009)
5. Campbell, D., Fishburn, P.: Anonymity conditions in social choice theory. Theory and Decision 12(1), 21–39 (1980)
6. Chaum, D.: The dining cryptographers problem: unconditional sender and recipient untraceability. J. Cryptol. 1(1), 65–75 (1988)
7. Daskalakis, C., Papadimitriou, C.: Computing equilibria in anonymous games. In: 48th Annual IEEE Symposium on Foundations of Computer Science, FOCS 2007, pp. 83–93 (2007)
8. Goranko, V., van Drimmelen, G.: Complete axiomatization and decidability of alternating-time temporal logic. Theor. Comput. Sci. 353(1-3), 93–117 (2006)
9. Halpern, J.Y., O'Neill, K.R.: Anonymity and information hiding in multiagent systems. J. Comput. Secur. 13(3), 483–514 (2005)
10. Jamroga, W., Dix, J.: Do agents make model checking explode (computationally)? In: Pěchouček, M., Petta, P., Varga, L.Z. (eds.) CEEMAS 2005. LNCS (LNAI), vol. 3690, pp. 398–407. Springer, Heidelberg (2005)
11. Parikh, R.: Social software. Synthese 132, 200–202 (2001)
12. Pedersen, T., Dyrkolbotn, S., Kaźmierczak, P., Parmann, E.: Concurrent game structures with roles. In: Mogavero, F., Murano, A., Vardi, M.Y. (eds.) Proceedings 1st International Workshop on Strategic Reasoning, Rome, Italy, March 16-17. Electronic Proceedings in Theoretical Computer Science, vol. 112, pp. 61–69. Open Publishing Association (2013)
13. Van Ditmarsch, H., Van Der Hoek, W., Kooi, B.: Dynamic epistemic logic, vol. 337. Springer (2007)
14. van Eijck, J., Orzan, S.: Epistemic verification of anonymity. Electron. Notes Theor. Comput. Sci. 168, 159–174 (2007)

Procedural Justice and 'Fitness for Purpose' of Self-organising Electronic Institutions

Jeremy Pitt, Dídac Busquets, and Régis Riveret

Department of Electrical & Electronic Engineering,
Imperial College London, Exhibition Road, London, SW7 2BT, UK
{j.pitt,d.busquets,r.riveret}@imperial.ac.uk

Abstract. In many multi-agent systems, it is a commonplace requirement to distribute a pool of collectivised resources amongst those agents. One way to meet this requirement is for the agents to mutually agree a set of rules to self-organise and self-regulate the distribution process; but there is no guarantee that any arbitrary set of rules is 'optimal' or congruent with the system environment. Therefore, we propose a framework for measuring the 'fitness for purpose' of such a set of rules, which encapsulates metrics for principles of participation, transparency and balancing, as derived from various conceptions of procedural justice. We define a metric for the empowerment dimension of the participation principle, and use this in a proof of concept of the framework, that this metric can reveal an inherent 'fairness' or 'unfairness' over time. We conclude that procedural justice metrics for evaluating 'fitness for purpose' are essential in adaptive institutions of both electronic and human varieties.

1 Introduction

It is a commonplace requirement, in many open multi-agent systems, for a common pool of collectivised resources to be distributed between the agents. Typical examples of such systems include automated irrigation management systems and 'smart' electrical power management systems, cloud and grid computing, and ad hoc, sensor and vehicular networks.

In open systems designed to meet this requirement, there are a number of desirable non-functional requirements of the distribution procedure and its outcomes, such as ensuring some degree of 'fairness', although there are many different metrics for evaluating fairness [16]. Equally, there are many potential pitfalls to avoid, such as free-riding, free-for-alls, and the tragedy of commons (whereby the common pool is depleted by self-interested behaviour intended to maximise utility in the short-term, even if this is in no-one's long-term interest).

One way of satisfying the desirable properties and avoiding the pitfalls is for the agents to reach a consensus on a set of rules to self-regulate and self-organise the distribution. This is the basis of an *institution*: a mutually-agreed, conventional and structured rule-set used to govern or regulate the behaviour of autonomous agents in a collective group organised for some common purpose, particularly regarding access to some shared (common-pool) resource [18].

G. Boella et al. (Eds.): PRIMA 2013, LNAI 8291, pp. 260–275, 2013.
© Springer-Verlag Berlin Heidelberg 2013

Ostrom [18] identified a set of eight 'institutional design principles' for self-governing (and enduring) institutions. These principles can be complemented by rules for resource provision and appropriation which correspondingly provide for 'fairness' in the distribution using a theory of distributive justice [24].

However, Ostrom could assume that people will apply collective choice rules to select provision and appropriation rules, and systems of graduated sanctions, which are congruent with the environment. Such assumptions cannot be made in multi-agent systems. As a result, if the agents have to learn and adapt, for and by themselves, specific rule sets for particular environmental circumstances – including their own adaptive behaviour – they need to have some way of evaluating the 'fitness for purpose' of these rule sets.

In this paper we propose an innovative framework for such an evaluation, based on *procedural justice*. The motivation for this approach is given in Section 2, in which conceptual definitions of procedural justice from different disciplines are considered, and three principles for measuring procedural justice are derived. Section 3 considers a formal representation of the structures, function and processes of institutions, and defines a new metric for evaluating institutional 'fitness for purpose' in terms of its distribution of institutionalised power [12]. A proof of concept is given Section 4 to show how this metric can reveal an inherent 'fairness' or 'unfairness' over time. We conclude in Section 5, commenting that procedural justice metrics for evaluating 'fitness for purpose' are essential in adaptive institutions of both electronic and human varieties.

2   Procedural Justice

Robert's Rules of Order [25] is a comprehensive manual of procedures for conducting business in a deliberative assembly, i.e. an institution, in which a collection of individuals form a group and make a decision about some policy or course of action, by mutually agreeing some conventional rules and procedures which regulate how that decision is to be made. Such rules can be used by a group of agents, who need to collectivise and distribute a common-pool resource, to agree on provision and appropriation rules to decide on the distribution of resources to agents, sanctions and appeals for non-compliance with the rules, etc.

Our concern in this paper is evaluating the 'fitness for purpose' of such institutions, in particular meeting Ostrom's second institutional design principle that the provision and appropriation rules should be congruent with the environment. There are (at least) three problems with undertaking such an evaluation. Firstly, the requirement to distribute resources *fairly* is a non-functional one and, given the proliferation of fairness metrics [16] and subjectivity of fairness norms [7], correspondingly harder to quantify and reach a common agreement on. Secondly, these institutions are meso-level structures intended to achieve a macro-level outcome by regulating the micro-level behaviour of autonomous individuals, who can not only participate in the selection of the meso-level rules but can also change their behaviour according to incentives implied by the rules. Assuring the connection between behaviour, rules and outcomes is extremely problematic (cf. evidence-based policy-making and legislation [26]). Thirdly, there is a temporal dimension as the environment and constitution of these meso-level structures changes over time, giving rise to various further complications like path dependency [6] and the Shirky Principle [14].

Given these problems, it is necessary to make a more oblique evaluation of 'fitness for purpose', by addressing questions such as: are the rights of members of the institution to participate in collective-choice arrangement adequately represented and protected? Is an institution where decisions are made by one actor who justifies its decision 'preferable' to an institution where the decision is made by a a committee that does not explain how the outcome was reached? Is an institution which expends significant resources on determining the most equitable distribution 'preferable' to one that uses a cheaper method to produce a less fair outcome, but has more resources to distribute as a consequences

To answer these questions, we propose a framework to formalise concepts of *procedural justice*. Procedural justice is of concern to many fields of human endeavour, including dispute resolution in political deliberation, law, public health, organisational psychology, and philosophy. In addition to Rawls' [22] graduated analysis (depending on whether there is a fairness criterion and/or a procedure guaranteeing a fair outcome according to the criterion), this has led to multiple analyses and definitions, for example, procedural justice is . . .:

- . . . a theory of fairness for civil dispute resolution [28], which ensures that the procedural arrangements provide 'adequate' participation and acceptable accuracy;
- . . . a requirement for a community to engage in a democratic process to determine which public health functions the authorities should maintain, with respect to a trade-off between costs and benefits [13] and a justification for their decisions [31];
- . . . a four-component relational model [3] based on subjective assessments of procedural function (evaluating rules and decisions) and source (evaluating the group authorities and their treatment of members).

Based on these definitions, this framework should evaluate 'fitness for purpose' according to three criteria of procedural justice, *participation, transparency* and *balancing*. These we informally define as follows:

The *participation principle* requires that arrangements for the allocation of resource, the selection of collective-choice methods and the resolution of disputes should be structured to provide each interested party (i.e. each appropriator) with the right to 'adequate' participation.

The *transparency principle* is the requirement for those making the decision to communicate the justification for their actions and allow for an appeal, by ensuring that any disinterested third party could validate the outcomes from a specification of the process and the given inputs.

The *balancing principle* is the requirement to select methods for 'fair' resource allocation and sanction which balance out the relative benefits and burdens (for example, in systems with endogenous resources, the most scrupulously fair method may be prohibitively expensive to compute).

The next section gives a more formal analysis of these principles for a formal framework for analysing procedural justice.

3   (Towards A) Formal Framework

We propose to use procedural justice to evaluate the 'fitness-for-purpose' of institutional rules. The previous section identified three principles of procedural justice according to which such an evaluation could be made. In this section, these principles are 'unpacked' to reveal a more detailed description of what each entails. Some different representations of institutional rules (from functional, structural and procedural perspectives) are considered, following which metrics for calculating (comparative) values for the three principles are given.

3.1   Unpacking the Principles

In this section, we unpack the different principles into a set of dimensions.

Dimensions of the Participation Principle. To measure the degree of participation or engagement afforded to the agents by a set of institutional rules, we can identify four dimensions, three of 'space' and one of time, that address the following questions:

- *Empowerment*: what is the distribution of institutionalised power [12] among the members of the institution?
- *Inclusivity*: how many of the agents affected by the rule have a saying on how to choose it?
- *Representation*: are the decisions made solely by agents affected by the rule, or is there any external influence?
- *Decision frequency*: how often a decision about the rule is made, in relationship to its application frequency?

Dimensions of the Transparency Principle. The more an institution is operating 'transparently', the 'easier' it is for its members (or outsiders) to see and understand what decisions are made, and why. This requires addressing aspects of:

- *Justifiability*: is membership of decision-making bodies disclosed, are their procedures available, and are their workings revealed?
- *Accountability*: do those who make the decisions benefit equally (rather than excessively) from the outcomes, and are they liable if they go wrong?
- *Equal Suffrage*: to what extent is the principle of 'one agent, one vote' upheld, or do some agents have multiple votes? Is there a 'golden share' which accounts for 51% of the votes (i.e. guaranteeing a veto)?
- *Temporality*: are decisions appealable, and are they repealable?

Dimensions of the Balancing Principle. In a system with endogenous resources, the balancing principle is particularly important in trading-off the cost of monitoring with its frequency [2]. In addition, there may be a trade-off between the cost of implementing a procedure and ensuring the correct outcome (this is a particular concern for systems of jurisprudence). Yet another aspect of 'balance' is ensuring that procedures give equal outcomes to every individual with comparable other conditions. Therefore the balancing principle should address aspects of:

- *Cost*: what is the cost (in whatever 'currency', which could be time) of operating a procedure?
- *Accuracy*: does the procedure ensure the correct outcome [22]?
- *Consistency*: does a procedure produce equal outcomes for different individuals under the same circumstances?

3.2 'Institution Science'

The previous section specified in which dimensions procedural justice in institutions should be measured; we now need a formal representation of 'an institution' in order define appropriate metrics. Unfortunately, there are many different representations offered by organisation theory, but minimally, for a meaningful measurement of the principles of procedural justice, there is a requirement to represent the structure, functions and processes of institutions (i.e. the objects of study in 'institution science').

In terms of structures the general case with which we are concerned is represented diagrammatically in Figure 1(a). This shows an action situation ([19], originally called a decision arena in [18]) to be regulated by a set of conventional rules, with clearly defined boundaries (determining who is and is not a appropriator belonging to the situation). Within any action situation there are 'decision groups' (here for example there are three). These sub-groups make decisions of conventional significance to the institution; that is to say, there is a procedure for making a decision, which is declared by a distinguished agent occupying an identified role and performing a designated action in the appropriate context, i.e. by the exercise of *institutionalised power* [12].

The relationship between the membership of the institution and any of the decision groups is shown in the 'participation space' shown in Figure 1(b). This 2-dimensional space 'plots' inclusivity against representation (inc × rep, see also Section 3.3), showing the possible relationships between A (institution membership) and DG (group membership). DG_1 and DG_2 are points on the line between ① and ②, whereas DG_3 is in the space 'near' ④. Note that $b \succeq a$ denotes that point b is preferred to point a, while $a \sim b$ denotes indifference between a or b.

In terms of functional representation, an institution's rules, can be divided into three levels, from lower to higher [18]: *operational-choice rules* (OC) are concerned with the provision and appropriation of resources, as well as with membership, monitoring and enforcement; *social collective-choice rules* (SC) drive policy making and management of the institution, including the choice of

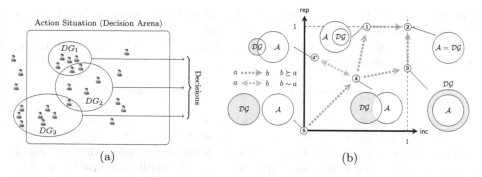

Fig. 1. (a) Action Situation (Decision Arena), (b) Participation Space

the operational choice rules; finally, *constitutional-choice rules* (CC) deal with governance and formulation of the institution.

To determine dependency between rules and the roles occupied by the agents in (members of) the institution, a graphical representation can be used, as illustrated in Figure 2, which shows the relationship between each of the rules, as well as their inputs and outputs.

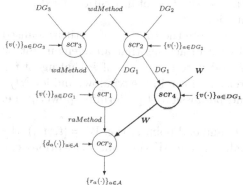

This structure shows an operational choice rule (ocr_2) which maps a set of demands d_a from each agent $a \in \mathcal{A}$ to a set of allocations. For the four social choice rules, scr_1 uses collective choice to select a resource allocation method ($raMethod$) used in ocr_2, scr_2 is the membership election of DG_1 and scr_3 is the vote for the winner determination method ($wdMethod$) to be used in scr_1, and scr_4 selects weights if the resource allocation method is based on legitimate claims (see later).

Fig. 2. Functional relationships between institutional rules

Finally, we need a formal representation of institutional processes which identifies their procedural, temporal and normative aspects, typically of concern in the study of social and organisational systems.

Computational logic can be used to represent these processes, using an Action Language for example the Event Calculus (EC) [15]. The EC is a logical formalism for representing and reasoning about actions or events and their effects based on a many-sorted first-order predicate calculus. An *action description* in EC includes axioms that define a narrative (the occurrence of actions), using the happens predicate; the effects of actions, using initiates and terminates predicates;

and the values of the fluents, using initially and holdsAt predicates. A fluent is a proposition whose values can change over time.

The set of institutional rules can be specified as an EC action description containing axioms of the form:

$$Action \quad \text{initiates} \quad F = V \quad \text{at} \quad T \quad \leftarrow \quad Conditions$$

which are read as stating: the occurrence of action $Action$ at time T initiates a period of time for which the value of fluent F is V, if the $Conditions$ are satisfied. These conditions will gnerally include the requirement that the agent performing the action should be empowered (has the institutionalised power) to do so. This is represented as:

$$\mathbf{pow}(Agent, Action(\ldots)) = true \quad \text{holdsAt} \quad T$$

3.3 Formal Metrics

This section defines metrics for different dimensions of the participation principle, and considers metrics for the transparency and balancing principles.

A Metric for Empowerment. The metric for empowerment is concerned with measuring the degree and variance in the distribution of institutionalised power within a self-organising electronic institution.

During a given time window W, let $\mathcal{P}$ denote the totality of institutionalised powers available to all the roles, i.e. the set of actions that an agent might be empowered to perform during W, let $\mathcal{P}(i)$ denote the subset of $\mathcal{P}$ that agent i is both empowered and permitted to exercise perform in the window, and let $N(p)$ be the number of agents with power and permission of performing power p (i.e. $N(p) = |\{i \mid p \in \mathcal{P}(i), i \in \mathcal{A}\}|$).

Then, for a window with start point t_s and end point t_e (i.e. $W = [t_s, t_e]$), the relative (institutionalised) power of each agent in W (in some institution) can be represented in the generic form:

$$\text{RelIP}_W = [\mathcal{P}; p_1, \ldots, p_n]_W$$

where (dropping the subscript W for the window as obvious from context):

$$p_i = \sum_{p \in \mathcal{P}(i)} \frac{w_p}{N(p)}$$

where w_p is the relative weight (importance) of power p. For the moment, we assume $w_p = 1$ for all p.

Metrics for Inclusivity and Representation. Let $\mathcal{DG}$ be a decision group in an institution, and let $\mathcal{A}$ be the non-empty set of institution members affected by the group's decisions. The degree of inclusivity of a decision group, $\text{inc}_{\mathcal{DG}}$, is the ratio of the number of appropriator agents in the relevant decision group to the number of appropriators:

$$inc_{\mathcal{DG}} = \frac{|\mathcal{A} \cap \mathcal{DG}|}{|\mathcal{A}|}$$

The maximum ratio of inclusivity, $inc_{\mathcal{DG}} = 1$ indicates that all the appropriator agents take part of the decision making, thus satisfying Ostrom's third principle: "those affected by the operational-choice rules participate in selection and modification of those rules". The minimum ratio, $inc_{\mathcal{DG}} = 0$, would indicate that no appropriator agents are involved in the decision outcome of the rule.

Inclusivity is a relative measure of the involvement of the appropriators in the decision groups. Its counterpart is representation, which is a relative measure of the involvement of those *not* affected by the rules yet who still participate in their selection. The degree of representation, $rep_{\mathcal{DG}}$ is the ratio of the number of appropriator agents in the decision group to the size of that group (assuming the group is valid, i.e. non-empty), e.g.:

$$rep_{\mathcal{DG}} = \frac{|\mathcal{A} \cap \mathcal{DG}|}{|\mathcal{DG}|}$$

A degree of representation of $rep_{\mathcal{DG}} = 1$ denotes that there is no external influence in the decision-making. This would partially fulfil Ostrom's seventh principle: "Existence of and control over their own institutions is not challenged by external authorities".

The inclusivity and representation metrics define, for each decision group, a 2-dimensional space (Figure 1(b)), and a point in that space is calculated by:

$$increp(\mathcal{DG}) = inc_{\mathcal{DG}} \times rep_{\mathcal{DG}}$$

If there are n decision groups in an institution, this defines an n-dimensional hypercube, and a point in this space – what we might call the 'Democratic Participation Index' (DPX) – during a window W, is computed by representing each decision-group's point in inclusivity/representation space in a vector, and the coefficient given by multiplying all the elements of the vector together:

$$\mathbf{DPX}_W = \langle increp(\mathcal{DG}_1), increp(\mathcal{DG}_2), \ldots, increp(\mathcal{DG}_n) \rangle$$
$$coeff(\text{DPX})_W = increp(\mathcal{DG}_1) \times increp(\mathcal{DG}_2) \times \ldots \times increp(\mathcal{DG}_n)$$

A Metric for Decision frequency. To account for the fact that the result of applying a rule may be used in various other rules, we proceed as follows. Let r be the rule being analysed. Then, for each rule $r' \in succ(r)$, where $succ(r)$ is the set of children of r (i.e. the edges of the graph in Figure 2), we compute how often a decision (i.e. use of rule r) about rule r' is made:

$$freq(r, r') = \frac{exec(r)}{exec(r')}$$

where $exec(r)$ indicates how many times rule r has been executed.

Metrics for Transparency. There are already metrics for measuring suffrage or enfranchisement, for example the Banzhaf power index for weighted voting systems. In weighted voting systems, not all votes in all elections count equally: for example Roman assembles allowed for voting according to wealth, and Athenian democracy allowed for delegation so that one person could cast many votes.

For justifiability, an EC specification could be useful, if the specification was made open and public, in order that a disinterested third party could replicate the deliberations and verify decisions of a particular group. The problem of accountability, however, is particularly complicated [29] and, in its totality, not necessarily directly addressable using these mechanisms; however there is progress towards action languages for collective action and agency, see [27].

The idea of temporality considers that, on the assumption that procedures may not be perfect, that decisions are not 'written in stone' but can be repealed if shown to be incorrect. Note that a guiding principle of Robert's Rules of Order [25] is that "anything goes unless someone objects", and that one of Ostrom's eight institutional design principles is that there should be an appeals procedure. Therefore the dimension of 'temporality' is a foundational principle of institutional design for Ostrom: therefore it should be possible to determine by inspection whether or not an institution has processes for appealing.

Metrics for Balancing. The Balancing Principle is important for monitoring procedures in a system with endogenous resources where the cost of monitoring is not free. It is possible to ruin a common-pool resource system by over-monitoring, thereby expending all the resources on monitoring and leaving little or nothing to distribute for 'real' tasks.

For the Balancing Principle, one approach would be to analyse the computational complexity of each of the procedures and protocols used by the decision groups. For example, there are many alternative winner determination methods for voting protocols. These vary in their robustness (i.e. resistance to strategic manipulation [30]), but also in their complexity, from plurality to instant runoff (which is up to 10 times more complex).

4   Proof of Concept

Some of the metrics have clearer functional definition than others, but none of these measures are *absolute* or binary, in the sense that they return either a "yes, fit for purpose" or "no, not fit for purpose" outcome. In other words, they need to be used as *relative* measures, for example in comparative assessments, or in evaluating trade-offs (especially the balancing principle).

This section describes a demonstrator system which uses the empowerment metric as a dimension of the Participation Principle to calculate the RelIP for an electronic institution. The experimental setting is a self-organising electronic institution for endogenous resource provision and appropriation. This is described next, followed by the specification of a test system which has been developed, and a presentation and evaluation of some observed experimental results.

4.1   Setting: Self-organising Resource Allocation

The experimental setting is concerned with self-organised resource allocation amongst a set of appropriator agents.

This situation has typically been studied as a variant of the Linear Public Good (LPG) game LPG' [21]. In the LPG' game, the provision and appropriation of resources occurs in a sequence of rounds. In each round, first the 'players' (i.e. the appropriators, which we will hereafter refer to as agents) provide and demand resources. Next, a resource-allocation method is used to compute an allocation to each agent. Each agent then appropriates its allocation. The process is regulated by a set of mutually-agreed, conventional rules, i.e., an institution.

There are many different resource-allocation methods that can be used, for example, ration, random, queue, etc. In [21], a method using legitimate claims based on a formalisation of Rescher's [24] theory of distributive justice was used. This method treats each legitimate claim to resources (based on need, provision, equal treatment, voluntary contribution, etc.) as a function which created a total order on the agents making demands. Each order was treated as a weighted vote in a candidate election to create a final order. Resources are allocated to those agents in this order until there were no resources to distribute. The agents themselves vote on the weight to be associated with the claims in the candidate election for the next round.

In this setting, three decisions need to be made through the collective action of a decision group:

- DG_1: Resource allocation – applies the resource-allocation method to compute a set of allocations;
- DG_2: Weights on legitimate claims – selects and applies an algorithm for winner-determination which computes a new weight for the legitimate claims;
- DG_3: Role assignment – selects and applies a role-assignment protocol to select an agent to occupy a role or to admit an agent to occupy that role.

For the resource-allocation method using legitimate claims, the following roles, empowered actions and decision-group 'contexts' can be identified:

Role	DG	Action
prosumer	A	*provide, demand, appropriate* (resources)
allocator	1	*announce* (candidate election result), *allocate* (resources)
head	2	*cfv* (call for votes), *declare* (weights on legitimate claims)
voter	2	*vote* (expressed preference for legitimate claims)
authorizer	3	*appoint* (assign agent to role)

The DG_1 function specifies the decision of a resource allocation, but it does not specify when or how this allocation is done, or who 'brings it about'. For this we need a role *allocator*, and the agent assigned to this role is empowered to declare the results of applying the resource allocation method. The *allocate* action initiates values for three EC fluents: an allocation to an agent, a reduction in the amount of pooled resource (*ifpool*) to allocate, and removing the agent from the front of the legitimate claim queue. A complete EC specification for the process is given in [21].

Example. Consider a self-organising electronic institution using an EC specification, with $\mathcal{A} = \{a, b, c, d, e\}$, all of whom occupy the role of *prosumer*. Suppose in some window W that a is assigned to the role of *allocator*, so it is empowered to perform *announce* and *allocate* actions; that b is assigned to the role of *head*, so it is empowered to perform *cfv* and *declare* actions; and that there are insufficient resources to satisfy e's demand so its allocation is zero ($r_e = 0$), so while e is empowered to *appropriate* it is not permitted to *appropriate*. Then:

	prosumer				allocator		head		p_i
	provide	demand	appropriate	vote	announce	allocate	cfv	declare	
a	✓	✓	✓	✓	✓	✓			2.85
b	✓	✓	✓	✓			✓	✓	2.85
c	✓	✓	✓	✓					0.85
d	✓	✓	✓	✓					0.85
e	✓	✓		✓					0.6
$1/N(p)$	0.2	0.2	0.25	0.2	1	1	1	1	

Therefore, for this window W:

$$\text{RelIP}_W = [\mathcal{P}; 2.85, 2.85, 0.85, 0.85, 0.6]_W$$

The RelIP can be analysed in various ways. One property to test for is 'fairness', for which the Gini index (coefficient) can be used. The Gini index measures the statistical dispersion of values in a frequency distribution, such as the number of institutionalised powers of a group of agents. The index of institutional power IPX for a window W is given by (where $\mu = mean(\{p_i\})$):

$$\text{IPX}_W = gini(\text{RelIP}_W) = \frac{1}{2} \frac{1}{\mu} \frac{1}{|\mathcal{A}|^2} \sum_{i=1}^{|\mathcal{A}|} \sum_{j=1}^{|\mathcal{A}|} |p_i - p_j|$$

and the cumulative IPX for a series of Windows $W_1, \ldots, W_n$ by:

$$\text{IPX}_{[W_1, W_n]} = gini \left(\frac{\sum_{i=1}^{n} \text{RelIP}_{W_i}}{n} \right)$$

An IPX coefficient of zero would indicate 'perfect' fairness (every agent has the same 'amount' of power), while a coefficient of one would indicate 'complete' unfairness (one agent has all the powers).

4.2   Demonstrator Testbed

The experimental testbed has three modules, LPG' Game Engine, the EC Engine, and the IPX Calculator.

The LPG' Game Engine module is initialised with a specification of M agents in $\mathcal{A}$. Its operation is shown in Algorithm 1. This also shows the sequence of

---

Algorithm 1: Algorithm for LPG' Game Engine

$A \leftarrow generate\_agents(M)$;
$W \leftarrow 1$ (set window to 1); $T \leftarrow 0$ (set ECtime to 0) ;
repeat

    update agent status $\longrightarrow$ happens(join(...), T) ;

    update arena roles $\longrightarrow$ happens(appoint(...), T) ;

    foreach *agent* $i \in C$ **do**

        provide resources $\longrightarrow$ happens(provide(...), T) ;

        demand resources $\longrightarrow$ happens(demand(...), T) ;

    end

    compute priority queue $\longrightarrow$ happens(announce(...), T) ;

    grant allocation $\{r_a(\cdot)\}_{a \in \mathcal{A}} \longrightarrow$ happens(allocate(...), T) ;

    foreach *agent* $i \in C$ **do**

        $r_i > 0 \rightarrow$ appropriate $\longrightarrow$ happens(appropriate(...), T) ;

    end

    call election $\longrightarrow$ happens(cfv(...), T) ;

    cast votes $\longrightarrow$ happens(vote(...), T) ;

    declare results $\longrightarrow$ happens(declare(...), T) ;

    $W \leftarrow W + 1$;

until $W = W_{lim}$;

---

events generated in the EC narrative ($\longrightarrow$ happens(...), T)) at each stage in the game. One full game round is played in each window W. Note that each time a new event happens, the EC time T is incremented by 1.

The EC Engine takes the narrative generated by the LPG' Game engine, the domain-dependent social constraints, and an initial state, and computes the social state (for each agent: what roles it occupies, what powers it has, what permissions it has) at each EC time point in the window.

The IPX Calculator accepts as input these social states and computes the IPX coefficient per window (i.e. IPX_W for each window W in isolation), and the cumulative IPX coefficient (i.e. $\text{IPX}_{[W_1, W_n]}$ over a series of n windows), as specified in Section 3.3.

4.3   Experimental Results

The system was run for a multi-agent, single institution model for 200 LPG' Game Rounds (so 200 windows generating over 23,000 EC events in the narrative), with the *head* and *allocator* roles being re-assigned every 2 rounds (implicitly by the agent occupying the role of *authoriser*, according to some designated role-assignment protocol). Four conditions were tested with 20 agents (enough to expose any significant variation with respect to the number of assigned roles, of which there were two):

- IN-TURN: agents take it in turns to be assigned both roles;
- RANDOM: both roles assigned at random;

– SAME-BOTH: the same agent always assigned to both roles;
– SAME-EACH: the same agent always assigned to each role.

The first two role assignment conditions ensure that the institutionalised powers are distributed between the members of the institution in IN-TURN and RANDOM, but in SAME-* it is concentrated with one or two agents. The experimental hypothesis is that the two intuitively 'fairer' conditions will present lower IPX coefficients than the two intuitively 'unfairer' conditions.

For each window W_i we computed IPX_{W_i} and $IPX_{[W_1,W_i]}$. The results are shown in Figure 3. The graphs show that:

– the IPX coefficient per window has a similar profile for all four conditions for role assignment. Taking each window in isolation, the distribution of institutionalised power is broadly indistinguishable and relatively 'neutral' (IPX ~ 0.5);
– however, a series of ostensibly 'neutral' IPX coefficients (per window) can reveal a pattern/trend towards fairness or (relative) unfairness over time, respectively diminishing towards a low IPX or by 'flatlining' respectively;
– the 'fair' average IPX coefficients are correlated with the intuitively 'fairer' role assignment conditions IN-TURN and RANDOM, and the 'unfair' average IPX coefficient are correlated with the intuitively 'unfairer' role assignment conditions SAME-*.

We conclude that the 'fair' role assignment conditions are distinguishable from the 'unfair' role assignment conditions, both in comparative magnitude (IPX ~ 0.1 compared to IPX ~ 0.45) and in 'trajectory'. The next question to consider is, what can agents do with this information?

4.4 Evaluation

The empowerment metric is an indicative, qualitative, and outcome-related metric. Used subjectively, it is much more informative for evaluating adaptation than a relative comparison of specifications based on distance, difference or cost/benefits, e.g. [1,11,17]. In this sense, our work has more in common with the idea of a socially useful laws [8] and selection between alternatives based on criteria such as minimality or simplicity.

In previous experiments with the LPG' game in an economy of scarcity and using legitimate claims as the resource allocation method [21], a measure of subjective 'satisfaction' was used by each agent to evaluate its benefit from belonging to an institution. If its subjective satisfaction fell below a personal threshold, the agent had no alternative but to 'vote with its feet'. However, this is too coarse to distinguish between unfair treatment and extreme scarcity. Similarly, it is not the case that a horizontal trajectory at mid-value IPX is necessarily 'bad' – a platonic benign dictator would show the same empowerment metric profile, but would distribute resources fairly.

This means a range of indices is required, which can be used as pointers to possible issues. In addition, to observe Ostrom's seventh principle (no intervention from external authorities), the agents themselves have to be able to use the

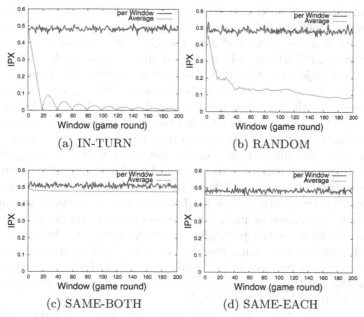

(a) IN-TURN   (b) RANDOM

(c) SAME-BOTH   (d) SAME-EACH

Fig. 3. IPX Coefficients for Different Role Assignment Conditions

metrics for evaluating 'fitness for purpose', by mapping its index observations to its own assessment. To leverage this assessment, the agents need to communicate with each other. A framework for interleaving gossiping and opinion formation, together with rules of social order and social choice, is presented in [20], which could form the basis of such an scheme to inform decision-making and rule adaptation.

5   Summary and Conclusions

In general, we are concerned with the problem of resource allocation in open multi-agent systems. We have proposed using the institutional design principles defined by Ostrom [18], conceptually formalised with dynamic norm-governed systems [1], to specify both the rules and the self-organisation of these rules.

Given the difficulty of directly correlating rules with outcomes in normative, complex and adaptive systems, in this paper we have proposed taking principles of procedural justice – for participation, transparency and balancing – and defining metrics for obliquely measuring the 'fitness for purpose' of an institution. We proposed a framework in which to measure: inclusivity and engagement using a form of participation principle inspired by [28], openness and transparency using a form of the transparency principle inspired by [3], and cost-effectiveness and efficiency using a form of balancing principle inspired by [13]. However, we also need to consider, as a source of principles and metrics, argumentation-based judicial processes [10] and methods to analyse resource distribution procedures (e.g. cake cutting, matching) and assess them in terms outcome 'fairness' [5].

In particular, we defined a metric for the distribution of (institutionalised) power as one dimension of the participation principle of procedural justice, what we called the IPX coefficient based on the Gini index for fairness assessment. We described an experiment which showed there was a marked difference (in magnitude and trajectory of the IPX) between institutions which had a 'fair' and an 'unfair' distribution of institutionalised power. However, there are a number of open questions which require further consideration: this includes the weight attached to powers (which might be a function of the number of fluents initiated and/or the inferences that can be derived from them, i.e. their relevance, cf. [9]), other aspects of time like duration and frequency of decision-making, and their degree of influence and control in the organisational hierarchy of decision groups.

Moreover, this metric alone might be indicative but not sufficient as an index of procedural justice. Future work needs to extend the participation principle with different dimensions of inclusivity, representation and decision frequency, and include metrics for the principles of transparency and balance, to leverage the full power of the formal framework for evaluating 'fitness for purpose'. Another direction of research is to examine formal methods for static (off-line) analysis of the institutional rules, to complement the work here which requires the institution to be be active (on-line).

In conclusion, the requirement to evaluate self-organising electronic institutions with respect to their 'fitness for purpose' is an important and pressing one, but it is a challenge of significant complexity. But, as the UK Royal Commission on Environmental Pollution's white paper on Adaptive Institutions [23] asserts, in order to address contemporary global challenges, it is also one that simply *has* to be addressed. A framework for evaluating procedural justice in self-organising electronic institutions could prove extremely valuable for evaluating procedural justice in adaptive (human) institutions; indeed, we are planning to use the framework for procedural justice in Serious Games using self-organising electronic institutions for resource allocation in SmartGrids [4].

References

1. Artikis, A.: Dynamic specification of open agent systems. Journal of Logic and Computation 22(6), 1301–1334 (2012)
2. Balke, T., de Vos, M., Padget, J.: I-ABM: combining institutional frameworks and agent-based modelling for the design of enforcement policies. Artificial Intelligence and Law (2013) 10.1007/s10506-013-9143-1
3. Blader, A., Tyler, T.: A four-component model of procedural justice: Defining the meaning of a "fair" process. Personality and Social Psychology Bulletin 29(6), 747–758 (2003)
4. Bourazeri, A., Pitt, J.: Serious game design for inclusivity and empowerment in smartgrids. In: First International Workshop on Intelligent Digital Games for Empowerment and Inclusion (2013)
5. Chevaleyre, Y., Endriss, U., Lang, J., Maudet, N.: A short introduction to computational social choice. In: van Leeuwen, J., Italiano, G.F., van der Hoek, W., Meinel, C., Sack, H., Plášil, F. (eds.) SOFSEM 2007. LNCS, vol. 4362, pp. 51–69. Springer, Heidelberg (2007)

6. Collier, R., Collier, D.: Shaping The Political Arena. Princeton University Press, Princeton (1991)
7. Elster, J.: Local Justice: How Institutions Allocate Scarce Goods and Necessary Burdens. Russell Sage Foundation (1992)
8. Fitoussi, D., Tennenholtz, M.: Choosing social laws for multi-agent systems: Minimality and simplicity. Artificial Intelligence 119(1-2), 61–101 (2000)
9. Gabbay, D., Kempson, R., Pitt, J.: Labelled abduction and relevance. In: Demolombe, R. (ed.) Non-standard Queries and Answers. OUP (1994)
10. Gordon, T.: The Pleadings Game: An Artificial Intelligence Model of Procedural Justice. Kluwer (1995)
11. Hoogendoorn, M., Jonker, C., Schut, M., Treur, J.: Modeling centralized organization of organizational change. Computational & Mathematical Organization Theory 13(2), 147–184 (2007)
12. Jones, A., Sergot, M.: A formal characterisation of institutionalised power. Journal of the IGPL 4(3), 427–443 (1996)
13. Kass, N.: An ethics framework for public health. American Journal of Public Health 91(11), 1776–1782 (2001)
14. Kelly, K.: The Shirky principle. The Technium (2010)
15. Kowalski, R., Sergot, M.: A logic-based calculus of events. New Generation Computing 4, 67–95 (1986)
16. Lan, T., Kao, D., Chiang, M., Sabharwal, A.: An axiomatic theory of fairness in network resource allocation. In: INFOCOM, pp. 1343–1351. IEEE Press (2010)
17. Martin, C., Barber, K.S.: Adaptive decision-making frameworks for dynamic multi-agent organizational change. Journal AAMAS 13(3), 391–428 (2006)
18. Ostrom, E.: Governing the Commons. Cambridge Univ. Press (1990)
19. Ostrom, E.: Understanding Institutional Diversity. Princeton Univ. Press (2005)
20. Pitt, J., Ramirez-Cano, D., Draief, M., Artikis, A.: Interleaving multi-agent systems and social networks for organized adaptation. Computational and Mathematical Organization Theory, 1–35 (2011)
21. Pitt, J., Schaumeier, J., Busquets, D., Macbeth, S.: Self-organising common-pool resource allocation and canons of distributive justice. In: 6th IEEE Conference on Self-Adapting and Self-Organising Systems (SASO), pp. 1–10 (2012)
22. Rawls, A.: A Theory of Justice (Revised Edition). Harvard University Press (1999)
23. RCEP: 28th report: Adapting institutions to climate change. Royal Commission on Environmental Protection, The Stationery Office Limited, UK (2010)
24. Rescher, N.: Distributive Justice. Bobbs-Merrill, Indianapolis (1966)
25. Robert, S.C., Robert, H., Evans, W.J., Honemann, D.H., Balch, T.J.: Robert's Rules of Order, Newly Revised, 10th edn. Perseus Publishing, Cambridge (2000)
26. Seidman, A., Seidman, R.: ILTAM: Drafting evidence-based legislation for democratic social change. Boston University Law Review 435 (2009)
27. Sergot, M.: Action and agency in norm-governed multi-agent systems. In: Artikis, A., O'Hare, G.M.P., Stathis, K., Vouros, G.A. (eds.) ESAW 2007. LNCS (LNAI), vol. 4995, pp. 1–54. Springer, Heidelberg (2008)
28. Solum, L.: Procedural justice. Southern California Law Review 78(181), 275–289 (2004)
29. Thompson, D.: Moral responsibility and public officials: The problem of many hands. American Political Science Review 74(4), 905–916 (1980)
30. Tideman, N.: Collective decisions and voting: the potential for public choice. Ashgate Publishing Ltd. (2006)
31. Uphsur, R.: Principles for the justification of public health intervention. Canadian Journal of Public Health 93, 101–103 (2002)

A Reliability Analysis Technique
for Estimating Sequentially Coordinated
Multirobot Mission Performance

John F. Porter[1], Kawa Cheung[2], Joseph A. Giampapa[2], and John M. Dolan[1]

[1] Robotics Institute, Carnegie Mellon University,
5000 Forbes Avenue, Pittsburgh, PA 15213-3890, USA
{johnporter,kawacheung}@cmu.edu, jmd@cs.cmu.edu
http://www.ri.cmu.edu/
[2] Software Engineering Institute, Carnegie Mellon University,
4500 Fifth Avenue, Pittsburgh, PA 15213-2612, USA
garof@sei.cmu.edu
http://www.sei.cmu.edu/

Abstract. This paper presents a quantifiable method by which the behaviors of robots, as determined by their performance in a cyber-physical context, can be captured and generalized so that accurate predictions of sequentially coordinated multirobot behaviors can be made. The analysis technique abstracts sequentially coordinated multirobot missions as a frequentist inference problem. Rather than attempt to identify and put into a causal relation all the hidden and unknown cyber-physical influences that can have an impact on mission performance, we model the problem as that of predicting multirobot performance as a conditional probability. This allows us to initially limit the testing and evaluation of robot performance to evaluations of atomistic behaviors, and to experiment mathematically with the combinations of predictive features and elementary performance metrics to derive accurate predictions of higher-level coordinated performance. Statistical tests on the goodness of the results are reported, as well.

Keywords: coordinated autonomy, coordinated multi-robot reliability analysis, robotics, reliability engineering, quantitative assurance, robotic de-mining.

1 Introduction

Autonomous non-teleoperated robots are becoming more ubiquitous and commercially viable. They are being utilized in applications as diverse as: agriculture [11], automated delivery systems [2], terrestrial and planetary exploration [9,3], water quality monitoring, flood disaster mitigation and depth buoy verification [19]. Most of these missions are designed to provide the two functionalities of scanning a surface, which we call *covering terrain*, and *detecting objects*. Common performance quality attributes of those services are time (e.g. *as quickly as*

G. Boella et al. (Eds.): PRIMA 2013, LNAI 8291, pp. 276–291, 2013.
© Springer-Verlag Berlin Heidelberg 2013

possible) and energy (e.g. *with the given energy resources*). Often it can be prohibitively expensive to design individual robots with near-perfect performance or wide-ranging capabilities so multirobot missions are configured to cost-effectively improve performance. Yet, the act of simply adding multiple robots to a mission does not necessarily improve overall mission results. As cyber-physical agents, robots need to share physical space or they get in the way of each other [16], hence coordination is introduced to manage the use of shared space for a given time. As a general performance modifier, coordination can help improve overall mission outcome by improving multirobot performance on task (e.g. terrain coverage, object detection), by improving the means by which the tasks are performed (e.g. quickly, energy-efficiently), and by avoiding unintended performance degradation by managing shared physical resources such as time and space.

Sequential coordination is a term that we coin to describe the common and simplistic form whereby either the robot operator or the robots themselves delay the order in which they deploy in the mission area. Both homogeneous and heterogeneous groups of robots can be coordinated in this way. For the same sequential physical deployment sequence, information can be aggregated according to different *policies* to improve the effectiveness of the multirobot mission.

The focus of this paper is to introduce a quantifiable method by which the behaviors of robots, as determined by their performance in a cyber-physical context, can be captured and generalized so that accurate predictions of sequentially coordinated multirobot behaviors can be made. This is what we refer to as *reliability analysis*. Reliability analysis seeks to understand systems quantifiably and predictively so that trade-off decisions can be made for all aspects of a system or application life cycle: design, development, testing, implementation, acquisition, maintenance and obsolesence. The results of such analyses and the methods for using them comprise the discipline of *reliability engineering* [8,10].

Multirobot reliability analysis is as yet a nascent engineering discipline [14] and in great demand as indicated by a recent report [1]. One body of work treats the robot as a physical component with its particular failure rate, and analyzes how to guarantee mission success in light of dynamic substitution or on-the-fly repair via cannibalization [18]. More recent work seeks to quantify energy usage and management [13] and devise acceptance tests via simulation for unmanned ground vehicles [12] applied to modeling component behavior such as torque motors. While not considered contributions to reliability engineering, the human factors community has invested much effort in analyzing human factors issues involved in human use of a robot and multirobot team, as exemplified by [7]. While researchers in coordinated multi-agent and multirobot systems provide validations of their systems through extensive mission-specific testing [15], their focus has been more on proving the viability of the implemented and deployed system rather than on contributing a reliability analysis technique.

Inspired by investigations in dependability metrics [6], probabilistic reliability engineering [17], and the work documented in [4,5], we developed an analysis technique that abstracts sequentially coordinated multirobot missions as a frequentist inference problem. Rather than attempt to identify and put into a

causal relation all the hidden and unknown cyber-physical influences that can
have an impact on mission performance, we model the problem as that of predicting multirobot performance as a conditional probability. That is, we identify
features in the cyber-physical environment, such as estimated likelihood of there
being a mine in the terrain, type of terrain, and policy for combining independent verifications, and probabilisticly evaluate the likelihood of any number of
performance metrics given those preconditions. This allows us to initially limit
the testing and evaluation of robot performance to evaluations of atomistic behaviors, and to experiment mathematically with the combinations of predictive
features — environmental influence as well as the policies for combining evidence during sequential coordination — and elementary performance metrics,
such as true/false positive and true/false negative rates of detection, to derive
accurate predictions of higher-level coordinated performance. Statistical tests on
the goodness of the results are reported, as well.

The paper is organized as follows. The sequentially coordinated minesweeping
scenario, involving real robots on a physical terrain, is described in Section 2.
Section 3 describes the performance of individual robots in two different modes
of operation; this simulates diversity of individual robotic capability. Section
4 describes the policies by which independent robot observations are combined.
Section 5 describes our conditional probabilistic models. Their predictive abilities
are described and evaluated in Section 6. Section 7 concludes the paper.

2   The Minesweeping Scenario

Minesweeping is an operation with salient characteristics in common with the
common sequentially coordinated multirobot missions mentioned in the Introduction. Covering terrain is as important as the ability to detect objects within
the terrain. Quality attributes are: *quick completion* and *best accuracy possible*,
that is, zero or near-zero false positive and false negative detection rates. Uncertainties are introduced by: unknown density of mines in the terrain, drift during
locomotion, imprecise localization within the mission area, and signal/noise confusion during mine detection. Within each of these categories of uncertainties,
variation and finer-grained details can be introduced, such as: terrain obstacles to
provide hard constraints, variation of soil type, variation of obstacle dimensions,
and subclassification of mine type.

A number of considerations inform the design of the virtual mine. The first
is the "terrain" in which the mines are placed. The terrain is simulated as an
8-square-by-8-square checkerboard of black and white tiles. Each of the resultant
sixty-four 5" x 5" tiles corresponds to the configuration space of an individual
robot. Similar discretizations of terrain are common in practice. The alternating
white/black checkerboard colors are chosen for two reasons: (1) as an artifact
of the experiment that assists the observability of the robot on the terrain, and
(2) the differences of terrain color roughly approximate soil types, which add
to the operational signal/noise confusion of a sensor operating on that terrain.
While the alternating colors are an experimental device, they introduce truly

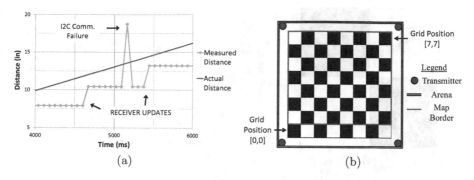

Fig. 1. (1a) Actual vs. Perceived Location with spike due to error. (1b) Minefield (red border) and the environment (checkerboard) within the arena (black border).

unpredictable and realistic uncertainty into the test environment terrain model, forming an analog to real world detection problems.

The second consideration is how to represent a mine. Each mine is represented as a simple color patch. By printing a desired shape, patten, and color intensity, various mine profiles can be created. For example, to simulate the strength of the mine detection signal due to material composition and/or depth in the ground, the color transparency of the simulated mines can be varied. The patch is most color-saturated in the center of the circle (i.e., 100% blue) and a linear gradient transforms the mine to the desired background color (i.e., 100% white or 100% black) towards the edge of the mine. A transparency is applied to the mine to change its color intensity. This allows some mines to be more easily detected than others. For our testing, a total of twelve mine types were created, 6 on a black background and 6 on a white background, with each of those six mines having a transparency varying from 0% to 75% in 15% increments. The diameter of the mine was set to 5", which corresponds to the size of the checkerboard tiles. A sample of the mines is provided in Fig. 2a.

The mine-to-background color intensity signal follows a predictable waveform pattern as the robot scans the terrain. A mine on a black background appears as a peak, whereas a mine on a white background appears as a valley. All mine types are distinct, i.e., each is defined by a large peak, and no two mines peak at the same value. The recorded profiles for mines drawn in blue are provided in Fig. 2b.

While this method is simple to implement and can quickly be altered by printing new mines and/or terrain, all printed objects are subject to variations in the saturation of printed (non-white) colors. Additionally, no two color sensors are perfectly matched and they may read slightly different values for the same patch of color. For the purposes of introducing signal-to-noise [SnR] confusion and uncertainty, the technique described is effective. It creates a non-trivial problem to solve that has a believable correspondence with real world robotic sensors.

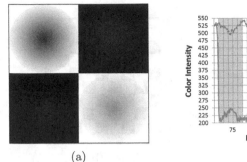 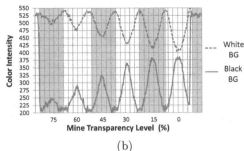

(a)   (b)

Fig. 2. (2a) Top Row: white & black background with 0% transparency. Bottom Row: black & white background with 45% transparency. (2b) Color intensity values based on transparency for black & white backgrounds.

There are two primary tasks for the minesweeping robot in this project. The first task is navigation, i.e., the robot must determine how to get from one way-point to another. The second task is mine detection. As the robot is navigating an environment, it must process color sensor data to determine if it traverses a virtual mine. To accomplish these tasks, the robot has been provided two primary subsystems: one for locomotion and the other for mine detection.

The color sensor is placed under the center of the robot. It allows the robot to see light intensity and color at an optimal range of approximately 3/4 inch (19.05mm). It is used as input to the mine detection algorithm, which will be described later. A holonomic driving base (multi-directional wheels) was chosen as the locomotion method to reduce the likelihood of drift while turning.

Two modes of operation have been defined for this robot. *Mode 1* provides a fast but inaccurate scan, where data analysis is limited to a few data points. *Mode 2* provides a slower but much more accurate scan. It attempts to collect significantly more data samples in order to form a full color intensity profile for every square that it scans. A result is provided only after a Mode 2 robot has collected enough data to understand the color intensity profile of the square.

While a number of metrics can be defined for mission evaluation, this research uses a 2x2 contingency table for its ability to provide statistical significance of binary classifications. A contingency table with its related terminology is provided in Table 1. Note that 'Predicted' describes how the robot has identified the grid locations (mine or no mine) while 'Actual' is the ground truth as tabulated across all of the printed minefields.

From this contingency table, the metrics of precision, recall and accuracy can be defined. Precision is the probability of a mine given that there is a detection. Recall is the probability of a detection given that there is a mine. Accuracy attempts to combine all of the results observed in the contingency table, though it is desensitized by the high number of true negatives inherent to this scenario. This metric is useful for examination but may not show the differences in the mine detection algorithm as clearly as the other metrics.

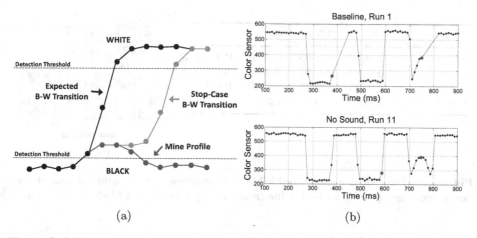

Fig. 3. (3a) Color intensity transition profiles for detecting mine on black background. (3b) Example detection errors due to thread starvation. Top: bad signal Bottom: good signal

Table 1. Contingency table definition

		Actual	
		Yes	No
Predicted	Yes	True Pos (TP)	False Pos (FP)
	No	False Neg (FN)	True Neg (TN)

$$Precision = \frac{TP}{TP+FP} \tag{1}$$

$$Recall = \frac{TP}{TP+FN} \tag{2}$$

$$Accuracy = \frac{TP+TN}{TP+FP+FN+TN} \tag{3}$$

Lastly, metrics related to mission duration are also considered. This includes the maximum, mean and minimum durations. Time is often a critical aspect of a mission, and this is especially true in mine detection scenarios, where mines must be identified as soon as possible to avoid accidental detonation.

Metric	Max	Mean	Min	Std
Precision	1.0000	0.6805	0.3900	0.1267
Recall	0.9200	0.7107	0.5000	0.0930
Accuracy	0.9500	0.8775	0.7700	0.0400
Duration (s)	167.54	150.91	138.60	6.03

(a)   (b)

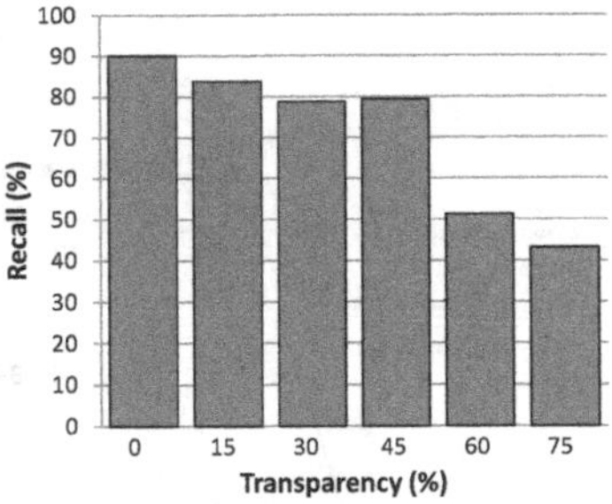

Fig. 4. (4a) Performance summary for Mode 1 operation. (4b) Combined mine detection percentages (recall) for each mine transparency level during Mode 1 operation.

3   Atomistic Performance Evaluation

Our initial investigations seek to determine if it is possible or not to predict team performance based on atomistic evaluations of the individuals. This involves quantifying the performance of individual team members. The evaluation results of each of the robots described in this paper are provided, below.

3.1   Mode 1 Individual Performance

Mode 1 operation consists of a fast but inaccurate mine detection algorithm combined with a lawnmower-type navigation scan pattern. A total of 80 data collection runs were completed to form a training data set. From these data, a contingency table was created for each run and the precision, recall and accuracy were computed. These results are combined in Table 4a, where the maximum, mean, and minimum of each metric are shown. Additionally, Fig. 4b breaks down the combined mine detection recall by the mine transparency level.

As expected, the Mode 1 mine detection algorithm is not very accurate. This is evident from the precision (brought down by a high proportion of false positives) and the recall (brought down by a low proportion of true positives). Fig. 4b, however, affirms the representation of our mine field, as highly saturated mines are detected much more frequently than high transparency mines. The only exception to this is the 45% transparency mines, which are detected slightly more frequently than the 30% transparency mines. This may be due to the distribution of the mines on the minefield and whether or not a mine was on a waypoint. It is anticipated that mines on a waypoint will have a higher probability of detection, as the navigation algorithm homes in on the center of the square.

Time to completion is a common robotic performance quality attribute. Table 4a summarizes mission duration values. The longest (worst) duration was 2.78 minutes, shortest (best) duration was 2.31 minutes, and the mean mission duration was 2.5 minutes.

Metric	Max	Mean	Min	Std
Precision	1.0000	0.9571	0.8000	0.0578
Recall	1.0000	0.9458	0.8333	0.0575
Accuracy	1.0000	0.9812	0.9375	0.0164
Duration (s)	559.02	530.70	511.73	11.255

(a)

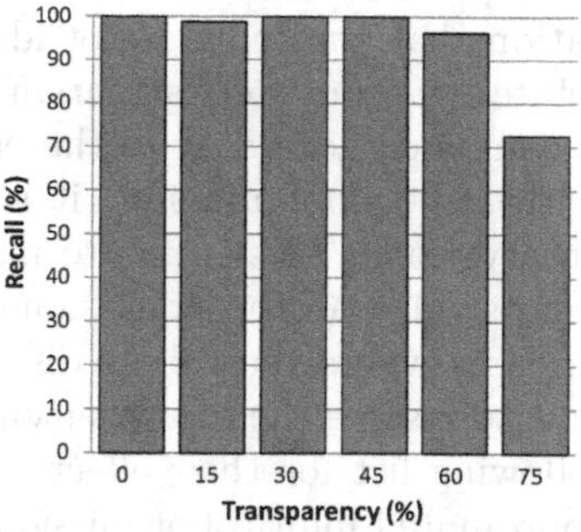

(b)

Fig. 5. (5a) Performance summary for Mode 2 operation. (5b) Combined mine detection percentages (recall) for each mine transparency level during Mode 2 operation.

3.2   Mode 2 Individual Performance

Mode 2 operation consists of a slower but more accurate mine detection algorithm than Mode 1. This algorithm only scans specified grid locations, and so it was provided with all 64 grid locations in order to scan the entire map. Due to the extended mission duration, only five runs were completed for each of 8 maps, yielding a total of 40 data collection runs. The mine detection metrics are computed as before, with the results provided in Table 5a and the breakdown of the mine detection levels in Fig. 5b.

These results affirm the accuracy of the improved detection algorithm. There is a very low number of false positives and false negatives, resulting in a much higher precision and recall. The detection levels for each of the individual mine types fit our expectations as well, though Fig. 4b shows considerably better performance than Mode 1 operation. These results do not come for free, however; this algorithm requires much more time to complete its mission, over 8 minutes. Depending on the mission objectives, the benefits of this algorithm may not warrant the increased run time.

4   Coordinated Missions

Two coordinated missions are evaluated. The first is a homogeneous team of Mode 1 robots with 2-4 members. The second is a heterogeneous team with one Mode 1 and one Mode 2 robot. In the homogeneous team, all members are tasked with scanning the minefield independently from one other. Deployment of each robot is staggered by 15 seconds to avoid collisions, and the final results are compiled once all robots have completed scanning the minefield. In the heterogeneous team, the Mode 1 robot assumes a scout role, scanning the minefield at the quicker of the two rates. The Mode 2 robot assumes a verification role. Its departure is delayed by 15 seconds from when it receives the way point of the square to scan from a scout. A Mode 2 robot will only scan the grid location that the scout robot identified as having a mine, and either confirm or refute the scout's classification. The evidence from the two robots' observations is combined according to the below policies.

In multirobot missions it is highly unlikely that all robots make the same observations. This is due to inaccuracies in the navigation system (i.e., no two robots will scan the exact same path) and variations in color sensor sensitivities. In cases where the robots disagree with one another, a decision must be made how to resolve the disagreement. We evaluated the three decision policies of the following list for their effectiveness at improving the mine detection results of coordinated multirobot missions. Policies 1 and 2 are applied only to the homogeneous team configuration, while Policy 3 is only applied to the heterogeneous team configuration.

Policy 1. All robots must be in agreement that there is a mine in a given location ('and' logic). The benefit of this policy is that the number of false positives should be greatly decreased, as not all robots will experience false positives in the same location. It is unlikely, however, that all robots will have detected all of the mines on the map and consequently, the number of true positives will therefore suffer.

Policy 2. Any robot can make a detection and it will be included in the aggregate result ('or' logic). The benefit of this policy is that everything is included and that the recall should increase. Unfortunately, every false positive is also included, thus decreasing the precision of the aggregate result. More conservative policies like this may be more beneficial in a real world mission due to the extremely high cost for missing even a single mine.

Policy 3. One robot's detection results are weighted more heavily than another. This is of value in heterogeneous teams where two robots perform very differently from one another, such as a team consisting of the two robots described in this paper. In that case, the robot with the better mine detection algorithm is probably more trustworthy and should be given extra consideration.

5   Predictions

Our hypothesis is that atomistic testing provides the necessary data to build predictive models. These models can then be used to make quality assurance statements about the reliability of coordinated missions. Predictions include probability distributions for the number of detections (as true or false positives) and derivative measures, such as precision, recall, and accuracy.

To explain our model, consider the example arenas in Fig. 6. The black and white squares represent the environment, where blue circles represent the presence of a mine and orange triangles represent the robot's waypoints. The red arrows denote the robot's projected path. It is desirable to achieve balance between the model's simplicity and accuracy, with each depending on the number of aforementioned features included. While all the details in the arena of Fig. 6

(left) can be included, only the presence of a mine is considered in the simplified arena of Fig. 6 (right). To demonstrate our prediction technique, the simplified arena will be used in the following equations.

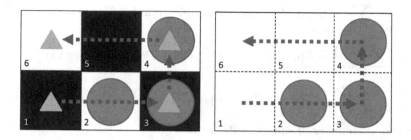

Fig. 6. A subset of an arena (left) and a simplified version (right)

The probability of a given set of detections for the example arena can be expressed as:

$$P(d_1, \dots, d_i, \dots, d_n \mid \text{example arena}) \tag{4}$$
$$\text{where } d_i : 1 \text{ for detection, } 0 \text{ for no detection}$$
$$i : \text{square number, in order of traversal of robot}$$
$$n : \text{total number of squares in arena (6 in Fig. 6)}$$

In this simplified example, the probabilities of a detection occurring in a specific square are assumed to be conditionally independent given that the existence of the mines are known. In other words, neither the square color, existence of a waypoint, nor the physical location of the squares is considered. This conditional independence allows Equation 4 to be written as:

$$P(d_1 \mid \{m_1 = 0\}) \times P(d_2 \mid \{m_2 = 1\}) \times P(d_3 \mid \{m_3 = 1\}) \times$$
$$P(d_4 \mid \{m_4 = 1\}) \times P(d_5 \mid \{m_5 = 0\}) \times P(d_6 \mid \{m_6 = 0\})$$
$$= P(d = 1 \mid \{m = 0\})^{d_1 + d_5 + d_6} \times (1 - P(d = 1 \mid \{m = 0\}))^{3 - d_1 - d_5 - d_6} \times$$
$$P(d = 1 \mid \{m = 1\})^{d_2 + d_3 + d_4} \times (1 - P(d = 1 \mid \{m = 1\}))^{3 - d_2 - d_3 - d_4} \tag{5}$$
$$\text{where } m : 1 \text{ for mine, } 0 \text{ for no mine}$$

To predict the total number of detections, we only require the conditional probabilities of detection given the existence of the mines. Using this, the probability of observing a given number of detections can be expressed as:

$P(\# \text{ detections} = N \mid \text{example arena})$

$\quad = P(d_1 + d_2 + ... + d_n = N \mid \text{example arena})$

$\quad = \displaystyle\sum_{d_1+...+d_n = N} P(d_1, d_2, ... , d_n \mid \text{example arena})$

$\quad = \displaystyle\sum_{i+j=N} [\binom{a}{i} \times P(d = 1 \mid \{m = 1\})^i \times (1 - P(d = 1 \mid \{m = 1\}))^{a-i} \times$

$$\binom{b}{j} \times P(d = 1 \mid \{m = 0\})^j \times (1 - P(d = 1 \mid \{m = 0\}))^{b-j}] \quad (6)$$

where a : number of squares with a mine

$\qquad b$: number of squares without a mine

$\qquad i$: number of true positives

$\qquad j$: number of false positives

$\qquad N$: predicted number of detections

For the multi-robot case, where individual observations are aggregated to determine collectively if a mine is detected, Equation 6 above can be modified by replacing $P(d = 1 \mid m = 1)$ and $P(d = 1 \mid m = 0)$ with the combined detection probabilities $P(d_{cmb} = 1 \mid m = 1)$ and $P(d_{cmb} = 1 \mid m = 0)$ respectively. This probability is dependent upon the decision policy used, so each of the three policies are presented below.

Policy 1. All robots must agree that there is a mine in a square ('and' logic).

$$P(d_{cmb} = 1 \mid \{m\}) = P(d_1 = 1 \mid \{m\}) \times ... \times P(d_r = 1 \mid \{m\}) \quad (7)$$

where r : number of robots

Policy 2. Any robot can identify a mine in a square ('or' logic). Note that Equation 8 presents the two robot case, though this can be generalized.

$$\begin{aligned} P(d_{cmb} = 1 \mid \{m\}) = &P(d_1 = 1 \mid \{m\}) \times P(d_2 = 1 \mid \{m\}) + \\ &P(d_1 = 1 \mid \{m\}) \times P(d_2 = 0 \mid \{m\}) + \\ &P(d_1 = 0 \mid \{m\}) \times P(d_2 = 1 \mid \{m\}) \quad (8) \end{aligned}$$

Policy 3. One robot's observations are weighed more heavily than the others. If operating independently, the combined probability would simply be the probability of the more heavily weighted robot. In our scout/verification role, however, robot 'b' (Mode 2) only scans the squares marked by robot 'a' (Mode 1) and verifies or dismisses the detections. This yields Equation 9. Note that robot 'a' observations could be made by a single Mode 1 robot or by multiple Mode 1 robots using decision policy 1 or 2.

$$P(d_{cmb} = 1|\{m\}) = P(d_a = 1|\{m\}) \times P(d_b = 1|\{m\}) \qquad (9)$$

It is observed that while policy 3 is operationally different from policy 1, they are mathematically equivalent due to robot 'b's dependence on robot 'a's initial detection of a mine.

While Equation 6 provides an implementation to predict the number of detections, the probabilities of our evaluation metrics (precision, recall, accuracy) can also be derived. To modify Equation 6 for these metrics, the summing criterion can be replaced with the corresponding expressions provided in equations 10-12. By exhaustively computing for all possible combinations of i and j, the probability distributions of these quantities can be generated and a mean and standard deviation produced.

$$Precision = \frac{i}{i+j} \qquad (10)$$

$$Recall = \frac{i}{a} \qquad (11)$$

$$Accuracy = \frac{i+b-j}{a+b} \qquad (12)$$

Mission duration is also important to the overall performance evaluation of a coordinated mission. As such, we have provided the following equations to predict the mission duration under the homogeneous and heterogeneous team configurations.

Homogeneous Mission. Mission duration for a homogeneous team will vary depending on how the robots are deployed. If robot deployment is staggered, and each robot will scan the entire minefield, mission duration will depend greatly on the deployment interval. An equation for estimated mission duration can be written as:

$$Mission\ Duration = X + Y * (Z - 1) \qquad (13)$$

$$\text{where } X : \text{single robot mission duration}$$
$$Y : \text{time between deployment}$$
$$Z : \text{number of robots}$$

If it is desirable to deploy the robots with each only scanning a subsection of the minefield, the expected mission time is X/Z. The difference between these two mission strategies is that deployment in subsections will not improve detection results, but only the mission duration. Deploying the robots in a staggered fashion will improve detection results, but will require slightly more time than an individual robot.

Heterogeneous Mission. With a single Mode 1 robot, and without considering a staggered time delay, the Mode 2 robot is able to begin scanning for mines immediately after it receives the coordinates of an observation to verify. Since this team of robots is operating in parallel, the mission time will be largely dependent upon the completion time of the first robot, with additional time requirements dependent on the distribution of observations. Should observations be made towards the end of the minefield, such as the very last square scanned by Mode 1, the Mode 2 robot will need time to 1) traverse to that square and 2) scan the square. Using the Mode 2 mission duration results, the average mission duration of 530.70 seconds can be divided by the 64 total squares scanned per run to yield a scan time of approximately 8.3 seconds per square. Because this robot is capable of traversing at the same speed as Mode 1, we can divide the average mission duration of 150.91 seconds by 64 squares to yield a traversal time of 2.3 squares per second. Also, because of the physical constraints of the minefield, the Mode 2 robot should be no more than 11.3 squares away from the final mine scanned (diagonal map distance). The expected run time is then equal to the Mode 1 scan time plus the traversal time plus the time to scan a mine. Assuming a reasonable worst case scenario (average Mode 1 run time, mine in last scanned position, Mode 2 furthest distance away) the expected run time for this combined mission is approximately 185.20 seconds. To reiterate, however, this is highly dependent on the distribution of mine detections within the minefield and may fluctuate greatly.

6   Coordinated Performance Evaluation

Coordinated missions were synthesized using the results from single robot runs. This is not an unrealistic simplification if one can presume highly reliable locomotion, collision avoidance, and very low probability of accidental mine detonation, and allows us to focus on the information-theoretic aspects of the multirobot coordination evaluations. For the homogeneous missions (Policies 1 and 2), 160 runs were completed to form a training/testing data set. These runs were combined as if they had been run together (i.e., 8 runs = four missions with 2 robots or two missions with 4 robots.). For the heterogeneous missions, an additional 160 runs were completed for the verifier role, while the homogeneous mission results provided the data for the scout role. This was completed to synthesize the timing of the communication of detections. It should also be noted that the predictions presented were created with the arena model including both mine existence and background color (cf. Section 5). Runs were partitioned into training and test sets. A set of 10 training runs was tested against 150 test runs; 20 training runs against 140 tests; and so on, until 80 training runs against 80 test runs were configured. The performance of our prediction algorithm across 10 train/test increments is illustrated by Fig. 7. Table 2 and Table 3 provide the predicted and observed performance of the homogeneous and heterogeneous missions.

Table 2. Homogeneous Mission Performance vs. Predictions

Policy	# Robots	Metric	Predicted		Actual	
			Mean	Std	Mean	Std
1	2	Precision	0.9458	0.0899	0.8657	0.1199
		Recall	0.5062	0.1443	0.6623	0.1129
		Accuracy	0.9016	0.0287	0.9153	0.0303
		Duration (s)	165.31	5.869	167.13	4.186
	3	Precision	0.9887	0.0786	0.9147	0.0981
		Recall	0.3601	0.1386	0.6159	0.1058
		Accuracy	0.8795	0.0261	0.9164	0.0256
		Duration (s)	180.31	5.869	178.72	6.042
	4	Precision	0.9706	0.1674	0.9295	0.0994
		Recall	0.2562	0.1260	0.5778	0.1198
		Accuracy	0.8605	0.0236	0.9125	0.0294
		Duration (s)	195.31	5.869	191.10	4.310
2	2	Precision	0.5753	0.0833	0.6155	0.1140
		Recall	0.9167	0.0798	0.8158	0.0481
		Accuracy	0.8523	0.0442	0.8618	0.0516
		Duration (s)	165.31	5.869	167.13	4.186
	3	Precision	0.4989	0.0665	0.5505	0.0937
		Recall	0.9760	0.0442	0.8370	0.0396
		Accuracy	0.8057	0.0484	0.8336	0.0530
		Duration (s)	180.31	5.869	178.72	6.042
	4	Precision	0.4406	0.0549	0.5002	0.0852
		Recall	0.9931	0.0240	0.8444	0.0430
		Accuracy	0.7561	0.0518	0.8052	0.0557
		Duration (s)	195.31	5.869	191.10	4.310

The most striking tendency that we observe is that the predictive capability of our algorithm is sensitive to the initial quality of sensing of the robot and the policy for combining evidence. Our algorithm was able to make better predictions for the heterogeneous mission than for the homogeneous missions. Policy 2 yielded better predictions than Policy 1. Policy 1 seemed to only perform tolerably well for the 2-robot mission. A χ^2 (Chi-Squared) goodness-of-fit test was completed, confirming that the predictions for Policy 1, teams 3 and 4, are untenable and can be disregarded with 95% confidence.

It is possible to make near-100% predictions with a Policy 3 team of robots, as the Mode 2 robot has near perfect detection capabilities. Predictions tend to slightly overestimate Policy 3 precision and underestimate recall and accuracy. With respect to Policy 2, it should be noted that performance improved uniformly for recall (both predicted and actual) as the number of robots increased, whereas both precision and accuracy showed an inverse trend (both predicted and actual) due to the policy favoring recall over precision. Interestingly, while Policy 2 lends itself to better predictions by our methods, its numeric performance estimates are less precise than actual.

Table 3. Heterogeneous Mission Performance vs. Predictions

Policy	# Robots	Metric	Predicted		Actual	
			Mean	Std	Mean	Std
3	2	Precision	0.9947	0.0250	0.9961	0.0203
		Recall	0.6729	0.1354	0.7177	0.0961
		Accuracy	0.9379	0.0256	0.9465	0.0182
		Duration (s)	185.20	11.255	170.40	22.83

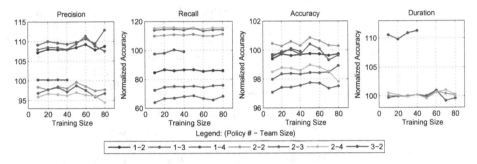

Fig. 7. Predictor performance as a function of training set size

Policy 1 showed the least tendency to be predictable. As could be expected, it favors precision at the expense of recall, but also seems to introduce variance that prohibits reliable predictions to be made as the number of robots increases. Team configurations of 3 and 4 robots failed the χ^2 test; only a team of 2 robots was not excluded. Although its overall predictions are not statistically significant, multirobot teams did show improved precision at detecting mines as the number of robots increased. Further, the numeric predictions were within one standard deviation of actual, unlike for recall for Policy 2.

7 Conclusions

In this article, we have proposed a method for predicting the behavior of a coordinated robotic mission. This was completed through the performance evaluation of an individual robot, where a specific set of behaviors could be quantitatively evaluated. Coordinated missions were then defined such that coordination involved the combination of observations from multiple robots. In defining how the robots make observational decisions, it was shown that reasonable predictions for the coordinated mission (relative to the atomistically evaluated behaviors) could be produced. In being able to predict the behavior of a coordinated mission, overall testing time is reduced (because only atomistic testing is required) while assurance statements can be made with regard to the performance of a coordinated team.

Acknowledgments. The authors thank David S. Kyle and Eric Whitman for their contributions to this research.[1]

References

1. The role of autonomy in DoD systems. Task force report, Department of Defense Defense Science Board (July 2012)
2. Aethon, Inc.: TUG: Automated delivery and tracking solutions. Datasheet (September 5, 2012)
3. Burgard, W., Moors, M., Stachniss, C., Schneider, F.: Coordinated multi-robot exploration. IEEE Transactions on Robotics 21(3), 376–386 (2005)
4. Chaki, S., Giampapa, J.A.: Probabilistic verification of coordinated multi-robot missions. In: Bartocci, E., Ramakrishnan, C.R. (eds.) SPIN 2013. LNCS, vol. 7976, pp. 135–153. Springer, Heidelberg (2013)
5. Chaki, S., et al.: Toward a quantitative method for assuring coordinated autonomy. Tech. Rep. CMU-RI-TR-13-12 (June 2013), ARMS 2013, at AAMAS 2013
6. Eusgeld, I., Freiling, F.C., Reussner, R. (eds.): Dependability Metrics: Advanced Lectures. Springer, Berlin (2008)
7. Howard, A.M.: A systematic approach to predict performance of human-automation systems. IEEE Trans. on SMC, Part C 37(4), 594–601 (2007)
8. Ireson, W.G., Coombs Jr., C.F.: Handbook of Reliability Engineering and Management. McGraw-Hill Book Company, New York (1988)
9. Jet Propulsion Laboratory: Five commercial rovers. Web (2013), http://www-robotics.jpl.nasa.gov/systems/system.cfm?System=4 (accessed September 2013)
10. Pham, H. (ed.): Handbook of Reliability Engineering. Springer (2003)
11. Qingchun, F., Xiu, W., et al.: A new strawberry harvesting robot for elevated-trough culture. Int. Jrnl. of Agricultural & Biological Eng. 5(2), 1–8 (2012)
12. Sadrpour, A., Jin, J., et al.: Simulation-based acceptance testing for unmanned ground vehicles. Int. Jrnl. of Vehicle Autonomous Systems 11(1), 62–85 (2013)
13. Sadrpour, A., et al.: Mission energy prediction for UGVs using real-time measurements and prior knowledge. Journal of Field Robotics 30(3), 399–414 (2013)
14. SAE International: Report on unmanned ground vehicle reliability. Surface Vehicle Information Report J2958 NOV2011, SAE International (November 2011)
15. Scerri, P., Velagapudi, P., et al.: Real-world testing of a multi-robot team (June 2012), ARMS 2012, at AAMAS 2012
16. Scerri, P., Vincent, R., Mailler, R.: Comparing Three Approaches to Large-Scale Coordination. In: Coordination of Large-Scale MASs, pp. 53–71. Springer (2006)
17. Shooman, M.L.: Probabilistic Reliability: An Engineering Approach, 2nd edn. Robert E. Krieger Publishing Company, Malabar (1990)
18. Stancliff, S.B.: Planning to Fail: Incorporating Reliability into Design and Mission Planning for Mobile Robots. PhD thesis, RI, CMU (2009)
19. Valada, A., et al.: Development of a low cost multi-robot autonomous marine surface platform. In: Int. Conf. on Field & Service Robotics 2012 (July 2012)

---

[1] This material is based upon work funded and supported by the Department of Defense under Contract No. FA8721-05-C-0003 with Carnegie Mellon University for the operation of the Software Engineering Institute, a federally funded research and development center. This material has been approved for public release and unlimited distribution. Carnegie Mellon®is registered in the U.S. Patent and Trademark Office by Carnegie Mellon University. DM-0000619

Strategy-Proof Mechanisms for the k-Winner Selection Problem

Yuko Sakurai[1], Tenda Okimoto[2], Masaaki Oka[3], and Makoto Yokoo[3]

[1] Kyushu University, JST PRESTO
ysakurai@inf.kyushu-u.ac.jp
[2] Transdisciplinary Research Integration Center
tenda@nii.ac.jp
[3] Kyushu University
{oka@agent.,yokoo@}inf.kyushu-u.ac.jp

Abstract. The goal of this paper is to develop a strategy-proof (SP) mechanism for the k-winner selection problem, which finds a set of (at most) k winners among participants. Here, we assume the winners can have positive/negative externalities with each other; the gross utility of a winner not only depends on whether she wins, but also on the other winners. If the types of agents, i.e., the gross utilities of agents, are known, we can obtain a Pareto efficient (PE) allocation that maximizes the sum of the gross utilities of winners in polynomial time, assuming k is a constant. On the other hand, when the types of agents are private information, we need a mechanism that can elicit the true types of agents; it must satisfy SP. We first show that there exists no SP mechanism that is PE, individual rational (IR), and non-deficit (ND) in a general setting where we put no restrictions on possible agent types. Thus, we need to give up at least one of these desirable properties.

Next, we examine how a family of Vickrey-Clarke-Groves (VCG) based mechanisms works for this problem. We consider two alternative VCG-based mechanisms in this setting, both of which are SP and PE. We show that one alternative, called VCG-ND, is ND but not IR, and the other alternative, called VCG-IR, is IR but not ND. Also, we show special cases where VCG-ND satisfies IR, or VCG-IR satisfies ND. Moreover, we propose mechanisms called VCG-ND+ and VCG-IR+, which can be applied to a general setting, where a mechanism designer has partial knowledge about the possible interactions among agents. Both VCG-ND+ and VCG-IR+ are SP, IR, and ND, but they are not PE. Finally, we present a concise graphical representation scheme of agent types.

1 Introduction

Mechanism design is a subfield of micro economics and game theory, which concerns with designing a collective decision making rule for multiple agents. Such a rule is expected to satisfy several desirable properties, such as social efficiency, while each agent cares her own utility, i.e., is self-interested. Due to the growing

G. Boella et al. (Eds.): PRIMA 2013, LNAI 8291, pp. 292–307, 2013.

needs for agent technology and the Internet's popularity, vigorous research on mechanism design has been conducted in artificial intelligence and multi-agent system research communities [16,18]. In this paper, we design mechanisms for the k-winner selection problem, where the goal is to find a set of (at most) k winners from participating agents. We assume there exist externalities among winners, i.e., each agent has her preference over a set of winners. More specifically, her gross utility depends on who wins with her as well as whether she actually can win. Such an externality can be either positive or negative, i.e., agent i might like/dislike another agent j to be selected together.

One motivating application of the k-winner selection problem is a sponsored search auction. When a user enters keywords into a search engine, advertisements related to them are displayed around the search results. A search engine applies an auction mechanism to determine how to rank the advertisements and how much to pay when a user clicks on a displayed advertisement. Mechanism design for sponsored search auctions has recently attracted considerable attention [3,7,9,17,19]. Most of existing works do not consider the externalities among advertisers. However, it is natural to assume that some externalities exist among advertisers. For example, a used car dealer would be happy if its advertisement is displayed with a large car manufacture, while a large company does not want its advertisement to be displayed with smaller companies to protect its brand image. Also, if k tickets of a package tour are available for club members, the value of participating the package tour can heavily depend on other members who participate the tour. The k-winner selection problem can formalize a variety of situations in which externalities exist among selected winners.

If a mechanism designer knows each agent's preference, the k-winner selection problem can be solved in time $O(n^k)$ when the number of agents is n. Thus, by assuming the valuation of an agent for any set of winners is given by oracle, we can find a Pareto efficient (PE) selection that maximizes the sum of (at most) k agent valuations in polynomial time to the number of agents n. However, in general, the preference of an agent is her private information. According to the revelation principle [5,15], we can restrict our attention to strategy-proof (SP) direct revelation mechanisms without loss of generality. Unfortunately, in this setting, there exists no SP mechanism that simultaneously satisfies PE, individual rational (IR), and non-deficit (ND).

Next, we examine how a family of the Vickrey-Clarke-Groves (VCG) based mechanisms works for the k-winner selection problem. First, we examine how the straightforward application of the VCG mechanism in this setting works. We assume each player has an option not to join the mechanism, thus the mechanism needs to satisfy IR. In this case, the mechanism does not satisfy ND since the gross utility of a winner can be negative and she must be paid some money. Next, we consider another variation of the VCG assuming that an agent cannot opt out of the mechanism. We call this mechanism VCG-ND, which achieves ND, but not IR. Furthermore, we develop mechanisms that utilizes partial knowledge of possible interactions among agents. These mechanisms satisfy SP, IR, and ND, by sacrificing PE.

Furthermore, we consider the communication complexity for running k-winner selection mechanisms. If an agent needs to naively declare the valuations of all sets of winners, she must declare her preference over 2^{n-1} combinations. This is impractical when n becomes large. We propose a concise representation scheme based on a graphical representation. This representation is general, i.e., it can represent any valuation of an agent by allowing hyper-edges. Also, the representation is concise when the (positive or negative) synergies among agents are sparse.

The remainder of this paper is organized as follows. Section 2 summarizes existing literature. Section 3 describes our model and the VCG mechanism. Section 4 shows the non-existence theorem, and Section 5 introduces a family of the VCG-based mechanisms. In Section 6, we propose a graphical representation as a concise representation of the k-winner selection problem. Section 7 shows our simulation results of the VCG and VCG-ND mechanisms. Section 8 concludes this paper.

2   Related Works

This section introduces several related works. Haghpanah et al. [11] showed that the problem of finding an optimal allocation to maximize an auctioneer's revenue is NP-hard in an auction where an agent can declare non-negative externalities. They proposed an approximate allocation algorithm.

Bhalgat et al. [1] proposed approximate algorithms to optimize social surplus when externality functions are restricted to either concave or convex. An agent's valuation of an item is affected by the set of other agents in the network possessing the item. Although this paper considers the problem of allocating multiple products when each agent is a unit-demand, it restricts externality functions to positive, monotone, and non-decreasing.

Krysta et al. [12] developed a bidding language for combinatorial auctions with externalities, which uses weighted logical formula to represent bidder valuation functions. They also investigated the complexity of the winner determination problem, and characterized the complexity of classifying the properties of valuation functions.

The following recent studies focus on externalities among advertisers in sponsored search auctions. Sakurai et al. [17] proposed a sponsored search auction mechanism called GSP with an Exclusive Right (GSP-ExR). In GSP-ExR, the number of winners can be either 1 or k, and an agent can exclusively allow displays of her advertisement when she is willing to pay a premium. In the real world, some advertisers who have more complicated preferences over their competitors vary their bidding prices with a set of winners.

Constantin et al.   [3] proposed a greedy algorithm under the assumption that there exits some constraints on relationships between the slot of an agent's advertisement and the slots of other agents' advertisements. Furthermore, they showed a condition under which their proposed algorithm satisfied strategy-proofness.

Fotakis *et al.* [9] studied the winner determination problem to maximize social surplus when users attention may be captured by any size c window of consecutive slots, within which externalities take effect among advertisers. In their model, the Click-Through Rate(CTR) of an advertisement depends on the set of other advertisements appearing in the sponsored list, on their relative order, and on their distance in the list.

3   Preliminaries

3.1   Model

This paper considers a k-winner selection problem among a set of agents $N = \{1, 2, \ldots, n\}$ which select a set of agent $S \subseteq N$ such that $|S| \leq k$ holds for a given $k \leq n$.

Agent i has preferences over any set of winners. Formally, we model this by supposing that agent i observes parameter (signal), θ_i, which determines her preferences. We refer to θ_i as the *type* of agent i and assume θ_i is drawn from set Θ_i. Let $v(\theta_i, S)$ indicate agent i's *gross utility/valuation* for a set of winners S. We assume each agent has quasi-linear utility where the utility of agent i with type θ_i is given as $v(\theta_i, S) - p_i$ and p_i is the payment of agent i. Also, we assume that if agent i is not a winner, her gross utility is 0; $\forall S \ni i$, $v(\theta_i, S) = 0$ holds. Note that the gross utility of agent i depends on who is going to be selected with her, i.e., agents have externalities with each other. These externalities can be either negative or positive; agent i might like/dislike another agent j to be selected together. Furthermore, we assume $v(\theta_i, \{i\}) \geq 0$ holds, i.e., becoming the sole winner never hurts the winner.

3.2   Desirable Properties

A mechanism consists of selection rule x and payment rule p. We denote the type profile of all agents except i as θ_{-i}. $x(\theta_i, \theta_{-i})$ and $p_i(\theta_i, \theta_{-i})$ represent a set of winners and the payment of agent i, respectively, when the declared type profile of other agents is θ_{-i} and the declared type of agent i is θ_i.

Strategy-proofness is defined as follows:

Definition 1 (Strategy-proofness). *A mechanism is strategy-proof (SP) iff the following condition holds:*

$$\forall \theta_i, \tilde{\theta}_i, \theta_{-i}, v(\theta_i, x(\theta_i, \theta_{-i})) - p_i(\theta_i, \theta_{-i}) \geq v(\theta_i, x(\tilde{\theta}_i, \theta_{-i})) - p_i(\tilde{\theta}_i, \theta_{-i}). \quad (1)$$

In other words, a mechanism is strategy-proof if for each agent, reporting her true type θ_i is a dominant strategy; it maximizes her utility.

The *revelation principle* guarantees that we can restrict our attention to direct revelation mechanisms that are strategy-proof without loss of generality [14]. In other words, if a certain property (e.g., PE) can be achieved using some mechanism in a dominant strategy equilibrium, i.e., the combination of the dominant strategies of all participants, the property can also be achieved using a SP direct revelation mechanism.

Definition 2 (Pareto efficiency). S^* *is Pareto efficient iff*

$$S^* = \arg \max_{\{S \mid S \subset N, |S| \leq k\}} \sum_{i \in N} v(\theta_i, S)$$

holds. Also, a mechanism is Pareto efficient (PE) if it is strategy-proof and obtains a Pareto efficient allocation when all agents declare their true types.

Pareto efficient allocation for the k-winner selection problem is an optimal allocation to maximize the sum of the valuations of winners.

When a mechanism designer knows all the agents' types, assuming $v(\theta_i, \cdot)$ is given by an oracle and k is fixed, we obtain S^* in $O(n^k)$. However, since agents' types are private information, we need a SP mechanism to achieve PE.

A mechanism is individually rational if an agent never suffers any loss as long as she reports her true type. Formally, we define this property as follows:

Definition 3 (Individual rationality). *A mechanism is individually rational (IR) iff the following condition holds:*

$$\forall i, \theta_i, \theta_{-i}, v(\theta_i, x(\theta_i, \theta_{-i})) - p_i(\theta_i, \theta_{-i}) \geq 0. \tag{2}$$

Finally, we define a non-deficit condition.

Definition 4 (Non-deficit). *A mechanism is non-deficit (ND) iff the following condition holds:*

$$\sum_{i \in N} p_i(\theta_i, \theta_{-i}) \geq 0. \tag{3}$$

If a mechanism continues to lose money, it cannot be sustained without continuous financial support from an external source, e.g., the government.

In the rest of this paper, when there is no ambiguity, i.e., we can assume all agents report their true types, since the mechanism is SP, we simply write $v_i(S)$ to represent $v(\theta_i, S)$, and p_i to represent $p_i(\theta_i, \theta_{-i})$. For a set of agents S, we write $V(S)$ to represent $\sum_{i \in N} v_i(S)$.

3.3   VCG Mechanism

We introduce a general mechanism called the Vickrey-Clarke-Groves (VCG) mechanism [2,20], which is also known as the Clarke mechanism or the Clarke tax. First, let us introduce the Groves mechanism, which is a generalization of VCG [10]. This mechanism can be applied to general social choice settings. Assume agents are going to choose one outcome o from a set of alternatives O. The gross utility of agent i for outcome o is given as $v_i(o)$. The Groves mechanism is defined as follows.

Definition 5 (Groves mechanism). *The mechanism chooses an optimal outcome $o^* \in O$, i.e.,*

$$o^* = \arg \max_{o \in O} \sum_{j \in N} v_j(o).$$

The payment of agent i is given as

$$p_i(\theta_{-i}) - \sum_{j \neq i} v_j(o^*). \tag{4}$$

Here, $p_i(\theta_{-i})$ can be any function of θ_{-i}, but its value must be determined independently from θ_i.

The Groves mechanism is guaranteed to be SP and PE. However, it cannot guarantee IR or ND in general.

Next, the VCG mechanism is defined as a special case of the Groves mechanism.

Definition 6 (VCG mechanism). *o^*_{-i} is given as $\arg\max_{o \in O} \sum_{i \neq j} v_j(o)$, i.e., the optimal outcome ignoring agent i. Then the payment of agent i is given as*

$$\sum_{j \neq i} v_j(o^*_{-i}) - \sum_{j \neq i} v_j(o^*). \tag{5}$$

The VCG payment of each agent equals the decrease of the social surplus except the agent, caused by the agent's participation. In other words, the payment is the externality imposed by an agent on the other agents. The VCG satisfies SP and PE, since it is one instance of the Groves mechanism. Also, from the definition of Equation 5, since we can choose $o^*_{-i} = o^*$, the first term is always larger than or at least equal to the second term. Thus, the VCG payment are always non-negative. As a result, the VCG is ND. On the other hand, the VCG cannot guarantee IR in general. If $v_i(o^*_{-i}) \geq 0$ holds for all i, the VCG is guaranteed to be IR. This condition means that agent i's gross utility is non-negative for optimal outcome o^*_{-i} of the other agents. This condition is trivially satisfied in a combinatorial auction, since by assuming free-disposal, for each agent, the valuation of any allocation is non-negative.

4 Non-existence Theorem

In this section, we show that there exists no SP mechanism that satisfies PE, IR, and ND simultaneously [1].

Theorem 1 (Non-existence theorem). *For the k-winner selection problem, there exists no SP mechanism that satisfies PE, IR, and ND at the same time.*

Proof. It is sufficient to show one instance where there exists no auction mechanism satisfies the prerequisites. We suppose 2-winner selection problem. Assume that there exist 2 agents: agent 1 and agent 2, each of whom declares her valuations for any set of winners in case 1 as follows. The vector indicates $(v_i(\{1\}), v_i(\{2\}), v_i(\{1, 2\}))$.

---

[1] Although a similar non-existence theorem holds in a more general social choice setting, it is worthwhile to check whether we can circumvent impossibility results in our more specialized setting of the k-winner selection problem.

- Agent 1: $(a, 0, b)$
- Agent 2: $(0, a, b)$

Assume that $0 < a, b$ and $a < 2b$ are satisfied. Based on PE, the mechanism designer chooses both agents as winners. Let p_1 denote agent 1's payment in this situation. Based on IR, inequality $p_1 \leq b$ should hold, and either p_1 or p_2 must be non-negative to guarantee ND. Here, without loss of generality, we assume $p_1 \geq 0$. These assumptions lead to $0 \leq p_1 \leq b$.

Next, we consider case 2 in which agent 1 submits $c < 0$ for a set of agents 1 and 2, instead of b. In other words, she declares negative externality for the set.

- Agent 1: $(a, 0, c)$
- Agent 2: $(0, a, b)$

Assume that the value of c is satisfied as $a < c + b$. Therefore, both agents must be winners to satisfy PE. Based on IR, agent 1's payment p_1' should be $p_1' \leq c$. Also, $p_1' \geq p_1$ should hold for SP; otherwise, in case 1, agent 1 has an incentive to declare that her type is $(a, 0, c)$.

Inequality $p_1' \geq p_1$ contradicts condition $p_1 \geq 0$, which must satisfy ND in case 1. Thus, there exists no SP mechanism that simultaneously achieves PE, IR, and ND for the k-winner selection problem.   □

5   VCG-Based Mechanisms for the k-Winner Selection Problem

Based on the non-existence theorem, we must relax at least one property of PE, IR, and ND of a SP mechanism. In this section, we examine how a family of the VCG-based mechanism works for the k-winner selection problem.

5.1   VCG-ND Mechanism

First, we show a straightforward application of the VCG mechanism to the k-winner selection problem, which is called VCG-ND. Let $\hat{S}_{-i}^*$ be the optimal winners when we ignore the utility of agent i. Formally, we define that

$$\hat{S}_{-i}^* = \arg \max_{\{S \mid S \subset N, |S| \leq k\}} \sum_{j \neq i} v_j(S).$$

The VCG-ND payment is calculated by

$$p_i = \sum_{j \neq i} v_j(\hat{S}_{-i}^*) - \sum_{j \neq i} v_j(S^*). \tag{6}$$

It is clear that the VCG-ND mechanism is clearly a straightforward application of the VCG to the k-winner selection problem. Thus, the following theorem holds since the VCG is SP, PE, and ND.

Theorem 2. *The VCG-ND mechanism guarantees SP, PE, and ND.*

Example 1. We assume that there are 3 agents and that the VCG-IR mechanism is executed for 2-winner selection problem. The following is the sequence of valuation $v(\theta_i, \cdot)$ declared by agent i: $(v(\theta_i, \{1\}), v(\theta_i, \{2\}), v(\theta_i, \{3\}), v(\theta_i, \{1,2\}),$ $v(\theta_i, \{2,3\}), v(\theta_i, \{1,3\}), v(\theta_i, \{1,2,3\}))$.

- agent 1: $(0, 0, 0, -5, 0, -3, -8)$
- agent 2: $(0, 0, 0, 7, 0, 0, 7)$
- agent 3: $(0, 0, 0, 0, 0, 4, 4)$

Each agent's valuation is 0 when she wins exclusively. Agent 1 has negative externality for the other set of winners. Her most important requirement is to become a sole winner. Otherwise, she requires a reward when she wins with other agents. On the other hand, agents 2 and 3 have positive externality for the other set of winners. The VCG-ND mechanism selects $S^* = \{1, 2\}$ in the same manner as the VCG. The VCG-ND payment for agent 1 is calculated by $7 - 7 = 0$, since $\hat{S}^*_{-1} = S^*$ holds. On the other hand, the VCG-ND payment for agent 2 is $(-3 + 4) - (-5) = 6$ which is identical to the VCG payment, since $\hat{S}^*_{-2} = \{1, 3\}$ holds. As a result, the VCG-ND satisfies the non-deficit condition, because the sum of payments becomes $0 + 6 = 6$. However, agent 1's utility is calculated by $-5 - 0 = -5$. This fact implies that the VCG-ND is not IR.

5.2   Sufficient Condition for the VCG-ND to Be IR

We show a sufficient condition where the VCG-ND is guaranteed to be IR.

Theorem 3. *The VCG-ND mechanism satisfies IR when*

$$v_i(S) \geq 0 \tag{7}$$

holds for any set of agents $S \subseteq N$.

Proof. Based on the definition of the VCG-ND mechanism, we calculate agent i's utility as

$$v_i(S^*) - p_i = v_i(S^*) - \sum_{j \neq i} v_j(\hat{S}^*_{-i}) + V(S^*) - v_i(S^*)$$

$$= V(S^*) - \sum_{j \neq i} v_j(\hat{S}^*_{-i}). \tag{8}$$

From the way of choosing S^* and $\hat{S}^*_{-i}$, $V(S^*) \geq v_i(\hat{S}^*_{-i}) + \sum_{j \neq i} v_j(\hat{S}^*_{-i})$ holds. Since we assume that $v_i(S) \geq 0$ holds for all S, $v_i(\hat{S}^*_{-i}) \geq 0$. Thus, $V(S^*) - \sum_{j \neq i} v_j(\hat{S}^*_{-i}) \geq v_i(\hat{S}^*_{-i}) \geq 0$. Therefore, agent i's utility is non-negative.   □

Furthermore, if the smallest value of $v_i(S)$ is bounded by $-\delta$, i.e., $v_i(S) + \delta \geq 0$ holds for all S, we can bound the maximum amount of the deficit when an agent (unwillingly) becomes a winner; the maximum deficit of an agent is bounded by δ.

5.3   The VCG-IR Mechanism

Next, we introduce an alternative way of applying the VCG to the k-winner selection problem, which we call VCG-IR. Let S^*_{-i} be the set of agents that maximizes the sum of the valuations that of except agent i, but the winners should not include agent i:

$$S^*_{-i} = \arg \max_{\{S \subset N \setminus \{i\}, |S| \leq k\}} \sum_{j \neq i} v_j(S). \tag{9}$$

The payment of agent i is defined using S^*_{-i} as follows:

$$p_i = \sum_{j \neq i} v_j(S^*_{-i}) - \sum_{j \neq i} v_j(S^*). \tag{10}$$

This mechanism is one instance of the Groves mechanism. Thus, it is guaranteed to be SP and PE. Furthermore, let us show that the VCG-IR is also IR. The utility of winner i is calculated by

$$v_i(S^*) - p_i = V(S^*) - \sum_{j \neq i} v_j(S^*_{-i}). \tag{11}$$

Since S^*_{-i} does not include i, based on how we choose S^* and S^*_{-i}, $V(S^*) \geq \sum_{j \neq i} v_j(S^*_{-i})$ holds. Thus, the VCG-IR guarantees IR,

However, the VCG does not satisfy ND. This is because the payment of agent i can be negative: she can be paid by the mechanism designer. This happens when other agents have positive externalities with agent i. Thus, by excluding agent i, the gross utilities of other agents become low. $\sum_{j \neq i} v_j(S^*_{-i})$ can be smaller than $\sum_{j \neq i} v_j(S^*)$. Thus, the payment can be negative.

Example 2. Consider an identical situation to Example 1. The VCG-IR mechanism chooses $S^* = \{1, 2\}$, since the optimal social surplus is calculated by $V(S^*) = -5+7 = 2$. The VCG-IR payment of agent 1 is calculated by $0-7 = -7$. This means that agent 1 obtains 7 as her reward by becoming a winner. Her utility is given by $-5 - (-7) = 2 > 0$. The VCG-IR payment of agent 2 is calculated by $(-3+4) - (-5) = 1 + 5 = 6$ and her utility is $7 - 6 = 1 > 0$. As a result, the auctioneer has a deficit, since the sum of payments is $-7 + 6 = -1$.

When we remove agent 1, the optimal social surplus for remaining agents is $V(S^*_{-1}) = 0$. From $V(S^*) - v_1(S^*) = v_2(S^*) = 7$, we obtain $0 = V(S^*_{-1}) < v_2(S^*) = 7$, and the payment becomes negative.

5.4   Sufficient Condition for the VCG-IR Mechanism to Be ND

Here, we define a sufficient condition under which the VCG-IR mechanism guarantees ND.

Theorem 4. *The VCG-IR mechanism satisfies ND, when the following condition holds:*

$$\forall j \in N, \forall S, S', \text{ where } S' \subset S \subseteq N, v_j(S') \geq v_j(S). \tag{12}$$

Proof. The VCG-IR mechanism satisfies ND when formula (12) holds. Consider the case where we choose $S^* \setminus \{i\}$ as winners. Since $v_j(S') \geq v_j(S)$ holds, we obtain

$$\sum_{j \neq i} v_j(S^* \setminus \{i\}) \geq \sum_{j \neq i} v_j(S^*).$$

Also, based on how we choose S^*_{-i}, we obtain

$$\sum_{j \neq i} v_j(S^*_{-i}) \geq \sum_{j \neq i} v_j(S^* \setminus \{i\}).$$

The payment of agent i is given by:

$$p_i = \sum_{j \neq i} v_j(S^*_{-i}) - \sum_{j \neq i} v_j(S^*) \geq \sum_{j \neq i} v_j(S^*) - \sum_{j \neq i} v_j(S^*) = 0.$$

As a result, the VCG-IR mechanism is ND. □

Formula (12) represents that the most preferred situation of each agent is that she wins exclusively. In other words, an agent has non-positive externalities for any set of winners including herself.

Furthermore, when an agent has some positive externalities, if the amount of the positive externalities is bounded, the auctioneer's deficit can be bounded. More specifically, assume the following condition holds:

$$\forall j \in N, \forall S, S', \text{ where } S' \subset S \subseteq N, v_j(S') + \epsilon \geq v_j(S). \tag{13}$$

The value of ϵ indicates the upper bound of the positive externalities from agent i to a set of winners. If an agent's valuation satisfies formula (13), the money paid to an agent from the mechanism designer never exceeds ϵ. Thus, the total deficit of a mechanism designer can be bounded by $k \cdot \epsilon$ for the k-winner selection problem.

5.5 Utilizing a Mechanism Designer's Information

Consider the case where a mechanism designer has a partial knowledge about the relation among agents.

Here, we classify the relation between two agents into the following four cases.

Definition 7 (Classification of Relation).

Independent: *agents i and j are independent if $\forall S \subseteq N \setminus \{i,j\}$, $v_i(S \cup \{i\}) = v_i(S \cup \{i,j\})$ and $v_j(S \cup \{j\}) = v_j(S \cup \{i,j\})$ hold.*

Negative relation: *agents i and j are negatively related if they are not independent, and $\forall S \subseteq N \setminus \{i,j\}$, $v_i(S \cup \{i,j\}) - v_i(S \cup \{i\}) \leq 0$ and $v_j(S \cup \{i,j\}) - v_j(S \cup \{j\}) \leq 0$ hold.*

Positive relation: *agents i and j are positively related if they are not independent, and $\forall S \subseteq N \setminus \{i,j\}$, $v_i(S \cup \{i,j\}) - v_i(S \cup \{i\}) \geq 0$ and $v_j(S \cup \{i,j\}) - v_j(S \cup \{j\}) \geq 0$ hold.*

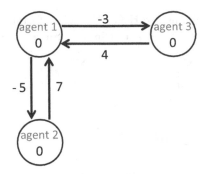

Fig. 1. Graphical Representation for examples 1 and 2

Bidirectional relation: *agents i and j are bidirectionally related if they are not independent or negatively or positively related.*

Assume that the mechanism designer has partial information about the possible relations between two agents; for a subset of agent pairs, the mechanism designer knows whether the relation between them is either independent or positively, negatively, or bidirectionally related. If the mechanism designer is not sure about the relation, she assumes it is bidirectional as a default value.

By using this partial knowledge of the mechanism designer, we can construct mechanisms that can be applied to general setting without putting any assumptions on the types of agents, that are required to guarantee that the VCG-ND is IR (or the VCG-IR is ND). These mechanisms are SP, IR, and ND. However, as implied by the impossibility theorem, they cannot be PE.

VCG-ND+: this mechanism is identical to the VCG-ND mechanism except that when choosing S^* and $\hat{S}^*_{-i}$, we choose agents so that each of them are either independent or positively related; choosing two agents who are negatively or bidirectionally related is prohibited. We guarantee that the VCG-ND+ is IR, and formula (7) is automatically satisfied for all S that are not prohibited since we assume that $v(\{i\}) \geq 0$ holds and no pair of agents with negative externalities can be selected together.

VCG-IR+: this mechanism is identical to the VCG-IR mechanism except that when choosing S^* and S^*_{-i}, we choose agents so that each of them are either independent or negatively related; choosing two agents who are positively or bidirectionally related, is prohibited. We guarantee that the VCG-IR+ is ND, since formula (12) is automatically satisfied for all S that are not prohibited.

6   Concise Representation

In this section, we consider the communication complexity for running k-winner selection mechanisms. If an agent need to naively declare the valuations of all sets of winners, she must declare her preference over 2^{n-1} combinations. When

n becomes large, this approach becomes quickly infeasible. Thus, in this section, we propose a concise representation scheme based on a graphical representation. This representation is general, i.e., it can represent any valuation of an agent by allowing hyper-edges. In the rest of this section, we assume an edge is defined between a pair of agents for notation simplicity. Generalizing the notation to allow hyper-edges is rather straightforward (though verbose). Also, the representation is concise when the positive or negative synergies among agents are sparse.

Let $G = (N, E)$ be a weighted directed graph, where N is a set of weighted vertices and E is a set of directed weighted edges among the vertices. A vertex indicates an agent, and a directed weighted edge indicates externality among agents. If a vertex has an outgoing edge, the agent of the node has an externality for the agent of the connected vertex. When there exists no edge from a vertex to another vertex, the externality is 0. The weight of a vertex represents a valuation when each agent wins exclusively. The weight of a directed edge is the value of the externality for the agent of a node with an outgoing edge.

We define agent i's valuation for a set of winners S as

$$v_i(S) = v_i(\{i\}) + \sum_{j \in S} e_i(\{j\}). \tag{14}$$

Here, $e_i(\{j\}) = e(\theta_i, \{j\})$ indicates the externality from agents i to j. Fig. 1 shows a graphical representation for examples 1 and 2. For example, $v_1(\{1,2\})$ is given by $v_1(\{1\}) + e_1(\{2\}) = 0 - 5 = -5$ and $v_1(\{1,2,3\})$ is given by $v_1(\{1\}) + e_1(\{2\}) + e_1(\{3\}) = 0 - 5 - 3 = -8$.

This representation resembles a graphical representation scheme for a characteristic function in cooperative games. The difference is that the value of a set of winner S depends on an agent in S. Thus we use a direct edge in a graph, which is a more complicated scheme than the graphical representation of a characteristic function formalized in [6].

The k-winner selection problem is a generalization of the densest k subgraph problem for finding the maximum density subgraph on k vertices for undirected graphs where the weight of an edge is 1. In such undirected graphs, the densest k subgraph problem is identical to find the maximum weighted induced subgraph on k vertices. Thus, we can map k-winner selection problem to the densest k subgraph problem. Although the densest k subgraph problem can be solved in polynomial time when k is a constant, it is known to be NP-hard by a reduction from the maximum clique problem in general cases [4,8]. We can apply a similar observation to the problem of finding PE allocation in this concise representation.

7   Experimental Evaluations

In this section, we experimentally evaluate the VCG-ND and VCG-IR mechanisms. In particular, the VCG-ND is not IR and the maximum deficit of an agent is at most δ, where $-\delta$ is the smallest value of $v_i(S)$. The VCG-IR is not ND and the maximum deficit of the mechanism designer is at most $k \cdot \epsilon$, where ϵ indicates the upper bound of the positive externalities. With simulations, we show that

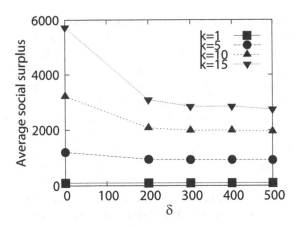

Fig. 2. Average social surplus obtained by VCG-ND

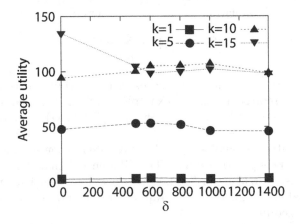

Fig. 3. Average utility obtained by VCG-ND

these bounds are rather pessimistic, where in the VCG-ND, an agent obtains a positive utility on average, and in the VCG-IR, the mechanism designer collects a positive amount of money on average.

We utilize our concise representation proposed in the previous section. Our winner determination problem can be formalized as the following integer programming problem:

$$
\begin{aligned}
\max \quad & \sum_i (x_i v_i(\{i\}) + \sum_j y_{ij} e_i(\{j\})) \\
\text{subject to} \quad & \sum_i x_i \leq k \\
& y_{ij} \leq x_i, \ \forall i \\
& y_{ij} \leq x_j, \ \forall j \\
& y_{ij} \geq x_i + x_j - 1, \ \forall i,j \\
& x_i \in \{0,1\}, \ \forall i \\
& y_{ij} \in \{0,1\}, \ \forall i
\end{aligned}
$$

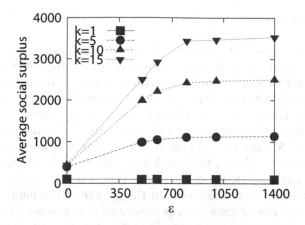

Fig. 4. Average social surplus obtained by VCG-IR

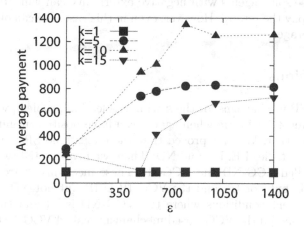

Fig. 5. Average revenue obtained by VCG-IR

We solved this problem with CPLEX version 12.1, a general-purpose mixed integer programming package.

We used the following problem setting for the agent's valuations:

- The weight of node $v_i(\{i\})$ was randomly chosen from $[0, 100]$.
- The externality $e_i(\{j\})$ is randomly selected from $[-100, 100]$.

For constructing a graph structure, we used the following settings: the existence of an edge is determined based on parameter $p \in [0, 1]$. In other words, p indicates the probability that that an edge will be added between two nodes. If we set p to 1, the graph structure is a complete graph. On the other hand, if p is set to 0, there exist no edges in a graph. Parameter p determines the connectivity. In our experiments, we set $n = 30$ and $p = 0.3$ and generated 100 problem instances based on the above models by varying the number of winners from 1 to 15.

Figures 2 and 3 show the average social surplus and the average utility of an agent obtained by the VCG-ND mechanism. We varied the value of δ from 0 to 500. When δ is set to 500, the problem setting is identical to the situation where we put no restrictions on the valuations an agent can declare. The average social surplus increases based on the growth of the number of winners. Also, an agent can obtain positive utility on average independently of the number of winners.

Figures 4 and 5 show the average social surplus and average revenue, respectively. When $\epsilon = 0$ holds, formula 5 is satisfied. On the other hand, when $\epsilon = 1,400$, the maximum deficit of the mechanism designer can be $1400 \times k$. The average social surplus increases based on the growth of the number of winners and the value of ϵ. The average revenue always retains non-negative values. The maximum average revenue can be obtained when $k = 10$ holds independently of the value of ϵ. The average revenue for $k = 15$ decreases compared to $k = 5$ and $k = 10$. Because some agents with negative externality can win, the mechanism designer must pay the reward. However, even in this case, she can obtain positive revenue on average.

8   Conclusions

We examined SP mechanisms for the k-winner selection problem, where the goal is to select at most k winners when agents can have positive/negative externalities with each other. We first proved that there exists no SP mechanism that simultaneously satisfies PE, IR, and ND. Then, we investigated two VCG-based mechanisms called VCG-ND and VCG-IR. These mechanisms are SP, PE. The VCG-ND is ND but not IR, and the VCG-IR is IR but not ND. Furthermore, we proved sufficient conditions where the VCG-ND is IR and the VCG-IR is ND. We also proposed the VCG-based mechanisms called VCG-ND+ and VCG-IR+ that achieve both IR and ND by sacrificing PE when a mechanism designer partially knows the relations between agents.

Future works will include evaluation of efficiency of VCG-ND+ and VCG-IR+ by computer simulations. We also want to propose a mechanism that is SP, ND, and IR and does not require any prior knowledge of the mechanism designer. Furthermore, we hope to generalize the formalization of the k-winner selection problem so that it can formalize combinatorial auctions where an agent might have allocative externalities, i.e., an agent cares not only what she obtains, but also what other agents obtain.

Acknowledgments. This research was partially supported by JST PRESTO and Japan Society for the Promotion of Science, Grant-in-Aid for Scientific Research (C), 23500166, 2011.

References

1. Bhalgat, A., Gollapudi, S., Munagala, K.: Mechanisms and allocations with positive network externalities. In: ACM EC 2012, pp. 179–196 (2012)
2. Clarke, E.H.: Multipart pricing of public goods. Public Choice (1971)
3. Constantin, F., Rao, M., Huang, C.C., Parkes, D.C.: On expressing value externalities in position auctions. In: AAAI 2011, pp. 644–649 (2011)
4. Cornell, D., Perl, Y.: Clustering and domination in perfect graphs. Discrete Applied Mathematics 9, 27–39 (1984)
5. Dasgupta, P.S., Hammond, P.J., Maskin, E.S.: The implementation of social choice rules: Some general results on incentive compatibility. Review of Economic Studies 46(2), 185–216 (1979)
6. Deng, X., Papadimitriou, C.H.: On the complexity of cooperative solution concepts. Mathematics of Operations Research 19(2), 257–266 (1994)
7. Edelman, B., Ostrovsky, M., Schwarz, M.: Internet advertising and the generalized second price auction: Selling billions of dollars worth of keywords. American Economic Review 97, 242–259 (2007)
8. Feige, U., Kortsarz, G., Peleg, D.: The dense k-subgraph problem. Algorithmica 29, 410–421 (2001)
9. Fotakis, D., Krysta, P., Telelis, O.: Externalities among advertisers in sponsored search. In: Persiano, G. (ed.) SAGT 2011. LNCS, vol. 6982, pp. 105–116. Springer, Heidelberg (2011)
10. Groves, T.: Incentives in teams. Econometrica 41, 617–631 (1973)
11. Haghpanah, N., Immorlica, N., Mirrokni, V., Munagala, K.: Optimal auctions with positive network externalities. In: ACM EC 2011, pp. 11–20 (2011)
12. Krysta, P., Michalak, T.P., Sandholm, T., Wooldridge, M.: Combinatorial auctions with externalities. In: AAMAS 2010, pp. 1471–1472 (2010)
13. Liazi, M., Milis, I., Pascual, F., Zissimopoulos, V.: The densest k-subgraph problem on clique graphs. Journal of Combinatorial Optimization 14, 465–474 (2007)
14. Mas-Colell, A., Whinston, M.D., Green, J.R.: Microeconomic Theory. Oxford University Press (1995)
15. Myerson, R.B.: Incentive compatibility and the bargaining problem. Econometrica 47(1), 61–73 (1979)
16. Nisan, N., Roughgarden, T., Tardos, E., Vazirani, V.V. (eds.): Algorithmic Game Theory. Cambridge University Press (2007)
17. Sakurai, Y., Iwasaki, A., Yokoo, M.: Keyword auction protocol for dynamically adjusting the number of advertisements. Web Intelligence and Agent Systems 8(4), 331–341 (2010)
18. Shoham, Y., Leyton-Brown, K.: Multiagent Systems: Algorithmic, Game-Theoretic, and Logical Foundations. Cambridge University Press (2008)
19. Varian, H.R.: Position auctions. International Journal of Industrial Organization 25(6), 1163–1178 (2007)
20. Vickrey, W.: Counter speculation, auctions, and competitive sealed tenders. Journal of Finance 16, 8–37 (1961)

Social Norm Recommendation for Virtual Agent Societies

Bastin Tony Roy Savarimuthu[1], Julian Padget[2], and Maryam A. Purvis[1]

[1] Department of Information Science, University of Otago, Dunedin, New Zealand
[2] Department of Computer Science, University of Bath, United Kingdom
.{tonyr,tehrany}@infoscience.otago.ac.nz,
jap@cs.bath.ac.uk

Abstract. Norms express expectations about behaviours of interacting entities in both human and software agent societies. While humans naturally possess the ability to recognize existing norms and learn new ones, software agents representing human users (e.g. avatars in virtual worlds) have to be endowed with such capabilities. Such a norm recognizing and learning agent, using observed actions and interactions of other agents in a situated environment, can be considered a *norm-aware* agent. This paper contributes to the agenda of creating a norm-aware agent, by proposing an architecture for social norm recommendation, comprising norm identification, norm classification, norm life-stage detection, and finally norm recommendation. These recommendations can then either be provided to a human user (e.g. the user of an embodied virtual agent in a new environment) or can be used by the agent itself for choosing appropriate actions. We use a simulation-based study to demonstrate how the four phases of the norm recommendation system work. The contributions of this paper are: (i) a comprehensive account of norm recommendation: identification, classification, life-stage detection and how to combine them into a recommendation, and (ii) a first evaluation of the approach, which advances the state of the art for this problem.

1 Introduction

Norms are of interest to researchers in multi-agent systems because they enable cooperation and coordination in software agent societies [1] and their smoother functioning by facilitating social order. Since norms can be used to help establish social order, MAS researchers have used this concept to build multi-agent systems.

Agents that know about norms in their societies do not need to recompute what the norms of the society are [4] and also do not often need to spend time in contemplating which actions are permitted, forbidden and obliged as they are aware of these norms. Also, agents that are aware of norms know that violating them has consequences. However, a new agent joining a society may not know the norms and needs to be equipped with some mechanism for recognizing them.

An agent may come to know about the norms of a society through several mechanisms: (i) an agent may ask another agent, (ii) it can also observe the actions and interactions of others and infer norms. In societies where norms are well-established and well-communicated, the agents know what the norms are. However, an agent may not know about norms where those of different communities are different or the norms

G. Boella et al. (Eds.): PRIMA 2013, LNAI 8291, pp. 308–323, 2013.

may be in a state of flux (i.e. norms might be emerging or changing). For example, in domains such as virtual worlds and multi-player online-games, apart from strict rules on what agents can or cannot do, that are usually encoded in the system at design-time, there might be norms that are generated at run-time, which do not exist *a priori*. For example, a specific reciprocity norm might be generated at run-time – derived from the generic "do unto others..." – in an online game, when one player who helps another escape from a dragon, expects reciprocal help [15] when another such a situation arises with roles reversed. Also, depending upon the population composition, norm may also change: for example, the influx of new agents might lead to norm change in the society. Additionally, when norms are in flux communication-based approaches for norm spreading may not be reliable since agents may miscommunicate what the norms are, or agents could lie about what the norms might be. Hence, there is a need for agents to recognize what the new norms are and also keep abreast with changing norms. One possible approach to recognize these norms is for agents to use an observation-based approach for inferring potential norms.

The problem of knowing the norms of a society is difficult because different societies have different norms and the uptake of different types of norms can vary. The work of Savarimuthu et al [9, 10] and of Oren and Meneguzzi [7] has focussed on the problem of norm identification. We believe that a more comprehensive norm recommendation architecture is necessary that not only identifies norms, but also recommends norms taking into account norm salience – how often does a violation get sanctioned and the life-stage of the norm, namely whether it is emergent, stable or decaying.

Thus, the objective of this paper is the proposition and evaluation of a high-level architecture for norm recommendation that takes these factors into account. An effective mechanism would mean a new agent (human or software) joining an agent society (e.g. a virtual world) could receive normative advice about expected behaviour. In a virtual world scenario, where human users interact with one another using their avatars, we foresee such users would then be able to receive advice from the avatar thanks to the norm recommendation module. The human users can subsequently decide whether to take the advice or not. We demonstrate the functioning of the architecture using synthetic data and focussing on prohibition norms and show how its effectiveness improves upon published work. As the literature suggests, the approach should be equally applicable for obligation norms.

Section 2 reviews existing work on norm identification, identifying five significant limitations, and outlines how the work in this paper concretely addresses all of them. Section 3 starts with an overview of the revised norm recommendation system, after which (i) section 3.1 presents the high-level details of the experimental design and also introduces the important parameters of the norm recommendation system which are then used in the subsequent sections (ii) section 3.2 presents the norm identification phase, highlighting in particular how this advances upon existing work both in principle and in practice (iii) section 3.3 presents the norm classification phase and (iv) section 3.4 presents the norm life-stage detection phase, then (v) the three phases are drawn together to make an heuristic-based norm recommendation system in Section 3.5. We conclude with some discussion, in which, despite the progress reported here, we identify a further five shortcomings that together set the agenda for future work in Section 4.

2 Background and Contribution

Sen [12], Savarimuthu [11] and Villatoro [14] all report on investigations into how norms might emerge in societies. Agents in these works employ one of several mechanisms such as imitation, advice-based learning (e.g. learning norms from leaders, peers etc.), and machine learning (e.g. Q-Learning) to learn a new norm. As norms are learnt by individual agents, this leads to norm emergence at the societal level. For an overview of norm learning mechanisms that facilitate norm emergence we refer the reader to [8]. Morales et al. [6] have investigated how new norms can be synthesized in the context of traffic domain. One observation on the above is that they consider only a limited number of actions (e.g. the work of Sen et al. [12] considers only two actions: whether an agent should give way to the left or to the right). Also, in most cases, only the emergence of a single norm is considered. However, in a more realistic setting, such as virtual worlds and massively multi-player games, where human users interact with other human or software agents, there are a large number of actions available for agents and also information (partial or complete) about other agents' actions might be available. For example, an agent in a virtual environment can observe actions that other agents perform and their interactions. Agents can employ data mining techniques to infer what the norms of the societies are based on the data on agent behaviour (obtained through observations). Corapi et al. [2] have explored how norms can be synthesized using an induction-based learning approach. This however is downstream from the problem addressed here: it describes a concrete method for revising a computational logic based norm representation that requires both the observations of actions related to the norm and the decision to revise the norm set have been made, which is exactly the purpose of the method outlined here.

The prohibition norm identification algorithm put forward in [10], in contrast to [12] above, considers up to four actions, associating those that occur $x\%$ of the time before the sanction event as having a causal relationship to the sanction. The exact value of x is controlled by a parameter called the Norm Inference Threshold (NIT), which is set by the (observing) agent. To illustrate the approach consider an agent that litters a park and which might receive a sanction from another agent. An observer, based on the actions and sanction it sees, can infer that littering is prohibited. More recently, Oren and Meneguzzi [7] have proposed algorithms for norm identification by means of Hierarchical Task Network (HTN) planning, however only conventions can be recognized using this approach since sanctions are not taken into account. The work of Criado et al. [3] proposes norm reasoning services for agents where agents can make use of a norm reasoning service to seek advice on norms. However, this work assumes that norms are known *a priori* as opposed to the situation in norm identification, where norms are not known ahead of time.

The approach to norm identification in [10] has several limitations that impact on the quality of the recommendations it makes:

L1: Focuses on norm identification that does not take into account potentially significant contextual information, such as: (i) determining the life-stage of a norm – that is whether it is emerging or decaying, for example – and factoring this into the recommendation process, and (ii) whether the norm is salient (i.e. how often does the violation of a norm actually result in a sanction).

L2: Infers norms from the punished event sequence (PES), without considering those occasions in which an action occurs, but does not lead to punishment (i.e. unpunished event sequence (UES)). Examples of PESs and UESs are provided in Figure 2 and are discussed in detail in Section 3.2. For example, if action A happens five out of ten times in the PES, while in the other five sequences another action (e.g. B) is the reason for the sanction to occur and action A does not appear in those sequences, then the punishment probability[1] is 0.5 (i.e. $PP(A) = 0.5$). However, there could have been n other instances (e.g. 15) in the UES where the action A happens, but is not punished. The algorithm in [10] calculates PP only based on PES, whereas here we take both PES and UES into account. Hence, $PP(A) = 0.25$ because action A is punished 5 out of 20 occurrences.

L3: The limited number of actions that agents can perform (as noted above) as set by the experiment designer. Whereas here the algorithm determines the number of actions to take into account based on the available data.

L4: Consideration of one type of probability distribution over actions – called predetermined – where there is a fixed probability assigned to each action in advance, to generate event sequences. The impact of other kinds of distribution (e.g. uniform, Gaussian) is not examined.

L5: High number of false positives when trying to identify multiple co-existing norms. This is directly related to the dependence (of the algorithm in [10]) on the norm inference threshold (NIT) parameter, which has to be lowered to the punishment probability of the lowest norm in order to detect (all) the norms. For example, if there are three norms such as prohibit(*walk on the grass*), prohibit(*litter*) and prohibit(*eat*) in the context of behaviour in a park, and if the punishment probability for violating each of these is 0.5 and 0.2 and 0.1 respectively, then NIT must be less than or equal to 0.1 to identify all three. However, lowering NIT is counter-productive, because it generates false positives. Even though the false positive problem can be resolved at the norm verification stage, because the agent (in [10]) checks with another agent that the norm it has inferred is indeed correct, it remains problematic since the other agent may not respond truthfully. The cited work assumes the agents are truthful.

The current work addresses the five limitations above. We present a comprehensive norm recommendation system consisting of four phases: (i) identification, (ii) classification (iii) life-stage detection (iv) recommendation. This addresses **L1** above by taking into account more elements of the bigger picture. An agent uses the formula above for punishment probability (**L2**). As noted above, the number of actions to consider is determined automatically (**L3**). The new algorithm is demonstrated using 20 randomly generated actions and the impacts of three different distributions (uniform, Gaussian

---

[1] **Punishment Probability (PP):** The punishment probability of an action A is the ratio of the number of punished occurrences of A to the total number of occurrences of A as expressed in the formula:

$$PP(A) = \frac{\text{Number of occurrences of A where it was punished}}{\text{Total number of occurrences of A}}$$

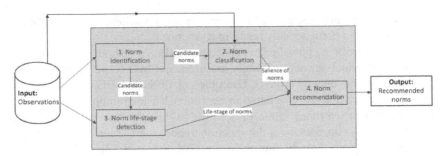

Fig. 1. Architecture of the norm recommendation system

and pre-determined) that are used to generate actions that agents perform in the simulations (**L4**). We also demonstrate that the algorithm reduces the number of false positives and false negatives (**L5** – details in Section 19). The new algorithm does not use NIT and also does not require the norm verification stage employed in [10], thus removing (i) a dependence on an arbitrary parameter and (ii) reliance on the veracity of other agents, so making the approach more robust and better decoupled.

3   Norm Recommendation Architecture

Existing approaches to norm identification, such as [9, 10], focus on how norms are identified and do not consider the importance of contextual aspects in providing norm recommendation, such as detecting norm salience and the life stage of the norm. This section provides an overview of a norm recommendation architecture that brings these factors into the process. The system comprises four phases, as shown in Figure 1. The input is the set of observations of an individual agent and the output is a set of norms and recommendations on each regarding whether an agent should follow or not. The norm recommendation system forms a part of an agent's reasoning process, in that one of the inputs to the agent's decision making process is the output of the recommendation system, along with beliefs, desires and goals.

1. **Norm identification:** The first phase identifies what we call candidate norms. The criterion is the ratio of violations for punishments to total occurrences for a given action (i.e. $PP(A)$). This is used in the algorithm discussed in Section 3.2.
2. **Norm classification:** The salience of the candidate norms (the extent to which norm violations are sanctioned) are then analyzed in the norm classification stage. Norm classification is based on punishment probability of the candidate norms obtained from the previous stage and the frequency of actions that are governed by the norms. This stage uses the frequency of an action (low, high) and probability of punishment for that action (low, high) to establish the salience category of a candidate norm. Hence, the four norm salience categories are very high, high, low and very low as depicted in Figs 5(a)–5(d), and discussed in more detail in Section 3.3. It must be noted that norm classification takes a short term view of the norm (i.e. the agent looks at the salience of the norm at the current time step). The longer term is addressed by the next phase.

3. **Norm life-stage deduction:** Based on any historical data that is available, it is possible to assign a life-stage to a candidate norm. We use a 5-stage categorisation: emerging, growing, maturing, declining or decaying (i.e. severely declining). For example, the norm against smoking virtually did not exist before the 1970s. In the 1990s, it might been said to be emergent, followed by growing rapidly in the 2000s. From such situations, we conclude it is useful for an agent to be able to take the life-stage of a norm into account in determining its reaction to it. The life-stage of a norm provides a longer-term perspective, in that it situates the current adoption of a norm in a historical context, by using a history of observed interactions between agents over as long a period of time as is recorded.

4. **Norm recommendation:** Heuristics are now used, driven by the short and long term information of the previous two phases, to make a recommendation on whether to follow a norm or not. For example, if salience is low and the life-stage is decaying, then the agent can be recommended not to follow the norm. However, if salience is very high and life-stage is emerging, then an agent might be recommended to follow the norm. To ground this: if the salience of the norm against smoking is high (i.e. smokers are punished with high probability), then the agent is recommended not to smoke.

3.1   Experiment Design

In this section we summarise the framework in which the experiments are conducted. We also describe the key parameters that are used in the sections discussing the phases and the results.

The approach taken for the simulation experiments is abstracted from any actual scenario. Thus, the agents have a vocabulary of actions available to them, denoted A–Z, while the system has a vocabulary of sanctions, denoted #, @, $. Agent action selection is based on a probability distribution; in this paper we work with three: (i) uniform, so each action is equally likely, (ii) Gaussian (or normal), so actions closer to the middle of the (ordered) action list are more likely than those further away and (iii) pre-determined, where actions are assigned probabilities in advance (useful for bespoke distributions and testing). The system is configured (for a given run) with prohibition norms, by specifying as many action sequences leading to a sanction event as the experimenter wishes. The task for the agents is to discover this configuration.

In an experiment, an agent acts as an observer, collecting data on the actions of another agent and whether there are any consequent sanctions. An agent has a configurable history length (HL) that determines the length of the observation sequence and within that uses a window size (WS) to determine how many actions to consider prior to a sanction event when trying to establish a correlation between action(s) and sanction. This window size ranges from 1 up to HL as the agent seeks to discover the violating action sequence. An illustration of an experiment appears in Figure 2, with HL=20, WS=4 and a uniform distribution for actions. The one remaining experiment parameter is the generation window size (GWS), which determines the maximum delay between a violation and a sanction which is set by the experimenter. If GWS is set to 10, then the violations will be punished within the next 10 actions. Other experiment parameters (numbers of runs etc. are given in the context of the experimental results).

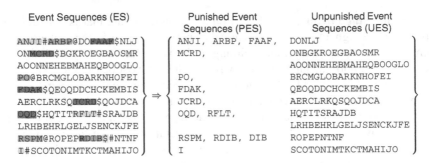

Event Sequences (ES)	Punished Event Sequences (PES)	Unpunished Event Sequences (UES)
ANJI#ARBP@DOPAAF$NLJ	ANJI, ARBP, FAAF,	DONLJ
ONMCRD$BGKROEGBAOSMR	MCRD,	ONBGKROEGBAOSMR
AOONNEHEBMAHEQBOOGLO		AOONNEHEBMAHEQBOOGLO
PO@BRCMGLOBARKNHOFEI	PO,	BRCMGLOBARKNHOFEI
FDAK$QEOQDDCHCKEMBIS	FDAK,	QEOQDDCHCKEMBIS
AERCLRKSQ#CRD$QOJDCA	JCRD,	AERCLRKQSQOJDCA
OQD$HQTITRFLT#SRAJDB	OQD, RFLT,	HQTITSRAJDB
LRHBEHRLGELJSENCKJFE		LRHBEHRLGELJSENCKJFE
RSPM@ROPEPRDIB$#NTNF	RSPM, RDIB, DIB	ROPEPNTNF
I#SCOTONIMTKCTMAHIJO	I	SCOTONIMTKCTMAHIJO

Fig. 2. An example of punished and unpunished event sequences

The next four sections (Sections 3.2 to 3.5) describe each of the four phases that lead to norm recommendation. Each of these sections present both the details of the corresponding phases and the experimental results obtained.

3.2 Norm Identification

The objective of the norm identification phase is to identify the candidate norms. The input is the history of actions that an agent observes over a period of time. When a new agent joins a society, it records the observed actions and interactions in a log. We assume that agents can recognize sanctions, but do not know the reason for the sanctions (i.e. do not know what norms were violated to have caused these sanctions).

The starting point for the algorithm is sanction recognition. Once sanctions are recognized, the reasons for these sanctions are investigated (i.e. norm violations are reasons for sanctions to occur). As noted earlier, the prohibition norm identification algorithm of [10] identifies those actions that occur $x\%$ of the time before the sanctions, but that does not take into account issues two to five as discussed in Section 2 and for which we now propose a revision (see Algorithm 1).

We start by computing the punishment probability through examination of episodes where sanctions follow and do not follow an action. An agent uses a fixed length history of event sequences, over which it runs a variable window size (WS). The agent looks into its history for a certain number of recent events that precede a sanction. For example, if the WS is set to 3, an agent creates an event episode with the last three events that were observed before the sanction. The sequence of events in this window is called the punishment event sequence (PES). The agent does not know the right window size, so it lets WS range over $[1, \text{HL})$ and calculates the punishment probabilities for all the actions. The actions are then sorted by PP, highest first, in order to identify a set of actions that precede the sanctions in all cases and may therefore be attributed with causing the punishment. If the WS range is $[1, 10)$ (i.e. HL=11), the agent has 10 sets of actions that circumstantially have a causal relationship with the sanction. Then, the agent computes the minimum set of actions from these 10 sets to identify actions that are most likely – by virtue of when the actions took place – to constitute the norms. We call this minimum set the candidate norms and it is the intersection of the action sets. The candidate norms thus identified become the input to the norm classification system.

Algorithm 1: Pseudocode to identify a minimum set of actions that are prohibited

---

Input: Event Sequences (ES) with punishments
Output: Minimum action set (a minimum set of actions that are prohibited)

1 List actionSetForEachWindowSize ⟵ ∅ ;   /* Contains a list of
   actionSets */
2 Set minimumActionSet ⟵ ∅
3 **for** *each window 1 to i in Window Size (WS)* **do**
4   **foreach** *action $(a_j) \in ES$* **do**
5 | Calculate Punishment Probability (PP_{aj});
6   **end**
7   Arrange actions by descending order of PP_{aj}
8   boolean actionSetForCurrentWSFound ⟵ false;
9   Set actionSetForCurrentWS ⟵ ∅;
10   **for** *each action $(a_j) \in ES$* **do**
11   actionSetForCurrentWS.add(a_j);
12   actionSetForCurrentWSFound ⟵
      checkIfActionSetResponsibleForSanctions (*actionSetForCurrentWS*) ;

13   **if** *actionSetForCurrentWSFound* **then**
14 | actionSetForEachWindowSize.add(actionSetForCurrentWS);
15 | break;
16   **end**
17   **end**
18 **end**
19 minimumActionSet = findIntersectingActions (*actionSetForEachWindowSize*)
   ;   /* intersection of all action sets */

In order to understand the norm identification process in detail, let us consider the event sequences shown in Figure 2. An event sequence (ES) is a sequence of actions that an agent observes another agent to be performing. The first line in the event sequences box on the left is the observation of another agent's actions and their consequences (HL=20 and WS=4). The observer sees an agent perform actions ANJI followed by a sanction (denoted by #). Subsequently, the observee performs ARBP and is sanctioned (@) and then it performs FAAF and is sanctioned again ($). The punishment event sequences (PES) occurring in a given history are listed in the middle, and are highlighted in the ES box on the left. There are three PES in the first observation. The unpunished event sequence (UES) in this case is the negation of the PES from the ES, yielding DONLJ. The input to Algorithm 1 is an ES list.

The agent can recognise a sanction. However, it does not know which action (or a set of actions in the case of multiple co-existing norms) has caused the sanction. To find out, it examines WSs 1 to HL-1, since it does know how long it is between violation and sanction (i.e. the delay between the two). For each WS the agent does the following: (i) extract the PES and UES from the history, (ii) calculate the punishment probabilities for all the unique actions in PES (line 5), (iii) order the actions in descending order of punishment probabilities (line 7). (iv) identify a set of actions that can account for all

Table 1. Action sets

Window Size	Action Set	Size of action set
1	[P, D, I, K, E, R, L, Q, G, M, J, H, A, C, S, B, F, N, O, T]	20
2	[D, I, P, S, R, B, T, C, M, G, F, K, L, J, O, N, H, Q, A, E]	20
3	[I, P, D, H, J, S, Q, O, N, T, B, A, K, E, G, F, R, M, L]	19
4	[P, D, I, O, T, M, F, K, G, A, J, B, N, E, L, H, C, Q]	18
5	[P, D, I, H, M, Q, O, R, C, F, J, T, K, N, G, E]	16
6	[P, I, D, N, K, R, F, J, O, B, S, G, T, M, Q, L]	16
7	[P, I, D, L, E, K, J, T, A, N, G, H, M, O, S]	15
8	[I, P, D, S, K, A, M, H, E, B, O, G, R]	13
9	[P, D, I, O, Q, G, E, K, F, A, T, M, S, R]	14
10	[P, D, I, O, K, H, J, B, G, R]	10
11	[P, D, I, J, E, S, O, K, F, Q]	10
12	[P, D, I, J, K, E, Q, A, O, N, F]	11
13	[P, D, I, Q, A, E, O, K]	8
14	[P, D, I, N, E, Q, J]	7
15	[P, D, I, E, R, S, F, K]	8
16	[P, D, I, N, E, J, R]	7
17	[P, D, I, O, E, R]	6
18	[P, D, I, Q, T]	5
19	[P, D, I]	3

violations (lines 10-18) by adding one action at a time starting with the one with the highest PP_{a_j}, (v) compute the intersection of the action sets (line 19). This intersection is the minimum set of actions that may account for the violations that have resulted in the sanctions.

Table 1 shows the actions sets obtained by ranging WS from 1 to 19 (i.e. HL=20) for an ES list containing 50000 entries. It shows three columns, the WS in column 1, the action set that was identified for the corresponding WS in column 2 and size of the action set in column 3. The minimum set of actions out of these 19 action sets is identified as the set of candidate norms. The minimum action set (i.e. the minimum set of prohibited actions) here is P, D and I identified at WS=19.

Note that this approach only identifies *potential* norms as an aggregate: that is, P, D and I *together* are considered responsible for the occurrence of the sanctions. It does not identify the salience of the individual norm violations. For example, it does not answer the question of whether P is punished more often than D. Addressing this question forms the focus of the next phase discussed in Section 3.3.

Results. We first compare the new algorithm against that is reported in [10]. For these experiments we use three data generation schemes: uniform, random and predetermined. The last was also used in [10], and thus provides us with a baseline reference against which to evaluate the new approach. A set of 20 actions are considered, with HL=20. At each time step, an agent picks an action to perform, governed by the underlying distribution.

Each experiment comprises three rounds in which the system is configured with one, two or three norms to be discovered. The number of norms in the system is known to the

Table 2. Comparison of two algorithms under different distributions

No.of. norms	FP or FN	Uniform Old	Uniform New	Gaussian Old	Gaussian New	Pre-determined Old	Pre-determined New
1	FP	0.003	0.000	5.623	0.130	3.033	0.000
1	FN	0.013	0.000	0.057	0.117	0.013	0.000
2	FP	0.003	0.000	5.570	0.043	3.967	0.000
2	FN	0.023	0.000	0.873	0.390	0.023	0.000
3	FP	0.000	0.000	5.187	0.053	1.877	0.000
3	FN	0.030	0.000	1.673	0.580	0.030	0.000

experimenter, but unknown to the norm identification system whose goal is to identify those norms. For each distribution, there are 100 runs each with low (p=0.1), medium (p=0.5) and high (p=0.9) punishment probability, making 300 runs in all. Finally, each run has 50,000 iterations, for each of which one event sequence of length HL is created. This process depends upon the punishment probability derived from the data set, to identify potential norms, in contrast to that of [10], which depends on the experimenter setting a hard Norm Inference Threshold (which is set to 0.25 here).

We compare the number of false positives (FP) and false negatives (FN) generated by the new and the published prohibition norm identification algorithm in experiments where the system is configured with one, two and three norms. The Generation Window Size (GWS) is set to 19. The results are shown in Table 2.

It can be observed that the new algorithm generally performs better, in that it significantly reduces the number of false positives and false negatives, except in the case of FNs in the one norm configuration under Gaussian distribution (an artifact of the behaviour of the Gaussian model that we explain below). The new algorithm does not produce any FPs or FNs under uniform and pre-determined distributions, while there are some under the normal (Gaussian) distribution. We explain this as follows: under normal distribution, there will be some actions (αs) that happen rarely and that get punished only a few times. Due to randomness there will be other actions (βs) that occur in the same windows as the αs (particularly when window sizes are large). Consequently, the βs can be identified as a reason for the sanction, rather than the αs.

For example, let us assume that there exists an action (γ) whose occurrence probability is low (say 0.0001) and when that action occurs it gets punished. In a run with 50000 iterations and generation window size of 19, this action would occur only 100 times[2]. When the WS is large (say 19), it could happen that another action (say ω) might co-occur with γ just by chance (e.g. ω could have a high occurrence probability). Hence, ω and α might be identified as two actions that are responsible for the sanctions to occur even though ω has nothing to do with sanctions (an error of commission – a false positive). On the other hand if ω is also a reason for a sanction and assuming that its PP is higher than that of γ, then, only ω could be identified as the norm (an error of omission – a false negative). Nevertheless, under Gaussian distribution, the new algorithm performs significantly better.

---

[2] 50000*19*0.0001=95.

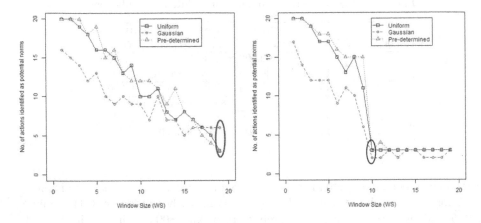

Fig. 3. Generation window size = 19   **Fig. 4.** Generation window size = 10

An agent inferring norms can also predict the delay between the violations and sanctions (i.e. how long after a violation does the sanction occur). In other words, the agent can identify the right WS for identifying the norms, simply by noting the WS at which the minimum action set is normally – because of the small probability of false positives/negatives – found. To illustrate the prediction of the correct WS consider Figures 3 and 4. They show the size of the action sets identified for WS=19 and 10 respectively. Each of the figures also show the comparisons of the sizes of norm sets that are identified when the underlying action generation distribution is varied (i.e. uniform, Gaussian and pre-determined).

The system was configured with three norms for all the three experiments and the HL was set to 20. Figure 3 shows that when the generation window size[3] was 19 the correct number of norms (i.e. three) is identified at WS=19 (x-axis) for uniform and pre-determined distributions, but under Gaussian there are two FPs (i.e. a total of five norms). Figure 4 shows the correct number of norms with WS=10 for uniform and pre-determined distributions, but Gaussian only identifies two norms (i.e. one FN). It should be noted that in all the three cases, the dip (i.e. the least number of action sets (norms) is found for the first time (highlighted using ellipses in the figures) – 3 in this experiment), occurs at the correct generation window size (19 and 10, respectively in Figures 3 and 4) for uniform and pre-determined distributions. It should be noted that for the Gaussian distribution the dip occurs at the correct generation window sizes (19 and 10). However, the sets of norms identified contain false positives in one case (Figure 3) and a false negative in another (Figure 4). Nevertheless, independent of the distributions, the window size at which the dip occurs has consequences for an agent. In all the three distributions an agent is able to determine the delay between an action and a sanction (i.e. the right WS). This has implications for the amount of processing

---

[3] To reiterate, the generation window size (GWS) is the delay between an action and the sanction that follows it. This delay is set by the experimenter.

an agent undertakes in order to identify norms. For example, upon discovering that all norms are punished within a window size of 10, an agent only needs to consider the 10 actions that precede a sanction for further processing (i.e. to identify norms). It does not have to consider window sizes 11 to 19, which it would otherwise for HL=20.

3.3   Norm Classification

Norm classification is based on norm salience. Norm salience is computed based on two axes: frequency of an action in the x-axis and the punishment probability in the y-axis. We propose a simple salience categorization containing four zones of salience (very high, high, low and very low). The graphical representation of the norm classification scheme is given in Figure 5(a).

The agent classifies the candidate norms identified in the previous stage. Figures 5(b), 5(c) and 5(d) show example norm classifications for the three distributions considered in this work. It can be observed in Figures 5(b) and 5(d) that all the three norms with which the system is configured (P, D and I) are classified as *very highly* salient norms (highlighted by dashed rectangles). However, under Gaussian distribution, P, D and I are *highly* salient norms, In order to provide a comparison of how normative actions (i.e. P, D and I) and non-normative actions fare on the norm classification scale, we have also presented all the other non-normative actions. It can be observed that there is a clear separation of normative and non-normative actions for uniform and pre-determined distributions, while for Gaussian distribution, the difference isn't clear. There are some actions that occur rarely, but appear along the sanctioned action more often (just by chance) in the gaussian distribution (e.g. action H in Figure 5(c)). Since Algorithm 1 arranges actions based on descending order of the punishment probability the action H will appear in the norms set in this case. This is an example of how false positives are included in the norms set in the case of Gaussian distribution.

Norm salience is a metric for the short term (i.e. how salient is the norm now) and does not account for whether a norm is stable or emerging etc. The purpose of the next step is to identify the life-stage of a norm.

3.4   Norm Life-Stage Detection

We propose that every potential norm should be considered in a historical context. Assuming that we have enough long-term information available, norm life-stage detection can be enabled. Based on historical data, an agent can identify whether a norm is emerging, growing, maturing, declining or decaying. The inspiration for this terminology comes from the life cycle stages of a product [13].

We define the life-stage function below. The function takes three inputs, the cumulative PP of a norm at regular time intervals, a threshold for norm emergence (α) and a threshold for norm growth (β). We specify the decision function in terms of whether: (i) the PP of a norm is higher, the same or lower than its value at the previous census point, (ii) the value of PP in relation to α and β (noting that $0 \leq \alpha < \beta \leq 1$). The life-stage labels are assigned according to the scheme outlined below, with the additional distinction between the start of the decline of a mature norm and the latter stages when

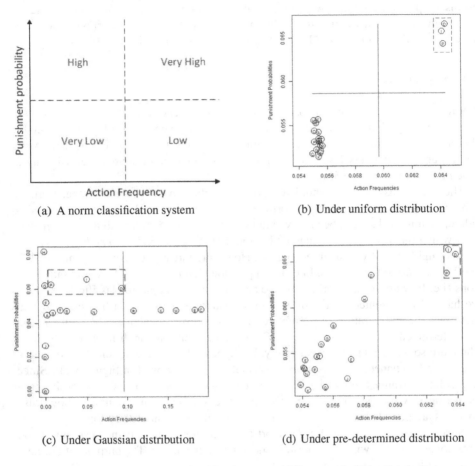

Fig. 5. Salience based norm classification across different probability distributions

its influence is greatly reduced, but not yet decaying. For each label, we also give an abbreviation that is used in Figure 6.

$$
\text{life\_stage}(PP, \alpha, \beta) = \begin{cases}
PP_t > PP_{t-1} \wedge PP_t \in [0, \alpha] \to \text{emerging: E} \\
PP_t > PP_{t-1} \wedge PP_t \in (\alpha, \beta] \to \text{growing: G} \\
PP_t > PP_{t-1} \wedge PP_t \in (\beta, 1] \to \text{maturing: M} \\
PP_t = PP_{t-1} \qquad\qquad\qquad \to \text{previous value} \\
PP_t < PP_{t-1} \wedge PP_t \in (\beta, 1] \to \text{declining but mature: D1} \\
PP_t < PP_{t-1} \wedge PP_t \in (\alpha, \beta] \to \text{declining and weak: D2} \\
PP_t < PP_{t-1} \wedge PP_t \in [0, \alpha] \to \text{decaying: D3}
\end{cases}
$$

Figure 6 shows how life-stages are identified for a sample set of datapoints (being the cumulative punishment probabilities for the violation of a norm (y-axis) over time (x-axis)) using the life-stage function. The values of α and β are set at 0.25 and 0.75,

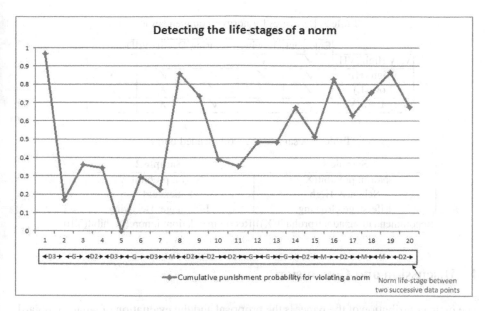

Fig. 6. An example of life stage detection for a sample norm

respectively. At time t_1 the punishment probability is 0.96. At t_2 the value falls to 0.17 which is less than α, giving a life-stage of decaying. The life-stage at time t_2 (between data points 2 and 3) is growing and the life-stage at time t_3 is declining. Using the life-stage function, we can identify the life-stages between the pairs of consecutive data points. The norm life-stages at various time points are shown at the bottom of Figure 6. Consideration of a sequence of time points to establish a trend is a task for future work.

3.5 Norm Recommendation

Using the results of the previous two stages, this stage can provide norm recommendation to software agents or to human users. A simple heuristic based recommendation is set out in Table 3. The tick marks represent occasions where a norm is recommended to an agent and the crosses represent occasions where a norm is not recommended to an agent. Two sample recommendations are given in Table 4. The first column corresponds to a situation where an agent has been advised to adopt the norm *prohibit(X)* (i.e. the agent has been advised to abstain from performing action X) whose salience is high and the norm is growing. The second column corresponds to a situation where an agent has been recommended to ignore the norm proscribing action Y (represented by *ignore(prohibit(Y))*) since the norm salience is low and the norm is decaying.

It should be noted that the heuristics used in this phase will be configured by the designer of the system. Also, the norm recommendations are provided to human users, who may or may not decide to honour these norms. The approach proposed here is a 'non-intrusive' approach where recommendation is provided to human agents without forcing them to abide to the norms (i.e. autonomous decision making is honoured).

Table 3. Heuristics for norm recommendation

	Emergent	Growing	Maturing	Declining	Decaying
Very High (VH)	✓	✓	✓	✓	✓
High (H)	✓	✓	✓	✓	✗
Low (L)	✓	✓	✓	✗	✗
Very Low (VL)	✗	✓	✓	✗	✗

Table 4. A sample of recommended norms

Sample 1	Sample 2
Norm: prohibit(X)	Norm: prohibit(Y)
Salience: High	Salience: Low
Life-stage:Growing	Life-stage: Decaying
Recommendation: adopt(prohibit(X))	Recommendation: ignore(prohibit(Y))

4   Discussion and Conclusion

The main contribution of the paper is the proposal and the evaluation of what we regard as a more realistic model for a norm recommendation system. This paper has presented a comprehensive four-phase approach for recommending norms in software agent societies. Based on the data observed by an agent, it first identifies candidate norms. Second, these norms are then classified based on their salience (i.e. the extent of punishments imposed for violations). Third, the life-stage of the norm is identified. Finally, based on salience and life-stage detection, a heuristic method is used to recommend norms. The recommended norms can then be used by human or software agents for choosing actions. The operationalization of the four phases of the recommendation system is evaluated using simulated data. Additionally, the paper also proposes a new algorithm for norm identification which overcomes the limitations of published work.

There are some shortcomings to the current work that we intend to address in the future. First, there could be a combination of actions that are the reason for a sanction (as opposed to just one action as assumed here). Second, the subject of the method described here is prohibition norms: it is technically fairly straightforward to apply this approach also to obligation norms. Third, the demonstration of the architecture is based on simulations. A concrete implementation in the context of an agent-based application is a desirable next step (e.g. in conjunction with the revision mechanism of Li et al. [5]). Fourth, different models for some of the phases of norm recommendation can be considered. For example, in the norm identification phase, norms are ordered based on the descending order of punishment probability. A weighted approach that ranks candidate norms not only based on punishment probability, but also the action frequency can be considered. Fifth, enabling agents to auto-tune parameters in certain scenarios will be beneficial. For example, an agent can decide that it is only interested in highly salient norms and may decide to ignore all the other norms. Hence, the agent will only identify the life-stages of those norms that are highly salient, thus eliminating additional computation required for evaluating other norms. Sixth, the norm life-cycle model presented in the paper is coarse grained using a small number of discrete stages. The discrete model could be replaced with a continuous model that the designer might specify by means of a malleable graph interface. What these points serve to highlight is that the contribution here is not just in the various decision procedures and the plausibility of the results they together deliver, but also in form of a framework into which alternative procedures can be plugged to explore a rich landscape of norm discovery.

References

1. Axelrod, R.: The complexity of cooperation: Agent-based models of competition and collaboration. Princeton University Press (1997)
2. Corapi, D., De Vos, M., Padget, J., Russo, A., Satoh, K.: Norm refinement and design through inductive learning. In: De Vos, M., Fornara, N., Pitt, J.V., Vouros, G. (eds.) COIN 2010. LNCS, vol. 6541, pp. 77–94. Springer, Heidelberg (2011)
3. Criado, N., Such, J.M., Botti, V.: Providing agents with norm reasoning services. In: Third International Workshop on Infrastructures and Tools for Multiagent Systems, ITMAS 2012 (2013)
4. Epstein, J.M.: Learning to be thoughtless: Social norms and individual computation. Computational Economics 18(1), 9–24 (2001)
5. Li, T., Balke, T., Vos, M.D., Padget, J., Satoh, K.: A model-based approach to the automatic revision of secondary legislation. In: The 14th International Conference on Artificial Intelligence and Law, Proceedings of the Conference, Rome, Italy, June 10-14, pp. 202–206 (2013)
6. Morales, J., López-Sánchez, M., Esteva, M.: Using experience to generate new regulations. In: Proceedings of the Twenty-Second International Joint Conference on Artificial Intelligence, vol. 1, pp. 307–312. AAAI Press (2011)
7. Oren, N., Meneguzzi, F.: Norm identification through plan recognition. In: Coordination, Organization, Institutions and Norms in Agent Systems, COIN 2013@AAMAS (2013)
8. Savarimuthu, B.T.R., Cranefield, S.: Norm creation, spreading and emergence: A survey of simulation models of norms in multi-agent systems. Multiagent and Grid Systems 7(1), 21–54 (2011)
9. Savarimuthu, B.T.R., Cranefield, S., Purvis, M.A., Purvis, M.K.: Obligation norm identification in agent societies. Journal of Artificial Societies and Social Simulation 13(4), 3 (2010)
10. Savarimuthu, B.T.R., Cranefield, S., Purvis, M.A., Purvis, M.K.: Identifying prohibition norms in agent societies. In: Artificial Intelligence and Law, pp. 1–46 (2012)
11. Savarimuthu, B.T.R., Cranefield, S., Purvis, M.K., Purvis, M.A.: Norm emergence in agent societies formed by dynamically changing networks. Web Intelligence and Agent Systems 7(3), 223–232 (2009)
12. Sen, S., Airiau, S.: Emergence of norms through social learning. In: Proceedings of the Twentieth International Joint Conference on Artificial Intelligence (IJCAI), pp. 1507–1512. AAAI Press (2007)
13. Theodore, L.: Exploit the product life cycle. Harvard Business Review 43, 81–94 (1965)
14. Villatoro, D., Sen, S., Sabater-Mir, J.: Topology and memory effect on convention emergence. In: WI-IAT 2009: Proceedings of the 2009 IEEE/WIC/ACM International Joint Conference on Web Intelligence and Intelligent Agent Technology, pp. 233–240. IEEE Computer Society, Washington, DC (2009)
15. Wang, C.-C., Wang, C.-H.: Helping others in online games: Prosocial behavior in cyberspace. Cyberpschology, Behavior, and Social Networking 11(3), 344–346 (2008)

A Methodology for Plan Revision
under Norm and Outcome Compliance

Simone Scannapieco[1,2,3], Guido Governatori[2,3],
Francesco Olivieri[1,2,3], and Matteo Cristani[1]

[1] Department of Computer Science, University of Verona, Italy
[2] NICTA, Queensland Research Laboratory, Australia*
[3] Institute for Integrated and Intelligent Systems, Griffith University, Australia

Abstract. Scholars understand an agent as a system acting in an environment. Such an environment is usually governed by norms, and the agent has to obey to such norms when pursuing her objectives. We report a non-monotonic modal logic able to describe the environment, the norms, and the agent's capabilities as well as her mental attitudes (e.g., desires, intentions). First, we show how such a logic is expressive enough to determine when the agent is compliant with respect to norms and objectives by extending it with a formal characterisation of the concepts of norm and outcome compliance. Then, in the case the agent violates some norms or does not achieve all her objectives, we propose a preliminary analysis of methodologies to revise the theory and restore compliance.

Keywords: Norm compliance, goal compliance, Defeasible Logic, business process, logic-based revision.

1 Introduction

An agent is a system which operates in the environment where she is embedded driven by a set of objectives. Typically, an agent is equipped with a library of plans and, based on her mental attitudes, she deliberates on the course of action to adopt to achieve her objectives [1].

We depart from the standard architecture proposed in [2,3,4] where an agent selects a plan from her plan library and instead we assume that the agent generates alternative plans to reach a particular set of objectives in the form of a *business process* (workflows), derived from the declarative specifications of the agent's knowledge base. This is in line with the classical definition of business process as the set of all the possible ways in which it can be executed, i.e., the set of its execution traces [5]. In turn, the notion of trace is compatible with the classical AI definition of plan as a sequence of actions that are triggered by pre-conditions and that generate some effects (post-conditions) [6].

The constraints imposed by the environment play an important role in choosing the most suitable plan for a given circumstance. In fact, the environment is usually governed

---

* NICTA is funded by the Australian Government as represented by the Department of Broadband, Communications and the Digital Economy, the Australian Research Council through the ICT Centre of Excellence program and the Queensland Government.

G. Boella et al. (Eds.): PRIMA 2013, LNAI 8291, pp. 324–339, 2013.

by a set of rules describing the "right way" of behaving, which are expressed in various forms (e.g., guidelines, norms, laws, regulations).

In this perspective, it is possible to consider scenarios where an agent is not able to achieve all her objectives without violating the norms. That is to say, there is no possible way for the process to be executed without either violating the norms, or achieving some objectives. In other words, the whole business process is not compliant [7,8].

Consider the following example. Robbie the Robot is downtown to deliver some mail for its boss, Carmen. It is just done with the task and thinking to get a (well-deserved) ice-cold oil-beer, when Carmen calls him: the meeting she was supposed to attend at 3pm has been anticipated and will start in one hour. Therefore, she tells him to bring some food at her office since she will not be able to have lunch at her favourite restaurant for lack of time. Moreover, Robbie cannot forget to pick up a suit for Carmen, which is necessary for the presentation she will hold during the meeting.

Robbie's internal system elaborates four plans. Plan A is to go to the dry-cleaner to get Carmen's favourite suit and then to a take-away, but to get all these things done in time, it needs to drive beyond the speed limit, thus violating the traffic laws. Plan A_1 is not to stop at the dry-cleaner, while plan A_2 is not to stop to get the food (not fulfilling one objective in both cases). Instead, Plan B involves going to Carmen's place to get another suit and then stop at a fast-food close by (Carmen's less favourite food). In this way, there is no time for the ice-cold oil-beer. Thus, whatever plan Robbie decides to adopt, either a violation of the norms occurs, or some of the objectives are not fulfilled.

The main aim of this paper is to start an analytical study on how to restore compliance of a business process with respect to objectives and obligations. More specifically, we search for a methodology to revise the knowledge base of the agent to obtain a new plan which complies with the governing norms and meets her objectives.

To integrate the previous example, suppose Robbie has recently been equipped with an (on-line) unit which can suggest alternative plans. Strangely enough, the unit informs Robbie that there is a grocery store close to Carmen's home. Just by downloading from the server the task-programmes *buy_groceries* and *make_a_sandwich*, Robbie may indeed buy all the necessary ingredients to prepare an healthy sandwich (which Carmen prefers to a fast-food burger), get an oil-beer six-pack and return to Carmen's office in time without driving fast. With great delight, Robbie opts for this plan, happy and proud of its new software.

To succeed in our endeavour, we start from the logic presented in [9] which is a modal variant of Defeasible Logic (DL) [10]. The logic is inspired by the BDI (Belief-Desire-Intention) architecture [2,3,4] and defines a framework to model rational agents, based on three kind of knowledge:

(i) the internal constraints guiding the agent (i.e., her mental attitudes);
(ii) the external constraints she has to obey to (i.e., norms);
(iii) her vision of the world (i.e., her beliefs) along with the actions she is able to perform in the form of *rules*; each action has its pre-conditions (inputs) and post-conditions (effects).

Equipped with this knowledge, the agent is able to choose different courses of action to reach the objectives she decides to achieve.

The paper is organised as follows. In Section 2, we first illustrate the logical formalism, and we end by discussing the notion of compliance with respect to norms and objectives (Subsection 2.3). Section 3 gives an overview of existing formalisms and suggests a methodology to address business process revision using the logical framework proposed. We summarise and comment some future works in Section 4.

2   Logic

Despite the traditional treatment of internal constraints in the BDI architecture, the logic proposed in [9] considers all mental attitudes (desires, goals, intentions, and social intentions) as facets of the same concept of *outcome*, which is regarded as something the agent would like to achieve. As a result, mental attitudes were modelled by using a single type of rule, called *outcome rule*, whose nature is very similar to that of *reparative chains* modelling the mechanism of norm violation/reparation [11]. Given the rule $r : \Gamma \Rightarrow o_1 \otimes o_2 \otimes \cdots \otimes o_n$, if the context described by Γ holds, then the obligation in force is o_1; in case o_1 is violated then the new obligation in force is o_2, and so on. Similarly, we use the same rationale to model an agent which ranks alternative outcomes by a *preference ordering*. Using only one type of rule to derive all agent's mental attitudes reflects a natural way to express alternatives to more preferred outcomes. The agent then deploys her knowledge of the environment to filter out the actual objectives she will commit to from all her preferences. For instance, consider the following setting. Alice, during her holidays, plans to pay a visit to her friend John, who lives close to her parents. A possible plan for Alice is described by the following modal outcome rule, where the notation $\Rightarrow_U$ denotes the fact that rule s is used to derive oUtcomes.

$$s : holiday \Rightarrow_U visit\_John \odot visit\_parents \odot stay\_home$$

The intended meaning is *"I shall come over to John's place to visit him, but if it is not possible (for instance, if he is not home), I am going to visit my parents. If this is not possible as well, I shall take some rest at home"*.

Four different types of mental attitudes were identified: desires, goals, intentions, and social intentions, whose meaning is the following.

Desires as acceptable outcomes. Consider an agent equipped with the outcome rules

$$r : a_1, \ldots, a_n \Rightarrow_U b_1 \odot \cdots \odot b_m \qquad s : a'_1, \ldots, a'_n \Rightarrow_U b'_1 \odot \cdots \odot b'_k$$

and that the situation described by $a_1, \ldots, a_n$ and $a'_1, \ldots, a'_n$ are mutually compatible but b_1 and b'_1 are not, namely $b_1 = \neg b'_1$. In this case $b_1, \ldots, b_m, b'_1, \ldots, b'_k$ are anyway all *acceptable outcomes*, including the incompatible outcomes b_1 and b'_1. *Desires* are expected or acceptable outcomes, independently of whether they are compatible with other expected or acceptable outcomes.

Goals as preferred outcomes. For rule r alone the preferred outcome is b_1, and for rule s alone it is b'_1. But if both rules are applicable, then the agent would not be rational if she considers both b_1 and $\neg b_1$ as her preferred outcomes. Hence, the agent has to decide if she prefers a state where b_1 holds to one where b'_1 (i.e., $\neg b_1$) holds, or the other way around. If the agent has no way to decide which is the most suitable option for her, then neither the chain of r nor that of s can produce preferred outcomes. Suppose that the agent opts for b'_1; this can be done if she establishes that the second rule overrides the first one, i.e., $s > r$. Accordingly, the preferred outcome is b'_1 for the chain of outcomes defined by s, and b_2 is the preferred outcome of r. b_2 is the second best alternative according to rule r: in fact b_1 has been discarded as an acceptable outcome given that s prevails over r.

Two degrees of commitment: intentions and social intentions. We now clarify which are the outcomes for an agent to commit to. Naturally, if the agent values some outcomes more than others, she should strive for the best, i.e., for the most preferred outcomes.

We first consider the case where only rule r applies. Here, the agent should commit to the outcome she values the most, i.e., b_1. But what if the agent *believes* that b_1 cannot be achieved in the environment, or she knows that $\neg b_1$ holds? Committing to b_1 would result in a waste of agent's resources; rationally, she should target the next best outcome, in this case b_2. Accordingly, the agent derives b_2 as her *intention*. Suppose, now, that b_2 is *forbidden*, and the agent is social (an agent is social if the agent would not knowingly commit to anything that is forbidden [12]). Once again, in this situation the agent has to lower her expectation and settle for b_3, which is considered her *social intention*.

To complete the analysis, consider the situation where both rules r and s apply and the agent prefers s to r. As we have seen before, $\neg b_1$ (b'_1) and b_2 are the preferred outcomes since the agent stated $s > r$. Assume that, this time, the agent knows she cannot achieve $\neg b_1$ (or equivalently, b_1 holds). If the agent is rational, she cannot commit to $\neg b_1$. Thus, the best option for her is to commit to b'_2 and b_1 (both regarded as intentions and social intentions), where she is guaranteed to be successful. In this scenario, the best course of action for the agent is where she commits herself to some outcomes that are not her preferred ones, or even that she would consider not acceptable based only on her preferences, but such that they influence her decision process given that they represent relevant external factors (either her beliefs or the norms that apply to her).

2.1 Language

Let PROP be a set of propositional atoms, $\text{MOD} = \{B, O, D, G, I, SI\}$ the set of modal operators, whose reading is B for *belief*, O for *obligation*, D for *desire*, G for *goal*, I for *intention* and SI for *social intention*. Let Lab be a set of arbitrary labels. The set $\text{Lit} = \text{PROP} \cup \{\neg p | p \in \text{PROP}\}$ denotes the set of *literals*. The *complementary* of a literal q is denoted by $\sim q$; if q is a positive literal p, then $\sim q$ is $\neg p$, and if q is a negative literal $\neg p$ then $\sim q$ is p. The set of *modal literals* is $\text{ModLit} = \{\Box l, \neg \Box l | l \in \text{Lit}, \Box \in \{O, D, G, I, SI\}\}$. We assume that modal operator "$\Box$" for belief B is the empty modal operator. Accordingly, a modal literal Bl is equivalent to literal l; the complementary of $B \sim l$ and $\neg Bl$ is l. We define a *defeasible theory* D as a structure $(F, R, >)$, where

(i) $F \subseteq \text{Lit} \cup \text{ModLit}$ is a set of *facts* or indisputable statements;
(ii) R contains three sets of *rules*: for beliefs, obligations, and outcomes;
(iii) $> \subseteq R \times R$ is a *superiority relation* to determine the relative strength of conflicting rules.

Belief rules are used to relate the factual knowledge of an agent (her vision of the environment), and defines the relationships between states of the world. As such, provability for beliefs does not generate modal literals. *Obligation rules* determine when and which obligations are in force. The conclusions generated by obligation rules are modalised with obligation. Finally, *outcome rules* establish the possible outcomes of an agent depending on the particular context. Apart from obligation rules, outcome rules are used to derive conclusions for all modes denoting possible types of outcomes: desires, goals, intentions, and social intentions.

Following ideas given in [11], rules can gain more expressiveness when a *preference operator* $\odot$ is used: an expression like $a \odot b$ means that if a is possible, then a is the first choice and b is the second one; if $\neg a$ holds, then the first choice is not attainable and b is the actual choice. This operator is used to build chains of preferences, called $\odot$-*expressions*. The formation rules for $\odot$-expressions are: (i) every literal is an $\odot$-expression; (ii) if A is an $\odot$-expression and b is a literal then $A \odot b$ is an $\odot$-expression. In this paper, we exploit the classical definition of *defeasible rule* in DL [10]. A defeasible rule is an expression $r : A(r) \Rightarrow_\square C(r)$, where

(i) $r \in \text{Lab}$ is the name of the rule;
(ii) $A(r) = \{a_1, \ldots, a_n\}$ with $a_i \in \text{Lit} \cup \text{ModLit}$ is the set of the premises (or the *antecedent*) of the rule;
(iii) $\square \in \{B, O, U\}$ represents the *mode* of the rule (from now on, we omit the subscript B in rules for beliefs, i.e., $\Rightarrow$ is used as a shortcut for $\Rightarrow_B$);
(iv) $C(r)$ is the *consequent* (or *head*) of the rule, which is a single literal if $\square = B$, or an $\odot$-expression otherwise. Notice that modal literals can occur only in the antecedent of rules: the reason is that the rules are used to derive modal conclusions and we do not conceptually need to iterate modalities. The motivation of a single literal as a consequent for belief rules is dictated by the intended reading of the belief rules, where these rules are used to describe the environment.

We use the following abbreviations on sets of rules: $R^\square$ ($R^\square[q]$) denotes all rules of mode $\square$ (with consequent q), and $R[q] = \bigcup_{\square \in \{B, O, U\}} R^\square[q]$. $R[q, i]$ denotes the set of rules whose head is $\odot_{j=1}^n c_j$ and $c_i = q$, with $1 \le i \le n$.

Notice that labelling the rules of DL produces nothing more but a simple treatment of the modalities, thus two interaction strategies between modal operators are analysed.

Rule conversions and conflict-detection/resolution. It is sometimes meaningful to use rules for a modality $\square$ as they were for another modality $\blacksquare$, i.e., to convert one type of conclusions into a different one. Formally, given rule $r : a_1, \ldots, a_n \Rightarrow_\square b$ and the situation where $\blacksquare a_1, \ldots, \blacksquare a_n$ hold, the asymmetric binary relation Convert$(\square, \blacksquare)$ permits to derive $\blacksquare b$. For instance, if statement $A =$ "buy a car" implies statement $B =$ "spend money" and we have the intention to buy a car, then we may conclude that we also have the intention to spend money (if $A \Rightarrow B$ and IA, then IB). In our framework, we consider Convert$(B, \square)$ with $\square \in \text{MOD} \setminus \{B\}$. Accordingly, we enrich the notation with $R^{B,\square}$, denoting the set of belief rules that can be used for a conversion to mode $\square$. The antecedent of all such rules is not empty, and does not contain any modal literal.

Moreover, it is crucial to identify criteria for detecting and solving conflicts between different modalities. Formally, we define an asymmetric binary relation Conflict $\subseteq$ MOD $\times$ MOD such that Conflict$(\square, \blacksquare)$ means 'modes $\square$ and $\blacksquare$ are in conflict and mode $\square$ prevails over $\blacksquare$'. In our framework, we consider Conflict $= \{(B, I), (B, SI)\}$ defining the realistic attitude of the agents [13], and Conflict $= \{(O, SI)\}$ defining the social attitude of the agents [12]. For instance, a social agent cannot have the social intention to smoke in a public place where it is forbidden to smoke.

There are two applications of the *superiority relation*. The first considers rules of the same mode. The latter compares two rules of different modes, with complementary literals and the two modes are related by the Convert relation.

2.2 Inferential Mechanism

A *proof P* of *length n* is a finite sequence $P(1), \dots, P(n)$ of *tagged literals* of the type $+\partial_\square q$ and $-\partial_\square q$, where $\square \in$ MOD. As a conventional notation, $P(1..i)$ denotes the initial part of the sequence P of length i. Given a defeasible theory D, $+\partial_\square q$ means that q is defeasibly provable in D with the mode $\square$, and $-\partial_\square q$ that it has been proved in D that q is not defeasibly provable in D with the mode $\square$. From now on, the term *refuted* is a synonym of *not provable* and we use $D \vdash \pm\partial_\square l$ iff there is a proof P in D such that $P(n) = \pm\partial_\square l$ for an index n.

To characterise the notions of provability for all modalities, it is essential to define when a rule is *applicable* or *discarded*. To this end, the preliminary notion of when a rule is *body-applicable/body-discarded* is needed, stating that each literal in the body of the rule must be proved/refuted with the suitable mode.

Definition 1. *Let P be a proof and* $\square \in \{O, D, G, I, SI\}$. *A rule* $r \in R$ *is* body-applicable *(at step $n + 1$) iff for all* $a_i \in A(r)$:

1. *if* $a_i = \square l$ *then* $+\partial_\square l \in P(1..n)$,
2. *if* $a_i = \neg\square l$ *then* $-\partial_\square l \in P(1..n)$,
3. *if* $a_i = l \in$ Lit *then* $+\partial l \in P(1..n)$.

A rule $r \in R$ *is* body-discarded *(at step $n + 1$) iff there is* $a_i \in A(r)$ *such that*

1. $a_i = \square l$ *and* $-\partial_\square l \in P(1..n)$, *or*
2. $a_i = \neg\square l$ *and* $+\partial_\square l \in P(1..n)$, *or*
3. $a_i = l \in$ Lit *and* $-\partial l \in P(1..n)$.

As already stated, belief rules allow us to derive literals with different modes. The applicability mechanism must take into account this constraint.

Definition 2. *Let P be a proof. A rule* $r \in R$ *is 1.* Conv-applicable, *2.* Conv-discarded *(at step $n + 1$) for* $\square$, $\square \in$ MOD $\setminus \{B\}$, *iff*

1. $r \in R^B$, $A(r) \neq \emptyset$ *and for all* $a \in A(r)$, $+\partial_\square a \in P(1..n)$;
2. $r \notin R^B$ *or* $A(r) = \emptyset$ *or* $\exists a \in A(r)$, $-\partial_\square a \in P(1..n)$.

As an example, consider theory $D = (\{a, b, Oc\}, \{r_1 : a \Rightarrow_O b, r_2 : b, c \Rightarrow d\}, \emptyset)$. Rule r_1 is applicable, while r_2 is not since c is not proved as a belief. Instead, r_2 is Conv-applicable for O, since Oc is a fact and r_1 proves Ob.

The notion of applicability gives guidelines on how to consider the next element in a given chain. Since a rule for belief cannot generate reparative chains but only single literals, we can conclude that the applicability condition for belief collapses into body-applicability. The same happens to desires, where we also consider the Convert relation. For obligations, each element before the current one must be a violated obligation. A literal is a candidate to be a goal only if none of the previous elements in the chain have been proved as a goal. For intentions, the elements of the chain must pass the wishful thinking filter, while social intentions are also constrained not to violate any norm.

Definition 3. *Given a proof P, $r \in R[q, i]$ is applicable (at index i and step $n + 1$) for*

1. *B iff $r \in R^B$ and is body-applicable.*
2. *O iff either: (2.1) (2.1.1) $r \in R^O$ and is body-applicable,*
      (2.1.2) $\forall c_k \in C(r), k < i, +\partial_O c_k \in P(1..n)$ and $-\partial c_k \in P(1..n)$, or
   (2.2) r is Conv-applicable.
3. *D iff either: (3.1) $r \in R^U$ and is body-applicable, or*
   (3.2) Conv-applicable.
4. *$\square \in \{G, I, SI\}$ iff either: (4.1) (4.1.1) $r \in R^U$ and is body-applicable, and*
      (4.1.2) $=\forall c_k \in C(r), k < i, +\partial_\blacksquare \sim c_k \in P(1..n)$ for some $\blacksquare$
      such that $\mathrm{Conflict}(\blacksquare, \square)$ and $-\partial_\square c_k \in P(1..n)$, or
   (4.2) r is Conv-applicable.
   For G there are no conflicts; for I we have $\mathrm{Conflict}(B, I)$, and for SI we have $\mathrm{Conflict}(B, SI)$ and $\mathrm{Conflict}(O, SI)$.

Conditions to establish that a rule is discarded correspond to the constructive failure to prove that the same rule is applicable, and follow the principle of *strong negation*. The strong negation principle is closely related to the function that simplifies a formula by moving all negations to an inner most position in the resulting formula, and replaces the positive tags with the respective negative tags, and the other way around [14].

We can now describe the proof conditions for the various modal operators; we start with those for desires:

$+\partial_D$: If $P(n+1) = +\partial_D q$ then
(1) $Dq \in F$ or
(2) (2.1) $\neg Dq \notin F$ and
    (2.2) $\exists r \in R[q, i]$: r is applicable for D and
    (2.3) $\forall s \in R[\sim q, j]$ either (2.3.1) s is discarded for D, or (2.3.2) $s \not> r$.

We say that a *desire* is each element in a chain of an outcome rule for which there is no stronger argument for the opposite desire. The proof conditions for $+\partial_\square$, with $\square \in MOD \setminus \{D\}$ are as follows:

$+\partial_\square$: If $P(n+1) = +\partial_\square q$ then
(1) $\square q \in F$ or
(2) (2.1) $\neg \blacksquare q \notin F$ for $\blacksquare = \square$ or $\mathrm{Convert}(\blacksquare, \square)$ and
    (2.2) $\exists r \in R[q, i]$: r is applicable for $\square$ and
    (2.3) $\forall s \in R^\blacksquare[\sim q, j]$ either
        (2.3.1) s is discarded for $\blacksquare$, or
        (2.3.2) $\exists t \in R^\diamond[q, k]$: t is applicable for $\diamond$ and either
            (2.3.2.1) $t > s$ if $\blacksquare = \diamond$, $\mathrm{Convert}(\blacksquare, \diamond)$, or $\mathrm{Convert}(\diamond, \blacksquare)$; or
            (2.3.2.2) $\mathrm{Conflict}(\diamond, \blacksquare)$.

To show that a literal q is defeasibly provable with modality $\Box$ we have two choices: (1) modal literal $\Box q$ is a fact; or (2) we need to argue using the defeasible part of D. In this case, we require that a complementary literal (of the same modality, or of a conflictual modality) does not appear in the set of facts (2.1), and that there must be an applicable rule for q for mode $\Box$ (2.2). Moreover, each possible attack brought by a rule s for $\sim q$ has to be either discarded (2.3.1), or successfully counterattacked by another stronger rule t for q (2.3.2). We recall that the superiority relation combines rules of the same mode, rules with different modes that produce complementary conclusion of the same mode through conversion (both considered in clause (2.3.2.1)), and conflictual modalities (clause 2.3.2.2). Obviously, if $\Box = \mathrm{B}$, then the proof conditions reduce to those of classical DL [10].

Again, the negative counterparts ($-\partial_\mathrm{D}$ and $-\partial_\Box, \Box \in \mathrm{MOD} \setminus \{\mathrm{D}\}$) are derived by strong negation applied to conditions for $+\partial_\mathrm{D}$ and $+\partial_\Box$, respectively.

Example 1. Let us consider the theory $D = (\{\neg b_1, \mathrm{O}\neg b_2, \mathrm{SI}b_4\}, \{r: \Rightarrow_\mathrm{U} b_1 \odot b_2 \odot b_3 \odot b_4\}, \emptyset)$. Then r is trivially applicable for D and $+\partial_\mathrm{D}b_i$ holds, for $1 \leq i \leq 4$. Moreover, we have $+\partial_\mathrm{G}b_1$ and r is discarded for G after b_1. Since $+\partial\neg b_1$, $-\partial_\mathrm{I}b_1$ holds (as well as $-\partial_\mathrm{SI}b_1$); the rule is applicable for I and b_2, and we are able to prove $+\partial_\mathrm{I}b_2$, thus the rule becomes discarded for I after b_2. Given that $\mathrm{O}\neg b_2$ is a fact, r is discarded for SI and b_2 and $-\partial_\mathrm{SI}b_2$ is proved, which in turn makes the rule applicable for SI at b_3, proving $+\partial_\mathrm{SI}b_3$. As we have argued before, this would make the rule discarded for b_4. Nevertheless, b_4 is still provable with mode SI (in this case because it is a fact, but in other theories there could be more rules with b_4 in their head).

In [9], authors showed the coherency and consistency of the logical apparatus.

2.3 Norm and Outcome Compliance

Our logic is able to model in a natural way the concepts of being compliant with respect to norms and outcomes. Consider the obligation rule $r: \Gamma \Rightarrow_\mathrm{O} o_1 \odot o_2 \odot o_3$ in a theory where $\mathrm{O}o_1$ and $\mathrm{O}o_2$ are the case. To be compliant with r, the agent has either to prove $\mathrm{B}o_1$, or to compensate by deriving $\mathrm{B}o_2$.

To formalise the concept of compliance, we first introduce a new literal $\bot$ whose interpretation is a not compliant situation, and we provide proof conditions to (defeasibly) derive it. We exploit the modal derivations of $\bot$ to formally characterise norm compliant ($-\partial_\mathrm{O}\bot$) and outcome compliant ($-\partial_\Box\bot, \Box \in \{\mathrm{G,I,SI}\}$) situations.

$-\partial_\mathrm{O}\bot$: If $P(n+1) = -\partial_\mathrm{O}\bot$ then
(1) $\forall r \in R^\mathrm{O} \cup R^{\mathrm{B,O}}$ either r is discarded or either
    (2.1) $\forall c_i \in C(r), -\partial_\mathrm{O}c_i \in P(1..n)$, or
    (2.2) $\exists c_i \in C(r)$ such that $+\partial_\mathrm{O}c_i \in P(1..n)$ and $+\partial c_i \in P(1..n)$.

To be norm compliant, all applicable rules producing an obligation are such that either all elements in the consequent are not actually active obligations (condition (2.1)), or one element c_i is an obligation in force and is fulfilled (condition (2.2)). The situation is slightly different when addressing outcome compliance.

$-\partial_\Box \bot$: If $P(n+1) = -\partial_\Box \bot$ ($\Box \in \{G, I, SI\}$) then

(1) $\forall r \in R^U \cup R^{B,\Box}$, Conflict($\blacksquare, \Box$), either r is discarded or

(2) (2.1) $\exists c_i \in C(r)$ such that $+\partial_\Box c_i \in P(1..n)$, $\forall c_j \in C(r), j < i, -\partial_\Box c_j \in P(1..n)$, and

   (2.2) $\exists c_k, k \geq i$ such that

   (2.2.1') (2.1.1.1') if $k = i$ then $+\partial c_k \in P(1..n)$, or

   (2.1.1.2') if $k \neq i$ then $+\partial c_k$ and $+\partial_D c_k \in P(1..n)$.

   (2.2.1'') $+\partial c_k \in P(1..n)$ and $-\partial_\Box \sim c_k \in P(1..n)$.

First, the agent chooses her level of commitment, that is the mode $\Box$ among G, I, or SI to comply with (notice that in some cases this process is not particularly meaningful, e.g., desires). Then, we select the first element proved with modality $\Box$ in the consequent of any applicable rule (element c_i in the proof condition (2.1)). We propose two variants of outcome compliance corresponding to sub-conditions (2.2.1') and (2.2.1'').

In the first case, we are compliant iff either c_i is proved as a belief (being the first element in the chain proved with modality $\Box$), or if there exists a following element c_k which has been proved as a desire as well as a belief. In the latter, we are outcome compliant with respect to r if an element c_k following c_i has been proved as a belief, and its opposite has not been chosen as an outcome to achieve. It may be the case that, semantically but not syntactically, if $\neg\Box\sim c_k$ is the case then $+\partial_D c_k$, but this is left to further analysis.

Again, the counterparts $+\partial_O \bot$ and $+\partial_\Box \bot, \Box \in \{G, I, SI\}$ are derived by strong negation applied to conditions for $-\partial_O \bot$ and $-\partial_\Box \bot$, respectively.

Example 2. We now formalise the "Robbie the Robot" example to show how compliance definitions work within our theoretical framework. For the sake of simplicity, we take the stance that whenever the unit suggests Robbie a plan, all the actions to perform are either derivable from the theory, or considered as additional facts.

F = { *Robbie_downtown, mail_delivered, early_meeting, lunch_time*},

R = { r_1 : *lunch_time* $\Rightarrow_U$ *restaurant* $\odot$ *take_away* $\odot$ *sandwich* $\odot$ *fast_food*,

   r_2 : *Robbie_downtown, mail_delivered* $\Rightarrow_U$ *oil-beer*,

   r_3 : *Robbie_downtown, dry_cleaner, take_away* $\Rightarrow$ *speed*,

   r_4 : $\Rightarrow_O$ $\neg$*speed*, r_5 : *early_meeting* $\Rightarrow_U$ *best_suit* $\odot$ *2nd_suit*,

   r_6 : *take_away* $\Rightarrow$ $\neg$*fast_food*, r_7 : *fast_food* $\Rightarrow$ $\neg$*take_away*,

   r_8 : *best_suit* $\Rightarrow$ *dry_cleaner*, r_9 : *best_suit* $\Rightarrow$ $\neg$*2nd_suit*,

   r_{10} : *2nd_suit* $\Rightarrow$ *go_home*, r_{11} : *go_home, fast_food* $\Rightarrow$ $\neg$*oil-beer*,

   r_{12} : *early_meeting* $\Rightarrow$ $\neg$*restaurant*}.

If Robbie decides to go to the take away and to give Carmen her best suit, then it must stop to the dry cleaner (r_8); this course of action (r_3) violates r_4. If Robbie decides to pick up the Carmen's second favourite suit from home (r_{10}) and then stop to a fast food, it will not get an oil-beer (r_{11}). In the first scenario, we are not compliant with respect to the norm stated by r_4, while in the second scenario we are not outcome-compliant since Robbie would not be able to derive as belief the conclusion of r_2.

3 Revision under Compliance

Norm and outcome compliance give rise to a non-trivial question: what to be done when a business process is not norm compliant or outcome compliant, or even both? To the best of our knowledge, no *effective approach* addresses the issue of how to revise non-compliant business processes.

We take on this challenge by taking inspiration from *business process revision*, which has received great attention in recent years given its crucial influence, for example, on organisation practices. The aim of the present section is twofold:

(i) to give a critical overview of the state of the art on business process revision and justify the proposed approach taking compliance into consideration;
(ii) to devise a methodology based on the logic proposed in Section 2 to afford revision under compliance.

Roughly speaking, all the efforts spent in the area of business process revision subscribe to two general approaches.

The first approach relies on modelling notations and languages which define the structural aspect of business processes and are extended with other formalisms to represent the behavioural aspects. As an example, BPMN enriched with semantic annotations is able to describe the effects implied by the execution of a particular task [7]. On the same grounds, several translations from modelling notations into other formalisms have been proposed, for example semantic nets [15] and business process graphs [16].

The second approach is instead based on pure logic formalisms, where revising a business process means revising the theory describing the business process itself. The underlying logical theory formally represents at the same time the structural and the behavioural aspects of the business process [17,18,19].

These two approaches capture different (and both interesting) meanings of compliance. The first aims at revising a business process at an higher level, in terms of removal, addition, swapping, and substitutions of tasks in the business process. On the other hand, the second one abstracts from the concepts of task and conditions that trigger (or are caused by) a task: they are all denoted by literals in the same theory and the main focus is on how they interact with each other to obtain other literals.

The most representative example of the first approach, given in [20] and then developed in [21], relies on the emerging trend of designing and thinking about business processes as related collections of *reusable modules* (or *fragments*). Reusable modules denote sets of standardised actions to be performed to achieve some fixed objectives (giving outcome compliance) that can be used with slight or no modifications also in other business processes. Modules are further augmented with built-in statements ensuring that the module is norm compliant according to the statements specified in the module.

The reusable modules approach is theoretically applicable both when a norm uncompliant process is given, or when it must be built from scratch and we have to ensure norm and outcome compliance at design time. For the first case, the algorithm for norm compliance checking proposed in [7] finds out the *exact* point in a business process where a violation of an obligation occurs. Thus, we can substitute the un-compliant part of the business process with a module that reaches the same objectives and compensates the previous violation(s). In the second case, we build the process starting from a given repository of modules, based on objectives to achieve and norms to comply with.

For many aspects, the reusable module approach recall the SOC paradigm that "promotes the idea of assembling application components into a network of services that can be loosely coupled to create flexible, dynamic business processes and agile applications" [22]. As such, the main advantage of this approach is the possibility of exploiting well defined techniques and methodologies developed through years of investigation in the field. Above all, *Web Service technology* is nowadays the most promising means for a widespread deployment of SOC-based architectures in on-the-net business process software development [23].

However, this approach is not free from drawbacks, especially in case of compliance recovery of a given business process. For example, the addition or substitution of a fragment in a business process may lead to a lack of resources, jeopardising the entire execution of the process. In fact, reusable fragments are intrinsically bound to a *localised* concept of compliance. Every fragment introduces potentially new effects in the business process and, consequently, other obligations or outcomes may be triggered. Thus, once a fragment has been added or replaced, there is no guarantee that the business process is *globally* compliant (with respect to norms and outcomes). Notice that the issue can be avoided in some cases when, for instance, the effects attached to executed modules are independent, or the execution of modules is mutually exclusive (when modules belong to different branches of XOR paths). Nevertheless, these cases represent a very limited part of the whole behavioural sphere of organisational practices.

Apart from the difficulties brought by the first family of approaches in managing compliance, a fully logic approach (like the one herein proposed) results much more appealing due to several factors:

(i)   the approach of revision based on module reuse is quite hypothetical at this moment, since no formal investigation has been yet carried out that looks at the possible ways to provide a correct and complete solution;

(ii)   a logic approach always comes with an inferential mechanism to reason about the underlying framework and to prove the computational properties like consistency and coherency;

(iii) it is particularly simple to map many different logic approaches existing in the current literature of the field into *graph models* and this is a promise for simplicity in the case we are dealing with too;

(iv)   a roadmap that can be considered useful aims at building real applications, and one possible target is a system that modifies a business process based upon preferences specified by the user. In this scenario, it is meaningful to provide a logic approach that extends execution environments (for example *Deimos* [24] and *SPINdle* [25]) where the schema is useful for deploying real systems.

3.1   Revision via Proof Tags Analysis

Rule-based nonmonotonic formalisms – like the one developed in this work – have been used in many types of reasoning given their predisposition to capture aspects from many domains of interest. As an example, in [26] authors address the problem of revising non-modal defeasible theories in the area of legal reasoning through an exhaustive analysis of proof tags. The major contribution of that work is the identification of three relevant cases, named *canonical*, where a revision operator could act by only changing the relative strength between pairs of rules.

First case. The revision operator acts on a defeasibly proved literal p and makes it not provable anymore, i.e., from $+\partial p$ to $-\partial p$;

Second case. The revision operator acts on a defeasibly proved literal p and makes its opposite defeasibly proved, i.e., from $+\partial p$ to $+\partial \sim p$;

Third case. The revision operator acts on a not defeasibly proved literal p and makes it defeasibly proved, i.e., from $-\partial p$ to $+\partial p$.

Additional proof tags other than those for classical defeasible proof ($\pm\partial$) are used to better identify all relevant situations. The new proof tags do not modify the expressive power of the logic itself, but they identify specific properties of literals within the theory, e.g., their reachability or being always derived.

There are three major reasons for using and extending the approach of proof tag analysis also in the framework at hand.

First, canonical cases clearly refer to the basic issue we address. For example, by definition of $+\partial_O \bot$, there exists at least one applicable rule r for obligations such that each element c_i defeasibly proved as an obligation in the chain is not derived as a belief, i.e., if $+\partial_O c_i$ holds, then $-\partial c_i$ holds as well. As this chain represents the consequent of a rule, there are two strategies to recover norm compliance with respect to r:

(i) By making one element c_i defeasibly provable as a belief, or
(ii) Acting on r, either by making the rule body-discarded in the sense of Definition 1, or by blocking the derivation of the first element in the chain as an obligation.

Case (i) represents a modal variant of the third canonical case, that is from $-\partial_\square p$ to $+\partial_\square p$, while case (ii) represent a modal variant of the first canonical case, that is from $+\partial_\square p$ to $-\partial_\square p$. Notice that in most cases, the first approach reflects a more intuitive way to address the problem. Indeed, it seems more reasonable to find a way to compensate an obligation (or the failure to achieve an outcome) rather than to make discarded the entire chain of obligations or outcomes.

Second, it is quite simple to align the additional proof tags introduced in [26] with a modal defeasible theory. As an example, the tagged literal $+\Sigma p$ means that there exists a reasoning chain supporting literal p. A more fine-grained definition of support can be given in our framework, that is, when a literal p is supported in a modal defeasible theory with modality $\square$ ($+\Sigma_\square p$). An analogous reasoning can be made for an unsupported literal p ($-\Sigma_\square p$).

$+\Sigma_\square$: If $P(n+1) = +\Sigma_\square q$ then
(1) $\square q \in F$ or
    (2) $\exists r \in R^\square[q,i]$ such that $\forall a \in A(r)$, $+\Sigma_B a \in P(1..n)$, and
            $\forall_\blacksquare b \in A(r)$, $+\Sigma_\blacksquare b \in P(1..n)$, or
    (3) $\exists r \in R^B[q]$ such that $\forall a \in A(r)$, $+\Sigma_\square a \in P(1..n)$

Third, the alignment of proof tags in a modal defeasible theory allows us to formally represent the conditions under which a revision operator could return a positive solution of the problem. To give an overall idea, we report in Figure 1 a conceptual tree representing the possible cases a revision operator could deal with in our framework. The schema is organised in levels, and every level sets up the parameters that the revision operator must obey to.

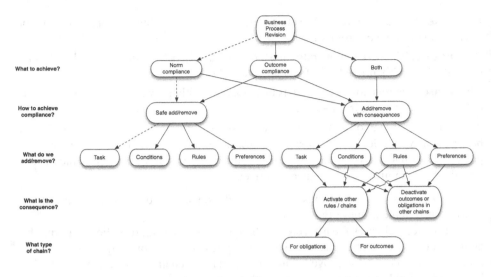

Fig. 1. Possible problems for a business process revision operator

The first level represents the type of compliance to be fulfilled; in the first two cases, we take the stance that a norm un-compliant business process is already outcome compliant, and the other way around.

The second level defines the possible actions the revision operator can perform in order to meet compliance. In our case, removal or addition of elements in the theory are the only feasible actions. At first glance, the combination of addition and removal could represent a potential candidate to define the operation of *swapping*: for example, to change the order between tasks t_1 and t_2, we just remove t_1 (resp. t_2) and then add it after t_2 (resp. before t_1).

The third level defines the elements (literals for tasks, literals representing conditions, rules, or preference relations between rules in the theory) the revision operator can manipulate based on the type of actions permitted. We define an addition or a removal *safe* if the operation does not make applicable any previously discarded rule in the theory, and does not deactivate obligations or outcomes previously in force. Otherwise, we define the operation *unsafe* or *with consequences*. In this case, we discriminate between the two types of consequences (fourth level), and in the first case, we specify which type of chain is activated (fifth level).

Intuitively, every path from the root to a leaf denotes a particular type of problem to be solved. For example, the dotted path in Figure 1 represents the problem of finding conditions under which we can revise a business process to recover norm compliance, remaining outcome compliant, only through safe addition or removal of tasks.

The schema aims at providing a combinatorial exploitation of the cases for a revision operator for business processes with compliance preservation. This analysis can be valued as exhaustive provided that we do not consider neither redundancy nor unfeasibility. These further aspects will be considered in the next step of this research.

Here follow some intuitive ideas, based on [27], on how to address the first (and second) canonical case by using rule addition/removal and preference manipulation.

Rule removal and exception addition. As the name suggests, the operation of *rule removal* contracts a literal p by simply removing rules in the theory directly deriving it. One of the proposed variants acts only on defeasible rules, and, unlike other variants, it has to take care of preserving minimality (in the sense of number of erased rules). The intuition here is to identify all rules that are essential to prove the literal at hand. This corresponds to remove only the applicable rules that are not inferiorly defeated, i.e., rules such that there is no stronger applicable rule for the opposite. Several variants of *exception addition* were discussed as well, and one of them consider only defeasible rules. In this case, the revision operator introduces a new conflicting defeasible rule for the opposite conclusion to block the conclusion we want to contract.

Preference addition/removal. This kind of contraction acts on the relative strength of rules, by making two complementary arguments of the same strength (and then both conclusions cannot be derived), or by making the opposite argument stronger than the argument for the literal to contract. When we deal with changing a theory by only modifying the superiority relation, we must switch perspective with respect to the operations of rule removal/addition and exception addition. The operations cannot anymore focus only on active/inactive chains for the literal we want to change, but they must take into account the entire theory. Moreover, one strong problematic that affects the contraction operation by modifying the superiority relation only is on the hardness of defining when a literal is absolutely unrefutable. Roughly speaking, a literal is absolutely unrefutable if it is true in every interpretation (and then we cannot contract it). We found examples on the structure of a theory where a non factual literal is absolutely unrefutable, and we proved that the problem of deciding if a literal is absolutely unrefutable is NP-hard. The proof is not reported in the present work for space reasons.

4   Conclusions and Further Work

This paper introduced a logical framework to represent objective-driven agents which deliberates her course of action based on constraints imposed by the environment. The logic deems the notions of desires, goals and intentions (and social intentions) as different nuances of the (more general) notion of outcome. The framework naturally describes and integrates the notion of being compliant with the notions of norms and outcomes. This allowed us to describe situations where the agent is able (or not) to reach all her objectives while not violating the norms. In addition, we proposed a preliminary analysis on how to devise a methodology to restore from un-compliant situations, covering the case of outcomes or norms. The analysis carried out in the previous sections points out several directions of research. We report the most valuable, referring to the case analysis reported in Figure 1.

Does a solution exist for each case? As already pointed out, one prior challenge to address is to study conditions under which the revision operator returns a positive answer to the case at hand. In this sense, proof tag analysis seems a good candidate for defining properties that describe the status of every literal in the theory. Moreover, this approach is compatible with a fully logical representation of business processes.

If a solution exists, what is the complexity of the problem instance? Once having established that at least a solution exists, another issue is to find algorithmic means that compute a particular (or all) solution(s). This is crucial for a better decision-making process with a view to automatic deployment. In fact, algorithms based on the logical system herein proposed could extend well-known execution environments, and that is a promise for the revision process to become a proper extension of the process for compliance checking, and could be fully integrated in the business process life-cycle.

Which is the minimum set of actions to obtain a solution? The trivial case is that a solution does not exist because the set of actions performed is too restrained. In this case, an interesting problem is to determine which action (or actions) the revision operator should be allowed to use in addition to solve the problem. In other terms, we define the revision operator as an entity with several *degrees of freedom* and we determine which is the minimum degree of freedom of the operator to solve each case.

In particular, the second problem deserves particular attention. Indeed, by its own nature a rule in our framework may have multiple antecedents, and a chain for obligations and outcomes with more than one element as a consequent. In the view of revision, a crucial aspect is defining the best point where to act during the process, be it in the antecedent or the consequent. This question naturally resembles the meaning of *minimal change* as a key tenet for the revision to be rational [28]. However, several criteria of minimality can be chosen, such as the degree of change in the extension of the theory, or based on the number of actions to be performed by the revision operator. In this respect, a method that exploits the concept of *literal dependency* could be useful. A literal l depends on another literal m if m appears in every reasoning chain supporting l. We are working on a complete formalisation of dependency property, and an algorithmic implementation to find out the dependency set of a literal in a theory is currently under development. Intuitively, if the revision operator decides to refute a (previously proved) literal l to be recover compliance, then in principle refuting a literal m on which l depends (if any) minimises the changes in the extension.

References

1. Wooldridge, M., Jennings, N.R.: Agent theories, architectures, and languages: A survey. In: Wooldridge, M.J., Jennings, N.R. (eds.) ECAI 1994 and ATAL 1994. LNCS, vol. 890, pp. 1–39. Springer, Heidelberg (1995)
2. Cohen, P.R., Levesque, H.J.: Intention is choice with commitment. Artificial Intelligence 42(2-3) (1990)
3. Rao, A.S., Georgeff, M.P.: Modeling rational agents within a BDI-architecture. In: Allen, J.F., Fikes, R., Sandewall, E. (eds.) KR. Morgan Kaufmann (1991)
4. Rao, A.S., Georgeff, M.P.: Decision procedures for bdi logics. Journal of Logic and Computation 8(3) (1998)
5. van der Aalst, W.M.P.: The application of Petri Nets to workflow management. Journal of Circuits, Systems, and Computers 8(1) (1998)
6. Ghallab, M., Nau, D., Traverso, P.: Automated planning - theory and practice. Elsevier (2004)
7. Governatori, G., Sadiq, S.: The journey to business process compliance. In: Handbook of Research on BPM. IGI Global (2008)
8. Governatori, G., Olivieri, F., Scannapieco, S., Cristani, M.: Designing for compliance: Norms and goals. In: Olken, F., Palmirani, M., Sottara, D. (eds.) RuleML - America 2011. LNCS, vol. 7018, pp. 282–297. Springer, Heidelberg (2011)

9. Governatori, G., Olivieri, F., Rotolo, A., Scannapieco, S., Cristani, M.: Picking up the best goal: An analytical study in defeasible logic. In: Morgenstern, L., Stefaneas, P., Lévy, F., Wyner, A., Paschke, A. (eds.) RuleML 2013. LNCS, vol. 8035, pp. 99–113. Springer, Heidelberg (2013)

10. Antoniou, G., Billington, D., Governatori, G., Maher, M.J.: Representation results for defeasible logic. ACM Transactions on Computational Logic 2(2) (2001)

11. Governatori, G., Rotolo, A.: Logic of violations: A gentzen system for reasoning with contrary-to-duty obligations. Australasian Journal of Logic 4 (2006)

12. Governatori, G., Rotolo, A.: BIO logical agents: Norms, beliefs, intentions in defeasible logic. Journal of Autonomous Agents and Multi-Agent Systems 17(1) (2008)

13. Broersen, J., Dastani, M., Hulstijn, J., van der Torre, L.: Goal generation in the BOID architecture. Cognitive Science Quarterly 2(3-4) (2002)

14. Antoniou, G., Billington, D., Governatori, G., Maher, M.J., Rock, A.: A family of defeasible reasoning logics and its implementation. In: Horn, W. (ed.) ECAI. IOS Press (2000)

15. Ghose, A., Koliadis, G.: Auditing business process compliance. In: Krämer, B.J., Lin, K.-J., Narasimhan, P. (eds.) ICSOC 2007. LNCS, vol. 4749, pp. 169–180. Springer, Heidelberg (2007)

16. Dijkman, R., Dumas, M., van Dongen, B., Käärik, R., Mendling, J.: Similarity of business process models: Metrics and evaluation. Inf. Syst. 36(2) (2011)

17. Governatori, G., Rotolo, A.: Norm compliance in business process modeling. In: [29], 194–209

18. van der Aalst, W., Pesic, M., Schonenberg, H.: Declarative workflows: Balancing between flexibility and support. Computer Science - R&D 23(2) (2009)

19. Rotolo, A.: Rule-based agents, compliance, and intention reconsideration in defeasible logic. In: Bassiliades, N., Governatori, G., Paschke, A. (eds.) RuleML 2011 - Europe. LNCS, vol. 6826, pp. 67–82. Springer, Heidelberg (2011)

20. Schumm, D., Leymann, F., Ma, Z., Scheibler, T., Strauch, S.: Integrating Compliance into Business Processes Process Fragments as Reusable Compliance Controls. Universitätsverlag Göttingen (2010)

21. Schumm, D., Turetken, O., Kokash, N., Elgammal, A., Leymann, F., van den Heuvel, W.-J.: Business process compliance through reusable units of compliant processes. In: Daniel, F., Facca, F.M. (eds.) ICWE 2010. LNCS, vol. 6385, pp. 325–337. Springer, Heidelberg (2010)

22. Leymann, F.: Combining web services and the grid: Towards adaptive enterprise applications. In: Castro, J., Teniente, E. (eds.) CAiSE Workshops (2). FEUP Edições, Porto (2005)

23. Weerawarana, S., Curbera, F., Leymann, F., Storey, T., Ferguson, D.: Web Services Platform Architecture: SOAP, WSDL, WS-Policy, WS-Addressing, WS-BPEL, WS-Reliable Messaging, and More. Prentice Hall PTR (2005)

24. Rock, A.: Deimos: Query answering defeasible logic system (2000)

25. Lam, H.P., Governatori, G.: The making of SPINdle. In: Governatori, G., Hall, J., Paschke, A. (eds.) RuleML 2009. LNCS, vol. 5858, pp. 315–322. Springer, Heidelberg (2009)

26. Governatori, G., Olivieri, F., Scannapieco, S., Cristani, M.: Superiority based revision of defeasible theories. In: [29], pp. 104–118

27. Governatori, G., Olivieri, F., Rotolo, A., Scannapieco, S.: Legal contractions: A logical analysis. In: Ashley, K.D., van Engers, T.M. (eds.) ICAIL. ACM (2013)

28. Alchourrón, C.E., Gärdenfors, P., Makinson, D.: On the logic of theory change: Partial meet contraction and revision functions. J. Symb. Log. 50(2) (1985)

29. Dean, M., Hall, J., Rotolo, A., Tabet, S. (eds.): RuleML 2010. LNCS, vol. 6403. Springer, Heidelberg (2010)

The Impact of Exchanging Opinions in Political Decision-Making on Voting by Using Multi-agent Simulation

Yuichiro Sudo, Shohei Kato, and Atsuko Mutoh

Dept. of Computer Science and Engineering, Graduate School of Engineering,
Nagoya Institute of Technology,
Gokiso-cho, Showa-ku, Nagoya-shi, 466-8555 Japan
{sudou,shohey}@katolab.nitech.ac.jp, atsuko@nitech.ac.jp
http://www.katolab.nitech.ac.jp

Abstract. Representative members who make laws and heads of local governments are elected by citizens in Japan. Therefore, elections are one of the most important factors in future political or economic trends. There are a lot of researchers, such as social psychologists and political scientists, focusing on voters' decision-making processes. It has been known that voters collect information from others or mass media to decide who to vote for. The rapid spread of information and communication technologies in recent years, such as the spread of the Internet, has increased the expansion of communication space. However, it is difficult to observe how voters make political decisions. In this paper, we propose a simulation model based on both Latane's dynamic social impact theory (DSIT) simulation model and Riker and Ordeshook's expected utility model of voting behavior to analyze political decision-making by using multi-agent simulation. Agents in the proposed model communicate with order utility that is based on ambiguity in communicating information. Agents are generated from a database of public opinion polls. Then, agents are given social attributes and values of political parties. The agents' communication space is a hierarchical network constructed by agents that have the same or similar attributes. In the experiment, we compared simulation results with the actual results from voting in an experiment and examined the validity of the proposed model. Moreover, we analyzed the effect of expanding communication space on voters' political decision-making in the experiment.

Keywords: Artificial Society, Multi-Agent Simulation, Complex Network, Political Decision-Making.

1 Introduction

Representative members who make laws and heads of local governments are elected by citizens in Japan. Therefore, elections are one of the most important factors in future political or economic trends [1]. There are a lot of researchers

G. Boella et al. (Eds.): PRIMA 2013, LNAI 8291, pp. 340–354, 2013.
© Springer-Verlag Berlin Heidelberg 2013

such as social psychologists and political scientists who focus on voters' decision-making processes. It has been known that voters collect information from others or mass media to decide who to vote for [2]. There have been previous studies that have analyzed the relationship between voting behavior and mass media [3]. The rapid spread of information and communication technologies in recent years, such as the spread of the Internet, has increased the expansion of communication space. Thus, we expect that the means or routes to obtain information will change. However, it is difficult to observe voters' making political decisions in the real world. Using multi-agent simulation is one technique for analyzing social phenomena, such as the distribution of public opinion, on a macroscopic level [4–7]. There have been previous studies that have analyzed the impact exchanging opinions and mass media have had by using Latane's Dynamic Social Impact Theory (DSIT) model [8]. Latane and Nowak conducted computer simulation of adaptive agent bound to network structure and found consolidation and clustering. They claimed minority could remain in the system by clustering. Ishiguro et al. suggested a model that extended the DSIT model and incorporated mass media, and they also demonstrated the possibility that minorities could have their opinions by using information from mass media in modern society [5]. There have been previous studies related to voting behavior. Riker and Ordeshook have suggested an expected utility model of voting behavior based on rational choice theory [9, 10]. Their model involved agents deciding whether to participate or not in voting by assessing profits from their voting. Sudo et al. [6] focused on elections in Japan and analyzed what impact exchanging opinions and mass media had by using multi-agent simulation. They found that communicating information from others or mass media was ambiguious in this study and attitudes were extremely similar among Japanese voters. They considered that ambiguity in communicating information was caused by differences in evaluation measures between individuals. Thus, it was difficult for people to accurately communicate their values to each other with words. However, the previous research did not deal with ambiguity in communicating information. As Ida points out, information receivers could identify the values of communicating information as evaluation orders [11]. In this paper, we thus formulate evaluation orders and extended the model suggested by Ishiguro et. al.. Ishiguro pointed out that social space is divided into substructures constructed by members who have the same or similar attributes [12]. Murakami and Murata analyzed the mechanism of Japanese public pension by using multi-agent simulation, and their social space is divided into substructures constructed by members who have the same or similar age [7]. Agents' communication space in proposal model represent a hierarchical network. Furthermore, we find that the frequency and variety of uses of mass media deffered between groups. For example, people who were younger tended to use the Internet more in Japan. Mass media were placed on each substructure to represent differences between them. We propose a simulation model in this paper based on both Latane's DSIT simulation model and Riker and Ordeshook's expected utility model of voting behavior. We analyzed political decision-making with the proposed model. Where agents communicate with order utility that is

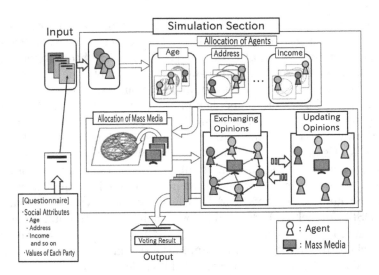

Fig. 1. Overview of simulations

based on ambiguity in communicating information. Agents were generated from a database of public opinion polls collected before and after the Japanese House of Councilors election in 2004. We compared simulation results with the actual vote results in an experiment and examined the validity of the proposed model. Moreover, we analyzed what effect expanding communication space had voters' political decision-making in the experiment.

2   Artificial Society Model

There is an overview of our simulation model in Fig. 1. Where agents are generated from a database of public opinion polls. Then, agents are given the social attributes and values of political parties. Agents belong to networks constructed by agents that have the same or similar attributes. The substructures of agents' communication space differ in each network. Acquaintances represent agents who are linked together. Agents exchange opinions with acquaintances and collect information from mass media, and then agents update their values. Agents vote after repeating these processes several times. This section describes agents and social space, mass media.

2.1   Agents

Social space is composed of N agents. Agent ag_i (i is the identifier) that represents voters collecting information is expressed by

$$ag_i = (AT_i, T_i, Su_i, Ra_i, Co_i), \tag{1}$$

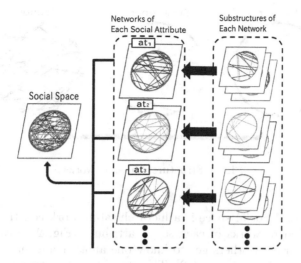

Fig. 2. Configurations for social space

where AT_i is its social attributes, T_i is its threshold to change its opinions, and Su_i is its evaluation values of political parties. Here, Ra_i is its evaluation orders of political parties, and $Co_i(0 \le Co_i \le 1)$ is the cost of participating in the vote. AT_i is defined as

$$AT_i = (at_{i1}, at_{i2}, ..., at_{iM}),\qquad(2)$$

where at_{ix} (x is the identifier) is a social attribute, such as age or address, and M is the number of social attributes. For example, the attribute of the address is an area in Japan. Agents' communication space is a hierarchical network constructed by agents that have the same or similar attributes. Agents in this model belong to M networks for every social attribute. Su_i and Ra_i are defined as

$$Su_i = (su_{i1}, su_{i2}, ..., su_{iK}), and\qquad(3)$$
$$Ra_i = (ra_{i1}, ra_{i2}, ..., ra_{iK}),\qquad(4)$$

where $su_{iy}(y$ is identifier) is an evaluation value, ra_{iy} is an evaluation order, $-10 \le su_{iy} \le 10$ and $1 \le ra_{iy} \le K$ satisfy this condition, and K is the number of political parties. Ra_i is decided by Su_i, and Ra_i is ranked according to Su_i when ag_i updates its evaluation values. Political parties that are higher in the sequence of evaluation orders (nearer to the first in line) obtain higher evaluation values from agents.

2.2   Social Space

Social space is represented by nodes and bidirectional links. Nodes represent agents, and bidirectional links represent the agent's relationships that mutually

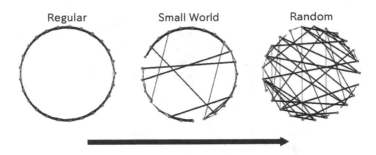

Fig. 3. Structures three networks

exchange opinions. Social space is a hierarchical network constructed with the M substructured networks of each social attribute (Fig. 2). People who have a lot in common with others get to know one another and have many opportunities of exchanging opinions [12]. Therefore, each substructure network has partial networks constructed by agents that hasve the same or similar attributes. For example, the substructure network of an address has partial networks constructed by agents that are in the same region in Japan, such as the Tohoku region or the Kanto region. Agents in the proposed model that have the same or similar attributes could have bidirectional links together in social space. In other words, agents that have the same or similar attributes have many opportunities of exchanging opinions in our model. The maximum number of links equals the number of social attributes M. Social space is able to represent sparse or dense interpersonal relationships that previous methods of generating networks could not represent. We are able to use methods of generating a network in the proposed model when each substructure network is generated. We generated a network of addresses by using the regular model and other networks by using the small world model that Watts and Strogatz suggested [13]. Here, we describe the parts of the regular model and small world model.

Regular Model. The regular model involves analyzing the impact of geographical factors [4, 5], and has a structure where each agent is linked to neighboring h agents. Agents that are arranged in an annular shape are linked to other h agent in the regular model (Fig. 3). Therefore, the total number of bidirectional links is $h \times N$ (N is the number of agents).

Small World Model. The small world model has a middle structure between the regular and random models. It is generated by replacing the links of the regular model for random links in the small world model with a displacement probability p (Fig. 3). As displacement probability p increases, the structure of the network becomes similar to that of the random model. As p increases in number, the structure of the small world model becomes similar to that of the Random model. When p is 0.01 to 0.1, the small world model's features are called "weak ties" [14]. Therefore, we used displacement probability $p = 0.01$ in this research.

2.3 Mass Media

Ishiguro et al. have defined mass media as informing each agent of information collected by all agents. However, people do not always obtain homogenized information from mass media. Because mass media have become more diversified with the expansion of the Internet and the start of satellite broadcasting, people have recently found it easy to select the information they require. The interpretation of information differs depending on who has what attributes [15]. Each substructure network therefore has different mass media, and each agent obtains information from them, which has the same or similar attributes to those of the agent. Individual mass media collect and transmit information to agents who belong to the same substructure network.

3 Political Decision-Making

Agents in the proposed model obtain the information from other agents and mass media, and then they vote after updating its values. This section describes agent's actions, i.e., collecting information, updating its values, and voting behavior.

3.1 Collecting Information

It is difficult for people to accurately communicate their values to one another with words because ambiguity in communicating information results from indefinite measures of evaluation. Agents in our proposed model exchange opinions by using its evaluation orders without definite measures of evaluation. Our model is called the order values model. However, people can communicate evaluation values with others if they have definite measures for evaluation. Here, we consider a model where agents exchange opinions by using their evaluation values. The model using evaluation values is called the cardinal values model. We describe both the order values and cardinal values models.

Order Values Model. This section describes the process where ag_i obtains ag_j's evaluation orders, and then decides the order values for political party y. The following three conditions are ag_i's values for political party y determined from a comparison with political party $k (k \neq y)$.

- $ra_{iy} \succ ra_{ik}$: ra_{iy} is higher than ra_{ik} in order.
- $ra_{iy} = ra_{ik}$: ra_{iy} equals ra_{ik}.
- $ra_{iy} \prec ra_{ik}$: ra_{iy} is lower than ra_{ik} in order.

Table 1 summarizes the definition of function $f_{i,j}(y, k)$, where $f_{i,j}(y, k)$ is when ag_i makes an assessment of ag_j's values for the political party y. $f_{i,j}(y, k)$ is

Table 1. Definition of $f_{i,j}(y, k)$

	$ra_{iy} \succ ra_{ik}$	$ra_{iy} = ra_{ik}$	$ra_{iy} \prec ra_{ik}$
$ra_{jy} \succ ra_{jk}$	0	1	1
$ra_{jy} = ra_{jk}$	-1	0	1
$ra_{jy} \prec ra_{jk}$	-1	-1	0

determined by the difference between ag_i's values and ag_j's values. If ag_j's values are higher than ag_i's values, $f_{i,j}(y, k)$ is high (equals 1), If ag_j's values are lower than ag_i's values, $f_{i,j}(y, k)$ is low(equals -1). Function $q_{ij}(y)$ is ag_j's evaluation orders of political party y defined as

$$q_{ij}(y) = \sum_{k=1}^{y-1} f_{ij}(y, k) + \sum_{k=y+1}^{K} f_{ij}(y, k), \tag{5}$$

where $q_{ij}(y)$ is the total sum of $f_{i,j}(y, k)$ in the order values model. We define that $q_{ij}(y) > 0$ when ag_i makes an assessment of ag_j having good opinions of political party y, and $q_{ij}(y) < 0$ when ag_i makes an assessment of ag_j having poor opinions of political party y. Mass media collect all agents' evaluation orders in the same substructure network. Mass media transmit the evaluation orders of political parties sequentially in the total sum to the number of agents that have the highest evaluation order to political parties. Here, the difference between the agent's opinion and the opinion that the agent obtains is called the opinion distance. The opinion distance is calculated with the agents' evaluation orders used in the proposed model. Function d_{ij} is the opinion distance between ag_i and ag_j. d_{ij} is defined as

$$d_{ij} = \sum_{k=1}^{K} (ra_{ik} - ra_{jk})^2, \tag{6}$$

based on Marden's knowledge [16]. The opinion distance of mass media is calculated similarly.

Cardinal Values Model. In the cardinal values model, $q_{ij}(y)$ equals ag_j's evaluation value for political party y. Mass media collect all agents' evaluation values in the same substructure network, and then transmit the average values for all agents' evaluation orders. The opinion distance is calculated with the agents' evaluation values. Function d_{ij} is the opinion distance between ag_i and ag_j. d_{ij} is defined as

$$d_{ij} = \sqrt{\sum_{k=1}^{K} |su_{ik} - su_{jk}|^2}, \tag{7}$$

based on the Euclidean distance.

3.2   Updating Values

The impact of exchanging opinions and mass media is called social impact [8]. Here, social impact is the total sum of impacts that an agent is influenced by from all sources of information. Social impact Imp_i is defined as

$$Imp_i = (imp_{i1}, imp_{i2}, ..., imp_{iK}), \tag{8}$$

where imp_{iy} is the social impact of political party y from exchanging opinions and mass media with political party y. imp_{iy} is defined as

$$imp_{iy} = E \cdot val_{iy}^{medias} + (1 - E)val_{iy}^{agents}, \tag{9}$$

where $E(0 \le E \le 1)$ is a weighting parameter of the mass media. val_{iy}^{agents} represents the social impact of exchanging opinions, and val_{iy}^{medias} represents the social impact of mass media. The set of agents that are linked to ag_i is classified into two types. Agents in set SA_i make assessments of those having good opinions of political party y by using ag_i, and agents in set DA_i make assessments of those having poor opinions of political party y by using ag_i. Also, the set of mass media that are linked to ag_i is classified into two types. Mass medias in set SM_i transmit good opinions of political party y, and mass medias in set DM_i transmit poor opinions of political party y. val_{iy}^{agents} and val_{iy}^{medias} are defined as

$$val_{iy}^{agents} = N_{SA_i}^{-\frac{1}{2}} \sum_{agent_u \in SA_i} \frac{q_{iu}(y)}{d_{iu}^2}$$

$$+ N_{DA_i}^{-\frac{1}{2}} \sum_{agent_v \in DA_i} \frac{q_{iv}(y)}{d_{iv}^2}, and \tag{10}$$

$$val_{iy}^{medias} = N_{SM_i}^{-\frac{1}{2}} \sum_{media_u \in SM_i} \frac{q_{iu}(y)}{d_{iu}^2}$$

$$+ N_{DM_i}^{-\frac{1}{2}} \sum_{media_v \in DM_i} \frac{q_{iv}(y)}{d_{iv}^2}, \tag{11}$$

based on Latane's DSIT. Where N_{SA_i} and N_{DA_i} are the numbers of each set of agents, N_{SM_i} and N_{DM_i} are the numbers of each set of mass media. Agents update their evaluation value su_{iy} according to function su_{iy}, which is defined as

$$su_{iy} \leftarrow \begin{cases} su_{iy} + 1 \ (imp_{iy} > su_{iy} + T_i) \\ \qquad \wedge (su_{iy} < 10) \\ su_{iy} - 1 \ (imp_{iy} < su_{iy} - T_i). \\ \qquad \wedge (su_{iy} > -10) \\ su_{iy} \qquad \qquad otherwise \end{cases} \tag{12}$$

All agents update evaluation values and evaluation orders after they have exchanged opinions.

3.3   Voting Behavior

Agents decide voting behavior bases on the Riker and Ordeshook model [9]. Riker and Ordeshook define as

$$R = P \cdot B - C + D, \tag{13}$$

to represent whether or not an individual will vote, where R is the reward that a voter will receive from voting, P is the probability that the vote cast will cause the preferred candidate wins, B is the differential benefit that a voter will receive if the preferred candidate wins, C is the costs of participating in the vote, and D is the various satisfactions that a voter gains from voting. Because it is difficult for the costs of participating in the vote to be measured in the election and adjusted with simulation, agents' voting behaviors in Sudo et al.'s model [6] are not faithfuly reproduced. Here, we expand their model by using Konishi et al.'s voting behavior model [10] as a reference. The rewards in the utility of voting are decided by an agent's evaluation values in the proposed model and the cost of participating in the vote is linked to agents' vote candidates. Agents decide whether to participate in the vote and which political party they will vote for with rewards in our model. Rewards R_i is defined as

$$R_i = (r_{i1}, r_{i2}, ..., r_{iK}), \tag{14}$$

where r_{iy} represents the reward in the utility of voting for political party y. r_{iy} is defined as

$$r_{iy} = \alpha \cdot U_{iy} - (1 - \alpha) \cdot Co_i, \tag{15}$$

where U_{iy} is the utility of voting for political party y, and $\alpha(0 \leq \alpha \leq 1)$ is the voting coefficient. We used the same reward for all agents discussed in this paper. Voting coefficient α is adjusted by tuning the parameters. U_{iy} is defined as

$$U_{iy} = pro_{iy} \times bene_{iy}, \tag{16}$$

where pro_{iy} is the probability that its vote matters, and $bene_{iy}$ is its benefits of having political party y win (compared to its evaluation values). Because more than five political parties contested seats in parliament throughout Japan, votes that were scattered between candidates easily became wasted. Therefore, pro_{iy} is decided by the number of political parties and other agents' values in the proposed model. Agents make an assessment that another agent's vote for a political party will have its highest value. We define political parties with highest values as agents' vote candidates. pro_{iy} is defined as

$$pro_{iy} = (K + \sum_{agent_w \in Z_{iy}} \frac{1}{N_{Cad_w}})^{-1}, \tag{17}$$

Table 2. Kinds of Social Attributes and Numbers of Substructures

Kinds of attributes	Numbers of social spaces
Sex and age	8
Income	7
Address	11
Total	26

where Cad_i is the ag_i's vote candidate's set, and Z_{iy} is the set of agents linked to ag_i with the highest value for political party y. Here, N_{Cad_w} is the number of Cad_w. pro_{iy} is lower as the number of Z_{iy} is higher. $bene_{iy}$ is defined as

$$bene_{iy} = su_{iy} - \min Su_i. \tag{18}$$

The cost is lower as Co_i approuches 0 in this paper. ag_i participates in the vote with $\max R_i > 0$, and $\max R_i \leq 0$ does not participate. Agents vote for the political party that has the highest evaluation value. If more than two political parties have the highest evaluation value, the agent chooses a political party from several political parties at random.

4 Experiments and Discussion

Agents were generated from a database of public opinion polls collected before and after the Japanese House of Councilors election in 2004. There was a large difference between previous public opinion polls and the results from the election of the Japanese House of Councilors in 2004. We assumed a factor in this difference was people vigorously exchanging opinions and collecting information. We used data that addressed all social attributes and values for political parties in public opinion polls in these experiments. There were 1283 agents, five political parties, and the weighting parameter for mass media E was 0.2. The social attributes and numbers of substructures are listed in Table 2. The political parties were the Liberal Democratic Party (LDP), and the Democratic Party of Japan (DP), the New Komeito (NK), the Japanese Communist Party (JCP), the Social Democratic Party (SDP). The substructures for sex, age, and income were generated by using the small world model, and the substructures for addresses were generated by using the regular model. Each agent's threshold to change its opinions were random numbers that had a Gaussian distribution with zero mean and a dispersion of one. Each agent's cost of participating in the vote were random numbers that had a Gaussian distribution with a 0.5 mean and a dispersion of one. Voting coefficient α was only identified once after social space was generated. Because 56.54% of people voted in the Japanese House of Councilors election in 2004, the same voting percentage was used in simulations is identified by α. We did not change voting coefficient α in the simulations. The values of political parties were collected with values from 0 to 100 in the database of public opinion, . Collected values were converted to values from -10 to 10. One

Table 3. Percentages of Votes and Voting Rate with Two Models

Party names	Initial state step =0	Cardinal values model step=100	Order values model step =100	Actual result
LDP	45.7	53.6	35.1	30.0
DP	33.3	36.3	34.5	37.8
NK	9.3	4.5	14.5	15.4
JCP	6.6	3.0	8.1	7.8
SDP	5.0	2.6	7.8	5.3
Voting rate	56.5	57.0	51.0	56.5

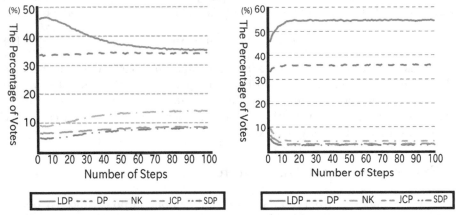

(a) Exchanging opinions with order values (b) Exchanging opinions with cardinal values

Fig. 4. Percentages of votes up to 100 steps

step was defined as a process where all agents exchanged opinions and updated values, and then mass media were updated. One trial ranged from starting the simulation to outputting the results up to 100 steps. Social space was initialized, and agents were relocated in social space at random in each trial. Because this simulation was for short term political decision making, the structure of social space did not change in the simulations.

4.1   Experiment 1

We compared the simulation results with the actual voting results in experiment 1 and examined the validity of the proposed model. Substructures were generated by using the regular or small world models of $h = 4$. The percentages of votes and voting and the actual percentages with each model are listed in Table 3 (rounded for double figures after decimal point). The results for the order values model had similarities, such as the percent who voted for the LDP or NK with the actual results in the election. Fig. 4(a) shows the process for the mean value

Table 4. Percentages of Votes and Voting Rate ($h = 4, 6, 8$, and 10)

Party names	$h = 4$	$h = 6$	$h = 8$	$h = 10$
LDP	35.1	30.0	26.3	24.1
DP	34.5	34.3	34.8	33.9
NK	14.5	16.0	16.6	17.0
JCP	8.1	9.8	11.1	12.7
SDP	7.8	9.8	11.2	12.3
Voting rate	51.0	47.8	44.8	43.2

of percentages of votes up to 100 steps with the order values model. Fig. 4(b) shows the process for the mean value of percentages of votes up to 100 steps with the cardinal values model. Comparing Fig. 4(a) and Fig. 4(b), the change in the voting percentages in 100 steps differs between the cardinal values and order values models. As the number of steps increases in the order values model, the voting percentages for LDA decreases. To focus on political parties that initially have similar voting percentages, such as NK, JCP, SDP and NK increased more than JCP and SDP, However, the voting percent for LDA greatly increased in the cardinal values model. NK continued to decrease in the same trace in the voting percentages for JCP and SDP. The change in the voting percentages for DP was small in the models. The results differed between the two models in the same feature of networks. Because we analyzed the factors where the simulation results from the order values model were similar to the actual results, we confirmed the amount of change in agents that had the highest evaluation values of political parties in its values to 100 steps from the initial state. We found the number of agents that had the highest evaluation values for the LDP obtained a majority of votes that did not increase. The number of agents that had the highest evaluation values for the DP and NK increased in the order values model. The number of agents that had the highest evaluation values for the JCP and SDP obtained a minority of votes that were larger in the order values model than in the cardinal values model. Therefore, agents' exchanging opinions with order utility was a contributing factor in the simulation to political decision-making.

4.2   Experiment 2

There was a possibility that expanding communication space would have great effects on political decision-making. Therefore, we analyzed the effects by using the proposed model in experiment 2. Substructures were generated in experiment 2 by using the regular and small world models that changed in four stages ($h = 4,6,8,$and 10). The percentages of votes and voting rates and actual result with each h are listed in Table 4 (rounded for double figures after the decimal point). The LDP and DP obtained a majority of votes had a low percentage of votes with the increase in h. However, the NK, JCP, and SDP obtained a minority of votes had a high percentage of votes with the increase in h. Fig. 5(a)

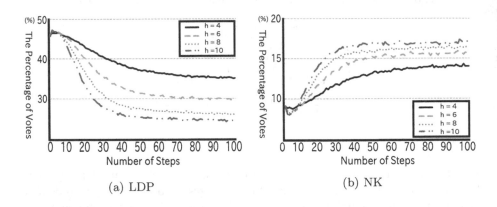

Fig. 5. Percentages of votes up to 100 steps ($h = 4, 6, 8$, and 10)

and Fig. 5(b) plot the process for each percentage (LDP and NK) of votes for the four values of h. Because the percentages of votes increasing or decreasing were in a similar range, we found that the percentages of votes were changed by a shift in votes between political parties in the simulations. We will discuss this from two standpoints of exchanging opinions and voting behavior. First, we will focus on exchanging opinions. Minority agents kept their opinions in expounded communication space because they had many opportunity of linking agents that had the same or similar opinions to themselves. However, majority agents lost propagation paths, which meant agents widely transmitted the majority's opinions, because agents that changed to the majority's opinions in social space (where h was a small value) did not change opinions. Next, we will focus on voting behavior. All agents could identify a lot of other agents' opinions because of expounding communication space. Majority agents identified many agents' opinions that were the same or similar to theirs. Therefore, agents' probabilities that their votes mattered were easy to decrease. For this reason, when agents had vote candidates, the political party that obtained a minority of votes was selected, which changed the percentages of votes. Finally, political parties that obtained a majority of votes had a low percentage of votes and political parties that obtained a minority of votes had a high percentage of votes because of expanding communication space.

5   Conclusion

We examined what the impact order utility in political decision-making had on voting by using multi-agent simulation. We demostrated the validity of the proposed model through experiment 1. Moreover, we analyzed what effect expanding communication space had on voters' political decision-making through experiment 2. Political parties that obtained a majority of votes had a low percentage of votes, and other political parties that obtained a minority of votes had a high percentage of votes with the increases in the experiment. These results revealed that the variety of opinions was maintained because of expanding communication space. We proposed a model of multi-agent simulation where agents communicated with order utility, and communication space represented a hierarchical network in the proposed model. The proposed model could not only be applied to political decision making but also to other fields such as artificial markets. However, the proposed model only extracted some elements in the political decision making process. Although we dealt fairly in this paper with other people's influences, Lazarsfield et al. argued that people called "opinion leaders" had a powerful effect or influence on others [17]. It will also be necessary for us to verify other networks such as the scale free model [14]. However, we presented important knowledge on political decision-making by using the regular and small world models. The structure of social space did not change in the simulations in this study because it was on short-term political decision making. Our future work will focus on changes to the structure of social space. In addition, we will extend the proposed model to focus on differences in people' influences and simulate political decision making by using other networks.

Acknowledgments. The data for this secondary analysis, "name of the survey, name of the depositor," was provided by the Social Science Japan Data Archive, Center for Social Research and Data Archives, Institute of Social Science, The University of Tokyo. This work was supported in part by the Ministry of Education, Science, Sports and Culture, Grant–in–Aid for Scientific Research under grant #25280100 and #25540146.

References

1. Adachi, T., Hizen, Y.: Political Economy Analysis of Mass Media and Voting Behavior: A Survey, KIER Discussion Paper, Institute of Economic Research, Kyoto University, vol. 1112 (2011) (in Japanese)
2. Downs, A.: An economic theory of democracy. Haper Collins, New York (1957)
3. Prat, A., Stromberg, D.: The Political Economy of Mass Media. CEPR Discussion Papers, No.DP8246 (2011)
4. Shimura, M., Kobayashi, T., Murakami, F.: Does extending social networks help a minority to survive?: On the introduction of information about distant others to a DSIT simulation. The Japanese Society of Social Psychology, Japanese Journal of Social Psychology (Before 1996, Research in Social Psychology) 21(1), 32–43 (2005) (in Japanese)
5. Ishiguro, I., Yasuno, S., Shibanai, Y.: Application of global information as generalized other to computer simulation of Dynamic Social Impact Theory. The Japanese Society of Social Psychology, Japanese Journal of Social Psychology (Before 1996, Research in Social Psychology) 16(2), 114–123 (2000) (in Japanese)
6. Sudo, Y., Mutoh, A., Kato, S.: Analyzing the impact of order utility in political decision-making on voting by using multi-agent simulatio. In: JAWS 2012, p. C4-1 (2012) (in Japanese)

7. Murakami, M., Tanida, N.: An Agent Based Modeling for the Formation of Public Opinion and its Effect on Japanese Public Pension System, Kansai University, vol. 59 (2008) (in Japanese)
8. Latané, B., Nowak, A., Liu, J.: Measuring emergent social phenomena: Dynamism,polarization,and clustering as order parameters of social systems. Behavioral Science 39, 1–24 (1994)
9. Riker, W., Ordeshook, P.: A Theory of the Calculus of Voting. American Political Science Review 62(1), 25–42 (1968)
10. Konishi, K., Murata, T., Natori, R.: Voting Simulation for Improving Voter Turnout and Reducing the Number of Polling Places. Japan Society for Fuzzy Theory and Intelligent Informatics 22(2), 203–210 (2010) (in Japanese)
11. Ida, M.: Possibility Valuation based on Oridinal Utility. Japan Society for Fuzzy Theory and intelligent informatics 7(6), 1175–1185 (1995) (in Japanese)
12. Ishiguro, I.: Attitude homophily and relational selectability: An analysis of dyadic data. The Japanese Society of Social Psychology, Japanese Journal of Social Psychology (Before 1996, Research in Social Psychology) 27(1), 13–23 (2011) (in Japanese)
13. Watts, D.J., Strogatz, S.H.: Collective dynamics of small-world networks. Nature 393(4), 440–442 (1998)
14. Masuda, N., Konno, N.: Introduction to complex networks. Sangyotosyo (2005) (in Japanese)
15. Tsuda, H.: Analysis about the Effect of the Internet to Constructing Process of Business Ethics. Bulletin of the Management Research Institute 15, 59–78 (2008) (in Japanese)
16. Marden, J.I.: Analyzing and Modeling Rank Data. Monographs on statistics and applied probability, vol. 64. Chapman & Hall (1995)
17. Lazarsfeld, P.F., Berelson, B., Gaudet, H.: The people's choice: how the voter makes up his mind in a presidential campaign, 3rd edn. Columbia University Press, Columbia University Press (1968)

SAT-Based Bounded Model Checking
for Weighted Interpreted Systems
and Weighted Linear Temporal Logic*

Bożena Woźna-Szcześniak, Agnieszka M. Zbrzezny, and Andrzej Zbrzezny

IMCS, Jan Długosz University
Al. Armii Krajowej 13/15, 42-200 Częstochowa, Poland
{b.wozna,a.zbrzezny,agnieszka.zbrzezny}@ajd.czest.pl

Abstract. We present a SAT-based bounded model checking (BMC) method for the weighted interpreted systems (i.e. interpreted systems augmented to include a weight function, one per each agent, that associates *weights* with actions, which are arbitrary natural numbers) and for properties expressible in the existential fragment of a weighted linear temporal logic with epistemic components (WELTLK). Since in BMC we translate both the system model and the checked specification to a propositional formula that is later analysed by a SAT-solver, we report on a propositional encoding of both the weighted interpreted systems and the WELTLK formulae. This encoding is designed specifically for managing weighted temporal operators and knowledge operators, which are commonly found in properties of multi-agent systems in models of which we assume that acting of agents may cost. We implemented the proposed BMC algorithm as a new module of VerICS, and we evaluated it by means of the following two examples: a weighted generic pipeline paradigm and a weighted bits transmission problem.

1 Introduction

Agents are autonomous and intelligent entities that can be engage in social activities such as coordination, negotiation, cooperation, etc. A multi-agent system (MAS) [16] is a distributed system composed of multiple interacting agents within an environment. There are variety of models of MASs, the most widely studied of which is the *interpreted system* (IS) [7], designed for reasoning about the agents' epistemic and temporal properties, and the *deontic interpreted system* (DIS) [12] that extends IS to make possible reasoning about correct functioning behaviour of MASs. An important assumption in this line of models is that there are no costs associated to agents' actions. The models become more expressive when this restriction is dropped. For example, the formalism of *weighted deontic interpreted systems* (WDISs) [17] extends DISs to make the reasoning possible about not only temporal, epistemic and deontic properties, but also about agents

---

* Partly supported by National Science Center under the grant No. 2011/01/B/ST6/05317.

G. Boella et al. (Eds.): PRIMA 2013, LNAI 8291, pp. 355–371, 2013.

quantitative properties. In the Kripke model of WDIS each transition is labelled not only by a joint action, but also by a positive integer value (e.g. 100 units) that represents the cost of acting agents. Such transitions could be simulated in the Kripke model of DIS by inserting 99 intermediate states. However, this increases the size of the Kripke model, and so it makes the model checking process more difficult.

Bounded model checking (BMC) [3,14] is one of the symbolic model checking techniques [4,16] that has gained popularity due to the immense success of SAT-solvers. In classical SAT-based BMC, we translate the existential model checking problem for a temporal epistemic logic to the satisfiability problem of a propositional formula. More precisely, we represent a counterexample of the bounded length by a propositional formula, and we check the satisfiability of the resulting propositional formula with a specialised SAT-solver. If this formula is satisfiable, then the SAT-solver returns a satisfying assignment that can be converted into a concrete counterexample showing the source of an error. Otherwise, the bound is increased until an error is found, or a pre-determined completeness threshold is reached (in practice, this is a rare case), or a pre-determined time/memory limits are reached.

Specification languages are most useful when they can be verified automatically. Therefore to model check the requirements of MASs various extensions of temporal logics [5] with epistemic (representing knowledge) [7], doxastic (representing beliefs) [10], and deontic (representing the distinction between ideal/correct behaviour and actual – possibly incorrect – behaviour of the agents) [12] components have been proposed. In this paper we aim at completing the picture of applying the SAT-based BMC techniques to MASs by looking at the existential fragment of the weighted LTLK (i.e. weighted LTL extended with epistemic components, called WLTLK), interpreted over the *weighted interpreted systems* (WISs), i.e. the WDISs formalism in which deontic properties cannot be expressed [17]. We restrict the presented BMC formalism to WISs, because adding the deontic modalities to the BMC method for the existential fragment of WLTLK that we present in the paper is straightforward.

The original contributions of the paper are as follows. First of all, we introduce the WLTLK language and its existential fragment, called WELTLK. In the second place, we propose a SAT-based BMC technique for WISs and for WELTLK. Finally, we report on the implementation of the proposed BMC method as a new module of VerICS [9], and evaluate it experimentally by means of a modified *generic pipeline paradigm* [13] and a modified *bit transmission problem* [1]. We would like to point out that to the best of our knowledge, this is the first work which provides a practical BMC algorithm for WELTLK interpreted over weighted interpreted systems. Moreover, the novelty with respect to [17] is the following: the language (WELTLK), a propositional encoding of WELTLK, a new propositional encoding of the weighted transition relation, an implementation, an experimental evaluation, and a new case study. Further, we do not compare our results with other model checkers for MASs, e.g. MCMAS [11] or MCK [8], simply because they do not support WELTLK and WIS.

The structure of the paper is as follows. In Section 2 we introduce WISs and WLTLK together with its existential fragment. In Section 3 we define a SAT-based BMC for WELTLK interpreted over WISs. In Section 4 we discuss our experimental results. In Section 5 we conclude the paper.

2   Preliminaries

Weighted Interpreted Systems. Let $Ag = \{1, \ldots, n\}$ denote the non-empty and finite set of agents, and $\mathcal{E}$ be a special agent that is used to model the environment in which the agents operate. The set of agents Ag together with the environment $\mathcal{E}$ constitute a multi-agent system (MAS). In the paper we use the weighted interpreted system (WIS), a formalism defined later on in the section, to model MAS. In the WIS formalism, each agent $\mathbf{c} \in Ag \cup \{\mathcal{E}\}$ is modelled using a non-empty set $L_\mathbf{c}$ of *local states*, a non-empty set $\iota_\mathbf{c} \subseteq L_\mathbf{c}$ of initial states, a non-empty set $Act_\mathbf{c}$ of *possible actions*, a *protocol function* $P_\mathbf{c} : L_\mathbf{c} \to 2^{Act_\mathbf{c}}$ that define rules according to which actions may be performed in each local state, a (partial) *evolution function* $t_\mathbf{c} : L_\mathbf{c} \times Act \to L_\mathbf{c}$ with $Act = Act_1 \times \cdots \times Act_n \times Act_\mathcal{E}$ (each element of Act is called a *joint action*), a *weight function* $d_\mathbf{c} : Act_\mathbf{c} \to \mathbb{N}$, and a *valuation function* $\mathcal{V}_\mathbf{c} : L_\mathbf{c} \to 2^{\mathcal{PV}}$ that assigns to each local state a set of propositional variables that are assumed to be true at that state. Further, we do not assume that the sets $Act_\mathbf{c}$ are disjoint for all $\mathbf{c} \in Ag \cup \{\mathcal{E}\}$.

Now for a given set of agents Ag, the environment $\mathcal{E}$ and a set of propositional variables $\mathcal{PV}$, we define the *weighted interpreted system* (WIS) as a tuple $(\{\iota_\mathbf{c}, L_\mathbf{c}, Act_\mathbf{c}, P_\mathbf{c}, t_\mathbf{c}, \mathcal{V}_\mathbf{c}, d_\mathbf{c}, \}_{\mathbf{c} \in Ag \cup \{\mathcal{E}\}})$. Next, for a given WIS we define: (1) a set of all *possible global states* $S = L_1 \times \ldots \times L_n \times L_\mathcal{E}$; by $l_\mathbf{c}(s)$ we denote the local component of agent $\mathbf{c} \in Ag \cup \{\mathcal{E}\}$ in a global state $s = (\ell_1, \ldots, \ell_n, \ell_\mathcal{E})$; and (2) a *global evolution function* $t : S \times Act \to S$ as follows: $t(s, a) = s'$ iff for all $\mathbf{c} \in Ag$, $t_\mathbf{c}(l_\mathbf{c}(s), a) = l_\mathbf{c}(s')$ and $t_\mathcal{E}(l_\mathcal{E}(s), a) = l_\mathcal{E}(s')$. In brief we write the above as $s \xrightarrow{a} s'$. Now, for a given WIS we define a *weighted model* (or a *model*) as a tuple $M = (\iota, S, T, \mathcal{V}, d)$, where

- $\iota = \iota_1 \times \ldots \times \iota_n \times \iota_\mathcal{E}$ is the set of all possible initial global state;
- S is the set of all possible global states as defined above;
- $T \subseteq S \times Act \times S$ is a transition relation defined by the global evolution function as follows: $(s, a, s') \in T$ iff $s \xrightarrow{a} s'$. We assume that the relation T is total, i.e. for any $s \in S$ there exists $s' \in S$ and a non empty joint action $a \in Act$ such that $s \xrightarrow{a} s'$;
- $\mathcal{V} : S \to 2^{\mathcal{PV}}$ is the valuation function defined as $\mathcal{V}(s) = \bigcup_{\mathbf{c} \in Ag \cup \{\mathcal{E}\}} \mathcal{V}_\mathbf{c}(l_\mathbf{c}(s))$;
- $d : Act \to \mathbb{N}$ is a "joint" weight function defined as follows: $d((a_1, \ldots, a_n, a_\mathcal{E})) = \sum_{\mathbf{c} \in Ag \cup \{\mathcal{E}\}} d_\mathbf{c}(a_\mathbf{c})$; note that this definition is reasonable, since we are interested in MASs, in which transitions carry some cost.

Given a WIS one can define the indistinguishability relation $\sim_\mathbf{c} \subseteq S \times S$ for agent $\mathbf{c}$ as follows: $s \sim_\mathbf{c} s'$ iff $l_\mathbf{c}(s') = l_\mathbf{c}(s)$. Further, a *path* in M is an infinite sequence $\pi = s_0 \xrightarrow{a_1} s_1 \xrightarrow{a_2} s_2 \xrightarrow{a_3} \ldots$ of transitions. For such a path, and for $j \leq m \in \mathbb{N}$, by $\pi(m)$ we denote the m-th state s_m, by π^m we denote the m-th suffix of the path π, which is defined in the standard way: $\pi^m = s_m \xrightarrow{a_{m+1}} s_{m+1} \xrightarrow{a_{m+2}}$

s_{m+2}.... Next, by $\pi[j..m]$ we denote the finite sequence $s_j \xrightarrow{a_{j+1}} s_{j+1} \xrightarrow{a_{j+2}} \ldots s_m$ with $m - j$ transitions and $m - j + 1$ states, and by $D\pi[j..m]$ we denote the (cumulative) weight of $\pi[j..m]$ that is defined as $d(a_{j+1}) + \ldots + d(a_m)$ (hence 0 when $j = m$). By $\Pi(s)$ we denote the set of all the paths starting at $s \in S$, and by $\Pi = \bigcup_{s^0 \in \iota} \Pi(s^0)$ we denote the set of all the paths starting at initial states.

The Logic WLTLK and Its Existential Fragment. WLTLK extends LTL with cost constraints on temporal modalities and with epistemic modalities. In the syntax of WLTLK we assume the following: $p \in \mathcal{PV}$ is an atomic proposition, $\mathbf{c} \in Ag$, $\Gamma \subseteq Ag$, I is an interval in $\mathbb{N} = \{0, 1, 2, \ldots\}$ of the form: $[a, b)$ and $[a, \infty)$, for $a, b \in \mathbb{N}$ and $a \neq b$, and $right(I) = b$ if $I = [a, b)$, otherwise $right(I) = \infty$. In the semantics we assume the following definitions of epistemic relations: $\sim_\Gamma^E \overset{def}{=} \bigcup_{\mathbf{c} \in \Gamma} \sim_\mathbf{c}$, $\sim_\Gamma^C \overset{def}{=} (\sim_\Gamma^E)^+$ (the transitive closure of $\sim_\Gamma^E$), $\sim_\Gamma^D \overset{def}{=} \bigcap_{\mathbf{c} \in \Gamma} \sim_\mathbf{c}$, where $\Gamma \subseteq Ag$.

The WLTLK formulae in the negation normal form are defined by the following grammar:

$$\varphi ::= \mathbf{true} \mid \mathbf{false} \mid p \mid \neg p \mid \varphi \wedge \varphi \mid \varphi \vee \varphi \mid X_I\varphi \mid \varphi U_I\varphi \mid \varphi R_I\varphi$$

$$\mid K_\mathbf{c}\varphi \mid \overline{K}_\mathbf{c}\varphi \mid E_\Gamma\varphi \mid \overline{E}_\Gamma\varphi \mid D_\Gamma\varphi \mid \overline{D}_\Gamma\varphi \mid C_\Gamma\varphi \mid \overline{C}_\Gamma\varphi$$

The temporal modalities X_I, U_I and R_I are, respectively, named as the *weighted next step*, the *weighted until* and the *weighted release*. The derived basic temporal modalities for *weighted eventually* and *weighted globally* are defined as follows: $F_I\varphi \overset{def}{=} \mathbf{true}U_I\varphi$ and $G_I\varphi \overset{def}{=} \mathbf{false}R_I\varphi$. Hereafter, if the interval I is of the form $[0, \infty)$, then we omit it for the simplicity of the presentation.

The epistemic modality $K_\mathbf{c}\varphi$ represents "agent $\mathbf{c}$ knows φ" while the modality $\overline{K}_\mathbf{c}\varphi \overset{def}{=} \neg K_\mathbf{c}\neg\varphi$ is the corresponding dual one representing "agent $\mathbf{c}$ considers φ possible". The epistemic modalities D_Γ, E_Γ, and C_Γ represent distributed knowledge in the group Γ, "everyone in Γ knows", and common knowledge among agents in Γ, respectively. The epistemic modalities $\overline{D}_\Gamma, \overline{E}_\Gamma$, and $\overline{C}_\Gamma$ are the corresponding dual ones. The WELTLK is the existential fragment of WLTLK, defined by the following grammar:

$$\varphi ::= \mathbf{true} \mid \mathbf{false} \mid p \mid \neg p \mid \varphi \wedge \varphi \mid \varphi \vee \varphi \mid X_I\varphi \mid \varphi U_I\varphi \mid \varphi R_I\varphi$$

$$\mid \overline{K}_\mathbf{c}\varphi \mid \overline{E}_\Gamma\varphi \mid \overline{D}_\Gamma\varphi \mid \overline{C}_\Gamma\varphi.$$

A WLTLK formula φ is true (valid) along the path π (in symbols $M, \pi \models \varphi$) iff $M, \pi^0 \models \varphi$, where the satisfaction relation $\models$ is defined inductively, with the classical rules for propositional operators and with the following rules for the temporal and epistemic modalities:

$M, \pi^m \models X_I\alpha$ iff $D\pi[m..m+1] \in I$ and $M, \pi^{m+1} \models \alpha$,

$M, \pi^m \models \alpha U_I\beta$ iff $(\exists i \geq m)(D\pi[m..i] \in I$ and $M, \pi^i \models \beta$ and $(\forall m \leq j < i)M, \pi^j \models \alpha)$,

$M, \pi^m \models \alpha R_I\beta$ iff $(\forall i \geq m)(D\pi[m..i] \in I$ implies $M, \pi^i \models \beta)$ or $(\exists i \geq m)$ $(D\pi[m..i] \in I$ and $M, \pi^i \models \alpha$ and $(\forall m \leq j \leq i)M, \pi^j \models \beta)$,

$M, \pi^m \models K_\mathbf{c}\alpha$ iff $(\forall\pi' \in \Pi)(\forall i \geq 0)(\pi'(i) \sim_\mathbf{c} \pi(m)$ implies $M, \pi'^i \models \alpha)$,

$M, \pi^m \models \overline{K}_\mathbf{c}\alpha$ iff $(\exists\pi' \in \Pi)(\exists i \geq 0)(\pi'(i) \sim_\mathbf{c} \pi(m)$ and $M, \pi'^i \models \alpha)$,

$M, \pi^m \models Y_\Gamma\alpha$ iff $(\forall\pi' \in \Pi)(\forall i \geq 0)(\pi'(i) \sim_\Gamma^Y \pi(m)$ implies $M, \pi'^i \models \alpha)$,

$M, \pi^m \models \overline{Y}_\Gamma \alpha$ iff $(\exists \pi' \in \Pi)(\exists i \geq 0)(\pi'(i) \sim_\Gamma^Y \pi(m)$ and $M, \pi'^i \models \alpha)$,
where $Y \in \{D, E, C\}$.

A WLTLK formula φ *existentially holds* in the model M (denoted $M \models \varphi$) iff $M, \pi \models \varphi$ for some path $\pi \in \Pi$. The *existential model checking problem* asks whether $M \models \varphi$.

3   Bounded Model Checking for WIS and for WELTLK

As usual we begin with defining the notion of k-paths and loops, which are required by the bounded semantics - the basis of each SAT-based BMC.

Let M be a model, and $k \in \mathbb{N}$ a bound. A k-*path* π_l is a pair (π, l), where π is a finite sequence $s_0 \xrightarrow{a_1} s_1 \xrightarrow{a_2} \ldots \xrightarrow{a_k} s_k$ of transitions. A k-path π_l is a *loop* if $l < k$ and $\pi(k) = \pi(l)$. Note that if a k-path π_l is a loop, then it represents the infinite path of the form uv^ω, where $u = (s_0 \xrightarrow{a_1} s_1 \xrightarrow{a_2} \ldots \xrightarrow{a_l} s_l)$ and $v = (s_{l+1} \xrightarrow{a_{l+2}} \ldots \xrightarrow{a_k} s_k)$. $\Pi_k(s)$ denotes the set of all the k-paths of M that start at s, and $\Pi_k = \bigcup_{s^0 \in \iota} \Pi_k(s^0)$.

Let $k \in \mathbb{N}$ be a bound, $0 \leq m \leq k$, $0 \leq l \leq k$, and φ a WELTLK formula. As in the definition of semantics we need to define the satisfiability relation on suffixes of k-paths, we denote by π_l^m the pair (π_l, m), i.e. the k-path π_l together with the designated starting point m. Further, $M, \pi_l^m \models_k \varphi$ denotes that the formula φ is k-true along the suffix $(\pi(m), \ldots, \pi(k))$ of π.

A WELTLK formula φ is k-true along the k-path π_l (in symbols $M, \pi_l \models_k \varphi$) iff $M, \pi_l^0 \models_k \varphi$, where where the bounded satisfaction relation $\models_k$ is defined inductively, with the classical rules for propositional operators and with the following rules for the temporal and epistemic modalities:

$M, \pi_l^m \models_k X_I \alpha$ iff $(m < k$ and $D\pi[m..m+1] \in I$ and $M, \pi_l^{m+1} \models_k \alpha)$ or
$\qquad (m = k$ and $l < k$ and $\pi(k) = \pi(l)$ and $D\pi[l..l+1] \in I$
$\qquad$ and $M, \pi_l^{l+1} \models_k \alpha)$,

$M, \pi_l^m \models_k \alpha U_I \beta$ iff $(\exists m \leq j \leq k)(D\pi[m..j] \in I$ and $M, \pi_l^j \models_k \beta$ and
$\qquad (\forall m \leq i < j) M, \pi_l^i \models_k \alpha)$ or $(l < m$ and $\pi(k) = \pi(l)$
$\qquad$ and $(\exists l < j < m)(D\pi[m..k] + D\pi[l..j] \in I$ and $M, \pi_l^j \models_k \beta$
$\qquad$ and $(\forall l < i < j) M, \pi_l^i \models \alpha$ and $(\forall m \leq i \leq k) M, \pi_l^i \models_k \alpha))$,

$M, \pi_l^m \models_k \alpha R_I \beta$ iff $(D\pi[m..k] \geq right(I)$ and $(\forall m \leq j \leq k)(D\pi[m..j] \in I$
$\qquad$ implies $M, \pi_l^j \models_k \beta))$ or $(D\pi[m..k] < right(I)$ and $\pi(k) = \pi(l)$
$\qquad$ and $(\forall m \leq j \leq k)(D\pi[m..j] \in I$ implies $M, \pi_l^j \models_k \beta)$ and
$\qquad (\forall l \leq j \leq k)(D\pi[m..k] + D\pi[l..j] \in I$ implies $M, \pi_l^j \models_k \beta))$ or
$\qquad (\exists m \leq j \leq k)(D\pi[m..j] \in I$ and $M, \pi_l^j \models_k \alpha$ and
$\qquad (\forall m \leq i \leq j) M, \pi_l^i \models_k \beta)$ or $(l < m$ and $\pi(k) = \pi(l)$
$\qquad$ and $(\exists l < j < m)(D\pi[m..k] + D\pi[l..j] \in I$ and $M, \pi_l^j \models_k \alpha$
$\qquad$ and $(\forall l < i \leq j) M, \pi_l^i \models \beta$ and $(\forall m \leq i \leq k) M, \pi_l^i \models_k \beta))$,

$M, \pi_l^m \models_k \overline{K}_c \alpha$ iff $(\exists \pi'_{l'} \in \Pi_k)(\exists 0 \leq j \leq k)(M, \pi'^j_{l'} \models_k \alpha$ and $\pi(m) \sim_c \pi'(j))$,

$M, \pi_l^m \models_k \overline{Y}_\Gamma \alpha$ iff $(\exists \pi'_{l'} \in \Pi_k)(\exists 0 \leq j \leq k)(M, \pi'^j_{l'} \models_k \alpha$ and $\pi(m) \sim_\Gamma^Y \pi'(j))$,
$\qquad$ where $Y \in \{D, E, C\}$.

Let m be a formula evaluation position, k a bound, and $p, q \in \mathcal{PV}$. An illustration of the bounded semantics is shown in Fig. 1.

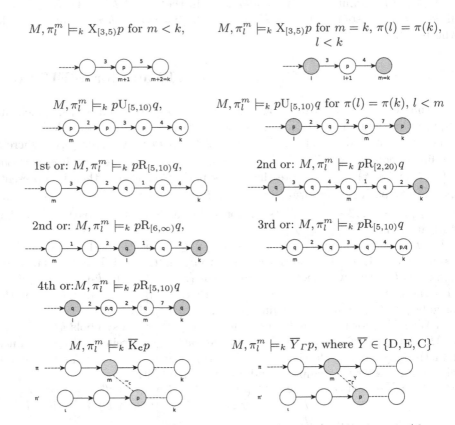

Fig. 1. Evaluation of temporal (the gray states are the same) and epistemic (the gray states are epistemically equivalent) formulae

Let M be a model, and φ a WELTLK formula. We use the following notations: $M \models_k \varphi$ iff $M, \pi_l \models_k \varphi$ for some $\pi_l \in \Pi_k$. The *bounded model checking problem* asks whether there exists $k \in \mathbb{N}$ such that $M \models_k \varphi$.

The following theorem states that for a given model and a WELTLK formula there exists a bound k such that the model checking problem ($M \models \varphi$) can be reduced to the bounded model checking problem ($M \models_k \varphi$). The theorem can be proven by induction on the length of the formula φ; we assume the size of M is the sum of the number of transitions and the number of states.

Theorem 1. *Let M be a model and φ a WELTLK formula. Then, the following equivalence holds: $M \models \varphi$ iff there exists $k \leq |M| \cdot |\varphi| \cdot 2^{|\varphi|}$ such that $M \models_k \varphi$.*

Note however that from the BMC point of view the bound k that makes the bounded and unbounded semantics equivalent is insignificant. This is because the BMC method for large k is unfeasible.

Translation to SAT. Let M be a model, φ a WELTLK formula, and $k \geq 0$ a bound. The presented propositional encoding of the bounded model checking problem for WELTLK is based on the BMC encoding of [18], and it relies on defining the propositional formula: $[M, \varphi]_k := [M^{\varphi, \iota}]_k \wedge [\varphi]_{M,k}$ which is satisfiable if and only if $M \models_k \varphi$ holds.

The definition of $[M^{\varphi, \iota}]_k$ assumes that the states and the joint actions of M, and the sequence of weights associated to the joint actions are encoded symbolically, which is possible, since both the set of states and the set of joint actions are finite. Formally, let $\mathbf{c} \in Ag \cup \{\mathcal{E}\}$. Then, each state $s \in S$ is represented by a vector $w = (\mathbf{w}_1, \ldots, \mathbf{w}_n, \mathbf{w}_{\mathcal{E}})$ (called a *symbolic state*) of *symbolic local states*, where each symbolic local state $\mathbf{w_c}$ is a vector of propositional variables. Next, each joint action $\mathfrak{a} \in Act$ is represented by a vector $\mathfrak{a} = (\mathfrak{a}_1, \ldots, \mathfrak{a}_n, \mathfrak{a}_{\mathcal{E}})$ (called a *symbolic action*) of *symbolic local actions*, where each symbolic local action $\mathfrak{a_c}$ is a vector of propositional variables. Next, each sequence of weights associated to a joint action is represented by a sequence $\delta = (d_1, \ldots, d_{n+1})$ of *symbolic weights*. The *symbolic weight* $d_{\mathbf{c}}$ is a vector $(\mathbf{d}_1, \ldots, \mathbf{d}_x)$ of propositional variables (called *weight variables*), whose length x depends on the weight functions $d_{\mathbf{c}}$. Further, in order to define $[M^{\varphi, \iota}]_k$ we need to specify the number of k-paths of the model M that are sufficient to validate φ. To calculate the number, we define the following auxiliary function $f_k : WELTLK \to \mathbb{N}$: $f_k(\mathbf{true}) = f_k(\mathbf{false}) = f_k(p) = f_k(\neg p) = 0$, where $p \in \mathcal{PV}$; $f_k(\alpha \wedge \beta) = f_k(\alpha) + f_k(\beta)$; $f_k(\alpha \vee \beta) = max\{f_k(\alpha), f_k(\beta)\}$; $f_k(\mathbf{X}_I \alpha) = f_k(\alpha)$; $f_k(\alpha \mathbf{U}_I \beta) = k \cdot f_k(\alpha) + f_k(\beta)$; $f_k(\alpha \mathbf{R}_I \beta) = (k+1) \cdot f_k(\beta) + f_k(\alpha)$; $f_k(\overline{\mathbf{C}}_\Gamma \alpha) = f_k(\alpha) + k$; $f_k(Y\alpha) = f_k(\alpha) + 1$ for $Y \in \{\overline{\mathbf{K}}_{\mathbf{c}}, \overline{\mathbf{D}}_\Gamma, \overline{\mathbf{E}}_\Gamma\}$. Now, since in the BMC method we deal with the existential validity, the number of k-paths sufficient to validate φ is given by the function $\widehat{f_k} : WELTLK \to \mathbb{N}$ that is defined as $\widehat{f_k}(\varphi) = f_k(\varphi) + 1$.

Given the above, the j-th symbolic k-path π_j is defined as the following sequence of transitions: $(w_{0,j} \xrightarrow{\mathfrak{a}_{1,j}, \delta_{1,j}} w_{1,j} \xrightarrow{\mathfrak{a}_{2,j}, \delta_{2,j}} \ldots \xrightarrow{\mathfrak{a}_{k,j}, \delta_{k,j}} w_{k,j}, u)$, where $w_{i,j}$ are symbolic states, $\mathfrak{a}_{i,j}$ are symbolic actions, $\delta_{i,j}$ are sequences of *symbolic weights*, for $0 \leq i \leq k$ and $1 \leq j \leq \widehat{f_k}(\varphi)$, and u is the *symbolic number* that is a vector $u = (\mathbf{u}_1, \ldots, \mathbf{u}_y)$ of propositional variables with $y = max(1, \lceil log_2(k+1) \rceil)$.

Let w and w' be two different symbolic states, δ a sequence of symbolic weighs, $\mathfrak{a}$ a symbolic action, and u be a symbolic number. We assume definitions of the following auxiliary propositional formulae: $p(w)$ - encodes the set of states of M in which $p \in \mathcal{PV}$ holds, $I_s(w)$ - encodes the state s of the model M, $\mathcal{T_c}(\mathbf{w_c}, (\mathfrak{a}, \delta), \mathbf{w'_c})$ - encodes the local evolution function of agent $\mathbf{c}$, $H(w, w')$ - encodes equality of two global states, $H_{\mathbf{c}}(w, w')$ - encodes the equivalence of two local states of agent $\mathbf{c}$, $\mathcal{N}_j^{\sim}(u)$ - encodes that the value j is in the arithmetic relation $\sim \in \{<, \leqslant, =, \geqslant, >\}$ with the value represented by the symbolic number u, $\mathcal{L}_k^l(\pi_n) := \mathcal{N}_l^{=}(u_n) \wedge H(w_{k,n}, w_{l,n})$, $\mathcal{B}_k^I(\pi_n)$ - encodes that the weight represented by the sequence $\delta_{1,n}, \ldots, \delta_{k,n}$ is less than $right(I)$, $\mathcal{D}_{a,b}^I(\pi_n)$ for $a \leq b$ - if $a < b$, then it encodes that the weight represented by the sequence $\delta_{a+1,n}, \ldots, \delta_{b,n}$ belongs to the interval I; otherwise, i.e. if $a = b$, then $\mathcal{D}_{a,b}^I(\pi_n)$ is true iff $0 \in I$, $\mathcal{D}_{a,b;c,d}^I(\pi_n)$ for $a \leq b$ and $c \leq d$ - if $a < b$ and $c < d$, then it encodes that the weight represented by the sequences $\delta_{a+1,n}, \ldots, \delta_{b,n}$ and $\delta_{c+1,n}, \ldots, \delta_{d,n}$ belongs to the interval I; if $a = b$ and $c < d$, then it encodes that the weight represented by the sequence $\delta_{c+1,n}, \ldots, \delta_{d,n}$ belongs to the interval I; if $a < b$ and $c = d$, then it encodes that the weight represented by the sequence $\delta_{a+1,n}, \ldots, \delta_{b,n}$ belongs to the interval I; if $a = b$ and $c = d$, then $\mathcal{D}^I_{a,b;c,d}(\boldsymbol{\pi}_n)$ is true iff $0 \in I$. $\mathcal{A}(\mathfrak{a})$ - encodes that each symbolic local action $\mathfrak{a}_\mathbf{c}$ of $\mathfrak{a}$ has to be executed by each agent in which it appears.

The formula $[M^{\varphi,\iota}]_k$, which encodes the unfolding of the transition relation of the model M $\widehat{f}_k(\varphi)$-times to the depth k, is defined as follows:

$$[M^{\varphi,\iota}]_k := \bigvee_{s \in \iota} I_s(w_{0,0}) \wedge \bigvee_{j=1}^{\widehat{f}_k(\varphi)} H(w_{0,0}, w_{0,j}) \wedge \bigwedge_{j=1}^{\widehat{f}_k(\varphi)} \bigvee_{l=0}^{k} \mathcal{N}_l^=(u_j) \wedge \qquad (1)$$

$$\bigwedge_{j=1}^{\widehat{f}_k(\varphi)} \bigwedge_{i=0}^{k-1} \mathcal{T}(w_{i,j}, (\mathfrak{a}_{i,j}, \delta_{i,j}), w_{i+1,j})$$

where $w_{i,j}$, $\mathfrak{a}_{i,j}$, $\delta_{i,j}$, and u_j are, respectively, symbolic states, symbolic actions, sequences of symbolic weights, and symbolic numbers, for $0 \le i \le k$ and $1 \le j \le \widehat{f}_k(\varphi)$. Moreover, $\mathcal{T}(w, (\mathfrak{a}, \delta), w')$ is defined as follows:

$$\mathcal{T}(w, (\mathfrak{a}, \delta), w') := \bigwedge_{\mathbf{c} \in Ag \cup \{\mathcal{E}\}} \mathcal{T}_\mathbf{c}(\mathbf{w_c}, (\mathfrak{a}, \delta), \mathbf{w'_c}) \wedge \mathcal{A}(\mathfrak{a}) \qquad (2)$$

Let $F_k(\varphi) = \{j \in \mathbb{N} \mid 1 \le j \le \widehat{f}_k(\varphi)\}$, and $[\varphi]_k^{[m,n,A]}$ denote the translation of φ along the n-th symbolic path $\boldsymbol{\pi}_n^m$ with the starting point m by using the set $A \subseteq F_k(\varphi)$. Then, the next step is a translation of a WELTLK formula φ to a propositional formula $[\varphi]_{M,k} := [\varphi]_k^{[0,1,F_k(\varphi)]}$.

Let A be a set of k-paths such that $|A| = \widehat{f}_k(\varphi)$. In order to define $[\varphi]_{M,k}$, we have to know how to divide the set A into subsets needed for translating the subformulae of φ. To accomplish this goal we use some auxiliary functions (g_l, g_r, g_s, h_k^U, h_k^R) that were defined in [18].

Definition 1 (Translation of the WELTLK formulae). *Let M be a model, φ a WELTLK formula, and $k \ge 0$ a bound. We define inductively the translation of φ over a path number $n \in F_k(\varphi)$ starting at the symbolic state $w_{m,n}$ as shown below, where $A \subseteq F_k(\varphi)$, $n' = min(A)$; we assume the classical rules for propositional operators.*

$$[\mathbf{X}_I \alpha]_k^{[m,n,A]} := \begin{cases} \mathcal{D}^I_{m,m+1}(\boldsymbol{\pi}_n) \wedge [\alpha]_k^{[m+1,n,A]}, & \text{if } m < k \\ \bigvee_{l=0}^{k-1}(\mathcal{D}^I_{l,l+1}(\boldsymbol{\pi}_n) \wedge \mathcal{L}_k^l(\boldsymbol{\pi}_n) \wedge [\alpha]_k^{[l+1,n,A]}), & \text{if } m = k \end{cases}$$

$$[\alpha \mathbf{U}_I \beta]_k^{[m,n,A]} := \bigvee_{j=m}^{k}(\mathcal{D}^I_{m,j}(\boldsymbol{\pi}_n) \wedge [\beta]_k^{[j,n,h_k^\mathrm{U}(k)]} \wedge \bigwedge_{i=m}^{j-1}[\alpha]_k^{[i,n,h_k^\mathrm{U}(i)]}) \vee$$
$$(\bigvee_{l=0}^{m-1}(\mathcal{L}_k^l(\boldsymbol{\pi}_n)) \wedge \bigvee_{j=0}^{m-1}(\mathcal{N}_j^>(u_n) \wedge [\beta]_k^{[j,n,h_k^\mathrm{U}(k)]} \wedge$$
$$\bigvee_{l=0}^{m-1}(\mathcal{N}_l^=(u_n) \wedge \mathcal{D}^I_{m,k;l,j}(\boldsymbol{\pi}_n)) \wedge$$
$$\bigwedge_{i=0}^{j-1}(\mathcal{N}_i^>(u_n) \to [\alpha]_k^{[i,n,h_k^\mathrm{U}(i)]}) \wedge \bigwedge_{i=m}^{k}[\alpha]_k^{[i,n,h_k^\mathrm{U}(i)]}),$$

$$[\alpha \mathbf{R}_I \beta)]_k^{[m,n,A]} := \bigvee_{j=m}^{k}(\mathcal{D}^I_{m,j}(\boldsymbol{\pi}_n) \wedge [\alpha]_k^{[j,n,h_k^\mathrm{R}(k)]} \wedge \bigwedge_{i=m}^{j}[\beta]_k^{[i,n,h_k^\mathrm{R}(i)]}) \vee$$
$$(\bigvee_{l=0}^{m-1}(\mathcal{L}_k^l(\boldsymbol{\pi}_n)) \wedge \bigvee_{j=0}^{m-1}(\mathcal{N}_j^>(u_n) \wedge [\alpha]_k^{[j,n,h_k^\mathrm{R}(k)]} \wedge$$

$$\bigvee_{l=0}^{m-1}(\mathcal{N}_l^{\neq}(u_n) \wedge \mathcal{D}_{m,k;l,j}^I(\pi_n)) \wedge$$
$$\bigwedge_{i=0}^{j}(\mathcal{N}_i^{>}(u_n) \to [\beta]_k^{[i,n,h_k^R(i)]}) \wedge \bigwedge_{i=m}^{k}[\beta]_k^{[i,n,h_k^R(i)]}) \vee$$
$$(\neg\mathcal{B}_k^I(\pi_n) \wedge \bigwedge_{j=m}^{k}(\mathcal{D}_{m,j}^I(\pi_n) \to [\beta]_k^{[j,n,h_k^R(k)]})) \vee$$
$$(\mathcal{B}_k^I(\pi_n) \wedge \bigwedge_{j=m}^{k}(\mathcal{D}_{m,j}^I(\pi_n) \to [\beta]_k^{[j,n,h_k^R(k)]}) \wedge$$
$$\bigvee_{l=0}^{k-1}[\mathcal{L}_k^l(\pi_n) \wedge \bigwedge_{j=l}^{k}(\mathcal{D}_{m,k;l,j}^I(\pi_n) \to [\beta]_k^{[j,n,h_k^R(k)]})]),$$

$$[\overline{K}_c\alpha]_k^{[m,n,A]} := \bigvee_{s\in\iota} I_s(w_{0,n'}) \wedge \bigvee_{j=0}^{k}([\alpha]_k^{[j,n',g_s(A)]} \wedge H_c(w_{m,n}, w_{j,n'})),$$
$$[\overline{D}_\Gamma\alpha]_k^{[m,n,A]} := \bigvee_{s\in\iota} I_s(w_{0,n'}) \wedge \bigvee_{j=0}^{k}([\alpha]_k^{[j,n',g_s(A)]} \wedge \bigwedge_{c\in\Gamma} H_c(w_{m,n}, w_{j,n'})),$$
$$[\overline{E}_\Gamma\alpha]_k^{[m,n,A]} := \bigvee_{s\in\iota} I_s(w_{0,n'}) \wedge \bigvee_{j=0}^{k}([\alpha]_k^{[j,n',g_s(A)]} \wedge \bigvee_{c\in\Gamma} H_c(w_{m,n}, w_{j,n'})),$$
$$[\overline{C}_\Gamma\alpha]_k^{[m,n,A]} := [\bigvee_{j=1}^{k}(\overline{E}_\Gamma)^j\alpha]_k^{[m,n,A]}.$$

The theorem below states the correctness and the completeness of the presented translation. It can be proven by induction on the complexity of the given WELTLK formula.

Theorem 2. *Let M be a model, and φ a WELTLK formula. Then for every $k \in \mathbb{N}$, $M \models_k \varphi$ if, and only if, the propositional formula $[M,\varphi]_k$ is satisfiable.*

Our encoding of the WELTLK formulae is defined recursively over the structure of a WELTLK formula φ, over the current position m of the n-th symbolic k-path, and over the set A of symbolic k-paths, which is initially equal to $F_k(\varphi)$. Next, our encoding does not translate looping and non-looping witnesses separately, but it combines both of them. Further, it is parameterised by the bound k, the set of symbolic k-paths, and closely follows the bounded semantics. Therefore, for fixed n, m, k and A, each subformula ψ of φ requires the constraints of size $O(k \cdot f_k(\varphi))$ using the encoding of ψ at various positions. Moreover, since the encoding of a subformula ψ is only dependent on m, n, k, and A, and, multiple occurrences of the encoding of ψ over the same set of parameters can be shared, the overall size can be bounded by $O(|\varphi| \cdot k \cdot f_k(\varphi))$. Further the size of the formula $[M, \varphi]_k$ is bounded by $O(|T| \cdot k \cdot f_k(\varphi) + |\varphi| \cdot k \cdot f_k(\varphi))$.

The main difficulty in defining of the extension of the BMC method for ELTLK and for the interleaved interpreted systems (IIS) [15] to the BMC method for WELTLK and for WIS is in the encoding of the weighted conditions and in the encoding of the global evolution function. This is because, in contrary to the BMC method of [15], in the WELTLK case we need to deal with joint actions and paths the transitions of which carry a cost. Thus, we have to take care of the following issues: (1) the cumulative weight is less/greater than the given bound k and the considered path is not a loop. (2) the cumulative weight is less/greater than the given bound k and the considered path is a loop. (3) the cumulative weight is counted for the joint actions. The translation has to reflect these possibilities. Further in the IIS case there is no need to encode joint actions together with the corresponding weights. Only local (or synchronised) actions and their weights are encoded. In the WIS case the encoding of the global evolution depends on both the joint actions and the "joint" weight function.

The main difficulties in the extension of the BMC method for WECTLK and for the WIS [17] to the BMC method for WELTLK and for WIS are in the encoding of the looping conditions. More precisely, in the WECTLK case the looping conditions are much simpler, since each epistemic and each temporal sub-formulae of a formula to be tested are evaluated over a new symbolic k-path that starts at an initial state, and therefore there is no possibility of getting different infinite paths from the same k-path. In the WELTLK case only epistemic sub-formulae can be evaluated over a new symbolic k-path that starts at the initial state. Thus, in the translation of X_I, U_I and R_I we cannot let different sub-formulae use different ways of bending a path into a loop, and thus, we have to disable the possibility of getting different infinite paths from the same k-path.

4   Experimental Results

In the section we experimentally evaluate the performance of our BMC en-coding for WELTLK and for WIS, which is implemented as extensions of our tool VerICS [9]. We have conducted the experiments using one classical multi-agent scenario, i.e. the (weighted) modified *bit transmission problem*, and one benchmark that is not yet so common in the multi-agent community, i.e. the *(weighted) generic pipeline paradigm*. Further, for all the considered examples we describe specifications as universal formulae, for which we verify the corre-sponding counterexample formulae that are interpreted existentially and belong to WELTLK. Moreover, for every specification given, there exists a counterex-ample, i.e. the WELTLK formula specifying the counterexample holds in the model of the benchmark.

We computed our experimental results on a computer with Intel Xeon 2 GHz processor and 4 GB of RAM, running Linux 2.6. We set the CPU time limit to 1800 seconds, and the memory limit to 2GB. Moreover, we used PicoSAT [2] in version 957 to test the satisfiability of the propositional formulae generated by our SAT-based BMC encoding.

Weighted Generic Pipeline Paradigm. We adapted the benchmark scenario of *a generic pipeline paradigm* [13], and we called it the *weighted generic pipeline paradigm* (WGPP). The model of WGPP involves Producer producing data, Consumer receiving data, and a chain of n intermediate Nodes that transmit data produced by Producer to Consumer. Producer, Nodes, and Consumer have different producing, sending, processing, and consuming costs.

This system is scaled according to the number of its Nodes (agents), i.e. the problem parameter n is the number of Nodes. Fig. 2 shows the local states, the possible actions, and the protocol for each agent. Null actions are omitted in the figure. Further, we assume that the following local states $ProdReady$-0, $Node_iReady$-0 and $ConsReady$-0 are initial, respectively, for Producer, Node i, and Consumer.

Given Figure 2, the local evolution functions of WGPP are straightforward to infer. Moreover, in the model we assume the following set of proposition variables: $\mathcal{PV}=\{ProdReady, ProdSend, ConsReady, ConsReceived\}$ with the following interpretation:

- $(M, s) \models ProdReady$ if $l_P(s) = ProdReady$-0

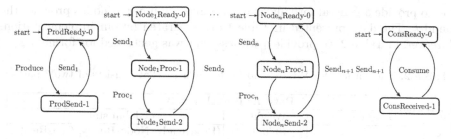

Fig. 2. The WGPP system

- $(M, s) \models ProdSend$ if $l_P(s) = ProdSend\text{-}1$
- $(M, s) \models ConsReady$ if $l_C(s) = ConsReady\text{-}0$
- $(M, s) \models ConsReceived$ if $l_C(s) = ConsReceived\text{-}1$

Let $1 \leqslant i \leqslant n$, and Min denote the minimum cost that is required to receive by Consumer the data produced by Producer. We have tested the WGPP with the following local weight functions: $d_P(Produce) = 4$, $d_P(send_1) = 2$, $d_C(Consume) = 4$, $d_C(send_{n+1}) = 2$, $d_{Ni}(send_i) = d_{Ni}(send_{i+1}) = 2$ and $d_{Ni}(Proc_i) = 2$, and their multiplications by 1,000 and 1,000,000 on the following specifications (universal formulae):

- $\varphi_1 = K_P G_{[Min,Min+1)} ConsReceived$, which expresses that Producer knows that always the cost of receiving by Consumer the commodity is Min.
- $\varphi_2 = K_P G(ProdSend \rightarrow F_{[0,Min-d_P(Produce))} ConsReceived)$, which states that Producer knows that always if she/he produces a commodity, then Consumer receives the commodity and the cost is less than $Min - d_P(Produce)$.
- $\varphi_3 = K_P G(ProdSend \rightarrow K_C K_P F_{[0,Min-d_P(Produce))} ConsReceived)$, which states that Producer knows that always if she/he produces a commodity, then Consumer knows that Producer knows that Consumer has received the commodity and the cost is less than $Min - d_P(Produce)$.
- $\varphi_4 = K_C G(ProdReady \rightarrow X_{[d_P(Produce),d_P(Produce)+1)} ProdSend)$, which expresses that Consumer knows that the cost of producing of a commodity by Producer is $d_P(Produce)$.

Table 1. WGPP with n nodes

Formula	(n, k) - n is the number of nodes, k is the bound	$\widehat{f_k}(\varphi)$
φ_1	(1,3), (2,5), (3,6), (4,6), (5,7), (6,8), (7,8), (8,9), (9,9), (10,10), (15,12), (20,14), (25,16), (30,18), (35,19), (40, 21), (45,22), (50,23)	2
φ_2	(1,3), (2,5), (3,6), (4,6), (5,7), (6,8), (7,8), (8,9), (9,9), (10,10), (11,11),(12,11), (13,12), (14,12), (15,12), (20,14), (25,16), (30,18), (31,18), (32,18), (33,19), (34,19), (35,19)	2
φ_3	(1,3), (2,4), (3,5), (4,6), (5,6), (6,7), (7,8), (8,9), (9,9), (10,10)	4
φ_4	$(n, 4)$ for $n \geq 1$	2

The size of the reachable state space of the WGPP system is $4 \cdot 3^n$, for $n \geq 1$. The length of the counterexamples, and the number of the considered k-paths for the above formulae are shown in Table 1; note that for formulae φ_1-φ_3 we are not able to provide a general formula that for a given number of nodes provides the bound k. The data presented in Table 1 are generated by our implementation. Moreover, in Table 2 we provide a witness that was generated for formula φ_1.

Table 2. The witness for WGPP and for formula φ_1 that consists of two 3-paths

		Path nr 0 with l = 3	
Step	Action	Weights	Global state
0		$\langle 0, 0, 0 \rangle$	$\langle \text{ProdReady, Node}_1\text{Ready, ConsReady} \rangle$
1	$\langle \text{Produce}, \varepsilon_{N1}, \varepsilon_C \rangle$	$\langle 4000, 0, 0 \rangle$	$\langle \text{ProdSend, Node}_1\text{Ready, ConsReady} \rangle$
2	$\langle \text{Send}_1, \text{Send}_1, \varepsilon_C \rangle$	$\langle 2000, 2000, 0 \rangle$	$\langle \text{ProdReady, Node}_1\text{Proc, ConsReady} \rangle$
3	$\langle \varepsilon_P, \text{Proc}_1, \varepsilon_C \rangle$	$\langle 0, 2000, 0 \rangle$	$\langle \text{ProdReady, Node}_1\text{Send, ConsReady} \rangle$
		Path nr 1 with l = 0	
0		$\langle 0, 0, 0 \rangle$	$\langle \text{ProdReady, Node}_1\text{Ready, ConsReady} \rangle$
1	$\langle \text{Produce}, \varepsilon_{N1}, \varepsilon_C \rangle$	$\langle 4000, 0, 0 \rangle$	$\langle \text{ProdSend, Node}_1\text{Ready, ConsReady} \rangle$
2	$\langle \text{Send}_1, \text{Send}_1, \varepsilon_C \rangle$	$\langle 2000, 2000, 0 \rangle$	$\langle \text{ProdReady, Node}_1\text{Proc, ConsReady} \rangle$
3	$\langle \text{Produce}, \text{Proc}_1, \varepsilon_C \rangle$	$\langle 4000, 2000, 0 \rangle$	$\langle \text{ProdSend, Node}_1\text{Send, ConsReady} \rangle$

The Weighted Bits Transmission Problem. We adapted the scenario of *a bit transmission problem* [1], and we called it the *weighted bits transmission problem* (WBTP). The WBTP involves two agents, a sender $\mathcal{S}$, and a receiver $\mathcal{R}$, communicating over a possibly faulty communication channel (the environment), and there are fixed costs c_S and c_R associated with, respectively, sending process of $\mathcal{S}$ and $\mathcal{R}$. $\mathcal{S}$ wants to communicate some information (e.g., the n-bit number) to $\mathcal{R}$. One protocol to achieve this is as follows. $\mathcal{S}$ immediately starts sending the n-bit number to $\mathcal{R}$, and continues to do so until it receives an acknowledgement from $\mathcal{R}$. $\mathcal{R}$ does nothing until it receives the n-bit number; from then on it sends acknowledgements of receipt to $\mathcal{S}$. $\mathcal{S}$ stops sending the n-bit number to $\mathcal{R}$ when it receives an acknowledgement. Note that $\mathcal{R}$ will continue sending acknowledgements even after $\mathcal{S}$ has received its acknowledgement. This system is scaled according to the number of bits the $\mathcal{S}$ wants to communicate to $\mathcal{R}$.

Each agent of the scenario can be modelled by considering its local states, local actions, local protocol, local evolution function, local weight function, and local valuation function. For $\mathcal{S}$, it is enough to consider 2^{n+1} possible local states representing the value of the n-bit number that $\mathcal{S}$ is attempting to transmit, and whether or not $\mathcal{S}$ has received an acknowledgement from $\mathcal{R}$. Thus, we have: $L_S = \{0, \ldots, 2^n - 1, 0\text{-}ack, \ldots, 2^n - 1\text{-}ack\}$. Further, $\iota_S = \{0, \ldots, 2^n - 1\}$. For $\mathcal{R}$, it is enough to consider $2^n + 1$ possible local states representing: the value of the received n-bit number, if any, and the circumstance in which no number has been received yet (represented by ϵ). Thus, we have $L_R = \{0, \ldots, 2^n - 1, \epsilon\}$, and $\iota_R = \{\epsilon\}$. For the environment $\mathcal{E}$, to simplify the presentation, we shall to consider just one local state: $L_{\mathcal{E}} = \{\cdot\} = \iota_{\mathcal{E}}$. Now we can define the set of possible global states S for the scenario as the product $L_S \times L_R \times L_{\mathcal{E}}$, and we consider the following set of initial states $\iota = \{(0, \epsilon, \cdot), \ldots, (2^n - 1, \epsilon, \cdot)\}$.

The set of actions available to the agents are as follows: $Act_S = \{sendbits, \lambda\}$, $Act_R = \{sendack, \lambda\}$, where λ stands for no action. The actions for $\mathcal{E}$ correspond to the transmission of messages between $\mathcal{S}$ and $\mathcal{R}$ on the unreliable communication channel. The set of actions for $\mathcal{E}$ is $Act_{\mathcal{E}} = \{\leftrightarrow, \rightarrow, \leftarrow, -\}$, where $\leftrightarrow$ represents the action in which the channel transmits any message successfully in both directions, $\rightarrow$ that it transmits successfully from $\mathcal{S}$ to $\mathcal{R}$ but loses any message from $\mathcal{R}$ to $\mathcal{S}$, $\leftarrow$ that it transmits successfully from $\mathcal{R}$ to $\mathcal{S}$ but loses any message from $\mathcal{S}$ to $\mathcal{R}$, and $-$ that it loses any messages sent in either direction. The set $Act = Act_{\mathcal{S}} \times Act_{\mathcal{R}} \times Act_{\mathcal{E}}$ defines the set of joint actions for the scenario.

The local weight functions of agents are defined as follows: $d_{\mathcal{S}}(sendbits) = a$ with $a \in \mathbb{N}$, $d_{\mathcal{S}}(\lambda) = 0$, $d_{\mathcal{R}}(sendack) = b$ with $b \in \mathbb{N}$, $d_{\mathcal{R}}(\lambda) = 0$, and $d_{\mathcal{E}}(\leftrightarrow) = d_{\mathcal{E}}(\rightarrow) = d_{\mathcal{E}}(\leftarrow) = d_{\mathcal{E}}(-) = 0$. We assume zero-weight for the actions of $\mathcal{E}$, since we wish to only count the cost of sending and receiving messages.

The local protocols of the agents are the following: $P_{\mathcal{S}}(0) = \ldots = P_{\mathcal{S}}(2^n - 1) = \{sendbits\}$, $P_{\mathcal{S}}(0\text{-}ack) = \ldots = P_{\mathcal{S}}(2^n - 1\text{-}ack) = \{\lambda\}$, $P_{\mathcal{R}}(0) = \ldots = P_{\mathcal{R}}(2^n - 1) = \{sendack\}$, $P_{\mathcal{R}}(\epsilon) = \{\lambda\}$, $P_{\mathcal{E}}(\cdot) = Act_{\mathcal{E}} = \{\leftrightarrow, \rightarrow, \leftarrow, -\}$.

It should be straightforward to infer the model that is induced by the informal description of the scenario we considered above together with the local states, actions, protocols, and weight functions defined above.

In the model we assume the following set of proposition variables: $\mathcal{PV} = \{0, \ldots, 2^n - 1, \mathbf{recack}\}$ with the following interpretation:

$(M, s) \models \mathbf{i}$ if $l_{\mathcal{S}}(s) = i$ or $l_{\mathcal{S}}(s) = i\text{-}ack$, for $i = 0, \ldots, 2^n - 1$

$(M, s) \models \mathbf{recack}$ if $l_{\mathcal{S}}(s) = 0\text{-}ack$ or $\ldots$ or $l_{\mathcal{S}}(s) = 2^n - 1\text{-}ack$.

We have tested the WBTP on the following specifications (universal formulae):

- $\varphi_1 = G_{[a+b, a+b+1]}(\mathbf{recack} \rightarrow K_{\mathcal{S}}(K_{\mathcal{R}}(\bigvee_{i=0}^{2^n-2} \mathbf{i})))$ - the property says that if an ack is received by $\mathcal{S}$, then $\mathcal{S}$ knows that $\mathcal{R}$ knows at least one value of the n-bit numbers except the maximal value, and the cost is $a + b$.
- $\varphi_2 = G_{[a+b, a+b+1]}(K_{\mathcal{S}}(\bigvee_{i=0}^{2^n-1}(K_{\mathcal{R}}(\mathbf{i})))$ - the property says that $\mathcal{S}$ knows that $\mathcal{R}$ knows the value of the n-bit number and the cost is $a + b$.

The size of the reachable state space of the WBTP system is $3 \cdot 2^n$ for $n \geq 1$. The number of the considered k-paths is the following: $\widehat{f}_k(\varphi_1) = 3$ and $\widehat{f}_k(\varphi_2) = 2^n + 2$. The length of the counterexamples for both formulae is equal to 2 for any $n > 0$.

4.1 Performance Evaluation

Table 3. The computation time and memory consumption

Formula	WGPP with 1 node						WBTP with 1 bit					
	Time (sec.)			Memory (MB)			Time (sec.)			Memory (MB)		
	x1	x10³	x10⁶	x1	x10³	x10⁶	x1	x10³	x10⁶	x1	x10³	x10⁶
φ_1	0.04	0.13	0.19	1.90	2.67	3.70	0.02	0.03	0.06	1.12	1.38	1.64
φ_2	0.04	0.11	0.16	1.90	2.82	3.78	0.03	0.05	0.10	1.12	1.66	1.92
φ_3	0.41	0.71	1.00	5.87	7.22	8.58	-	-	-	-	-	-
φ_4	0.09	0.22	0.34	1.91	3.18	4.25	-	-	-	-	-	-

The experimental results show that our SAT-based BMC method is slightly sensitive to scaling up the weights (see Fig. 3 and Fig. 4). To be more precise, we observed that when we scale up the weights for both benchmarks and for all properties, the computation time and the memory usage grows linearly, regardless of the considered number of nodes or n-bit integer value. For example, we refer the reader to Table 3 for the detailed results we have for WGPP/WBTP with one node/bit and with the basic weights and their multiplication by 10^3 or 10^6. The sensitivity to growing weights follows from the encoding of the cumulative weight. Namely, the number of bits that is required to encode the cumulative weights depends on the number of agents, on the length of the counterexample (i.e. the bound k) and the maximal weight that appear in the whole system.

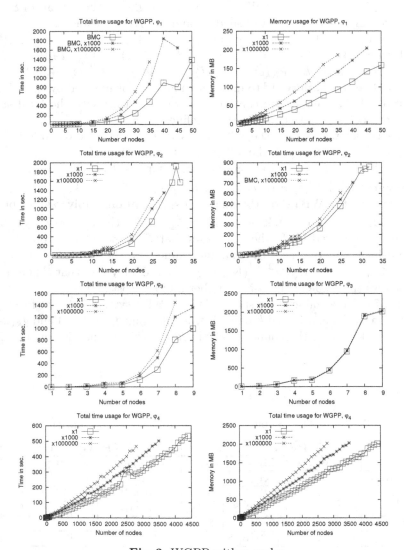

Fig. 3. WGPP with n nodes

As one can see from the line charts in Fig. 3 for WGPP with the basic weights, in the time limit set our method is able to verify the formulae φ_1 - φ_4, respectively, for 50, 32, 9, and 4400 nodes. The high efficiency of our method in the case of the formula φ_4 results from the constant length of the counterexample. In all the other cases we can observe that our method is sensitive to scaling up the size of benchmarks. This is because the length of the counterexamples grows with the number of the components, and the efficiency of the SAT-based BMC strongly depends on the length of the counterexamples. Further, in the case of the formula φ_3 we get results for 9 nodes only. This follows from the fact that apart from the growing length of the counterexample we need to consider as many as four k-paths.

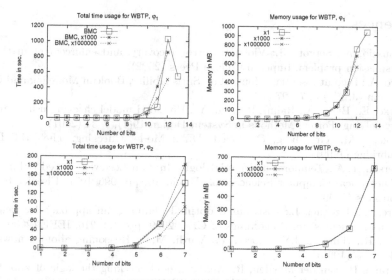

Fig. 4. WBTP with n bits integer value

As one can see from the line charts in Fig. 4 for WBTP with the basic weights (i.e. $a = 1$, $b = 2$), in the time limit set our method is able to verify the formulae φ_1 and φ_2, respectively, for 13 and 7 bits integer value. The inferiority of our method in the case of this benchmark results from the fact that our method has do deal with the model which has the exponential number of initial states. Observe that this is not the case in the WGPP benchmark.

5   Conclusions

We have defined and implemented the SAT-based BMC method for WELTLK and for WISs. The experimental results show that our method is slightly sensitive to scaling up the weights. Concerning the sensitivity of our SAT-based BMC encoding to growing size of the checked system, we can observe that it is rather standard, i.e. the method is not so efficient if many symbolic k-paths are encoded, and the length of the counterexample grows with the number of agents.

The BMC for WELTLK and for WISs may also be performed by means of Ordered Binary Diagrams (OBDD) and Satisfiability Modulo Theories (SMT). This will be explored in the future. Moreover, our future work includes a comparison of the OBDD- SMT- and SAT-based BMC method for WISs. Further, we would like to point out that the proposed BMC method can be used for solving some planing problems that can be formulated in terms of weighted automata. Namely, we can formalize the notion of the agent as a weighted automaton, and then apply our BMC technique for WIS that are generated by a given network of weighted automata. A planning problem defined in terms of weighted automata was considered, e.g. in [6].

References

1. Lomuscio, A., Sergot, M.: Violation, error recovery, and enforcement in the bit transmission problem. Imperial College Press (2002)
2. Biere, A.: Picosat essentials. Journal on Satisfiability, Boolean Modeling and Computation (JSAT) 4, 75–97 (2008)
3. Clarke, E., Biere, A., Raimi, R., Zhu, Y.: Bounded model checking using satisfiability solving. Formal Methods in System Design 19(1), 7–34 (2001)
4. Clarke, E.M., Grumberg, O., Peled, D.A.: Model Checking. The MIT Press, Cambridge (1999)
5. Emerson, E.A.: Temporal and modal logic. In: van Leeuwen, J. (ed.) Handbook of Theoretical Computer Science, vol. B, ch. 16, pp. 996–1071. Elsevier Science Publishers (1990)
6. Fabre, E., Jezequel, L.: Distributed optimal planning: an approach by weighted automata calculus. In: Proceedings of CDC 2009, pp. 211–216. IEEE (2009)
7. Fagin, R., Halpern, J.Y., Moses, Y., Vardi, M.Y.: Reasoning about Knowledge. MIT Press (1995)
8. Gammie, P., van der Meyden, R.: MCK: Model checking the logic of knowledge. In: Alur, R., Peled, D.A. (eds.) CAV 2004. LNCS, vol. 3114, pp. 479–483. Springer, Heidelberg (2004)
9. Kacprzak, M., Nabialek, W., Niewiadomski, A., Penczek, W., Półrola, A., Szreter, M., Woźna, B., Zbrzezny, A.: VerICS 2007 - a model checker for knowledge and real-time. Fundamenta Informaticae 85(1-4), 313–328 (2008)
10. Levesque, H.: A logic of implicit and explicit belief. In: Proceedings of the 6th National Conference of the AAAI, pp. 198–202. Morgan Kaufman (1984)
11. Lomuscio, A., Qu, H., Raimondi, F.: MCMAS: A model checker for the verification of multi-agent systems. In: Bouajjani, A., Maler, O. (eds.) CAV 2009. LNCS, vol. 5643, pp. 682–688. Springer, Heidelberg (2009)
12. Lomuscio, A., Sergot, M.: Deontic interpreted systems. Studia Logica 75(1), 63–92 (2003)
13. Peled, D.: All from one, one for all: On model checking using representatives. In: Courcoubetis, C. (ed.) CAV 1993. LNCS, vol. 697, pp. 409–423. Springer, Heidelberg (1993)
14. Penczek, W., Lomuscio, A.: Verifying epistemic properties of multi-agent systems via bounded model checking. Fundamenta Informaticae 55(2), 167–185 (2003)
15. Penczek, W., Woźna-Szcześniak, B., Zbrzezny, A.: Towards SAT-based BMC for LTLK over Interleaved Interpreted Systems. Fundamenta Informaticae 119(3-4), 373–392 (2012)

16. Wooldridge, M.: An introduction to multi-agent systems. John Wiley (2002)
17. Woźna-Szcześniak, B.: SAT-based bounded model checking for weighted deontic interpreted systems. In: Correia, L., Reis, L.P., Cascalho, J. (eds.) EPIA 2013. LNCS, vol. 8154, pp. 444–455. Springer, Heidelberg (2013)
18. Zbrzezny, A.: A new translation from ECTL* to SAT. Fundamenta Informaticae 120(3-4), 377–397 (2012)

Emotional Multiagent Reinforcement Learning in Social Dilemmas

Chao Yu, Minjie Zhang, and Fenghui Ren

School of Computer Science and Software Engineering
University of Wollongong, Wollongong, 2522, NSW, Australia
cy496@uowmail.edu.au, {minjie,fren}@uow.edu.au

Abstract. Social dilemmas have attracted extensive interest in multiagent system research in order to study the emergence of cooperative behaviors among selfish agents. Without extra mechanisms or assumptions, directly applying multiagent reinforcement learning in social dilemmas will end up with convergence to the Nash equilibrium of mutual defection among the agents. This paper investigates the importance of emotions in modifying agent learning behaviors in order to achieve cooperation in social dilemmas. Two fundamental variables, individual wellbeing and social fairness, are considered in the appraisal of emotions that are used as intrinsic rewards for learning. Experimental results reveal that different structural relationships between the two appraisal variables can lead to distinct agent behaviors, and under certain circumstances, cooperation can be obtained among the agents.

1 Introduction

Cooperation is ubiquitous in the real world and can be observed at different scales of organizations ranging from microorganisms and animal groups to human societies [1]. Solving the puzzle of how cooperation emerges among self-interested entities is a challenging issue that has motivated scientists from various disciplines including economics, psychology, sociology and computer science for decades. The emergence of cooperation is often studied in the context of social dilemmas, in which selfish individuals must decide between a socially reciprocal behavior of cooperation to benefit the whole group over time and a self-interested behavior of defection to pursue their own short-term benefits. Social dilemmas often arise in many situations in Multi-Agent Systems (MASs), e.g., file sharing in peer-to-peer (p2p) systems and load balancing/packet routing in wireless sensor networks [2]. For this reason, mechanisms that promote the emergence of cooperation in social dilemmas are of great interest to researchers in MASs.

Although various mechanisms, such as kin selection, reciprocal altruism and spatial selection [3], have been proposed to explain the emergence of cooperation in recent years, most of these mechanisms are based on Evolutionary Game Theory (EGT) [4], with a focus either on the macro-level population dynamics using replicator functions or on the agent-level strategy dynamics based on predefined imitation rules. Real animals and humans, however, do not simply replicate or

G. Boella et al. (Eds.): PRIMA 2013, LNAI 8291, pp. 372–387, 2013.

mimic others, but can learn efficient strategies from past interaction experience. In fact, this experience-based learning capability is important in building intelligent agents that can align human behavior, particularly when designers cannot anticipate all situations that the agents might encounter.

A major family of experience-based learning is Reinforcement Learning(RL) [5], which enables an agent to learn an optimal strategy through trial-and-error interactions with an environment. When multiple agents conduct their learning at the same time, which is called Multi-Agent Reinforcement Learning (MARL) [6], each agent faces a non-stationary learning environment and therefore each agent's individually optimal strategy does not necessarily guarantee a globally optimal performance for the whole system. In the setting of social dilemmas, directly applying distributed MARL approaches will end up with convergence to the Nash equilibrium of mutual defection among the agents if no additional mechanisms are implemented. The convergence to the Nash equilibrium occurs because both agents adopt the best-response actions during learning. As a result, neither agent can achieve a dominant position by choosing defection to exploit its opponent because the opponent will eliminate such dominance by also choosing defection, resulting in an outcome of mutual defection between the agents.

The rational behavior that ends up with mutual defection contradicts our daily observations of altruistic cooperative behaviors among humans. In fact, psychology and behavioral economics have provided convincing evidence that humans are not purely rational and self-interested, but generally express considerations for others and make decisions with bounded rationality [7,8]. Recent research in artificial intelligence and cognitive science has shown that emotions can be an important heuristic to assist humans' bounded rationality for effective decision-making [9]. Emotions play a fundamental role in learning by eliciting physiological signals that bias our behaviors toward maximizing reward and minimizing punishment. Therefore, MARL mechanisms, in essence, should rely on some emotional cues to indicate the advantage or disadvantage of an event.

In this paper, we investigate the importance of emotions in modifying agent rationality in MARL in order to achieve cooperation in social dilemmas. We focus on spatial versions of social dilemmas by considering topological structures among agents to study the impact of local interactions on the emergence of cooperation. An emotional MARL framework is proposed to endow agents with internal cognitive and emotional capabilities that can drive these agents to learn reciprocal behaviors in social dilemmas. Two fundamental variables, individual wellbeing and social fairness, are considered in the appraisal of emotions. Different structural relationships between these appraisal variables can derive various intrinsic emotional rewards for agent learning. Experimental results reveal that different ways of appraising emotions and various structural relationships between emotional appraisal variables can lead to distinct agent behaviors, and under certain circumstances, cooperation can be obtained among the agents.

Although emotion-based concepts and mechanisms have been widely applied in agent learning [10,11,12], most of these studies focus primarily on exploiting emotions to facilitate learning efficiency or to adapt a single agent to dynamic and complex environments. The other line of research [13,14] has examined the evolution of cooperation in social dilemmas by implementing an emotion mechanism based on rule-based emotional frameworks (i.e., not from learning perspective). Our work, therefore, bridges these two directions of research by incorporating emotions into agent learning to study the evolution of cooperation in social dilemmas. We claim this effort to be the main contribution of this paper.

The remainder of this paper is organized as follows. Section 2 describes social dilemmas. Section 3 introduces the emotional MARL framework. Section 4 gives the experimental studies. Section 5 lays out some related work. Finally, Section 6 concludes this paper with some directions for future research.

2   Social Dilemmas

This paper uses the well-known Prisoners' Dilemma (PD) game as a metaphor to study social dilemmas among self-interested agents. In PD, each player has two actions: 'cooperate' (C), which is a socially reciprocal behavior and 'defect' (D), which is a self-interested behavior. Consider the typical pay-off matrix of the PD game in Table 1. The rational action for both agents is to select D because choosing D ensures a higher pay-off for either agent no matter what the opponent does. In other words, mutual defection (DD) is the unique Nash equilibrium and both agents have no incentive to deviate from this equilibrium. As can be seen from Table 1, however, DD is not the Pareto optimal because each agent would be better off (i.e., $R > P$) and both agents together would receive a higher social reward (i.e., $2R > T + S$) if both agents select C. Therefore, when played repeatedly, which is called the Iterated Prisoner's Dilemma (IPD), it may be beneficial for an agent to cooperate in some rounds, even if this agent is selfish, in the hope of a reciprocal cooperative behavior to bring benefits in the long run. IPD has been widely used for studying the emergence of cooperation among selfish individuals in a variety of disciplines including artificial intelligence, economics and social sciences, etc. [15].

Table 1. Payoff matrix of the PD game (payoff of the row player is shown first)

	Cooperate (C)	Defect (D)
Cooperate (C)	R(= 3),R(= 3)	S(= 0),T(=5)
Defect (D)	T(=5),S(= 0)	P(= 1),P(= 1)

This paper uses spatial IPD by considering the topological structure among the agents to study the impact of local interactions on the emergence of cooperation. Three types of networks are used to represent a spatial IPD. They are (1) Grid networks GR_N, where N is the number of nodes, (2) Small-world networks $SW_N^{k,\rho}$, where k is the average size of the neighborhood of a node and ρ is the re-wiring probability to indicate the different orders of the randomness of the network, and (3) Scale-free networks $SF_N^{k,\gamma}$, where γ is an exponent indicating that the probability of an node having k neighbors is roughly proportional to $k^{-\gamma}$. A more detailed explanation of these networks is given by [16].

3   Emotional MARL in Social Dilemmas

This section introduces the emotional MARL framework and its implementation in social dilemmas based on previous appraisal theories of emotions.

3.1   Emotional MARL Framework

In recent years, researchers in artificial intelligence, cognition and psychology have shown increasing interest in defining the source and nature of rewards in RL [17]. It has been pointed out that the standard view of defining rewards in RL simply as an output of a "critic" from the external environment (Fig. 1(a)) is seriously misleading and thus not suitable as a reflection of real-life human and animal reward systems [18]. The environment of an RL agent should not simply be identified with the external environment where the agent is physically located, but should also include the agent's internal environment constituted by multiple intrinsic emotion circuits and drives. A novel framework called Intrinsically Motivated Reinforcement Learning (IMRL) [18] has been proposed to implement intrinsic motivation systems in learning agents by clarifying the rewards into "extrinsic rewards" that define a specific task related to an agent's external goal or cost, and "intrinsic rewards" related to an agent's internal emotion circuits and drives. The IMRL framework provides a computationally sound approach to better reflect the reward systems in real human and animals, and thus enables a learning agent to achieve more adaptive behaviors by overcoming its perceptual limitations. Most work on the IMRL framework, however, focused mainly on single-agent scenarios, in which the motivational system is used to drive a single agent to learn adaptive behaviors in complex environments. In addition, most previous work lacks an explicit description of how to derive the intrinsic rewards for learning, especially by using an emotion system.

To this end, we propose an emotional MARL framework in Fig. 1 (b), which extends the IMRL framework by implementing an emotion-driven intrinsic reward system based on the computational component appraisal models of emotions [19]. The framework consists of two parts: an agent and its external environment. The agent takes an action on the external environment and receives sensations and extrinsic rewards from the environment. An internal environment, including an emotion appraisal derivation model and an emotion derivation model, exists inside an agent to generate the emotions, which are then used in an emotion consequent model for adapting learning behaviors.

The emotion appraisal derivation model transforms an agent's belief about its relationship with the environment into a set of quantified appraisal variables. The appraisal variables correspond to a set of judgments that the agent can use to produce different emotional responses. Two variables are used to appraise

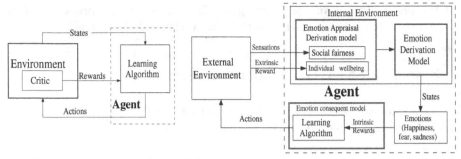

(a) The standard view [5]   (b) The proposed framework (adapted from [18,19]).

Fig. 1. The standard RL framework and the proposed emotional MARL framework

emotions by considering not only the agent's individual wellbeing, which is derived through extrinsic rewards from the environment, but also its sense of social fairness, which is derived from the agent's sensations of its neighbors' decisions.

The emotion derivation model maps the appraisal variables to an emotional state, and specifies how an agent reacts emotionally once a pattern of appraisals has been determined. By combining the variables using different emotion derivation functions, different agent personalities can be defined. For example, if the function is defined in such a way that social fairness is the core factor to determine an agent's final emotional state, the agent can then be considered as a socially aware agent. On the contrary, the agent is more like an egoist who cares about its own wellbeing more than the social fairness.

The emotion consequent model maps emotions into some behavioral or cognitive changes. In the framework, the consequent emotions generated in the internal environment are simply used as intrinsic rewards for agent learning. The learning model consists of general RL approaches [5] that can be directly used to update learning information using the emotional intrinsic rewards. In this research, the widely used Q-learning algorithm is used as the basic RL approach.

Many studies [10,11,12] claimed that RL mechanisms in nature should rely on emotional cues rather than on direct exogenous stimuli from the environment to indicate the advantage or disadvantage of an event. The proposed framework takes this position by differentiating an agent's external and internal environment, and defining a new reward system that endows agents with internal emotional capabilities to drive them towards more complex and adaptive behaviors. The following subsections show in detail how to implement the proposed framework in spatial IPD so that agents can learn to achieve cooperative behaviors.

3.2   Appraisal of Emotions

One way of explaining how emotions are generated according to one's relationship with the environment is by developing appraisal theories of emotions [20]. The appraisal on the elicitation and differentiation of emotions is based on an agent's individual evaluation of the significance of events and situations for itself along a set of judgments. These judgments, formally referred to appraisal variables, are used to produce different emotional responses by the agents. As Ellsworth and Scherer [20] pointed out, emotions can generally be considered to be composed of interacting elementary variables from two main dimensions: the basic/motivational dimension dealing with individual goals, needs and pleasantness, and the social dimension dealing with social norms, justice and fairness. Two fundamental appraisal variables, social fairness and individual wellbeing, therefore, are adopted in the appraisal of emotions in this research.

Appraisal of Social Fairness. Research in the field of behavioral economics has shown that humans are not purely self-interested, but care strongly about fairness [21]. Humans generally show a remarkable ability to solve social dilemmas due to their tendency to consider fairness to other people. In order to evaluate the social fairness, an agent needs to assess its own situation in its neighborhood context. We define a focal agent's neighborhood context C as:

$$C = \frac{1}{N} \sum_{i=1}^{i=N} \left(\frac{n_c^i - n_d^i}{M} \right), \tag{1}$$

where n_c^i and n_d^i are the counts of C actions and D actions adopted by neighbor i in M steps[1], respectively, and N is the number of neighbors of the focal agent.

An agent's neighborhood context $C \in [-1, 1]$ indicates the extent of cooperativeness of the environment, with $C = 1$ indicating a fully cooperative environment, $C = -1$ indicating a fully defective environment, and $C = 0$ indicating a neutral environment. An agent's sense of fairness is then to evaluate its own situation in such a neighborhood context, which can be given by:

$$F = C \times \frac{n_c - n_d}{M}, \tag{2}$$

where $F \in [-1, 1]$ represents the agent's sense of social fairness, n_c is the count of C actions and n_d is the count of D actions adopted by the agent in M steps.

From Equ. 2, we can see that when the environment is cooperative ($C > 0$), the agent senses fair if it cooperates more often ($n_c > n_d$) and unfair if it defects more often ($n_c < n_d$). Similar analysis applies when the environment is uncooperative ($C < 0$).

Appraisal of Individual Wellbeing. Agents also need to care about their own individual wellbeing in terms of maximizing utilities and achieving goals. Three different approaches are used to appraise an agent's individual wellbeing.

- **Absolute value-based approach**: A straightforward way to appraise an agent's individual wellbeing is to use the agent's absolute wealth as an evaluation criteria, which can be given by Equ. 3.

---

[1] In this research, a learning episode consists of several interaction steps, which means that the learning information will be updated only at the end of M interaction steps.

$$W = \frac{R_t}{M \times (T - S)}, \tag{3}$$

where R_t is the accumulated reward collected during M interaction steps at learning episode t, and $T - S$ is the difference between temptation and sucker's reward (refer to Table 1) to confine W to the range of $[-1, 1]$.

- **Variance-based approach**: It is argued, however, that low wealth does not necessarily imply a negative reaction and high wealth does not imply a positive reaction to the agents [11]. In fact, this phenomenon can be observed in the real world where rich people are not necessarily happier than poor people, but an increase in wealth can often cause a positive reaction. Therefore, we define the individual wellbeing as the positive and negative variations of an agent's absolute wealth, which can be given by Equ. 4.

$$W = \frac{R_{t+1} - R_t}{M \times (T - S)}, \tag{4}$$

where R_t and R_{t+1} are the accumulated reward collected at learning episode t and the following episode $t + 1$, respectively.

- **Aspiration-based approach**: In reality, people will be satisfied if their intrinsic aspirations can be realized [8]. The aspiration-based approach thus appraises the agent's individual wellbeing by comparing the reward achieved with an adaptive aspiration level, which is given by Equ. 5.

$$W = \tanh[h(\frac{R_t}{M} - A_t)], \tag{5}$$

where $\tanh(x) = \frac{e^x - e^{-x}}{e^x + e^{-x}}$ is the hyperbolic tangent function, $h > 0$ is a scalable parameter, and A_t is the aspiration level, which can be updated by:

$$A_{t+1} = (1 - \beta)A_t + \beta \frac{R_t}{M}, \tag{6}$$

where $\beta \in [0, 1]$ is a learning rate and $A_0 = (R + T + S + P)/4$.

3.3   Derivation of Emotions

This research aims to study the effects of various structural relationships between social fairness and individual wellbeing on the derivation of emotions, and how such emotional reactions affect agent learning behaviors in social dilemmas. To this end, we first differentiate the roles of the two appraisal variables in determining the final emotional states. Simith et al. [22] proposed a structural model of emotion appraisal to explain the relation between appraisals and the emotions they elicit. The appraisal process is broken up into two different categories, primary appraisal and secondary appraisal, with primary appraisal concerning whether and how the encounter is relevant to the person's motivational goals and secondary appraisal concerning the person's resources and options for coping with the encounter [22]. The structural model of appraisal allows researchers to formulate which emotions will be elicited from a certain set of circumstances by examining an individual's appraisal of a situation, and therefore allows researchers to define different appraisal processes that lead to different emotions.

Based on the differentiation of the emotion appraisal process, we define an appraisal variable to be a core appraisal variable (denoted as c) or a secondary appraisal variable (denoted as s). The core appraisal variable determines the desirability of an emotion through the agent's evaluation of its situation, while the secondary appraisal variable indicates the intensity of such an emotion based on the agent's evaluation of its coping ability. An emotion derivation function of emotion x, $F_x(c, s)$, therefore, can be formally defined as follows:

Definition 1. *Let c, s be the core and secondary appraisal variable, respectively, $0 \leq D_x \leq 1$ be the desirability of emotion x, and $-1 \leq I_x \leq 1$ be the intensity of emotion x, an* **emotion derivation function** *can be defined as $F_x(c, s) := E_x(c, s) = f(D_x) \cdot g(I_x)$, where $0 \leq E_x(c, s) \leq 1$ is the overall state of emotion x, $0 \leq f(D_x) \leq 1$ is the core derivation function that increases monotonically with the desirability of emotion $x (D_x)$, and $0 \leq g(I_x) \leq 1$ is the secondary derivation function that increases monotonically with the intensity of emotion x (I_x).*

In reality, people react to things differently. Even when presented with the same or a similar situation, people will react in slightly different ways based on their appraisals of the situation. These appraisals elicit various emotions that are specific to each person. Based on Definition 1, two different kinds of emotion derivation functions can be defined as follows:

- **Fairness-Wellbeing (FW) Emotion Derivation Function**: An agent that derives its emotions using the FW function puts social fairness F as the core appraisal variable ($c \leftarrow F$) and then derives its emotions based on its sense of its own wellbeing W ($s \leftarrow W$). More formally:

$$((F \geq 0 \Rightarrow D_{joy} = F) \wedge I_{joy} = W) \Rightarrow E_{joy}(F, W) = f(F) \cdot g(W); \quad (7)$$

$$((F < 0 \Rightarrow D_{fear} = -F) \wedge I_{fear} = W) \Rightarrow E_{fear}(F, W) = f(-F) \cdot g(W); \quad (8)$$

$$((F < 0 \Rightarrow D_{anger} = -F) \wedge I_{anger} = -W) \Rightarrow E_{anger}(F, W) = f(-F) \cdot g(-W); \quad (9)$$

An agent using the FW function to derive its emotions is a socially aware agent that pays more attention to social fairness than to individual wellbeing in appraising its emotions. As the first priority of an FW agent is to pursue social fairness, when the agent senses that the environment is fair ($F > 0$, Equ. 7), the agent will be in a positive emotional state of *joy* because the situation is consistent with the agent's motivational goal. The fairer the environment, the higher the desirability of emotion *joy*. Desirability D_{joy} is then equivalent to the core derivation variable of F. The intensity of emotion *joy* is then based on the increase or decrease in the agent's sense of its own wellbeing. An increase in the individual wellbeing in a fair environment indicates an easy coping situation. The socially aware agent, therefore, is in a positive emotional state because the agent can achieve selfish interest while at the same time pursue its core motivational goal of social fairness. The final state of the emotion of *joy*, then, can be calculated as $f(F) \cdot g(W)$. On the contrary, when an FW agent senses that the environment is unfair ($F < 0$), the agent will feel negative because the situation is inconsistent with the agent's goal of pursuing social fairness. The unfair environment can be caused by two reasons: the agent defects more often in a cooperative environment (Equ. 8) and the agent cooperates more often in a defective environment (Equ. 9). The socially aware agent will feel *fear* in the former case because it is exploiting its neighbors by choosing defection, while in the latter case, the agent will be in *anger* because it is being exploited by its neighbors. In both cases, desirability of the negative emotion is equivalent to the core derivation variable of $-F$. The secondary appraisal of emotion *fear* considers one's expectations of change in the motivational congruence of a situation [22]. If the agent is in *fear*, the intensity of emotion *fear* then increases monotonously with the wellbeing state of the agent ($I_{fear} = W$), because the socially aware agent realizes that it is exploiting its neighbors for an increase in its own wellbeing. The higher the wellbeing, the higher intensity of emotion *fear* of the agent. The final state of emotion *fear* can be then calculated as $f(-F) \cdot g(W)$. In contrast, if the agent is in *anger*, the intensity of emotion *anger* then increases inversely with the wellbeing state of the agent ($I_{anger} = -W$), because a lower wellbeing will result in a higher intensity of emotion *anger*. The final state of the emotion of *anger* can then be calculated as $f(-F) \cdot g(-W)$.

– **Wellbeing-Fairness (WF) Emotion Derivation Function**: In contrast to the FW function, an agent that derives its emotions using the WF function puts its own wellbeing W as the core derivation variable ($c \leftarrow W$) and then derives its emotions based on the social fairness F ($s \leftarrow F$). More formally:

$$((W \geq 0 \Rightarrow D_{joy} = W) \wedge I_{joy} = F) \Rightarrow E_{joy}(W, F) = f(W) \cdot g(F); \quad (10)$$

$$((W < 0 \Rightarrow D_{sadness} = -W) \wedge I_{sadness} = F) \Rightarrow E_{sadness}(W, F) = f(-W) \cdot g(F); \quad (11)$$

An agent using the WF function is more like an egoist that pays more attention to its own wellbeing than to social fairness to determine its emotions. Equ. 10 formulates how to generate the emotion of *joy*. As the first priority of a selfish WF agent is to pursue its own benefits, when the agent senses that its wellbeing is high ($W > 0$), the agent will be in a positive state of *joy* because the situation is consistent with the agent's motivational goal. The desirability of emotion *joy*, D_{joy}, is then equivalent to the value of core derivation variable W. The intensity of emotion *joy* is then based on the agent's sense of social fairness. A high social fairness (associated with a high individual wellbeing) indicates that the selfish agent is in a positive emotional state because the agent can achieve fairness while at the same time pursue its core motivational goal of staying in high wellbeing. The final state of the emotion of *joy*, therefore, can be calculated as $f(W) \cdot g(F)$.

On the contrary, when a WF agent senses that its wellbeing is low ($W < 0$, Equ. 11), the agent will be in *sadness* because the situation is inconsistent with the agent's goal of pursuing individual benefits. The desirability of the emotion of *sadness*, $D_{sadness}$, is then equivalent to the value of $-W$. The intensity of emotion *sadness* is then based on the increase or decrease in the agent's sense of social fairness. A low wellbeing in a fair environment indicates a difficult coping situation for a selfish WF agent. The final state of the emotion of *sadness* can be calculated as $f(-W) \cdot g(F)$.

Agents interact concurrently and simultaneously with all of their neighbors. Each agent keeps a Q-value table $Q_i(s_i, a_i)$, in which s_i and a_i are the local state and individual action of agent i, respectively. We use the stateless version of Q-learning that does not consider the transitions between states of agents. At each learning episode, agent i chooses action a_i (cooperation or defection) based on its Q-values and plays its action with each of its neighbors. Each pairwise interaction results in a reward for the agent. Agent i can observe its neighbors' actions to appraise the social fairness and rely on its average reward to appraise its sense of wellbeing. The agent then updates its Q-values using the intrinsic reward R_{int}, which is derived from the valenced emotions as follows:

$$R_{int} = \begin{cases} E_x(e,t) & \text{if emotion } x \text{ is positve,} \\ -E_x(e,t) & \text{if emotion } x \text{ is negative.} \end{cases} \tag{12}$$

where emotion is positive if it is *joy* and negative if it is *fear*, *anger* or *sadness*.

4 Experiments

We use the typical values of payoffs in Table 1 to represent a social dilemma game. The Watts-Strogatz model [23] is used to generate a small-world network, and the Barabasi-Albert model [16] is used to generate a scale-free network. To use the Barabasi-Albert model, we start with 5 agents and add a new agent with 1 edge to the network at every time step. This network evolves into a scale-free network following a power law with an exponent $\gamma = 3$. Learning rate α is 0.5 and discount factor γ is 0. Exploration rate ε is 0.1 in the ε-greedy exploration strategy. Scalable parameter h in the aspiration-based approach is 10 and learning rate β to update aspiration level is 0.5. We choose linear functions $f(D_x) = D_x$ and $g(I_x) = (1 + I_x)/2$ to map the value of D_x and I_x to $[0,1]$. All results are averaged over 100 independent runs.

Fig. 2 shows the learning dynamics in network GR_{100} using the variance-based approach to appraise the individual wellbeing. Fig. 2(a) shows the learning dynamics of average population reward using different emotion derivation functions. In the figure, R Agents (*Rational Agents*) represent those agents using the learning approach based on the traditional MARL framework, F Agents and W Agents represent agents using the social fairness and individual wellbeing to be

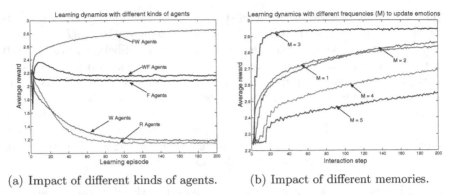

(a) Impact of different kinds of agents.   (b) Impact of different memories.

Fig. 2. Learning dynamics in the proposed emotional MARL framework

the emotional intrinsic rewards, respectively. From the results, we can see that different kinds of agents can learn distinct behaviors. As expected, R Agents end up with mutual defection among them, causing a final average reward around $P = 1$. W Agents learn a similar behavior as R agents. Both the F Agents and WF agents can learn to achieve a certain level of cooperation among them, which is still much lower than that of FW Agents. These results confirm that both social fairness and individual wellbeing are fundamental factors in the appraisal of emotions, but to guarantee a high level of cooperation, social fairness must be considered to be the core appraisal variable. The results provide an explanation of real-life phenomenons when people are social beings and often care about social fairness more than their own interests in order to achieve mutually beneficial outcomes [21]. For example, in the Ultimatum Game, people usually refuse an unfair offer, even this decision will cause them to receive nothing, and in the Public Goods Game, people are usually willing to punish free riders, even though this punishment imposes a cost on themselves.

Fig. 2(b) gives the learning dynamics when FW agents use different frequencies to update emotions. We can see that the frequency of updating intrinsic emotional states has a significant impact on the emergence of cooperation among the agents. A higher updating frequency (smaller interaction step M) causes a more dynamic extrinsic environment, which accordingly slows the emergence of cooperation, while a too low updating frequency (large interaction step M) will bring about a delay for the agents to catch up with the changing environment, causing a slow convergence of cooperation among the agents.

We are also interested in the impacts of network topological structures and different ways of appraising the individual wellbeing on the emergence of cooperation. We carried out extensive experiments by applying the proposed emotional learning approach in the three kinds of networks with different sizes of population and found that the patterns of results do not differ greatly. As an illustration, we plot the learning dynamics in three different networks with 100 agents in Fig. 3. From the results, we can see that in all three kinds of networks, the emotional FW Agents can learn to achieve cooperation using the different approaches of

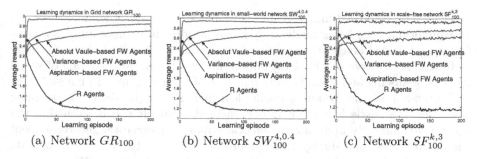

(a) Network GR_{100} (b) Network $SW_{100}^{4,0.4}$ (c) Network $SF_{100}^{k,3}$

Fig. 3. Learning dynamics of using different approaches to appraise the wellbeing

appraising the wellbeing. The variance-based and aspiration-based approaches, however, outperform the absolute value-based approach in terms of a quicker convergence speed and a higher level of cooperation among the agents.

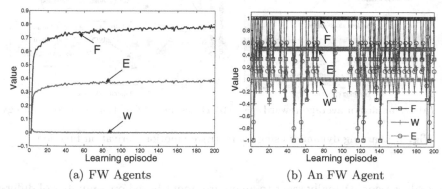

(a) FW Agents   (b) An FW Agent

Fig. 4. Dynamics of appraisal variables and resultant overall emotional state

Fig. 4 shows the learning dynamics of appraisal values and the resultant overall emotional state in grid network GR_{100}. Fig. 4 (a) gives the values of all FW Agents averaged in 100 runs. As learning proceeds, the value of F increases because more and more agents have chosen to cooperate in a cooperative environment. The value of W increases dramatically at the beginning and then stabilizes around 0 (This is because the difference between average reward 2.25 and final cooperation reward 3 is very minor. This difference is then normalized by $T - S = 5$, causing a final value of W close to 0). The overall state of emotion joy, E_{joy}, also increases during the learning process and finally stabilizes around 0.38, which means the agents cannot reach a fully joyful state ($E_{joy} = 1$). To reach the most joyful state ($E_{joy} = 1$), the agents must sense the highest fairness ($F = 1$) and remain in the highest wellbeing state ($W = 1$) at the same time. However, being very wealthy will result in others' defection so that the agent will feel unfair ($F < 0$) again in this case and will be fearful of being revenged by their neighbors (refer to Equ. 8). The reciprocal altruistic behaviors of cooperation require agents to forsake their own short-term benefits for long-term group benefits. The stabilized final level of emotional state of *joy*, therefore, becomes an equilibrium (i.e., being moderately joyful in order to achieve mutually satisfactory outcomes) among the agents, where no one has the incentive to deviate. Note that each curve in Fig. 4 (a) only indicates the overall variation of social fairness, wellbeing and overall emotional state of all the agents. To have a better understanding of the dynamics during learning, Fig. 4 (b) shows the learning dynamics in a single FW agent in one particular run. It can be seen that the agent is dynamically updating the emotion appraisal variables and consequent emotional states, and during this dynamical updating, the agent can bias its learning behavior to achieve cooperation with other co-learning FW agents.

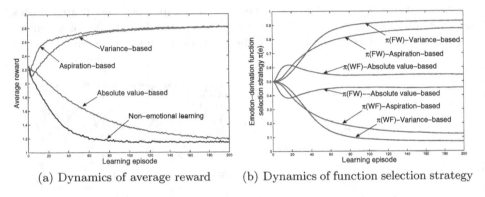

(a) Dynamics of average reward   (b) Dynamics of function selection strategy

Fig. 5. Learning dynamics using competitive emotion derivation functions

In reality, people usually react to an environment based on a number of different emotional cues. After a certain period of interaction, however, certain type of cues will emerge as the primary cause of emotional reactions in an individual. To model this phenomenon, we let each agent derive its emotions based on both FW and WF function at the same time. These two functions compete with each other in order to dominate the derivation of an agent's emotions through a meta-level inner-layer learning process. This means that the emotional intrinsic rewards are not only used to update the Q values associated with each function, but also used to update the strategy of selecting each function. The Weighted Policy Learner (WPL) algorithm [24] is used to indicate different learning rates of selecting the emotion derivation functions in the inner-layer learning process. Fig. 5(a) shows the learning dynamics in network GR_{100}. In the figure, non-emotional learning represents the traditional MARL approach used by rational agents, and other three approaches represent the learning approaches in the emotional MARL framework. As can be seen, different learning approaches produce different patterns of learning behaviors. The variance-based and aspiration-based approaches can greatly boost the emergence of cooperation among the agents, while the absolute value-based approach, however, cannot bring about cooperation among the agents, causing a similar learning curve to the non-emotional learning approach. This result confirms that the absolute wealth of an agent cannot reflect the agent's real emotional state regarding its own wellbeing.

Fig. 5(b) plots the dynamics of strategy to select emotion derivation functions in network GR_{100}, in which $\pi(e)$ indicates the probability of selecting emotion derivation function e (FW or WF) to derive emotions of the agents. As can be seen, when the learning process moves on, the strategy of selecting the functions differs significantly. When agents adopt the satisfaction-based or the variance-based approach, the FW function gradually emerges as a dominant function with a probability close to 100% to derive emotions of the agents. When agents adopt the absolute value-based approach, however, none of the functions can dominate each other to derive emotions of agents. The probability of selecting the WF function is only a bit higher than that of selecting the FW function. The results in Fig. 5(b) indicate that, through the competition of agents' emotion derivation functions in the inner-layer learning, the socially reciprocal behavior using the FW function can override the selfish egoistic behavior using the WF function, which correspondingly facilitates the cooperation among the agents.

5 Related Work

MARL in social dilemmas has been of great interest to researchers in MASs for decades. Sandholm and Crites [25] pioneered this area by investigating a Q-learning agent playing the IPD game against an unknown opponent. They reported that mutual cooperation did not occur when both agents did not take their past actions into account and that the exploration rates had a major impact on the level of cooperation. Vrancx et al. [26] used a combination of replicator dynamics and switching dynamics to model multi-agent learning automata in multi-state PD games. In addition, many other researchers investigated MARL in social dilemmas based on the aspiration-based approaches [8,27]. All these studies, however, focus on analyzing learning dynamics between two agents and understanding in which conditions naive RL agents could learn to achieve cooperation in social dilemmas. In contrast, our work incorporates an emotion mechanism into MARL in spatial social dilemmas to study the impact of local interactions on the emergence of cooperation.

Numerous studies [10,11,12] have incorporated an emotion-based concept and mechanism into RL. Most of these studies, however, focused primarily on exploiting emotions to facilitate learning efficiency or to adapt a single agent to dynamic and complex environments. Several studies examined the evolution of cooperation in spatial IPD by implementing an emotion mechanism. For example, a rule-based system, which enabled the synthesis and generation of cognition-related emotions, was proposed in order to improve the level of cooperation in spatial IPD [13]. Szolnoki et al. [14] proposed an imitation mechanism that could copy the neighbors' emotional profiles and found that this imitation could be capable of guiding the population towards cooperation in social dilemmas. All these studies, however, are based on rule-based emotional frameworks, in which the way of eliciting emotions must be predefined so that agents can adapt their behaviors of whether to cooperate directly based on their emotional states. This is in contrast to our work, in which emotions are used as intrinsic rewards to bias agent learning during local repeated interactions in spatial social dilemmas.

Bazzan *et al.* [15] used social attachments (i.e., belonging to a hierarchy or to a coalition) to lead learning agents in a grid to a certain level of cooperation. Although our work solves the same problem, we focus on exploiting emotions in modifying agent behaviors during learning, and do not impose assumptions of hierarchical supervision or coalition affiliation on the agents.

6 Conclusion and Future Work

This paper studied the emergence of cooperation in social dilemmas by using emotional intrinsic rewards in MARL. The goal of this work is to investigate whether such emotional intrinsic rewards, derived through the appraisals of social fairness and individual wellbeing, can bias agents' rational learning so that cooperation can be achieved. Experimental results revealed that different structural relationships between the emotional appraisal variables could lead to distinct agent behaviors in the whole system, and under certain circumstances, cooperation could be obtained among the agents.

This paper provides some directions for future research. For example, the impact of varying topological structures on the emergence of cooperation under the proposed learning framework is not the focus of this paper, but still needs to be further investigated. Also, it is interesting to study social dilemmas in heterogeneous societies, in which each agent is endowed with a different emotion derivation function, to model real-life situations where people usually have different emotional reactions to the same environmental changes.

References

1. Hofmann, L., Chakraborty, N., Sycara, K.: The evolution of cooperation in self-interested agent societies: a critical study. In: The 10th International Conference on Autonomous Agents and Multiagent Systems, pp. 685–692 (2011)
2. Salazar, N., Rodriguez-Aguilar, J., Arcos, J., Peleteiro, A., Burguillo-Rial, J.: Emerging cooperation on complex networks. In: The 10th International Conference on Autonomous Agents and Multiagent Systems, pp. 669–676 (2011)
3. Nowak, M.: Five rules for the evolution of cooperation. Science 314(5805), 1560–1563 (2006)
4. Perc, M., Szolnoki, A.: Coevolutionary games–a mini review. BioSystems 99(2), 109–125 (2010)
5. Sutton, R., Barto, A.: Reinforcement learning: An introduction. MIT Press, Cambridge (1998)
6. Busoniu, L., Babuska, R., De Schutter, B.: A comprehensive survey of multiagent reinforcement learning. IEEE Trans. Syst. Man Cybern. C. Appl. Re. 38(2), 156–172 (2008)
7. Conlisk, J.: Why bounded rationality? J. Econ. Lit. 34(2), 669–700 (1996)

8. Stimpson, J., Goodrich, M., Walters, L.: Satisficing and learning cooperation in the prisoner's dilemma. In: International Joint Conference on Artificial Intelligence, pp. 535–544. AAAI Press, California (2001)
9. Rumbell, T., Barnden, J., Denham, S., Wennekers, T.: Emotions in autonomous agents: comparative analysis of mechanisms and functions. J. Auton. Agents Multi-AG 25(1), 1–45 (2012)
10. Ahn, H., Picard, R.: Affective cognitive learning and decision making: The role of emotions. In: Proceedings of the 18th European Meeting on Cybernetics and Systems Research, pp. 1–6. North-Holland, Amsterdam (2006)
11. Salichs, M., Malfaz, M.: A new approach to modeling emotions and their use on a decision-making system for artificial agents. IEEE Trans. Affec. Comput. 3(1), 56–68 (2012)
12. Sequeira, P., Melo, F., Paiva, A.: Emotion-based intrinsic motivation for reinforcement learning agents. In: D'Mello, S., Graesser, A., Schuller, B., Martin, J.-C. (eds.) ACII 2011, Part I. LNCS, vol. 6974, pp. 326–336. Springer, Heidelberg (2011)
13. Bazzan, A., Bordini, R.: A framework for the simulation of agents with emotions. In: Proceedings of the 5th International Conference on Autonomous Agents, pp. 292–299. ACM, New York (2001)
14. Szolnoki, A., Xie, N., Wang, C., Perc, M.: Imitating emotions instead of strategies in spatial games elevates social welfare. Europhys. Lett. 96(3), 38002 (2011)
15. Bazzan, A., Peleteiro, A., Burguillo, J.: Learning to cooperate in the iterated prisoner's dilemma by means of social attachments. J. Braz. Comp. Soc. 17(3), 163–174 (2011)
16. Albert, R., Barabási, A.: Statistical mechanics of complex networks. Rev. Mod. Phys. 74, 47–97 (2002)
17. Singh, S., Lewis, R., Barto, A.: Where do rewards come from. In: Proceedings of the Annual Conference of the Cognitive Science Society, pp. 2601–2606. Cognitive Science Society, Inc., Austin (2009)
18. Singh, S., Lewis, R., Barto, A., Sorg, J.: Intrinsically motivated reinforcement learning: An evolutionary perspective. IEEE Trans. Auton. Mental Develop. 2(2), 70–82 (2010)
19. Marsella, S., Gratch, J., Petta, P.: Computational models of emotion. Blueprint for Affective Computing: A Source Book. Oxford University Press, Oxford (2010)
20. Ellsworth, P., Scherer, K.: Appraisal processes in emotion. Oxford University Press, New York (2003)
21. de Jong, S., Tuyls, K.: Human-inspired computational fairness. J. Auton. Agents Multi-AG 22(1), 103–126 (2011)
22. Smith, C.A., Lazarus, R.S.: Appraisal components, core relational themes, and the emotions. Cognition and Emotion 7(3-4), 233–269 (1993)
23. Watts, D., Strogatz, S.: Collective dynamics of 'small-world' networks. Nature 393(6684), 440–442 (1998)
24. Abdallah, S., Lesser, V.: Learning the task allocation game. In: Proceedings of the Fifth International Joint Conference on Autonomous Agents and Multiagent Systems, pp. 850–857 (2006)
25. Sandholm, T., Crites, R.: Multiagent reinforcement learning in the iterated prisoner's dilemma. Biosystems 37(1-2), 147–166 (1996)
26. Vrancx, P., Tuyls, K., Westra, R.: Switching dynamics of multi-agent learning. In: the 7th International Joint Conference on Autonomous Agents and Multiagent Systems, pp. 307–313. ACM Press, New York (2008)
27. Tanabe, S., Masuda, N.: Evolution of cooperation facilitated by reinforcement learning with adaptive aspiration levels. J. Theor. Biol. 293, 151–160 (2011)

On the Development of an MAS Based Evacuation Simulation System: Autonomous Navigation and Collision Avoidance

Leonel Enrique Aguilar Melgar[1], Wijerathne Maddegedara Lalith Lakshman[2], Muneo Hori[2], Tsuyoshi Ichimura[2], and Seizo Tanaka[2]

[1] Department of Civil Engineering, University of Tokyo, Bunkyo, Tokyo 113-8656
[2] Earthquake Research Institute, University of Tokyo, Bunkyo, Tokyo 113-0032
{leaguilar,lalith,hori,ichimura,stanaka}@eri.u-tokyo.ac.jp

Abstract. This paper presents implementation, verification and validation of autonomous navigation and collision avoidance algorithms in a multi agent based evacuation simulation code. The code is being developed with the aim of evaluating the effectiveness of different means to make time critical evacuation process, in large complex urban areas, fast and smooth. Implementation and verification of an autonomous navigation algorithm, which enable both the agents with and without a pre-defined path to reach far visible high grounds, are presented. The Optimal reciprocal collision avoidance scheme, by Berg et al. [1], is adopted for the collision avoidance. The collision avoidance implementation is validated by comparing the numerical results with field observations reported in literature.

1 Introduction

Considering the fact that a large number of lives are exposed to fatal dangers, detailed models have to be used in simulating time critical large urban area evacuations. Tsunami triggered evacuation of large coastal cities, which are located close to the tsunami source, is such a time critical evacuation for which detailed models of the environment and complex agents have to be used. The existing multi agent based large urban area evacuation simulations use too simplified models of agents and environment in which the environment is modelled as a network consisting of one dimensional elements [2]. The use of high resolution 2D models of environment in simulating areas of $1 - 100 km^2$ poses several difficulties: require complex agents capable of identifying the features of the environment and act accordingly; involves large amount of data; require high performance computing to meet the computational demand, etc.

This paper presents details of the implementations, verifications and validations of autonomous navigation and collision avoidance algorithms, which are implemented in a multi agent based large urban area evacuation simulator. The target application of this code is simulating time critical tsunami triggered evacuation of $1-100km^2$ areas, with the aim of evaluating the effectiveness of different

G. Boella et al. (Eds.): PRIMA 2013, LNAI 8291, pp. 388–395, 2013.

means for making the evacuation process fast and smooth. The environment is modelled as a two dimensional grid of $1m \times 1m$ sized cells so that details like damages due to earthquake can be modelled in details. Using radar like scanning, agents perceive the features, like paths, in their visible surrounding. The implemented autonomous navigation algorithm makes both agents with and without paths to reach far visible destinations, just as a real resident or visitor can do. Collision avoidance is implemented based on the optimal reciprocal collision avoidance algorithm (ORCA) [1].

The rest of the paper is organized as follows. Section 2 presents a brief overview of the multi agent system while the section 3 presents details of the autonomous navigation and collision avoidance algorithms. The verifications and validations of these algorithms are presented in the section 4. Finally the section 5 presents some concluding remarks.

2   The Agents and Environment

The agents represent the people evacuating on foot and by vehicles. Agents with different abilities, responsibilities and information are implemented to model the heterogeneous populations consisting of residents, visitors, police officers and volunteers.

The environment is modelled with a high resolution two dimensional grid consisting of $1m \times 1m$ sized cells, and, in a lower hierarchy, a graph with its edges representing available paths. The grid cells hold one of three different states: occupied, unoccupied or exit. The links of the graph hold approximate width of the roads, and the nodes hold the neighbouring cell status like exits. This hybrid vector/raster model is chosen to conveniently exploit the advantages of each model. The grid has advantages like the ability to model the available open waling spaces in detail, highly localized changes to the environment can be easily introduced, etc. The graph is efficient to perform route planning in large domains, prevent movements towards already traversed or blocked roads, etc.

3   Autonomous Pedestrian Navigation: Vision, Navigation and Collision Avoidance

Making agents navigate long distances through a large and complex urban environment, which is modelled as a grid, is a challenging task. For the target problem the agents require the ability to evacuate to a far visible high ground or tall building, even if an agent does not possess any information of the environment except what lies within its visible horizon (i.e. a visitor agent). This is an ability every human counterpart has.

When it comes to the navigation, the agents can be categorized into two groups: visitors and residents. A visitor agent possesses only the information of its visible surroundings ($30m$ to $100m$) and additionally the direction to a far visible destination like a high ground, if any. Resident agents know the paths to their desired destination and their paths are defined by a few landmark points, which can be a few hundred meters apart.

3.1 Vision

To perceive the environment, an agent's vision scans the grid environment like radar and identifies his boundary of visibility and a list of visible neighbour agents. The radar scanning is limited to each agents sight distance which can vary between 30 to 100 meters. Analysing the boundary of visibility, an agent identifies three main features, *exits*, *open paths* and *probable paths*. The region visible up to the maximum sight distance of an agent is categorized as an open path while sudden jumps are categorized as probable paths (see Fig. 1(a)).

If an agent gets too close to corners of obstacles, it's vision gets severely obstructed. In order to prevent this, agents movements towards the corners of obstacles are controlled by defining a set of target points which are located $0.5m$ away from a corner, see Fig. 1(b). These bounds are not too artificial; there is always at least half the shoulder width distance between an obstacle and the eye of a person.

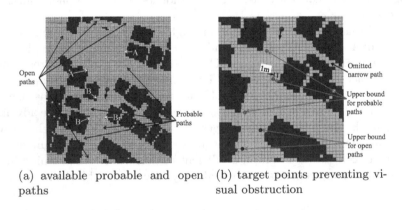

(a) available probable and open paths

(b) target points preventing visual obstruction

Fig. 1. An agent's boundary of visibility and the identified features

3.2 Navigation

Agents navigation uses the open and probable paths identified by the vision and the direction to the desired next destination. The desired next destination for a resident is the next landmark point in his path while that for a visitor is its final destination. Out of all the available paths, an agent chooses the path with most likelihood to lead him to his desired next destination (see Algorithm 1). The selected *next path*, the set of visible neighbours and the desired moving direction are then used as input for the collision avoidance algorithm to produce an ideally collision free movements.

Algorithm 1: Algorithm for autonomous visual based navigation

---

input : Agents properties, desired moving direction $\mathbf{v}_d$ (far visible destination or landmark direction)
output: Next moving direction: $\mathbf{v}_n$

```
/* vision.IdentifyFeatures() Processes the information available in the vision object, and
outputs vectors of open/probable paths and identified exits                              */
```

$vision.\texttt{IdentifyFeatures}(front/back\_open\_paths,\ front/back\_probable\_paths)$;
$next\_opening.\texttt{clear}()$

while not *Frozen* **do**
   if $front\_exits.\texttt{size}() > 0$ **then**
      $next\_opening \leftarrow \texttt{ClosestExit}(front\_exits, \mathbf{v}_d)$;
      $front\_exits.\texttt{clear}()$
   else if $back\_exits.\texttt{size}() > 0$ **then**
      $next\_opening \leftarrow \texttt{ClosestExit}(back\_exits, \mathbf{v}_d)$;
      $back\_exits.\texttt{clear}()$
   else if $\texttt{BestPath}(next\_opening, front\_open\_paths, front\_probable\_paths, \mathbf{v}_d, min\_jump)$ **then**
   else if $\texttt{BestPath}(next\_opening, back\_open\_paths, back\_probable\_paths, \mathbf{v}_d, min\_jump)$ **then**
   else   `/* agent has no paths */`
      Freeze the agent
   end
   if not $next\_opening.\texttt{empty}()$ **then break**
end

if not $\texttt{FindVelocity}(\mathbf{v}_n, next\_opening, Agent\ Properties)$ **then** Freeze the agent; `/* No satisfactory` $\mathbf{v}_n$
`found */`
return $\mathbf{v}_n$

Function BestPath

---

input : $next\_opening$, open and probable paths in the font or back; $open\_paths$, $probable\_paths$, $\mathbf{v}_e$,
       $\mathbf{v}_d, min\_jump$
output: Whether the openings have been exhausted and the $next\_opening$ if found

```
/* BestProbablePath() and BestOpenPath() find the probable and open path closest to the
direction of destination, avoiding narrow paths                                          */
```

$dot\_max = dot\_max\_p \leftarrow \text{-}1$;   `/* max(`$\mathbf{v}_d.\mathbf{v}$`) of all the directions, v, considered */`
$jump \leftarrow 0$;   `/* size of the jump which defines a probable path */`
if $open\_paths.\texttt{size}() > 0$ **and** $probable\_paths.\texttt{size}() > 0$ **then**
   $next\_opening \leftarrow \texttt{BestOpenPath}(open\_paths, \mathbf{v}_d, dot\_max)$;
   $next\_opening\_p \leftarrow \texttt{BestProbablePath}(probable\_paths, \mathbf{v}_d, dot\_max\_p, jump)$;
   $open\_paths.\texttt{clear}()$;
   if $dot\_max\_p > dot\_max$ **and** $jump > min\_jump$ **then** $next\_opening \leftarrow next\_opening\_p$;
else if $open\_path.\texttt{size}() > 0$ **then**
   $next\_opening \leftarrow \texttt{BestOpenPath}(open\_paths, \mathbf{v}_d), open\_paths.\texttt{clear}()$;
else if $probable\_path.\texttt{size}() > 0$ **then**
   $next\_opening \leftarrow \texttt{BestProbablePath}(probable\_paths, \mathbf{v}_d).probable\_paths.\texttt{clear}()$;
else return *false*

return *true*

Function FindVelocity

---

input : Agents properties, $next\_opening, \mathbf{v}_n$
output: Whether finding a velocity is successful, next moving direction: $\mathbf{v}_n$

$half\_planes.\texttt{clear}()$;
$\texttt{FindNaviPlanes}(half\_planes, next\_opening)$;   `/* Creates half-planes with the openings */`
$min\_navi\_planes \leftarrow half\_planes.\texttt{size}()$;
$\texttt{TuneParameters}(crowd\_density)$;   `/* Chooses the parameters for the ORCA planes creation */`
$\texttt{FindORCAPlanes}(half\_planes, neighbours\_info, \mathbf{v}_c, r)$;   `/* Creates an neighbour ORCA planes */`
while not $\texttt{LPSolver}(half\_planes, \mathbf{v}_n)$ **do**   `/* If no feasible solution found relax conditions */`
   $half\_planes.\texttt{pop\_back}$
end
```
/* min_navi_planes is the minimum threshold to consider LPSolver() to have failed.
Currently allows momentary collisions with other agents and disallows collisions with the
environment                                                                              */
```
if $half\_planes.\texttt{size}() < min\_navi\_planes$ **then return** *false*;
return *true*

3.3   Collision Avoidance

In order to model ideally collision free agent movements, the Optimal Reciprocal Collision Avoidance algorithm [1] is adopted. This scheme is based in generating collision free half-spaces based on each agent's neighbours and solving the resulting polytope using linear programming techniques.

3.4   Implementation of Collision Avoidance

In order to avoid collisions with the environment, two navigational half-planes are generated from the two target points of the *next path* and the agent's current position. In order to give the agents freedom in their mobility, these half-planes are moved away from the agent, using the target points of the *next path* as pivots. Only neighbors within $5m$ distance in an agent's front are considered in collision avoidance, although this value is dependent on the simulation time-step size and the properties of the the agents such as dimensions and velocity. The parameters for the ORCA planes detection are chosen based on the crowd density, and kinematics is enforced by limiting the maximum acceleration.

The ORCA scheme possesses some limitations as it finds the target agent's velocity considering each individual neighbours local optimum. This sometimes prevents an agent overtaking slow moving small groups. In order to prevent this problem neighbours close to each other are treated as a group and a *group-half-planes* is produced, instead of one half plane per each individual agent.

4   Verification and Validation

Both the verification and validation are indispensable in numerical simulations. However, only the verification is considered for the navigation algorithm due to the lack of observed data. Both the verification and validation are considered for the collision avoidance.

4.1   Verification of Autonomous Navigation

In order to verify the autonomous navigation algorithm, a fictitious setting consisting in 4000 agents in a part of Kochi City, Japan, is considered. The selected area is $1.6 \times 1.2 \ km^2$ and has a mountain, at the left edge, which is visible from any location in the selected domain. Two different cases are considered; all the agents in case 1 are residents while those of case 2 are visitors. The agents' initial positions and each individual agents properties are the same in both of the cases. Collision avoidance is disabled to make the problem well posed and each agent is assigned a constant velocity of $1 \ m/s$.

The macroscopic behaviour of the agents' movements is verified by comparing the theoretically expected number of agents with the simulation results. Knowing the agents' initial position, the shortest path to the closest evacuation point is calculated using the theta* algorithm [3] on the grid. The theoretically expected time is obtained from the length of the shortest path.

As is seen in Fig. 2(a), the resident agents are able to follow the optimal path with almost no deviations, which allowed them to reach the desired destination at the expected ideal travel time. Figure 2(a) shows how visitor agents evacuation time deviates from the ideally expected time. Compared to the ideal, there is a maximum difference of 260 agents at 1600s. Furthermore, figure 2(b) shows the distribution of the difference between visitor agents' evacuation time and the ideal. As can be seen most of the agents have a delay of 10s to 230s from their individual expected ideal evacuation time while the maximum ideal evacuation time is 30 minutes.

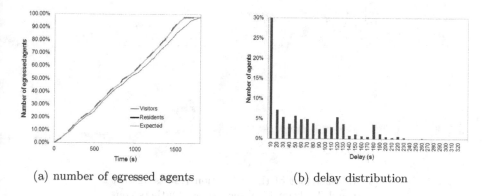

(a) number of egressed agents   (b) delay distribution

Fig. 2. Results of macroscopic comparisons for verifying agents' navigation

As a test of the microscopic details, the path taken by each individual resident agent is compared with its ideal path. This comparison shows that resident agents have only slight deviations from their ideal path. On the other hand detailed inspection of the paths taken by visitor agents show that only a few have taken a path close to the ideal one. However a few of them get lost, but only for a short time. All the visitor agents can reach the destination.

The results of the macroscopic and microscopic comparisons verify the resident agents' navigation algorithm. Although there is no ideal solution to verify visitor agents navigation, the microscopic and macroscopic comparisons show that the visitors navigation algorithm produces reasonable results; all the visitor can reach their destinations and the average delay time is reasonable compared to our experiences.

4.2   Verification and Validation of Collision Avoidance

The collision avoidance algorithm is verified by comparing outputs against those of other available codes. To validate the collision avoidance implementation, the results of the simulations are compared with field observations reported by Mori et al. [4]. Although these field observations present sidewalks with different widths, what's relevant for the validation is the relation between the average walking speed and the crowd density. To reproduce the field observation settings in the simulation, a target agent is positioned among a crowd, with a given maximum speed. Then this agent and its surrounded crowd are set to evacuate in a unidirectional flow, and its average speed is recorded. For each of considered crowd density, a Monte Carlo Simulation (MCS) is performed. Each MCS consisted in 100 simulations. The average speed of the target agent is recorded for each simulation and its distribution is presented as a whisker-box plot per MCS along with the data by Mori et al., see fig. 3(a). This shows that the numerical results are in good agreement with their observations.

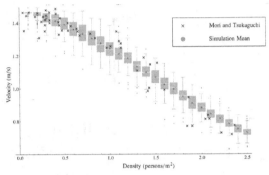

(a) Whisker plot of the validation results against Mori and Tsukaguchi observations. Outliers considered as further than 1.5 inter quartile range are plotted as black dots.

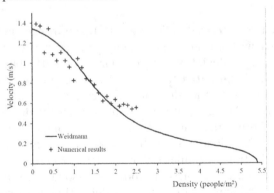

(b) Validation with Weidmann observations.

Fig. 3. Comparisons of numerical and observed data for the validation of collision avoidance algorithm

Further, as a part of validation, the simulations results are compared with the observations reported by Weidmann [5]. Weidmann reported observations encompassing a large amount of data with different flow and boundary conditions. Figure 3(b) compares the numerical results with the reported observations.

As is seen, the numerical results are once again in good agreement with their reported observations.

The objective of the target application is to evaluate the effectiveness of strategies to make evacuation process smooth and fast. For this reason, the validity for the densities above 2.5 $people/m^2$ isn't checked; any evacuation strategy producing high density crowds is out of the scope of the target application.

5 Concluding Remarks

This paper presents autonomous navigation and collision avoidance algorithms for multi agent based large urban area evacuation simulation. The environment is modelled as a high resolution $2D$ grid and radar based vision is implemented to make the agents perceive their visible neighbourhood. A vision based autonomous navigation algorithm, which makes both resident and visitor agents to navigate through complex urban environments, is implemented. The autonomous navigation algorithm for resident agents is verified by comparing the simulation results with the ideally expected, both in macroscopic and microscopic details. The visitor agents also produced reasonable navigation behavior. The ORCA based collision avoidance algorithm implementation is validated by comparing the numerical results with field observations by Mori et al and a data set by Weidmann, producing results in good agreement with the observed data.

Acknowledgments. This work was supported by JSPS KAKENHI Grant Number 24760359. Part of the results is obtained by using the K computer at the RIKEN Advanced Institute for Computational Science.

References

1. van der Berg, J., Guy, S.J., Lin, M., Pradalier, D.M.C., Siegwart, R., Hirzinger, G.: Reciprocal n-body collision avoidance. In: The 14th International Symposium on Robotics Research, ISRR. Springer Tracts in Advanced Robotics, vol. 70, pp. 3–19. Springer (May 2011)
2. Saito, T., Kagami, H.: Simulation of evacuation behavior from tsunami untilizing multi agent simulation. In: Proceedings ot the 13th World Conf. on Earth- Quake Engineering, Vancouver (2004)
3. Nash, A., Daniel, K., Koenig, S., Felner, A.: Theta*: any angle path planning on grids. In: Proceedings of the AAAI Conference on Artificial Intelligence, pp. 1177–1183 (2007)
4. Mori, M., Tsukaguchi, H.: A new Method for Evaluation of Level of Service in Pedestrian Facilities. Transp. Res.-A 21(3), 223–234 (1987)
5. Weidmann, U.: Transporttechnik der Fussgnger, Transporttechnische Eigenschaften des Fussgngerverkehrs (Literturauswertung), Schriftenreihe des IVT Nr. 90, Zweite, ergnzte Auage, Zrich (Mrz 1993) (109 Seiten)

Prosperity and Decline of Online Communities

Kimitaka Asatani[1], Fujio Toriumi[1], Hirotada Ohashi[1],
Mitsuteru Tashiro[2], and Ryuichi Suzuki[2]

[1] Graduate School of Enginireeing, Univirsity of Tokyo
7-3-1, Hongo, Bunkyoku, Tokyo, Japan
{asatani,torix,ohashi}@crimson.q.t.u-tokyo.ac.jp
[2] Nifty Corporation, Japan
Shinjuku Front Tower 21-1, Kita-shinjuku 2-chome, Shinjuku-ku, Tokyo
{tashiro.mitsuteru,ryuichi.suzuki}@nifty.co.jp

Abstract. On the basis of analyzing user behavior using the actual data of online communities, we constructed a model of user behavior in an online community. We found two fundamental characteristics (diversity and motivation of participants (content-oriented or friendship-based)) that majorly affect the time evolution of online communities. In addition, the model reproduced what happens in reality, such as time-scale transition of the number of posts and distribution of the number of posts in all periods.

Keywords: Online Community/Game Theory/Data Mining.

1 Introduction

Various online communities exist on the Internet. There are two types of online communities: content-based communities such as YouTube and friendship-based communities such as Facebook. The user motivations to join these types of communities are different. Michael Steve [1] has shown that the people's activities in the community on YouTube strongly depend on the content providers and contents themselves. It is considered that content-oriented communities decline quickly soon after their participants lose interest in the contents. On the other hand, the data analysis of the friendship-based communities demonstrated a fat tail distribution of connection[2] in all friendship-based communities and a long-term decline process over several years [3]. According to all this research, friendship-based communities continue for longer and decline more gradually than content-based communities. Although these independent researchers have demonstrated the difference between the friendship-based and content-oriented communities, when they treated communities as different types of architecture (content format, functions such as recommendations, etc.) and targeted country, the difference was not clear.

To reveal differences between these communities, we analyzed the data of Nifty-Serve, which provides a collection of more than 500 communities on the same architecture. Nifty-Serve was a big social network in Japan that had 500

G. Boella et al. (Eds.): PRIMA 2013, LNAI 8291, pp. 396–404, 2013.

thousand users and 40 million postings. Because Nifty-Serve has already declined, its cradle-to-grave data can explain the formation-prosperity-decline process. Nifty-Serve included both friendship-based and content-oriented communities. Therefore, we can observe the whole lives of different types of online communities simultaneously.

In this paper, we extract the behavioral characteristics of users in the community to create a communication model of Nifty Serve to simulate user behaviors. We verify the simulation results with actual data, and clarify the relationship between motivations and the macroscopic dynamics of the online community.

In addition, we reveal how online communities decline and evaluate their resiliency. Previous researchers[3] focused on resilience using the network analysis. By contrast, we focus on the resiliency using indicators of diversity along with the user motivations to participate in the community. We simulated online communities under various conditions to clarify the factors for their collapse.

2   Related Works

Life of online communities follows the process of formation - prosperity - decline. Data analysis of the formation - prosperity process has already been developed [6][7]. It has been revealed that all online communities consist of statistical properties such as the power-law distribution of response time and posting count.

Recently, some studies focused on the decline process. For example, G. Dror [4] clarified that there is a stylized fact that cannot be explained by the diffusion process. In addition, data analysis of a declined SNS (Friendster) support the hypothesis that a user who has a big k-core does not tend to leave the community.

Subsequently to data analysis, agent-based models have been proposed that focus on user behavior. For example, Foudalis et al. [8] focus on the behavioral characteristics and the backgrounds of the users. However, few models represent the decline process. Liu et al. [5] showed the predictable rise and fall in the future by classifying the behavior of users in SNS and simulating transitions. However, the treated range of this model is limited to static conditions, excluding exogenous or endogenous sudden changes. In addition, they did not explain why users come to take the actions. The goal of our study is to clarify what user motivation will affect the macroscopic properties of the community.

3   Online Community Log Mining

3.1   Data Set

We analyzed all records of Nifty-Serve, an online community that existed for 17 years until 2006 in Japan. There were more than 500 independent communities and 40 million posts. All online communities of Nifty Serve had bulletin boards with the same architecture. Nifty-Serve had no function for gfriendingh other users, unlike Facebook. We construct a relationship network on the basis of the posted data that received replies.

3.2   User Behavior on Nifty-Serve

To construct a user behavior model in an online community, we investigated when users gain benefits. A user who obtains more benefits is considered to stay longer in online communities. Thus, we analyzed the relationship between the behavior of individual users and staying duration.

Table 1. Correlation coefficient between average staying duration and indexes

Index	R	Index	R
The number of users responded to	0.390	Participation threads (>10 postings)	0.315
The number of postings	0.236	Participation threads	0.190
The number of responses received	0.227	PageRank	0.026

The correlation coefficient of the number of users who received a response and staying duration (0.390) is higher than the coefficient of the number of posts and staying duration (0.236). The results suggest that a user would have felt a higher gain from receiving responses from other users than writing numerous posts. In addition, since the number of responses (0.227) was a low value, the user seemed to obtain greater benefit from receiving responses from many users rather than multiple responses from the same user. Furthermore, the correlation coefficient of "Participation threads that have more than 10 posts" (0.315) is greater than that of "Participation threads" (0.190). These results suggests that a user who receives a large number of responses tends to stay in the online communities.

On the other hand, correlation between staying duration and PageRank is low. This fact shows that people in the center of the conversation structure of online communities do not always stay longer.

4   Model of User Behavior

By using the results of the data analysis, we built an agent-based model. The model consisted by topics, agents, and interests. Each community has its own topic, and each agent has own interest, which is represented by L-length bits.

In this model, when the topic on the community fits the interest of user, the user commits to the community. During a simulation, agents do not change its interest. On the other hand, topics change parameters representing the content in topics. After the topics change, some agents leave the community because of mismatches of topic and interest. This model is defined as a game that user selects one of three behaviors: Post / Surf / Wait. The flow is described in below.

The first step of the simulation contains one or more topics and users. Interests of each user are determined completely at random if diversity is high ($div = 1$) and permanently fixed if diversity is low ($div = 0$). Initially, all bit sequences of all users are 0. Then, all bits of all users are changed to 1 in probability div. When $div = 0$, the value of all bit strings is all 0. On the other hand, when $div = 1$, all bits are set as random. The processes are detailed in follow.

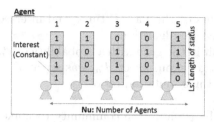
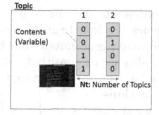

Fig. 1. Agent and topics in the model. Left figure shows users have bit string of interest, and right one shows topics have bit string of contents.

Calculation of benefit

Benefit of the agent can be explained by topic and friendship. The first is important in content-oriented communities, and the second in friendship-based ones. To express them continuously, we defined the degree of friendship Fri. Benefits of Post, Surf, and Wait can be written as follows using the benefit by topic B_{Topic}, benefit by friends B_{Friend}, cost of posting C_{Post}, and cost of surf C_{Surf}.

$$B_{Post} = (1 - Fri) * B_{Topic} + Fri * B_{Friend} - C_{Post} \qquad (0 < Fri < 1)(1)$$
$$B_{Surf} = (1 - Fri) * B_{Topic} - C_{Surf} \qquad (C_{Surf} < C_{Post}) \qquad (2)$$
$$B_{Wait} = 0 \qquad (3)$$

Benefit by topic B_{Topic} was to be proportional to the degree of similarity of the attributes of the user and topic. Similarity is expressed in (5) in the range between -1 - 1. In the previous section, a user who receives many responses obtains high benefit from the community. So, benefit by topic B_{Topic} was defined as (4) using the number of posting P.

$$B_{Topic} = Similarity * \log(P + 1) \qquad (4)$$
$$Similarity = \frac{\sum_{i=1}^{L} \delta_{Topic_i Agent_i} * 2 - 1}{L} \qquad (5)$$

Benefit by friend relationship B_{Friend} is defined using the percentage of friends who posted on the topic. Friends are defined as people who wrote on the same topic in the past P_t times. This definition corresponds to the data analysis results that correlation coefficient of user's PageRank and staying duration is different in each communities.

Leaving

The user leaves when the sum of the benefit from the past P_t times is less than the tolerance Tol.

Update the strategy

Each user updates his/her strategy to make it similar to the strategy of users who obtain large benefits. First, half the gene expresses the probability of Surf or Post, and the other half expresses the probability of a Post when the first half expresses Surf or Post. Users choose one agent with a probability proportional to the sum of benefits of the Past P times and intersect with the genes of selected agents in genetic algorithm.

In addition, a gene mutates one bit in the gene with a probability of P_m. This probability means sensitivity of exogenous effect. P_m was set at $P_m < 0.01$ on the basis of the genetic algorithms mutation ratio.

Perform actions

The agent changes one bit of the topic in the community to make a new topic that fits the agent better. If the created topic has not been posted to the community, the agent posts the topic to the community.

Bit String of Topic Changes

After all agents post topics, the community topic changes to one of them randomly. By the change in topics, we can express the boring of agents. For example, in a community made up of agents with close statuses, if a topic changes a lot, most agents lose interest in the topic and leave the community.

5   Verification of Model

5.1   Classification of Online Communities Using the Log

We classified 509 communities on Nifty using two indicators ("friendship-base" and "diversity of users' interests".) corresponding to parameters in our model.

The index "friend-base" is represented by a correlation coefficient between staying duration and PageRank. In completely content-oriented communities, the number of friends does not change the benefits of users. On the other hand, in friendship-based it does so. Thus, the index can be treated as an indicator of "friendship-base" corresponding to Fri in our model.

For an indicator of the diversity of users' interests, we adopted the average number of threads to which a user posts in a month. This indicator shows the range of user interests. The results of the classification are shown in fig. 2.

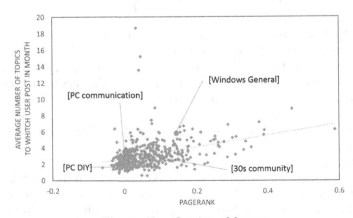

Fig. 2. Classification of forums

We picked out four communities on the basis of high/low intensity of the "friendship-base" and the strength/weakness of the diversity. All four communities have around 2000 (close to the median) specific users. Fig 3 plots time-series variation of the number of users and the distribution of the number of posts. In section 5.3, we will compare the actual data and simulation results.

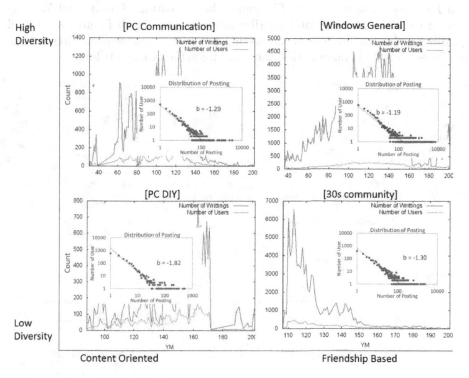

Fig. 3. Posting and user count of typical forums

5.2 Long-Term Transition of the Community by Simulation

To verify the model and actual data, we performed the simulation in conditions in which the agent continues to join every step in the communities. Then, we observed the long-term characteristics and decline of communities. We conducted

Table 2. Parameter of Simulation

	Parameter	Value			Parameter	Value
N_u	Number of Users	Variable		L	Length of bit string	10
N_t	Number of Topics	1			The number of steps	
Div	Diversity of Users	Variable(0-1)		P_t	looking back to the past	5
Fri	Friendship	Variable(0-1)		Tol	Tolerance to leaving	-0.4
C_{Post}	Cost of Post	0.4		N_g	Bit length of gene	6
C_{Surf}	Cost of Surf	0.2		P_m	Mutation ratio of gene	0.01

a simulation of 1000 steps. In this subsection, we describe simulation results, and in the next section, we compare the simulation results and actual data.

Before presenting simulation results, we list the simulation conditions in Table 2. The number of users is able to be added step-by-step. Simulations were performed while the ratio of friendship and diversity of the users was varied.

Fig. 4 shows results of the simulation for condition of Fri was set to 0.1 or 0.5, and Div was set to 0.2 or 0.8. The figure shows Posting, Surfing, and Waiting count time series and the total distributions of posts (Small Figure). Under all conditions, the distributions of the posting counts follow power-low distribution. In content-oriented communities, the absolute value of slope is large.

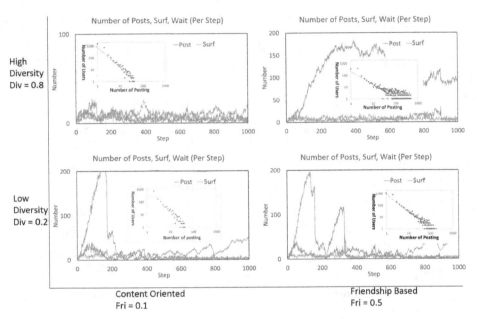

Fig. 4. Communities' development and decline depending on Fri and Div

The number of posts is small in the communities on the left in Fig. 4. Furthermore, friendship-based communities in the right-hand side graphs have larger numbers of postings than contents-oriented communities except for the peak at step 300. This fact suggests that friendship prolongs community life.

In communities that have low diversity, regardless of whether they are content-oriented or friendship-based, the number of posts in the significant peak and other states differs greatly. Diversity of users' interests is thus required for the continuous survival of online communities.

5.3   Verifying Simulation Results with Data

By comparing the results in Section 5.2 and actual data, some statistical properties seems to be similar. High diversity makes the distribution fat-tailed. This is evidence that the model represents the statistical properties of the actual data.

The upper-left graph in Fig. 3 is a content-oriented forum of latest information about technology. In this community, the number of posts changes greatly over time. The slope of distribution of g is gentle (1.19). In the corresponding simulation results (upper-left in Fig. 4). In low diversity communities, increase or decrease in the number of posts is more intense in the "PC DIY" (lower-left in Fig. 3) and simulation results (lower-left in Fig. 4).

These content-oriented communities have the characteristics of exogenous burst. In simulation results (left-hand side in Fig. 4), a small number of people post repeatedly. This means that almost all users stay for a short time.

In friendship-based communities, the forum like "Windows general" (upper-right in Fig. 3) lasts long. Friendship stabilizes the community and users' wide-ranging interests can support long-term prosperity. These characteristics are the same as those in the simulation results (upper-right in Fig. 4)

In addition, it is possible to find out nature of user behavior like surfing history by fitting simulation results to actual data which include only the action of posting. In "PC DIY" (lower-left of Fig. 3), many users surfes around $YM = 180$ because corresponding simulation results show there is a large number of surfing users near the peak. In this case, most people are considered just to want information. On the other hand, there are few surfing users in the "Windows General" (upper-right of Fig. 3), because of the corresponding simulation results (upper-right of Fig. 4).

6 Conclusion

We demonstrated by simulation and data analysis that the diversity of users' interests and the strength of friendship indicate the features of communities.

Results of the data analysis of user behavior show two features. One is that user benefit is more strongly related to the number of users who make responses than number of posts users makes. The other is that correlation between PageRank and user benefit is significantly difference depending on communities. On the basis of these results, we defined a utility function of the user and proposed an agent-based model of communication in the online community.

One objective of future study is to improve the fitting accuracy of the data. We need to increase the number of parameters, for example, user tolerance and cost of posting. Another objective is to measure the resiliency of a community to exogenous and endogenous impacts. The ultimate goal is to predict the future community under various conditions using the proposed model.

References

1. Laine, et al.: User Groups in Social Networks: An Experimental Study on YouTube. In: 44th Hawaii International Conference on System Sciences (HICSS). IEEE (2011)
2. Ahn, Y., Han, S., et al.: Analysis of Topological Characteristics of Huge Online Social Networking Services. In: 16th International Conference on W3C. ACM (2007)
3. Garcia, D., Mavrodiev, P., Schweitzer, F.: Social Resilience in Online Communities: The Autopsy of Friendster. arXiv preprint arXiv:1302.6109 (2013)

4. Dror, G., Pelleg, D., et al.: Churn Prediction in New Users of Yahoo! Answers. In: Proceedings of the 21st International Conference Companion on WWW. ACM (2012)
5. Liu, H., Nazir, A., et al.: Modeling/predicting the Evolution Trend of Osn-Based Applications. In: Proceedings of the 22nd International Conference on WWW (2013)
6. Backstrom, L., et al.: Group Formation in Large Social Networks: Membership, Growth, and Evolution. In: 12th ACM SIGKDD International Conference. ACM (2006)
7. Zheleva, E., Sharara, H., Getoor, L.: Co-Evolution of Social and Affiliation Networks. In: 15th ACM SIGKDD International Conference. ACM (2009)
8. Foudalis, et al.: Modeling social networks through user background and behavior. In: Anonymous Algorithms and Models for the Web Graph. Springer (2011)

Information Dependencies in MCS: Conviviality-Based Model and Metrics*

Patrice Caire[1], Antonis Bikakis[2], and Yves Le Traon[1]

[1] Luxembourg University, Interdisciplinary Center for Security,
Reliability and Trust (SnT)
firstname.lastname@uni.lu
[2] Department of Information Studies, University College London
a.bikakis@ucl.ac.uk

Abstract. Information exchange among heterogenous entities is common in most distributed systems. To facilitate information exchange, we first need ways to evaluate it. The concept of conviviality was recently introduced to model and measure cooperation among agents. In this paper, we use conviviality to model and measure information dependencies in distributed systems modeled as Multi-Context Systems. Then, we apply our findings to resolve inconsistencies among participating entities.

1 Introduction

Today's distributed information systems are characterized by multiple forms of cooperation between heterogeneous entities including information exchange. Examples include distributed databases, Linked Data, P2P systems, sensor networks and others. One approach to model such systems is with *Multi-Context Systems (MCS)* [18,17,7]. MCS are logical formalizations of distributed context theories connected through bridge rules, which enable information flow between contexts.

Intuitively, MCS can be used as a representation model for any information system involving distributed, heterogeneous knowledge agents such as peer-to-peer systems and distributed ontologies. Applications developed on top of MCS and other logic-based context formalizations are numerous, e.g.,[22,6,23,1,2]. Such systems consist of individual entities cooperating through information sharing. Reasoning with the information they import, they derive new knowledge and take more informed decisions. These features are enabled by MCS notions of contexts, bridge rules and contextual reasoning. But, how can we evaluate the ways in which systems enable cooperation? How can we characterize a MCS based on the opportunities for information exchange that it provides to its contexts?

In previous work [11], we model *conviviality* in a version of MCS called Contextual Defeasible Logic. In this paper we extend our model to the general MCS model[18,17,7], and introduce measures for information dependencies based on

---

* The present research is supported by the National Research Fund, Luxembourg, CoPAInS project (code: CO11/IS/1239572).

G. Boella et al. (Eds.): PRIMA 2013, LNAI 8291, pp. 405–412, 2013.

this notion of conviviality. Defined by Illich as "individual freedom realized in personal interdependence" [20], conviviality has been introduced as a social science concept for multiagent systems [9] to highlight soft qualitative requirements like user friendliness of systems. Conviviality is measured by counting the possible ways to cooperate, indicating degree of choice or freedom to engage in coalitions [10]. The authors' coalitional theory is based on dependence networks, labeled directed graphs where nodes represent agents, and each labeled edge represents that the former agent depends on the latter to achieve some goal. In distributed information systems, individual freedom is linked to the choice of keeping personal knowledge and beliefs at the local level, while interdependence is understood as reciprocity, i.e. cooperation.

In MCS as in mutliagent systems, participating entities depend on each other to achieve their goals; in MCS, the enrichment of local knowledge. This leads to our research question: *How to evaluate and improve the exchange of information in MCS with the use of conviviality model and measures?* In this paper, we first propose a formal model to represent *information dependencies* in MCS modeled as dependence networks. Then, we define conviviality measures for MCS. Finally, we apply our findings to address inconsistency resolution in MCS.

2   Multi-Context Systems: Definitions and Example

We define a MCS as in [7]: A *MCS* $M = (C_1, \ldots, C_n)$ is a set of contexts $C_i = (L_i, kb_i, br_i)$, $1 \leq i \leq n$. $L_i = (\mathbf{KB}_i, \mathbf{BS}_i, \mathbf{ACC}_i)$ is a logic, where $\mathbf{KB}_i$ is the set of well-formed knowledge bases of L_i and each element of $\mathbf{KB}_i$ is a set of formulae; $\mathbf{BS}_i$ is the set of possible belief sets, and an element of a belief set is a set of formulae; and $\mathbf{ACC}_i$: $\mathbf{KB}_i \rightarrow 2^{\mathbf{BS}_i}$ is a function describing the semantics of the logic by assigning to each knowledge base a set of acceptable belief sets. $kb_i \in \mathbf{KB}_i$ is a knowledge base, and br_i a set of L_i-bridge rules over $(L_1, \ldots, L_n)$. A *bridge rule* can add information to a context, depending on the belief sets accepted by other contexts. An L_k-bridge rule r over L is of the form

$$r = (k : s) \leftarrow (c_1 : p_1), \ldots, (c_j : p_j),$$
$$\mathbf{not}(c_{j+1} : p_{j+1}), \ldots, \mathbf{not}(c_m : p_m). \tag{1}$$

where c_i, $1 \leq c_i \leq n$, refers to a context in M, p_i is an element of some belief set of L_i, and k refers to the context receiving information s. We denote by $h_b(r)$ the belief formula s in the head of r. By $br_M = \bigcup_{i=1}^{n} br_i$ we denote the set of bridge rules in M. For each $H \subseteq \{h_b(r) | r \in br_i\}$ it holds that $kb_i \cup H \in \mathbf{KB}_{L_i}$, i.e. bridge rule heads are compatible with knowledge bases.

Example 1. Consider a MCS M, through which three distributed software agents exchange information and classify research articles they retrieve from the web. Contexts $C_1 - C_3$ in M encode the knowledge of the three agents. The knowledge bases of the three contexts are respectively:

$$kb_1 = \{sensors, corba, centralizedComputing \leftrightarrow \neg distributedComputing\}$$
$$kb_2 = \{prof A\}$$
$$kb_3 = \{ubiquitousComputing \subseteq ambientComputing\}$$

C_1 states in propositional logic that the article is about sensors and corba, and that centralized computing and distributed computing are opposite concepts. C_2 states (also using propositional logic) that the article is written by $prof A$. C_3 is an ontology about computing written in a basic description logic, according to which ubiquitous computing *is a type of* ambientComputing. The three agents use bridge rules r_1-r_4 to associate their local knowledge. For example, with r_1, C_1 classifies middleware (defined by C_2) as a centralized computing technology.

$$r_1 = (1 : centralizedComputing) \leftarrow (2 : middleware)$$
$$r_2 = (1 : distributedComputing) \leftarrow (3 : ambientComputing)$$
$$r_3 = (2 : middleware) \leftarrow (1 : corba)$$
$$r_4 = (3 : ubiquitousComputing) \leftarrow (1 : sensors), (2 : prof B)$$

A belief state of a MCS is the set of the belief sets of its contexts. Formally, a *belief state* of $M = (C_1, \dots, C_n)$ is a sequence $S = (S_1, \dots, S_n)$ such that $S_i \in \mathbf{BS}_i$. Intuitively, S is derived from the knowledge of each context and the information conveyed through applicable bridge rules. A bridge rule of form (1) is applicable in a belief state S iff for $1 \leq i \leq j$: $p_i \in S_{c_i}$ and for $j < l \leq m$: $p_l \notin S_{c_l}$. Equilibrium semantics selects certain belief states of a MCS $M = (C_1, \dots, C_n)$ as acceptable. Intuitively, an equilibrium is a belief state $S = (S_1, \dots, S_n)$ where each context C_i respects all bridge rules applicable in S and accepts S_i. Formally, S is an equilibrium of M, iff for $1 \leq i \leq n$,

$$S_i \in \mathbf{ACC}_i(kb_i \cup \{h_b(r) | r \in br_i \text{ applicable in } S\}).$$

Example 2. In our example, M has one equilibrium:

$$S = (\{sensors, corba, centralizedComputing\}, \{prof A, middleware\}, \emptyset).$$

3   MCS Conviviality Property: Model and Measures

To capture the notions of *context* and *bridge rules*, we build on [10] and define a dependence network for MCS as follows:

Definition 1 (Dependence network for MCS). *A dependence network corresponding to a MCS M, denoted as $DN(M)$, is a tuple $\langle C, br_M, dep, \geq \rangle$ where: C is the set of contexts in M; br_M is the set of bridge rules in M; $dep : C \times C \rightarrow 2^{br_M}$ is a function that is constructed as follows: for each bridge rule r (in the form of (1)) in br_M add the following dependencies: $dep(k, c_i) = \{r\}$ where k is the context appearing in the head of r and c_i stands for each distinct context appearing in the body of r; and $\geq : C \rightarrow 2^{br_M} \times 2^{br_M}$ is for each context a total pre-order on sets of its bridge rules.*

Furthermore, based on the conviviality measures defined for multi agent systems in [10], we define the conviviality of a MCS as:

$$\Theta = \sum_{L=2}^{L=|C|} P(|C| - 2, L - 2) \times d_M^L, \tag{2}$$

$$\Omega = |C|(|C| - 1) \times \Theta, \tag{3}$$

$$\mathrm{Conv}(M) = \frac{\displaystyle\sum_{c_i, c_j \in C, i \neq j} \mathrm{coal}(c_i, c_j)}{\Omega} \tag{4}$$

where $|C|$ is the number of contexts in M, L is the cycle length, P is the usual permutation defined in combinatorics, $\mathrm{coal}(c_i, c_j)$ for any distinct $c_i, c_j \in C$ is the number of cycles that contain the ordered pair (c_i, c_j) in $DN(M)$, such that the cycles do not represent logical loops, i.e., for any participating literals, we assume no other inference ways, and Ω denotes the maximal number of pairs of contexts in cycles. d_M is the maximum number of dependencies that a context in M may have on each of the other contexts in M:

$$d_M = \max_{k \in M} \sum_{i=1}^{|C|} dep(k, c_i) \tag{5}$$

To summarize, the conviviality of the MCS is obtained by computing the sum of all cycles containing any ordered pair of contexts in the network, over the maximal number of contexts pairs potentially in cycles. (A value of 0 indicating an unconnected graph, i.e., no conviviality, and a value of 1 indicating a fully connected graph, i.e., maximal conviviality).

Figure 1 visualizes the dependence network corresponding to MCS M in Example 1: each node corresponds to a context in M; dependencies are derived from the four bridge rules of M. Per Eq. 2 and assuming $d_M = 1$, then $\mathrm{Conv}(M) = 7/\Omega = 0.58$, where $\Omega = 12$. We note that $\mathrm{Conv}(M)$ is almost maximal as adding only one bridge rule, namely from C_2 to C_3, results in a fully connected graph, i.e., maximal conviviality.

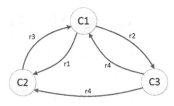

Fig. 1. The dependence network $DN(M)$ of MCS M of the running example

4   Application: Inconsistency Resolution

Even if contexts are locally consistent, bridge rules may render a whole MCS inconsistent. This is formally described in [7] as a *lack of an equilibrium*. All inconsistency resolution techniques proposed so far are based on the same intuition: for the entire system to be consistent again, a subset of the bridge rules causing inconsistency must be invalidated and another subset unconditionally applied. For nonmonotonic MCS, it is formally defined in [14] as diagnosis:

"Given a MCS M, a *diagnosis* of M is a pair (D_1, D_2), $D_1, D_2 \subseteq br_M$, s.t. $M[br_M \backslash D_1 \cup heads(D_2)] \not\models \perp$". $D^{\pm}(M)$ is the set of all such diagnoses, while with $M[R]$ we denote the MCS obtained from M by replacing its bridge rules br_M with R; therefore $M[br_M \backslash D_1 \cup heads(D_2)]$ is the MCS obtained from M by removing the rules in D_1 and adding the heads of the rules in D_2.

If we deactivate the rules in D_1 and apply the rules in D_2 in unconditional form, M becomes consistent. In a MCS, more than one diagnosis may restore consistency. We propose using the conviviality of the resulted system as a criterion for selecting a diagnosis. For each diagnosis we measure the conviviality of the system that is derived after applying the diagnosis, and select the diagnosis that minimally decreases conviviality. The intuition is that the system should remain as *cooperative* as possible. This is achieved by maximizing the number of agents involved in the derivation of a conclusion or a decision and the number of potential ways in which a conclusion may be drawn.

Diagnoses contain two types of changes applicable to bridge rules: invalidation of a rule, and unconditional application of a rule, i.e., removing the body of the rule. When invalidating or adding unconditionally rule r (as defined in (1)) in a MCS M, all the dependencies labeled with r are removed from the dependence network of M. Assuming that $D_i = (D_{i1}, D_{i2})$ is a diagnosis that may be applied in M, and $M(D_i)$ is the MCS obtained M after applying D_i, the optimal diagnosis is the one that maximizes the conviviality of $M(D_i)$:

$$D_{opt} = \{D_i : \mathrm{Conv}(M(D_i)) = max\}$$

Example 3. Consider the case, illustrated Figures 2-5: prof B is identified by C_2 as a co-author of the paper under examination. In this case kb_2 would also contain prof B: $kb_2 = \{prof A, prof B\}$, which would cause an inconsistency in kb_1 due to the activation of rules r_4 and r_2. To resolve the conflict, one of the four bridge rules r_1-r_4 must be invalidated.

Using the diagnosis definition presented above, this is formally described as:

$$D^{\pm}(M) = \{(\{r_1\}, \emptyset), (\{r_2\}, \emptyset), (\{r_3\}, \emptyset), (\{r_4\}, \emptyset)\}.$$

Figures 2-5 depict the four dependence networks $DN(M(D_i))$, which are derived after applying D_i, where $D_i = (\{r_i\}, \emptyset)$. Dashed arrows represent the dependencies that are dropped in each $DN(M(D_i))$ compared to $DN(M)$.

Following Equation 2 and the four dependence networks (Figures 2-5) the conviviality of each DN is:

$$\mathrm{Conv}(M(D_1)) = 5/\Omega = 0.42 \text{ and}$$
$$\mathrm{Conv}(M(D_j)) = 2/\Omega = 0.17 \text{ with } j = 2, 3, 4 \text{ and } \Omega = 12$$

Applying D_1 (Figure 2), removes one cycle only $\{(C_1, C_2, r_1), (C_2, C_1, r_3)\}$ from the initial dependence network $DN(M)$, while applying any of diagnoses D_2-D_4 (Figures 3-5), two cycles are removed. Hence the optimal diagnosis is D_1.

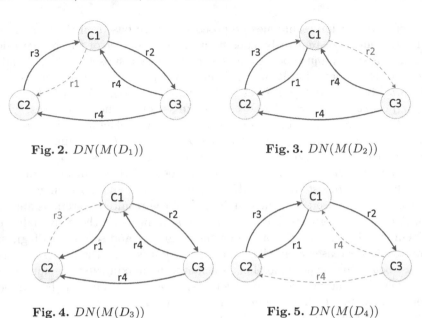

Fig. 2. $DN(M(D_1))$ **Fig. 3.** $DN(M(D_2))$

Fig. 4. $DN(M(D_3))$ **Fig. 5.** $DN(M(D_4))$

5 Related Research

The present work takes as a starting point the notion of social dependence and dependence graphs introduced by Castelfranchi et al. [13,26] and further developed, with a more abstract representation similar to ours, in Boella et al. [5]. In this context the concept of conviviality is defined as reciprocity, in Caire et al. [9,10,12]. Dependence based coalition formation is analyzed by Sichman [25], while other approaches are developed in [24,16,4]. Similarly to Grossi and Turrini [19], our approach brings together coalitional theory and dependence theory within multiagent systems social cooperation study. However, our approach differs as it does not hinge on agreements, and we extend it to MCS.

Various criteria have been proposed for the choice of diagnosis in inconsistency resolution: *i.*) number of bridge rules contained in diagnosis, e.g., subset-minimal diagnoses [14]; *ii.*) local preferences on proposed diagnoses [15]; and *iii.*) local preferences on contexts and provenance information in Contextual Defeasible Logic [3]. Our approach differs in that we take into account a global property of the system, conviviality, with the goal of maximizing its cooperativeness. Our solution is based on the assumption of a central entity that monitors information dependences, and can be combined with any of these approaches. For example, one can apply the conviviality-based approach only to those diagnoses that comply with some local constraints representing user-defined criteria [15], or define hybrid criteria, which combine preferences on diagnoses, as explicitly defined in [15] or derived from local preferences on contexts as in [2], with conviviality-based criteria.

6   Conclusion and Future Work

Multi-Context Systems (MCS) are logical formalizations of distributed context theories connected through a set of bridge rules that enable information flow between contexts. Contexts, represented as individual agents, cooperate by sharing information through their bridge rules. By reasoning on the imported information, they are then able to derive new knowledge. Hence, it is extremely useful to evaluate the ways in which system enable cooperations, and to characterize MCS based on the opportunities they provide to exchange information. In this paper, we introduce into MCS the concept of conviviality, previously proposed to model and measure potential cooperations among agents in multiagent systems. We describe how conviviality can be used to model cooperation in MCS. Based on the intuition that agents depend on the information they receive from other agents to achieve their goals (e.g. to take more informed decisions), we define dependence networks for MCS. The aim for MCS is to be as cooperative as possible, and for agents to have as many choices as possible to cooperate with other agents. We compare the conviviality of MCS, with pairwise conviviality measures. Finally we propose to use conviviality as a property of MCS to resolve inconsistencies resulting from importing mutually inconsistent knowledge from different contexts. Our approach is based on the idea that the optimal solution is the one that minimally decreases the conviviality of the system.

In further research, we plan to label dependencies among system contexts by using the heads of the rules these dependencies are derived from, rather than the rules themselves. Our intuition is that the aim of applying a rule is actually to derive the conclusion that labels the head of the rule. This will require a redefinition of dependence networks to capture both disjunction (among rules that support the same conclusion) and conjunction (among the premises of each rule). We will also address the relation between the preference order on goals, part of our dependence networks definition, and preferences on rules, contexts or diagnoses. Furthermore, we plan to combine conviviality-based inconsistency resolution with the preference-based approaches of [15] and [2], and develop hybrid criteria for inconsistency resolution, taking into account both local preferences and the conviviality of the system. Finally, we will look into how the concept and tools for conviviality can be used in other distributed knowledge models, such as Linked Data, E-connections [21] and managed MCS [8], and distributed systems (e.g. indoor intelligent environments), and study the tradeoff between conviviality and other system properties such as privacy and trust.

References

1. Antoniou, G., Papatheodorou, C., Bikakis, A.: Reasoning about Context in Ambient Intelligence Environments: A Report from the Field. In: Proceedings of KR 2010, pp. 557–559. AAAI Press (2010)
2. Bikakis, A., Antoniou, G.: Defeasible Contextual Reasoning with Arguments in Ambient Intelligence. IEEE Trans. on KDE 22(11), 1492–1506 (2010)

3. Bikakis, A., Antoniou, G., Hassapis, P.: Strategies for contextual reasoning with conflicts in Ambient Intelligence. KIS 27(1), 45–84 (2011)
4. Boella, G., Sauro, L., van der Torre, L.: Algorithms for finding coalitions exploiting a new reciprocity condition. Logic Journal of the IGPL 17(3), 273–297 (2009)
5. Boella, G., Sauro, L., van der Torre, L.W.N.: Power and dependence relations in groups of agents. In: IAT, pp. 246–252. IEEE Computer Society (2004)
6. Bouquet, P., Giunchiglia, F., van Harmelen, F., Serafini, L., Stuckenschmidt, H.: C-OWL: Contextualizing ontologies. In: Fensel, D., Sycara, K., Mylopoulos, J. (eds.) ISWC 2003. LNCS, vol. 2870, pp. 164–179. Springer, Heidelberg (2003)
7. Brewka, G., Eiter, T.: Equilibria in Heterogeneous Nonmonotonic Multi-Context Systems. In: Proceedings of AAAI 2007, pp. 385–390 (2007)
8. Brewka, G., Eiter, T., Fink, M., Weinzierl, A.: Managed Multi-Context Systems. In: IJCAI, pp. 786–791 (2011)
9. Caire, P., Villata, S., Boella, G., van der Torre, L.: Conviviality masks in multiagent systems. In: AAMAS 2008, May 12-16, pp. 1265–1268 (2008)
10. Caire, P., Alcade, B., van der Torre, L., Sombattheera, C.: Conviviality measures. In: AAMAS 2011, Taipei, Taiwan, May 2-6 (2011)
11. Caire, P., Bikakis, A.: Enhancing Cooperation in Distributed Information Systems Using Conviviality and Multi-Context Systems. In: Sombattheera, C., Agarwal, A., Udgata, S.K., Lavangnananda, K. (eds.) MIWAI 2011. LNCS, vol. 7080, pp. 14–25. Springer, Heidelberg (2011)
12. Caire, P., van der Torre, L.: Convivial ambient technologies: Requirements, ontology and design. The Computer Journal 3 (2009)
13. Castelfranchi, C.: The micro-macro constitution of power. Protosociology 18, 208–269 (2003)
14. Eiter, T., Fink, M., Schüller, P., Weinzierl, A.: Finding Explanations of Inconsistency in Multi-Context Systems. In: Proceedings of KR 2010. AAAI Press (2010)
15. Eiter, T., Fink, M., Weinzierl, A.: Preference-Based Inconsistency Assessment in Multi-Context Systems. In: Janhunen, T., Niemelä, I. (eds.) JELIA 2010. LNCS, vol. 6341, pp. 143–155. Springer, Heidelberg (2010)
16. Gerber, A., Klusch, M.: Forming dynamic coalitions of rational agents by use of the dcf-s scheme. In: AAMAS, pp. 994–995 (2003)
17. Ghidini, C., Giunchiglia, F.: Local Models Semantics, or contextual reasoning=locality+compatibility. Artificial Intelligence 127(2), 221–259 (2001)
18. Giunchiglia, F., Serafini, L.: Multilanguage hierarchical logics, or: how we can do without modal logics. Artificial Intelligence 65(1) (1994)
19. Grossi, D., Turrini, P.: Dependence theory via game theory. In: AAMAS 2010, pp. 1147–1154 (2010)
20. Illich, I.: Tools for Conviviality. Marion Boyars Publishers, London (1974)
21. Kutz, O., Lutz, C., Wolter, F., Zakharyaschev, M.: E-connections of abstract description systems. Artificial Intelligence 156(1), 1–73 (2004)
22. Lenat, D.B., Guha, R.V.: Building Large Knowledge-Based Systems; Representation and Inference in the Cyc Project. Addison-Wesley Longman Publishing Co., Inc., Boston (1989)
23. Sabater, J., Sierra, C., Parsons, S., Jennings, N.R.: Engineering Executable Agents using Multi-context Systems. J. of Logic and Computation 12(3), 413–442 (2002)
24. Shehory, O., Kraus, S.: Methods for task allocation via agent coalition formation. Artif. Intell. 101(1-2), 165–200 (1998)
25. Sichman, J.S.: Depint: Dependence-based coalition formation in an open multi-agent scenario. J. Artificial Societies and Social Simulation 1(2) (1998)
26. Sichman, J.S., Conte, R.: Multi-agent dependence by dependence graphs. In: Procs. of the First Int. Joint Conference AAMAS 2002, pp. 483–490. ACM (2002)

Model and Algorithm for Dynamic Multi-Objective Distributed Optimization

Maxime Clement[1], Tenda Okimoto[3,4], Tony Ribeiro[2], and Katsumi Inoue[4]

[1] Pierre and Marie Curie University (Paris 6), Paris, France
maxime.clement@etu.upmc.fr
[2] The Graduate University for Advanced Studies, Tokyo, Japan
[3] Transdisciplinary Research Integration Center, Tokyo, Japan
[4] National Institute of Informatics, Tokyo, Japan
{tony-ribeiro,tenda,inoue}@nii.ac.jp

Abstract. Many problems in multi-agent systems can be represented as a Distributed Constraint Optimization Problem (DCOP) where the goal is to find the best assignment to variables in order to minimize the cost. More complex problems including several criteria can be represented as a Multi-Objective Distributed Constraint Optimization Problem (MO-DCOP) where the goal is to optimize several criteria at the same time. However, many problems are subject to changes over time and need to be represented as dynamic problems. In this paper, we formalize the Dynamic Multi-Objective Distributed Constraint Optimization Problem (DMO-DCOP) and introduce the first algorithm called DMOBB to handle changes in the number of objectives.

1 Introduction

A *Distributed Constraint Optimization Problem* (DCOP) [6, 8, 9] is a fundamental problem that can formalize various applications related to multi-agent cooperation. A DCOP consists of a set of agents, each of which needs to decide the value assignment of its variables so that the sum of the resulting costs is minimized. In the last decade, various algorithms have been developed to efficiently solve DCOPs, e.g., ADOPT [8], BnB-ADOPT [11], DPOP [9], and OptAPO [6]. Many multi-agent coordination problems can be represented as DCOPs, e.g., distributed resource allocation problems including sensor networks [4], meeting scheduling [5], and the synchronization of traffic lights [3].

A *Multi-Objective Distributed Constraint Optimization Problem* (MO-DCOP) [2, 7] is an extension of a mono-objective DCOP. Algorithms for solving an MO-DCOP provide all the solutions that offer an interesting trade-off between the different objectives Compared to DCOPs, there exists only two MO-DCOP algorithms, the Bounded Multi-Objective Max-Sum algorithm (B-MOMS) [2] and a distributed search method with bounded cost vectors [7] generalizes ADOPT for MO-DCOPs.

Now consider a dynamic environment where many changes can occur. Many real world problems take place in such environment but the previous models

G. Boella et al. (Eds.): PRIMA 2013, LNAI 8291, pp. 413–420, 2013.
© Springer-Verlag Berlin Heidelberg 2013

(DCOP and MO-DCOP) do not take changes into account. There exists some works for dynamic DCOPs [1, 12], however, as far as the authors are aware, there exists no work on considering multiple criteria in a dynamic environment.

As an example, imagine a set of unmanned vehicles searching for survivors while maintaining a wireless communication network between them. Those vehicles care about several objectives such as the fuel consumption, the quality of the communication network, the distance to the base, etc. We do not know if changes to the problem might occur but assume the topology of the problem (the agents and their ordering) will not change. Now, while searching for survivors, the vehicles are warned about several dangerous areas in their research zone. The vehicles need to react to this new information in order to avoid dangerous spots and new solutions are required to take every objectives into account.

In this paper, we first propose a Dynamic Multi-Objective Distributed Constraint Optimization Problem (DMO-DCOP) which is the extension of an MO-DCOP and a dynamic DCOP. Furthermore, we develop the first algorithm called Dynamic Multi-Objective Branch and Bound (DMOBB) for solving a DMO-DCOP. This algorithm focuses on a change in the number of objectives and utilizes (i) a special graph structure called a *pseudo-tree*, which is widely used in DCOP algorithms, (ii) a Decentralized Synchronous Branch and Bound. We adapted it for MO-DCOPs and DMO-DCOPs.

The remainder of this paper is organized as follows. Section 2 and 3 provides some preliminaries on DCOPs and MO-DCOPs. Section 4 formalizes a DMO-DCOP and introduces a novel algorithm for solving a DMO-DCOP which can guarantee to find all Pareto solutions. Section 5 empirically evaluates our proposed algorithm. Finally, we conclude in Section 6 and provide some perspectives for future work.

2 DCOP

A *Distributed Constraint Optimization Problem* (DCOP) [8, 9] is a fundamental problem that can formalize various applications for multi-agent cooperation.

A DCOP is defined with a set of agents S, a set of variables X, a set of constraint relations C, and a set of reward functions O. An agent i has its own variable x_i. A variable x_i takes its value from a finite, discrete domain D_i. A constraint relation (i, j) means there exists a constraint relation between x_i and x_j. For x_i and x_j, which have a constraint relation, the reward for an assignment $\{(x_i, d_i), (x_j, d_j)\}$ is defined by a reward function $r_{i,j}(d_i, d_j) : D_i \times D_j \to \mathbb{R}^+$. For a value assignment to all variables A, let us denote

$$R(A) = \sum_{(i,j) \in C, \{(x_i, d_i), (x_j, d_j)\} \subseteq A} r_{i,j}(d_i, d_j), \tag{1}$$

where $d_i \in D_i$ and $d_j \in D_j$. Then, an optimal assignment A^* is given as $\arg\max_A R(A)$, i.e., A^* is an assignment that maximizes the sum of the value of all reward functions. A DCOP can be represented using a constraint graph, in which a node represents an agent/variable and an edge represents a constraint.

Table 1. Example of MO-DCOP

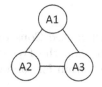

A_1	A_2	cost	A_2	A_3	cost	A_1	A_3	cost
a	a	(5,2)	a	a	(0,1)	a	a	(1,0)
a	b	(7,1)	a	b	(2,1)	a	b	(1,0)
b	a	(10,3)	b	a	(0,2)	b	a	(0,1)
b	b	(12,0)	b	b	(2,0)	b	b	(3,2)

3   MO-DCOP

A *Multi-Objective Distributed Constraint Optimization Problem* (MO-DCOP)
[2, 7] is the extension of a mono-objective DCOP. An MO-DCOP is defined
with a set of agents S, a set of variables X, multi-objective constraints $C = \{C^1, \ldots, C^m\}$, i.e., a set of sets of constraint relations, and multi-objective functions $O = \{O^1, \ldots, O^m\}$, i.e., a set of sets of objective functions. For an objective
l $(1 \leq l \leq m)$, a cost function $f_{i,j}^l : D_i \times D_j \to \mathbb{R}$, and a value assignment to all
variables A, let us denote

$$R^l(A) = \sum_{(i,j) \in C^l, \{(x_i, d_i), (x_j, d_j)\} \subseteq A} f_{i,j}^l(d_i, d_j), \text{ where } d_i \in D_i \text{ and } d_j \in D_j. \quad (2)$$

Then, the sum of the values of all cost functions for m objectives is defined
by a cost vector, denoted $R(A) = (R^1(A), \ldots, R^m(A))$. Finding an assignment
that minimizes all objective functions simultaneously is ideal. However, in general, since trade-offs exist among objectives, there does not exist such an ideal
assignment. Thus, the optimal solution of an MO-DCOP is characterized by using the concept of *Pareto optimality*. Because of this possible trade-off between
objectives, the size of the Pareto front is exponential in the number of agents,
i.e., every possible assignment can be a Pareto solution in the worst case. An
MO-DCOP can be also represented using a constraint graph.

Definition 1 (Dominance). For an MO-DCOP and two cost vectors $R(A)$
and $R(A')$ obtained by assignments A and A', we say that $R(A)$ *dominates*
$R(A')$, denoted by $R(A) \prec R(A')$, iff $R(A)$ is partially less than $R(A')$, i.e., (i)
it holds $R^l(A) \leq R^l(A')$ for all objectives l, and (ii) there exists at least one
objective l', such that $R^{l'}(A) < R^{l'}(A')$.

Definition 2 (Pareto solution). For an MO-DCOP and an assignment A, we
say A is the *Pareto solution*, iff there does not exist another assignment A', such
that $R(A') \prec R(A)$.

Definition 3 (Pareto Front). For an MO-DCOP, the *Pareto front* is the set
of cost vectors obtained by the Pareto solutions. *Solving an MO-DCOP is to
find the Pareto front.*

Example 1 (MO-DCOP). We show a bi-objective DCOP using the example represented with Table 1. The table shows three cost tables among three agents.
The Pareto solutions of this problem are $\{\{\{(A_1, a), (A_2, a), (A_3, a)\} \to (6,3)\}$,
$\{\{(A_1, a), (A_2, b), (A_3, b)\} \to (10,1)\}\}$.

4 Dynamic Multi-Objective Distributed Constraint Optimization Problem

In this section, we formalize a Dynamic Multi-Objective Distributed Constraint Optimization Problem (DMO-DCOP). Furthermore, we develop the Dynamic Multi-Objective Branch and Bound (DMOBB), the first algorithm for solving a DMO-DCOP and provide its complexity.

4.1 Model

A *Dynamic Multi-Objective Distributed Constraint Optimization Problem* (DMO-DCOP) is the extension of an MO-DCOP. A DMO-DCOP is defined by a sequence of MO-DCOPs.

$$< MO\text{-}DCOP_1, MO\text{-}DCOP_2, ..., MO\text{-}DCOP_k > . \qquad (3)$$

In this paper, we assume that

- only the number of objective functions changes,
- the number of agents/variables, domains, and costs for current constraints does not change.

Solving a DMO-DCOP is to find a sequence of Pareto front

$$< PF_1, PF_2, ..., PF_k >, \qquad (4)$$

where PF_i $(1 \leq i \leq k)$ is the Pareto front of $MO\text{-}DCOP_i$. Since we do not know how many objective functions will be removed/added in the next MO-DCOP, it is a reactive approach.

Definition 4 (Evolution of the Pareto Front). For an MO-DCOP$_i$ and its corresponding Pareto front PF_i, *adding* objectives to MO-DCOP$_i$ will result in a new Pareto front PF_{i+1} such that for all unique cost vectors in PF_i, one of the assignment yielding this cost will still be a Pareto solution in PF_{i+1}. However, if different assignments yield a same cost in PF_i, there is no guarantee that all assignments will still yield Pareto Solutions in PF_{i+1}. Similarly, in case several objectives are *removed*, there is no guarantee that all Pareto solutions of MO-DCOP$_i$ are also the Pareto solutions in MO-DCOP$_{i+1}$.

4.2 DMOBB Algorithm

To run DMOBB, we first order the agents into a *pseudo-tree* [10].

A pseudo-tree is a special graph structure widely used in DCOP algorithms. In a pseudo-tree, there exists a unique root node, and each non-root node has a parent node. For each node/agent i, we denote the parent node, and children of i as follows:

- $parent_i$, the parent of the agent i.

Algorithm 1. Search Algorithm for agent a_i

1: i: integer (agent id)
2: $children$: list of agents
3: PF: set of pairs of assignment and cost vector (local PF for all $context$)
4: $currentPF$: set of pairs of assignment and cost vector (local PF front for the current $context$)
5: PF_c: set of pairs of assignment and cost vector (children Pareto front)
6: $context$: vector of integers (ancestors assignment)
7: UB: set of cost vectors (local upper bounds)
8: $response$: integer
9: d_i: current value from domain D_i being explored
10: $currentPF \leftarrow \emptyset$
11: **if** Root agent **then**// Root agent
12:     **for** each value d_i of D **do**
13:         $UB \leftarrow computeUB()$
14:         send $(d_i, \emptyset, UB)$ // Send Value message
15:         $response \leftarrow 0$;$PF_c \leftarrow \emptyset$
16:         **while** $response < |children|$ **do** // Receive Cost messages
17:             **if** message $= (PF_{c_i})$ **then**
18:                 $PF_c \leftarrow (PF_c \oplus PF_{c_i}) + \delta_{assignment \cup d_i}$
19:                 $response \leftarrow response + 1$
20:         $currentPF \leftarrow (currentPF \uplus PF_c)$
21:     send TERMINATE to all children
22: **else**
23:     **while** $message \neq$ TERMINATE **do**
24:         $message \leftarrow receive()$ // Receive Termination message
25:         **if** $message =$ TERMINATE **then**
26:             send TERMINATE to all children
                // Receive Value message
27:         **if** $message = (new\_context, \gamma_{new\_context}, UB_p)$ **then**
28:             $context \leftarrow new\_context$; $currentPF \leftarrow \emptyset$; $PF_c \leftarrow \emptyset$
29:             **for** each value d_i of D **do**
30:                 $UB \leftarrow computeUB()$
31:                 $assignment \leftarrow context \cup d_i$
32:                 $\gamma_{assignment} \leftarrow \delta_{assignment} + \gamma_{new\_context}$
33:                 **if** $\gamma_{assignment}$ is not dominated by UB **then** // Check bounds
34:                     send $(assignment, \gamma_{assignment}, UB)$ to all children
35:                     **if** Leaf agent **then** // Leaf agent
36:                         $currentPF \leftarrow (currentPF \uplus \delta_{assignment})$
37:                     **else**
38:                         $response \leftarrow 0$;$PF_c \leftarrow \emptyset$
39:                         **while** $response < |children|$ **do** // Receive Cost messages
40:                             **if** message $= (PF_{c_i})$ **then**
41:                                 $PF_c \leftarrow (PF_c \oplus PF_{c_i})$
42:                                 $response \leftarrow response + 1$
43:                         $currentPF \leftarrow (currentPF \uplus (PF_c + \delta_{assignment}))$
44:             send $currentPF$ to parent // Send Cost message
45:         add $currentPF$ to PF

Algorithm 2. Algorithm to build UB

46: UB: set of cost vectors (local upper bounds)
47: UB_p: set of cost vectors (upper bounds received from the parent)
48: $currentPF$ set of pairs of assignment and cost vector (local Pareto front for the current $context$)
49: $previousPF$ set of pairs of assignment and cost vector (local Pareto front for the previous search)
50: $context$: vector of integers (ancestors assignment)
51: $addedObjMax$: vector of integers with the local maximal value for each newly added objectives.
52: $UB \leftarrow currentPF \uplus UB_p$
    //Find the maximal acceptable cost for the new objectives
53: **for** each added objective m **do**
54:     **for** each $cost \in UB$ **do**
55:         $addedObjMax[m] \leftarrow max(addedObjMax[m], cost[m])$
    //Reuse previous bound
56: **for** each $(assignment, cost) \in previousPF$ **do**
57:     **if** $assignment$ compatible with $context$ **then**
58:         $UB \leftarrow UB \uplus (cost \cup addedObjMax)$

– $children_i$, the set of children of i.

We assume that this operation is done as a preprocessing step. Since adding or removing objectives has no impact on the topology of the problem, the ordering will stay the same throughout the execution.

We show the pseudo-code of DMOBB in Algorithm 1 and 2. During the search phase, the solution space will be explored to completely determine the Pareto solutions. The search can start without any prior knowledge or it can use the Pareto front found during the previous search.

To communicate information between the agents in the pseudo-tree, we use the following three message types :

Value message: Sent from an agent i to its children, it contains the *context* currently being explored, the gamma cost $\gamma_{context}$ and the bounds used by the parent (UB_p).

Cost message: Sent from an agent i its parent, it contains the local Pareto front $PF_{context}$ found for the given context *context*.

Terminate message: Sent from parent to children to indicate the search is over.

Furthermore, we define 2 operators, the first one is the direct sum for two Pareto fronts which makes use of the direct sum between two vectors.

$$PF_1 \bigoplus PF_2 = \left\{ \forall (X, Y) \in PF_1 \times PF_2, X \bigoplus Y \right\} \tag{5}$$

The second operator is the union of two Pareto fronts that keeps only the non-dominated cost vectors.

$$A \uplus B = A \cup B \setminus \{a < b\} \cup \{b < a\}, a \in A, b \in B. \tag{6}$$

We also define the delta cost $\delta_{context+d_i}$ and the gamma cost $\gamma_{context+d_i}$. The delta cost is the sum of constraint costs of all constraints that involve both i and one of its ancestors for the current value d_i and the values of ancestor agents contained in the current *context*. The gamma cost is the sum of ancestors' delta cost plus the local delta cost for context $context + d_i$.

Theorem 1. *With DP the DMO-DCOP we want to solve, n the number of variables, m the number of objectives and $|d|$ the domain size for the variables, the memory use of an agent to solve DP is given by $O(2m|d|^n)$. The total time required to solve DP is given by $O(m^2|d|^{3n}|DP|)$.*

5   Experimental Evaluation

In this section, we evaluate the performances of DMOBB and compare them with the naive method where each MO-DCOP is solved independently. All the tests are made with a domain size of 2 and a density of 1 (a variable always share a constraint with all the other variables). We show the results obtained when

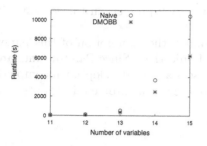

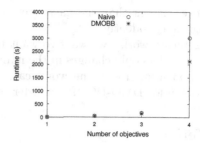

Fig. 1. Varying number of variables   **Fig. 2.** Varying number of objectives

varying the number of variables and when varying the number of objectives. We implemented our algorithm in Java using the Jade framework and all tests were run on 6 cores running at 2.6GHz with 12GB of RAM.

Varying Variables Figure 1 shows the runtime when varying the number of nodes. Those results are obtained for the complete solving of a $DMO\text{-}DCOP =< MO\text{-}DCOP_1, MO\text{-}DCOP_2, MO\text{-}DCOP_3 >$ with the first MO-DCOP having 3 objectives, the second one 4 and the last one 5. We can see the expected exponential growth of the runtime making larger problems quickly uncomputable. However, we can see that the growth when using DMOBB is reduced. The costliest operation in our algorithm is the comparison of Pareto fronts. Our algorithm, even in the worst case, can prune some solutions in the leaf nodes. This reduces the size of the Pareto fronts that comes up the tree, decreasing the runtime significantly. We now consider the influence of the number of objectives on the runtime. For this test, we solved a $DMO\text{-}DCOP =< MO\text{-}DCOP_1, MO\text{-}DCOP_2 >$ such that $MO\text{-}DCOP_1$ has m objectives and $MO\text{-}DCOP_2$ has $m+1$ objectives. We show in figure 2 the runtime it takes to solve $MO\text{-}DCOP_2$ for a problem with 14 variables. We varied m from 1 to 4 and we can see that with bigger m the improvement compared to the naive method increases. DMOBB has almost no impact for small problems but we see that we get 30% speedup when solving a problem with 5 objectives and reusing the previous solutions.

To conclude the experimental part, we have shown that the larger the problems, the more efficient DMOBB is compared to the naive resolution. However, on smaller problems, DMOBB offers no advantages compared to the naive method and can even be less efficient. Note that those results were obtained on the worst case (random cost vectors and density 1) and that depending on the problem, better results can be expected.

6   Conclusion

In this paper, we introduced the Dynamic Multi-Objective Distributed Constraint Optimization Problem (DMODCOP) and proposed DMOBB, the first algorithm to solve such problem in a reactive approach. We showed how DMOBB is more efficient than the naive method where each problem in the sequence is solved independently.

As future works, we want to want to abandon the assumption of this paper that considers only changes in the number of objectives. Since Pareto fronts are of exponential size in the worst case, we also want to develop an incomplete algorithm for DMO-DCOPs in order to solve large-scale problem instances.

References

[1] Billiau, G., Chang, C.F., Ghose, A.: SBDO: A new robust approach to dynamic distributed constraint optimisation. In: Desai, N., Liu, A., Winikoff, M. (eds.) PRIMA 2010. LNCS, vol. 7057, pp. 11–26. Springer, Heidelberg (2012)

[2] Fave, F.M.D., Stranders, R., Rogers, A., Jennings, N.R.: Bounded decentralised coordination over multiple objectives. In: Proceedings of the 10th International Conference on Autonomous Agents and Multiagent Systems, pp. 371–378 (2011)

[3] Junges, R., Bazzan, A.L.C.: Evaluating the performance of DCOP algorithms in a real world, dynamic problem. In: Proceedings of the 7th International Conference on Autonomous Agents and Multiagent Systems, pp. 599–606 (2008)

[4] Lesser, V., Ortiz, C., Tambe, M. (eds.): Distributed Sensor Networks: A Multiagent Perspective, vol. 9. Kluwer Academic Publishers (2003)

[5] Maheswaran, R.T., Tambe, M., Bowring, E., Pearce, J.P., Varakantham, P.: Taking DCOP to the real world: Efficient complete solutions for distributed multi-event scheduling. In: Proceedings of the 3rd International Conference on Autonomous Agents and Multiagent Systems, pp. 310–317 (2004)

[6] Mailler, R., Lesser, V.R.: Solving distributed constraint optimization problems using cooperative mediation. In: Proceedings of the 3rd International Conference on Autonomous Agents and Multiagent Systems, pp. 438–445 (2004)

[7] Matsui, T., Silaghi, M., Hirayama, K., Yokoo, M., Matsuo, H.: Distributed search method with bounded cost vectors on multiple objective dcops. In: Proceedings of the 15th International Conference on Principles and Practice of Multi-Agent Systems, pp. 137–152 (2012)

[8] Modi, P., Shen, W., Tambe, M., Yokoo, M.: Adopt: asynchronous distributed constraint optimization with quality guarantees. Artificial Intelligence 161(1-2), 149–180 (2005)

[9] Petcu, A., Faltings, B.: A scalable method for multiagent constraint optimization, pp. 266–271 (2005)

[10] Schiex, T., Fargier, H., Verfaillie, G.: Valued constraint satisfaction problems: Hard and easy problems. In: Proceedings of the 14th International Joint Conference on sArtificial Intelligence, pp. 631–639 (1995)

[11] Yeoh, W., Felner, A., Koenig, S.: BnB-ADOPT: An asynchronous branch-and-bound DCOP algorithm. Journal of Artificial Intelligence Research 38, 85–133 (2010)

[12] Yeoh, W., Varakantham, P., Sun, X., Koenig, S.: Incremental dcop search algorithms for solving dynamic dcops. In: AAMAS, pp. 1069–1070 (2011)

Lightweight Distributed Adaptive Algorithm for Voting Procedures by Using Network Average Consensus

Clement Duhart[1,2], Michel Cotsaftis[1], and Cyrille Bertelle[2]

[1] LACSC, ECE Paris School of Engineering, France
{duhart,mcot}@ece.fr
[2] LITIS, Havre University, France
cyrille.bertelle@univ-lehavre.fr

Abstract. Consensus Seeking (CS) is an important research area in which this work contributes by proposing a new distributed algorithm to solve Voting Procedures (VP) problems in mobile networks with link failures under strong constraints on communication capacity.

Keywords: Multi Agent System (MAS), Network Average Consensus (NAC), Wireless Sensor Network (WSN), Voting Procedures (VP).

Introduction

Synopsis. In Multi Agent Systems (MASs) research community, Consensus Seeking (CS) has been an attractive domain for a long time with recent emphasis on using new approaches through the Network Average Consensus (NAC) framework. Initially applied in Dynamic System (DS) and particularly in non-holonomic systems, NAC is a very powerful framework ensuring coordination on autonomous mobile networks performing distributed tasks like in Multi-Vehicle Systems. From good properties in terms of robustness according to switching communication topologies and transmission time delay issues, it is interesting to explore NAC's approach on data fusion applied in distributed statistical Decisions Theory (DT). Moreover, this framework does not require complex network protocols with extra semantic concepts which introduce protocol overhead. Therefore application of MAS running on networks with restricted communication capacity is investigated with an interest on network load costs for Wireless Sensor Network (WSN) implementation. *This paper focuses on preference aggregation to allow a set of agents to select a common, consistent and unique decision in dynamic networks with constrained communication capacity in a fully distributed way.* As NAC is an asymptotic approximation of consensus equilibrium, finite time convergence issue is addressed by using a multi-scale adaptive algorithm which ensures likewise discrete result values. The paper is organized as follows. Section 1 presents the theoretical background of the proposed algorithm. Section 2 defines implementation requirements. Section 3 presents an example application with associated results and some discussions. Conclusion and future works appear in Section 4.

G. Boella et al. (Eds.): PRIMA 2013, LNAI 8291, pp. 421–428, 2013.
© Springer-Verlag Berlin Heidelberg 2013

Literature Review. NAC has been studied initially in DS and Control Theory (CT) e.g. Synchronization of Coupled Oscillators, Flocking Theory, Fast Consensus, Rendez-vous in Space or Distributed Formation Control around issues concerning continuous versus discrete time consensus and undirected or directed graphs [5] and references herein. Several contributions have demonstrated the insensitivity of NAC convergence according to given conditions for Time Delay, Switching Topologies [6,8] and Network costs in real applications with localized in time communication failures [4,7]. After robustness study, convergence time has been explored [3] according to network topology (regular lattive, random network, smallworld [5] and free-scale network [10]) to define a performance indicator λ_2 called algebraic connectivity. Finally, other update schemes are currently studied for finite time convergence [1] and the definition of general function operators framework [2]. This brief outline is not comprehensive regarding the amount of work on NAC, but illustrates its possibility for new kinds of distributed algorithms in MAS, especially for Voting Procedures (VP).

1   Theoretical Background

This paper proposes a way to perform Voting Procedures (VP) in Multi Agent System (MAS) by a distributed approach. Each node has its own preference order which must be aggregated with those of the other nodes to represent the whole network preference order. Preferential model uses a utility function to model numerically the preference order for each node. Each of these utility functions are aggregated by executing Multi-Network Average Consensus (NAC) on them to build a unique aggregated utility function on which decision rules are applied. Present work proposes a distributed algorithm which guarantees convergence to a unique preference order produced by the consensus. This allows nodes to take the same decision at the end of the algorithm without using extra mechanisms to ensure consistency and uniformity of node decisions. Network agents are distributed and constrained by their communication capacity such as in Wireless Sensor Network (WSN) applications. Their ability to communicate with agent community is limited to their neighbours which excludes full broadcast exchanges producing network overload.

1.1   Preference Model

The agent community is composed of N nodes which must select a common profile among a set $\rho_0, \rho_1 \ldots \rho_M$ of size M without centralization of all node preferences. Notice that "A is preferred to B by the node i" is denoted $A \underset{i}{\succ} B$. Each node should define a partial order of their profile preferences by defining vector $u^i(t) = \{u_1^i, \ldots, u_M^i\}$, $u_j^i(t)$ is the monotonic discrete utility function of profile ρ_j for the node i at the time t and $\dot{u}_j^i = \lim_{t \mapsto +\infty} u_j^i(t)$. The whole network profile preference order is defined by Eq. 1.

$$\exists j \; / \; \forall i, k, \rho_j \underset{i}{\succ} \rho_k \iff \exists j \; / \; \forall k, \rho_j \succ \rho_k \iff \exists j \; / \; \forall i, k, \dot{u}_j^i > \dot{u}_k^i \qquad (1)$$

1.2 Distributed Aggregation Process

Based on the discrete utility function $u^i(0)$ of each node i, the aggregation process must build an aggregated utility function $\dot{u}$ representative of the whole network. The utility functions are discrete, so the aggregation process can be executed independently. Global aggregation process is composed of a set of elementary aggregations by using NAC algorithm [9]. In Eq. 2, $(\dot{u}_0, \ldots, \dot{u}_M)$ represents the result values of consensus on each profile j which has its final value $\dot{u}_j$ equal to the means of the utilities $u_j^i(0)$ weighted by their relevant node importance w^i. So, as NAC algorithm is a decentralized algorithm, the global aggregation process is also decentralized because it is composed of M NAC executed simultaneously. NAC algorithm has an asymptotic convergence to the initial value of node's utility by using gradient-descent algorithm with error approximation ε.

$$\dot{u} = (\dot{u}_0, \ldots, \dot{u}_M) = \frac{1}{N} \sum w^i u_j^i(0) \Longrightarrow \forall i, j \left| \dot{u}_j - \dot{u}_j^i \right| < \varepsilon \qquad (2)$$

The analytic form of iterative algorithm NAC is reminded in Eq. 3 under the necessary condition of convergence given in [5]: $\forall i, w^i < \frac{1}{\Delta}$; $\Delta = max(\#\Upsilon_i)$ with $\#\Upsilon_i$ is the degree of vertex i and Δ the graph's degree.

$$u_j^i(t+1) = u_j^i(t) - w^i \sum_{k=0}^{N} \left(u_j^i(t) - u_j^k(t) \right) \qquad (3)$$

By applying NAC on each profile, each node obtains the same profile utility function according to error interval $]-\varepsilon + \dot{u}; \dot{u} + \varepsilon[$ produced by asymptotic convergence. Unfortunately, this error interval is unknown and cannot be computed analytically without full knowledge of the problem data. This theory limitation is bypassed, by using an upper bound function as discussed in Section 2.1.

1.3 Consistent Decision Rules

After the execution of the aggregation process, nodes must choose the best profile. According to the convergence error, some cases cannot be accurately determined. Consequently, Th. 1 gives conditions under which interval between utility values is large enough to choose without ambiguity. Else, Def. 1 proposes decision-making which ensures its uniqueness for each node.

Theorem 1. *If and only if there exists a profile utility function u_j^i greater than any other profile utility function u_k^i over 4ε for any decision makers i estimated by network average consensus, then this profile is preferred to any other profile by all decision makers.*

$$\forall i, k, \exists j \;/\; u_j^i > u_k^i \text{ and } \left| u_j^i - u_k^i \right| > 4\varepsilon \Longleftrightarrow \forall i, \exists j \;/\; \rho = \rho_j \qquad (4)$$

Proof. Network average consensus converge to average value $\dot{u}$ of node initial value $u(0)$ for any network topology if convergence rate of gradient-descent algorithm is limited to $\frac{1}{\Delta}$ with $\Delta = max(\#\Upsilon_i)$ [5]. Average value $\dot{u}$ is unique by definition, so the set of utility order $u_0^i(0) > \cdots > u_M^i(0)$ of each node i will evolve to a unique average utility order $\dot{u}_k > \cdots > \dot{u}_j$, $k, j \in [0, M]$ according to convergence error ε which defines an error interval $]-\varepsilon + \dot{u}; \dot{u} + \varepsilon[$. Assume that there exists a node which prefers a profile j different from the other node preferences. This can happen if and only if the interval error of this preference utility is juxtaposed to another interval error of another near preference utility $:]-\varepsilon + \dot{u}_j, \dot{u}_j + \varepsilon[\cap]-\varepsilon + \dot{u}_k, \dot{u}_k + \varepsilon[\neq \emptyset$ with $\dot{u}_j^i \in]-\varepsilon + \dot{u}_j, \dot{u}_j + \varepsilon[$ and $\dot{u}_k^i \in]-\varepsilon + \dot{u}_k, \dot{u}_k + \varepsilon[$. Now, if $|\dot{u}_j^i - \dot{u}_k^i| > 4\varepsilon$, it is obvious by using triangle inequality that $]-\varepsilon + \dot{u}_j, \dot{u}_j + \varepsilon[\cap]-\varepsilon + \dot{u}_k, \dot{u}_k + \varepsilon[= \emptyset$. Thus, if a node has other preference than the other nodes, its preference utility cannot be spaced from its other preference utility by more than 4ε.

Definition 1. *Two profiles ρ_i and ρ_j are defined as equivalent if the distance between their estimated aggregated utility value is inferior to 4ε.*

$$\rho_j \sim \rho_k \iff |u_j^i - u_k^i| < 4\varepsilon \tag{5}$$

Based on Th. 1 and Def. 1, a uniqueness profile decision rule can be defined such as in Eq. 6. Th. 1 guarantees that it is possible to build a unique aggregated order of preferences which is representative of all nodes' profile preference where the interval is sufficiently accurate. Def. 1 defined equivalence state if it is a partial order. Finally, space U^i is the set of equivalent best aggregated profile preference utility on which is applied an arbitrary rule to select one unique and common profile ρ.

$$\rho = \begin{cases} U^i \in \mathbb{N} \ / \ j, k \in U^i \text{ if } \forall l, i, \ \rho_j \underset{i}{\sim} \rho_k \underset{i}{\succ} \rho_l \\ \rho_i = \min(U^i) \end{cases} \tag{6}$$

2   Algorithm Implementation

2.1   Time Convergence Estimator

Previous theoretical background presents a convergence process under infinite time. Also, it is assumed that it is possible to determine a cone distance ε around an ideal average value $\dot{u}_j$ where each estimated value u_j^i is inside it. But, as each node cannot know the utility values of other nodes, it is impossible for them to know when consensus is reached. Banach fixed point theorem can give a bounded time to reach it because NAC uses a gradient-descent algorithm which has a q-linear convergence and so it is a k-lipschitzien function such as defined in Eq. 7.

$$\left| u_j^i(t+1) - \dot{u}_j \right| \le k \left| u_j^i(t) - \dot{u}_j \right| \ , \ k \in [0,1] \Longrightarrow \varepsilon \le \frac{k^n}{(1-k)} \left[\max(u_j^i) - \min(u_j^i) \right] \tag{7}$$

Unfortunately to the best of our knowledge, there is no analytical method to determine value k without knowing about the network's topology (like algebraic connectivity λ_2) and nodes initial values. Indeed, based on initial values, the graph Laplacian matrix L and the algebraic value λ_2, it is possible to determine an upper bounded value of required iterations [1]: $\frac{||Lu_j(0)||_2}{\lambda_2}$.

2.2   Multi-Scale Adaptive Accuracy

Implementation is limited by hardware accuracy and finite time requirement. In this case, the algorithm must refine its equivalence Def. 1 between two utility values and its stop condition for the processing. As ε determines maximum error interval for a given utility value for all nodes, after enough iterations their equivalence according to ε and encoding base q is defined by Eq. 8.

$$\forall i, \exists j, k \ / \ \left\lceil \frac{(u_j^i - u_k^i)}{(q+1)\,\varepsilon} \right\rceil = 0 \Longrightarrow \rho_j \sim \rho_k \tag{8}$$

Even with Eq. 8, two profiles can be equivalent without equality of their utility values according to ε because of a lack of significant digits. To increase the accuracy of the estimated utility value, the refining process is executed NAC with a decreasing error interval $\varepsilon = \frac{\varepsilon}{q}$. The refining process must continue until it is possible to guarantee that utility values are accurate enough for allowing each node to extract the same U^i space defined in Eq. 6. As node decisions must be consistent by defining the common U space, the process of estimation refining must stop if each node has its set U distant enough from the other utility values according to ε error interval and encoding limitations as defined in Eq. 9.

$$\forall i, \exists j, k \ / \ u_j^i \in U^i, u_k^i \notin U^i, |u_j^i - u_k^i| > q\varepsilon + \varepsilon \Longleftrightarrow \forall i, U = U^i \tag{9}$$

2.3   Voting Procedure Algorithm

The algorithm is composed of two main steps: the aggregation of utility values and the selection of the profile. During the aggregation step, nodes communicate with each other by broadcasting their current utility value $u^i(t)$ to their neighbours. This step is called with a decreasing ε until the aggregated utility values are spaced enough according to convergence error to d utility values.

Algorithm 1. Algorithm executed on each node i.

Data: $u^i(0)$, w^i Result: ρ
begin
 $\varepsilon \leftarrow 1$;
 repeat
  $\varepsilon \leftarrow \varepsilon * 0.1$;
  repeat
   foreach $j=1 \ldots M$ do
    $u_j^i(t+1) \leftarrow u_j^i(t) - w^i \sum_{k=0}^{N}[u_j^i(t) - u_j^k(t)]$
   until $\frac{k^n}{(1-k)}[\max(u_j^i) - \min(u_j^i)] < \frac{\varepsilon}{2}$;
   $[value, k] \leftarrow max(u)$;
   DONE $\leftarrow$ true;
   foreach $j=1 \ldots M$ do
    if $|value - u_j| < (q+1)\,\varepsilon$ and $\left\lceil \frac{(value - u_j)}{(q+1)\,\varepsilon} \right\rceil \neq 0$ then
     DONE $\leftarrow$ false;
  until $!\ DONE$;
  $[value, \rho] = \max(u)$;
  foreach $j=1 \ldots M$ do
   if $\left\lceil \frac{(value - u_j)}{(q+1)\,\varepsilon} \right\rceil = 0$ then
    $\rho \leftarrow \min(\rho, j)$

---

3   Experimental Application

The application considered here is a set of WSN agents which have to select a common profile ρ together. A random network topology of degree 5 is considered in the proposed experimentation in which 25 nodes should select the best profile among a list of 10 profiles with their utility value defined such as $u\rho_0 \succ_i \rho_1 \iff u_0^i(0) = u_1^i(0) + 1$. But, this proposal is absolutely not a requirement since it can be modelled by other functions which must be monotonic, discrete and bounded. Resulting utility functions are reported on Figure 1 for each node at time 0. As illustrated on Figure 2, convergence time of the proposed algorithm is 50 iterations composed of three Multi Network Average Consensus (MNAC) loop. Figure 3 shows the adaptive error criterion such as common space U is not distant enough from other utility values at first loops to ensure consistency of node decisions. Finally, utility functions of each node on Figure 4 are equal according to last ε value.

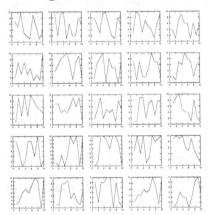

Fig. 1. Node's utility functions $u^i(0)$

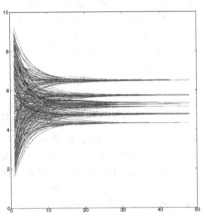

Fig. 2. Convergence to utility $\dot{u}$

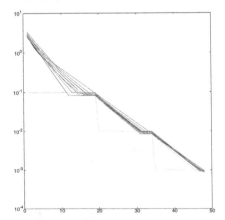

Fig. 3. Mean estimated error ε

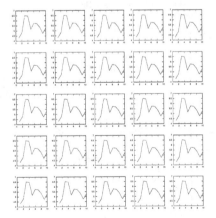

Fig. 4. Final utility function $\dot{u}$

3.1   Byzantine Threats and Voting Veto Discussions

The proposed algorithm is interesting by its properties inherited from Network Average Consensus (NAC) for Voting Procedures (VP). Indeed, VP can require veto possibilities concerning some profile alternatives for application reasons. NAC algorithm solves alignment problem when a single agent (called the leader) keeps its value unchanged. In this case, all other agents will asymptotically agree with it [5]. This alignment property allows agents to veto on a given profile by keeping its value unchanged. If an agent cannot allow a profile to be selected by the community, should then bypass the update scheme of the concerned NAC and use the minimal utility value instead. Unfortunately, this property of alignment can be undesirable in case of Byzantine threats. Byzantine threats should be detectable by comparing utility value evolution from neighbour agents which should have a q-linear convergence as previously presented. In this case, nodes just have to exclude this node from their NAC update scheme to eliminate the threat.

4   Conclusion

This paper proposes a new distributed algorithm for Voting Procedures (VP) in Multi Agent System (MAS). It is composed of a distributed preferences aggregation step with adaptive refining according to the requirements of the selection step. The latter is realized by each agent individually selecting the profile preferred by the agent community according to a common decision function. As the result's consistency is ensured at the aggregation step, the selection step is not required to verify if all agents have taken the same decision.

The alignment property of Network Average Consensus (NAC) allows the chosen preference model to be extended by adding Veto possibility. A veto is a node's behavior which allows a profile to be excluded of the Voting Procedures (VP). If any node keeps the utility value of a profile unchanged and low, the community will converge asymptotically to an agreement of exclusion. But, Byzantine agent can try to exploit this property in order to change the profile preferred by the community. Either way, nodes decisions stay consistent with or without a Byzantine agent in the community.   Moreover, the proposed Voting Procedures (VP) algorithm is interesting because of its good properties inherited from Network Average Consensus (NAC) research on mobile networks constraints such as robustness in switching topology and large scale network but also time delay. This algorithm is simply based on a utility function of preferences for each node and does not require any extra information about the network's topology other than a list of its neighbours. As this algorithm converges asymptotically and exponentially as observed on Figure 2, it requires several iterations and exchanges over the network. But these exchanges remain localized in local neighbours area, which allows network load balancing. As these exchanges have a very small payload with a null overhead (it just contains utility vector of the node), this algorithm is very interesting in Wireless Sensor Network (WSN) applications which are extremely limited in their communication capacity.

However, aggregation operator studied in this paper is the arithmetic mean for min or max operator decision function which can limit application case. Future works will be focused on studying this algorithm on general functions for reaching consensus during the aggregation step. J.Cortes [2] proposes several new NAC update schemes which will be explored such as the minimum and maximum operator, the harmonic mean, the geometric mean, the arithmetic mean and the root mean square. A study of Ordered Weighted Average operator as a generic decision function will also extend algorithm genericity.

Acknowledgements. The authors thank M. Zitouni, M. Courbin and M. Papastefanakis for their discussions and reviews during the development of this work.

References

1. Cortés, J.: Finite-time convergent gradient flows with applications to network consensus. Automatica 42(11), 1993–2000 (2006)
2. Cortés, J.: Distributed algorithms for reaching consensus on general functions. Automatica 44(3), 726–737 (2008)
3. Hatano, Y., Mesbahi, M.: Agreement over random networks. IEEE Transactions on Automatic Control 50(11), 1867–1872 (2005)
4. Kar, S., Moura, J.: Distributed consensus algorithms in sensor networks with imperfect communication: Link failures and channel noise. IEEE Transactions on Signal Processing 57(1), 355–369 (2009)
5. Olfati-Saber, R., Fax, J.A., Murray, R.M.: Consensus and cooperation in networked multi-agent systems. Proceedings of the IEEE 95(1), 215–233 (2007)
6. Olfati-Saber, R., Murray, R.M.: Consensus problems in networks of agents with switching topology and time-delays. IEEE Transactions on Automatic Control 49(9), 1520–1533 (2004)
7. Patterson, S., Bamieh, B., El Abbadi, A.: Distributed average consensus with stochastic communication failures. In: 2007 46th IEEE Conference on Decision and Control, New Orleans, Louisiana, USA, pp. 4215–4220 (December 2007)
8. Ren, W., Beard, R.W.: Consensus of information under dynamically changing interaction topologies. In: Proceedings of the 2004 American Control Conference, Boston, USA, vol. 6, pp. 4939–4944. IEEE (June 2004)
9. Ren, W., Beard, R.W., Atkins, E.M.: A survey of consensus problems in multi-agent coordination. In: Proceedings of the 2005 American Control Conference, Portland Oregon, USA, pp. 1859–1864 (June 2005)
10. Wang, H., Guo, Y.: Consensus on scale-free network. In: American Control Conference, Seattle, Washington, USA, pp. 748–752. IEEE (June 2008)

nADICO: A Nested Grammar of Institutions

Christopher Frantz, Martin K. Purvis,
Mariusz Nowostawski, and Bastin Tony Roy Savarimuthu

Department of Information Science, University of Otago, New Zealand
{cfrantz,mpurvis,mnowostawski,tonyr}@infoscience.otago.ac.nz

Abstract. We propose a refined institutional scheme derived from Crawford and Ostrom's *Grammar of Institutions* (GoI) that has been refined to provide a more comprehensive representation of conventions, norms, and rules, which extends to describing institutions in more detail but also allowing the expression of fuzzy aspects (e.g. the uncertainty about a sanction's occurrence). After initially reviewing the GoI grammar structure (also referred to as ADICO), we discuss its adoption as well as limitations. We introduce selected extensions and refinements that enable the grammar's ability to describe institutions in more detail, but also to capture more complex institutions as well as characteristics of institutions themselves, such as institutional regress.

Central features of our *Nested ADICO* (nADICO) include:

- A notion of nesting monitored and consequential ('Or else') statements, and
- a refined differentiation between norms and rules.

nADICO both enables a more comprehensive expression of institutions and extends the use of the original grammar into various application domains, while taking the initial step towards a more dynamic perpective on institutional modelling.

Keywords: Grammar of Institutions, Nested ADICO, nADICO, Institutions, Norms, Rules, Institutional Statements, Policy Modelling, Multi-Agent Systems

1 Introduction

Crawford and Ostrom's *Grammar of Institutions* [2] (GoI) is an approach to unify the expression of different kinds of manifestations of social behaviour (institutions), such as shared strategies (or conventions), social norms, and codified rules, while maintaining the ability to discriminate between these different types. To do so, it consists of five components, *Attributes, Deontic, AIm, Conditions* and an *Or else* - ADICO in short - that are necessary to specify *institutional statements*, such as rules. By restricting constitutive components to a minimum, this syntax offers a wide scope for the expression of institutional statements representing the different kinds of institutions, which we refer to as institution types for the remainder of the paper.

The generality of ADICO enables researchers to express various institutional views, including *institutions as stabilised equilibria* (e.g. [6], favoured by economics analysts), *institutions from a normative perspective* (e.g. [13], which concentrates on the behavioural perspective and is favoured by many researchers in the multi-agent systems community (e.g. [9])), and *institutions as rules* (e.g. [7], a central subject of study in the New Institutional Economics movement).

G. Boella et al. (Eds.): PRIMA 2013, LNAI 8291, pp. 429–436, 2013.

In this work, we revise the grammar to extend its ability to capture institutions in more detail, while reviewing its interpretation of different institution types with the intent to offer interpretational prescriptions that are more faithful to the nature of the institutions the grammar represents.

In the next section (Section 2) we review Crawford and Ostrom's grammar and its adoption in different fields. Then in Section 3 we present Nested ADICO (nADICO).

2   The Institutional Grammar

2.1   Overview

The ADICO grammar consists of five components. Those include:

- *Attributes* – describe the attributes and characteristics of social entities (which can be individuals or groups) that are subject to the institutional statement (e.g. shared strategy, norm, rule). If not specified explicitly, all individuals (or members of a group/society) are implied.
- *Deontics* – a deontic primitive that describes either an *obligation* (e.g. represented as **must**), *permission* (**may**), or a *prohibition* (**must not**).
- *AIm* – the aim describes an action or outcome associated with the institutional statement. Only constraint put on an aim instance is that the action or outcome it describes must be physically possible, so their non-/compliance can be determined [2,14].
- *Conditions* – capture the circumstances under which the statement applies. This can include spatial, temporal and procedural elements. If not further constrained, the *conditions* component default to "at all times and in all places" [2].
- *Or else* – describes consequences that are associated with the violation of the institutional statement, i.e. the combination of all other components used in that statement. In Crawford and Ostrom's grammar, this component has constitutive role in classifying statements as rules. [1]

Using three statement types, one can construct institutional statements of increasing prescriptiveness. Parsing an institutional statement in the form of a *shared strategy* (*convention*) with this grammar yields an AIC statement:

Drivers (A) hand their driver's license to the police officer (I) when stopped in traffic control (C).

It effectively reflects a description of drivers' commonly observable behaviour when facing the request to hand over their licenses. From a normative perspective, this can be interpreted as a descriptive norm.

---

[1] Crawford and Ostrom specify three requirements for an 'Or Else' statement: 1) It needs to result from a decision-making process by a collective that has the power to do so; 2) it requires the 'Or Else' component to be supported by another norm or rule statement that modifies the assigned deontic under the condition that the first rule is violated; 3) it requires the specification of a rule that specifies the responsibilities of a monitor.

In GoI parlance, a *norm* would extend a shared strategy with a prescription, expressed as ADIC:

Drivers (A) *must (D)* **hand their driver's license to the police officer (I) when stopped in traffic control (C).**

This represents an unambigious instruction to the driver who might feel threatened by an uncertain consequence of violation, or (if taking a strictly deontological perspective) perceives it as his duty to present his driver's license, independent of any threatening consequences.

Finally, a *rule* (ADICO) would introduce consequences for non-compliance:

Drivers (A) must (D) hand their driver's license to the police officer (I) when stopped in traffic control (C), *or else the police officer must enforce it based on traffic law (O).*

Here the driver faces explicit consequences, which, depending on the nature of his refusal, can result in material (e.g. fines) or physical sanctions (e.g. arrest).

2.2 Application Fields, Refinements and Limitations

The ADICO grammar provides a semi-formal description of institutional rules that make them accessible for economic analysis (e.g. using game-theory, as done by Crawford and Ostrom [2]) and structured policy coding [11]. In the area of multi-agent simulation, Smajgl et al. [12] have used the grammar to model endogenous changes of ADICO rule statements in the context of water usage. Significant recent contributions that use the grammar in more depth include Ghorbani et al.'s MAIA framework [4], which represents a comprehensive attempt to translate Ostrom's Institutional Analysis and Development Framework [8] into an agent-based model. Earlier, Ghorbani et al. [3] explored the notion of shared strategies as a fundamental statement type and differentiated their application across common, shared, and collective strategies.

Apart from a wide range of uses, the grammar has attracted some suggestions for refinement [10]. Our own interests in this area concern how to make the grammar more comprehensive, flexible and dynamic. There are two key issues in this context which we wish to emphasise.

First, the existing ADICO differentiation between shared strategies, norms, and rules (differing grammar components are used in those separate contexts) seems to compartmentalise this domain artificially to provide a neat match between grammar and institution types. In original ADICO terms, rules are assumed to have sanctions, whereas norms do not [2].

Second, in ADICO the notions of prohibition and obligation norms are mapped into a 'discrete' perspective. Other authors already have pointed out this limitation and claimed that a more continuous perspective [10] would be more applicable. It would seem that modelling the progression across differing institutional types requires more flexibility in specifying norms, beyond the discrete **may**'s, **must**'s, and **must not**'s. More flexible boundaries are desirable to support continuous adaptation so that a new and different norm may gradually emerge from or replace an existing one.

In this work, we take the initial step and address the first issue by introducing a nested approach to institutional statements, in the form of Nested ADICO.

3   Nested ADICO (nADICO)

In our work we shift the focus from the classification and isolated analysis of institutional types over to a more integrated view on institutions, smoothening their boundaries. Although this blurs the strict categorisation of the ADICO grammar, our refinements offer (a) the potential of capturing institutions in greater detail and their full complexity, (b) a refined interpretation between different institution types so as to prepare the modelling of institutional transitions.

3.1   Nested Institutional Statements

Vertical Nesting (Institutional Regress) – We introduce the notion of nested institutional statements. These provide a more detailed, operational description of the consequences of actions (corresponding to the 'Or else' component of the ADICO grammar). We replace the original unstructured ADICO 'Or else' statement with a nested institutional statement. The first part of this statement (the 'ADIC') is what we call the *monitored statement* with respect to the second, nested part of the statement (the 'O' in the original GoI), which we call the *consequential statement*. Using vertical nesting one can express consequences using the same structural components as the monitored statement, thereby supporting a nested structure and hence a multi-level modelling of institutions, allowing the representation of institutional regress. That is, consequential statements may be interpreted as comprising their own *second-order monitored statements* backed by their own *second-order consequential statements*. This can support the interrelation and dependencies among connected institutions - certain additional institutions may be invoked and activated as a social consequence of failure to comply with some higher-level monitored statement. We call this nesting across different statement levels *vertical nesting*. Recall the example from Section 2:

Drivers (A_1) must (D_1) hand their driver's license to the police officer (I_1) when stopped in traffic control (C_1),

OR ELSE ———————————— *2nd level* ————————————
the police officer (A_2) must (D_2) enforce this (I_2) under any circumstances (C_2),

OR ELSE ———————————— *3rd level* ————————————
internal investigators (A_3) must (D_3) follow up on this issue (I_3) in any case (C_3).

Decomposing this into its syntactic elements, the structure for this rule instance can be interpreted as `ADIC(ADIC(ADIC))`. "Drivers" represent a *first-order violator*, while the police officer (A_2) is *first-order sanctioner (reactor)*. In the case of violation at this level, however, the police officer becomes a *second-order violator*, and internal investigators (A_3) become *second-order sanctioners (reactors)*, and potential *third-order violators*. This supports the more realistic expression of interrelated rules and, in principle, enables a generative approach to rule establishment.

Horizontal Nesting (Statement Combinations) – Violating a rule may often have multiple consequences - or, in the case of norms, the types of reactions and their occurrences may be unspecified or vague. Thus a strict 1:1 mapping will not be adequate for a generalisable institutional grammar. To accommodate this required generality, we propose the expansion of statements on a given level, labelled as *horizontal nesting*, and introduce three logical operators for the combination of institutional statements: *and* (logical conjunction), *or* (inclusive disjunction), and *xor* (exclusive disjunction). Rephrasing the previous example in more detail in this format results in the following statement:[2]

Drivers (A_1) must (D_1) hand their driver's license to the police officer (I_1) when stopped in traffic control (C_1),

OR ELSE ———————————————— *2nd level* ————————————————

the police officer ($A_{2a/b/c}$) must (D_{2a}) enforce this (I_{2a}) under any circumstances (C_{2a}) **and,**

depending on severity ($C_{2b/c}$), must ($D_{2b/c}$)
  either fine the driver (I_{2b})
  or arrest him (I_{2c}),
  OR ELSE ————————————— *3rd level* —————————————
  internal investigators (A_3) must (D_3) follow up on this issue (I_3) in any case (C_3).

The structure of this statement is `ADIC((ADIC and (ADIC xor ADIC))ADIC)`, and it depicts the clear specification of sanctions as a key characteristic for rules.

or-combinations are useful to express uncertainty associated with sanction diversity and occurrence in the context of social norms. Referring to the norm to keep well-mowed lawn in American neighbourhoods, we could express:

American home owners (A_1) must (D_1) mow their lawns (I_1) under any circumstances (C_1),
OR ELSE ———————————————— *2nd level* ————————————————
their neighbours (A_{2a}) may (D_{2a}) address that negligence (I_{2a}),
or they (A_{2b}) may (D_{2b}) feel the need to explain themselves (I_{2b}),
or their neighbourhood (A_{2c}) may (D_{2c}) reject them (I_{2c}).

The respective nADICO expression is `ADIC(ADIC or ADIC or ADIC)`.

Nesting in Monitored Statements – It should be noted that not only can the consequences be combined by operators, but also the monitored statements:

- `(ADIC and ADIC)(ADIC)` requires the co-occurrence of conditions to activate the consequence;
- `(ADIC or ADIC)(ADIC)` requires one or both statements to match;
- `(ADIC xor ADIC)(ADIC)` exclusively requires the match of a single monitored statement.

As with consequential statements, monitored statements can include combinations of multiple operators (e.g. `(ADIC and (ADIC xor ADIC))(ADIC)`) to achieve horizontal nesting. Note that each of the individual monitored statements can optionally have its own vertical nesting structure (i.e. individual consequences), such as `(ADIC(ADIC)`

---

[2] We extend the index indicating the nesting levels along with letters that associate grammar components with the respective consequential statement(s) on that level. In this example, the second level comprises three statements (a, b and c), all of which share a common sanctioner A_2, expressed as $A_{2a/b/c}$, but only b and c share the same *Conditions* ($C_{2b/c}$) and so on.

and ADIC(ADIC *or* ADIC))(ADIC), however, when combined they additionally have a compound consequence.[3] Alternatively to the examples shown here, nADICO statements can be terminated by AIC statements (shared strategies/conventions), which are descriptive (e.g. to reflect behaviour change of individuals) in case of violations instead of prescribing behaviours.[4]

Figure 1 shows the complete nADICO grammar in the Extended Backus–Naur Form (EBNF) [5] capturing all nADICO statements, including the elementary ADICO institution types AIC (convention) and ADIC (sanction-less norm).

```
attributes  =   "A" ;
deontic     =   "D" ;
aim         =   "I" ;
conditions  =   "C" ;
aic         =   attributes , aim , conditions ;
adic        =   attributes , deontic , aim , conditions ;
and         =   "and" ;       (* conjunction *)
or          =   "or" ;        (* inclusive disjunction *)
xor         =   "xor" ;       (* exclusive disjunction *)
ws          =   " " ;         (* whitespace *)
LB          =   "(" ;
RB          =   ")" ;
nadico      =   adic | (* individual norm statement without sanction *)
                [ nadico [ , LB , ( nadico | aic ) , RB ] ] | (* vertical nesting *)
                [ LB ( nadico | aic ) , ws , and , ws , ( nadico | aic ) RB ] | (* combinations *)
                [ LB ( nadico | aic ) , ws , or , ws , ( nadico | aic ) RB ] |
                [ LB ( nadico | aic ) , ws , xor , ws , ( nadico | aic ) RB ] ;
statement   =   aic | nadico ; (* nADICO statement (including conventions) *)
```

Fig. 1. nADICO grammar in EBNF

3.2   Revised Interpretation of Institution Types

The extensions to the original GoI affect the rigid classification principles the grammar offers. Given that we integrate the representation of social consequences of norm violation into the grammar, we lose the ability to differentiate between norms and rules based on the mere existence of an 'Or else' component. Instead we use characteristics that are not directly reflected in the original grammar. This includes the nature of the monitor. In Crawford and Ostrom's conceptualisation, monitors are essential to constitute rules, along with the previous process of collective action (see Section 2).

The requirement for a monitor is a useful criterion; however, we must equally assume that monitors exist for norms, as supported by a wide range of literature [1]. The GoI [2] only prescribes monitors for rules, in accordance with the GoI's assumption of sanctions only for rules, and its focus on explicitly formalised aspects of an institution. For a more inclusive perspective, however, it seems necessary to consider the nature of monitors also for normative statements. The inclusion of the monitor for norms has equally been discussed by Schlüter and Theesfeld [10], who suggest a set of monitor types but are not explicit about their association with norms and rules.

---

[3] As an example imagine the case suggesting that drivers should not speed, but also should not drive drunk, for both of which we assume individual consequences. However, if combined, both actions can have consequences beyond the individual sanctions, such as driver's license suspension based on demerit points.

[4] Note that conventions in ADICO are equivalent to descriptive norms, while the norms in ADICO are of injunctive nature.

Table 1. Monitor types

Monitor type	Institution type
Internal monitor	Personal Norm
Social monitoring Informally assigned monitor(s)	Social Norm
Formally assigned by private entities Formally assigned by legislative body	Rule

We interpret the existence of a structured and clearly specified collective action[5] process, such as majority-based group decision-making, with an outcome that is known to potential violators as a differentiation criterion between norms and rules. This allows the classification of the suggested monitor types as shown in Table 1.

A limitation of the work of Crawford and Ostrom [2] and Schlüter and Theesfeld [10] is the lack of *clear differentiation between institution monitor and enforcer/sanctioner.* The grammar presupposes that the monitor is also the enforcer, which can be sufficient in some cases. However, for rules we would generally assume a potential differentiation between an entity that monitors an institution and an entity enforcing it, such as a government as regulative body that assigns enforcement duties to specialised enforcement entities such as the police (and in principle an even more refined differentiation by assigning the task of sanctioning to a judicial body). The effectiveness for social norms, in contrast, oftentimes relies on both the fact that a) the monitor is *not* clearly specified, and b) that monitor and enforcer are generally a unified entity[6] that considers itself directly affected by norm violations and thus feels inclined to act as an enforcer. A core motivation for the specification of rules, in contrast, is the clearly specified duties of both monitor and enforcer (which can either be captured as role descriptions or be expressed in great detail using nADICO statements themselves). A further aspect for the differentiation of norms in contrast to rules is the *uncertainty about the consequences involved*, the fuzziness of which we see as a strong motivator to comply with norms. We thus think that those characteristics – the clear vs. fuzzy interpretation of 1) monitor/enforcer and 2) consequences – are more significant for a distinction between norm and rule in a general grammar of institutions than the mere existence of a sanction.

This has consequences for the interpretation of nADICO statements. For rules we expect a *clear specification of the sanctioner* and/or its attributes (which are often implicitly captured by specifying roles), and, if differentiated from sanctioner, the specification of the monitor. Secondly, an indicator for the existence of rules when analysing nADICO expressions is the *clear specification of consequences*, and, if statement combinations (*horizontal nesting*) are used, the use of *and* as well as *xor* operators (e.g. to express graduated sanctions). For norms, in contrast, we would initially expect *a fuzzy specification of sanctioners*. This becomes a generic placeholder for the *attributes* component of a consequential statement (such as '*'') implying *social monitoring*, or (an) *informally assigned sanctioner(s)*, such as a person that is affected by norm violation and simply acts as self-assigned sanctioner. Over time the nature of the sanctioner can transition between those types (see Table 1). However, unlike in the rule case (and specified by Crawford and Ostrom [2]), no collective action is involved. If horizontal

---

[5] Recall that collective action is another ADICO criterion to constitute rules (see Section 2; [2]).

[6] Note that the differentiation into monitor and enforcer for rules may not always hold (e.g. police officer as monitor and enforcer); in any case we would still expect a clear specification/characterisation in case of such a unified representation.

nesting is used for norms, the *uncertainty about the sanctions involved* is expressed by the use of *or* statements that combine possible (e.g. experienced) sanctions and express the fuzziness of sanctions that are applied in a non-exclusive manner (e.g. an individual's misstep can be sanctioned multiple times by different sanctioners applying the same or different sanctions, or not be sanctioned at all). Using this revised interpretation, nADICO enables a more comprehensive representation *of* and more nuanced differentiation *between* norms and rules.

4   Conclusion and Future Work

In this paper we have introduced nADICO, an extension of the Grammar of Institutions. We have extended the original grammar's expressive power and generalisability of its application by introducing the notion of nested monitored and consequential ('Or else') statements and a refined differentiation between norms and rules. To operationalise the grammar, in future work we will introduce a fluid notion of deontics that allow the modelling of transitions between different institution types.

References

1. Conte, R., Dignum, F.: From Social Monitoring to Normative Influence. Journal of Artificial Societies and Social Simulation 4(2) (2001)
2. Crawford, S.E., Ostrom, E.: A Grammar of Institutions. In: Understanding Institutional Diversity, ch. 5, pp. 137–174. Princeton University Press, Princeton (2005)
3. Ghorbani, A., Aldewereld, H., Dignum, V., Noriega, P.: Shared Strategies in Artificial Agent Societies. In: Aldewereld, H., Sichman, J.S. (eds.) COIN 2012. LNCS, vol. 7756, pp. 71–86. Springer, Heidelberg (2013)
4. Ghorbani, A., Bots, P., Dignum, V., Dijkema, G.: MAIA: a Framework for Developing Agent-Based Social Simulations. Journal of Artificial Societies and Social Simulation 16(2) (2013)
5. ISO. ISO/IEC 14977 – Information technology - Syntactic metalanguage - Extended BNF (December 1996) (accessed on July 1, 2013)
6. Menger, C.: Problems in Economics and Sociology. University of Illinois Press (1963)
7. North, D.C.: Institutions, Institutional Change, and Economic Performance. Cambridge University Press, Cambridge (1990)
8. Ostrom, E.: Understanding Institutional Diversity. Princeton University Press, Princeton (2005)
9. Savarimuthu, B.T.R., Cranefield, S.: Norm creation, spreading and emergence: A survey of simulation models of norms in multi-agent systems. Multiagent and Grid Systems 7(1), 21–54 (2011)
10. Schlüter, A., Theesfeld, I.: The Grammar of Institutions: The challenge of distinguishing between strategies, norms, and rules. Rationality and Society 22, 445–475 (2010)
11. Siddiki, S., Weible, C.M., Basurto, X., Calanni, J.: Dissecting Policy Designs: An Application of the Institutional Grammar Tool. The Policy Studies Journal 39, 79–103 (2011)
12. Smajgl, A., Izquierdo, L., Huigen, M.G.A.: Rules, knowledge and complexity: how agents shape their institutional environment. Journal of Modelling and Simulation of Systems 1(2), 98–107 (2010)
13. Ullmann-Margalit, E.: The Emergence of Norms. Clarendon Library of Logic and Philosophy. Clarendon Press, Oxford (1977)
14. von Wright, G.H.: Norm and Action: A Logical Enquiry. Routledge & Kegan Paul (1963)

Towards Semantic Merging of Versions of BDI Agent Systems

Yingzhi Gou, Hoa Khanh Dam, and Aditya Ghose

School of Computer Science and Software Engineering
University of Wollongong
New South Wales 2522, Australia
{yg452,hoa,aditya}@uow.edu.au

Abstract. Modern software development environment is based on developers' ability to work in parallel on the same codebase and perform concurrent changes, which potentially need to be merged back together. However, state-of-the-art merging systems follow text-based algorithms that focus only on modifications to text but completely ignore the semantic of the code written. This limitation significantly restricts developers' ability to perform and merge concurrent changes. In this paper, we propose a merging technique that fully understands the programming language structure of typical BDI agent systems. In addition, our approach effectively captures the semantic of an agent system using the notion of semantic effects of goals, plans and actions constituting the agent system.

1 Introduction

Engineering large, complex software systems is inherently a collaborative process since it requires the participation of teams of people who may work on the same product independently and concurrently (creating different versions of it). As a result, merging is a critical functionality in existing versioning systems which support the optimistic versioning process that enables different developers to work concurrently on the same set of software artefacts (e.g. source code) rather than pessimistically locking each artefact when it is changed by one developer. However, software merging remains a highly challenging and complicated process since merging should heavily depend on the syntax and semantic of the software artefacts [5]. State-of-the-art versioning systems (e.g. CVS, Subversion or Git) are usually based on textual merging techniques. Since any software program (including agent programs) can be seen as a piece of text, text-based merge tools have been dominantly used for merging software code. This flexibility however comes with a cost in which text-based merge tools do not take the specific syntax, structure and semantic of agent programs into account and thus the merging may often result in unnecessary conflicts or a merged version which has syntax errors and inconsistent semantic behavior.

Since the 1980s, intelligent agent technology has attracted an increasing amount of interest from the research and business communities, and the practical utility of agents has been demonstrated in a wide range of domains such

G. Boella et al. (Eds.): PRIMA 2013, LNAI 8291, pp. 437–444, 2013.

as weather alerting, business process management, holonic manufacturing, e-commerce, and information management. This number continues to increase since there are compelling reasons to use intelligent agent technology. However, to the best of our knowledge, there has been no work on merging versions of an agent program. If we are to be successful in the development of large-scale agent systems which requires the participation of teams of people who may work on the same product independently and concurrently, the research community must provide solutions and insights that will improve the practice of merging versions of agent software.

The main purpose of this paper is to contribute towards filling that gap. We propose a merging technique specifically for Belief-Desire-Intention (BDI) agent systems. Our approach captures the essential semantic of a BDI agent system by computing the *cumulative effects* of plan execution from the *immediate effects* of the actions constituting the plan. We then merge the semantic effects of the revisions, and use them to establish a merged version. In the remaining of the paper, we will describe an example to illustrate the limitations of existing text-based merging approach, and present in detail our approach and how it overcomes those issues.

2   Illustrative Example

Most of today's version controlling systems uses text-based merging techniques which consider software programs (regardless of the programming language which they are written in) merely as text files. The most common approach is to use line-based merging where lines of text are considered as indivisible units [5]. Line-based merging however cannot handle two concurrent modifications to the same line very well, which will be shown in the following scenario.

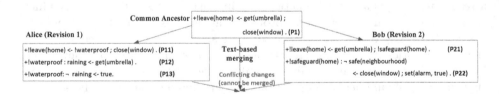

Fig. 1. An example of classical, text-based merging (unnecessary conflicts)

Figure 1 illustrates an example of two developers, Alice and Bob, concurrently work on the same agent program written in AgentSpeak(L) [6], a well-known, abstract BDI agent programming language. BDI agents' behaviour is mostly determined in terms of their plans to handle events or achieve goals. Each plan is typically of the form $G : [C] \leftarrow P$, meaning that the plan is an applicable plan for achieving goal G when context condition C is believed true. Plan P typically contains a sequence of actions that are meant to be directly executed in the world (e.g. *get*(*umbrella*) in plan P1 in Figure 1) or subgoals (written as !*G*) (e.g. !*waterproof* in plan P11) to be resolved by further plans. Both Alice and Bob check out the same piece of code (the common ancestor), which in this example, a plan (P1) to achieve goal *leave*(*home*), and make different changes to it. Alice replaces the first action of the plan with a subgoal *waterproof* and creates two plans (P12 and P13) to resolve the subgoal. In the meanwhile, being unaware of Alice's changes, Bob replaces action *close*(*window*) with a subgoal *safeguard*(*home*) and creates a plan (P22) to resolve it. When both developers check in their own revision, existing versioning systems (which mostly rely on text-based merging) would detect unnecessary conflicts since parallel modifications has made to the same lines of code in the common ancestor. In general, text-based merging fails in these scenarios since they are heavily dependent on the position of the texts being modified and they do not consider any syntactic or semantic information in the agent code.

3   Semantic Effects

A BDI agent program is built around a plan library, a collection of pre-defined hierarchical plans indexed by goals. As a result, the semantic of a BDI agent program is mostly determined by the semantic of its plans, which can essentially be captured by the semantic effects achieved by the plans. Such effects can be expressed in terms of *declarative goals* that the plans are meant to achieve. However, mainly due to practical concerns, goals in BDI agent programming languages are mostly *procedural* where a goal is a set of tasks or processes that are to be completely carried out [7]. Therefore, a description of effects achieved by a plan has to be explicitly established from the effects of its constituting steps in a *context-sensitive* manner. We note that such a description will necessarily be non-deterministic, i.e., there might be alternative effects achieved, which is due to the following reasons. First, there might be different paths in plan execution since there might be multiple ways of achieving a (sub-)goal. Second, the effects of certain plan steps might "undo" the effects of prior process steps. This is often described as the belief update or knowledge update problem – multiple alternative means of resolving the inconsistencies generated by the "undoing" of effects is another source of non-determinism.

Each action has a precondition under which an action can be successfully executed and its effect (or postcondition) on the environment. The semantic effect of action a, denoted as $e(a)$, is a *conjunctive* set of belief literals since the action's effect on the environment may eventually be perceived by the agent. The effect of action *get*(*umbrella*) in the example in the previous section is the set $\{on(umbrella, hand)\}$, and the effect of action *set*(*alarm*, *true*) is $\{alarm(on)\}$. Many agent programming languages (e.g. 3APL [4]) require an explicit specification of actions in terms of both preconditions and effects. However, our work *only* focuses on leveraging action effects to establish semantical representations of agent systems and use them for merging. A BDI agent also has a belief base $\mathcal{B}$ which encodes what the agent believes about the world. An agent's belief base may also contain rules, which allows for new knowledge to be deduced from existing knowledge. For simplicity, in this paper we assume that the context condition is expressed as a conjunctive set of belief literals, which is similar to a semantic effect.

The effect specification of actions allows us to determine, at design time, the (cumulative) effects of plan execution. We now define a number of basic definitions that are used in the procedure for computing the cumulative effects.

Definition 1. *For two effects e_1 and e_2, and the belief base $\mathcal{B}$, if $e_1 \not\models \perp$ and $e_2 \not\models \perp$, then the cumulative effects $acc(e_1, e_2)$ (accumulating es_2 onto es_1) is defined as:*

$$acc(e_1, e_2) = \{e_2 \cup e \mid e \subseteq e_1 \wedge e \cup e_2 \cup \mathcal{B} \not\models \perp \wedge$$
$$\textit{if there exists } e' \textit{ such that } e \subset e' \subseteq e_1,$$
$$\textit{then } e' \cup e_2 \cup \mathcal{B} \models \perp\}$$

We note that the result of $acc()$ on a pair of effects is a disjunctive set of effects, each of which represents a distinct way in which potential inconsistencies between the effects to be accumulated are resolved. For example, if $e_1 = \{m, n\}$ and $e_2 = \{x, y\}$ and there is a rule $m \wedge n \rightarrow \neg y$ in the belief base $\mathcal{B}$, then $acc(e_1, e_2) = \{\{m, x, y\}, \{n, x, y\}\}$.

Definition 2. *The cumulative effects of the two disjunctive sets of effects ES_1 and ES_2 are defined as:*

$$ES_1 \oplus ES_2 = \bigcup_{es_i \in ES_1, es_j \in ES_2} acc(es_i, es_j)$$

The operator $\oplus$ performs the pair-wise effect accumulation $acc()$ on every pair of $(es_i, es_j) \in ES_1 \times ES_2$ to form a new disjunctive set of effects. For example, if $ES_1 = \{e_1\}$ and $ES_2 = \{e_2\}$, then $ES_1 \oplus ES_2 = \{\{m, x, y\}, \{n, x, y\}\}$. The cumulative effects of a plan are represented as a disjunctive set of effects where each effect (also called an effect scenario) corresponds to a particular path of the plan execution (i.e. a particular scenario). In order to compute a plan's cumulative effects, we need to simulate the plan execution, particularly the context-sensitive subgoal expansion and plan selection. For example, assume that a plan has executed a number of actions, which gives cumulative effects $ES = \{\{m, x, y\}, \{n, x, y\}\}$, and is about to expand a subgoal g, which can be resolved by plan P under the context condition $c = \{\neg n\}$. Since only the effect scenario $\{m, x, y\}$ is consistent with the context condition, the cumulative effects just before plan P is executed would be $ES \ominus c = \{\{m, x, y, \neg n\}\}$. The operator $\ominus$ which eliminates effects that are inconsistent with a plan's context condition is defined as below.

Definition 3. *The effect elimination of ES with regard to context condition c (which is a set of literals and can be considered as an effect) is defined as:*

$$ES \ominus c = \bigcup_{es_i \in ES} \{es_i \cup c\}, \textit{where } es_i \cup c \not\models \perp$$

Algorithm 1. Computing semantic effects for a given node in the goal-plan tree (initial call is *SemanticEffect*(*root*, $\varnothing$))

1: **procedure** SEMANTICEFFECT(n, *ES*)
2:     **if** n is a **plan** node **then**
3:         $ES \leftarrow ES \ominus context(n)$
4:         **if** $ES \neq \varnothing$ **then**
5:             **for each** child n' of n from left to right **do**
6:                 $ES \leftarrow SemanticEffect(n', ES)$
7:             **end for**
8:         **end if**
9:     **else if** n is an **action** node **then**
10:         $ES \leftarrow ES \oplus \{e(n)\}$
11:     **else if** n is a **goal** node **then**
12:         $ES' \leftarrow \varnothing$
13:         **for each** child n' of n **do**
14:             $ES' \leftarrow ES' \cup SemanticEffect(n', ES)$
15:         **end for**
16:         $ES \leftarrow ES'$
17:     **end if**
18:     **return** *ES*
19: **end procedure**

A BDI agent program can be represented as a number of goal-plan trees where each goal has as children the plans that are relevant to it, and each plan has as children its actions and/or subgoals. The goal-plan tree is an "and-or" tree: each goal is realised by one of its relevant plans ("or") and each plan needs all of its actions to be executed and its sub-goals to be achieved ("and"). Therefore, computing semantic effects for a BDI agent program is reduced to computing semantic effect for a goal-plan tree. Algorithm 1 describes how we traverse a goal-plan tree to compute the cumulative effects for a particular node in the tree. The cumulative effects are stored in the set *ES* which are accumulated as we visit each node of the tree in the depth-first search manner. If the node n is a plan node (lines 2–8), we obtain the context condition of the plan (i.e. *context*(*n*)) and apply the effect elimination operator $\ominus$ onto the set of cumulative effects *ES*. If the outcome is *not* an empty set, reflecting there exists at least a scenario in which the plan is applicable, we visit each node of the plan's children (i.e. which is either an action or subgoal node) to accumulate its semantic effects. If the node is an action node (lines 9–10), we simply use the operator $\oplus$ to accumulate the action's effect. Finally, if the node is a goal node (lines 11–16), we visit each node of the goal's children (i.e. which are plan nodes), compute its semantic effects and add them into the set of cumulative effects.

Figure 2 shows the goal-plan trees for the agent program and its two revisions in Figure 1. Using the procedure described in Algorithm 1, we can compute that the cumulative effects of goal $+!leave(home)$ in the ancestor version are $ES_{base} = \{\{on(umberalla, hand), window(closed)\}\}$, and in revisions 1 and 2 are $ES_1 = \{\{raining, on(umberalla, hand), window(closed)\}, \{\neg raining, window(closed)\}\}$

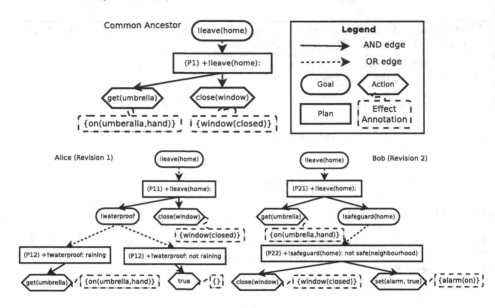

Fig. 2. Goal plan trees annotated with semantic effects for programs in Figure 1

and $ES_2 = \{\{on(umberalla, hand), \neg safe(neighbourhood), window(closed),$
$alarm(on)\}\}$.

4 Semantic Merging

We now outline the process of merging two BDI agent programs using semantic effects. Our approach follows the popular three-way merging [5] which requires a common ancestor program as the base and two revisions.

1. Compute the semantic effects of the (common) ancestor agent program and its two revisions, which gives us three set of semantic effects ES_{base}, ES_1 and ES_2.
2. Use those semantic effects to identify the essential differences between the ancestor and the revisions. The difference of two semantic effects ES_i and ES_j is defined as $\delta(ES_i, ES_j) = ES_j \backslash ES_i$, which contains the semantic effects that are in ES_j but not in ES_i. Note that δ is asymmetric, that is $\delta(ES_i, ES_j) \neq \delta(ES_j, ES_i)$.
3. Compute the merged semantic effects $ES_{merge} = (ES_{base} \cup \Delta^+) \backslash \Delta^-$ where $\Delta^+ = \delta(ES_{base}, ES_1) \cup \delta(ES_{base}, ES_2)$ and $\Delta^- = \delta(ES_1, ES_{base}) \cup \delta(ES_2, ES_{base})$. Intuitively, Δ^+ is the effects newly created in the revisions, and Δ^- is the effects that are removed in the revisions. The merged version therefore has the behaviours in the base program that are preserved in both revisions and the new behaviours coded in the revisions. Note that the order of merging is not important since merging is done here in terms of set union.
4. Construct the merged program from the merged semantic effects.

We now illustrate how a merged version can be obtained in our running example by following the above steps. In the previous section, we have computed the semantic effects ES_{base}, ES_1 and ES_2. Now, we compute the semantic differences $\delta(ES_1, ES_{base})$ and $\delta(ES_2, ES_{base})$ which are the same, and equal to $\{\{on(umberalla, hand), window(closed)\}\}$. The set of merged semantic effects are then computed as follows.

$$ES_{merge} = (ES_{base} \cup \Delta^+)\backslash\Delta^- = (ES_1 \cup ES_2)\backslash\Delta^-$$
$$= \{\{raining, on(umberalla, hand), window(closed)\},$$
$$\{\neg raining, window(closed)\},$$
$$\{on(umberalla, hand), \neg safe(neighbourhood), window(closed), alarm(on)\}\}$$

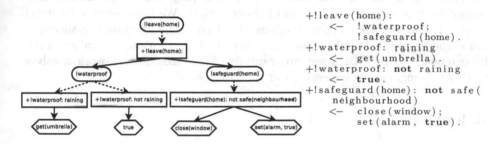

+!leave(home):
    <-   !waterproof;
          !safeguard(home).
+!waterproof: raining
    <-   get(umbrella).
+!waterproof: **not** raining
    <-   **true**.
+!safeguard(home): **not** safe(
    neighbourhood)
    <-   close(window);
          set(alarm, **true**).

Fig. 3. A merged goal-plan tree and program for the example in Figure 1

The final step of the merging process involves reconstructing a program from the merged semantic effects. This involves reconstituting a *feasible* goal-plan tree such that the semantic effects of this tree, denoting ES_r, satisfy the following condition: $\forall es \in ES_{merge}, \exists es' \in ES_r, es' \cup \mathcal{B} \models es$. Figure 3 shows a feasible goal-plan tree whose semantic effects $ES_r = \{\{raining, on(umberalla, hand), \neg safe(neighbourhood), window(closed), alarm(on)\}, \{\neg raining, \neg safe(neighbourhood), window(closed), alarm(on)\}\}$ satisfy the above condition. If we cannot reconstitute any feasible goal-plan tree from the merged semantic effects, there must be conflicting changes made in the revisions that need to resolved. Our future work involves identifying those conflicting changes using the semantic effects. We also note that there may be more than one feasible goal-plan tree and they should be presented to the software engineers for selection. Future work would involves developing a search algorithm to find all of those feasible goal plan trees. Computing the differences and the merged semantic effects are essentially set operations, which grow linearly with the size of the programs. The number of ways to resolve conflicts is constrained within the changes made in the revisions to be merged. Therefore, we expect the approach does scale to standard programs.

5   Conclusions

Although there have been some recent work on providing support for the maintenance and evolution of agent systems (e.g. [2,3]), there is still a big gap in addressing the versioning and merging issues of agent systems. Text-based merging is the dominant approach used in most today's versioning systems. Due to its limitations, a number of approaches (e.g. [1] or see [5] for a comprehensive survey) have been proposed to merge classical programs (e.g. procedural or object-oriented) in a semantical manner. Recently, there have been some work (e.g. the recently released commercial SemanticMerge software[1]) on refactoring-aware merge (which preserves the semantics), but they are limited to object-oriented programming languages. Such approaches are not readily applied to a BDI agent program due to its distinct syntax, structure and semantics. In addition, traditional approaches which rely on program slicing or dependency graph do not really capture the true semantics of agent programs. In particular, they cannot capture the semantic effects of agent actions. We have proposed a novel approach that enables merging versions of a BDI agent program semantically. Since the approach is built upon an abstract BDI notation, it can generally be extended to any BDI agent programming languages. Future work involves further refining and implementing our merge approach.

References

1. Berzins, V.: Software merge: semantics of combining changes to programs. ACM Trans. Program. Lang. Syst. 16(6), 1875–1903 (1994)
2. Dam, H.K., Ghose, A.: Automated change impact analysis for agent systems. In: Proceedings of the 27th IEEE International Conference on Software Maintenance, ICSM 2011, pp. 33–42. IEEE, Washington, DC (2011)
3. Dam, K.H., Winikoff, M.: Cost-based BDI plan selection for change propagation. In: Padgham, Parkes, Müller, Parsons (eds.) Proceedings of the 7th International Conference on Autonomous Agents and Multiagent Systems (AAMAS 2008), Estoril, Portugal, pp. 217–224 (May 2008)
4. Dastani, M., Birna Riemsdijk, M., Meyer, J.-J.: Programming multi-agent systems in 3APL. In: Bordini, R., Dastani, M., Dix, J., Fallah Seghrouchni, A. (eds.) Multi-Agent Programming. Multiagent Systems, Artificial Societies, and Simulated Organizations, vol. 15, pp. 39–67. Springer US (2005)
5. Mens, T.: A state-of-the-art survey on software merging. IEEE Transactions on Software Engineering 28(5), 449–462 (2002)
6. Rao, A.S.: AgentSpeak(L): BDI agents speak out in a logical computable language. In: Perram, J., Van de Velde, W. (eds.) MAAMAW 1996. LNCS (LNAI), vol. 1038, pp. 42–55. Springer, Heidelberg (1996)
7. Sardina, S., Padgham, L.: A BDI agent programming language with failure handling, declarative goals, and planning. Autonomous Agents and Multi-Agent Systems 23(1), 18–70 (2011)

---

[1] http://www.semanticmerge.com/

A New Ant Colony Optimization Method Considering Intensification and Diversification

Mitsuru Haga and Shohei Kato

Dept. of Computer Science and Engineering, Graduate School of Engineering,
Nagoya Institute of Technology,
Gokiso-cho, Showa-ku, Nagoya-shi, 466-8555 Japan
{haga,shohey}@katolab.nitech.ac.jp
http://www.katolab.nitech.ac.jp

Abstract. Ant colony optimization (ACO) is a meta-heuristic algorithm inspired by foraging behavior of ants and is one of the most well known swarm intelligence algorithms for solving the Traveling Salesman Problem (TSP) because of its simpleness and quality. In this paper we will propose an ACO based algorithm called ASwide that adds simple but powerful factors in the pheromone updating formula. To check the efficiency of our algorithm we did several computer experiments and confirmed that ASwide generates an acceptable solution stably compared with other methods.

Keywords: Ant Colony Optimization, Traveling Salesman Problem, Swarm Intelligence, Combinatorial Optimization.

1 Introduction

Ant Colony Optimization (ACO) is a method inspired by the foraging behavior of ants used and studied in various types of complicated problems including the Traveling Salesman Problem (TSP) with significant efficiencies [1,6]. For these metaheuristic algorithms the balance between intensification and diversification will play an important roll in the quality of its solution. In recent studies lots of significant research has been done by adjusting the pheromone tables or by setting several colonies using $\mathcal{MAX} - \mathcal{MIN}$ Ant System [17,14,18,22]. But using $\mathcal{MAX} - \mathcal{MIN}$ Ant System has a problem in that it needs a preliminary preparation by using another method such as nearest neighbour algorithm [9], 2-opt [3] to the pheromone table which greatly affects solution's quality.

In this paper we will propose a method called ASwide which outputs solutions with high precision in an acceptable time aiming in the field of car navigations and network routings. ASwide which is an improvement of ACO adds a ratio of the best solution the system found so far and the length of the trail the ant agents moved to the ACO's pheromone updating formula. In addition, we will also propose a method to make the system converge faster with maintaining diversification using λ-branching factor. In the next section, we will explain the ACO algorithm and some other algorithms improved form the ACO. In Section

G. Boella et al. (Eds.): PRIMA 2013, LNAI 8291, pp. 445–452, 2013.

Algorithm 1. A typical ACO algorithm

- Initialize all ant agents and the pheromone

while Termination condition are not satisfied **do**

    1. Every ant agents selects the next city to move stochastically using the city selection formula

    2. Calculates the amount of pheromone each ant agent secrete to the trail using the pheromone calculation formula

    3. Updates the pheromone field using the pheromone updating formula

    end while
- Outputs the best ant's trail found in the system

---

3 and Section 4 we will do some computer experiments and consideration with our proposed method and other traditional methods. Finally in Section 5 we will conclude our study.

2   An Outline of ACO

Recently, studies on swarm intelligence which models the habits and behaviours of a particular creature especially social insects and natural phenomenons are commonly done [21,15]. One of the major and famous method in swarm intelligence is the Ant Colony Optimization (ACO) which ant agents secrete pheromones to communicate and cooperate food retrieval with other ant agents.

The most basic and common ACO named as the Ant System (AS) was introduced by Dorigo to solve complex combinatorial optimization problems especially the TSPs [5].

Traveling Salesman Problem (TSP) is one of the typical NP-hard problem in combinatorial optimization which you need to find the shortest possible route that visites each city exactly once and return to the origin city when the list of cities and the distances between each pair of cities are given.

Most studies on ACOs done today such as ASelite [8], ASrank [2], Ant Colony System [7], $\mathcal{MAX} - \mathcal{MIN}$ Ant System [17] is a method improved from the Dorigo's Ant System. Algorithm 1 shows the basic Ant System's algorithm.

3   ASwide

In Bullnheimer's study [2] the pheromone value of ASrank is weighted $(\sigma - \mu)$ times according to the rank of the elite ants. In addition to that the ratio of the maximum pheromone value that a single ant agent can secrete and the ant agent's tour length is also weighted the the pheromone calculation. We think there is a problem in this method. There is a bad influence on the system when all the elite ant's evaluation were not good since it will be weighted $(\sigma - \mu)$, not considering the tour length found beforehand.

So in our proposed method ASwide, we will add another weighting to the ASrank to solve the problem mentioned above. The added weight will be the

Table 1. Comparison Using eil51.tsp at Tour 300 (Best solution:426)

	ACO	ASelite	ASrank	ASwide
Best Solution	450	437	**429**	431
Relative Error	5.33	2.52	**0.67**	1.16
Average	474.2	458.9	444.6	**440.4**
Relative Error	10.16	7.17	4.18	**3.27**
Worst Solution	487	475	472	**451**
STDEV	9.73	11.86	9.39	**5.98**

Table 2. Comparison Using qa194.tsp at Tour 300 (Best solution:9352)

	ACO	ASelite	ASrank	ASwide
Best Solution	11814	11392	9883	**9855**
Relative Error	20.84	17.91	5.37	**5.10**
Average	12134.0	11838.5	10171.9	**10124.4**
Relative Error	22.93	21.00	8.06	**7.63**
Worst Solution	12373	12187	10656	**10463**
STDEV	**161.09**	229.03	227.95	162.61

ratio of the best solution the system found so far and the tour length the elite ant traveled. By adding this weight the system can give the ant agents proper rewards either negative or in positive even if all the elite ants' evaluation were no good. The system can also give extra pheromone to the ant agent that has broken the record of the best solution found so far. We think by this ASwide could do the weighting better than ASrank and other methods and reflects it to the solution's quality. ASwide's pheromone calculation formula $\Delta \tau_{ij}^{\mu}$ is shown in Formula (1).

$$\Delta \tau_{ij}^{\mu} = \begin{cases} (\sigma - \mu) \frac{Q \cdot L^*}{(L_{\mu}(t))^2} & \text{if } (i, j) \in T^{\mu}(t) \\ 0 & \text{else} \end{cases} \tag{1}$$

Where μ represents the rank of the elite ants which is ranked by the length of their route, σ as a value added one to the number of the elite ants, L^* as the best length of the route the system found so far, $L_{\mu}(t)$ as the μ-th elite ant's length of the route at the t-th tour, Q as the maximum value of pheromone a single ant can secrete in a single tour, $T^{\mu}(t)$ as the μ-th elite ant's route at the t-th tour.

3.1 Computer Experiments

In this section we would have done some experiments focusing on intensification to confirm the effectiveness of ASwide by comparing the results with other ACOs using few TSP problems. For our computer experiments we used eil51.tsp which has 51 cities provided from the "TSPLIB" [20] and qa194.tsp which has 194 cities provided from the "The Traveling Salesman Problem" [19]. For our comparative approach we used ACO, ASelite and ASrank which all of the methods promotes intensification. Defining the number of cities in the TSP as x, parameters for our computer experiments are as follows: number of ant agents m are $x - 1$, number of elite ants σ are $x/10$, α and β are both 1, maximum pheromone value Q is 100 and the evaporation rate ρ is 0.005. In this paper we considered 300 tours as a reasonable time to solve the problem which is an early searching period for the ACOs. Each simulation resultes until 300 tours are shown in Table 1 and Table 2. The best solution, worst solution, average, standard deviation (STDEV) are the results from 30 simulations and the relative error is calculated from the best known solutions from each benchmark, 426 for the eil51.tsp and 9352 for the qa194.tsp.

From the two tables Table 1 and Table 2 we can confirm that ASwide outperforms other methods when solving both eil51.tsp and qa194.tsp. This is because we think ASwide was able to give an appropriate reward both negative and positive to the elite ants which lead to the results. In addition other than the best average and the best solution, the standard deviation was in the smaller which means ASwide can output good solutions stably compared to other methods.

From the computer experiments we confirmed that ASwide outperforms other methods with a stable and a good quality of solution, only adding a simple ratio of the maximum pheromone value that a single ant agent can secrete and the ant agent's tour length to the pheromone calculation formula.

4   Control in Diversification

In ACO's searching process ant agents secrete pheromone to the path they traveled to communicate the route with other ant agents. But there is a problem with ACO that in the latter stage of the search it easily falles into a localized solution which makes the system to stop searching. Maintaining diversity is a very important factor for improving the ACO and a lot of studies have been done to maintain diversity mainly by making some ants randomly select cities [13,16,11,10,12]. Selecting the suitable random rate for the system in very difficult since the best random selection rate differs in every problem. So, in this paper we will introduce a method applying random selection after the system converges instead of applying the random selection from the beginning of the search which most of the studies have done.

4.1   Introducing Random Selection

Random selection enables the system to maintain diversity by ant agents randomly selecting their next city to travel. Randomly selecting the next city means not to use heuristic, pheromone information nor the length between the two cities, but to select the next city to visit all in the same probability.

In Nakamichi's study [13] the random selection above is held at the beginning of the search, but in this paper random selection will be introduced only after it satisfies the convergence inequality. We will use the λ-branching factor [4] which examines the deviation of the pheromone in the field for our convergence inequality.

4.2   Lambda-branching Factor

λ-branching factor [4] was introduced by Dorigo to verify whether the system needs to continue the search by checking the convergence to set the termination condition automatically. In this paper we will use λ-branching factor for our convergence inequality to determine the timing to apply random selection. λ-branching factor is a method that calculates the deviation of the pheromone by taking the average number of the cities from city i to city j which exceeds the threshold a user defines.

The formula which $\Lambda(t)$ represents the average number of cities exceeding the threshold in time t is shown in Formula (2).

$$\Lambda(t) = \frac{1}{n} \sum_{1 \leq i \leq n} \sum_{1 \leq j \leq n, j \neq i} \epsilon_{ij}(t) \tag{2}$$

Where n represents the number of cities, ϵ_{ij} as a function determining whether the pheromone from city i and city j exceeds the threshold which is detailed in Formula (3).

$$\epsilon_{ij}(t) = \begin{cases} 1 & \text{if } \tau_{ij}(t) > \lambda(\tau_i^{max}(t) - \tau_i^{min}(t)) + \tau_i^{min}(t) \\ 0 & \text{else} \end{cases} \tag{3}$$

Where τ_{ij} represents the value of pheromone secreted in cities between i and j, λ as a constant on how severely you want to make the convergence that satisfies $(0 \leq \lambda \leq 1)$, $\tau_i^{max}(t)$ as the maximum pheromone value that goes out from city i in time t and $\tau_i^{min}(t)$ as the minimum pheromone value that goes out from city i in time t.

4.3   Sensitivity Experiments Using Random Selection

In this section we will examine how diversity control will affect to the system. We prepared 4 methods for the computer experiments. ASwide$_{RS}$ and ASrank$_{RS}$ a method which adds the random selection from the beginning to ASwide and ASrank. ASwide$_\lambda$ and ASrank$_\lambda$ which adds random selection only after it satisfies the convergence inequality by λ-branching factor to ASwide and ASrank. To determine the best random selection rate for the 4 methods we did a sensitivity experiment. Since it is impossible the determine the "best" random selection rate we prepared 14 random selection rates to compare, 0.1 to 1.0 at intervals of 0.1 and 1.0 to 5.0 at intervals of 1.0. All the parameters used in this simulation are same as the computer experiment in Section 3 and the parameter λ was set to 0.001. Also to check the best threshold value we changed the threshold value Λ from 2.2 to 4.0 at intervals of 0.2 and used the best value for our comparison.

Table 3. Comparison between the 4 Methods

	ASrank$_{RS}$	ASwide$_{RS}$	ASrank$_\lambda$	ASwide$_\lambda$
Random Selection Rate	0.8	0.6	0.7	0.7
Λ	-	-	3.4	3.8
Best Solution	9649	**9501**	9585	**9495**
Relative Error	3.08	**1.57**	2.49	**1.51**
Average	9797.8	**9724.8**	9843.7	**9822.7**
STDEV	141.36	**138.61**	117.51	**107.09**

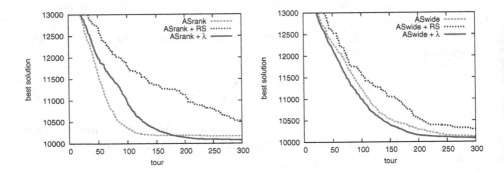

Fig. 1. Best solution found using ASrank   **Fig. 2.** Best solution found using ASwide

The experiment results for the 4 methods ASwide$_{RS}$, ASrank$_{RS}$, ASwide$_\lambda$ and ASrank$_\lambda$ using the best paramaters from the sensitivity experiment with 10000 tours is shown in Table 3. The computer experiments results were results by doing 30 simulations using qa194.tsp.

From Table 3 we confirmed that ASwide outperforms other methods not only focusing on intensification by weight control but also with maintaining diversification using random selection. In addition, compared from the results in Section 3 introducing random selection to maintain diversification improves the result of not only ASwide but also ASrank. Also from the same Table we can see that ASwide$_\lambda$ and ASrank$_\lambda$ both has 0.7% as the best average with 3.8 and 3.4 for the threshold of Λ. From the best solution, relative error and average we can confirm that ASwide$_\lambda$ and ASrank$_\lambda$ has better results than ASwide$_{RS}$ and ASrank$_{RS}$ from Table 3.

Fig. 1 and Fig. 2 shows the result until 300 tours which had the best average and also with the original ASwide and ASrank's average. From the two figures we can confirm that random selection introduced using λ-branching factor converges faster than introducing it at the beginning of the search. From the previous experiment we had confirmed that ASwide$_\lambda$ and ASrank$_\lambda$ had better results. Therefore, we conclude that the timing of random selection using λ-branching factor is an attractive method which intensifies at the beginning at the search and diversifies after it converges, making the system to maximizing the quality of the solution in any period of the search.

In addition we also did the same experiments with eil51.tsp and all 4 methods were able to output the best known solution 426. In other experiments we were able to get the mostly the same property as the experiments using qa194.tsp.

5 Conclusion

In this paper we proposed a method called ASwide which adds the ratio of the maximum pheromone value that a single ant agent can secrete and the ant agents tour length to the pheromone calculation formula. From the computer experiments using TSP we confirmed that ASwide was able to give an appropriate reward to the system. In addition we confirmed ASwide outputs better solutions in large numbers of cities.

In Section 4 we proposed a new way of introducing random selection using λ-branching factor. From the results of ASwide$_\lambda$ and ASrank$_\lambda$ which adds random selection by using λ-branching factor, over half of the results were able to output a solution that has a relative error less than 3.0% and confirmed that it could outperform the Nakamichi's method. In addition we also confirmed that by introducing λ-branching factor it could maximize the quality of the solution in any period of the search.

In the future we would like to introduce random selection using λ-branching factor in other ACO based algorithms such as $\mathcal{MAX} - \mathcal{MIN}$ Ant System [17] and Ant Colony System [7], and reducing some parameters for the system. In addition we would also like to introduce random selection dynamically according to the value of Λ, and use the system to a TSP in a larger number of cities.

Acknowledgment. This work was supported in part by the Ministry of Education, Science, Sports and Culture, Grant–in–Aid for Scientific Research under grant #25280100 and #25540146.

References

1. Arora, T., Moses, M.E.: Ant Colony Optimization for power efficient routing in manhattan and non-manhattan VLSI architectures. In: IEEE Swarm Intelligence Symposium, SIS 2009, pp. 137–144. IEEE (2009)
2. Bullnheimer, B., Hartl, R.F., Strauss, C.: A new rank based version of the Ant System. A computational study (1997)
3. Croes, G.: A method for solving traveling-salesman problems. Operations Research 6(6), 791–812 (1958)
4. Dorigo, M., Stützle, T.: Ant colony optimization. A Bradford Book (2004), http://books.google.co.jp/books?id=_aefcpY8GiEC
5. Dorigo, M.: Optimization, learning and natural algorithms. Ph. D. Thesis, Politecnico di Milano, Italy (1992)
6. Dorigo, M., Caro, G.D., Gambardella, L.M.: Ant algorithms for discrete optimization. Artificial Life 5(2), 137–172 (1999)

7. Dorigo, M., Gambardella, L.M.: Ant colony system: A cooperative learning approach to the traveling salesman problem. IEEE Transactions on Evolutionary Computation 1(1), 53–66 (1997)
8. Dorigo, M., Maniezzo, V., Colorni, A.: Ant system: optimization by a colony of cooperating agents. IEEE Transactions on Systems, Man, and Cybernetics, Part B: Cybernetics 26(1), 29–41 (1996)
9. Gutin, G., Yeo, A., Zverovich, A.: Traveling salesman should not be greedy: domination analysis of greedy-type heuristics for the TSP. Discrete Applied Mathematics 117(1), 81–86 (2002)
10. Haga, M., Kato, S.: ASwide: An Ant System Adapting Penalty by Using the Ratio of Best Solution found. In: JAWS 2012 (2012) (in Japanese)
11. Haga, M., Kato, S.: ASwide: An Efficient Ant System for Solving the Traveling Salesman Problem. In: RENGO 2012 pp. D3–D6 (2012) (in Japanese)
12. Haga, M., Kato, S.: Maintaining Diversity in Ant Colony Optimization using λ-branching factor. In: Kansei Robotics Symposium 2013, pp. 89–96 (2013) (in Japanese)
13. Nakamichi, Y., Arita, T.: The Effects of Diversity Control Based on Random Selection in Ant Colony Optimization. Transactions of Information Processing Society of Japan 43(9), 2939–2946 (2002)
14. Rong-Long, W., Li-Qing, Z.: Ant colony optimization with memory and its application to traveling salesman problem. IEICE Transactions on Fundamentals of Electronics, Communications and Computer Sciences 95(3), 639–645 (2012)
15. Shah-Hosseini, H.: The intelligent water drops algorithm: a nature-inspired swarm-based optimization algorithm. International Journal of Bio-Inspired Computation 1(1), 71–79 (2009)
16. Shimomura, S., Sugimoto, M., Haraguchi, T., Matsushita, H., Nishio, Y.: Behavior of Ant Colony Optimization with Intelligent and Dull Ants. Institute of Electronics, Information, and Communication Engineers 110(83), 157–160 (2010) (in Japanese)
17. Stutzle, T., Hoos, H.H.: MAX-MIN ant system. Future Generations Computer Systems 16(8), 889–914 (2000)
18. Tsai, C.W., Hu, K.C., Chiang, M.C., Yang, C.S.: Ant colony optimization with dual pheromone tables for clustering. In: 2011 IEEE International Conference on Fuzzy Systems (FUZZ), pp. 2916–2921. IEEE (2011)
19. TSP, T.: The Traveling salesman problem (2013), http://www.tsp.gatech.edu/index.html
20. TSPLIB: TSPLIB (2013), http://comopt.ifi.uni-heidelberg.de/software/TSPLIB95/
21. Wong, L.P., Low, M.Y.H., Chong, C.S.: A bee colony optimization algorithm for traveling salesman problem. In: Second Asia International Conference on Modeling & Simulation, AICMS 2008, pp. 818–823. IEEE (2008)
22. Zhou, X., Zhao, L., Xia, Z., Wang, R.: A Max-Min Ant System with two colonies and its application to Traveling Salesman Problem. In: 2012 IEEE Fifth International Conference on Advanced Computational Intelligence (ICACI), pp. 319–323 (2012)

Evaluating the Impact of the Human-Agent Teamwork Communication Model (HAT-CoM) on the Development of a Shared Mental Model

Nader Hanna, Deborah Richards, and Michael Hitchens

Computing Department, Macquarie University, Australia
{nader.hanna,deborah.richards,michael.hitchens}@mq.edu.au

Abstract. It is well known that the development of a Shared Mental Model (SMM) leads to better teamwork performance. Communication of shared knowledge is considered a crucial factor in successful teamwork. In this paper, we evaluate the impact of applying a proposed Human-Agent Teamwork Communication Model, namely HAT-CoM, on the development of SMM between human and agent teammates. Another aim of the paper is to investigate the impact of an implausible or unreasonable request on the SMM. The results show that HAT-CoM is effective in assisting the human and agent teammates to develop SMM. In addition, the results show that an implausible request breaks the developed SMM.

Keywords: Shared Mental Model, Multimodal Communication, Human-Agent Collaboration, Human-Agent Communication.

1   Introduction

Shared Mental Model (SMM) refers to the state among team members where the members have overlapping knowledge and beliefs. SMM was introduced by Cannon-bowers et al. [1] in the context of teamwork between humans. Later, it became apparent that SMM is not only important in human teams, but also in human-agent teams [2]. Hence, it has gained the attention of many researchers in psychology, social sciences and artificial intelligence. Many researchers who have been studying SMM classified the shared knowledge into two categories: knowledge about the team and knowledge about the task [1].

Communication is considered as a catalyst in successful teamwork [3]. Many researchers agreed that a SMM could be created via the experience of team members who work together [4] and/or communication between them. Stout et al. [5] assumed that SMM among team members enabled them to utilise communication strategies efficiently during high-workload conditions. On the other hand, effective communication positively affects the degree of coordinated performance attained by teammates which in turn fosters the development of SMM [6].

As many researchers have been interested in the development of SMM in the human team, Sycara and Sukthankar [7] stated that the biggest challenge in human-agent

G. Boella et al. (Eds.): PRIMA 2013, LNAI 8291, pp. 453–460, 2013.

team work is to establish a SMM. In recent years, many researchers have been interested in extending the concept of SMM to include the teamwork of agents or situations that combine the human and the agent in one team. The greatest challenge in designing agents as a teammate for a human lies in communicating their intent and making results intelligible to them [8].

We proposed the Human-Agent Communication Model (HAT-CoM) to aid communication in a human-agent collaborative environment. This communication model extends an agent planner (for more details about the communication model see [9]), and so every response made or perceived by the agent depends on agent planning. The communication model includes both verbal communication (i.e. textual communication) and non-verbal communication (i.e. behavioural communication). Interaction between the human and the agent involves alternating between textual and behavioural communication. That is to say, the human will send a request message to the agent, and the agent will reply with acceptance or rejection depending on its plan. The agent may also send a request message to the human user asking for help to achieve the task. The human user may reply with acceptance or rejection. The rejection of the agent's request by the human user will lead the agent to modify its plan to the new state of the task. Behavioural communication is also handled in an alternating fashion, and it relies on the agent planning process. As part of behavioural communication, the agent has to monitor the surrounding environment, observe the actions of the human teammate and continuously adapt his/her plan to the new changes.

The aim of this study is to verify the impact of HAT-CoM on the development of a SMM between human and agent as teammates. The study asks the following two research questions:

Research Question 1: What is the impact of applying HAT-CoM on the development of the SMM between the human and the agent as represented in the outcomes of SMM? The outcomes are measured in terms of anticipating a teammate's decisions, reduced explicit communication, match in cognitive perspective and competence in decision-making (ease of flow of decisions).

Research Question 2: What is the impact of an implausible request between the team members on the SMM as represented in the outcomes of the SMM?

The paper is organized as follows. Section 2 presents the literature review. The methodology used to evaluate the impact of HAT-CoM on the SMM is presented in section 3. The results will be given in section 4 and the discussion will come in section 5. Finally, section 6 presents conclusions.

2   Literature Review

A limited amount of research has focused on human-agent communication during collaboration to help developing a SMM. Extending their agent architecture, called CAST [10], which enables a team of agents to establish a computational shared mental model, Yen et al. [11] studied the impact of SMM-supported decision-making on an agent's communication of required information with another teammate and the overall performance of a team of agents or humans. In addition, the authors assumed that designing agents with an understanding of the behaviour of individuals in a team of agents and humans could be used to address the challenges that face teams.

In order to design an agent's cognitive structure especially for human-agent teamwork, Fan and Yen [12] developed a system called Shared Mental Models for all - SMMall. SMMall implements a hidden Markov model (HMM) to help the agent to predict its human partner's cognitive load status. However, SMMall does not support communication. Our proposed model enables agents on the one hand, to deduce the humans' intention and on the other hand, to communicate their internal state.

Many researchers present SSM for multi-agent systems. However these often are agent-only systems, for example the model of Xu and Volz [13] neglected the human in agents' teamwork. Having a shared mental model is common in multi-agent systems with agent-to-agent collaboration without a human component [14].

3   Methodology

Sixty-six undergraduate university students participated in the study. Concerning participants' linguistic skills, 92.42% were English native speakers. The non-native English speakers have been speaking English on a daily basis on average for 14.4 years. Regarding computer skills, 21.21% of the participants described themselves as having basic computers skills, 16.67% as having advanced skills, while 62.12% said they have proficient computer skills. Concerning their experience in using games and other 3D application, the participants answered the question "How many hours a week do you play computer games?" with times ranging between 0 to 30 hours weekly (mean=4.24, SD=6.66).

Data was collected by two means: Automatic data logging was used to track human utilization; in addition, a survey was used to collect participants' perception about SMM with the agent.

3.1   The Scenario

In order to demonstrate the effect of the proposed communication model on developing SMM between the human and the agent, the model was implemented in a collaborative task-based scenario. In the task, the human and the agent should collaborate together to trap an animal for scientific research. The animal is surrounded by eight regions (four pairs of regions). Both the human and the agent should select one region at a time to build a fence around the animal, and then observe each other's action, i.e. non-verbal behaviour. Meanwhile, they exchange verbal messages to convey their intention and request a recommended selection from the other counterpart. The human and the agent should be able to select only neighbouring regions. A neighbouring region is one that is before or after the already selected regions. We call the process of selecting each pair of regions out of the four pairs a cycle. That is to say, there are four cycles. Each cycle includes the human and the agent selecting a region. Except for the first cycle, they should exchange requests and replies verbally.

As a means to observe the effect of an implausible request on the SMM, we created a situation where a subset of the participants was asked to take a step that seems unreasonable. We made the agent ask the human to go and select a region which has already been selected before and there is a fence built in this requested region. The human participant is in a situation where on the one hand, he/she successfully collaborated with the agent to complete the task and experienced plausible requests from the agent, and on the other hand, he/she has to carry out a request that seems unreasonable, we called this last cycle an 'implausible cycle'.

4   Result

The outcomes of establishing a SMM between team members could be used as evidence of successful development of the SMM between team members. To evaluate the development of SMM, five outcomes were used. These outcomes are anticipating teammate's plan, the reduction of explicit communication, Match in cognitive perspective, Competence in decision-making and the involvement with teammate [15].

Concerning *Anticipating teammate's plan*, estimating how the human's request matched the agent's plan tends to show the closeness in understanding the requirements of the task. Fig. 1 shows a continuous increase in agent's acceptance of the human's request from 17.24% in the first cycle, to 85.19% in the last cycle in the normal phase.

Another outcome of the development of a SMM between teammates is *the reduction of explicit communication* while achieving the shared goal. According to some researchers, e.g. [16], the result of anticipating the plan of another team member is that explicit communication will be less, and the more the team members will share each other's understanding about the goal. To estimate the explicit communication between the human and the agent, a tracking mechanism was used to register the human's explanation requests to the agent, when the agent asks the human to take a certain step. Fig. 1 shows that in the first cycle 67.80% of the participants asked the agent to explain the proposal that the agent made to the human teammate. In the following cycles, the ratios continuously dropped to 32.20% and 25.86% of the participants.

To evaluate *Match in cognitive perspective*, the verbal requests made by the agent were tracked and the ratios of acceptance and rejection of these requests were calculated during each cycle. Fig. 2 shows the percentage of the human's acceptance of the agent's verbal requests in each cycle. The results show that the human's behaviour reflects an acceptance level in cycle1, cycle2 and cycle3 to what the agent has requested of 76.27%, 67.80% and 70.69% respectively with an average 71.59%.

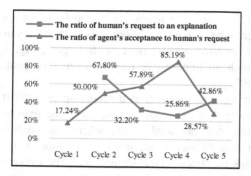
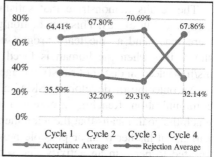

Fig. 1. The ratios of agent's acceptance of the human's requests and human's request to explain

Fig. 2. The ratios of the human's acceptance of the agent's verbal requests

Regarding *Competence in decision-making*, the progress of the human's performance to complete the different cycles was evaluated through recording the average time to complete each cycle. Fig. 3 shows that the average time the human participant needs to complete the first cycle is 51.1 seconds. The time decreased in the consecutive cycles to be 40.66 and 33.78 seconds in the second and the third cycles respectively.

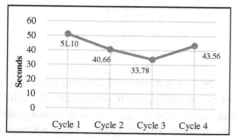
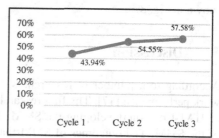

Fig. 3. The average time to complete each normal cycle including the implausible cycle

Fig. 4. The ratios of recommending next step in each cycle

To evaluate *the involvement of the human with the agent teammate*, we calculated the ratio of the participants who recommended a possible next step that the agent can take. Fig. 4 shows that in the first cycle only 43.94% of the human participants proposed recommendations for a possible next step that the agent can take. The ratios increased to 54.55% and 57.57% in the second and the third cycles.

4.1 Breaking the Shared Mental Model

A SMM is created using effective communication and plausible directions while conducting the actions to complete the shared goal. The plausible directions foster trust between team members. To investigate the effect of proposing unreasonable directions on SMM as demonstrated by its outcomes, we present the results of an additional cycle (fourth cycle) where the agent asks the human to select a region that is already selected before.

The results demonstrate that satisfaction with the agent continuously increases along the four cycles. This satisfaction grew when reasonable requests from the agent were made and as the team progressed towards achievement of their goal. Fig. 1 shows that when the human is faced with an implausible request from the agent, his/her selection does not satisfy the agent's plan.

An outcome of developing SMM among team member is a reduction in explicit communication. Reaching a common understanding about the goal, and the plan to reach the goal, means that the team member does not need to keep asking his counterpart about his/her plan or possible next step. However, when a team member is requested to perform an activity that seems unrelated to the shared goal, the explicit communication to ask for more explanation would be a sign of expressing disagreement. Fig. 1 shows that 42.86% of the participants clicked 'Reason' button to seek explanation from the agent about his implausible request.

The average of the human's acceptance to the agent's requests in the first three cycles was 71.59%. Fig. 2 shows that 32.14 % of the participants accepted the implausible request from the agent compared to 70.69 % in the previous cycle that had a reasonable request. The time needed to complete each cycle dropped continuously from 51.1 seconds to 33.78 seconds to complete cycle one to three. The result shows that the average time needed to complete the implausible cycle is 43.56 seconds, as shown in Fig. 3.

5   Discussion

According to a number of researchers, the development of a SMM improves teamwork performance [17]. The first research question was posed to investigate the effect of HAT-CoM on developing the SMM. This effect appears in the common outcomes of the SMM. The outcomes of SMM that we studied are anticipating the teammate's decisions; reduction in explicit communication; match in cognitive perspective; and competence in decision-making.

When evaluating the ratio of the agent's acceptance to the human's requests, the result shows that over the consecutive cycles of the collaborative task the acceptance ratio increases. The increase in the agent acceptance ratio is a sign of having a mutual agreement on the steps to achieve the task. Another outcome of the SMM is the reduction in the explicit communication as the team members go on conducting the task. The result shows that the optional communication regarding the inquiries about the agent's decision is reduced over the cycles. This reduction is assumed to be because of the human's realization of how the agent is making his decisions. A third outcome of the SMM that we investigated is the match in cognitive perspective. The result shows that the rate of the agent's acceptance slightly increased from one cycle to another. This finding is consistent with other studies [18] and confirms the development of SMM between teammates is accompanied with forming a similar expectation and perspective about the outcome of the shared task. The fourth outcome of SMM is the competence in making a decision while carrying out the shared task. Competence could be represented as efficiency in the time to complete the task.

The time to complete each cycle was recorded and an improvement in the efficiency in the time needed to complete the shared task was registered. The result is consistent with other research work that assumed that developing a SMM helps teammates to reach decisions more easily [19]. The last outcome of SMM is the involvement in the shared task. We found that the ratio of the participants who optionally recommended steps for the agent to take increased over the cycles as a sign of the human's desire to collaborate more with the agent. Our findings about the involvement in the shared task is consistent with the assumption of a number of studies [20] which claimed that developing SMM makes team members more positive about the shared purpose. Our findings in studying the impact of HAT-CoM on the development of SMM demonstrate improvement in the considered outcomes. These findings answer the posed second research question.

Relying on our findings in the implausible cycle, we conclude that an implausible request between the team members while participating in a collaborative activity will result in the degradation of the developed SMM. This degradation is apparent in some of the SMM features such as inaccurate anticipation of the plan of the teammate, increase in the explicit communication, mismatch in cognitive perspective and difficulty in taking decisions.

6   Conclusion

In this paper, we aimed to verify the impact of our human-agent communication model on the development of the SMM between a human and an agent. Our results showed that elements of HAT-CoM had a positive impact on the development of the SMM as witnessed by the participants. The inductive evaluation aimed to verify the impact of HAT-CoM on the development of the SMM through tracing the changes on the outcomes of the SMM. The results showed that HAT-CoM had a positive impact on the development of the SMM as demonstrated in the improvements in SMM features. These improvements witnessed abrupt decline, when the participants faced an implausible request from the agent teammate.

References

1. Cannon-Bowers, J.A., Salas, E., Converse, S.: Shared Mental Models in Expert Team Decision-Making. In: Castellan, J.J. (ed.) Individual and Group Decision Making, pp. 221–246 (1993)
2. van de Kieft, I., Jonker, C.M., van Riemsdijk, M.B.: Explaining Negotiation: Obtaining a Shared Mental Model of Preferences. In: Mehrotra, K.G., Mohan, C.K., Oh, J.C., Varshney, P.K., Ali, M. (eds.) IEA/AIE 2011, Part II. LNCS, vol. 6704, pp. 120–129. Springer, Heidelberg (2011)
3. Smith-Jentsch, K.A., Johnston, J.H., Payne, S.C.: Measuring Team-Related Expertise in Complex Environments. In: Cannon-Bowers, J.A., Salas, E. (eds.) Decision Making Under Stress: Implications for Individual and Team Training, pp. 61–87. American Psychological Association, Washington, DC (1998)

4. Tsuchiya, T., Tsuchiya, S.: Policy Exercise: an Essential Enabler of Virtual Corporation. International Journal of Production Economics 60-61(1), 221–228 (1999)

5. Stout, R.J., et al.: Planning, Shared Mental Models, and Coordinated Performance: An Empirical Link Is Established. Human Factors: The Journal of the Human Factors and Ergonomics Society 41(1), 61–71 (1999)

6. Espevik, R., et al.: Shared Mental Models and Operational Effectiveness: Effects on Performance and Team Processes in Submarine Attack Teams. Military Psychology 18, 23–36 (2006)

7. Sycara, K., Sukthankar, G.: Literature Review of Teamwork Models, technical report, CMU-RI-TR-06-50, Robotics Institute, Carnegie Mellon University, Pittsburgh, PA (2006)

8. Lewis, M.: Designing for Human-Agent Interaction. AI Magazine 19(2) (1998)

9. Hanna, N., Richards, D.: "Come and Join my Team": Extending the Collaborative Ability of Virtual Agents in a Multi-Agent System. In: Proceedings of International Workshop on Cognitive Agents for Virtual Environments (CAVE 2012), Workshop at the 11th International Conference on Autonomous Agents and MultiAgent Systems (AAMAS 2012), Valencia, Spain (2012)

10. Yin, J., et al.: A Knowledge-Based Approach for Designing Intelligent Team Training Systems. In: Proceedings of the Fourth International Conference on Autonomous Agents 2000, pp. 427–434. ACM, Barcelona (2000)

11. Yen, J., et al.: Agents with Shared Mental Models for Enhancing Team Decision Makings. Decision Support Systems, Special Issue on Intelligence and Security Informatics 41(3), 634–653 (2006)

12. Fan, X., Yen, J.: Modeling Cognitive Loads for Evolving Shared Mental Models in Human-Agent Collaboration. IEEE Transactions on Systems, Man, and Cybernetics, Part B: Cybernetics 41(2), 354–367 (2011)

13. Xu, D., et al.: Modeling and Verifying Multi-Agent Behaviors Using Predicate/Transition Nets. International Journal of Software Engineering and Knowledge Engineering 13(1), 103–124 (2003)

14. Jones, R.M., et al.: Automated Intelligent Pilots for Combat Flight Simulation. AI Magazine 20(1), 27–41 (1999)

15. Kraiger, K., Wenzel, L.H.: Conceptual Development and Empirical Evaluation of Measures of Shared Mental Models as Indicators of Team Effectiveness. In: Brannick, M.T., Salas, E., Prince, C. (eds.) Team Performance Assessment and Measurement: Theory, Meothds, and Applications, pp. 63–84. Lawrence Erlbaum, Mahwah (1997)

16. Espevik, R., Johnsen, B.H., Eid, J.: Outcomes of Shared Mental Models of Team Members in Cross Training and High-Intensity Simulations. Journal of Cognitive Engineering and Decision Making 5(4), 352–377 (2011)

17. Rouse, W.B., Cannon-Bowers, J.A., Salas, E.: The Role of Mental Models in Team Performance in Complex Systems. IEEE Transactions on Systems, Man and Cybernetics 22(6), 1296–1308 (1992)

18. Banks, A.P., Millward, L.J.: Running Shared Mental Models as a Distributed Cognitive Process. British Journal of Psychology 91, 513–531 (2000)

19. Noordzij, M., Postma, A.: Categorical and Metric Distance Information in Mental Representations Derived from Route and Survey Descriptions. Psychological Research 69, 221–232 (2005)

20. Carpenter, S., et al.: Studying Team Shared Mental Models. In: Proceedings of the 3rd International Conference on the Pragmatic Web: Innovating the Interactive Society (ICPW 2008), pp. 41–48. ACM, Uppsala (2008)

Repeated Auctions for Reallocation of Tasks with Pickup and Delivery upon Robot Failure

Bradford Heap and Maurice Pagnucco

ARC Centre of Excellence for Autonomous Systems and NICTA
School of Computer Science and Engineering
The University of New South Wales
Sydney, NSW, 2052, Australia
{bradfordh,morri}@cse.unsw.edu.au

The task allocation problem with pickup and delivery is an extension of the widely studied *multi-robot task allocation (MRTA) problem* which, in general, considers each task as a single location to visit. Within the robotics domain distributed auctions are a popular method for task allocation [4]. In this work, we consider a team of autonomous mobile robots making deliveries in an office-like environment. Each robot has a set of tasks to complete, and each task is composed of a pickup location and a delivery location. The robots seek to complete their assigned tasks either minimising distance travelled or time taken according to a global team objective. During execution, individual robots may fail due to malfunctioning equipment or running low on battery power.

A common approach for reacting to task execution delays and changes in the system is to repeatedly auction and redistribute tasks that are not completed, either at certain time intervals or upon each single task completion [6,12]. Reallocating and replanning tasks can be costly in terms of computational power and time. While arbitrary replanning may not be the most efficient approach, knowing when to reallocate and how much of the system should be reallocated is a challenging problem.

In this paper we consider the reallocation of a failed robot's assigned tasks to the remaining operating robots using sequential single-item auctions (SSI auctions) [11,8]. We consider two different approaches to the reallocation of tasks amongst the remaining operating robots: a) partial reallocation in which the failed robot's uncompleted tasks are auctioned—this results in the remaining operating robots modifying their existing task execution plans to incorporate additional tasks—b) global reallocation of the failed robot's uncompleted tasks plus all remaining tasks yet to be picked up. This results in a re-assignment of the task set across all remaining operating robots and new task execution plans to be generated. Despite a global reallocation requiring more computation, inter-robot communication and time, it can be expected that this approach would produce lower distance and/or task execution times as more task assignment combinations are considered. However, our empirical results show that partial allocations, on average, produce final results that are equivalent to the results for global reallocation. The aim of this paper is to explore this surprising result.

G. Boella et al. (Eds.): PRIMA 2013, LNAI 8291, pp. 461–469, 2013.

1   Problem Definition

We expand the problem formalisation given by Koenig *et al.* [9] to include tasks with pickup and delivery. Given a set of robots $R = \{r_1, \ldots, r_m\}$ and a set of tasks $T = \{t_1, \ldots, t_n\}$. A partial solution to the MRTA problem is given by any tuple $\langle T_{r_1}, \ldots, T_{r_m} \rangle$ of pairwise disjoint task subsets: $T_{r_i} \subseteq T$ with $T_{r_i} \cap T_{r_{i'}} = \emptyset$, $i \neq i'$, $\forall i = 1, \ldots, m$. Each task subset T_{r_i} is then assigned to a single robot $r_i \in R$. To determine a complete solution we need to find a partial solution where all tasks are assigned to task subsets: $\langle T_{r_1} \ldots T_{r_m} \rangle$ with $\cup_{r_i \in R} T_{r_i} = T$.

When a robot fails, we remove it from the set of operating robots: $R \leftarrow R \backslash \{r_{fail}\}$. As a consequence of this, if $T_{r_{fail}} \neq \emptyset$, the previous complete solution to the problem $\cup_{r_i \in R} T_{r_i} = T$ no longer holds. A new complete solution can be found by re-assigning the set of tasks assigned to the failed robot $T_{r_{fail}}$ to the remaining operating robots. We wish to investigate if it is better for these remaining operating robots to keep their existing commitments or to start from scratch.

Multi-robot routing is considered the standard testbed for MRTA problems [4]. For tasks with pickup and delivery, the structure of each task t is a tuple $t = \langle l_p, l_d \rangle$ of a pickup location l_p and a delivery location l_d. We consider a robot to be executing a task once it has visited its pickup location up until it reaches its delivery location. Robots may have capacity constraints in the number of tasks are able to execute at any moment in time. This is representative of real robots which may have a fixed maximum number of items they can carry.

Each robot always has private knowledge of its current location and can calculate the cost λ to travel between locations. The cost to travel between any two locations is equal across all robots. The robot cost $\lambda_{r_i}(T_{r_i})$ is the minimum cost for an individual robot r_i to visit all locations T_{r_i} assigned to it. There can be synergies between tasks assigned to the same robot, such that: $\lambda_{r_i}(\{t\}) + \lambda_{r_i}(\{t'\}) \neq \lambda_{r_i}(\{t\} \cup \{t'\})$. This allows robots, when calculating bids for additional tasks, to consider the cost of completing additional tasks relative to their current commitments. A positive synergy is when the combined cost for a robot to complete two tasks is lower than the individual costs for the robot to complete each task: $\lambda_{r_i}(\{t\} \cup \{t'\}) < \lambda_{r_i}(\{t\}) + \lambda_{r_i}(\{t'\})$.

Team objectives are used to provide additional guidance in the search for solutions to the task allocation that meet certain criteria. Lagoudakis *et al.* discusses team objectives in detail and their application to MRTA [11]. In this work we use two commonly considered team objectives:

MiniSum $\min \sum_{r_i \in R} \lambda_{r_i}(T_{r_i})$ that is to minimise the sum of the paths of all robots in visiting all their assigned pickup and delivery locations.

MiniMax $\min \max_{r_i \in R} \lambda_{r_i}(T_{r_i})$ that is to minimise the maximum distance any individual robot travels.

2   Related Work

Market-based distributed auction algorithms are popular in the robotics community for solving MRTA problems [4,7]. Common auction types include *combinatorial auctions*, *parallel auctions* and *sequential auctions*. In NP-complete single-round combinatorial auctions [1] each robot bids on all subsets of the tasks on offer. This generates optimal allocations of tasks to robots. However, in most scenarios, the computation tends to be intractable and is generally not feasible for any but the most simple problems. In parallel auctions, robots generate bids for each task in isolation, with no consideration given to inter-task synergies, and the auctioneer then allocates the tasks all at once. The computational complexity is minimal but solutions are often extremely sub-optimal [8].

Sequential single-item auctions which allocate tasks over multiple rounds are a popular middle ground [11,8]. In each auction round, each robot submits a bid for a task of its choosing, and one task is awarded to the lowest bidder. A key strength of SSI auctions is their ability to build upon inter-task synergies during each task bidding round. However, when robots have few tasks allocated, robots bidding for tasks using SSI auctions have a greedy bias towards tasks that are close to their initial locations. This can see two tasks, that in an optimal solution would be allocated to one robot, split and allocated to two different robots. Previous work on repeated auctions has demonstrated the benefits of reallocating tasks during execution [12,13]. Additionally, a variety of further improvements and extensions to SSI auctions have been studied which trade off allocation time against overall team costs [7].

2.1   Robot Failure and Task Reallocation

A variety of approaches for task reallocation upon robot failure have been studied. Botelho and Alami [2] consider the problem of robot failure in Smith's contract net protocol (CNP) [14]. In this work, when a robot is about to fail, it sends out an emergency distress message to all other robots and one robot will come to its aid and complete the failed robot's task. However, in this work no inter-task synergies are explored as each additional task is allocated only after the completion of a previous task. This approach also means that, regardless of robot failure, an optimal solution to the task allocation problem is unlikely to be achieved. Dias *et al.* [3] consider various forms of robot failure: communication, partial robot malfunction, and robot death. Their approach to task reallocation is to do a partial reallocation of tasks in the system from the robot that has failed. This is followed by a global reallocation of all tasks at a later moment in time. Gerkey and Mataric [6] deal with robot failures by repeatedly auctioning all uncompleted tasks at set time intervals. While this solution works where tasks are single points, it does not work for tasks with pickup and delivery. Robots may be halfway through the transport of one or more tasks and they would not be able to switch to a different task. Nanjanath and Gini [12] consider repeated auctions upon robot delay. Their approach is that, upon each task completion, all uncompleted tasks across all robots are offered up for reallocation.

Robot failure is closely related to the problem of dynamic task insertion. In dynamic task insertion, additional tasks are inserted into a running system resulting in a need to reallocate tasks. Previous work by Schoenig and Pagnucco [13] has considered SSI auctions with dynamically inserted tasks and compared the costs of robots bidding only for the new task versus a full new auction of all uncompleted tasks. Their results show, despite a large trade-off in computation time, a global reallocation of tasks gives the best results.

2.2 Tasks with Pickup and Delivery

In the field of transport logistics, Fischer, Müller and Pischel apply the CNP to transportation scheduling with fixed time windows [5]. In this work trucks bid for tasks from a central controller and can also make one-for-one swaps with other trucks before they begin to execute their plans. During the execution of plans, the trucks may face traffic delays and, as such, they can locally replan their routes or auction their uncompleted tasks. Their results show that global reallocation of uncompleted tasks provides a large reduction in distance travelled. However, Kohout and Erol argue that Fischer, Müller and Pischel's generation of an initial allocation is poor and therefore global reallocation will produce much better results than local replanning [10]. In their analysis they study problems where multiple items can be transported together and additional jobs are announced sequentially. When a new job is announced, each vehicle bids for the job according to the cost of completing the additional job relative to their existing commitments. To avoid problems where inserting additional tasks has large impacts on the completion time of other tasks, upon each task insertion, already scheduled tasks are permitted to be reallocated to other vehicles. In their empirical analysis they compare this approach to a popular operations research based approach [15]. Overall, they show that their distributed approach is statistically equivalent to this centralised technique.

3   Task Reallocation upon Robot Failure

When a robot detects a problem, for instance, low battery power, it should let other robots know and safely shutdown. A failing robot broadcasts a message to all other operating robots containing its present location and the list of its uncompleted tasks. Any tasks that have not been picked up are able to be immediately auctioned. However, tasks that are under execution when the robot fails must be modified. Because the robot has already visited the pickup location of these tasks, other robots must travel to the location of the failed robot and collect the task from it. To do this the pickup location l_p of all initialised tasks $T_{r_{init}} \subseteq T_{r_{fail}}$ must be updated to the present location of the failed robot $l_p = l_{r_{fail}}$. During reallocation robots continue executing their current task.

   A partial reallocation only auctions the task set assigned to the failed robot. The remaining operating robots calculate the bids for these tasks taking into consideration their existing task commitments. Using the cheapest insertion heuristic, each robot's existing task execution plan is modified to include any additional task assignments. This approach allows robots to consider inter-task synergies between their existing commitments and tasks they are bidding for that may not have been considered during the previous allocation. For instance, if in a previous allocation the task $t \in T_{r_{fail}}$ was assigned during the very first round of bidding, no other robot would have been able to consider its synergy with other tasks. Partial reallocations also, generally, have smaller communication overheads than a global reallocation of all tasks. In a distributed SSI auction the total number of messages sent between all robots is $|\bar{T}| * |R|^2$. The number of tasks for auction in a partial reallocation will always be $|T_{r_{fail}}| \leq |T|$.

A global reallocation considers all of the tasks from the failed robot and all uninitialised tasks across all remaining operating robots $\bar{T} \leftarrow T_{r_{fail}} \cup T \backslash T_{init}$. Uninitialised tasks are tasks where a robot has not visited the pickup location of the task. Each robot retains the tasks that it has picked up $T_r \leftarrow T_{r_{init}}$. When calculating bids for additional tasks, the completion of these retained tasks is taken into consideration. It is important to note that, the previous task allocations were generated under conditions and constraints in the number of robots available and the tasks available for bidding in each round which have now changed. Allowing robots to give up tasks previously allocated under these prior circumstances enables them to completely regenerate their plans and consider previous unexplored inter-task synergies. As a result, we expect that this approach will generate solutions with lower costs than partial reallocations.

4 Experiments

To contrast the differences between partial and global reallocations, we simulate an office-like environment with 16 rooms (in a 4x4 grid), each containing four interconnecting doors that can be independently opened or closed to allow or restrict travel between rooms. This environment has become the standard testbed in recent literature [9]. In each experiment, the doors between different rooms and the hallway are either open or closed. We test on 25 randomly generated configurations of opened and closed doors with each robot starting in a different random location. Robots can only travel between rooms through open doors and they cannot open or close doors. However, it is guaranteed that there is at least one path between each room and every other room. For each configuration we test with 10 identical robots, 60 tasks, and from two to eight robot failures. We compare these results to an initial cost which is the cost to complete all tasks without any robot failures or reallocations of tasks. Robots fail at random intervals after arriving at a pickup or dropoff location. We test with the MiniSum and MiniMax team objectives and with capacity constraints of 1, 3, and 5.

In both reallocation approaches the total distance travelled decreases as the capacity constraint is increased. This is not surprising as, the larger the capacity constraint, the more flexibility robots have in executing multiple tasks in unison. We also note, as the number of robots failing increases, the distance required for the remaining robots to travel increases.

To further analyse these results we looked at the distribution of the final costs for both reallocation techniques. Fig. 1 is a plot of the distribution of one standard deviation around the mean for the capacity constraint of one. The other two capacity constraints tested follow a similar trend. One can observe in

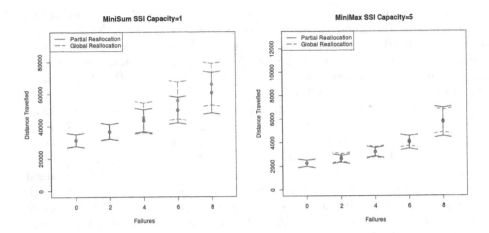

Fig. 1. Distribution of MiniSum team objective results for capacity 1

Fig. 2. Distribution of MiniMax team objective results for capacity 5

t_{r_1}	t'_{r_1}	r_1 $\overset{}{\leftarrow}$	r_2 $\overset{}{\rightarrow}$	t_{r_2}	t'_{r_2}	r_3 $\overset{}{\rightarrow}$	t_{r_3}	t'_{r_3}

Fig. 3. Reallocation example with three robots and six tasks. r_1 is travelling to the left, r_2 and r_3 to the right. Tasks are point locations $l_p = l_d$.

this plot that, as the number of failed robots increases, the standard deviation becomes much larger. This indicates that in some of the configurations tested the final costs remained low despite the large number of robot failures, however, in other configurations the final costs became extremely large. When the number of robot failures remains less than four there is very little difference in means and distributions between partial and global reallocations. However, as the number of robot failures becomes large there is a clear benefit in using partial reallocations.

For the MiniMax team objective, again, there are trends that, as the capacity constraint is increased, the cost decreases and, as the number of failed robots increases, the cost increases. The plot in Fig. 2 shows one standard deviation around the mean for the MiniMax team objective with a capacity of five initialised tasks at any one time. This plot shows a different distribution to that of the MiniSum team objective. Our first observation is that the results for both partial and global reallocations completely overlap. At no point does one technique offer an advantage over the other. Our second observation is that the standard deviation remains small in all but the extreme case of eight failed robots. Our logs suggest this is due to robots with lower costs than the robot with the maximum cost taking on additional tasks from failed robots without impacting the overall maximum cost.

Overall, these results are surprising. Our expectations were that global reallocation would outperform partial reallocation. For instance, consider three robots travelling along a horizontal line. The first robot is travelling to the left,

Table 1. Mean MiniSum Team Objective Computation Time (s) (percentage increase in time after reallocation compared to initial time in brackets)

Capacity	Failures	Initial Allocation	Partial Reallocation	Global Reallocation
1	2	209	250 (19.3%)	330 (57.6%)
1	4	209	265 (25.9%)	439 (110.0%)
1	6	209	280 (33.3%)	510 (143.0%)
1	8	209	302 (44.3%)	579 (176.4%)
3	2	211	261 (23.8%)	339 (60.9%)
3	4	211	284 (36.1%)	419 (100.8%)
3	6	211	314 (48.4%)	493 (133.5%)
3	8	211	340 (61.3%)	553 (162.4%)
5	2	213	269 (25.3%)	343 (59.4%)
5	4	213	307 (44.2%)	433 (103.1%)
5	6	213	358 (68.7%)	509 (140.0%)
5	8	213	398 (86.7%)	615 (188.9%)

the middle robot to the right, and a third robot also travelling to the right (Fig. 3). The first robot then fails. In a partial reallocation the middle robot would need to continue doing tasks to its right and then complete the tasks on its left. However, in a global reallocation the middle robot could give up its tasks to the right and travel to the left and complete the failed robot's tasks. In this situation you would expect that the global reallocation would result in a smaller task cost than the partial allocation.

Finally, we consider the overall computation time required for generating an initial allocation and for reallocation. Table 1 presents the mean timings for the MiniSum team objective (we omit the MiniMax team objective data as it is nearly identical). These results show that the time required for partial reallocation is much lower than for global reallocation. We note that, for the initial allocation, the capacity constraint has almost no impact on the time required. For partial reallocation, as the capacity constraint increases, there is a smaller increase in the time taken, however, this trend is not seen in global reallocation. As the number of failed robots increase, both reallocation techniques require more computation time. In particular, the time required for global reallocation grows at a very rapid rate as the number of failed robots increases. Overall, from this data and the previous results, we can conclude that partial reallocations are a viable technique for handling robot failure. Their resultant costs are at least equal to global reallocation and they have much faster computation times.

5   Discussion

Our experimental results are unexpected and appear to contradict previous results on reallocation of tasks using auctions. We can classify previous work into two groups, the first being work that presents algorithms for task reallocation

[2,3,6,12], and the second dealing with task reallocation upon new task insertion [13,16]. We are unaware of previous work comparing partial and global reallocation of tasks using repeated auctions.

In our related work section we stated that dynamic task insertion is a very similar problem. Naively, one can assume that adding a new task to the set of tasks: $T \leftarrow T \cup \{t_{new}\}$ and removing a robot from the set of robots: $R \leftarrow R \backslash \{r_{fail}\}$ would affect the task allocation problem in the same way as the complete solution: $\cup_{r_i \in R} T_{r_i} = T$ relies on both R and T. However, a key difference between dynamic task insertion and robot failure is the location of the tasks for reallocation. Most dynamic task insertion approaches assume that the task location is random. However, in the case of a robot failure, despite a robot failure occurring at random, the tasks for auction are not randomly distributed. They are generally geographically close and also contain tight inter-task synergies.

6 Conclusion

This work has studied task reallocation in a robot team upon the failures of teammates. We explored two techniques for task reallocation: partial reallocation which considers only a subset of the total tasks in the system; and, global reallocation which considers almost all tasks in the system. Our empirical evaluations show that, despite global reallocation considering more inter-task synergies, partial reallocations, on average, performed at least as well. Furthermore, partial reallocations require much less computation time.

References

1. Berhault, M., Huang, H., Keskinocak, P., Koenig, S., Elmaghraby, W., Griffin, P.M., Kleywegt, A.J.: Robot exploration with combinatorial auctions. In: IROS, pp. 1957–1962 (2003)
2. Botelho, S., Alami, R.: M+: A scheme for multi-robot cooperation through negotiated task allocation and achievement. In: ICRA, pp. 1234–1239 (1999)
3. Dias, M.B., Zinck, M., Zlot, R., Stentz, A.: Robust multirobot coordination in dynamic environments. In: ICRA, pp. 3435–3442 (2004)
4. Dias, M.B., Zlot, R., Kalra, N., Stentz, A.: Market-based multirobot coordination: A survey and analysis. Proceedings of the IEEE 94(7), 1257–1270 (2006)
5. Fischer, K.: Cooperative transportation scheduling: An application domain for dai. Applied Artificial Intelligence 10(1), 1–34 (1996)
6. Gerkey, B.P., Matarić, M.J.: Sold!: auction methods for multirobot coordination. IEEE Transactions on Robotics 18(5), 758–768 (2002)
7. Koenig, S., Keskinocak, P., Tovey, C.A.: Progress on agent coordination with cooperative auctions. In: AAAI (2010)
8. Koenig, S., Tovey, C.A., Lagoudakis, M.G., Markakis, E., Kempe, D., Keskinocak, P., Kleywegt, A.J., Meyerson, A., Jain, S.: The power of sequential single-item auctions for agent coordination. In: AAAI, pp. 1625–1629 (2006)
9. Koenig, S., Tovey, C.A., Zheng, X., Sungur, I.: Sequential bundle-bid single-sale auction algorithms for decentralized control. In: IJCAI, pp. 1359–1365 (2007)

10. Kohout, R.C., Erol, K.: In-time agent-based vehicle routing with a stochastic improvement heuristic. In: AAAI, pp. 864–869 (1999)
11. Lagoudakis, M.G., Markakis, E., Kempe, D., Keskinocak, P., Kleywegt, A.J., Koenig, S., Tovey, C.A., Meyerson, A., Jain, S.: Auction-based multi-robot routing. In: Robotics: Science and Systems, pp. 343–350 (2005)
12. Nanjanath, M., Gini, M.L.: Repeated auctions for robust task execution by a robot team. Robotics and Autonomous Systems 58(7), 900–909 (2010)
13. Schoenig, A., Pagnucco, M.: Evaluating sequential single-item auctions for dynamic task allocation. In: Australasian Conference on Artificial Intelligence, pp. 506–515 (2010)
14. Smith, R.G.: The contract net protocol: High-level communication and control in a distributed problem solver. IEEE Trans. Computers 29(12), 1104–1113 (1980)
15. Solomon, M.M.: Algorithms for the vehicle routing and scheduling problems with time window constraints. Operations research 35(2), 254–265 (1987)
16. Van Duin, J., Tavasszy, L., Taniguchi, E.: Real time simulation of auctioning and re-scheduling processes in hybrid freight markets. Transportation Research Part B: Methodological 41(9), 1050–1066 (2007)

Decentralized Area Partitioning
for a Cooperative Cleaning Task

Chihiro Kato and Toshiharu Sugawara

Department of Computer Science and Eng., Waseda University, Tokyo 1698555, Japan
c.kato@isl.cs.waseda.ac.jp, sugawara@waseda.jp

Abstract. We describe a method for decentralized task/area partitioning for coordination in cleaning domains. Ongoing advances in computer science and robotics lead to robot applications for large areas that require coordinated tasks by multiple robots. We focused on a cleaning task to be performed by multiple robots with potentially different performances and developed a method for partitioning the target area to improve the overall efficiency through their balanced collective efforts. Agents autonomously decide how the task/area is to be partitioned by taking into account the characteristics of the environments. Experiments showed that the proposed method can adaptively partition the area among the agents so that they can keep it clean effectively and evenly.

1 Introduction

Continuing advances in computers and robotic technologies should lead to applications combining computers, sensors, and robots that perform tasks normally done by people. In these applications such as cleaning and patrolling tasks in a certain environment, coordination and cooperation using multiple agents are required to cover a large areas. Additionally, the real-world environments are diverse. For example, in cleaning tasks, some locations are easy to accumulate dirt. So robots for cleaning must visit the locations in the area with different frequencies accordance with the characteristics of the environment. The agents must therefore work cooperatively by taking into account these differences in order to efficiently perform the tasks in more balanced manner.

There are two conventional approaches to implementing coordinated and cooperative patrolling activities for cleaning. The first is for the agents to share the working area and clean it in a coordinated manner. For example, agents could patrol the area by using different cleaning algorithms or different visitation cycles to uniformly cover the entire area [2,4,5,7]. The second approach is to divide the area into a number of subareas and make each agent responsible for a different subarea [1,3]. However, performing fair division is not trivial; if the characteristics of the area are not uniform, equal-size subareas are inappropriate.

We thus propose the method in which the agents autonomously decide their subareas so as to divide the task fairly on the basis of their capabilities and the characteristics of the each subarea. The key idea is that each agent monitors the locations it recently visited and calculates its *expansion power*, which is based on the the expected amount of dirt remaining in its subarea so represents the degree of task completion. It then negotiates with adjacent agents to determine which agents should expand their current subarea so as to balance the cleanliness levels of the area.

G. Boella et al. (Eds.): PRIMA 2013, LNAI 8291, pp. 470–477, 2013.

2 Model and Problem Definition

2.1 Models of Agent and Environment

We assume that an agent has a map (graph) of the area and the likelihood of dirt accumulation at each location that described by a probability distribution. Such information may often be unknown. However, many algorithms for creating a map and identifying agent locations have been proposed ([6]), and a simple learning method to identify such probability distributions can be added to the agents. Because we focus on autonomous learning for area partitioning for balanced work, we use these assumptions here.

Let A be a set of agents. The area in which the agents work is described by connected graph $G = (V, E)$, where V and E are sets of nodes and edges, respectively. The edge connecting $v_i, v_j \in V$ is expressed by $e_{i,j}$. We introduce a discrete time with a unit called a *tick*. Without the loss of generality, we can assume that the length of an edge in E is one (by adding dummy nodes if necessary), so any agent can move from a node to another along an edge and then clean the visited node in one tick.

Let positive integers B_{max}^i and $b^i(t)$ be the maximal capacity and the remaining power of the battery in agent i at time t. Agent i consumes a constant amount of power per tick, B_{drain}^i. Thus, $b^i(t)$ is updated by $b^i(t+1) \leftarrow b^i(t) - B_{drain}^i$. Agent i can thus continuously operate at most $\lfloor B_{max}^i / B_{drain}^i \rfloor$ ticks, which is called the *maximum running time* and is denoted by M_i. Agent i charges its battery at its charging base, $v_{base}^i \in V$. The required time for a full charge starting from time t, $T_{charge}^i(t)$, is proportional to the battery power consumed: $T_{charge}^i(t) = k_{charge}^i(B_{max}^i - b^i(t))$, where $k_{charge}^i(> 0)$ is the proportionality factor indicating the speed of charge. Hereafter, $B_{max} = B_{max}^i$, $k_{charge} = k_{charge}^i$, and $B_{drain} = B_{drain}^i$ are assumed to be independent of i for simplicity. Agents with a full battery start to move around and perform cleaning; they return to their bases and recharge their batteries. Agents iterate this *cleaning cycle* to keep their assigned area clean.

For any node $v \in V_t^i$, i calculates the *potential*, which is the minimal capacity of battery required to return to i's charging base v_{base}^i. The potential of v for i is denoted by $\mathcal{P}(v)$ and calculated by $\mathcal{P}(v) = d(v, v_{base}^i) \cdot B_{drain}$, where $d(v, v')$ is the shortest path length. We say that node v is *safe* for i to move at time t if $b^i(t) \geq \mathcal{P}(v) + d(v_t^i, v) \cdot B_{drain}$, where v_t^i is the node where i is currently located. Agent i moves to only safe nodes; if the next node is not, i returns to v_{base}^i along the shortest path and then recharges.

2.2 Model of Dirt Accumulation

For node $v \in V$, the rate of dirt accumulation is represented by event probability $p_v (0 \leq p_v \leq 1)$ per tick, which is called the *dirt accumulation probability* for v. Then the *amount of accumulated dirt* at v at time t, $L_t(v)$, is updated using

$$L_t(v) \leftarrow \begin{cases} L_{t-1}(v) + 1 & \text{if dirt is present (with probability } p_v) \text{ at } t \\ L_{t-1}(v) & \text{otherwise} \end{cases} \tag{1}$$

However, if an agent has visited v at t, $L_t(v) = 0$. Agent i cannot know the actual value of $L_t(v)$. However, since we assume that agents know p_v for $\forall v \in V$, i can estimate it as the expected amount of accumulated dirt on v, which is $E(L_t(v)) = p_v \cdot (t - t_v^i)$, where t_v^i is the most recent time at which i visited and cleaned v for $v \in V_t^i$. We also define $L_t(V_0) = \sum_{v \in V_0} L_t(v)$ and $E(L_t(V_0)) = \sum_{v \in V_0} E(L_t(v))$ for the subset of nodes $V_0 (\subset V)$.

Each agent has a *responsible area* (RA) to keep clean. The RA of agent i at time t is the connected subgraph $G_t^i = (V_t^i, E_t^i)$, where $V_t^i \subseteq V$ and $E_t^i = \{e_{i,j} \in E \mid v_i, v_j \in V_t^i\}$. We assume that $v_{base}^i \in V_t^i$, and if $i \neq j$, V_t^i and V_t^j are disjoint. An agent may change the size of its RA, which is $|V_t^i|$, to keep the area evenly clean through balanced cooperative work.

One evaluation measure is the performance of the agents' collective tasks, which is represented by the *sum of the amounts of accumulated dirt* for the whole area at certain intervals of time. This is defined as

$$D_{t_s, t_e} = \sum_{v \in V} \sum_{t=t_s}^{t_e} L_t(v)/(t_e - t_s), \tag{2}$$

where positive integers t_s and t_e are the start and end times of the interval. We also pay attention to the sizes of the RAs and the expected amounts of accumulated dirt in RAs.

3 Proposed Method

3.1 Expansion Power

Agent i calculates its *expansion power* for the current RA when it returns to the charging base at time t. First, i calculates the expected amount of accumulated dirt in the RA

$$E(L(G_t^i)) = \sum_{v \in V_t^i} E(L_t(v)) = \sum_{v \in V_t^i} p_v \cdot (t - t_v^i), \tag{3}$$

where t_v^i is the most recent time when i visited node $v \in V_t^i$; if i never visited v, t_v^i is the time when v was included in G_t^i. Then, the expansion power $\xi(i, t)$ of i at time t is defined as the inverse of the expected value, i.e., $\xi(i, t) = E(L(G_t^i))^{-1}$. Since $p_v > 0$, $E(L(G_t^i)) \neq 0$, so $\xi(i, t)$ is computable unless $V_t^i = \emptyset$. Agents retain their calculated expansion power until the next calculation time.

The cleaning cycle of each agent starts when it leaves its base node with a fully charged battery to clean its RA. If it determines that it has mostly cleaned the RA, it may decide to expand its RA. For this decision, agent i calculates the expected amount of accumulated dirt in its RA at a certain future time, $E(L_{t_0+\gamma}(G_{t_0}^i))$, when i leaves from v_{base}^i at time t_0, where γ is a positive integer. Agent i also stores the number of visited nodes, $N_{vis}(t)$, and the amount of vacuumed dirt, $N_d(t)$, at $t(> t_0)$ during the current cleaning cycle, which started from t_0. It then tries to expand its current RA, V_t^i, if the following conditions are fulfilled.

$$N_{vis}(t) \geq R_1 \cdot |V_t^i| \quad \text{and} \quad N_d(t) \geq R_2 \cdot E(L_{t_0+\gamma}(G_{t_0}^i)), \tag{4}$$

where $0 \leq R_1, R_2 \leq 1$, and $0 \leq \gamma \leq M_i$ are the parameters used by agents to determine if they have cleaned most of the current RA. Note that we introduce parameter γ, which specifies the expected amount of dirt in the RA at a certain future time, because dirt will continue to accumulate while the agents move around.

3.2 Expansion Strategy

When Conditions (4) are satisfied, agents believe that they can clean a larger area. Hence, they start an *area expansion trial* (AET), which is the process of trying to expand an RA to cover other nodes that are not covered by other agents or are in the RAs of busier agents. When agents expand their RAs, we have to consider a number of factors, such as the distances from their bases because these factors may affect the agents' and thus the system's overall performances. We also try to avoid frequent failures of expansion in a certain direction in which unbusy agents operate.

Suppose that agent i finds that Conditions (4) are satisfied at time t during its cleaning cycle. It then initiates an AET, which consists of two parts. First, i identifies the nodes I^i that should be included in its RA using the *expansion strategy*. It then negotiates to decide which agent should take charge of the identified nodes, assuming that part of I^i is in the RAs of other agents.

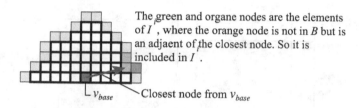

The green and organe nodes are the elements of I, where the orange node is not in B but is an adjaent of the closest node. So it is included in I.

v_{base} Closest node from v_{base}

Fig. 1. Expansion strategy (nearest boundary expansion). Squares with bold lines represent the current RA, and yellow and green squares are boundary of subarea. Blue node is the base.

The expansion strategy depends on the distance from the charging base. First, agent i identifies B, the set of boundary nodes of its current RA (B and the RA is disjoint). Agent i selects I^i_{inc} from B, which is the set of $k_{inc}(>0)$ nodes that are not in I^i_{avoid} (this will be defined below) and are closest from base, v^i_{base}. It then defines I^i as the nodes in I^i_{inc} and their adjacent (north, south, east, and west) nodes that are not in V^i_t and not in I^i_{avoid}. For example, in Fig. 1, where the environment G is a grid, V^i_t is the set of nodes (squares) with bold lines, and the boundary B consists of the yellow and green colored nodes. The green and orange nodes express I^i when $k_{inc} = 1$ and $I^i_{avoid} = \emptyset$. If $I^i = \emptyset$, the AET ends, and no nodes are added to i's RA. To avoid frequent failures of the AET, i stores into I^i_{avoid} the nodes that it failed to take and does not select them as elements of I^i in the next k_{avoid} times of AET, where k_{avoid} is a positive integer.

3.3 Negotiation for Expanding Responsible Areas

After i identifies I^i, it starts negotiation to determine which agent nodes in I^i should be included in its RA. This process is as follows:

(0) Revise the responsible area: V^i_t is set to $V^i_{t-1} \cup I^i$.
(1) Send request message for area expansion: Agent i broadcasts I^i with its current expansion power $\xi = \xi(i, t)$.

(2) Accept/Reject area expansion request: Suppose that agent j has received a request message for area expansion from i at time t. If $V_t^j \cap I^i = \emptyset$, j does nothing. Otherwise, j compares j's expansion power, $\xi(j, t)$, with ξ.

(2.1) If $\xi(j, t) \geq \xi$, j sends a rejection message with $V_t^j \cap I^i$ and $\xi(j, t)$ to i.

(2.2) If $\xi(j, t) < \xi$, j sends an acceptance message with $V_t^j \cap I^i$ and $\xi(j, t)$ to i. Then j revises its RA to $V_t^j = V_t^j \setminus I^i$.

(3) Expand responsible area: If i has received an acceptance message, it continues to set the current RA (it has already been extended). If i has received a rejection message from j, it excludes the nodes from V_t^i and stores the excluded nodes with j's expansion power. These nodes are stored into I_{avoid}^i and are not be included in I^i in the next k_{avoid} times of AET to avoid frequent failures.

Note that during these message exchanges, i continues to clean the current RA. We assume that AET is invoked only once per cleaning cycle even if i has enough battery to continue in order to avoid excess expansion.

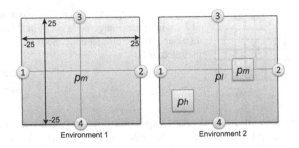

Fig. 2. Experimental environments

4   Experimental Evaluation

4.1   Environments

We call the proposed method *performance-based partitioning* (PBP). We evaluated the PBP method using two simulated environments, as shown in Fig. 2, to clarify the performance and features of our proposed method. Cleaning area G is defined as a 51×51 grid. Node v is expressed by (x, y), where $-25 \leq x, y \leq 25$. Four agents $A = \{a_1, a_2, a_3, a_4\}$ move around G starting from v_{base}^i ($i = 1, 2, 3, 4$).

Agents move around the RAs by using the *(random) depth-first exploration* algorithm, which is a simple depth-first search; i selects the first target node randomly, moves to it along the shortest path, and pushes the node on top of its stack. It then randomly selects one of the adjacent nodes except for previously visited ones, moves to it, and pushes it on top of its stack. This process is iterated as long as i can select an unvisited node. If i cannot select it, i pops the top node from its stack and backtracks one step. It then tries to select another unvisited node. If i returns to the first target node after repeating this movement, it returns to v_{base}^i.

The dirt accumulation probabilities for all nodes are shown in the figure, where parameters p_l, p_m, and p_h are defined as $p_l = 2 \cdot 10^{-6}, p_m = 2 \cdot 10^{-5}, p_h = 2 \cdot 10^{-4}$. Whereas dirt accumulates uniformly in the first environment (Env. 1), there are rectangular regions that more easily accumulate dirt in the second environment (Env. 2). The encircled integers indicate the locations of the charging bases; for example, the charging base of a_1 is at $(-25, 0)$. The subarea whose dirt accumulation probability is p_h in Env. 2 referred to here as a the *easy-to-dirty* subarea.

We set $B_{max} = 900$, $B_{drain} = 1$, and $k_{charge} = 3$. Thus, the maximum length of a cleaning cycle is 3600 ticks. The parameters for selecting AET were defined as $R_1 = 0.7$, $R_2 = 0.7$, and $\gamma = 300$ ($= M_i/3$). Control parameters k_{inc} and k_{avoid} used in the AET were set to 15 and 7. We then stored, every 3600 ticks up to 1,000,000 ticks, the sum of the amounts of accumulated dirt, D_{t_s,t_e} and the sizes of the RAs, $|V_t^i|$. The experimental results are the average values for 30 trials. We compare these results with those of a conventional distributed partitioning method [3], in which agents try to divide the area into equal-size subareas by comparing the current sizes of their RAs.

4.2   Experimental Results: Performance of Cleaning and Sizes of RAs

The purpose of the experiment was to compare cleaning performance, i.e., the sum of the amounts of accumulated dirt D_{t_s,t_e}, between environments. The average values of D_{t_s,t_e} observed between 800,000 and 1,000,000 ticks in Env. 1 and Env. 2 are listed in Table 1. For Env. 1, it is reasonable that the dirt accumulation probabilities p_v (for $\forall v \in V$) are constant and that the area divisions are equal in size. Hence, the difference between the PBP and conventional methods was small (a delta of 6.61) although PBP exhibited slightly better performances. For in Env. 2, the proposed method resulted in a much smaller D_{t_s,t_e}, and the delta was 19.52, because it partitioned the area in accordance with the characteristics of the environment.

Table 1. Sum of the amounts of accumulated dirt between 800,000 and 1,000,000 ticks

	Conventional method	Proposed PBP method	Difference (delta)
D_{t_s,t_e} in Env. 1	138.7	132.1	6.61
D_{t_s,t_e} in Env. 2	97.4	77.9	19.52

We plotted the sizes of the RAs of agents a_i for the PBP method in Figs. 3 (a) and (b) for Envs. 1 and 2 to investigate how the RAs expanded in accordance with the characteristics of the environment. In Env. 1, because the environment was uniform, the agents divided the area into almost equal-size RAs, about 650 nodes each (Fig. 3 (a)). In contrast, because there is a easy-to-dirty subarea in Env. 2, the equal-size partitioning is inappropriate. This is evident in Fig. 3 (b); for example, agents a_1 and a_4 had bases near the easy-to-dirty subarea, so their RAs were smaller than those of the others. The RA of a_3 was the largest (about 830) because there was no easy-to-dirty subarea near its charging base. Note that we do not show how the sizes of the RAs of agents using the conventional method changed over time, but the results were almost identical to

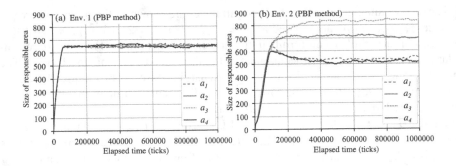

Fig. 3. Sizes of RAs $|V_t^i|$

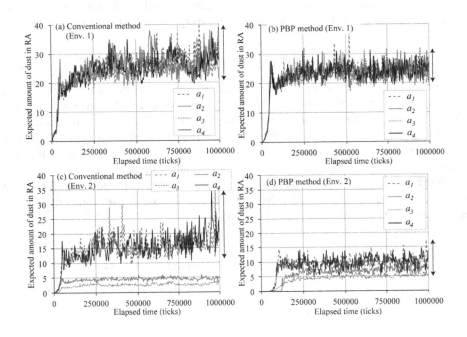

Fig. 4. Expected values of dirt in RAs

those in Fig. 3 (a) for both environments (and in all the experiments below) because the method tries to divide the area into equal-size subareas.

We plotted the expected amounts of accumulated dirt in the RAs when the agents returned to their bases; these values are the inverses of the expansion powers. The results for Env. 1 are shown in Figs. 4 (a) and (b), and those for Env. 2 are shown in Figs. 4 (c) and (d). As shown in Figs. 4 (a) and (b), both the conventional and PBP methods kept their RAs equally clean (although the amplitude widths were smaller for the PBP method). Note that the sum of the expected amounts of dirt in the four RAs is smaller than the result shown in Table 1 because the expected values in these graphs were calculated only when the agents returned their bases while D_{t_s,t_e} is the average amount of dirt in a certain interval of time.

Figure 4 (c) shows that the agents did not keep the RAs equally clean with the conventional method. Because the RAs of a_1 and a_4 included an easy-to-dirty subarea in which the dirt accumulation probabilities were 10- to 100-times higher than in the other RAs, the RAs of a_1 and a_4 were not sufficiently cleaned. The RA of a_3 was the most cleaned because dirt barely accumulated there. In contrast, with the PBP method, the agents kept the RAs almost equally clean (Fig. 4 (d)). This is because, as shown in Fig. 3 (b), the PBP method partitioned the area appropriately by taking into account the characteristics of the environment.

5   Conclusion

We have presented a decentralized area-partitioning method for cleaning tasks. It uniformly keeps clean the environment by dividing RAs in accordance with the characteristics of the environment. We described the proposed method in which agents try to expand their responsible areas and negotiate with adjacent agents to determine which agents should clean the identified boundary nodes. Experimental results demonstrated that the proposed method can effectively divide an area fairly and appropriately in accordance with the efficiency of agents and the characteristics of the environment. As a result, unbalanced tasks are resolved, and the task is completed in a balanced and efficient manner. Our future work is to speedup the convergence of learning for a larger environment large-scale systems by introducing additional control into robots.

References

1. Ahmadi, M., Stone, P.: Continuous Area Sweeping: A Task Definition and Initial Approach. In: Proc. of the 12th Int. Conf. on Advanced Robotics, pp. 316–323 (2005)
2. Chevaleyre, Y.: Theoretical Analysis of the Multi-agent Patrolling Problem. In: Proc. of Intelligent Agent Technology, pp. 302–308 (2005)
3. Elor, Y., Bruckstein, A.M.: Multi-a(ge)nt Graph Patrolling and Partitioning. In: Proc. of the 2009 IEEE/WIC/ACM Int. Joint Conf. on Web Intelligence and Intelligent Agent Technologies, pp. 52–57 (2009)
4. Kurabayashi, D., Ota, J., Arai, T., Yoshida, E.: Cooperative Sweeping by Multiple Mobile Robots. In: Proc. on IEEE Int. Conf. on Robotics and Automation, pp. 1744–1749 (1996)
5. Mead, R., Weinberg, J.B., Croxell, J.R.: An implementation of robot formations using local interactions. In: Proc. of AAAI 2007, pp. 1989–1990 (2007)
6. Wolf, D.F., Sukhatme, G.S.: Mobile Robot Simultaneous Localization and Mapping in Dynamic Environments. Autonomous Robots 19(1), 53–65 (2005)
7. Yoneda, K., Kato, C., Sugawara, T.: Autonomous Learning of Target Decision Strategies without Communications for Continuous Coordinated Cleaning Tasks. In: 2013 IEEE/WIC/ACM Int. Conf. on Web Intelligence and Intelligent Agent Technology (2013)

A Computational Agent Model of Influences on Physical Activity Based on the Social Cognitive Theory

Julia S. Mollee and C. Natalie van der Wal

VU University Amsterdam, The Netherlands
{j.s.mollee,c.n.vander.wal}@vu.nl

Abstract. A computational agent model of social and cognitive influences on physical activity based on Bandura's Social Cognitive Theory is proposed. The utility of this model is twofold. First, it is used to run simulations of many different scenarios, that cannot be manipulated easily in reality, and that can possibly lead to new hypotheses about how social and cognitive factors influence physical activity. Second, as a next step, this computational model will be deployed in a real world coaching agent. The coach will use the current model to reason about the social and cognitive influences on the user's physical activity and derive which coaching strategy fits the user best.

Keywords: Computational modelling, social cognitive theory, physical activity.

1 Introduction

Unhealthy lifestyles are a major public health issue, as they increase the risk of disease and fatal illness. For instance, smoking and physical inactivity account for 18% and 12% of all deaths in developed societies respectively [1]. The increasingly sedentary nature of Western culture cultivates unhealthy lifestyles. It is important to develop novel and effective means to stimulate people to improve their lifestyle.

Physical activity is an important means to lower the risk of disease and premature death [2]. Physical activity can be increased significantly through self-monitoring and the use of pedometers, but whether these changes are durable over the long term is still undetermined [3], [4]. Furthermore, internet- and e-mail-based systems that promote physical activity, or other healthy lifestyles, can increase cost-effectiveness and accessibility of an intervention, but often have low adherence rates [5-7]. If no efficient methods are developed that stimulate physical activity and other healthy lifestyles on the long term, developed societies are threatened by rapidly increasing disease prevalence and related health care costs.

The current research serves as the first step towards such an innovative method to effectively increase physical activity. We present a computational model of the social and cognitive factors that influence one's level of physical activity, according to Albert Bandura's Social Cognitive Theory [8], [9]. The purpose of this work is the future integration of this domain model in a smartphone app coaching agent. This agent will gather physical, cognitive and social data about the user, and apply the current

G. Boella et al. (Eds.): PRIMA 2013, LNAI 8291, pp. 478–485, 2013.
© Springer-Verlag Berlin Heidelberg 2013

computational model and intelligent reasoning techniques to these data, in order to predict the most effective coaching strategy to stimulate the user to exercise more.

Up to our knowledge, this work is the first computational model of the Social Cognitive Theory. It could lead to new testable hypotheses, that are interesting for other disciplines such as Social Sciences and Psychology. Our aim is to simulate many scenarios of different personalities and other factors influencing physical activity and to find emerging properties leading to new hypotheses for future experiments. As a case study, we use the model to investigate how impediments and facilitators influence one's exercise behaviour.

The paper is organised as follows: Section 2 describes the proposed computational model. Section 3 describes the simulations performed with the model. Section 4 addresses the analysis of the model through automated property verification. Finally, Section 5 concludes the paper and discusses possible refinements and future work.

2   Social Cognitive Computational Agent Model for Exercise Behaviour

In this section, the computational model based on the Social Cognitive Theory is described both conceptually and formally.

The Social Cognitive Theory addresses both social and cognitive factors that influence health behaviour [8], [9]. The key cognitive factor is the concept of *self-efficacy*: the confidence in one's own ability to achieve goals. It plays a fundamental role in achieving motivation and action for healthy behaviour. The *behaviour* stands for the level of physical activity that someone is engaged in. However, people may have different perceptions of their behaviour. This subjective notion is called the *satisfaction*. It depends on whether someone's behaviour has met the related *intentions*, and on the *impediments* and *facilitators* they experience. Another factor contributing to engagement in physical activity concerns the *outcome expectations* for the behaviour, which comes in three types: the expected social outcomes, the expected personal outcomes and the expected physical outcomes.

The motivation to base the current computational agent model on Bandura's Social Cognitive Theory is threefold. First of all, this theory is well-established in the literature of behaviour change: it has shown to explain a large part of the variance observed in physical activity [10] and it served as basis for many studies investigating the determinants of physical activity [11], [12]. Second, in [8] and [9], the theory was specifically applied to health promotion and health behaviour. Considering the objective of this research, the promotion of physical activity, the theory is very suitable to this particular endeavour. Third, the Social Cognitive Theory explains health behaviour by a combination of self-regulative processes and social context. Both of these factors are particularly relevant to the final aim of this research: the former is perfectly suited to be individually supported through a smartphone app, and the latter is available through information and interactions on social media.

2.1   Computational Model of Physical Activity Behaviour

The dynamic relationships between all concepts are depicted in graphical form in Figure 1 and formalised with the differential equations below. All concepts are modelled numerically, as real values in the interval [0,1].

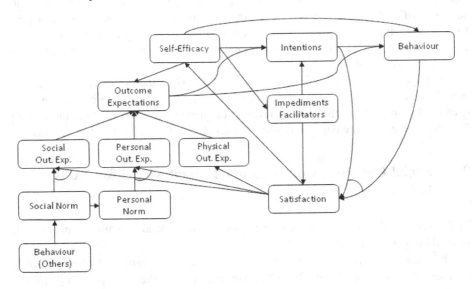

Fig. 1. Graphical Overview of Relations between Concepts

Self-Efficacy (SE). The self-efficacy is largely based on the behavioural satisfaction. A positive evaluation of one's own behaviour helps to build trust in the efficacy, whereas a feeling of failure undermines it. These effects are formalised by updating the self-efficacy beliefs with a fraction of the difference between the self-efficacy and the satisfaction: if the value of the satisfaction is higher than the self-efficacy, then this will lead to increased feelings of efficacy, and vice versa. In order to guarantee that the resulting value stays within the interval from 0 to 1, the adjustment is multiplied with SE(t) in case of a decrease and $(1 - \text{SE}(t))$ in case of an increase.

If $\text{SE}(t) \geq \text{Sat}(t)$: $\text{SE}(t + \Delta t) = \text{SE}(t) + \beta_{\text{Sat,SE}} \cdot (\text{Sat}(t) - \text{SE}(t)) \cdot \text{SE}(t) \cdot \Delta t$
If $\text{SE}(t) < \text{Sat}(t)$: $\text{SE}(t + \Delta t) = \text{SE}(t) + \beta_{\text{Sat,SE}} \cdot (\text{Sat}(t) - \text{SE}(t)) \cdot (1 - \text{SE}(t)) \cdot \Delta t$

Impediments (Imp). The self-efficacy plays a role in how insurmountable one views his/her impediments. Therefore, the 'objective' impediments are adjusted based on the difference between the values of the self-efficacy and the impediments.

If $\text{SE}(t) \geq \text{Imp}(t)$: $\text{Imp}(t + \Delta t) = \text{Imp}(t) - \beta_{\text{SE,Imp}} \cdot (\text{SE}(t) - \text{Imp}(t)) \cdot \text{Imp}(t) \cdot \Delta t$
If $\text{SE}(t) < \text{Imp}(t)$: $\text{Imp}(t + \Delta t) = \text{Imp}(t) - \beta_{\text{SE,Imp}} \cdot (\text{SE}(t) - \text{Imp}(t)) \cdot (1 - \text{Imp}(t)) \cdot \Delta t$

Facilitators (Fac). Similar to the impediments, the facilitators are adjusted according to the self-efficacy.

If $\text{SE}(t) \geq \text{Fac}(t)$: $\text{Fac}(t + \Delta t) = \text{Fac}(t) + \beta_{\text{SE,Fac}} \cdot (\text{SE}(t) - \text{Fac}(t)) \cdot (1 - \text{Fac}(t)) \cdot \Delta t$
If $\text{SE}(t) < \text{Fac}(t)$: $\text{Fac}(t + \Delta t) = \text{Fac}(t) + \beta_{\text{SE,Fac}} \cdot (\text{SE}(t) - \text{Fac}(t)) \cdot \text{Fac}(t) \cdot \Delta t$

Intentions (Int). The intentions are updated by the difference between the intentions and the self-efficacy and between the intentions and the outcome expectations: the higher the self-efficacy and/or the outcome expectations, the more ambitious the intentions. Also, the intentions are adjusted for the facilitators and the impediments.

$$\text{Change\_Int}(t) = \quad \beta_{SE,\,Int} \cdot (SE(t) - Int(t)) + \beta_{SOE,Int} \cdot (SOE(t) - Int(t)) + \beta_{Fac,Int} \cdot Fac(t)$$
$$- \beta_{Imp,Int} \cdot Imp(t)$$

If $\text{Change\_Int}(t) \geq 0$: $Int(t + \Delta t) = Int(t) + \text{Change\_Int}(t) \cdot (1 - Int(t)) \cdot \Delta t$
If $\text{Change\_Int}(t) < 0$: $Int(t + \Delta t) = Int(t) + \text{Change\_Int}(t) \cdot Int(t) \cdot \Delta t$

Behaviour (Beh). The behaviour indicates one's activity level: a value of 0 denotes that someone is not physically active at all and a value of 1 denotes that someone is maximally active. The value is updated by comparing its previous value to the self-efficacy, the outcome expectations and the intentions, and by adjusting it for the facilitators and the impediments that a person is facing.

$$\text{Change\_Beh}(t) = \quad \beta_{SE,Beh} \cdot (SE(t) - Beh(t)) + \beta_{OE,Beh} \cdot (OE(t) - Beh(t)) + \beta_{Int,Beh} \cdot$$
$$(Int(t) - Beh(t)) + \beta_{Fac,Beh} \cdot Fac(t) - \beta_{Imp,Beh} \cdot Imp(t)$$

If $\text{Change\_Beh}(t) \geq 0$: $Beh(t + \Delta t) = Beh(t) + \text{Change\_Beh}(t) \cdot (1 - Beh(t)) \cdot \Delta t$
If $\text{Change\_Beh}(t) < 0$: $Beh(t + \Delta t) = Beh(t) + \text{Change\_Beh}(t) \cdot Beh(t) \cdot \Delta t$

Satisfaction (Sat). The satisfaction, i.e. the evaluation of one's behaviour, is implemented by updating its value with the difference between the intentions and the behaviour, and by accounting for the presence of facilitators and impediments.

$$\text{Change\_Sat}(t) = \beta_{Int\&Beh,Sat} \cdot (Beh(t) - Int(t)) + \beta_{Imp,Sat} \cdot Imp(t) - \beta_{Fac,Sat} \cdot Fac(t)$$

If $\text{Change\_Sat}(t) \geq 0$: $Sat(t + \Delta t) = Sat(t) + \text{Change\_Sat}(t) \cdot (1 - Sat(t)) \cdot \Delta t$
If $\text{Change\_Sat}(t) < 0$: $Sat(t + \Delta t) = Sat(t) + \text{Change\_Sat}(t) \cdot Sat(t) \cdot \Delta t$

Social Norm (SN). The social norm is implemented as the weighted average of the behaviour of all relevant friends, where closer and more influential friends contribute more to the social norm than more distant or less influential friends.

$$SN(t) = \sum_{i=1}^{n}(Beh_i(t) \cdot \omega_i) / \sum_{i=1}^{n}(\omega_i)$$

Personal Norm (PN). The personal norm is partly based on the social norm and partly on a personality trait, which is called the static personal norm.

$$PN(t) = \alpha_{SN,PN} \cdot SN(t) + (1 - \alpha_{SN,PN}) \cdot \text{Static\_PN}$$

Expected Social Outcomes (SOE). By comparing the behavioural satisfaction with the social norm, the social outcome expectations are calculated. The second half of the formula allows for outcome expectations that are not dependent on the satisfaction. The parameter $\alpha_{Sat,SOE}$ specifies to what extent someone is influenced by the social norm.

$$SOE(t) = \alpha_{Sat,SOE} \cdot \min(Sat(t)/SN(t)/2, 1) + (1 - \alpha_{Sat,SOE}) \cdot \text{Static\_SOE}$$

Expected Personal Outcomes (POE). The personal outcome expectations are calculated similarly to the expected social outcomes.

$$POE(t) = \alpha_{Sat,POE} \cdot \min(Sat(t)/PN(t)/2, 1) + (1 - \alpha_{Sat,POE}) \cdot Static\_POE$$

Expected Physical Outcomes (PhOE). The physical outcome expectations are formalised by combining two parts as well: one part is determined by the satisfaction, and the other part allows for expectations based on new experiences.

$$PhOE(t) = \alpha_{Sat,PhOE} \cdot Sat(t) + (1 - \alpha_{Sat,PhOE}) \cdot Static\_PhOE$$

Outcome Expectations (OE). The three types of outcome expectations are aggregated into one concept: the outcome expectations. First, the three sets of expected outcomes are combined in a weighted average. Subsequently, the outcome expectations are adjusted based on the feelings of self-efficacy.

$$OE^*(t) = (\omega_{SOE} \cdot SOE(t) + \omega_{POE} \cdot POE(t) + \omega_{PhOE} \cdot PhOE(t)) / (\omega_{SOE} + \omega_{POE} + \omega_{PhOE})$$

If $OE^*(t) \geq SE(t)$: $OE(t + \Delta t) = OE^*(t) + \beta_{SE,OE} \cdot (SE(t) - OE^*(t)) \cdot OE^*(t) \cdot \Delta t$
If $OE^*(t) < SE(t)$: $OE(t + \Delta t) = OE^*(t) + \beta_{SE,OE} \cdot (SE(t) - OE^*(t)) \cdot (1 - OE^*(t)) \cdot \Delta t$

The values of all parameters (αs, βs and ωs) can be adjusted by the modeller and appropriate settings were chosen by the authors.

2.2   Expert Opinion on the Computational Model

The first step towards validation of our computational model was to ask an expert in the field of Physical Activity Research her opinion on our model. She is familiar with many psychosocial theories about physical activity, which she applies in her research to validate coaching strategies to increase the level of physical activity in children and young adults. She proved to be able to reason about the concepts and the dynamic relationships at the conceptual level, and provided us with insightful feedback. After careful analysis of our chosen concepts, relations and formulas, the expert agreed on all of our relations and the way they were modelled. She evaluated our model as very plausible. A possible refinement based on her advice is discussed in Section 5.

3   Simulations

The computational model, which was implemented in Matlab, contains 21 parameters. These are the result of representing Bandura's theory in a computational model without losing details of the original model. A total of 160 simulation scenarios were carefully set up by the authors to investigate many hypotheses about Bandura's model.

Four characteristic person types for physical activity were determined beforehand, with the advice of an expert in the field of physical activity. The initial values of the relevant concepts are either 0.5 (neutral person), 0.9 (active person) or 0.1 (inactive person), with some exceptions. The person recovering from an injury is similar to an active person, but has low values for behaviour and satisfaction. All simulations were analysed manually and interpreted by the authors. All data is available upon request.

3.1   Scenario 5-28: Impediments Only

Impediments were varied in three different strengths over all four person types with either a high or low value for $\beta_{Imp,Beh}$, resulting in a set of 4×3×2 = 24 simulations. The simulations show that for an active person and during the presence of impediments: the higher the impediments, the lower the behaviour. This effect is more apparent for a high $\beta_{Imp,Beh}$. On the contrary, the presence of impediments causes a boost in the behaviour of an inactive person. (See Figure 2.) The effect is greater for a low $\beta_{Imp,Beh}$. This suggests that encountering (and overcoming) obstacles might in some cases lead to an increase in confidence and as a result an increase in physical activity.

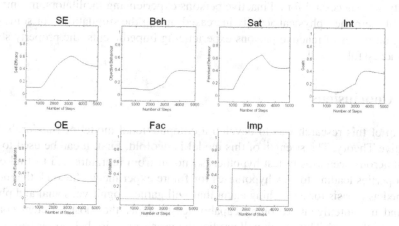

Fig. 2. Scenario 18: Inactive Person, Average Impediments, Low $\beta_{I,mp,Beh}$

4   Verification of Computational Agent Model

The presented computational model was analysed by specification and verification of properties expressing dynamic patterns that are expected to emerge. The purpose of such verification is to automatically check whether the model behaves correctly, by running a large number of simulations and verifying such properties against the simulation traces. This process would be very time consuming if done by hand, and it enables verifying complex properties that require deep logical thinking automatically.

Several dynamic properties have been identified to check basic model issues or were based on hypotheses from the researchers or from literature. The properties were formalised in the Temporal Trace Language (TTL) and checked automatically [13]. Below, we present an example of such a property. It checks whether the physical activity level is increased at the end of the simulation.

4.1   P1: Increase of Physical Activity During Simulation

There exists a timepoint t1 at the beginning of the trace, at which behaviour has value x, and a timepoint t2 at the end of the trace, at which behaviour has value y and y > x.

∃m: TRACE, ∃t1, t2:TIME , ∃x, y: REAL

state(m,t1) |= Beh(x) & state(m, t2) |= Beh(y) & y>x

Property P1 can be used to verify if the physical activity is increased at the end of the simulation. This is interesting to find out for many simulation scenarios at the same time. One can find out which combination of the interaction between the social and cognitive processes with the impediments and/or facilitators leads to an increase or decrease in physical activity. This property can be verified for all concepts, simply by changing Beh(x) into another concept, such as SE(x). This property was verified for many simulation traces. For example, the property did not succeed for all active persons that experience impediments and injured persons experiencing facilitators, meaning their behaviour decremented or remained stable during the simulation. The property was successful for all inactive persons experiencing facilitators, meaning that for all of them their physical activity increased during the simulation. For some of the simulation traces of inactive persons experiencing impediments, the property showed to be successful as well.

5   Conclusions

The aim of this research was to develop a computational model of Bandura's Social Cognitive Theory. The strength of this model is twofold. First, it can be used to simulate numerous scenarios to test hypotheses known from literature and to find emerging properties leading to new hypotheses for future experiments. Second, the model is designed as a basis for a coaching agent that will gather cognitive, social and physical data and use intelligent reasoning capabilities to apply the most efficient coaching strategy to the user. This coach will predict the user's exercise behaviour based on the measured data and it will reason with the current computational model to apply different coaching strategies on the user in order to stimulate him/her to exercise more.

In order to draw strong conclusions or make predictions based on the current computational model, it should be validated. Although an expert in the field of physical activity found our computational model plausible, and the model was also verified successfully through checking many dynamic properties over all simulations, we plan to gather empirical data of the model's concepts over time to tune the parameters and to test whether the patterns generated by the model are supported by real world data.

A possible improvement of the model identified by the expert was preventing the self-efficacy to drop below the value for the actual behaviour. It can be questioned whether it is possible in real life to be physically active, but have low feelings of self-efficacy. A property was created to test this, which revealed that the model does enable it. The empirical data gathered for the validation of the model could be used to find indications whether this artefact is desirable, or whether it should be avoided.

Acknowledgements. This research is supported by Philips and Technology Foundation STW, Nationaal Initiatief Hersenen en Cognitie NIHC under the Partnership program Healthy Lifestyle Solutions. We would like to thank dr. Saskia te Velde for her insightful feedback on our computational model.

References

1. Murray, C.J., Lopez, A.D.: On the Comparable Quantification of Health Risks: Lessons from the Global Burden of Disease Study. Epidemiology 10(5), 594–605 (1999), http://www.ncbi.nlm.nih.gov/pubmed/10468439
2. Warburton, D.E., Nocol, C.W., Bredin, S.S.: Health benefits of physical activity: the evidence. Canadian Medical Journal 174(6) (2006), doi:10.1503/cmaj.051351
3. Bravata, D.L., Smith-Spangler, C., Gienger, A.L., Lin, N., Lewis, R., Stave, C.D., Olkin, I.: Using Pedometers to Increase Physical Activity A Systematic Review. The Journal of the American Medical Association 298(19), 2296–2304 (2007), doi:10.1001/jama.298.19.2296
4. Lubans, D.R., Morgan, P.J., Tudor-Locke, C.: A Systematic Review of Studies Using Pedometers to Promote Physical Activity among Youth. Preventive Medicine 48(4), 307–315 (2009)
5. Davies, C.A., Spence, J.C., Vandelanotte, C., Caperchione, C.M., Mummery, W.K.: Meta-analysis of Internet-delivered Interventions to Increase Physical Activity Levels. The International Journal of Behavioral Nutrition and Physical Activity 9, 52 (2012), doi:10.1186/1479-5868-9-52
6. Eysenbach, G.: The law of attrition. Journal of Medical Internet research, 7(1) 11 (2005), doi:10.2196/jmir.7.1.e11
7. Wangberg, S.C., Bergmo, T.S., Johnsen, J.A.K.: Adherence in Internet-based Interventions. Patient Preference and Adherence 2, 57–65 (2008)
8. Bandura, A.: Health promotion from the perspective of social cognitive theory. Psychology and Health, 37–41 (October 2012), http://www.tandfonline.com/doi/abs/10.1080/08870449808407422 (retrieved)
9. Bandura, A.: Health promotion by social cognitive means. Health education & behavior: the official publication of the Society for Public Health Education 31(2), 143–164 (2004), doi:10.1177/1090198104263660
10. Rovniak, L.S., Anderson, E.S., Winett, R.A., Stephens, R.S.: Social Cognitive Determinants of Physical Activity in Young Adults: A Prospective Structural Equation Analysis. Annals of Behavioral Medicine 24(2), 149–156 (2002)
11. Dzewaltowski, D.A., Noble, J.M., Shaw, J.S.: Physical Activity Participation: Social Cognitive Theory Versus the Theories of Reasoned Action and Planned Behavior. Journal of Sport and Exercise Psychology 12, 388–405 (1990)
12. Petosa, R.L., Suminski, R., Hortz, B.: Predicting vigorous physical activity using social cognitive theory. American Journal of Health Behavior 27(4), 301–310 (2003)
13. Bosse, T., Jonker, C.M., van der Meij, L., Sharpanskykh, A., Treur, J.: Specification and Verification of Dynamics in Agent Models. International Journal of Cooperative Information Systems 18, 167–193 (2009)

Agent's Strategy in Multiple-Issue Negotiation Competition and Analysis of Result

Shota Morii and Takayuki Ito

Nagoya Institute of Technology,
Gokiso-cho, Showa-ku, Nagoya, Aichi, 466-8555
morii.shouta@itolab.nitech.ac.jp
ito.takayuki@nitech.ac.jp

Abstract. The Automated Negotiation Agents Competition (ANAC201 2) was organized. It is likely that the strategies of an agent can be applied to real-life negotiation problems. Therefore, this paper deals with a new scenario of multiple-issue negotiation problems. The advantage of the proposed scenario in comparison with existing ones is being close to real-life negotiation problems. In this paper, we present our agent (AgentMRK2) strategy and investigate the effects of strategy that uses the negotiation history in the ANAC2013 qualifying rounds. Moreover, we discuss a change of acquired utility by repeating the negotiations. The study revealed the existence of correlations between the number of bids and the average of utilities.

Keywords: Multi-Agent System, Multi-issue Negotiation, Automated Negotiation Competition.

1 Introduction

Automated negotiating agents used to be widely studied in multi-agent systems research (e.g., [1,2,3,4,5,6]). Automated agents can be used side-by-side with a human negotiator embarking on an important negotiation task. There may even be situations in which automated negotiators can replace the human negotiators. Thus, success in developing an automated agent with negotiation capabilities has great advantages and implications.

Motivated by the challenges of bilateral negotiations between people and automated agents, the Automated Negotiating Agents Competition (ANAC) was organized. The purpose of the competition is to facilitate research in the area of bilateral multi-issue closed negotiation. The first ANAC was held in 2010 in conjunction with the Ninth International Conference on Autonomous Agents and Multi-Agent Systems (AAMAS2010). ANAC2011 was held in AAMAS2011, and 18 agents participated. At ANAC2012 our agent (AgentMR) got through the qualifying rounds. ANAC2013 has been organized in this year.

In this paper, we develop a new agent (AgentMRK2) that can negotiate on various negotiation problems. Additionally, we analyze the multiple bilateral multi-issue closed negotiation problem that was introduced in ANAC2013.

G. Boella et al. (Eds.): PRIMA 2013, LNAI 8291, pp. 486–493, 2013.

This problem can take into account the negotiation history, and agents can conduct efficient negotiation by utilizing this history. We conduct an analysis of effect based on negotiation time or agreement rate at the ANAC2013 qualifying rounds. Moreover, we investigate the relation between the number of bids and the average of utilities by repeating the negotiations.

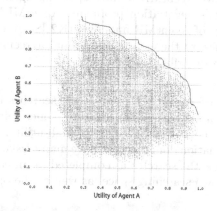

Fig. 1. Negotiation Domains of ANAC

2 Automated Negotiating Agents Competition (ANAC)

2.1 Purpose of ANAC

The purpose of the competition is to steer research in the area of bilateral multi-issue closed negotiation. Closed negotiation, when opponents do not reveal their preferences to each other, is an important class of real-life negotiation.

Negotiating agents designed using a heuristic approach require extensive evaluation, typically through simulations and empirical analysis, since it is usually impossible to predict precisely how the system and constituent agents will behave in a wide variety of circumstances.

In ANAC2012, participants designed negotiation domains (Figure 1) that adopted problems close to real-life negotiation. Thus, the main idea of simulation in these domains is to develop an agent's strategy for real-life negotiation.

2.2 Negotiation Platform

To facilitate research in the area of bilateral multi-issue negotiation, the GENIUS system was developed [7]. It allows easy development and integration of existing negotiating agents. GENIUS can be used to simulate individual negotiation sessions as well as tournaments between negotiating agents in various scenarios. It allows the specification of negotiation domains and preference profiles by means of a graphical user interface. GENIUS can be used to train human negotiators by means of negotiations against automated agents or other humans. Furthermore, it can be used to teach the design of generic automated negotiating agents.

3   Developing Automated Agents in Multiple-Issue Negotiation Problems

3.1   Implementing Automated Agents (AgentMRK2)

In this study, we improve AgentMR to develop a new agent (AgentMRK2) that can negotiate on various negotiation problems. AgentMRK2 is an agent that combines the strategies of AgentMR and AgentK2 [8]. AgentK2 has a strategy that tries to compromise to the estimated optimal agreement point. The basic strategy of the agent is described as follows.

Searching Strategy of AgentMR. AgentMR searches the bid based on the heuristic that one's own bid has similar utilities. Concretely, when a certain bid changes one point at issue, this bid has similar high utility. This searching strategy is effective in negotiation domains that have many *issues*. This strategy leads to early agreement since the search was completed at an early stage. Moreover, AgentMR searches it own searching space, as well as the opponent's space.

Compromising Strategy of AgentK2. AgentK2 estimates the alternatives the opponent will offer in the future based on the history of the opponent's offers. In particular, we estimate it using the values mapping the opponent's bids to our own utility function. The agent works at compromising to the estimated optimal agreement point.

Concretely, our behavior is decided based on the following:

$$emax(t) = \mu(t) + (1 - \mu(t))d(t) \tag{1}$$
$$target(t) = 1 - (1 - emax(t))t^\alpha \tag{2}$$

$emax(t)$ means the estimated maximum utility of a bid the opponent will propose in the future. $emax(t)$ is calculated by $\mu(t)$ (the average of the opponent's offers in our utility space), $d(t)$ (the width of the opponent's offers in our utility space) when the timeline is t. $d(t)$ is calculated based on the deviation. We can see how favorable the opponent's offer is based on the deviation ($d(t)$) and the average ($\mu(t)$).

If we assume that the opponent's offer is generated based on uniform distribution $[\alpha, \alpha + d(t)]$, the deviation is calculated as follows:

$$\sigma^2(t) = \frac{1}{n}\sum_{i=0}^{n} x_i^2 - \mu^2 = \frac{d^2(t)}{12} \tag{3}$$

Therefore, $d(t)$ is defined as follows:

$$d(t) = \sqrt{12}\sigma(t) \tag{4}$$

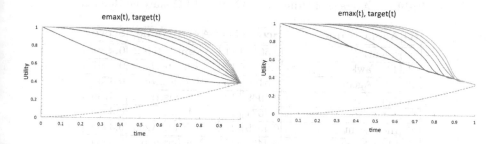

Fig. 2. *target(t)* when *emax(t)*

Fig. 3. *target(t)* when *emax(t)* based on *g(t)*

Figure 2 is an example of *target(t)* when α is changed from 1 to 9. *emax(t)* is $\mu(t) = \frac{1}{10}t$, $d(t) = \frac{1}{3}t^2$. The horizontal axis shows the passage of time of the negotiation. The vertical axis indicates the effect value that the agent obtains. The curve that increases with time passage is *emax(t)*, and the curve that approaches *emax(t)* with time passage is *target(t)*.

3.2   Negotiation Strategy in Multiple-Issue Negotiation Problems

The main idea of strategy is to compute concessions of the opponent in order to grasp the characteristics of the opponent. Concretely, a concession of the opponent is calculated as follows. Let $\mathcal{D}$ be our set of domains. Agent A negotiates with B on domain $D \in \mathcal{D}$ if they reach a certain outcome ω, in which a concession degree of B on utility space of A is defined as expression (5).

$$\lambda = \frac{U(\omega) - U(\omega_{rivalFirst})}{U(\omega_{myMax}) - U(\omega_{rivalFirst})} \tag{5}$$

$U(\omega_{myMax})$ means the bid of one's own highest utility, and $U(\omega_{rivalFirst})$ means the first bid of the opponent on its own utility space. If we assume that the concession degree of the opponent is λ_k in the negotiation of kth number, AgentMRK2 has the set of concession degree: $\Lambda = \{\lambda_1, \lambda_2, \ldots, \lambda_n\}$. On domain D, the opponent can take maximum utility as follows:

$$U_{rivalMax} = U(\omega_{rivalFirst}) + (U(\omega_{myMax}) - U(\omega_{rivalFirst})) \cdot \bar{\Lambda} \tag{6}$$

$\bar{\Lambda}$ means the average of the set of concession degree (Λ). We calculated the agent's own minimum concession of degree on domain D by expressions (4) and (6) . Figure 3 is an example of *target(t)* based on *g(t)* when α is changed from 1 to 9. Figure 3 shows concession faster than Figure 2. Therefore, this strategy can concede at an early stage to match the concession of the opponent.

Table 1. Average of Utilities in ANAC2013 Qualifying Rounds

ID	Agent Name	Score	ID	AgentName	Score
1	AgentKF	0.5616	11	**AgentMRK2**	**0.4298**
2	TheFawkes	0.5221	12	Elizabeth	0.3867
3	TMFAgent	0.5160	13	ReuthLiron	0.3736
4	MetaAgent	0.4949	14	BOAconstrictor	0.3735
5	AgentG	0.4571	15	Pelican	0.3586
6	InoxAgent	0.4549	16	OrielEinatAgent	0.3498
7	SlavaAgent	0.4467	17	MasterQiao	0.3454
8	VAStockMarketAgent	0.4460	18	EAgent	0.3376
9	RoOAgent	0.4320	19	ClearAgent	0.3149
10	AgentTalex	0.4307			

Table 2. Factor Patterns after *Promax Rotation*

Element Name	Factor1 Z_1	Factor2 Z_2
Agreement Rate	**1.066**	0.1467
Acquired Utility	**0.8333**	-0.1929
Number of Bid	0.1324	**0.9080**
Negotiation Time	-0.2265	**0.6506**
Factor Contribution	1.8748	1.3634

4   Analysis of Characteristics of ANAC2013

4.1   Considerations of Agent Characteristics by Factor Analysis

Average of utilities for each agent at ANAC2013 qualifying rounds are given in Table 1. As can be seen from Table 1, AgentMRK2 got an average score. We show the analysis results based on this result.

In this analysis, we compute the number of bids, negotiation time, acquired utilities, and agreement rates. Moreover, we investigate the effect of each agent by these indexes using factor analysis. In factor analysis, the initial estimate is calculated by Squared Multiple Correlation (SMC) method, and we use *promax rotation* to rotate factor axis.

Table 2 shows factor patterns after promax rotation. Figure 4 also reveals a scatter diagram of factor patterns at Factor 1 (Z_1) and Factor 2 (Z_2). It is clear from Table 2 that Z_1 contributed agreement rates and acquired utilities, and Z_2 contributed the number of bids and negotiation time. In other words, agreement rates and acquired utilities have positive correlation. Similarly, the number of bids and negotiation time also have positive correlation. Figure 4 depicts the value of each element at Z_1 and Z_2 on a two-dimensional graph. Moreover, Figure 5 gives the value of each agent based on the scatter diagram of factor patterns (Figure 4). In this figure, each agent corresponds to the number of Table 1's ID.

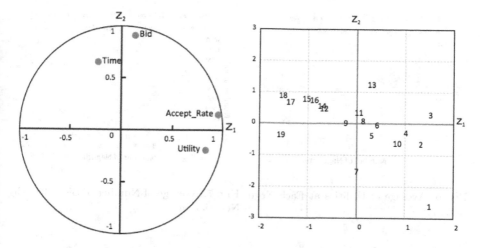

Fig. 4. Scatter diagram of Factor Patterns

Fig. 5. Scatter diagram of Score after *Promax Rotation*

Figure 5 corresponds to Figure 4's factor of each axis. Therefore, Figure 5 shows that agreement rate and acquired utilities are high if the value of Z_1 approached 1. On the other hand, the number of bids and negotiation time are high if the value of Z_2 approached 1. By way of example, AgentMRK2 (11), which acquired the average utilities, sits at the center at the graph. AgentKF (1), which acquired highest utilities, can be found at the lower right. It follows from this that AgentKF is an agent for which the number of bids and negotiation time are exceedingly small. The agent that got the high utilities constitutes a characteristics feature and has the high value at the Z_1 axis. In contrast, there is not a great difference among the agents at the number of bids and negotiation time since many agents had a value in-between -1 to 1 at the Z_2 axis. The results of investigation of factor analysis lead to the following conclusions.

- In ANAC2013, acquired utilities are high if there is high agreement rate. Therefore, it is important that we try to achieve high agreement rate by utilizing negotiation history.
- There is not a great difference among the agents for the number of bids and negotiation time. This result shows that the agents have some strategies in common.
- AgentKF is an agent for which the number of bids and negotiation time are exceedingly short. For this reason, there is a greater chance of increasing the acquired utilities if we reduce the number of bids and negotiation time.

4.2   Influence by Utilizing the Negotiation History

This study discussed characteristics among the agents that got through the qualifying rounds (including AgentMRK2). The purpose of this consideration is to

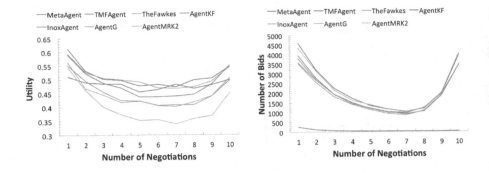

Fig. 6. Average of Utilities at Each Nego- **Fig. 7.** Average of Number of Bids at Each
tiation   Negotiation

reveal the change of the acquired utilities or the number of bids by repeating
the negotiation. Note that each agent negotiates 10 times at the same domain
with the same opponent.

Figures 6 and 7 show the average of utilities and the average of bids among
the agents at each negotiation. The horizontal axis shows the number of times of
negotiation. The vertical axis indicates the utilities that the agent obtains. The
result in Figure 6 indicates that the utilities of many agents decrease through
the negotiations repeatedly. Moreover, the utilities increase again with the passing of the negotiations. According to Figure 7, all agents except for AgentKF
decrease the number of bids through the negotiations repeatedly. Similarly, the
number of bids increases again with the passing of the negotiations. There is an
analogy between the average of utilities and the number of bids. Therefore, it
is possible to reduce the number of bids by searching efficiently by utilizing the
negotiation history. It is also to be noted that diminution of the number of bids
does not contribute to the rise of the acquired utilities. These findings present
the following conclusions.

- In the first time negotiation, an agent tends to search for many bids since
  we do not know agent information.
- By using the history in the negotiation, the number of bids was decreased.
  However, each agent takes a hard stance in order to try to get the more
  utilities. As a result, the utilities were decreased.
- Although each agent takes a hard stance at repeating the negotiation, the
  agent takes a cooperative stance if a certain limit is reached.

As can be seen from Figures 6 and 7, many agents have a similar strategic
model that extracts a concession from the opponent. The strategy of a hard
stance was also confirmed to provide efficient negotiation in ANAC2012 [9]. It
is one of the features of ANAC2013 that many agents had a similar strategy.

5   Conclusion

In this paper, we described the rules of ANAC. Then, we argued a basic strategy for AgentMR and AgentK2. Moreover, we developed a new agent (AgentMRK2) that is more effective than our existing agent. Third, we introduced the characteristics of ANAC2013 using factor analysis. As a result of analysis, we confirmed that agreement rate is an important factor, and we found the existence of similarities among the agent's strategies. Finally, by examining the average of utilities and the number of bids, we investigated the effects of utilizing the negotiation history. The study revealed the characteristics that the utilities of many agents decrease through the repeated negotiations. Moreover, it is noteworthy that the utilities increase again with the passing of negotiations. We obtained the agent's model that each agent tends to take a hard stance by introducing the negotiation history.

In the future, a strategic model that has negotiation history also needs to be discussed in more detail. Specifically, we will analyze a strategy like a AgentKF's, in which the acquired utilities hardly change.

References

1. Kraus, S.: Strategic Negotiation in Multiagent Environments. MIT Press (2001)
2. Fatima, S.S., Wooldridge, M.J., Jennings, N.R.: Multi-issue negotiation under time constraints. In: 1st International Joint Conference on Autonomous Agents and Multi-Agent Systems, pp. 143–150 (2002)
3. Jennings, N.R., et al.: Automated negotiation: prospects, methods and challenges. Group Decision and Negotiation 10(2), 199–215 (2001)
4. Minghua, H., Jennings, N.R., Leung, H.F.: On agent-mediated electronic commerce. IEEE Transactions on Knowledge and Data Engineering 15(4), 985–1003 (2003)
5. Xudong, L., et al.: KEMNAD: a knowledge engineering methodology for negotiating agent development. Computational Intelligence 28(1), 51–105 (2012)
6. Li, P., et al.: A Two-Stage Win-Win Multiattribute Negotiation Model: Optimization and Then Concession. In: Computational Intelligence (2012)
7. Lin, R., Kraus, S., Baarslag, T., Tykhonov, D., Hindriks, K., Jonker, C.M.: Supporting the design of general automated negotiators. In: Proceedings of the Second International Workshop on Agent-based Complex Automated Negotiations, ACAN 2009 (2009)
8. Kawaguchi, S., Fujita, K., Ito, T.: Agentk2: Compromising strategy based on estimated maximum utility for automated negotiating agents. In: Complex Automated Negotiations: Theories, Models, and Software Competitions, pp. 235–241 (2012)
9. Morii, S., Kawaguchi, S., Ito, T.: Analysis of agent strategy based on discount utility in Automated Negotiating Agents Competition (ANAC 2012). In: JAWS (Joint Agent Workshop and Symposium) (2012)

Estimating Arrival Time of Pedestrian Using Walking Logs

Yui Okuda and Yasuhiko Kitamura

Department of Informatics
School of Science and Technology
Kwansei Gakuin University
2-1 Gakuen, Sanda 669-1337, Japan
ykitamura@kwansei.ac.jp
http://ist.ksc.kwansei.ac.jp/~kitamura/

Abstract. Recent advances in sensor technology, wireless communication, and hand held computing devices enable location-aware services and agents that provide appropriate information and services depending on the location of the user. To provide better quality services, it is required to know and predict accurately the behavior of the user based on the data acquired from the sensors. We propose a method to estimate the arrival time of pedestrian using walking logs obtained by the GPS and stored in a database. It can be applied for pedestrian navigation and just-in-time information retrieval with high accuracy. The method retrieves walking trajectories similar to the user's one from the database and estimates the arrival time to her destination. In the evaluation experiment, we collected walking trajectories of pedestrians who walked the same route, and compared our method with conventional ones based on the average arrival time and the extrapolation method. As a result, the estimation error of our method was smaller than that of the conventional ones. In particular, our method shows a better estimation for a route that includes a slope where the walking pattern of pedestrians drastically change.

Keywords: location-aware servicesCpedestrian navigation, just-in-time information retrievalCestimation of arrival time, GPS.

1 Introduction

Recent advances in sensor technology, wireless communication, and hand held computing devices enable location-aware services [1] and agents [2] which provide appropriate information and service depending on the location of the user. Typical location-aware services are car navigation [3], pedestrian navigation [4], tourist guides [5], museum guides [6], shopping assistance [7] and just-in-time information retrieval [8], to name a few.

To provide better quality services, it is required to know and predict accurately the behaviour of the users based on the data acquired from the sensors [9]. By utilizing data from sensors like GPS, we can estimate the location and/or

G. Boella et al. (Eds.): PRIMA 2013, LNAI 8291, pp. 494–501, 2013.

movement of users [10], transportation routines (walk, bus, or train) [9], their activities (home, work, or lunch) [11], and furthermore their intent and plan [12].

We, in this paper, propose a method to estimate the arrival time of the user when she walks a route. It is especially an important function for just-in-time information retrieval agents with high accuracy. For example, when a user goes to a station on foot to take a train, whether she can catch the train in time significantly affects her plan later. If she could not catch the train, the agent sends an e-mail about that to her friends because she cannot be in time for the meeting. Thus, it is important for the agent to estimate exactly when the user arrives at the station.

Conventional methods to estimate the arrival time have been developed mainly for logistic and car navigation systems [13,14]. They calculate the average speed of cars and estimate the arrival time based on the distance to the destination and the congestion information on the route. However, it is difficult to estimate the arrival time of pedestrians by using the conventional method because each pedestrian has a different walking pattern. We need to estimate the arrival time depending on the walking pattern of the user.

We, in this paper, propose a method to estimate the arrival time of pedestrian using walking logs obtained by the GPS and stored in a database. In the method, we retrieve walking trajectories similar to the user's one from the database and estimate the arrival time to her destination.

In Section 2, we propose our method to estimate the arrival time of pedestrian using walking logs. In Section 3, we evaluate our method using actually collected walking logs and compare it with conventional methods. In Section 4, we conclude this paper with our future work.

2   Estimating the Arrival Time of Pedestrian

2.1   Walking Trajectory

A walking trajectory is represented as P^s and is stored in a walking log database $\Omega = \{P^1, P^2, \cdots, P^n\}(1 \leq s \leq n)$. It is composed of a sequence of points $P^s = \langle p_1^s, p_2^s, \cdots, p_m^s \rangle$ where p_1^s is the starting point of the trajectory and p_m^s is the goal [15]. A point is represented as $p_k^s = \langle x_k^s, y_k^s, t_k^s \rangle$ where x_k^s is the longitude of the point, y_k^s is the latitude, and t_k^s is the time measured by the GPS. We assume $t_1^s < t_2^s < \ldots < t_m^s$.

To make our discussion simple, we assume that the walking trajectories stored in the database are collected from pedestrians who walked the same route though the walking time may be different depending on each. Namely, $\forall P^i, P^j \in \Omega, 1 \leq k \leq m : x_k^i = x_k^j \wedge y_k^i = y_k^j$. We also assume that every distance interval between two points in a trajectory is the same. Namely, $\forall P^i \in \Omega, 1 \leq k \leq m - 1 : \sqrt{(x_k^i - x_{k+1}^i)^2 + (y_k^i - y_{k+1}^i)^2} = d$, where d is a constant distance. How to obtain such trajectories is discussed in Section 2.3.

Figure 1 shows an example of walking trajectory. A part of walking trajectory is represented as $P_{a,b}^s = \langle p_a^s, p_{a+1}^s, \cdots, p_b^s \rangle$ $(1 \leq a < b \leq m)$. For example, a partial walking trajectory $P_{2,5}^s$ is colored in red in Figure 1.

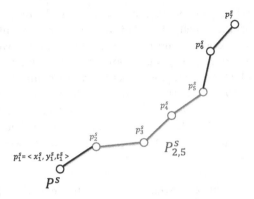

Fig. 1. Walking trajectory

2.2   Estimating Arrival Time

When a partial walking trajectory $P_{a,b}^q$ of $P^q = \langle p_1^q, p_2^q, \cdots, p_m^q \rangle$ is given, we estimate the arrival time t_m^q by using a walking log database Ω. We first retrieve a walking trajectory P^j which is similar to $P_{a,b}^q$ from Ω as given by

$$P^j = argmin_{P^s \in \Omega} D(P_{a,b}^q, P_{a,b}^s) \qquad (1)$$

where $D(P_{a,b}^q, P_{a,b}^j)$ is the degree of difference between two trajectories $P_{a,b}^q$ and $P_{a,b}^j$ as defined below.

$$D(P_{a,b}^q, P_{a,b}^j) = \frac{|T(P_{a,b}^j) - T(P_{a,b}^q)|}{T(P_{a,b}^q)}, \qquad (2)$$

where $T(P_{a,b}^q)$ is the walking time of $P_{a,b}^q$, namely $t_b^q - t_a^q$.

Then, we estimate the arrival time t_m^q to the goal as follows.

$$t_m^q = t_b^q + T(P_{b,m}^j) \cdot \frac{T(P_{a,b}^q)}{T(P_{a,b}^j)} \qquad (3)$$

Namely, we estimate the walking time between p_b^q and p_m^q to be the product of the walking time between p_b^j and p_m^j and the ratio of the walking time of P^q to P^j between p_a^q and p_b^q.

For example, when $P_{2,5}^q$ is given as in Figure 2, we can estimate that the arrival time t_7^q is $1:00:50$ by using P^j.

2.3   Resampling Walking Trajectory

We, in this paper, assume that walking trajectories in the walking log database are collected from pedestrians who walked the same route and that the distance

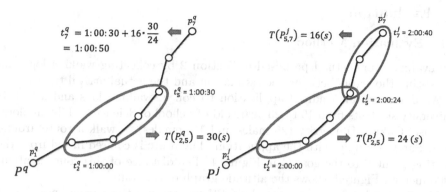

Fig. 2. Example of the arrival time estimation

between every pair of connecting points is also the same. However, when we actually collect walking trajectories using the GPS, the distance between two connecting points is not always the same, or we may have missing data. As a remedy to cope with this problem, we resample the trajectory to make the distance of every pair of connecting points be a constant. Resampling may cause additional measuring errors, but the errors are not significant if the sampling rate is high enough.

Figure 3 shows an example of resampling to make the distance of every pair of connecting points to be 10. In the original walking trajectory P^s, the distance between the points p_1^s and p_2^s is 8. We add a new point $p_2^{\prime s}$ on a line between p_2^s and p_3^s to make the distance between p_1^s and $p_2^{\prime s}$ to be 10. Then, we make the distance between $p_2^{\prime s}$ and p_3^s to be 10, but the distance is less than 10, so we add a new point $p_3^{\prime s}$ on the line between p_3^s and p_4^s as before. By repeating the above process, we obtain a walking trajectory $< p_1^s, p_2^{\prime s}, p_3^{\prime s}, \ldots >$ in which the distance between every pair of connecting points is 10.

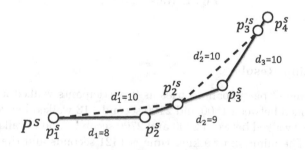

Fig. 3. Resampling walking trajectory

3   Evaluation

3.1   Evaluation Method

We evaluate our method proposed in Section 2 by collecting walking logs and measuring the errors between the estimation and the actual arrival time.

We developed an Android application to collect walking logs and asked 38 university students from 19 to 23 years old of School of Science and Technology, Kwansei Gakuin University (25 males and 13 females) to walk a route around Kobe Sanda Campus with the application. The route is colored in red from the starting point S to the goal G in Figure 4. The distance of this route is about 3000 meters. Figure 5 shows the altitude graph of the route.

The Android application uses the GPS to measure the current position of the walker every 10 seconds. After collecting the walking logs, we resampled the trajectories to make the distance d between two connecting points to be 1 meter.

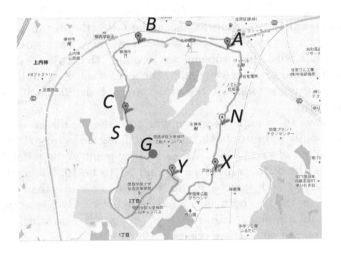

Fig. 4. Walking route

3.2   Evaluation Results

The walking time of participants varies as 2 participants walked less than 1800 seconds, 10 walked between 1800 and 2100 seconds, 13 walked between 2100 and 2400 seconds, 10 walked between 2400 and 2700 seconds, and 3 walked more than 2700 seconds. The minimum walking time is 1421 seconds and the maximum is 3260 seconds.

We estimated the arrival time using the 38 walking logs. We first select $P_{a,b}^q$ from the walking logs and leave the rest to be Ω, then we estimate the arrival time t_m^q by using Ω. We repeated the estimation 38 times by changing $P_{a,b}^q$.

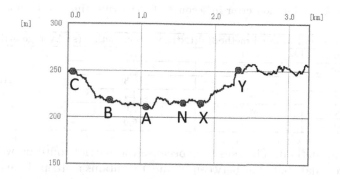

Fig. 5. Altitude graph of walking route

The base point N, which corresponds to p_b^q, in Figure 4 is 1600 meters away from the starting point and we evaluated how the estimation error changes depending on the distance between p_a^q and p_b^q and that between p_b^q and the goal.

For a comparison with conventional methods, we compared our method with estimations by the average arrival time and by the extrapolation method. The average arrival time is calculated by averaging the time taken to the goal of walking logs in Ω. Namely, $t_m^q = t_b^q + \frac{\sum_{s \in \Omega} T(P_{b,m}^s)}{|\Omega|}$.

The extrapolation method estimates the arrival time by assuming that the pedestrian walks in the future at the same walking speed in the past. Given a walking trajectory P^s, the walking speed of pedestrian is calculated as

$$v_{a,b}^q = \frac{d \cdot (b - a)}{T(P_{a,b}^q)}, \tag{4}$$

where d is the distance interval of resampling, so the arrival time t_m^q is estimated as

$$t_m^q = t_b^q + \frac{d \cdot (m - b)}{v_{a,b}^q}. \tag{5}$$

Given a walking log $P_{a,b}^q$, our method retrieves the similar walking logs from the database and estimates the arrival time. There are statistical variations among the walking logs actually, it is better to estimate the arrival time by using multiple walking logs than by using a single log. We use walking logs whose degree of difference, defined in Section 2, is less than 0.05, considering a preliminary experiment we have performed.

Table 1 shows estimation errors when the distance of $P_{a,b}^q$ is 500 meters (p_a^q at A), 1000 meters (p_a^q at B) and 1500 meters (p_a^q at C) and the goal is at X, which is 250 meters away from N. It shows that the estimation error of the average arrival time is large and the difference between the proposed method and the extrapolation method is small.

Table 2 shows estimation errors when the goal is at Y, which is 750 meters away from N. It shows that the error of our method is smaller than that of the

Table 1. Estimation error in seconds of the arrival time to the point X

	Average/Median	Proposed method(s)	Extrapolation method(s)	Average arrival time(s)
A	Average	7.9	7.4	
	Median	6.1	4.8	
B	Average	6.4	6.3	21.4
	Median	4.6	4.4	
C	Average	8.9	7.6	
	Median	7.3	5.9	

extrapolation method. The reason is because the partial route between N and X is relatively flat, but that between N and Y contains a steep slope and makes the walking speed of pedestrians change. Our method can detect the walking speed change due to the topography and produce better estimations.

Table 2. Estimation error in seconds of the arrival time to the point Y

	Average/Median	Proposed method(s)	Extrapolation method(s)	Average arrival time(s)
A	Average	30.0	40.8	
	Median	24.0	35.8	
B	Average	27.1	44.9	69.8
	Median	20.5	38.1	
C	Average	27.0	46.8	
	Median	17.6	36.9	

4   Summary and Future Work

We, in this paper, propose a method to estimate the arrival time of pedestrians, which can be applied for pedestrian navigation and just-in-time information retrieval with high accuracy. Considering a variety of walking patterns of pedestrians, the method estimates the arrival time using a walking log database. In the evaluation experiment, we collected walking trajectories of pedestrians who walked the same route and estimated the arrival time by using the log. As a result, the estimation error of our method is smaller than the conventional methods (the average arrival time and the extrapolation method). In particular, our method shows a better estimation for a route that includes a slope where the walking pattern of pedestrians change. The estimation of our method will be improved if we can use more walking logs. We would like to analyze the improvement of estimation depending on the number of walking logs in our future work. In addition, we plan to improve our method to estimate the arrival time for long routes by using a dynamic probability network [16].

Acknowledgement. This work is partly supported by the MEXT-Supported Program for the Strategic Research Foundation at Private Universities, 2010-2014.

References

1. Kaasinen, E.: User needs for location-aware mobile services. Personal and Ubiquitous Computing 7(1), 70–79 (2003)
2. Lee, J., Mateo, R.M.A., Gerardo, B.D., Go, S.-H.: Location-aware agent using data mining for the distributed location-based services. In: Gavrilova, M.L., Gervasi, O., Kumar, V., Tan, C.J.K., Taniar, D., Laganá, A., Mun, Y., Choo, H. (eds.) ICCSA 2006. LNCS, vol. 3984, pp. 867–876. Springer, Heidelberg (2006)
3. Fujita, Y., Nawaoka, T., Hirohata, E.: Development of a mapping and guidance database for automobile navigation system. In: Proceedings of the 41st IEEE Vehicular Technology Conference, pp. 869–874. IEEE (1991)
4. Arikawa, M., Konomi, S., Ohnishi, K.: NAVITIME: Supporting pedestrian navigation in the real world. IEEE Pervasive Computing 6(3), 21–29 (2007)
5. Cheverst, K., Davies, N., Mitchell, K., Friday, A., Efstratiou, C.: Developing a context-aware electronic tourist guide: some issues and experiences. In: Proceedings of the SIGCHI Conference on Human Factors in Computing Systems, pp. 17–24. ACM (2000)
6. Bieber, G., Giersich, M.: Personal mobile navigation systems – design considerations and experiences. Computers & Graphics 25(4), 563–570 (2001)
7. Fano, A.E.: Shopper's eye: using location-based filtering for a shopping agent in the physical world. In: Proceedings of the 2nd International Conference on Autonomous Agents, pp. 416–421. ACM (1998)
8. Rhodes, B.: Using physical context for just-in-time information retrieval. IEEE Transactions on Computers 52(8), 1011–1014 (2003)
9. Liao, L., Patterson, D.J., Fox, D., Kautz, H.: Learning and inferring transportation routines. Artificial Intelligence 171(5), 311–331 (2007)
10. Ashbrook, D., Starner, T.: Using GPS to learn significant locations and predict movement across multiple users. Personal and Ubiquitous Computing 7(5), 275–286 (2003)
11. Liao, L.: Location-based activity recognition. PhD thesis, University of Washington (2006)
12. Bui, H.H., Venkatesh, S., West, G.: Policy recognition in the abstract hidden Markov model. JournalofArtificial Inteligence Research 17, 451–499 (2002)
13. Rice, J., Van Zwet, E.: A simple and effective method for predicting travel times on freeways. IEEE Transactions on Intelligent Transportation Systems 5(3), 200–207 (2004)
14. Lin, H.-E., Zito, R., Taylor, M.A.: A review of travel-time prediction in transport and logistics. In: Proceedings of the Eastern Asia Society for Transportation Studies, vol. 5, pp. 1433–1448 (2005)
15. Trajcevski, G., Wolfson, O., Hinrichs, K., Chamberlain, S.: Managing uncertainty in moving objects databases. ACM Transactions on Database Systems (TODS) 29(3), 463–507 (2004)
16. Jula, H., Dessouky, M., Ioannou, P.A.: Real-time estimation of travel times along the arcs and arrival times at the nodes of dynamic stochastic networks. IEEE Transactions on Intelligent Transportation Systems 9(1), 97–110 (2008)

A Computational Model of Affective Moral Decision Making That Predicts Human Criminal Choices

Matthijs A. Pontier[1], Jean-Louis Van Gelder[2], and Reinout E. de Vries[3]

[1] Center for Advanced Media Research Amsterdam (CAMeRA@VU)
Buitenveldertselaan 3, Amsterdam, 1081HV, The Netherlands
matthijspon@gmail.com
[2] Netherlands Institute for the Study of Crime and Law Enforcement (NCSR)
JvanGelder@nscr.nl
[3] VU University Amsterdam, Faculty of Psychology and Education
re.de.vries@vu.nl

Abstract. In the present paper we show that a computational model of affective moral decision making can fit human behavior data obtained from an empirical study on criminal decision making. By applying parameter tuning techniques on data from an initial sample, optimal fits of the affective moral decision making model were found supporting the influences of honesty/humility, perceived risk and negative state affect on criminal choice. Using the parameter settings from the initial sample, we were able to predict criminal choices of participants in the holdout sample. The prediction errors of the full model were fairly low. Moreover, they compared favorably to the prediction errors produced by constrained variants of the model where either the moral, rational or affective influences or a combination of these had been removed.

Keywords: Moral Reasoning, Mathematical Modeling, Cognitive Modeling, Criminal Decision Making, Affective Decision Making, Machine Ethics, Empirical Data.

1 Introduction

1.1 Ratio and Affect in Criminal Decision Making

Although there is substantial evidence that emotions are fundamental inputs in the criminal decision making process [1], references to the role of emotions have largely remained confined to narrative or interpretative approaches and rarely made it into choice models of offending. These approaches are limited in terms of gaining insight into the decision making process, as they do not specify the psychological mechanisms according to which they operate [18] or how emotions influence the criminal calculus and alter concerns regarding risk.

The possible interplay between cognition and affect has been prominent in dual-process theories of information processing [5]. Van Gelder [18] argues that criminal decision making processes, perceived as a particular kind of risk taking, may also be insightfully portrayed as invoking these two types of processing. According to the

G. Boella et al. (Eds.): PRIMA 2013, LNAI 8291, pp. 502–509, 2013.

hot/cool perspective of criminal decision making, the cognitive, 'cool', processing mode is sensitive to risk considerations and is therefore likely to respond to notions of sanction severity and certainty, as suggested by deterrence theorists [18]. The cognitive mode is also responsible for balancing costs against benefits and making projections about the long-term consequences of decisions and, consequently, functions much in accordance with the logic assumed by rational choice theory. The affective mode, on the other hand, remains largely unresponsive to probabilities [21]. The dual-process approach applied to criminal decision making can illuminate why notions such as severity of punishment in general have little or no effect on crime rates, why the effect of punishment certainty is only modest, and why recidivism rates are as high as they are.

The present study focuses on the relationship between personality, ratio, affect and criminal behavior. Our point of departure is the HEXACO model. Recently, reanalyses of the same lexical data that have yielded the Big Five model have suggested that instead of five, there are six main dimensions of personality. In the HEXACO model, a sixth cross-culturally corresponding personality dimension named *Honesty–Humility* is added [6]. This trait refers to individual differences in the tendency to be interpersonally genuine, to be unwilling to take advantage of others, to avoid fraud and corruption, to be uninterested in status and wealth, and to be modest and unassuming. Recent research by Van Gelder and De Vries [20] suggests that the HEXACO model and its Honesty-Humility dimension in particular, is also a strong predictor of criminal behavior.

1.2   Predicting Criminal Behavior Using a Computational Model

To be able to predict human criminal behavior, we created a computational model of affective moral decision making. To our knowledge, no agent models that also include affect and personality to predict crime have so far been proposed. As a first step in this direction, we integrated a moral reasoning system that matched the decision of medical ethical experts [12] and an empirically validated model of affective decision making [7]. We extended the affective moral decision making module so that the agent can take into account anticipatory emotions during the decision making process. The section below will explain the model in more detail.

We obtained empirical data to test whether the model can predict human criminal behavior. In simulation experiments, we optimized the weights for the moral, rational and affective influences in the decision making process and the morality of the criminal choice, based on the first half of the sample, using parameter tuning, similar to [2]. With the obtained weights, we tested the predictions for the holdout sample (i.e., the remaining half of the participants) using seven different versions of the model: the full model and constrained versions of the model, in which one or two of the three influences in the decision making process (i.e., personality, ratio and affect) were removed. We hypothesized that the full model would fit the data the best. Because of the generic form of the model, we expect that if the model successfully predicts human affective moral decision making (i.e., criminal behavior), it can also be used to simulate human affective ethical decision making.

2   The Computational Model of Affective Moral Decision Making

In the rational moral reasoning system [12], the agent tries to estimate the morality of actions by holding each action against the moral principles inserted in the system and picking actions that serve these moral goals best. The moral goals inserted into the system are (1) autonomy, (2) beneficence, (3) non-maleficence and (4) justice. The agent calculates the estimated level of Morality of an action by taking the sum of the ambition levels of the moral goals multiplied with the beliefs that the particular actions facilitate the corresponding moral goals:

$$\text{Morality(Action)} = \Sigma_{\text{Goal}}(\text{ Belief(Action facilitates Goal))} * \text{Ambition(Goal))} \qquad (1)$$

This can be represented as a weighted association network, where moral goals are associated with the possible actions via the belief strengths that these actions facilitate the four moral goals.

However, only focusing on balancing principles through rational argumentation may lead to the underexposure of the role of social processes of interpretation and communication [10]. To be able to capture these human moral decision making processes, we integrated the moral reasoning system of Pontier and Hoorn [12] with Silicon Coppélia [8], a computational model of emotional intelligence that is capable of affective decision making. During the process, the agent retrieves beliefs about actions that facilitate or inhibit the desired or undesired goal-states. This is to calculate an *ExpectedUtility* [0, 1] of each action. Actions that facilitate desired goals or inhibit undesired goals will have a high ExpectedUtility [8]. In an affective decision-making module, affective and rational influences are combined in the decision-making process. By combining moral reasoning and affective decision making into Moral Coppélia, human moral decision making processes could be simulated that could not be simulated using the moral reasoning system alone [15].

In the previous affective decision making module in Moral Coppélia, emotions were only implicitly regulated, by picking actions that lead to desired goals. To be able to account for *Negative State Affect* in Moral Coppélia, we added *ExpectedEmotionalStateAffect* (EESA) [0, 1] to the affective moral decision making module. Here, a high EESA indicates that an action is expected to improve the emotional state of the agent, whereas a low EESA indicates that an action is expected to worsen the emotional state. Hereby, we more explicitly add the emotion regulation strategy *situation selection* of Gross' model of emotion regulation [4] to the system.

For calculating the EESA, we added *ActionEmotionBeliefs* (AEB) [0, 1] to the system. An AEB(action, emotion) represents the belief that an action will lead to a certain level of emotion. For example, an AEB(shoplifting, excitement) of 0.6 represents the belief that shoplifting will lead to a level of excitement of 0.6. The ExpectedEmotion (EE) [0, 1] is calculated using formula 2:

$$\text{EE(action, emotion)} = (1-\beta) * \text{AEB(action, emotion)} + \beta * \text{current\_emotion} \qquad (2)$$

In this formula, the persistency factor β is the proportion of emotion that is taken into account to determine the EE. The new contribution to the emotion response level is determined by taking the appropriate AEB.

To determine the EESA of an action, a weighed sum of the discrepancy between desired emotions and expected emotions after performing the action is subtracted from 1. For simplification, the weights $w(i)$ were set to the same level for all emotions added to the system:

$$EESA(action) = 1 - (\sum_{n}^{0} W(i) * (Desired(emotion(i)) - EE(action, i))) \qquad (3)$$

To determine the *ExpectedSatisfaction* [0, 1] of a criminal choice, a weighed sum is taken of the Morality, the rational ExpectedUtility and the emotional EESA of the action:

ExpectedSatisfaction(action) =
W_{mor} *   Morality(action) +
W_{rat} * ExpectedUtility(action) +
W_{emo} · ExpectedEmotionalStateAffect(action)   (4)

3   Matching the Data to the Model

153 undergraduate psychology and educational science students from a university in the Netherlands were approached by email to participate in a short scientific study about dilemmas. Two scenarios were used to measure the mediating and outcome variables. Both scenarios described illegal behavior that can be classified as common, minor crime, i.e., illegal downloading and insurance fraud. Both scenarios were followed by a set of items measuring anticipated sanction probability and severity, negative affect, and criminal choice. For more information about the scenarios and the procedure, see [20].

For matching the data to the model, we transformed all obtained data to the domain [0, 1]. Subsequently, we populated a virtual environment with agents that estimated the probability of making a criminal choice. Each agent was coupled to a participant. The goals inserted into the system were 'profit from a criminal choice' and 'not getting caught'. The emotions inserted into the system were 'hope', 'fear', 'joy' and 'sadness'. For each agent, the rational beliefs about actions relating to goals were set to a level so that the ExpectedUtility of an action matched the Perceived Risk of the participant. Additionally, the beliefs about actions relating to emotions were set to a level that the EESA of the criminal choice matched the Negative State Affect. The weight of the morality in the decision-making process was set proportional to the level of the trait 'Honesty-Humility' in the participant. To divide the remaining weight for calculating the expected satisfaction of a criminal choice, the rational and emotional influence were each assigned a part of the remaining weight, where we made sure that $part_{rat} + part_{emo} = 1$. In formula 5 and 6, w_{rat_opt} and w_{emo_opt} represent the optimal weights found with parameter tuning for the rational and affective influences in the decision making process.

$$W_{rat} = (1 - W_{mor}) + part_{rat} * W_{rat\_opt} \quad (5) \qquad W_{emo} = (1 - W_{mor}) + part_{emo} * W_{emo\_opt} \quad (6)$$

With the found weights, we tested the predictions for the holdout sample (i.e., the remaining half of the participants) using seven different versions of the model: the full model and constrained versions of the model, in which one or two of the three influences in the decision making process (i.e., personality, ratio and affect) were removed.

The quality of fit was determined by investigating the discrepancy between the expected satisfaction of the agents (i.e., their prediction of the behavior of their human counterparts) and the likelihood of criminal choice as reported by the participants. The coefficient of determination R^2 [17] was calculated to determine the quality of the fit (the closer to 1 the better). The match was called satisfactory when the quality of fit did not increase anymore for several time steps. If the matching process seemed to be stuck into a local optimum, the parameters were adjusted by intuition to check whether the match could be improved.

4   Results

Table 1 shows the results of the simulation experiments. In experiment 1, we tried to predict the criminal choice of the participants by agents using only the rational expected utility in the decision making process. This resulted in an R^2 of 0.719 for the holdout sample. In experiment 2, only making use of the Expected Emotional State Affect (EESA) of a criminal choice resulted in an R^2 of 0.906 for the holdout sample. In experiment 3, optimally tuning a combination of ratio and affect resulted in a $part_{rat}$ of 0.34 and a $part_{emo}$ of 0.66, leading to an R^2 of 0.9323 for the holdout sample. In experiment 4, using only moral reasoning resulted in an R^2 of 0.9281 for the holdout sample. In experiment 5, an optimally tuned combination of moral reasoning and ratio resulted in an R^2 of 0.9803 for the holdout sample. In experiment 6, an optimally tuned combination of moral reasoning and affect resulted in an R^2 of 0.9778 for the holdout sample. Experiments 5, 6 and 7 found similar values for the morality of the criminal choice (mor_{cc}).

Table 1. Simulation results

	Exp 1	**Exp 2**	**Exp 3**	**Exp 4**	**Exp 5**	**Exp 6**	**Exp 7**
mor_{cc}	0	0	0	0.68	0.42	0.453	0.435
w_{mor}	0	0	0	1.00*hh	0.96*hh	0.97*hh	0.87*hh
$part_{rat}$	1	0	0.34	0	1	0	0.64
$part_{emo}$	0	1	0.66	0	0	1	0.36
R^2 initial	0.7553	0.8792	0.9222	0.9336	0.9871	0.9798	0.9881
R^2 holdout	**0.7192**	**0.9060**	**0.9323**	**0.9281**	**0.9803**	**0.9778**	**0.9821**

The optimal fit was found in experiment 7. Here, we tested the full model, including moral reasoning, ratio and affect in the decision-making process. Parameter tuning led to a $part_{rat}$ of 0.64 and a $part_{emo}$ of 0.36, resulting in an R^2 of for the simulation of the 0.9881. The R^2 for the predictions of the holdout sample was 0.9821.

5   Discussion

We asked the participants to estimate the probability of making a criminal choice in two scenarios, and assessed their perceived risk and the negative state affect with respect to different criminal choices using a scenario design. Additionally, we measured the personality dimension Honesty-Humility of the participants.

We extended a model of affective moral decision making, Moral Coppélia [15], and matched the participants to agents equipped with the model. We applied parameter tuning techniques and found optimal parameter settings to fit the initial sample. Using the obtained parameter settings, we predicted the criminal choice of the participants in the holdout sample. The prediction errors that were found turned out to be fairly low. Thereby we have shown that an extended version of Moral Coppélia can fit empirical data. This can be seen as a form of ecological validation.

Moreover, we compared the prediction errors with those produced by constrained variants of the model where either the moral, rational or affective influences or a combination of these had been removed. The best predictions were produced by the full model, which confirms our hypothesis.

This is an important indication that making a criminal choice is dependent on the participants' personality, rational choice considerations, as well as emotions. This corresponds with recent informal models of criminal decision making [18, 19, 20]. Thereby the current findings strengthen these informal models. We show that the models can be used to reproduce and predict human criminal decision making.

There are many applications in which a combination of moral reasoning, rational choice considerations as well as emotions is useful. In the first place, the model can be used to predict criminal behavior in humans. Additionally, Moral Coppélia can be used to develop intelligent agents for a wide variety of applications, such as (serious) digital games, tutor and advice systems, or coach and therapist systems. Another possible use is in software and/or hardware that interacts with a human and tries to understand this human's cognitive and emotional states and processes and responds in an intelligent manner. The system can combine sensor data as input to project Moral Coppélia in the user to maintain their emotional state. This can enable the system to adapt the type of interaction to the user's needs.

Additionally, there are many applications in which agents should not behave ethically 'perfect' in a rationalist sense. They should be able to distinguish between right and wrong. In a training simulation or serious game, police officers may not always be effective when they 'play it nicely.' Sometimes they have to break the moral rules (e.g., lie or cheat) to achieve a higher goal (e.g., prevent a murder). The need to be context-sensitive and not rigidly follow rational principles is crucial in all human interaction.

Furthermore, Moral Coppélia can be used to develop agents for interactive storytelling. A trend in developing virtual stories is the movement from stories with a fixed, pre-scripted storyline toward emergent narratives; i.e., stories in which only a number of characters and their personalities are fixed, rather than the precise script of the story. In emergent narratives, ideally, all the designer (or writer) has to do is to determine which (types of) characters will occur in the play, although usually it is still needed to roughly prescribe a course of events. To accomplish complex personalities with human-like properties such as emotions and theories of mind, researchers have started to incorporate cognitive models within agents (e.g., [3]). Moral Coppélia can be seen as a next step into this direction. The agent can combine moral reasoning with rationality and emotions to make decisions on its own. The agent can simulate emotions, and regulate them upwards as well as downwards using various emotion regulation strategies.

Agents telling stories are not only useful to make the elderly feel less lonely. Autonomous agents that can affectively make moral decision are also applicable in an entertainment context (e.g., computer games, see [13]). Additionally, the use of autonomous agents also proved to be useful for clinical experts in the treatment of behavior problems, family counseling, and training [11], education [16], or in persuasive contexts (e.g., science and health communication), or clinical therapy [9].

In particular, agents can play a useful role in the interaction between human and computer in a Web context. One of the application areas foreseen is in self-help therapy, in which humans with psychological disorders are supported through applications available on the Internet and virtual communities of persons with similar problems. An agent equipped with Moral Coppélia can respond empathically toward the user. Together with expert knowledge, the agent can use the model to behave emotionally intelligent and give 'the right response at the right moment'.

As is, the moral reasoner with rational and affective components only allows choosing from given decision options in scenarios. In future research, we additionally want to explore what happens if the Caredroid makes use of computational creativity to propose alternatives that include more information than the offered decision options. Finally, we would like to extend autonomy in the moral reasoning system to be able to distinguish positive and negative autonomy [14]

Acknowledgements. This study is part of the SELEMCA project within CRISP (grant number: NWO 646.000.003).

References

1. Athens, L.: Violent encounters, violent engagements, and tiffs. Journal of Contemporary Ethnography 34, 631–678 (2005)
2. Bosse, T., Brenninckmeyer, J., Kalisch, R., Paret, C., Pontier, M.A.: Matching Skin Conductance Data to a Cognitive Model of Reappraisal. In: Proceedings of of the 33th International Annual Conference of the Cognitive Science Society, CogSci 2011, pp. 1888–1893 (2011)
3. Bosse, T., Pontier, M., Siddiqui, G.F., Treur, J.: Incorporating emotion regulation into virtual stories. In: Pelachaud, C., Martin, J.-C., André, E., Chollet, G., Karpouzis, K., Pelé, D. (eds.) IVA 2007. LNCS (LNAI), vol. 4722, pp. 339–347. Springer, Heidelberg (2007)
4. Bosse, T., Pontier, M.A., Treur, J.: A Computational Model based on Gross' Emotion Regulation Theory. Cognitive Systems Research Journal 11, 211–230 (2010)
5. Chaiken, S., Yaacov, T.: Dual-Process Theories in Social Psychology. Guilford Press, New York (1999)
6. De Vries, R.E., Ashton, M.C., Lee, K.: De zes belangrijkste persoonlijkheidsdimensies en de HEXACO Persoonlijkheidsvragenlijst. Gedrag en Organisatie 22, 232–274 (2009)
7. Hoorn, J.F., Pontier, M.A., Siddiqui, G.F.: When the user is instrument to robot goals. In: Proceedings of the Seventh IEEE/WIC/ACM International Conference on Intelligent Agent Technology, IAT 2008, pp. 296–301 (2008)
8. Hoorn, J.F., Pontier, M.A., Siddiqui, G.F.: Coppélius' Concoction: Similarity and Complementarity Among Three Affect-related Agent Models. Cognitive Systems Research Journal, 33–49 (2012)

9. Lee, E., Leets, L.: Persuasive storytelling by hate groups online: examining its effects on adolescents. American Behavioral Scientist 45, 927–957 (2002)
10. Ohnsorge, K., Widdershoven, G.A.M.: Monological versus dialogical consciousness - two epistemological views on the use of theory in clinical ethical practice. Bioethics 25(7), 361–369 (2011)
11. Painter, L.T., Cook, J.W., Silverman, P.S.: The effects of therapeutic storytelling and behavioral parent training on noncompliant behavior in young boys. Child and Family Behavior Therapy 21(2), 47–66 (1999)
12. Pontier, M.A., Hoorn, J.F.: Toward machines that behave ethically better than humans do. In: Miyake, N., Peebles, B., Cooper, R.P. (eds.) Proceedings of of the 34th International Annual Conference of the Cognitive Science Society, CogSci 2012, pp. 2198–2203 (2012)
13. Pontier, M.A., Siddiqui, G.F.: An Affective Agent Playing Tic-Tac-Toe as Part of a Healing Environment. In: Yang, J.-J., Yokoo, M., Ito, T., Jin, Z., Scerri, P. (eds.) PRIMA 2009. LNCS, vol. 5925, pp. 33–47. Springer, Heidelberg (2009)
14. Pontier, M.A., Widdershoven, G.A.M.: Robots that stimulate autonomy. In: Papadopoulos, H., Andreou, A.S., Iliadis, L., Maglogiannis, I. (eds.) AIAI 2013. IFIP AICT, vol. 412, pp. 195–204. Springer, Heidelberg (2013)
15. Pontier, M.A., Widdershoven, G., Hoorn, J.F.: Moral Coppélia - Combining Ratio with Affect in Ethical Reasoning. In: Pavón, J., Duque-Méndez, N.D., Fuentes-Fernández, R. (eds.) IBERAMIA 2012. LNCS, vol. 7637, pp. 442–451. Springer, Heidelberg (2012)
16. Schlosser, R.W., Lloyd, L.L.: Effects of initial element teaching in a story-telling context on Blissymbol acquisition and generalization. J. of Speech and Hearing Research 36, 979–995 (1993)
17. Steel, R.G.D., Torrie, J.H.: Principles and Procedures of Statistics, pp. 187–287. McGraw-Hill, New York (1960)
18. Van Gelder, J.L.: Beyond rational choice: The hot/cool perspective of criminal decision making. Psychology, Crime & Law 19, 745–763 (2013)
19. Van Gelder, J.L., De Vries, R.E.: Traits and states: Integrating personality and affect into a model of criminal decision making. Criminology 50, 637–671 (2012)
20. Van Gelder, J.L., De Vries, R.E.: Rational misbehavior? Evaluating an integrated dual-process model of criminal decision making. Journal of Quantitative Criminology (2012)
21. Van Gelder, J.L., De Vries, R.E., Van der Pligt, J.: Evaluating a dual-process model of risk: affect and cognition as determinants of risky choice. J. Behavioral Decision Making 22, 45–61 (2009)

Context-Aware Mobile Augmented Reality for Library Management

Adrian Shatte, Jason Holdsworth, and Ickjai Lee

School of Business, James Cook University, QLD, Australia

Abstract. Mobile augmented reality applications aim to simplify everyday tasks by providing additional information to increase efficiency. There are many challenges facing the field, including efficient and accurate methods for providing context-awareness. It is believed that research in the field of multi-agent systems can assist such applications in reducing the complexity of everyday tasks. To determine the benefits of using software agents to support mobile augmented reality, we develop a prototype titled Libagent for library management tasks. Our experimental results indicate that Libagent provides benefits to users by reducing errors.

Keywords: Agent programming, Augmented reality, Mobile computing, Library Management, Context-awareness.

1 Introduction

Due to the increased computing power of mobile devices and the high-quality cameras built-in to such devices, a fast growing field is mobile Augmented Reality (AR). The major benefits of portable and ubiquitous devices for AR means that context-aware, visual information can assist users in reducing the complexity of everyday tasks and minimize errors. However, current mobile AR systems lack a robust method for gaining contextual information based on visual data. Researchers in the field of agent programming have long posited that software agents have the potential to solve many programming challenges, including the delivery of personalized content on both a small and large scale [1]. Recent studies have determined that current agent-based frameworks are efficient enough to deliver solutions for these challenges [1].

In this paper, we describe the development of a modern mobile AR prototype that is supported by agents. Our prototype, dubbed Libagent, is designed to be used as a library management system for sorting and searching tasks. We validate the usefulness and effectiveness of Libagent by conducting two experiments, described in Section 4.

2 Preliminaries

2.1 Agent Programming

Agent programming is a software paradigm first proposed in the 1990s that takes concepts from theories in the field of artificial intelligence and applies those

G. Boella et al. (Eds.): PRIMA 2013, LNAI 8291, pp. 510–517, 2013.
© Springer-Verlag Berlin Heidelberg 2013

theories to the field of distributed theories [2]. The definition of the term 'agent' varies throughout the literature, due to the differing importance of certain agent characteristics in different applications (e.g. databases, networking, or robotics). Most researchers view the common thread in agency to be the characteristic of autonomy [3], which is the ability of agents to complete a task without direct input from a human user or other entity.

Jennings and Wooldridge [4] classified three distinct classes of agent: *gopher*, *service performing*, and *predictive*. Gopher agents are simple and execute straight-forward tasks according to pre-specified rules and assumptions. Service performing agents act in a goal-oriented manner to fulfil well-defined requests from users. Finally, predictive agents are more complex and, based on their own decision making, aim to provide information or services to users at an appropriate time. The prototype presented in this paper utilizes agents that could be classified as being gopher agents and service performing agents. These agents are described in Section 3.

2.2   Agent-Based Mobile AR

AR is defined by the enhancement or diminishment of a live, real-world image with virtual content [5]. This real-world image is viewed through a camera and displayed or projected onto an interface (e.g. mobile device screen) with the virtual imagery overlayed on top. The characteristics of agents make them ideal candidates for providing context-awareness in mobile AR applications. Recently, research has started to explore the use of agent programming to assist in adaptability and context-awareness for computing systems [6]. One potential advantage of using agents for context-awareness is that they can reduce the complexity of human tasks that require the use of short-term memory. The average person's short-term memory has the capacity to hold five to seven items for around fifteen to thirty seconds [7]. This has great implications for sorting and searching tasks in environments with a large search space like a library.

Two examples of agent augmented reality applications with context-awareness are presented in [8]. While this research provides evidence for the benefits of combining AR technology with software agents, there is no focus on error reduction. Additionally, the AR technology used in these studies is now outdated, so it is important to reconsider this research using modern mobile devices.

3   Development of Libagent

3.1   Framework

The proposed framework, Libagent, consists of an AR application with an agent-based backend. Libagent runs on a mobile device and utilizes the hardware camera to detect and recognise 2D markers attached to book spines. Using the metadata gained from these markers, the systems embedded agents can query a remote database for additional content. In our prototype, the remote database

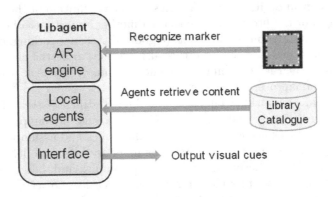

Fig. 1. Libagent framework

is a library catalogue, allowing the application to gain information such as book location, call number, or similar titles. Figure 1 displays the structure of the framework:

Libagent is split into three main functions: sorting, searching, and context-based shelf information. The sorting feature can recognize the markers attached to each book and display visual cues (a tick or a cross) to indicate whether there are currently errors on that shelf. The search feature allows a user to query the local library catalogue and select a desired result. Libagent then highlights that marker on the shelf and greys out all other markers to allow for easy location at a glance. The context-based shelf information can recognize whether books are missing from the shelf or detect which books are currently on loan from a given subset of books on a shelf. This information is displayed as a list to the user.

3.2   Development Tools

The implementation of Libagent utilized three main software packages for development: Vuforia (for augmented reality), JADE [Java Agent Development Framework] (for agent programming), and Blender (for 3D modelling). This selection of software packages was chosen based on simplicity, open source, and interoperability. This section of the paper will justify our choice of JADE for agent programming. JADE [1], developed by Telecom Italia, is a software framework that aims to simplify the implementation of multi-agent systems. The software libraries provided with JADE are written in the Java programming language. For this reason, we decided to build the Libagent prototype on the Android platform (which is also heavily Java-based), with JADE handling the agent-based features. Library catalogues are usually stored on local servers within a library, so in this situation the central computer-based nature of JADE is an advantage.

---

[1] http://jade.tilab.com/

3.3 Agents in Libagent

For the current prototype, three agents are deployed. These agents are described in Table 1.

Table 1. Agents used in our prototype

Agent Title	Description
BookDBAgent	Responsible for querying a database that contains a catalogue of books mapped to AR markers. Assists other agents to determine the context of a shelf.
ShelfStateCheckerAgent	Responsible for providing information about the current state of the shelf being viewed through the camera. Collaborates with BookDBAgent to relay information about the ID numbers of currently visible markers and determines number of books on loan, number of books missing, and metadata for those books.
RecommendationsAgent	Responsible for providing recommendations about similar books to the user based on search terms.

3.4 Algorithms

Based on the major Libagent features described in Section 3.1, the following algorithms were generated. Note that these algorithms are performed autonomously (based on the input data) by the software agents described in Section 3.3.

Book Sorting. The fact that each frame marker has a unique ID can be exploited for the purposes of sorting. Vuforia does not provide this functionality, so we developed the following method. Assuming that the position of the camera represents a fixed horizontal reference point of zero, then a frame marker that is located directly in line with the camera will also have a horizontal coordinate of zero. Conversely, a marker positioned to the left or right of centre will respectively have a negative or positive x-coordinate. Using simple Java sorting methods, Libagent can compare these coordinates against marker IDs (mapped to books in the catalogue) to provide sorting cues to the user (Figure 2).

Context-Sensitive Information. Utilizing the same information that the sorting algorithm obtains, the software agents can determine context-sensitive information about missing books and books on loan. The first step of this process is to query the library catalogue to determine shelf location, based on the currently visible minimum marker and the currently visible maximum marker (in terms of ID value). The agents download this data and compare the results with the visible markers. Books on loan are determined easily as this metadata is already part of the library catalogue (i.e. checked in *vs.* checked out). On the

Fig. 2. Libagent sorting process (left: the tick-cross output visual cue mode; middle and right: the number output visual cue mode)

other hand, missing books are determined by comparing the remaining book IDs to the currently visible IDs. For this system to work, Libagent ensures that the shelf is sorted first.

Searching for Books. The search algorithm utilizes the same data as the context-sensitive information. Based on the search terms, a remote library catalogue is queried (using a simple MySQL-based web service). The results of the search are displayed to the user in a list on the screen. Once the user selects the desired result, the AR component of the application resets all of its textures, setting a yellow exclamation mark for the desired book and graying out all other textures.

4   Experimental Results

4.1   Hardware

The device used for testing in the studies was a Samsung Galaxy Nexus smartphone running Android 4.1.2. This device was selected for its larger screen size and memory capacity, which are beneficial for AR. The device has the following relevant specifications: a display of 4.65" HD (1280 × 720), memory of 1GB RAM, OS of 1.2GHz dual core processor, a camera of 5MP continuous auto focus, LED flash and zero shutter lag, and sensors of accelerometer, gyro, compass, and proximity/light.

4.2   Correctness of Context-Aware Agents

The first study involves testing the correctness of the ShelfStateCheckerAgent, which works in collaboration with the BookDBAgent. Recall that these agents are used within the system to determine the contextual state of the shelf (or any given subsection of the shelf) in terms of missing books and books on loan. Various combinations of books are presented to the application (starting with no missing books), and gradually books are removed from the shelf. The number of missing books that Libagent calculated is recorded and compared to the real number of missing books (known by the experimenter). Initially, the shelf started with 30 total books, and the agents are tested for correctness over four scenarios.

The difficulty of these scenarios (in terms of real world applicability) varied from simple (common situation) to extreme (rare situation). The results of this study are presented in Table 2. In all four conditions, the application provides the correct information about missing books, which demonstrates the robustness of Libagent. No false positives and false negatives are identified with Libagent, and 100% reall and precision are recorded.

Table 2. Libagent's performance on missing books

Condition	Results
Simple (one book missing)	0 book loaned, 1 book missing
Intermediate (five books missing)	0 book loaned, 5 books missing
Difficult (ten books missing)	0 book loaned, 10 books missing
Extreme (twenty books missing)	0 book loaned, 20 books missing

Based on the results of our experiments, it is clear that there are benefits of using agents to support an AR library management application. The first study concluded that our agent-based AR system for library management is accurate at providing context-sensitive information about the state of a shelf. This information reveals very quickly (< 1 second) the number of books missing or on loan from the current shelf space, and also provides the metadata for these items. This information can be highly valuable to both library users and librarians alike.

While experienced library staff may have an increased ability to recognize a missing item, such skills require an intimate knowledge of the catalogue and the numbering system. The majority of library users will not have this knowledge, and will benefit from the speed of recognition provided by Libagent. Additionally, librarians (and all humans) are limited in terms of short-term memory capacity, which means that Libagent will be faster in scenarios that involve a large number of missing items (e.g. the difficult and extreme conditions in our experiment). For this reason, we can conclude that the agents can assist in overcoming cognitive limitations in library-based tasks.

4.3 Libagent *vs.* JCU Tropicat

The second study aimed to determine the effectiveness of an agent-based AR system at improving efficiency and reducing errors in library-based tasks. Libagent is compared to a current library system (JCU Tropicat, a computer-based system installed at James Cook University library). Tropicat allows users to search keywords to retrieve a listing of relevant books from the catalogue in Dewey decimal format (e.g. 139 RAN).

Twenty-one participants were sampled from JCUs student population in Townsville, North Queensland. Participants' ages range from eighteen to sixty, with frequency of library usage ranging from rare to frequent. In order to control extraneous variables, a replica of a subsection of the JCU library catalogue was created using thirty markers. Additionally, a local database of books was created for Libagent to use. The information in this database includes book title, author, catalogue number, and marker ID. Participants were provided with a demonstration of each system (Libagent and Tropicat) and then asked to complete tasks using each system. The first task is a *seek and sort* task, whereby a random book is placed in the incorrect position. In the Tropicat condition, participants are required to find the erroneous book and place it back in the correct position using only the call numbers on the spine. In the Libagent condition, participants are required to seek out the erroneous book using AR, and then sort it back to the correct position using recommendations provided by Libagent. Randomization was used to account for differences in cognitive ability.

The second task is a *search* task, whereby a participant is required to search for and locate different books on the shelf. In the Tropicat condition, participants are required to find the target book by first searching the JCU Tropicat system to find the call number, and then search the shelf for that call number. In the Libagent condition, participants are asked to search for a book using the application's search interface and then seek it through the viewfinder of the phone. The target book is randomized per condition, and the order of conditions is also randomized per participant. Each condition is repeated twice per participant. Table 3 shows the means and standard deviations for the sorting and searching tasks. Note that two outliers are removed from the sorting task and one outlier is removed from the search task to meet the normality assumption. A repeated

Table 3. Means and StDevs for the sorting/searching tasks

Task	Mean (seconds)	StDev
Sorting (Tropicat)	34.20	9.55
Sorting (Libagent)	36.34	10.56
Searching (Tropicat)	30.84	11.31
Searching (Libagent)	31.19	10.59

measures t-test for the sorting task found no significant difference between the mean time taken to complete the sorting task with Libagent and without it ($t_{18} = -.629$, $p = .537$) with 95% of confidence. Similarly, no significant difference is found between the mean time taken to complete the searching task with Libagent and without it ($t_{19} = -.105$, $p = .917$) with 95% of confidence. Other noteworthy findings from this study were that the application provided accurate and correct results in both the sorting and searching tasks (no false positives and false negatives). While some participants made mistakes during the Tropicat sorting task (which took additional time to recover from), no mistakes were recorded during the Libagent sorting condition.

Discussions. While our second study did not provide evidence for our system being more efficient than traditional methods, there are some methodological concerns that may have contributed. First, the participants of the experiment may not have had enough time to become proficient with Libagent. In contrast, many users will have searched for a book using traditional methods, so this task may have been faster in the circumstances. While an agent-based AR system may not save time for users in sorting and searching tasks (according to our results), there are still great benefits for the system to reduce errors. The sorting task completed by the participants in this experiment reported accurate results.

5   Final Remarks

The current study aimed to investigate the benefits of software agents for improving efficiency and reducing errors in a mobile AR library management system. We designed and developed a prototype, Libagent, to assist users when completing basic library-based tasks such as searching and sorting. Our final prototype is able to assist with difficult sorting tasks, search for books, as well as provide context-specific information about missing books and books on loan. While users do not appear to benefit from the agents in terms of efficiency, Libagent is able to provide correct results all of the time a better result than humans performing the tasks alone. Overall, the outcomes of the research presented in this paper are promising for the future collaboration of AR and agents. However, further research is to determine the applicability of our system in a real-world library. Additionally, future research could focus on including a greater number of agents in the system to further minimize errors by reducing the cognitive load on a user.

References

1. Chmiel, K., Gawinecki, M., Kaczmarek, P., Szymczak, M., Paprzycki, M.: Efficiency of jade agent platform. Scientific Programming 13(2), 159–172 (2005)
2. Fabio, B., Giovanni, C., Dominic, G., et al.: Developing multi-Agent systems with JADE. Wiley (2007)
3. Keeble, R.J., Macredie, R.D.: Software agents and issues in personalisation: Technology to accommodate individual users. Personal Technologies 2(3), 131–140 (1998)
4. Jennings, N., Wooldridge, M.: Software agents. IEE Review 42(1), 17–20 (1996)
5. Zhou, F., Duh, H., Billinghurst, M.: Trends in augmented reality tracking, interaction and display: A review of ten years of ismar. In: 7th IEEE/ACM International Symposium on Mixed and Augmented Reality, ISMAR 2008, pp. 193–202. IEEE (2008)
6. Zaslavsky, A.: Mobile agents: can they assist with context awareness? In: Proceedings of the 2004 IEEE International Conference on Mobile Data Management, pp. 304–305. IEEE (2004)
7. Miller, G.: The magical number seven, plus or minus two: Some limits on our capacity for processing information. The psychological review 63, 81–97 (1956)
8. Nagao, K.: Agent augmented reality: Agents integrate the real world with cyberspace. In: Ishida, T. (ed.) Community Computing: Collaboration over Global Information Networks. John Wiley & Sons (1998)

Using Agent Technology for Ambient Assisted Living

Nikolaos I. Spanoudakis[1] and Pavlos Moraitis[2]

[1] Applied Mathematics and Computers Laboratory, Technical University of Crete, Greece
nispanoudakis@isc.tuc.gr
[2] Laboratory of Informatics Paris Descartes (LIPADE), Paris Descartes University, France
pavlos@mi.parisdescartes.fr

Abstract. The goal of this paper is to provide some arguments in favor of the use of agent technology in real word applications. It does so through the, as much as possible, detailed description of a multi-agent system in the context of a real world application in the domain of ambient assisted living. It discusses development issues involving the use of the platform JADE and integrating computational argumentation and web services. It also gives some feedback concerning the experience of engineering such systems, especially when integrated in a more complex system with other components, but also concerning the perception of real users when using the system in an everyday life context.

Keywords: Multi-Agent Systems, Ambient Assisted Living, Argumentation, Alzheimer disease.

1 Introduction

This paper aims to present an agent-based architecture for addressing the non-trivial task [12] of engineering an Ambient Assisted Living (AAL) information system. AAL is about creating products and services that provide unobtrusive support for daily life based on context and the situation of the assisted person. It is currently one of the most important and well-funded research and development areas. The reason is the increasing average age of the total population, especially in the developed countries, that augments costs for the public, but also for individuals, for the care for the elderly people at home. As a consequence, the quality of life reduces for those people as their social skills diminish [8, 12].

The HERA project [24], co-funded by the AAL Joint Programme [17], built an AAL system to provide cost-effective specialized assisted living services for the elderly people suffering from Mild Cognitive Impairment (MCI), mild/moderate Alzheimer's Disease (AD), or other diseases (diabetes, cardiovascular) with identified risk factors, aiming to significantly improve the quality of their home life and extend its duration. HERA provided to its end users the following main categories of services:

- *Cognitive Exercises*, the end users play cognitive reinforcement games
- *Passive communication*, the end user can select (or receive a pro-active suggestion) to watch informative videos and news items related to his/her disease

G. Boella et al. (Eds.): PRIMA 2013, LNAI 8291, pp. 518–525, 2013.
© Springer-Verlag Berlin Heidelberg 2013

- *Pill and Exercise reminders*
- *Reality orientation*, e.g. date and time are visible on screen
- *Blood pressure and weight monitoring*

Previous works in this area [3, 5] introduced agent based systems for AmI for assisting in taking care of people with Alzheimer but on one hand they required the aid of a nurse or caregiver and on the other hand they used RFID tags [5] or NFC technology [3]. Both technologies are used to identify the location of the user using radio frequency identification technologies that require the use of sensors in different places at home and the use of another sensor on the user's body for identifying his location. Another application for medicine usage management using agent technology which might concern different health problems is the one proposed by Hoogendoorn et al. [6]. This application explores and analyses possibilities to use automated devices such as an automated medicine box, servers and cell phones as non-human agents, in addition to human agents such as the patient and a supervisor doctor. What is missing from such systems and which we had to address in HERA is to increase the autonomy of the user, to automate the ambient assistance (without requiring the use of managers, caregivers or nurses), to act unobtrusively and to minimize the use of hardware, aiming to a commercial solution to home care for people suffering from dementia and having cognitive problems.

The HERA overall system service oriented architecture and evaluation process is presented in [13]. Briefly, to address the above challenges we used a combined agent- and service-oriented approach. For the agents decision making we chose argumentation [1], as it allows for decision making using conflicting knowledge, thus different experts can express their opinion that can be conflicting. Argumentation has been used successfully in the last years in similar situations, e.g. for deliberating over the needs of a user with a combination of impairments in an AmI application [11], or for group decision making in a more general setting in ambient intelligence environments [10]. The latter proposes a multi-agent (simulator) argumentation based system whose aim is to simulate group decision making processes. The use of the TV set and remote control for Human-Machine Interaction allowed for a quick learning curve for our users. We used a service oriented architecture based on web services that allowed the different sub-systems to be connected in a plug and play standardized way.

In this paper we focus in presenting the intelligent part of the HERA system, which is a multi-agent system. We aim to show that agent technology is useful for modeling real world AAL systems through presenting and discussing the architecture and use of technology for HERA.

2 System Architecture

The MAS is a module in the overall HERA system architecture [13] that interacts with the Human-Machine Interface (HMI) and the back-office. It participates in a service oriented architecture where every module can offer services over the web. The

MAS module is responsible for learning the user's habits, personalizing services such as the pill reminder and the passive communication, and for reminding him to do his daily tasks. These needs were identified during the requirements analysis phase [16].

The MAS module was developed using the Agent Systems Engineering Methodology (ASEME [14]), an Agent Oriented Software Engineering (AOSE) methodology. ASEME supports a modular agent design approach and introduces the concepts of intra- and inter-agent control. The first defines the agent's behavior by coordinating the different modules that implement his capabilities, while the latter defines the protocols that govern the coordination of the society of the agents. ASEME uses the Agent Modeling Language (AMOLA), which provides the syntax and semantics for creating models of multi-agent systems covering the analysis and design phases of a software development process. ASEME, uniquely among other AOSE methodologies, a) caters for the integration of the inter-agent control model to the intra-agent control model, and b) provides a set of graphical and transformation tools that not only allow for getting from requirements down to implementation but also initialize each new phase model based on the existing information in previous phases models (for a detailed discussion the reader can consult [14]). The analysis and development process for HERA using ASEME is presented in [9].

During the analysis phase, we defined an architecture for the MAS module using Interface and Personal Assistant agent types [15]. The *Interface* (INT) agent is used for connecting with other modules. Thus, the interface agent is the only one exposing the MAS services to the other modules. This agent gets all requests for service and delegates them to the interested personal assistant agent.

The *Personal Assistant* (PA) agent is the most complex role and it serves a registered user, stores and manages his/her profile and personal data and uses the requests' history in order to adapt the services to his/her habitual patterns. A different PA agent is active for each user. The PA is persistent and retains a schedule for the user's tasks. These tasks are assigned by the doctors that monitor the specific user, using the services' back-office system. The following tasks are achieved by the PA:

- When the user's scheduled time for taking pills arrives the PA reasons on the quantity to be taken. The doctors are able to assign specific conditions when assigning pills to a patient. For example, if the blood pressure exceeds a limit then he has to take two pills (while normally he is assigned one pill)
- The agent learns the user's preferred time for the same type of activity (e.g. cognitive training). The algorithm searches for a pattern in recent acts, thus:
  - If the user did the same activity at the same time (differing by a few minutes) for this day of the week on the last two weeks then the agent proposes this time.
  - Else if the user did the same activity at the same hour on the last two days, then the agent proposes this time
- When an item is inserted or is rescheduled the agent reasons on the priority of possibly conflicting tasks. Specifically, when the user has been assigned more than one tasks for the same time (e.g. by different caregivers) or he has specific preferences (e.g. to watch a TV series at a particular time of day) the following priorities will hold:

- Priority no1: take the assigned pills
- Priority no2: watch his favorite TV series
- Priority no3: engage with the cognitive reinforcement exercises
- Priority no4: engage with the physical reinforcement exercises
• Once a week the agent selects a piece of information (video) to propose to the user.

For developing the MAS module, we chose the Java Agent Development Framework (JADE), as it is the most popular agent platform [2] that complies with the FIPA [18] standards, and as the adoption of ASEME allows for semi-automatic code generation.

For the agents decision making we chose argumentation as it is very well suited for implementing decision making mechanisms dealing with the dynamic nature of possibly conflicting actions due to different situations or contexts. The framework we used [7] is based on object level arguments representing the decision policies and then it uses priority arguments expressing preferences on the object level arguments in order to resolve possible conflicts. Subsequently, additional priority arguments can be used in order to resolve potential conflicts between priority arguments of the previous level. This framework has been applied in a successful way in different applications (see e.g. [11]) involving similar scenarios of decision making and it is supported by the Prolog-based Gorgias open source software [19]. The different components participating in the HERA MAS server are identified in the architecture diagram presented in Figure 1. All the agents communicate using FIPA Agent Communication Language (ACL)-based communication protocols and messages.

For exposing interfaces of services offered by the MAS, we used the Web Service Integration Gateway (WSIG) JADE add-on, which provides support for invocation of JADE agent services from Web service clients. The WSIG servlet exposes the web services and the WSIG agent transforms them to ACL messages using the MAS ontology and sends them to the interface agent. The latter decides if he needs to create a new personal assistant or to forward the request to one of the existing personal assistants.

For defining the interfaces of the MAS module with the other modules and also the inter-agent messages we defined an ontology (i.e. a list of concepts). The ontology was developed using the bean generator add-on of the Protégé open source ontology editor [22]. The process involves the generation of a suitable WSDL (Web Services Definition Language) file for each service-description registered with the Directory Facilitator (DF) agent.

Regarding security, the MAS module uses only the user's username in all transactions. Thus, the MAS module is never aware of the user identification data other than those of the username. Security in communication is achieved through the use of secure layer protocols (e.g. HTTPS) and through allowing only the HERA back-office to access the web services through the firewall.

The JADE Persistence add-on allows for saving the state of agents (recover user profiles and learned data in the case that the system crashes), using the HSQL relational database. Hibernate [20] was used for automating the transformation of the agents' data structures to relational database tables.

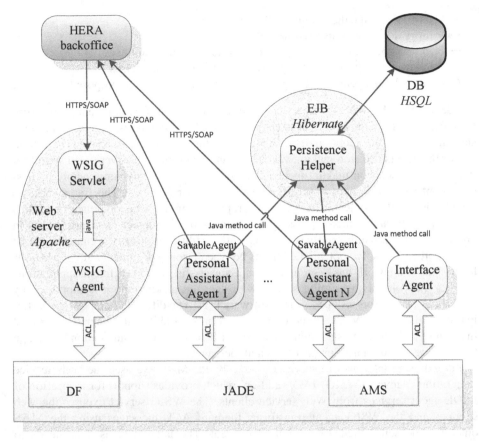

Fig. 1. HERA MAS Architecture

3   Validation and Evaluation

For validating the MAS server functionality, we defined specific scenarios of tests in four levels. Firstly, we validated the learning algorithms and the Prolog rule base against test data. Then, in a second level, we tested the individual agent types for their conformance in the defined protocols and tested their algorithms again using specific ACL messages. In the third level we tested the functionality of the MAS using a web services client to send specific service requests. Finally, after integrating all the HERA components in the application platform, we tested complete predefined usage scenarios using the HMI. Then the system was evaluated by the end users with the objective to assess (with metrics) the added value of HERA. The Process of Evaluation of Software Products [4] has been used for evaluating the HERA services.

The HERA services related to the MAS module were put under trial in Greece. The pilot operation took place at the Hygeia hospital [21]. We focused in two categories of users: the end-users (who use the HERA services), and the Medical Personnel (who configure the HERA services and assess the end users' progress). A total of 30 end-users (10 healthy elderly, 8 suffering from MCI, 8 from mild AD, and 4 from moderate AD) were selected to participate in the project trials phase, along with 10 medical experts. The equipment installed included a set-top-box (small PC), a TV-set and a remote control. Both end users and medical experts were trained at the hospital. Then they completed questionnaires. That was the end of the first phase.

For the second phase two helpdesks were setup. The main one was the 24/7 help-desk at Hygeia hospital, which was equipped with trouble shooting steps to be fol-lowed at each kind of problem. If the problem was not resolved, then it was forwarded to the Singular Logic [23] helpdesk either through email or voice mail. Then, the equipment was installed to the end-users' homes. They were also equipped with a 3G internet providing stick if the end-users did not have an ADSL connection. The HERA equipment stayed at the user's home for a minimum period of 15 days. Final-ly, the MAS module was connected to the HERA system for adapting the service to each user's habits and needs. An Hygeia representative from the memory clinic vi-sited the user to get him/her to fill the questionnaire. As soon as a doctor's users all finished their trial usage, the doctor also filled in the questionnaire. The evaluation criteria reflected the way of achieving the objectives. They were the following:

- Performance (C1), measures the capability of the system to produce valid and ac-curate results.
- Usability (C2), measures the satisfaction of the user with regard to his experience in using the system and the ease of achieving his tasks.
- Flexibility (C3), refers to the ease of troubleshooting and of moving from one ser-vice to another.
- Security and Trust (C4), refers to the user perception of whether sensitive data are securely handled and remain confidential, also to whether the user trusts the system when it proposes a course of action.

Figure 2 compares the system's performance during the second trial phase to its performance during the first phase for the end-users group. In the first phase, the end users saw a substantial performance gap in the Performance criterion. This is reasonable considering that, during the trials at the hospital the bandwidth was very low resulting in problems with viewing videos. Usability and Security and Trust criteria performance is considered satisfactory (both over 80%). However, the users showed skepticism on whether they are able to use this system at home (see the performance of the C3-Flexibility criterion). This was mainly due to the fact that the level of cognitive impairment directly affects the end users' views on their ability to use HERA at home: the wider the extent of cognitive impairment, the lower the perceived ability to use the system without assistance. Additionally, the vast majority of the end users (as most Greek elderly) were technologically illiterate and exhibited fear, doubt and uncertainty when asked to use technology-based services, even if, in the case of HERA, they were offered through a regular TV set, which they were familiar with.

Looking at the phase two bars, the reader can notice the substantial improvement in the Performance criterion. One of the reasons was the software agents that assisted the users as in the first phase there was no learning or personalization. The usage of the 3G USB sticks and the ADSL broadband connections helped in remedying the low bandwidth situation at the hospital. Furthermore, the original skepticism that the users showed on whether they will be able to use this system at home (see the performance of the Flexibility criterion) was finally dispersed. We believe that the use of the familiar remote control along with the setup of the help center in the Hygeia hospital helped substantially, since the end users at home did not need to talk to technicians if they had a problem, but a person from the hospital.

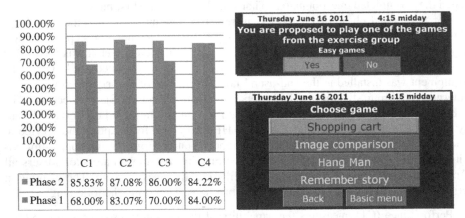

Fig. 2. The 1st and 2nd trial phases system performance (end users) on the left side, and two screenshots of the system in use on the right side: a) the user is reminded to play cognitive games (top), and, b) the user selects one game to play (bottom)

4   Discussion and Conclusion

Our goal in this paper was to provide the reader with information on how to engineer a real-world agent-based system and integrate it to a more general Service-oriented Architecture (in this case using the web services paradigm). We showed how to combine the WSIG and Persistence add-ons of JADE in an architecture with the interface and personal assistant agent types.

We also provided some state of the art information on agent-based systems for the ambient assisted living (AAL) domain. Related to that, in HERA we managed to increase the autonomy of the user, to automate the ambient assistance (without requiring the use of managers, caregivers or nurses), to act unobtrusively and to minimize the use of hardware, achieving a commercial solution for home care for people suffering from dementia and having cognitive problems.

We believe that the presented information can be exploited in a wider range of application domains as the agent types that we used are widely used and have been proposed as generic agent types by the agent technology community.

References

1. Bench-Capon, T.J.M., Dunne, P.E.: Argumentation in artificial intelligence. Artificial Intelligence 171(10-15), 619–641 (2007)
2. Bordini, R.H., et al.: A Survey of Programming Languages and Platforms for Multi-Agent Systems. Informatica 30, 33–44 (2006)
3. Bravo, J., López-de-Ipiña, D., Fuentes, C., Hervás, R., Peña, R., Vergara, M., Casero, G.: Enabling NFC Technology for Supporting Chronic Diseases: A Proposal for Alzheimer Caregivers. In: Aarts, E., Crowley, J.L., de Ruyter, B., Gerhäuser, H., Pflaum, A., Schmidt, J., Wichert, R., et al. (eds.) AmI 2008. LNCS, vol. 5355, pp. 109–125. Springer, Heidelberg (2008)

4. Colombo, R., Guerra, A.: The Evaluation Method for Software Product. In: Proceedings of the 15th International Conference on Software & Systems Engineering & Applications, Paris (2002)
5. Corchado, J., et al.: Intelligent environment for monitoring Alzheimer patients, agent technology for health care. Decision Support Systems 44(2), 382–396 (2008)
6. Hoogendoorn, M., Klein, M.C.A., Treur, J.: Formal Design and Simulation of an Ambient Multi-agent System Model for Medicine Usage Management. In: Mühlhäuser, M., Ferscha, A., Aitenbichler, E. (eds.) AmI 2007 Workshops. CCIS, vol. 17, pp. 207–217. Springer, Heidelberg (2008)
7. Kakas, A., Moraitis, P.: Argumentation based decision making for autonomous agents. In: Proceedings of the second International Joint Conference on Autonomous Agents and Multi-Agent Systems (AAMAS 2003), pp. 883–890. ACM Press, New York (2003)
8. Kleinberger, T., Becker, M., Ras, E., Holzinger, A., Müller, P.: Ambient Intelligence in Assisted Living: Enable Elderly People to Handle Future Interfaces. In: Stephanidis, C. (ed.) UAHCI 2007 (Part II). LNCS, vol. 4555, pp. 103–112. Springer, Heidelberg (2007)
9. Marcais, J., Spanoudakis, N., Moraitis, P.: Using Argumentation for Ambient Assisted Living. In: Iliadis, L., Maglogiannis, I., Papadopoulos, H., et al. (eds.) EANN/AIAI 2011, Part II. IFIP Advances in Information and Communication Technology, vol. 364, pp. 410–419. Springer, Heidelberg (2011)
10. Marreiros, G., Santos, R., Novais, P., Machado, J., Ramos, C., Neves, J., Bula-Cruz, J.: Argumentation-Based Decision Making in Ambient Intelligence Environments. In: Neves, J., Santos, M.F., Machado, J.M., et al. (eds.) EPIA 2007. LNCS (LNAI), vol. 4874, pp. 309–322. Springer, Heidelberg (2007)
11. Moraitis, P., Spanoudakis, N.: Argumentation-Based Agent Interaction in an Ambient-Intelligence Context. IEEE Intelligent Systems 22(6), 84–93 (2007)
12. Nehmer, J., et al.: Living assistance systems: an ambient intelligence approach. In: Proceedings of the 28th International Conference on Software Engineering, Shanghai, China, pp. 43–50 (2006)
13. Spanoudakis, N., et al.: A novel architecture and process for Ambient Assisted Living - the HERA approach. In: Proceedings of the 10th IEEE International Conference on Information Technology and Applications in Biomedicine. IEEE (2010)
14. Spanoudakis, N., Moraitis, P.: Using ASEME Methodology for Model-Driven Agent Systems Development. In: Weyns, D., Gleizes, M.-P. (eds.) AOSE 2010. LNCS, vol. 6788, pp. 106–127. Springer, Heidelberg (2011)
15. Sycara, K., Zeng, D.: Coordination of Multiple Intelligent Software Agents. International Journal of Cooperative Information Systems 5(2-3), 181–211 (1996)
16. The HERA Consortium: Project Deliverable D2.1: State-of-the-art and Requirements Analysis (2010), http://w3.mi.parisdescartes.fr/hera
17. Ambient Assisted Living Joint Programme, http://www.aal-europe.eu
18. Foundation for Intelligent Physical Agents (FIPA), http://www.fipa.org
19. Gorgias general argumentation framework, http://www.cs.ucy.ac.cy/~nkd/gorgias
20. Hibernate Object/Relational persistence and query service, http://www.hibernate.org
21. Hygeia hospital, http://www.hygeia.gr
22. OntologyBeanGenerator,
    http://protegewiki.stanford.edu/wiki/OntologyBeanGenerator
23. SingularLogic Software and Integrated IT Solutions Group,
    http://www.singularlogic.eu
24. The HERA project (AAL-2008-1-079), http://w3.mi.parisdescartes.fr/hera

A Framework
for Analyzing Simultaneous Negotiations

Yoshinori Tsuruhashi and Naoki Fukuta

Graduate School of Informatics, Shizuoka University, Japan
{gs12027@s,fukuta@cs}.inf.shizuoka.ac.jp

Abstract. Automated negotiation among agents is a technology that
can find out an agreement point without fully revealing their utility
spaces. In multi-agent negotiation scenarios, an agent can use various
forms of a negotiation. When there is a change in an agent's utility
space, there could be various patterns of generating a counter offer in
a negotiation. When an agent changed his behavior, there could be a
case that an agent only obtains lower utility while another negotiation
had a chance to have higher utility. To consider the above situation, we
need to see and reproduce negotiations among multiple agents. This paper presents a framework for analyzing simultaneous negotiations among
agents, including dynamic utility space changes and corresponding strategy changes.

1 Introduction

Automated negotiation among agents is a technology that can find out an agreement point without fully revealing their utility spaces [24]. Various researches
have been done for better negotiations among agents [3–7, 9–14, 17, 18, 20].
Sometimes an auction mechanism is used in obtaining agreements among three
or more agents. Although an auction mechanism can handle a large number of
agents, a naive auction approach cannot be applied for finding a good agreement
point in multiple issue negotiations [19].

In multi-agent negotiation scenarios, an agent can use various forms of a negotiation. For example, regardless of an offer is accepted or not in a negotiation,
the agent's utility can be changed due to the surrounding situation [5]. This
will also cause the change of an agent's strategy. When there is a change in an
agent's utility space, there could be various patterns of generating a counter
offer in a negotiation. This also makes the change of the expected utility with
the proposed offer.

In multiple simultaneous negotiation situation, negotiating agents might
change their behavior dynamically. When an agent is negotiating to multiple
agents, regardless of changing his behavior, there could be a case that the agent
only obtains lower utility compared to even a bilateral negotiation scenario since
in every time another negotiation had a chance to have higher utility. To consider the above situation, agents will need a meta strategy [27], which controls
the whole negotiations among multiple agents. Such a meta-strategy could be

G. Boella et al. (Eds.): PRIMA 2013, LNAI 8291, pp. 526–533, 2013.

designed as a different form compared with an ordinary strategy for a simple bilateral negotiation [1, 2, 15, 16].

In such a situation, frameworks and analysis tools for bilateral negotiations between two agents cannot be directly applied, and at least a system which enables an observation of behaviors of negotiating agents and the changes of the expected utilities on such simultaneous negotiations should be prepared. Also when we allow the agents to make dynamic changes of their negotiation strategies for bilateral negotiations in multiple simultaneous negotiations among two or more agents, it may cause further changes of other agents' strategies. Despite such a complex behaviors in multiple simultaneous bilateral negotiations, there are few systems or frameworks for analyzing the behaviors and the effect of meta-negotiation strategies applied to such a situation.

This paper presents a framework for analyzing simultaneous negotiations among agents, including dynamic utility space changes and corresponding strategy changes.

2 Preliminaries

2.1 Related Work

Simultaneous negotiation is one of the most active areas of negotiation research and there are a lot of mechanism or definition of question about negotiation. Since doing multiple negotiations simultaneously is very common in the real world, many systems and models have been developed [8, 23, 25, 26].

For example, in [26], Sim proposed a model and some strategy to apply it to e-Market for grid resource allocation, and presented a comparison to existing systems. Although they considered simultaneous negotiations using coordinators that can mediate negotiating agents, there is a gap to apply their specific model to many other real-world application scenarios. For example, there could be a case to consider a negotiation scenario without any coordinators. To apply simultaneous negotiation techniques without assumptions about existence of mediators or some other special mechanisms among them, we should consider the case with only having a simple simultaneous negotiation protocol.

Simultaneous negotiations among agents can be applied in various situations. For example, there is a case that the agents seek one shared agreement. In another case, the agents may try to obtain agreements among several agents independently, but there are some inter-relations among certain specific issues in their goals. In this paper, we will consider the latter case. The each negotiating agent has its own aim. When an agent obtained an agreement and commit the agreement (e.g., assign certain amount of resources to that, etc.), the agent's situation will be changed and thus the definition of its utility space could also be changed. Because of the changes, the agent could also change its own strategy for negotiations that are still in progress.

Pan et al. [21] proposed a model and an algorithm to find a better agreement point during a negotiation by using a two-stage negotiation protocol. They argued that the proposed method could search the most suitable agreement point with minimum information reveals about opponent's utility using the proposed algorithm.

However, in our case, since we consider the situation that the definition of utility space would be changed during the negotiation, it is difficult to directly apply these algorithms or mechanisms to our case.

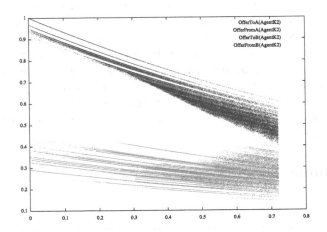

Fig. 1. The process of simultaneous negotiation (AgentK2)

2.2 Negotiation Model

In this paper, we will use a very simple negotiation protocol as a starting point of our discussion. In order to realize negotiations among two or more agents, we provide a platform that can perform two or more concurrent bilateral negotiation among agents, i.e., an agent can perform bilateral negotiation to two or more agents concurrently. In a negotiation among two agents, we will use a negotiation protocol that is called alternating offers [6, 11], which is also used in Automated Negotiating Agents Competition 2013 (ANAC2013[1]). In the alternating offer protocol, one side proposes an offer (bid) to an opponent first. Then, another side chooses an action, such as proposing an alternating offer, abandoning the negotiation, or agreeing to the offer. The negotiation is repeated until the negotiating agent refuses continuing the negotiation or agrees on both sides.

Here, we consider the case that two or more bilateral negotiations between two agents using alternating offer protocol are performed in parallel among three or more agents. Figures 1 and 2 show the negotiation processes on simultaneous negotiations with different negotiation strategies. Here, we used two bilateral negotiation strategies: AgentK2, which was used in ANAC2011 competition,

---

[1] http://www.itolab.nitech.ac.jp/ANAC2013/

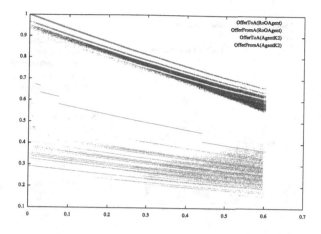

Fig. 2. The process of simultaneous negotiation (AgentK2 and RoOAgent)

and RoO, which was used in ANAC2013 competition. We can see that the process deeply depends on negotiating strategies. As shown in those figures, on our framework, we can re-use the negotiation strategies which are developed in ANAC as a bilateral negotiation strategy in simultaneous negotiations.

In this paper, we try to solve this issue by preparing a framework for analyzing such simultaneous negotiations. Therefore, we implemented a prototype system which makes it easy to analyze the appropriateness of the strategy in the multi-agent concurrent negotiations from a case of simple weighted-sum linear utility to more complicated cases, a kind of non-linear utility space for negotiating agents.

3   Interactive Analyzer for Multi Agents Negotiation

In this paper, to realize a better analysis using a meta strategy, we implemented a visual analyzer that can view and operate behaviors of agents in the actual negotiation on simultaneous negotiations. The system enables us to observe the behavior of agents and their expected utility to be obtained in each negotiation during simultaneous negotiations. Moreover, in order to realize deeper analysis of the negotiation process, it should have a capability to adjust the used parameters in the meta strategy to interactively create and reproduce some specific situations manually. Figure 3 shows the architecture of the implemented system.

3.1   Negotiation Platform

There exists several good negotiation analysis platforms designed to analyze one-by-one bilateral negotiations, such as GENIUS [6, 11]. In our proposing framework, to handle multiple simultaneous negotiations, each bilateral negotiation platform is controlled by the framework. The platform can manage parallel

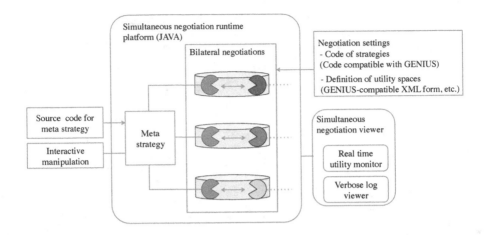

Fig. 3. System architecture

negotiations among agents that have various strategies or utility spaces, and also they might have different response speeds for offers. The platform also manages the simultaneous negotiations based on the defined rules. For example, when we assumes that an agent can only commit a single agreement among agents and a negotiation reaches an agreement, the agent at first sends a message that notifies the completion of the negotiation. Then, the framework broadcasts a message to all other negotiating agents to force them abandon their negotiations.

3.2 Handling Simultaneous Negotiations

Figure 4 (①) shows the changes of expected utilities in each negotiation process and its logs viewed from the agents' own utility spaces at the time of negotiations among two or more agents. In our framework, we implemented a graphical interface to observe and touch the parameters used in the meta-strategy.

3.3 Handling Strategies and Utility Spaces

To provide a mechanism to modify a opponent agent's utility space during the negotiation, the graphical user interface for operating the weight for each issue is prepared on the system (Figure 4 (②)). First, we can choose an agent's strategy, weight of issues in utility space, etc. to modify them. When a change is made to a slider while negotiating, the change can be reflected instantly to the definition of an actual agent's utility space. It can also modify a strategy to negotiate to a counterpart agent.

Furthermore, for observing the strategy shifts due to a change of utility space definition, the graphical interface can display the expected utility values from a corresponding opponent's utility space and the changes of such expected utility

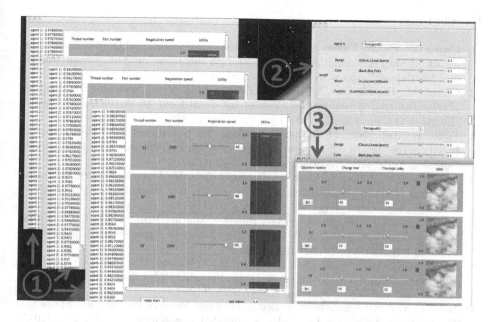

Fig. 4. Overview of the system

values when the alternating offer is accepted (Figure 4 (③)). To reproduce the changes in utility spaces, we proposed a mechanism to modify a specified utility space at the specified time.

4 Conclusions

In this paper, we proposed a system that can observe multiple simultaneous negotiations that consider dynamic changes of utility spaces. The proposed system can be applied to monitor and evaluate meta-strategies with dynamic changes of negotiation behavior to treat dynamically changing utility spaces in multiple simultaneous negotiations.

As we mentioned, there have been many researches about forming better agreements by various negotiation techniques. The use of considered simultaneous negotiations using coordinators that mediate negotiating agents, is one of challenging approaches to form better agreements [8, 22, 23, 25, 26, 28, 29]. When mediator agents exist in a concurrent negotiation environment, it has to consider that how a mediator works in the agreement process and it should be analyzed. Furthermore, it could be a good help to analyze in which case a kind of mediator works well in what kind of agreement processes. In our future work, we will expand our system to handle a case that is using mediator agents for such analyses.

References

1. Chang, M., He, M., Ekárt, A., Luo, X., Zhang, S.: Bi-directional Double Auction for Financial Market Simulation. In: Proc. of 12th Int. Conf. on Autonomous Agents and Multiagent Systems, AAMAS 2013 (2013)
2. Chang, M., He, M., Luo, X.: AstonCAT-Plus: An Efficient Specialist for the TAC Market Design Tournament. In: Proc. of Int. Joint Conf. on Artificial Intelligence (IJCAI 2011), pp. 146–151 (2011)
3. Fujita, K.: Automated Mediation Technologies for Non-monotonic Utility Function based on Tree-height Adjustments. In: Proc. of 6th Int. Workshop on Agent-based Complex Automated Negotiations, ACAN 2013 (2013)
4. Haberland, V., Miles, S., Luck, M.: Using Adjustable Fuzzy Inference for Adaptive Grid Resource Negotiation. In: Proc. of 6th Int. Workshop on Agent-based Complex Automated Negotiations, ACAN 2013 (2013)
5. Hara, K., Ito, T.: Effects of Dis GA Based Mediation Protocol for Utilities that Change over Time. In: Proc. of 6th Int. Workshop on Agent-based Complex Automated Negotiations, ACAN 2013 (2013)
6. Hindriks, K., Jonker, C.M., Kraus, S., Lin, R., Tykhonov, D.: Genius - Negotiation Environment for Heterogeneous Agents. In: Proc. of 8th Int. Conf. on Autonomous Agents and Multiagent Systems, AAMAS 2009 (2009)
7. Ilany, L., Gal, K.: Algorithm Selection in Bilateral Negotiation. In: Proc. of 6th Int. Workshop on Agent-based Complex Automated Negotiations, ACAN 2013 (2013)
8. Ishikawa, T., Fukuta, N.: A Prototype System for Federated Cloud-based Resource Allocation by Automated Negotiations using Strategy Changes. In: Proc. of 6th Int. Workshop on Agent-based Complex Automated Negotiations, ACAN 2013 (2013)
9. Ito, T., Klein, M., Hattori, H.: Multi-issue Negotiation Protocol for Agents: Exploring Nonlinear Utility Spaces. In: Proc. of the 20th Int. Joint Conf. on Artificial Intelligence (IJCAI 2007), pp. 1347–1352 (2007)
10. Kong, Y., Zhang, M., Ye, D., Luo, X.: A Negotiation Method for Task Allocation with Time Constraints in Open Grid Environments. In: Proc. of 6th Int. Workshop on Agent-based Complex Automated Negotiations, ACAN 2013 (2013)
11. Lin, R., Kraus, S., Baarslag, T., Tykhonov, D., Hindriks, K., Jonker, C.M.: GENIUS: An Integrated Environment for Supporting the Design of Generic Automated Negotiators Computational Intelligence (2012), doi:10.1111/j.1467-8640.2012.00463.x
12. Raz, L., Gev, Y., Kraus, S.: Facilitating Better Negotiation Solutions using AniMed. In: Proc. of 4th Int. Workshop on Agent-based Complex Automated Negotiations (ACAN 2011), pp. 64–70 (2011)
13. Lopez-Carmona, M.A., Marsa-Maestre, I., Velasco, J.R., de la Hoz, E.: A Multi-issue Negotiation Framework for Non-monotonic Preference Spaces. In: Proc. of 9th Int. Conf. on Autonomous Agents and Multiagent Systems, AAMAS 2010 (2010)
14. Lopez-Carmona, M.A., Marsa-Maestrey, I., Klein, M.: Consensus Policy Based Multi-agent Negotiation. In: Proc. of 4th Int. Workshop on Agent-based Complex Automated Negotiations (ACAN 2011), pp. 1–8 (2011)
15. Luo, X., Miao, C., Jennings, N.R., He, M., Shen, Z., Zhang, M.: KEMNAD: A Knowledge Engineering Methodology for Negotiating Agent Development. Computational Intelligence 28(1), 51–105 (2012)
16. Luo, X., Jennings, N.R., Shadbolt, N., Leung, H., Lee, J.H.: A Fuzzy Constraint Based Model for Bilateral, Multi-issue Negotiations in Semi-competitive Environments. Artificial Intelligence 148(1-2), 53–102 (2003)

17. Marsa-Maestre, I., Ito, T., Klein, M., Fujita, K.: Balancing Utility and Deal Probability for Auction-based Negotiations in Highly Nonlinear Utility Spaces. In: Proc. of the 22th Int. Joint Conf. on Artificial Intelligence (IJCAI 2009), pp. 214–219 (2009)

18. Marsa-Maestre, I., Lopez-Carmona, M.A., Velasco, J.R., de la Hoz, E.: Avoiding the Prisoner's Dilemma in Auction-based Negotiations for Highly Rugged Utility Spaces. In: Proc. of 9th Int. Conf. on Autonomous Agents and Multiagent Systems, AAMAS 2010 (2010)

19. Mizutani, N., Fujita, K., Ito, T.: Effective Distributed Genetic Algorithms for Optimizing Social Utility. In: Proc. The First Int. Workshop on Sustainable Enterprise Software, SES 2011 (2011)

20. Okumura, M., Fujita, K., Ito, T.: Implementation of Collective Collaboration Support System Based on Automated Multi-agent Negotiation. In: Proc. of 4th Int. Workshop on Agent-based Complex Automated Negotiations (ACAN 2011), pp. 71–76 (2011)

21. Pan, L., Luo, X., Meng, X., Miao, C., He, M., Guo, X.: A Two-stage Win-Win Multiattribute Negotiation Model: Optimization and then Concession. Computational Intelligence (2012)

22. Rahwan, I., Kowalczyk, R., Pham, H.H.: Intelligent Agents for Automated One-to-Many e-Commerce Negotiation. In: Proc. 25th Australian Comput. Sci. Conf., pp. 197–204 (2004)

23. Ren, F., Zhang, M., Luo, X., Soetanto, D.: A Parallel, Multi-issue Negotiation Model in Dynamic E-Markets. In: Wang, D., Reynolds, M. (eds.) AI 2011. LNCS, vol. 7106, pp. 442–451. Springer, Heidelberg (2011)

24. Shoham, Y., Leyton-Brown, K.: Multiagent Systems: Algorithmic, Game-theoretic, and Logical. Cambridge University Press (2009)

25. Sim, K.M.: Consurrent Negotiation and Coodination for Grid Resource Coallocation. IEEE Transactions on Systems, Man, and Cybernetics-Part B: Cybernetics 40(3), 753–766 (2010)

26. Sim, K.M.: Complex and Concurrent Negotiations for Multiple Interrelated e-Markets. IEEE Transactions on Systems, Man, and Cybernetics-Part B: Cybernetics 40(1), 230–245 (2013)

27. Tsuruhashi, Y., Fukuta, N.: A Preliminary Toolkit for Analyzing Meta-strategies in Simultaneous Negotiations among Agents. In: Proc. IIAI Int. Symposium on Applied Informatics, pp. 26–29 (2012)

28. Tsuruhashi, Y., Fukuta, N.: An Analysis Framework for Meta Strategies in Simultaneous Negotiations. In: Proc. of 6th Int. Workshop on Agent-based Complex Automated Negotiations, ACAN 2013 (2013)

29. Williams, C.R., Robu, V., Gerding, E.H., Jennings, N.R.: Towards a Platform for Concurrent Negotiations in Complex Domains. In: Proc. of 5th Int. Workshop on Agent-based Complex Automated Negotiations (ACAN 2012), pp. 26–33 (2012)

Author Index